I0822076

Systems upgrade

(Re)fabricating tectonic prototypes.

Leire Asensio Villoria & David Mah

New Module 1.3_ Associative Model 7 based_01

for Naia & Lucas

Content

Calmness as design research

Hanif Kara

I have long been interested in the junctures between science and art, as well as those between engineering and architecture. I have also learned that there is no universally agreed-upon definition of architectural design research, and that one is not needed to afford us productive transactions in this liminal territory.

Nevertheless, it is daunting to begin writing about this book—a book in which the authors have positioned many years of their own journey and work as a resource for others to incorporate and integrate into practice and education. They join a long tradition of scholars who have advanced architectural discourse through design research conducted by drawing, modeling, and writing. The authors make no claim that anything they present is revolutionary—to the contrary, there is a tacit assertion that their speculations are rooted in the histories of architecture, engineering and art. Thus, this opportunity given to me presents the dilemma of choosing which lens to speak from. Nonetheless, in my opinion it is judicious of the authors to invite me, as a structural engineer, to make a contribution.

It is important to acknowledge at the outset that I have worked with both authors in practice and at the academy. We have shared more than 20 years of exchanges through a variety of collaborations and intersections, in teaching as well as practice.

The common ground between us lies in our motivation to speak to audiences from different design disciplines and across generations. We have also been shaped by many colleagues who have influenced us. To write this, I look beyond the text alone. I have read between the lines wherever possible, to detect the slippages into many years of conversations I have had with the authors. The book offers a good view of the role played by these personal histories; allowing the authors to build several bridges between design and research.

The distinction I make is that the work presented here does not merely emphasize quantitative techniques, optimal solutions or experiments in materials that demand a background in numeracy. Rather, the authors conduct experiments through a conversation between making and drawing as well as between practice and the academy. The work acknowledges the emergence of technological production processes and methods (such as 3D printing and generative design) that help to accelerate these transfers and close the gap between digital and physical formats. Although their work may be enhanced by technology, the authors also resist the oversimplifications it can facilitate, managing to do so through the use of well-chosen thinkers and artefacts as references that punctuate the narrative of the book intentionally—but also, when viewed from my lens, fortuitously.

This enriches their work but also becomes particularly accented by the institutions and places they have been fortunate to live and teach in. It is also informed by a reaction and discomfort they have with the positions some of these places had adopted toward design research. Some separate it from the history of architecture while others might misuse technology in search of a formal "newness" or "uniqueness." This is pertinent, as the time spanned by the work in the book has seen a sea change in architectural practice and education. Many parts of the world now embrace design research as a legitimate research area in its own right. This has not always been the case; the authors have evidently had to confront some resistance to their position as they have moved around the globe over the years.

From reading parts of the manuscript I have learned that research, in the minds of these authors, is neither wholly intuitive nor based on "rule of thumb" processes. Instead, it takes a different starting point in each chapter, seeking to sharpen what we may already know and construct new bridges between research approaches that neither ignore nor depend too much on systematic knowledge. The range of work addressed in the book, and the ways in which the authors analyze it, reveals their own process. It is a process advanced through organizing and examining artefacts while studying a set of "cherry-picked" designers whom they respect, allowing them to amplify particular interpretations of this legacy without shame.

Another important question the work raises relates to how this book may engage the now ubiquitous cliché of the "digital native" generation that has never known a world without computation and the World Wide Web. But such speculation obscures the purpose of the book. The authors operate at the interstices between digital fluency and a more physical materiality with equal consistency. In fact, in some of the outcomes they present in the book, one recognizes a disorderly aesthetic that shows signs of a hybrid or collective intelligence.

In my opinion, by incorporating influences that are personal, while at the same time also learning from their experiences in the many places they have taught in, the authors make a broader contribution to design research. The book speculates openly about what the authors consider a model of design research that can be applied to architecture without the insecurity of emulating "scientific research." This offers some insights into processes that may be considered by the next generations of practitioners.

The role of architecture, both in education and practice, is once again under scrutiny. Given the ecological and socio-economic challenges we face, is it fit for purpose? I have been able to trace a productive aura of learning in this book that is born out of a deep respect for the histories of architecture and design research though a combination of the authors' own work and the references they adopt to illustrate the two worlds: the digital and the craft. The work offers compelling outcomes and suggests productive possibilities for interaction between these two worlds for academics and practitioners alike—even those who may seek a source of progress in computer-aided techniques to create new forms.

Superposition of Enneper surfaces

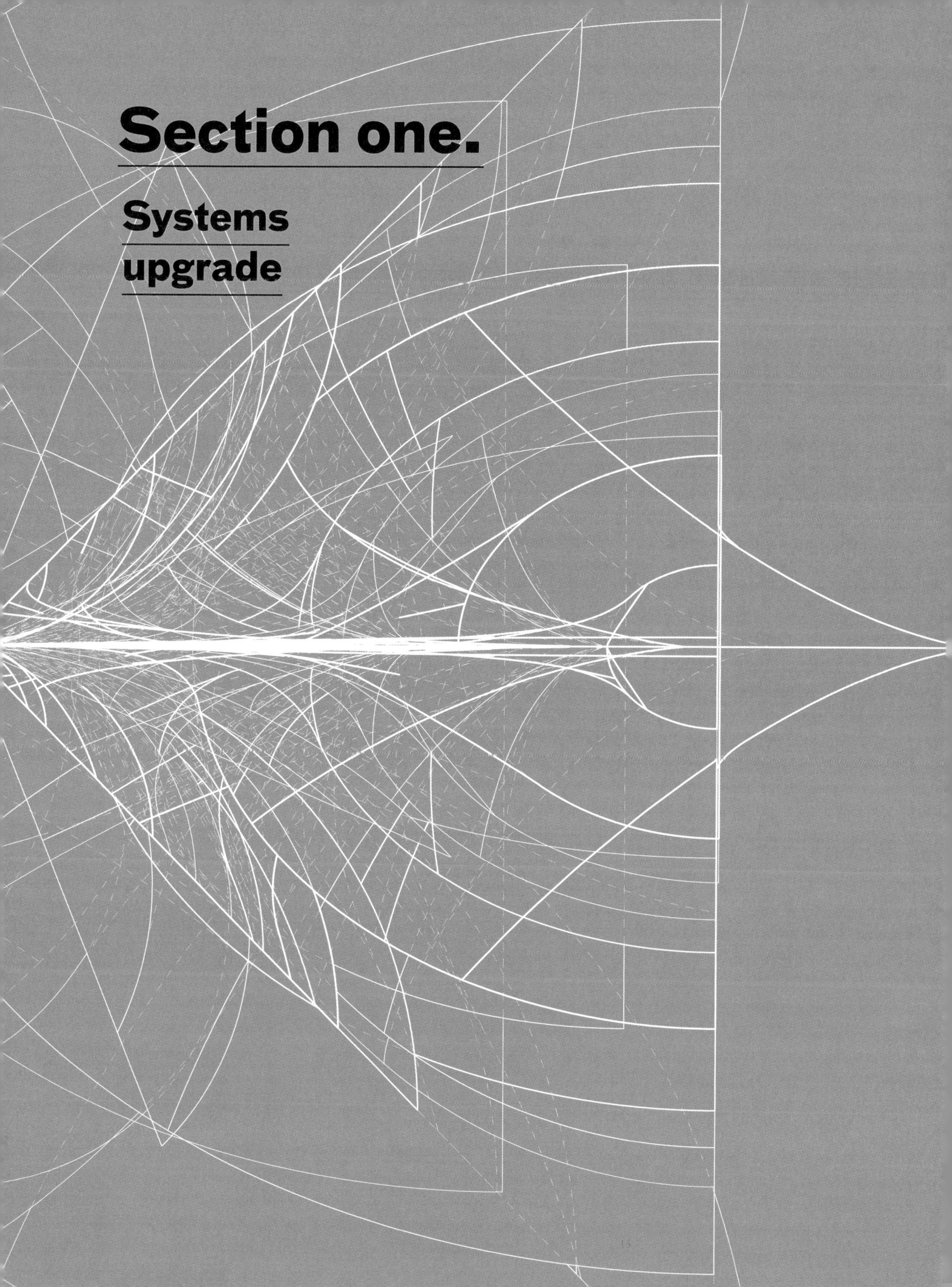

Section one.

Systems upgrade

From things as they are to things as they ought to be.

01_New Module 4.2_Enneper + Tetrahedron_3d printed model_perspective view

Learning from objects and things

The study of design history can never be complete without the dedicated study of its material artifacts. Different narratives, biographies and theories can be woven together to ascribe meaning as well as significance to the material products of design history. However, this book argues that a focus on examining and describing the material things themselves may also offer us an immediate and tangible window into the many concerns, sensibilities, preoccupations and know-how that have informed their creation.

The way in which the study of design history is undertaken can be influenced by a wide field of motivations, approaches, and frames of reference. However, the public and disciplinary imaginations are typically captured by the explication of design artifacts relative to their place within larger stylistic periods or through their significance within authors' biographical narratives. The longstanding focus has often been on the personal influences that compel designers, or on a contextualization of these works within an associated zeitgeist. Works are always discussed from and given meaning through their positioning within the authorial context or, often, by relating the work to abstract ideas, concepts and philosophies external to the "mundane" technical and material concerns of design practice. Uncovering lessons primarily from the focused study of design material artifacts, in and of themselves, is a less common model of contemporary design or art historical investigation.

However, recent investment in learning through an engagement with historical artifacts as "things" or objects has gained currency in a diverse roster of teaching and research institutions. On one hand, object-based learning is becoming widely practiced in different academic contexts. This has helped to elevate the material artifacts of history (or their replicas) as rich repositories of knowledge and information. The active use of objects in the process of learning has been motivated by acknowledgement of the capacity of objects to transmit a wide array of information, from "an object's date and location of origin, method of manufacture, artistic style" to its "original purpose and function." Objects are said to be "imbued with meaning and can be read much like a text."[1]

On the other hand, "things" have also achieved an elevated status for some historians across art and science who have come to recognize a capacity for reframing historical research around the specifics of "things that talk." As offered in the introduction to a collection of essays edited by Lorraine

1. Jamieson, A. (June, 2017). *Object-based learning: A new way of teaching in Arts West.* University of Melbourne Collections, Issue 20.

Daston, things "do not merely repeat, they are not instruments for the recording and playing back of the human voice."[2] For Daston and her collaborators, the study of things is pursued to open up new ways of accessing history, revealing new insights into art and scientific history through the deep study of material artifacts. This compulsion to frame historical exploration through a deep engagement with things is "to make things eloquent without resorting to ventriloquism or projection" and "explores the meaning of things in-situ, gaze fixed firmly on this or that thing in particular rather than on the ontology of things in general."[3]

2. Daston L. (ed.), (2004). *Things that Talk: Object lessons from Art and Science*, New York: Zone Books, p. 11

3. Daston L. (ed.), (2004). Ibidem. p. 9

Learning from the description of objects and things

Echoing the differing aims of object-based learning and "things that talk," the work described in this book is invested in the idea that a deep and sustained study of material artifacts constitutes a valuable study of design history. This pursuit of material knowledge also affords us the capacity to draw many different lessons from the specific design practices undertaken to deliver these artifacts, complementing wider contextual research on design history.

Although we began with the idea that, because the relationships between design and the material world are largely mediated by representational tools, the study of design history can never be complete without the dedicated study of its material artifacts, it may be more accurate to say that the study of design history can never be complete without the dedicated study of its material artifacts and the techniques or approaches we use to describe them. Here, we focus on the more direct and technical ways in which we describe the direct material qualities of artifacts, their forms, shapes and organizations. More precisely, the study of design history elaborated here is a reflection on the history of designing. The focus is on the conversation between the materialized work and the ways in which it may be materialized through our technical tools of description. A reflection on this relationship between material objects and the means through which they are materialized often reveals insights into the act of design.

The process of research and documenting material history (specifically in archaeological practice) is conducted using the same mediums of measured drawings or models of descriptive geometry used in design, and is underpinned by the same conventions. These mediums and practices are employed in two ostensibly opposed practices: the creative act of design on the one hand and the more "objective" research practices of analyzing existing historic artifacts on the other.

Interestingly, it is also through a deliberate and thoughtful use of these shared geometric and drawing mediums that an exercise in analysis may become the means through which we upgrade design history so that it may be applicable in contemporary design practice. In both the design and archaeological fields, the widespread adoption of digital tools such as 3D modeling has helped to extend these design and research practices. Through the virtual documentation of objects, there is the added capacity to contribute towards building extensive digital archives while also providing a more operative historical knowledge. While a digital archaeology of design artifacts may extend our knowledge on the history of design, it can also be leveraged to upgrade these historical antecedents for contemporary practice.

The sharing of these practices signals a potential role for contemporary representational methods and media to further empower these bridges between design history and practice. Digital mediums can be leveraged to enhance such crossing points between design history and its potential future practices. This process centers around studying the embedded information or the underlying "procedural codes" that govern the definition of the forms and materialization of design artifacts.

Re-describing and re-constructing design artifacts affords us access to design and production know-how embedded in the material artifacts themselves. This archaeology and archiving of material history profits from an attentiveness to the ways in which objects may be (re)drawn or (re)modeled, allowing for the articulation and explication of detailed material and design knowledge.

Reverse engineering: A digital design archaeology

> *"Reverse engineering, also called back engineering, is the process by which a man-made object is deconstructed to reveal its designs, architecture, or to extract knowledge from the object; similar to scientific research."*
> Eilam, E., 2005, Reversing: Secrets of Reverse Engineering. John Wiley & Sons.

One of the established processes for documenting existing artifacts or systems is the practice of reverse engineering. This process is deployed for a wide array of reasons ranging from conservation practices to industrial espionage. Reverse engineering involves analyzing and reconstructing existing objects or systems, typically without access to original documentation, codes or drawings. As explained, this process is carried out by different disciplines for different ends; however, the process itself is simply the analysis of existing artifacts for the sake of accessing a deeper understanding of the process that informed their conception or materialization. In effect, the process of reverse engineering is aimed at locating some of the underlying codes that determine structure and operability.

In the case of information systems, reverse engineering can be carried out to crack codes for the illegal duplication of proprietary software, or to construct viruses or malware that exploit weaknesses in existing systems. Yet there are other, less devious incentives for carrying out this process, such developing interfaces that enable greater flexibility and interoperability between different computing systems.

This understanding of the practice and purpose of reverse engineering could be adopted as an operative analogue that informs the construction of bridges between legacy design knowledge and the capacity to extend this information for future practice relevance. Knowledge of the codes that define material structure, form, and performance allows for the potential of design upgrades of historical designs through a re-contextualization or manipulation of these underlying codes.

Modeling from history

The use of reverse engineering in the study of historic artifacts has also been adopted as a method by archaeologists, and it shares some notable overlaps with the methods of design history scholars. Reverse engineering in design history has been pursued to support various types of projects, from the reconstruction of damaged or lost objects of anthropological value to the completion of unfinished architectural projects such as Dresden Cathedral in Germany.[4]

4. Rehberg, K.-S & Neutzner, M. (2015). *The Dresden Frauenkirche as a contested symbol: The architecture of remembrance after war.* DOI: 10.1017/CBO9781107444911.005.

02 & 03_Dresden cathedral 1880 - 2013

Interestingly, despite their great divergence in scales, the use of digital tools in the reverse engineering process allows these respective restoration and archaeological teams to be able to practice a very sophisticated reconstruction. These tools and processes support the sophisticated capacity to integrate fragments of the original material fabric into these reconstructed objects, making more accessible a process that previously would have been an exceedingly intricate undertaking.

In this wide spectrum of cases, the use of measured drawing and digital modeling techniques has been crucial in establishing conduits between investigative phases and the construction or restoration processes of these historic pieces. The modeling of the design for Dresden Cathedral and the scanning of the rubble remaining after its bombing in the Second World War allowed for the strategic re-integration of these original pieces of stones into the reconstructed cathedral. These digital 3D models allowed for this elaborate undertaking and were enabled through cross referencing with the original building plans. A complete reconstruction would likely have been sufficiently facilitated by the plans alone, but the deliberate embedding of original materials into the reconstituted cathedral necessitated a digitally aided reverse-engineered solution.

Another notable case in which the study of historic artifacts has been used to gain deep insights into the design histories and ambitions embedded in material forms is the ongoing construction of the Sagrada Familia Cathedral in Barcelona.[5] However, in this instance, the absence of comprehensive documentation on the design intentions of the cathedral's designer, Antoni Gaudi, has necessitated deep investigation of several surviving process models.

5. Burry, M., Grifoll, J. C., Gómez Serrano, J. (2008). *Sagrada Familia s. XXI: Gaudi ara/ahora/now*. Barcelona: Edicions UPC.

The establishment of a protocol for re-generating and re-constructing Gaudi's design, uncorroborated by construction drawings, has been aided by lessons offered by a deep immersion into the forms of the remaining models with a special focus on the associated geometries deployed to construct them.

Reverse engineering of the residual models developed by Gaudi was facilitated and accelerated by the use of digital three-dimensional modeling. The discovery of an association between geometric description with the material expression as well as performance specific to Gaudi's work emerged from this exploration, enabling a deeper understanding of Gaudi's design approach and a highly operative knowledge that supported the ongoing delivery of the cathedral.

The Sagrada Familia project is especially significant as an exemplar of how the knowledge gleaned from material artifacts can enable the continuity of an interrupted design legacy. In this sense, the construction of the cathedral in Barcelona is a tangible lesson in the potential for bridge-building or migration between traditional research and creative practice, facilitated through a digitally enhanced reverse engineering process.

Drawing: Design

Uncovering or approximating the specific techniques used in re-documenting historical objects and "things" can provide the means to access either the actual or analogous practices undertaken by its creators. This is particularly pertinent in relation to the study of drawing or modeling processes.

The process of materializing a design is primarily mediated by descriptive practices such as drawing and modeling, which help bridge the distance between designer and the construction/production process. One of the most lucid illuminations of this relationship is encapsulated in Robin Evans' essay, "Translations From Drawing to Building."[6] This critical intermediary between the design and materialization processes infers that drawing and modeling approaches are one of the most critical codes we would need to consider so that we may gain insight into the creation processes behind the legacy artifacts.

The widespread adoption of drawing as the authoritative notation system for communicating design intentions and coordinating the act of material assembly places the design field's activity into the category of the allographic arts.

This categorization of the arts as either autographic or allographic is offered by American philosopher Nelson Goodman as a measure of how authenticity may be attributed to works in different art forms.[7] For Goodman, the way that authenticity is determined should be differentiated between art practices that have an immediate relationship to material production (autographic) and those that are mediated by notation (allographic arts). This differentiation allows us to distinguish between art practices such as painting and music. In painting, the actual work executed by the artist (or their assistants) is afforded the status of the original, whereas disciplines such as music and dance can posit a different relationship between author and artwork.

The materialization of architecture, landscape and urban design frequently requires the involvement of large groups of diverse actors over long periods of time. Like music, this process of materialization has typically been coordinated using an assortment of visual documents. In architecture, this has more recently been complimented by digital building information models. The generative design phases are typically isolated from the actual construction procedure such that these two processes do not enjoy the instantaneous relationship associated with autographic arts like painting or sculpture.

6. Evans R. (1997). *Translations From Drawing to Building and Other Essays*. London: The Architectural Association Press.

7. Goodman, N. (1976). *Languages of Art*. London: Hackett Publishing Company.

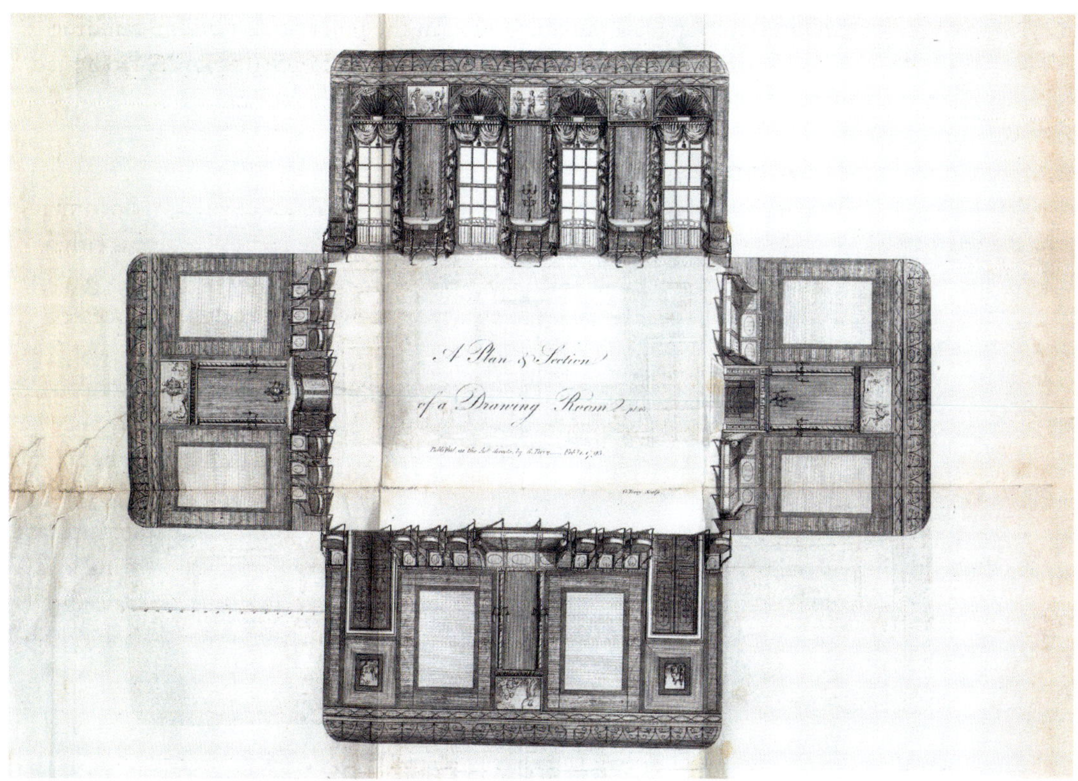

04_Developed surface drawing of a room from Thomas Sheraton, The Cabinet Maker and Upholsterer's Drawing Book, 1793

Resonating with allographic art practices, designers construct documents that translate projected material reality into visual symbols and graphic conventions. Traditionally, much of the significance attributed to a design is captured by a set of descriptive drawings, models and diagrams.

This systematic separation between designing and making as a common professional and disciplinary practice was consolidated during the Renaissance, when drawing was established as the convention in Western architectural history. However, the role of drawing or modeling has also been highly instrumental in the creative process despite its predominant professional role in design documentation. Different drawing approaches or techniques have been critical operative tools that structure and frame the ways in which a design is elaborated and refined for material realization. The manner in which geometry is defined and assembled, the ways in which the parts of a design are organized into wholes, and ways in which this is communicated to the other collaborators are all informed and mediated by drawing.

The strategic use of these drawing techniques and mediums is also crucial because of the ways in which they abstract the material world. Such strategic use is significant because it regulates the aspects which are made visible and those which are either obscured or omitted in the process.

Consequently, this propensity for abstraction—the question of how a method of description reframes the material world—is one of the most important considerations when pursuing material research as well as in design practice.

In another of his essays, "The Developed Surface," Robin Evans makes a clear argument for the agency of drawing as an influential and transformative accomplice in design exploration. He articulates the caveat that representational or notational techniques can operate as mediums that "affect the architect's field of visibility" and "its power to represent is always partial."[8] In this essay, Evans focuses specifically on the developed surface: a drawing technique made fashionable for describing architectural interiors in eighteenth-century England. He exposes the role of drawing in guiding design ambitions by "providing a range of subject-matter made visible in the drawing, as opposed to all the other possible subject-matter that is left out of the drawing or is not so apparent from it," Developed surface drawing is a technique that deliberately emphasizes the autonomy of the interior by removing any representation of the room's exterior while also focusing design attention to a chamber's enveloping surfaces, establishing a strong bias in the definition of these interior spaces and the ways in which they may be inhabited.

8. Evans R. (1997). Ibidem. p. 199

Although Evans' essay is an explication of this particular drawing style, it would be fair to extend this capacity for framing the designer's attention to most other forms of representation. The vital capacities of drawing to describe and coordinate, from a remote position, what are often complex processes of materialization, are also balanced by the limitations of drawing techniques to obscure different aspects of design consideration. A meticulous and earnest designer may endeavor to utilize a spectrum of drawing techniques that cast a wider view to achieve a more considered and holistic proposal but, nevertheless, the nature of drawings and their abstraction tends towards restraining our attentions. This is why an engagement with the description of material artifacts of history can also allow us to gain an understanding of the ways in which a designer's creative process was framed while at the same time affording creative practitioners the possibility of locating novel ways to reconsider these legacies.

Drawing: Research

The obligation to provide measurability as well as repeatability in research overlaps with the same requirements used in the transmission of design ideas for construction. In both cases, the prevailing standards are technical drawings that embed measure and are easily reproduced. More specifically, the descriptive technical drawings are generally underpinned by the strategic deployment of the conventions of descriptive geometry. Descriptive geometric techniques and conventions are what allow for the conversion of graphic modes of description into the form of measurable documents.

The role of these drawings is to communicate and focus on the formal, organizational, spatial and constructive information.

A longer-spanning, yet sporadic history of orthogonal projection in drawing practice predates the formalization and consolidation of the science of descriptive geometry in the eighteenth century by French mathematician Gaspard Monge. Like many historic technological innovations, the invention of descriptive geometry was hastened by a demand for military applications, specifically the systematization of designing and constructing defensive structures such as forts. This systematic knowledge was kept as a French state secret for many years; to divulge it was a crime punishable by death. What the French wanted to guard was the critical capacity of imparting a reliable metric precision to graphic techniques. Descriptive geometry established a dependable bridge between the abstract practices of drawing and geometric definition with the more tangible processes of actualization in the material world, and it remains the prevalent convention for technical drawing in practice.

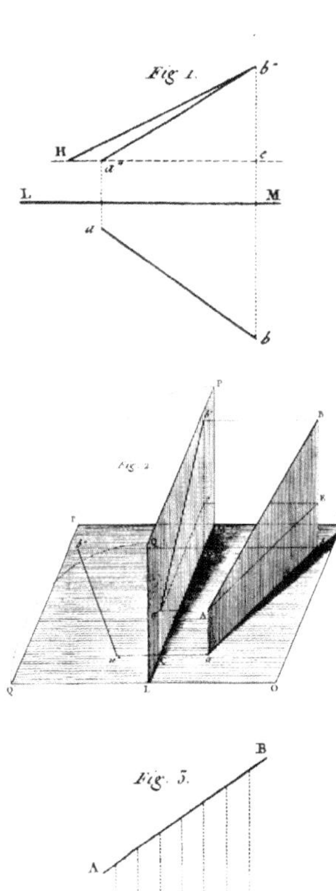

05 _Diagram of projection in Monge Geometrie Descriptive

Contemporary technical descriptive techniques have steadily expanded away from the dominance of orthographic two-dimensional drawing towards three-dimensional descriptions of the material world. This momentum has been made more accessible through the ubiquity of 3D modeling and has also affected the process of manufacturing and construction documentation. Although this digital representation medium is often credited with enabling a more faithful spatial description of the material world, the bases for these tools are still framed by descriptive geometry. The process of codifying material information in CAD or 3D modeling files retains many of the conventions of traditional technical drawings that predate computation.

However, in the same way that drawing techniques may focus a designer's view on certain concerns, the ways in which models are constructed remain an important consideration for how they also frame our creativity. The kinds of drawing or modeling approaches, the types of geometries that are used, or the ways in which these geometries are assembled, all reveal an attitude and sensibility towards the organization of the material world.
For the digital archaeological process, this competence over geometry is equally important where the same procedure of codifying material information into geometric notation can be said to be operating, but in the opposite vector. The process of "reverse-engineering" existing material objects demands an in-depth consideration of how descriptive geometry can be used in re-description. This protocol for assembling geometry, composed as drawings or models that describe a design, can be regarded as a vital component of the underlying code.

The specific nature of this geometric code can provide us with a range of latent information. For designers, geometry is the stand-in for material form. If an analysis of material forms yields learning and knowledge, then this is also a study of their geometric definition.

To further contextualize this bridge between the analysis of the material world with contemporary creative practice and the notion of form as a source of knowledge, a brief sidebar into another unlikely intersection between research and creative practice offers some potentially vital insight.

Form as embedded information

A shared understanding of form that underpins two very different design and research approaches in architecture indicates a larger revitalization of interrogating the description of the material world. Although parametric design and forensic architectural research do not necessarily share common motivations, both approaches regard material forms as repositories of information.

In both approaches, the generation of material organizations (in the case of parametric design) or the study of material evidence (in the case of forensic architecture) is underpinned by the notion of form as an index of information. The formation process is predicated on a focus on forces or associative criteria as factors that impose a formative influence on its creation. A succinct description of the material and formal ideas shared by these seemingly opposing architectural cultures reverberates with second-order cybernetician Gregory Bateson's description of form as embedded information.

We can see the resonances with this notion of form in the different descriptions of material offered by these different practice cultures. On one hand, the analysis of the index of forces on matter affords researchers the capacity to build up material evidence. The information embedded in the form is reverse-engineered to better understand the circumstances of its creation and to help build cases in legal trials. An example is the study of topographic irregularities in places of conflict, which have helped to locate the sites of mass graves associated with major war crimes. Surface irregularities registered on the ground through LIDAR scanning have allowed research groups to identify these sites usually hidden to the naked eye.[9] On the other hand, the information-matter relationship is operationalized as a design practice that uses data as the defining parameters, which drives the formation of material organizations. In this case, a geometric transformation or formal definition is associated with information and the resulting material organization can be seen as an index of the different parameters that have been adopted in the design process.[10]

9. Weizman, E. (2017). *Forensic Architecture: Violence at the Threshold of Detectability*. New York: Zone Books.

10. A similar explanation offered by the American theorist Jeffrey Kipnis when discussing the work of FOA and their contemporaries can be found in Kipnis, J. (2000). Performance Anxiety? 2G, no. 16 (4).

> *"Recently, speculative research has shifted its attention from the power of material arrangements to represent to the more general problem of how information causes material arrangements to reorganize…*
> *…as complex material arrangements index more and more information, resonating and rearranging with ever increasing subtleties to the super-positions and harmonics of new flows of information, new forms and unexpected behaviors emerge."*
> Kipnis J., 2000, Performance Anxiety?, 2G Foreign Office Architects, vol. 4, no. 16, p. 6

> *"If material deformations are a building's response to changing environmental force fields, then, inversely, the formal mutations a building undergoes are processes of recording: deformations as matter in formation are also information."*
> Weizman E., 2017, Forensic Architecture: Violence at the Threshold of Detectability, Zone Books, New York, p. 52

During a public lecture at Harvard's Graduate School of Design in 2012, Eyal Weizman, a principal in the Forensic Architecture Research Group, explicitly describes this seemingly counterintuitive intersection while also calling for a more concerted effort to bridge between the practice-based research work of parametric design and the more explicitly analytical and evidence-focused work of the forensic architecture research agency.

> *"Too often, those of us that were seen more as social architects [were considered to be opposed to] the other group, who were the formalists. Those kinds of polemics really divided the field in an unproductive way. I would find myself, methodologically much closer to the parametric world where you would say form is derived from forces. And there is a kind of scientific process…..In a certain sense, I think those two strands have to marry again..."*
> Weizman E., 1/10/2012, Forensic Architecture: The Place of Law in War, public lecture at Harvard's Graduate School of Design

Even more pertinent to the work outlined in this book is Weizman's declaration of an extension of these approaches towards reconsidering the ways in which the study of architectural history distinguishes itself from the existing norms in architectural historiography through a deep engagement with material evidence.

> *"In considering buildings as historical documents, forensic architecture has a claim to the history of architecture, especially at a time when the field has largely disavowed the materiality of buildings in favor of the history of architectural practitioners and the documents that they leave behind.*

> *It can also potentially extend architecture's historiographical methods, because it gives accounts of the history of buildings as material things beyond the history of their human conception with a biography that is beyond that of an architect."*
>
> Weizman E., 2017, Forensic Architecture: Violence at the Threshold of Detectability, Zone Books, New York, pp. 52–54

This unexpected convergence between seemingly disparate design practice and research concerns echoes the primary ambitions and methods of the investigations showcased through this book. The work is underpinned by the mandate to define a bridge between the exploration of the material design history of objects or "things" to inform future creative practice. Weizman also speculates that this mandate may also yield vital knowledge and information from the material world that does not require the validation of the original authors' declared intentions. It suggests that we may yet discover new knowledge by reframing our view of what exists. This characterization of the potentials of studying the material artifacts from design history summarizes a major ambition of the research addressed in this book.

Applied geometries

Following on from the idea of material form as a register of information, there is the implication that a close study of material organization offers an understanding of some of the processes and drivers that have propelled the formation of these artifacts. The established standard of utilizing drawn geometries as proxies for the material world suggests that the careful review of this mediated process is especially critical for acquiring information from form. Explorations in design history framed by this conceptual framework benefit from a careful attendance to the different kinds of drawing and geometric approaches deployed for the definition and realization of forms. As articulated in Evans' essays, the way in which geometry is used is particularly important because of the ways in which it can impact a design researcher or practitioner's capacities to view and imagine material forms.

So how best to broach this subject of drawing and geometry? How do we uncover drawn geometry's formative influences on material form? Design and art history already appear to offer a substantial body of knowledge that can be used as a reference. Some scholarly design history traditions have associated different proclivities for geometric forms and sensibilities to tendencies in wider creative and social practice. In the Western art-historical traditions of formalism, there is the assumption that prevalent uses of specific formal or geometric assemblies can be generalized and associated with particular styles or periods. A persistent example is the pivotal work on the Renaissance and the Baroque by eminent Swiss art historian Heinrich

Wolfflin,[11] who offered five pairs of concepts that help to distinguish between the forms of those two styles. These five concept pairs establish a broad view that the Renaissance could be characterized by an inclination towards the clear composition and articulation of regular geometries. The intended appearance of repose projected by Renaissance art and architecture had been accomplished through a part-to-whole logic that discretized the overall composition and privileged legible geometries. Individual elements were clearly articulated or separated, and Wolfflin defined the style through its linearity, planarity, closed forms and multiplicity.

In Wolfflin's concept pairings, Renaissance forms can be distinguished from the Baroque, where this relationship between the parts and whole were said to have adopted a more amorphous or massive quality. Baroque architecture has generally been associated with movement[12] as well as a more massive and elusive sensibility towards architectural articulation. The propensity for these qualities in the Baroque was manifested in the tendency towards a more ambiguous enunciation between the architectural elements, subordinating these individual elements to the massiveness of the whole. Assuming the lens of this formal tradition, material artifacts in themselves may reveal information that, despite its singularity as an art work, can be contextualized within a particular social, cultural and political moment. It has been argued that despite Wolfflin's association with formalism in art history, his characterization of the part-to-whole relationships and forms of the Renaissance and Baroque resonate with the political and social climates of the time.[13]

> *"Architectural historians, in an effort to let architecture speak, have tended to suppress the distinction that exists between a representation and what it represents."*
>
> Evans R., 1995, The Projective Cast: Architecture and Its Three Geometries, The MIT Press, London, Cambridge, p. 44

Robin Evans has questioned some of these seemingly simple and obvious associations with an idealized conception of the use of geometry.[14] By interrogating the historical theorization of Renaissance central-plan churches, exemplified by the contrasting positions of Wolfflin's formalism and Rudolf Wittkower's symbolic readings,[15] Evans destabilizes both positions. He argues for an attendance to form which is more focused on the actual geometric practices likely to have been employed by the designers and to be equally precise in studying their nuanced materialized effects. Evans argues that imprecise descriptions of the actual material organizations and forms of Renaissance churches offered by Wolfflin and Wittkower allow them to reinforce this generalization about centrality. Evans speculates that they may also be relying on a reading of the churches that is primarily mediated by a reading of their drawings. The church plans, if viewed as visual proof,

11. Wolfflin H., Simon K. (Trans) & Murray P. (1979). *Renaissance and Baroque.* New York: Cornell University Press.

12. This association between a moving subject and the Baroque is supported by Allen S. Weiss' description of the anamorphic nature of Le Notre's Vaux Le Vicomte in Weiss S. A. (1997). *Mirrors of infinity: The French formal garden and 17th-century metaphysics*, New York: Princeton Architectural Press.

13. For an extensive reflection on this relationship see Levy E. (2015). *Baroque and the Political Language of Formalism (1845 – 1945): Burckhardt, Wolfflin, Gurlitt, Brinckmann, Sedlmayr.* Basel: Schwabe Verlag.

14. See Evans' essay, Perturbed Circles, in Evans R. (1995). *The projective cast: Architecture and its three geometries.* Cambridge: The MIT Press.

15. Wittkower R., (1965) *Architecture Principles in the Age of Humanism.* London: Random House.

support the notion of the singular centrality of these churches. In both Wolfflin and Wittkower's positions, Evans unpacks the generalizations that prevent a more multivalent understanding of the capacities offered by the translation of geometry into matter. He overturns these academic claims by focusing on interrogating the material itself.

Rather than a single centrality perceivable in a plan, Evans' description of an immersive reading of these spaces reveal multiple centers. The precision he adopts in studying the relationship between the abstract geometries that aided in determining these forms, as well as the actual church spaces themselves, allows Evans to articulate another way of engaging with the study of material history. In "Perturbed Circles," he deliberately looks for what the actual works reveal about the capacities of creative and material practice rather than relying on the ideas that we ascribe to them. Even though this uncovers an ambivalent relationship between symbolism and actual material practice, this clarification contributes to a history of designing. Evans offers us a design history that does as much to stimulate and illuminate creative practice as it does to expand our knowledge of precedent.

In "Translations From Drawing to Building," Evans expounds on another compelling geometric practice, which was applied in the Royal Chapel at Anet by Philibert del'Orme. Studying patterns carved into the dome, Evans manages to reveal the actual geometric ingenuity employed by del'Orme in this design. Interestingly, "all drawings made of the chapel, from the sixteenth to the late nineteenth century are manifestly incorrect."[16] Compounding this error is the misleading description of the techniques employed to define the geometry of the pattern in del'Orme's own writings.

16. Evans R. (1997). Ibidem p. 175.

17. Evans R. (1997). Ibidem p. 180.

Evans reveals an ingenious geometric strategy that explicates the final form of the dome tracery. Rather than determining these patterns metrically, the actual techniques used exploit orthographic projection. The net-like patterns are also a consequence of arraying regular circles around another center at the circles' edge. In Evans' words, Philibert del'Orme's geometric play at the chapel offers "architectural drawing in a new mode, more abstract in appearance, more penetrating in effect, capable of a more unsettling, less predictable interaction with the conventional inventory of forms...suggestive of a perverse epistemology in which ideas are not put in things by art, but released from them."[17]

To make "things talk," an immersion in assessing geometry and its relationship to stewarding the movement of design intent to materialization would profit from greater attentiveness to geometries are actually applied in practice. What else may we learn from things beyond being able to surmise "an object's date and location of origin, method of manufacture, artistic

06_Château_d'Anet, France_
Author: Binche

style" as well as its "original purpose and function"? If objects are "imbued with meaning and can be read much like a text,"[18] these investigations do not need to focus on culturally ascribed meanings or symbolism; rather, they can be deliberations on how designers have come to define the specific material qualities and conditions of these artifacts together with their immediate and tangible effects.

By sidestepping the academic historicization of geometry and form either as symbolic meaning or through its contextualization within wider stylistic categories, we can focus on the operative use of geometry. This gives us access to the creative process in a more immediate fashion. As illustrated by Evans' description of the Royal Chapel at D'Anet,[19] it also obviates what are sometimes misleading "declarations of original intentions." A detailed analysis of the many inventive ways in which a designer may approach the generation and communication of design intent can help to uncover evidence of their formal preoccupations, material sensibilities and embedded know-how in the material outcome itself. Such an analysis also opens up the possibility of "reframing our view" and uncovering other lessons and opportunities from "what exists." Much of the tacit knowledge deployed in the practical act of designing and describing a design is likely to be embodied in the conversation between the material "thing" and how it arrived at this state via drawing.

18. Jamieson, A. (June, 2017). Ibidem.

19. Evans R. (1997). Ibidem

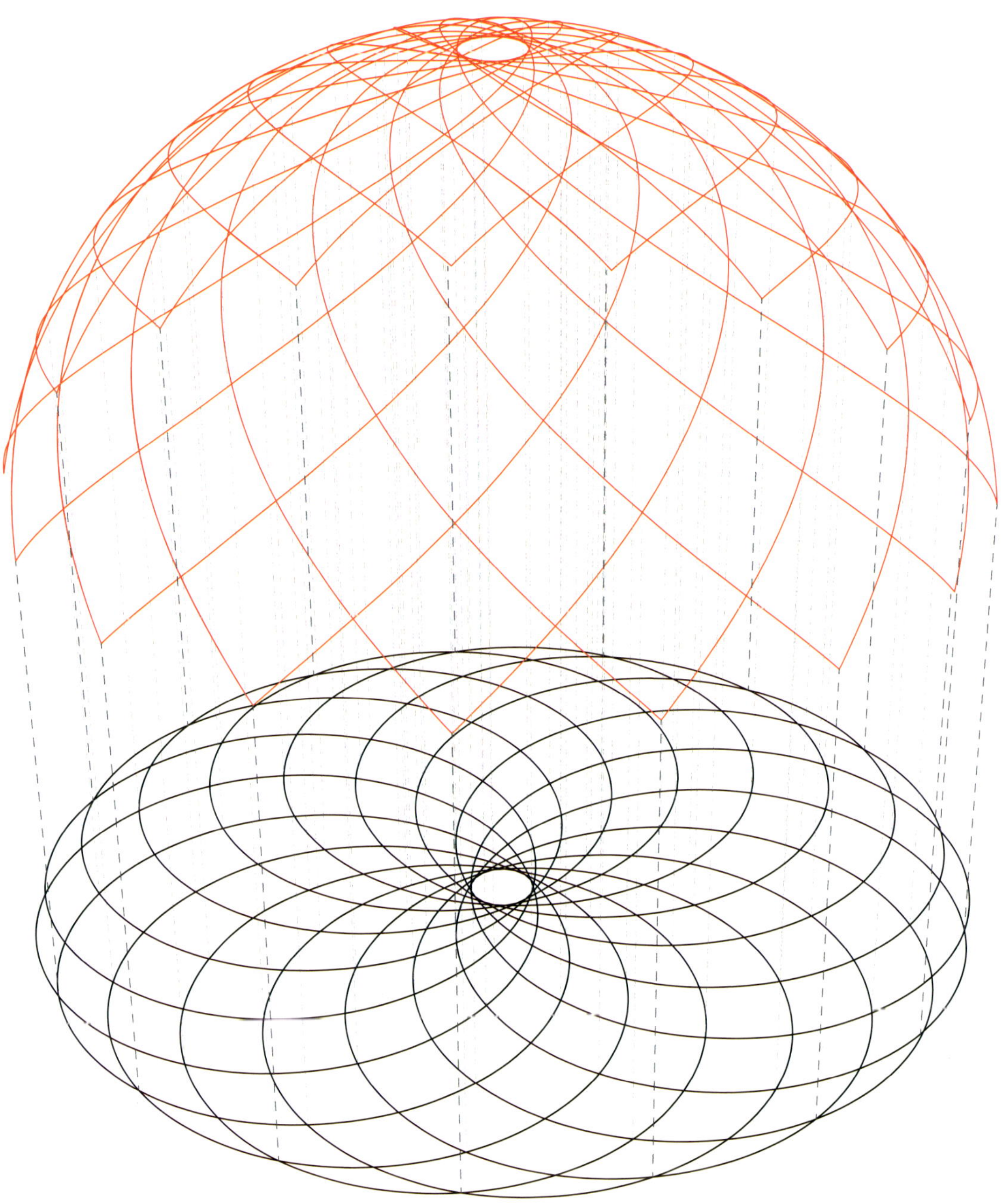

07_Diagram of Chapel at Anet projection as per Robin Evans' description_ drawn by asensio-mah (assisted by Candela de Bortoli)

A number of illustrative cases are reflected on here to better articulate the specific ways in which this relationship between drawing, matter and materialization has the capacity to provide another model for studying history and applying it into contemporary creative practice. In many ways, the model proposed here is a deep dive into the history of designing, rather than a design history.

A practiced geometry

How do we study history through an engagement with geometry? An engagement with geometry—particularly practical, technical and descriptive geometry—signals that the focus is on the precise ways in which designers define and discipline their ideas for translation to building. Following on from this principle, it is crucial that the preoccupations and demands associated with this process of transposition help inform our engagement with geometry.

Enric Miralles and Eva Prats' visual essay, "How to Lay Out a Croissant,"[20] offers a potent illustration of a geometric approach that may help illuminate this model of inquiry. In this exercise, there is a rendering of technical drawing and descriptive geometry as having a dual role. The exercise involves discretizing the complex formal qualities of material realities into manageable and repeatable operations on one hand, while also being a means to better advance and articulate design sensibilities on the other.

20. Miralles, E. & Prats, E. (2002). How to lay out a croissant. In Enric Miralles 1983-2000. El Escorial: *El Croquis*, pp. 192–193.

Miralles and Prats' croissant is drawn with their own unmistakable sensibilities. But its strategic use of geometry as a composite grouping of regular figures also resonates with the dominant manufacturing constraints contemporary to the time of writing of the essay. This manner of discretizing the overall form into an assembly of smaller geometric figures is a graphic codification of how a croissant form may be described and re-described.

Constructing forms, organizations and spaces at architectural or landscape scales generally involves a strategy for discretization. Buildings and constructed landscapes are largely constructed from an assembly of components, many still made from standardized elements. Assembling parts into larger wholes or, conversely, the subdivision of totalities, still remains a fundamental aspect of the design and delivery process. Design itself is often described as a process of organizing the different elements of a project into larger assemblies. An understanding of discretization is fundamental to this process of constructing part-to-whole relationships.

Composite geometries like Miralles and Prats' croissant drawings are a reliable way for both generating and re-describing material forms. The conversion of this composite geometric approach into digital associative models gives us the added capacity for explicitly coding these forms. It also provides an important resource in the specific design archaeology and history topic covered in this book.

Adopting associative models of composite geometries addresses the conventional research and technical expectations for repeatability while also allowing for a coherent management of the complex form description process. An associative model, particularly one that can also be described in a coded form (whether it be through conventional or visual programming), offers a very direct and explicit format for retaining and visualizing the protocol used to arrive at a particular form. This reverberates with a vital overlap between design process and important concepts of computation. Christopher Alexander's Notes on the Synthesis of Form[21] offers a compelling description of how complex design problems may be resolved through the discretization of challenges into smaller yet interrelated steps. His described process is a modularization of larger design challenges into smaller interconnected explorations. This discretization of complex problems became an important reference in the definition of object-oriented programming and is a rare instance in which ruminations on the design process have contributed so critically to computer science. The codification of a design process leading to the definition of a design artifact can be seen as the modularization of geometric operations into manageable and repeatable steps.

21. Alexander C. (1964). *Notes on the Synthesis of Form*. Cambridge: Harvard University Press.

Formatting the geometric code of these precedents as associative models also provides the framework for extending this embedded design knowledge into contemporary design practice through its seamless link to parametric or associative design approaches. This scope for interaction between analysis and speculation enables the rapid generation of new instantiations of an underlying-precedent organizational scheme. These iterative transformations, while reliant on the variability of the geometric associations of the model, can also be guided by different parameters and, conversely, evaluated according to an array of criteria. These triggers or drivers span between aesthetic judgment to quantifiable performance indicators.

A seamless movement between analysis, design and simulation is also supported by the way that the model is defined. Although this modeling process offers a tangible and immersed view into the organizational, spatial and formal priorities of the designer, it is also the construction of the model which allows for evaluating or constructing digital simulations and analysis that reframe or open up another view or dimension of the design for consideration.

Digital simulations and evaluations exploit the capacity for rapid calculation in computation, allowing for large discretized samples of calculation points to offer readings of wider, often continuous patterns in their aggregation.

Fluid dynamics, structural analysis, and lighting and solar studies are just a few conventional simulations offering a view of dynamic phenomena that influence our experiences of the material world. It is important to acknowledge the operational need for discretization or partitioning that is shared across these quite different practices. Each leverages the possibility of approaching intricacy or complexity through the calculated organization of the way our material world is framed and how its different parts and dimensions are managed.

This research covered by this book outlines the use of associative modeling as a key partner in the study of material artifacts from design history. This approach offers a way to document the material history of design archetypes by deciphering the concrete ways in which these forms have been—or can be—explained in a technical, graphic format. However, this is done to capture a wider scope of knowledge beyond constructing a digital archive. In contrast to techniques that can more directly capture a faithful recording of the literal physical fabric of artifacts, such as through three-dimensional scanning, this model of study is invested in design exploration that both reflects on how precedents may be objectively described and, more importantly, helps to articulate how they may be conceived. The aim is not simply an ostensibly objective history, but rather a contextualization of these forms from history within the practices and processes that facilitate their genesis.

Models and the multiverse

This book aims to elaborate on a process for linking design history and practice through a shared operative and technical medium. Although the research is anchored in a rigorous engagement with the geometric description of the material world, the resulting codified format of the associative model also becomes the medium through which new actors may engage with an inherited material legacy and take it into new streams of exploration.

We may take some reference from the notion of design models that have been elaborated by Bruno Latour and Albena Yaneva[22] that seek to place the process and outcomes of design practice within a "multiverse." "Only by generating earthly accounts of buildings and design processes, tracing pluralities of concrete entities in the specific spaces and times of their co-existence, instead of referring to abstract theoretical frameworks outside architecture, will architectural theory become a relevant field for architects, for end users, for promoters, and for builders." Latour and Yaneva see the disciplinary focus on drawing as an impoverished and overly objectified view of design. For them, "architectural anthropology" would need to cast a wider net to capture all the different mediums and non-human actors that form this larger creative network. For Latour, drawing and descriptive geometry describe design as static objects and suspend them in Euclidean space.

22. Latour B. & Yaneva A. (2008) Give me a gun and I will make all buildings move: An ANT's view of architecture. In Geiser, R. & Yaneva A. (ed.). *Explorations in Architecture: Teaching, Design, Research.* (pp. 80–89). Basel: Birkhäuser.

This expanded view of design beyond the Euclidean involves the larger recursive process of iteration and feedback between different constraints being imposed on the design, as well as a larger conversation between drawings, diagrams, models, prototyping and the ongoing life of the buildings and all the other actors that the design process interacts with to constitute a wider environment and network.

To conduct this research, there still must be a central space for drawing and descriptive geometry, for it remains the technology and medium that has long helped designers establish a proficiency for generating and communicating space, organization and form. To exclude it would be to remove one of the key actors in this wider network of design history and practice. However, it is crucial to re-situate these geometric objects into a wider multiverse—something closer to the associative models that can iteratively index a multitude of considerations and be thrown into conversations with simulated environments.

For Yaneva, models act as the material surrogates for the design process, where the model forms are "shaped by constraints, expectations, demands, attitudes and other sorts of concerns."[23] In their aggregate, an array of models registering different dimensions and concerns of the building offer a more expanded view of the "multiverse" that the building participates in. In effect, "...the model houses not only different elements but also the discussion for their definition and characterization."[24] This is a capacity that is becoming increasingly possible with digital associative models. The ease with which analysis and simulation can be coupled with rapid iteration facilitates the transformation of geometric objects into multi-dimensional "things." Extending these dimensions of consideration even further, the addition of digital manufacturing tools to the existing array of fabrication methods enables what is widely known as "rapid prototyping." Materializing design prototypes in the course of design and inquiry offers yet another view and dimension into the network of design history and practice. Prototyping invites us to share even more closely in the original authors' experiences and actions along the extended design path from ideas to materialization. Gaining an understanding of the imposition of manufacturing, material and logistical constraints on the materialized design is an invaluable feedback mechanism that deepens learning as well as design know-how. Exploring other possible approaches for actualizing these designs in more efficient, intelligent, sustainable and compelling ways of making—or in other materials—is another valuable branch of exploration that promises to expand the possibilities for upgrading these systems.

23. Yaneva A. (2005). A building is a multiverse. In Latour B. & Weibel P. (E ds.), *Making Things Public: Atmospheres of Democracy* (p. 530). Cambridge: The MIT Press.

24. Yaneva A. (2005) Ibidem, p. 531.

Beyond simply characterizing an authorial signature or style, geometry has often been used as an instrument that helps to resolve material and construction challenges. The Miralles and Prats croissant embeds a great deal of construction know-how in the geometric approach outlined in their essay.[25] Economizing the construction of complex forms can often be done through a geometric disciplining of the surfaces.[26]

25. See essay: The Associative Croissant.

26. See essay: The Sphere and The Vectorial Grid.

Digital fabrication techniques are also strongly tied to geometric description. One of the early precursors to the CNC mill was the relief pantograph machine developed by Karl Wenschow. The translation of topographic data from contour lines into a three-dimensional relief model was achieved through the pairing of a small drill on one side of a frame to a nib on the other end. By tracing the contour lines with the nib, the path of the drill on the pantograph would carve a corresponding geometric path into the model. Today, CNC milling machines are also controlled by toolpaths that are defined geometrically before being translated into machine code. In the pantograph and the contemporary mill, the overall form intended for fabrication is discretized into geometric toolpaths.

Other fabrication technologies, such as additive 3D printing or robotic arms, are also determined by geometrically re-describing an intended form in a manner that corresponds with the movements of the associated machines. In effect, the physical operations required for the machine to produce a form are translated into composites of geometric figures. At this late phase of the design materialization process, the geometric description of form remains an important consideration—perhaps even more so than in the earlier schematic phases. An immersion in these modes of description associated with making affords us yet another dimension through which we may view and re-view design artifacts.

Engaging geometric description, associative modeling and simulations together with prototyping offers a multi-faceted focus for—and a detailed view of—the design process. In other words, these different lenses used to look at things from the past offer a wider view on design history. They also offer an enrichment of current and future creative practice. The work presented in this book seeks to make design history available as things capable of making new connections in the world, rather than as rarefied historical objects. In this way, the knowledge embedded in these models transforms an artifact or object into an active model, affording us a way to imagine and bring to light many other possible realities. The geometric descriptions, models, simulations and prototypes all reopen the design code of an embedded design and material intelligence to transformation and experimentation. Through this opening-up, there exists the possibility to migrate these existing systems to other functionalities or into new environments. In that sense, these techniques expose these design codes to a "multiverse" and an expansion in the ways in which these artifacts from history may be reimagined. It grants a renewed significance to systems that were once seen as closed and exhausted.

Things as they are and things as they ought to be

The research focus in this book is part of a larger project that has been sustained over several years across academic inquiry, teaching and design practice. Our efforts to highlight methods that illuminate an understanding of precedent and its latent practical applicability have been advanced through a simultaneous engagement with history together with creative practice. It has also benefited from a diffusion within different streams and contexts. Resonating with Latour's proposition of a need to open up design and its material outcomes to a multiverse, this research has benefitted from immersion in different capacities and fields of action.

This book outlines the processes, outcomes and conclusions that emerged from two key projects in this larger network of action. Through graduate design courses taught by the book's authors from 2010 to 2017, a large collection of design work and research has been built that provides a robust sampling of projects that can be evaluated individually or in the aggregate. These courses were shaped by a desire to bridge contemporary and historical design practice as well as research. This sustained activity has yielded a collection of methods, techniques and novel outcomes grounded in history—yet openly speculative in outlook. It is hoped that these outcomes will contribute towards the definition of an evolving body of knowledge and a common exploratory framework for histories of design, as well as an evolution of our own capacities as design practitioners.

Systems Upgrade also extensively illustrates several important phases of a design research project that was directed by the authors to provide a detailed view of how the bridge between analysis and creative practice may be achieved. An in-depth demonstration of techniques as well as design and analytical approaches using the Austrian American sculptor Erwin Hauer's mid century designs as a case study to provide information and relevance to readers interested in design research and teaching. While we have been mindful about offering as precise interpretation and re-description of these works as possible, we fully acknowledge that these are interpretations and do not claim to be Hauer's and Rosado's actual processes. This book is intended as an opportunity for readers to be immersed in a detailed description of one of the most exceptional design and artistic oeuvres in recent history while also gaining an insight into the ways in which this interpretation and transformation may serve as the springboard toward future creative practice. It is a bridge between explaining "things as they are" and working towards "things as they ought to be."[27]

27. Simon, H. A. (1969). *The Sciences of the Artificial* (1st ed.). Cambridge: MIT Press.

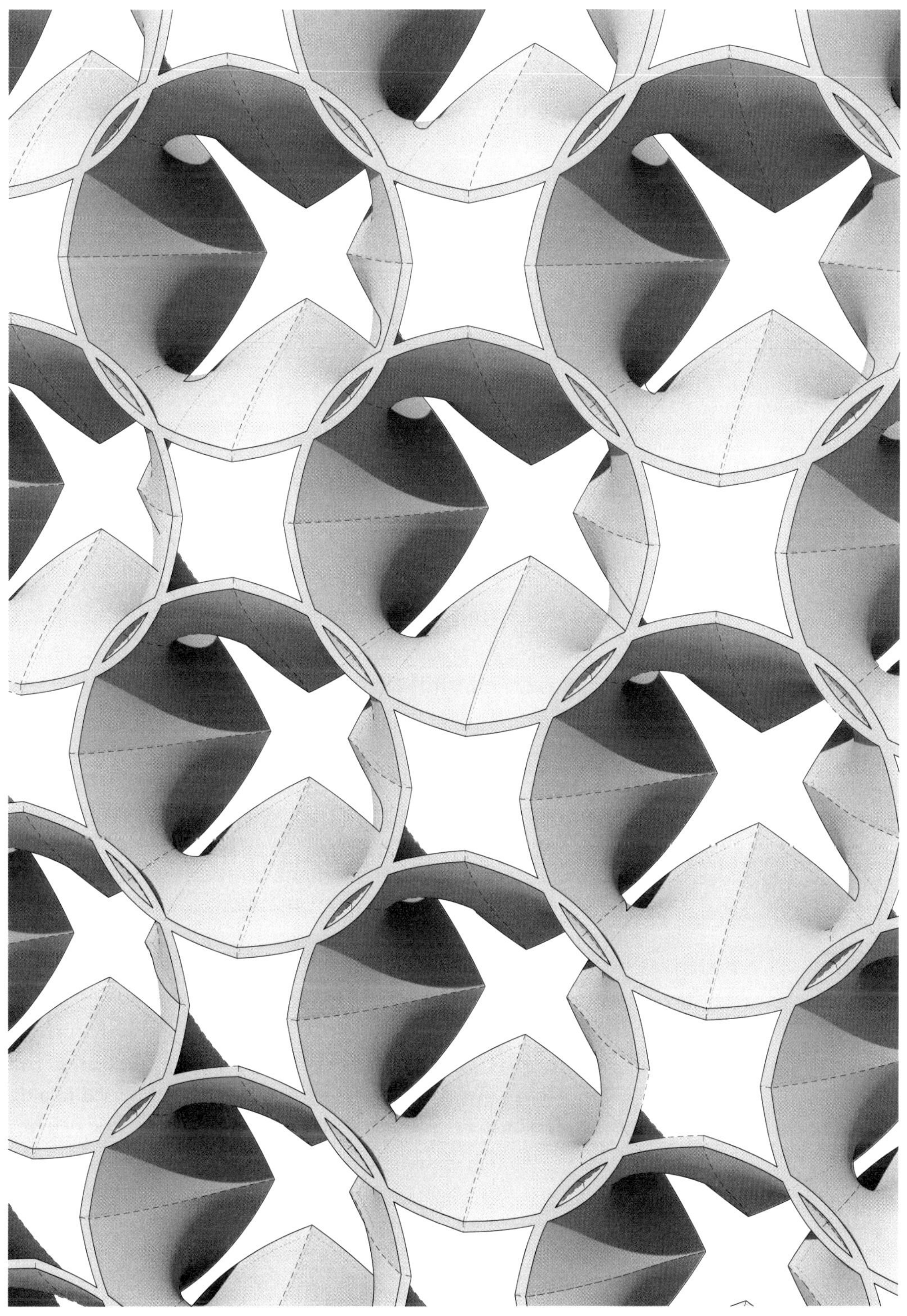

08_New Module 4.2_Enneper + Tetrahedron_perspective view

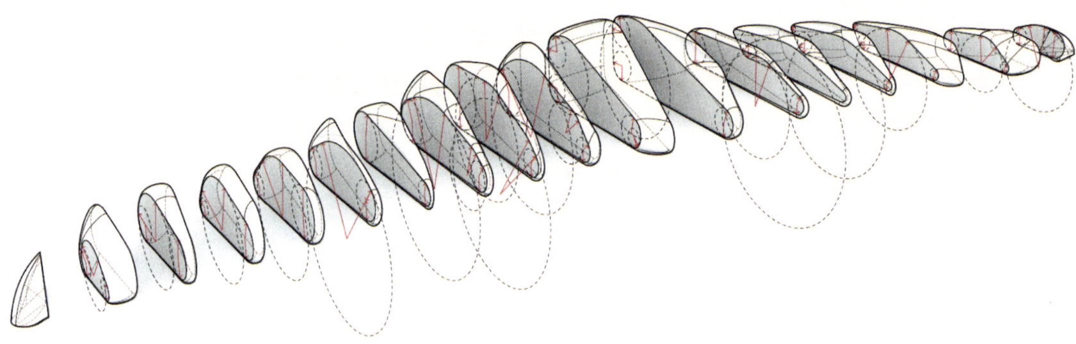

09_Segments of a croissant by asensio-mah

An associative croissant

A notable exercise in leveraging descriptive geometry to describe irregular forms is the visual essay "How To Lay Out a Croissant" by Enric Miralles and Eva Prats. The exercise is a deceptively modest one, due its association with a familiar everyday object. However, the complexity of the croissant form is revealed through the intricate assemblage of complex geometries deployed by Miralles and Prats. Composites of regular arcs, tangential lines and triangular control geometries are arranged in a manner that approximates the pastry's profile, in plan and sequential sections cut throughout specific parts of the croissant.

Interestingly, the sensibilities and techniques used to tame complex formal projects, such as the pergolas on the Avenida Icaria in Barcelona, Spain, are hinted at in these descriptive drawings of the croissant. Through these drawings we also catch a glimpse of the operational approaches, design sensibilities, and culture cultivated by Miralles and his various collaborators through this revealing account of how they approach the description and generation of material objects. In fact, this essay reveals considerably more about how these architects approach and generate design than it does about anything to do with the actual nature of croissants. Many of the construction and fabrication practices contemporary to this essay are accounted for in the strict adherence to composites and segments of regular geometries. This geometric description process was required by the methods related to bending steel and the necessary segmentation of complex forms with regular construction elements prevalent at the time.

Furthermore, a designer's work is mediated by geometry, whereas pastry chefs work directly with matter. The geometries deployed in these drawings resonate much more with building and construction constraints than the acts of folding and rolling the pliable ingredients associated with baking.

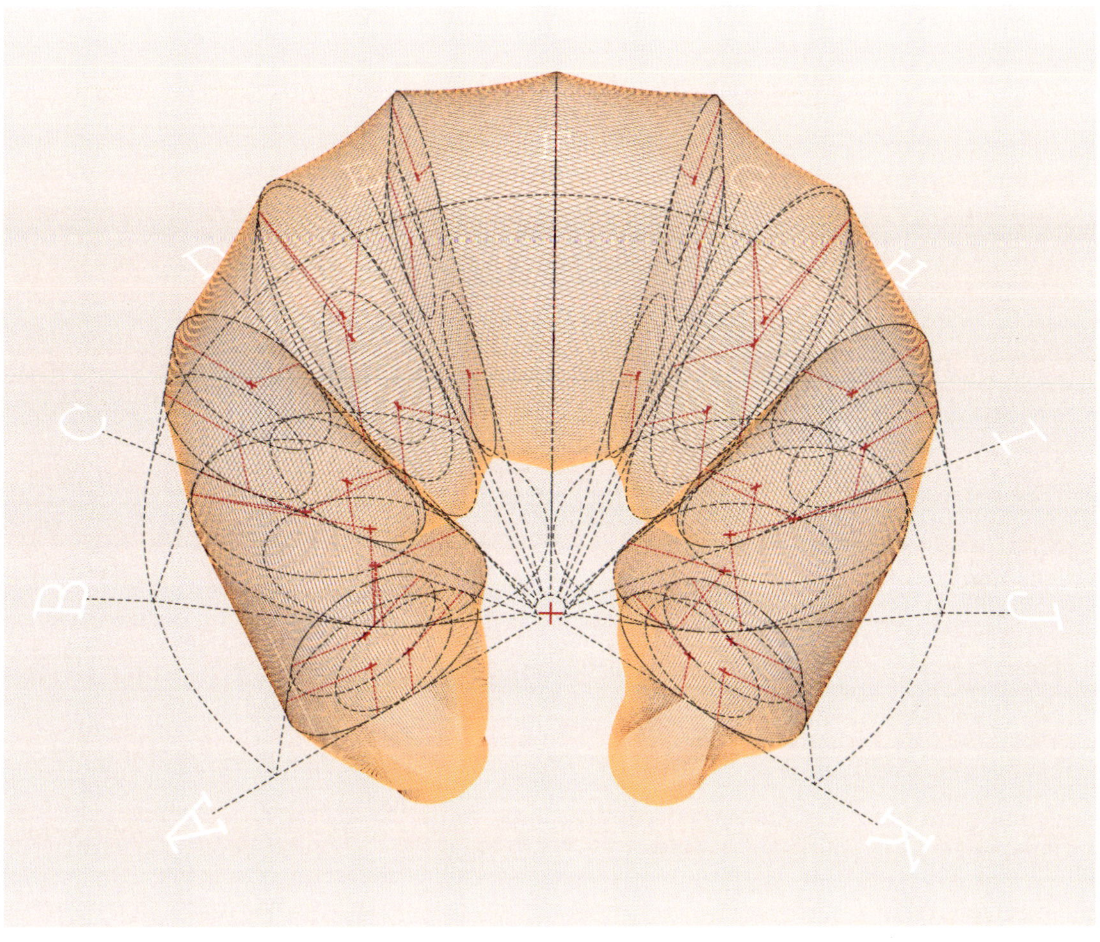

10_Associative model of a croissant by asensio-mah

A differentiable associative model of a croissant is an exercise that we have developed as an introduction to graduate representation courses. Extending the careful arrangement of regular geometries via Miralles and Prats' masterful use of descriptive geometry into an associative three-dimensional model, the exercise offers both a system of description as well as a generative mechanism. The exercise adopts the careful discretization of complexity into manageable regular geometries and nests them within a hierarchy of relationships in a consistent three-dimensional arrangement. Although these geometries are coordinated into an assembly that approximates the form of a croissant, the associations across the different scales of the model permit the retention of a consistent global relationship while also allowing for variability across different scales of the model.
Modifications in variables at local scales may influence an associated transformation at higher order levels in the model, while differences in large-scale configurations are achievable without compromising connections lower down the hierarchy. The associative croissant leverages the accessible complexification of formal description offered by three-dimensional and relational modeling while also providing a clear continuity with the descriptive rigor revealed by Miralles and Prats. The croissant illuminates the relationship between the shared exploitation of geometry for design and representational purposes by reconsidering an inspiring exercise in translating something that is existing into a "vectorial" model that can generate many possible croissants.

The sphere and the vectorial grid

The practical delivery and documentation phases of design can be highly illuminating and crucial creative moments. These seemingly mundane aspects of creative practice can also be instrumental in generating new design cultures. The typical overinvestment in theory, philosophy or academic historization obfuscates the ability to recognize the cultivation of exemplary creative practice from the simple pragmatics of technical practice.

Two architectural projects completed twenty-nine years apart, the Sydney Opera House by Jorn Utzon and Yokohama International Port Terminal by Foreign Office Architects, highlight two different approaches in the strategic use of technical geometry for describing and resolving built form and material organization.

What is significant about these examples is the subsequent transformative influence that the delivery processes undertaken for these buildings would have over their respective architects' modes of working. The inventive design techniques devised to resolve challenging practical aspects of these projects are significant for the ways in which they helped to evolve the focus of each author's creative practice.

It could be argued that, rather than being able to neatly attribute these projects to larger stylistic or theoretical categories, the resourcefulness employed to materialize them helped to identify other design ideas and concerns that generated their own design cultures and sensibilities. Neither project remained completely faithful nor followed a logical path towards realizing the forms suggested in the earlier, more schematic phases of the project.
The project at Yokohama, particularly in its early design phases, could easily be associated with the fashionable interest in "single-surface" organizations of the time. Single-surface organizations came into focus in architectural practice and academia during the late 1990s and stimulated considerable attention from theorists, educators and practitioners. Practices such as the Office for Metropolitan Architecture spearheaded a revitalized focus on these fluid or formless spatial organizations through a number of highly circulated projects. Coinciding with a widespread uptake of digital tools in the design world, the single-surface fad catalyzed an arms-race aimed at building works that could exemplify this larger design exploration into seamless architectural organizations approximating a more landscape-like modality of spatial articulation.

Jorn Utzon's 1956 Sydney Opera House competition entry suggested heroic forms reminiscent of the innovative thin-shell concrete structural constructions of Eero Saarinen and Heinz Isler. The free form promised in the early design phases pointed towards the adoption of in-situ concrete construction associated with these antecedents. Utzon's initial ambitions for the project were likely to have been highly informed by Saarinen's works, compounded by the fact that Saarinen himself was also on the jury for the architectural competition. Despite the divergent methods of its final realization, Utzon's competition submission was likely to have been associated with the innovative thin-shell and structurally expressive research of the time.

In both cases, these earlier associations and the seemingly self-evident path towards realization swerved into very different paths during the practical delivery of the buildings. Both deviations were triggered by the ingenuity that came with the practical application of geometry to resolve construction challenges.

The development of what is known as Utzon's spherical solution for the Sydney Opera House shells was instrumental in articulating a relationship between complexity and standardization that would go on to be a major theme in his ensuing work. This solution was a geometric technique devised for resolving the main shells of the Sydney Opera House. It would initiate both the resolution of the complex problem of constructing the shells of the design as well as a more focused line of design exploration in his office.

During the delivery process for the building, a discussion between the architect, Utzon, and Ove Arup's engineering team highlighted a tension between achieving a complex form on one hand while having the pressure of constraining its components to standardized and repeated elements on the other. Utzon's spherical solution, developed with Spanish architect Rafael Moneo as an assistant, involved the segmentation of a sphere into different-sized shells that approximated the earlier forms of the design. Through this segmentation of a sphere, the team was able to generate different-sized shells for the project while also ensuring that all the curvatures were standardized, allowing for regularizing the structural ribs as well as tiling the shells.

In effect, the project development involved the rationalization of a form to fit the industrial logic of standard repetition. In this case, a larger regular geometric object is subdivided into discrete elements of varying sizes. This process of subdividing, or moving from a global reference geometry down into smaller constituent parts, maintains a shared constant single curvature,

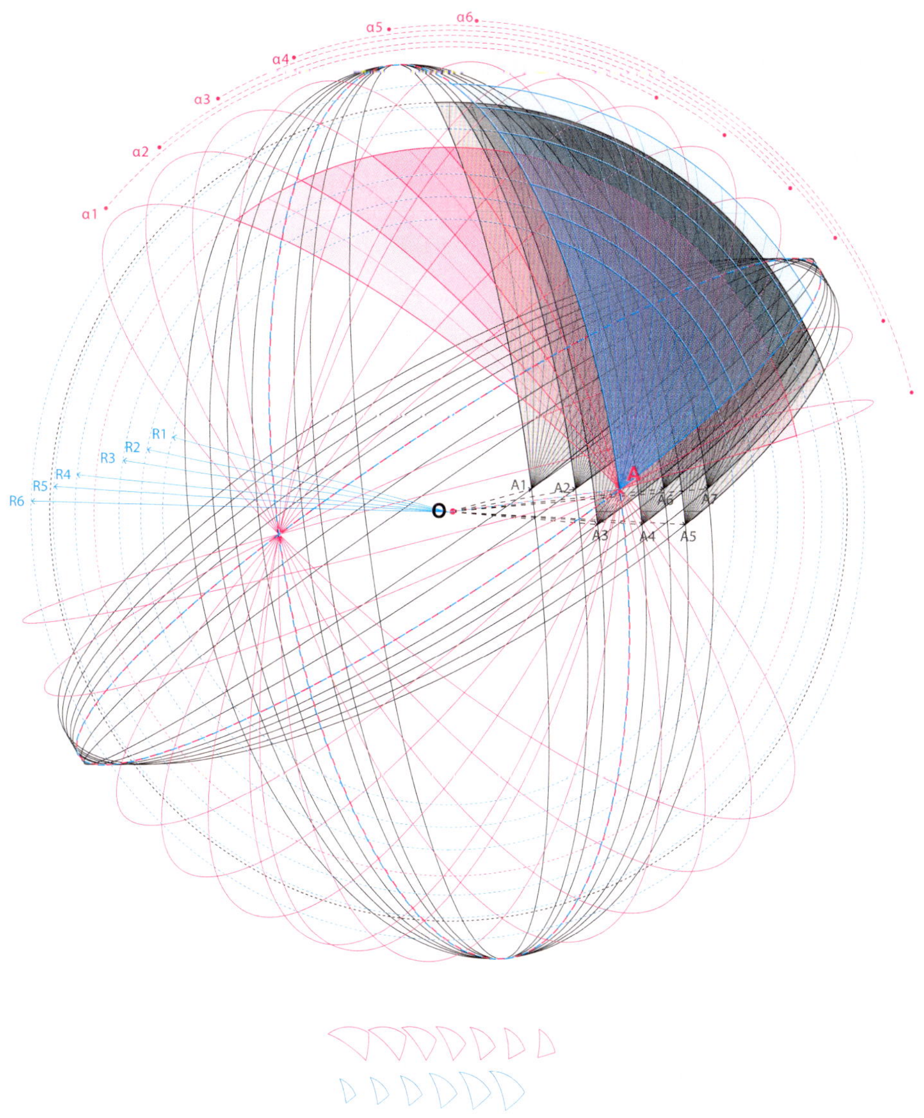

11_In pink: iterations of different opening angles. In light blue: iterations of different cutting radii. In black: iterations of different decentered points. Utzon's Great Circles associative model by asensio-mah (assisted by Xun Liu).

regardless of size. The possibility of subdivision allows for flexibility in determining the sizes of the shells, but in many ways, each consequent shell would simply be segment variations in partitioning the same identical geometry. Incidentally, testing the shells' performance was one of the earliest uses of computers in studying structural forces to inform design.

The Sydney Opera House was Utzon's most focused and greatest foray into standard prefabrication and design research into organizing larger complex architectural wholes from the clever arrangement of identical (or near-identical) parts. This would define much of his later production. Utzon's design research and practice could be seen to shift from its association with the works of Saarinen, Candela and Nervi towards taming heroic Modern forms for prefabrication and industrial production.

For Utzon, the possibility of variation, flexibility and adaptability through the arrangement of standard components compelled his sustained interest in an architectural practice that would more closely resonate with the capacity for growth and transformation seen in some vernacular practices and natural systems. His subsequent investment in prefabrication and additive architecture was informed by the prevalence of industrial production at the time, where standardization was a mandate, but was also informed by his familiarity with older Chinese building traditions.

During the development of the construction systems for FOA's Yokohama International Port Terminal, there was also a noticeable shift in the way in which the structural system would be geometrically described and, consequently, how it would be constructed. In many ways, the Japanese infrastructure project is similar to the Australian example, in that the initial forms suggested by the competition-winning scheme was transformed considerably under the pressures of delivery.

The terminal's single-surface, landform-like organization suggested a more topographic and topological approach towards its material resolution. At the early phases of design development, the design team explored the possibility of a non-hierarchical structural system wherein a single structural module or material operation would be repeated and locally differentiated to formulate the whole structure. Differentiated spaceframes and corrugated structural modules were explored as early solutions, and this approach seemed to resonate more explicitly with the topological surfaces of the competition project.

The ensuing pivot to alternative solutions was an operative transition from "raster space to a vectorial space" for determining the construction as well as spatial logic for the design resolution. The initial strategies of controlling the surface geometry through sequential parallel sections or a superimposed conventional structural grid still depended on a global coordinate system to organize the material components. This would make way for a "topological grid" at the later stages of resolution.

Emerging out of pragmatic concerns related to facilitating and managing the delivery of a highly differentiated structural and landscape system, the geometric techniques were redirected away from "a geometry that is fundamentally Cartesian, referenced to an orthogonal axial system...to the topological grid...more referred to the moment in which pieces are joined, becoming more locally referenced." Resonating with rollercoaster construction, FOA's exploration in consistent differentiation is informed by the pragmatic resolution of technical conflicts.

The building's final resolution involved the introduction of a quasi-symmetrical organization in plan and the discretization of the structure between two longitudinal girders and a folded steel roof section spanning in between. The resolution of the folded, origami-like roof and the girder structures highlights the trajectory from raster to vectorial. Despite this swing towards a seemingly conventional compositional approach, the local differentiations of these systems would offer a more explicitly pragmatic use of topology. In the case of the folded structure, the practical push towards standardizing the joints (keeping all connections between the folded plate and girders perpendicular) while allowing an easier installation of the differentiated folded trusses, results in a highly localized and relational system for organizing the structural and material resolution. The girders more closely follow the logic of rollercoaster construction, where sections are rolled along a trajectory. This was undertaken to limit the surfaces of the girders to flat or developable panels, thereby rationalizing and economizing the construction of the project.

It is clear that a line of creative research evolved out of this experience, and that a sustained and deep engagement with material practice emerged. As the terminal's architects reflected, "these kinds of discoveries are the ones that can turn processes of a purely technical nature back toward an architectural discourse based on material agency."

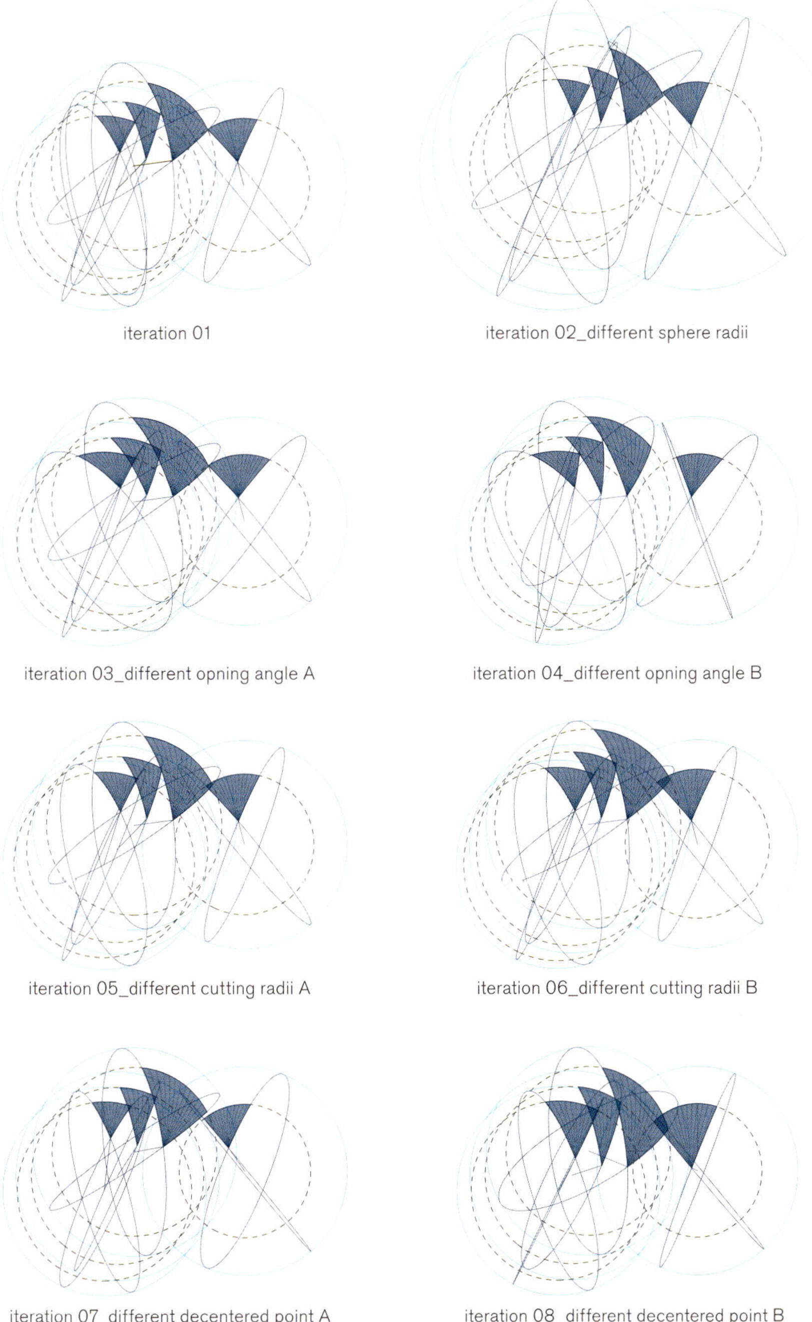

12_Iterations of shells generated by Utzon's Great Circles associative model by asensio-mah (assisted by Xun Liu)

13_Echinocereus engelmannii_ drawn by Benoit, M.

The geometry of the glass flowers

Over a period of five decades, Germans Leopold and Rudolf Blaschka created the Glass Flowers for Harvard University's Museum of Natural History. This vast collection of more than 4,000 glass models of over 830 plant species was originally commissioned by George Lincoln Goodale in 1887 for use as didactic instruments. These flower replicas were conceived of as scientific models for the purpose of botanical instruction, offering a tangible representation of the morphology and appearance of flora species that would otherwise have been challenging to preserve or cultivate in the New England context.

The Blaschkas painstakingly replicated the forms and colors of a vast array of plant species in glass, meticulously and expertly deploying common glassmaking techniques such as lampworking. Despite its fragile or brittle associations, glass was seen as a more long-lasting material than wax, which at the time was another material commonly used for similar projects.

The undeniable difficulty in replicating these natural forms within such a challenging and rigorous medium has afforded the flowers their distinction as exemplary material artifacts. For reasons described by Lorraine Daston, the Glass Flowers' value as teaching instruments diminished over time and their consequent prestige as artifices of exceptional craft came to supplant their original scientific function. Interestingly, the exceptionally faithful reproduction of authentic plant specimens that provides the wonder associated with these objects was also among the reasons for their diminished status as scientific instruments. The propensity for scientists to value a more structural study of plants resulted in the privileging of the principles of plant morphology rather than the idiosyncrasies of any individual plant specimen. What became valued was the communication of overall consistency in the structuring of species morphologies. However, despite this shift in scientific focus, the Glass Flowers continue to astound as archetypes of representational prowess, allowing them to retain their importance within the museum's collection and within a wider public imagination.

When considering the value of the Glass Flowers as exercises in representation or as craft, it is

14_Echinocereus engelmannii_ drawn by Benoit, M.

important to recognize that the working process followed by the Blaschkas was carried out through an autographic material practice.

However, if such an exercise were reconsidered within the context of approaches typically adopted by architects and designers, the translation of these natural forms into another material assembly would typically involve a mediating notational process, which would in turn involve translating the actual material form of these specimens into visual or graphic information requiring different degrees of abstraction. Rather than willfully shaping matter into form, there is a need to strategize how geometry and graphic conventions may be carefully arranged and deployed in combination to approximate specific forms.

An exercise based on the geometric three-dimensional modeling of flowers from the Blaschka collection was part of a course on representation offered to first-year students within the graduate landscape architecture professional program at Harvard. In this exercise, established by the book's authors, students recorded artifacts from the Glass Flowers collection in photographs or sketches and subsequently translated these visual observations into a fully composed three-dimensional model. The exercise was explicitly limited to the use of composites of regular geometries.

A key aim of the exercise was the development of strategies for breaking down the natural flowing forms characteristic of the flowers into manageable subdivisions that can be described with simple geometric elements. Geometric transformations such as moving, rotating, mirroring and arraying these elements were explored. These young designers were challenged to achieve the complexity offered "for free" by spline curves through a more considered approach of assembling a geometric composition. A series of associations and relationships between these elements needed to be carefully cultivated in order to approximate or describe the flowers.

BIBLIOGRAPHY

1- Daston.L.(ed), (2004), *Things that Talk: Object Lessoons from Art and Science*, Zone Books
2- Mikami.Y., (2001), *Utzon's Sphere. Sydney Opera House, How it was designed and built*, Shokokusha
3- Miralles.E. & Prats.E. "Como acotar un croissant", in *El Croquis 49-50*, 1991
4- Zaera Polo.A. & Moussavi.F.(2002), *The Yokohama Project*, Actar

Proto-typical

May 21, 1963 E. F. HAUER **3,090,163**

LIGHT DIFFUSING WALLS AND THE LIKE

Filed July 15, 1957 2 Sheets-Sheet 1

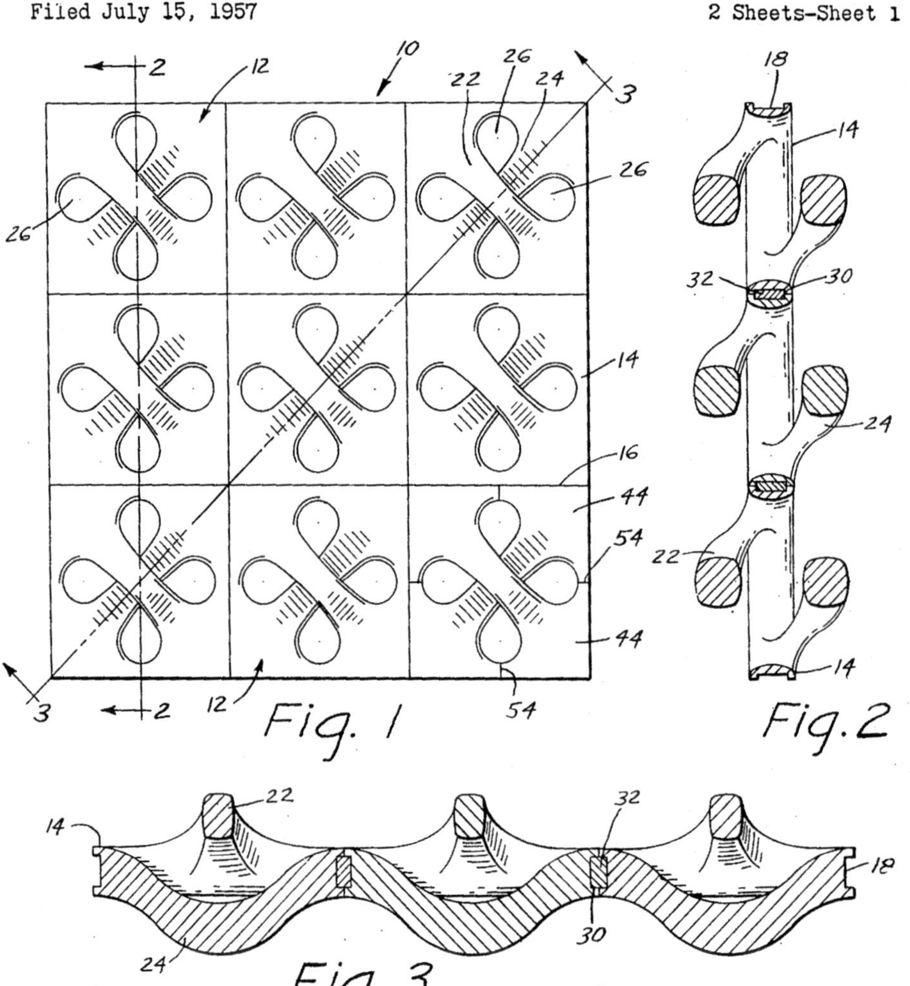

01_Erwin Hauer_Design 1 patent_1963

The discipline and profession of architecture can be seen as principally preoccupied with the singular and exceptional, sponsoring an unbalanced focus on the extraordinary aspects of the built environment. Design systems and prototypes are rarely considered a privileged model of creative practice in architecture. Despite the implications of its allographic practice, where the necessity for transposing design ideas into drawings can be seen to support standardization or replication, the architectural discipline is most celebrated for its one-off masterpieces. Authenticity and excellence in architecture are generally afforded to an architectural work for its status as a remarkable and unique building, rather than for a design aimed at mass implementation or widespread adoption.

Today, architecture has generally emphasized and theorized its capacity for addressing the particular. It has long idealized its capacities to offer specific responses to unique sites, clients and briefs. Much of the discipline's attention is afforded to differentiation, from customized buildings, genius loci ("spirit of place") to the spectacular and iconic. This tendency helps to explain why celebrated architectural systems designed for mass production, such as Buckminster Fuller's Dymaxion houses and Jean Prouve's axial portal frame, are often noted as exceptions in the discipline. This disciplinary neglect of systematic approaches has its foundation in a history of engagement with such ideas that has come to be regarded as a vexed legacy.[1]

1. The reaction against the orthodoxy of Modern architecture was supported by the criticism of its generally lack of contextual sensitivity, the standardization as well as perceived generic nature of its international deployment. Some architectural critics such as Charles Jencks were also critical of its social ambitions and more specifically, its perceived inability to deliver on its aims.

However, there is certainly a considerable body of work on systematic architecture that can be extracted and studied from design history. The generation of a critical mass of design systems focused on addressing larger economies of scale was most extensively supported by Modernist creative practices. Reverberating with the ascendancy of industrialization together with the massive war mobilizations and post-war rebuilding efforts, these endeavors at a systematic recalibration of the material world upended many aspects of architectural practice and culture. The pedagogic models privileged by the discipline were also transformed, introducing a more explicitly technical driver for design and fostering a more explicit engagement with new Modern technological, cultural and artistic sensibilities. The polytechnic model of architectural education in late eighteenth century, stewarded in France by such figures as Jean Louis Nicolas Durand, as well as the pivotal didactic models gestated at the Bauhaus in early-twentieth-century Germany, were instrumental in establishing new pedagogic mandates and methodologies responding to the industrial revolution.

With the maturing of the industrial revolution into its second phase, the advent of mass production emblematized by Fordist production lines, and the emergence of novel construction technologies such as reinforced concrete, it was seen as necessary by some for architectural culture to engage with this zeitgeist. Le Corbusier's manifestos, elevating the engineer as the figure of the times and promulgating a machine sensibility for Modern architecture, remain one of the most symbolic declarations of this transition. Much of Le Corbusier's work was propelled by this polemic; his Citrohan House (1920), Dom-Ino House (1914), the Unité d'Habitation (1957), the Museum of Unlimited Growth (1931), and the Venice hospital (1964) are just a few examples of a prototypical ambition.

Le Corbusier's prototypical objectives would even fuel the elaboration of systems for organizing larger urban transformations; the Cité Frugès in Pessac, a regulated model for industrial housing estates, is one of his earliest realized urban projects.

This favoring of prototypes mirrored the second industrial revolution economies predicated on standardization and invests in the possibility of enacting a wider systemic change in architectural practice and urbanization. Through the conception of architecture or cities as systems, there is the prospect for realizing universality and pervasive applicability. The deliberate reverberation of industrial production in architectural and urban practice can also be contextualized by the scale and velocity of urbanization together with the technological advancement experienced in the West at the time. Particularly in the first half of the twentieth century, the speed of technological and scientific advances enabled by industrialization was further accelerated by the advent of the military–industrial complex. Its vigorous research programs, compelled by what were perceived as existential threats during the world wars, ushered in a series of technological and scientific innovations that would lay the groundwork for what are now being dubbed the third and fourth industrial revolutions.

02_Charles Eames_Laminated Splint patent_1951

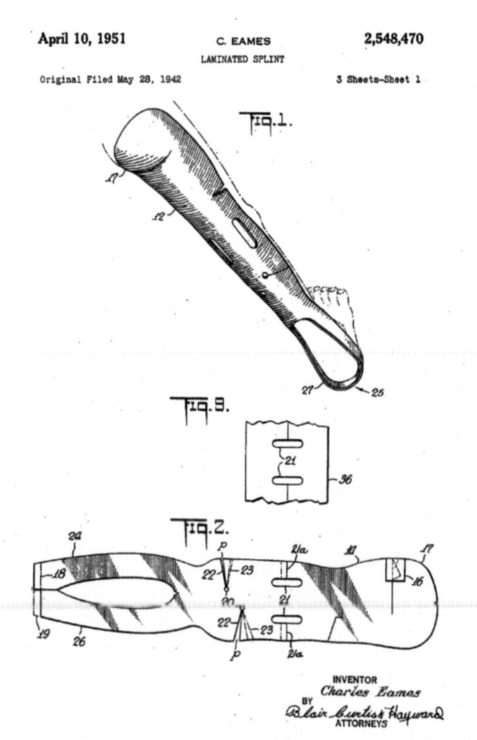

The material-industrial complex

On one hand, this wartime industrialization offered explicitly material opportunities for designers. The material reality of warfare generally drives arms races for material and technological inventions aimed at performing tangible operations with higher degrees of efficiency and precision. Such material innovations adopted by the military–industrial complex during the world wars included the enhancement of plywood manufacturing through the introduction of water-resistant synthetic glues. This industrialization of an ancient material process rendered plywood ubiquitous and was used to build sophisticated battle machinery such as the Mosquito and H-4 Hercules aircraft. Early in their careers, the designers Ray and Charles Eames contributed their skills to the war effort.

This included their design of medical equipment that exploited plywood and other material inventions for active use on the front line. Molded plywood splints for wounded soldiers were early material experiments in their careers that would later be redeployed for some of their most celebrated postwar furniture designs. The Second World War was also the major catalyst for the inventive and extensive applications of plastics, a further material advancement exploited by Ray and Charles Eames to devise some of their mass-produced furniture.

Another wartime material exploration that would ripple through celebrated prototypical design experiments was the application of geodetics or geodesics for structural functions. The geodesic structural system was devised in the 1920s by German engineer Walter Bauersfeld[2] for domed planetarium buildings. Built instantiations of these prototypical structures were first conceived for the German campus of the Zeiss industrial optics company. These structural and media innovations became a source of curiosity and interest for the fledgling Bauhaus community whose founder, Walter Gropius, had direct knowledge of Bauersfeld's domes. His practice partner, Adolf Meyer, was also an architect on the planetarium.

These early experiments were likely sources of inspiration for the patented domes of American futurist Buckminster Fuller. The Bauhaus émigré community in the United States were the likely bridge to these earlier German buildings; Walter Gropius along with Josef and Ani Albers were key members of the leadership at Black Mountain College during Fuller's tenure there. It was during this residency at Black Mountain College that Fuller developed the definitive prototypes for his patented geodesic dome.[3]

Many of Fuller's inventions and designs, including his variants on the geodesic dome, found a supportive client in the US military and benefitted from manufacturing capabilities mobilized for the war effort. His prototypical Dymaxion and Wichita houses, predating his geodesic experiments, were conceived of as mass-produced transportable housing and were prefabricated using the capabilities of aircraft factories. Fuller's Dymaxion House and geodesic domes were considered by the US military for their potential as light and rapidly deployable structures. Subsequent material variations of the geodesic logic using plywood, catenary tensile elements, and fiberglass fabrication yielded structural inventions that can be credited to Fuller, such as the laminar dome, geodesic catenary tent and the Fly's Eye Dome. In these cases, Fuller was able to build upon the geodesic system and migrate it into new material applications.

In parallel to the early architectural applications of geodesics, British engineer Barnes Wallis[4] labored on analogous material problems for military hardware. His adaption of geodetic structures for aviation

2. See Fernández-Serrano, M. & López, J. (2019). Projecting Stars, Triangles and Concrete. *Architectura* (vol 47(1-2)), pp. 92-114.

3. Fernández-Serrano, M. & López, J. (2019). Ibidem.

4. Jesse Reiser and Nanako Umemoto have written about Barnes and geodetics in their books: Reiser J. & Umemoto N. (2006). *Atlas of Novel Tectonics*. New York: Princeton Architectural Press; Reiser J. & Umemoto N. (2019) *Projects and Their Consequences*. New York: Princeton Architectural Press.

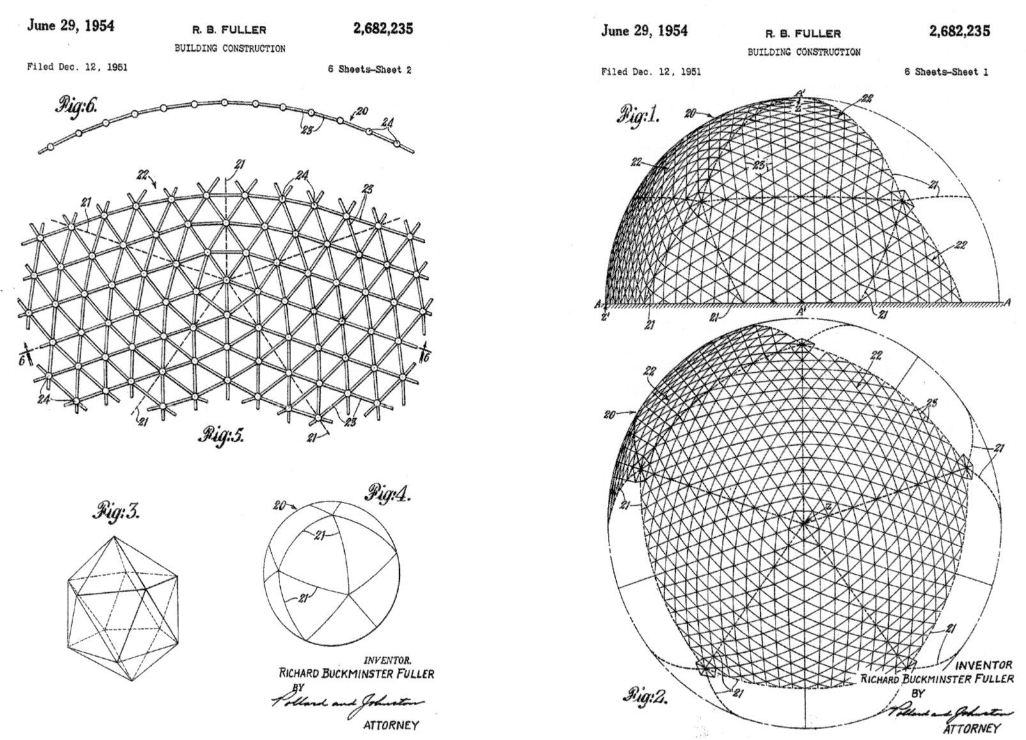

03&04_Buckminster Fuller_Geodesic Dome patent_1954

engineering informed the production of bomber aircraft for the Second World War. The redundant material patterning of his metal basket-weave constructions imbued the aircraft with a structural resilience and supported a larger structure-free interior. The complications in defining a truly mass-produced version of the planes, compounded with a subsequent shift towards monocoque construction, would render these geodetic models redundant. However, these explorations in geodetics reverberate with Bauersfeld and Fuller's applications of these material practices in architecture. This larger material research has since found disparate lines of renewal through the work of Foster and Partners, Reiser and Umemoto, and others. As geodesics and geodetics migrate through different designers, there have been regular re-contextualizations of this material technology to address different concerns and produce novel effects while also being motivated by a range of impulses—from combat to Fuller's environmental mandate, and from structural efficiency to enabling new forms and organizations.

Computed combat

The military–industrial complex also fostered intense investigation into systems, and was also a particularly productive forum for the advancement of diverse scientific investigations that contributed to today's prevalence of computation. In addition to producing material innovations intended for deployment in combat, abstract explorations into systems were also an area of intense study. Two key examples are described below.

Norbert Weiner's formulation of cybernetics[5] benefited from his engagement with the US military on efforts to devise automated rapid-fire anti-aircraft artillery. Weiner was tasked with formulating systems adept at pairing rapid mechanical operations with a capacity to automatically track and aim at moving targets. This seemingly pragmatic directive would lead him to deliberate on self-regulating systems operating through information feedback loops. The influence of cybernetics' primary focus on the control of complex systems was a vital progenitor of contemporary computer science and systems theory.

5. Weiner N. (1948) *Cybernetics: Or control and communication in the animal and the machine.* Cambridge: MIT Prcss.

6. See Kepes G. (1963). *The new landscape in Art and Science.* New York: Paul Theobald and Co. and Kepes G. (1965). *Structure in Art and in Science.* New York: George Braziller.

On the other side of the Atlantic, Alan Turing's involvement in cryptographic operations for the British during the Second World War led to the construction of "Bombe" machines, which have come to be regarded as proto-computers. The capacity for rapid calculation and information retrieval offered by Turing's machines facilitated the deciphering of intercepted coded messages. Turing's other mathematical explorations into codes and patterns further contributed to a wide array of knowledge, including morphogenesis—the scientific study of the processes that give rise to biological forms. This research helped to explicate many developmental biological processes as algorithmic propagations of patterns, offering a computational logic for form generation.

The beginnings of the elaboration of systems and information theory, computer science, artificial intelligence and robotics can be traced back to this period and are associated with the aggregation of various groundbreaking explorations. These scientific advancements in the study of systems and structuring logics would also find an audience in the worlds of design and art.

The material innovations, industrial manufacturing processes, and the influences of new sciences provided designers with opportunities for a significant transformation of design practice. A design culture and practice invested in leveraging the opportunities presented by new science and technologies began to gain momentum, accompanied by a corresponding flow of design system inventions.

Gyorgy Kepes' books, as well as his exhibition titled "The New Landscape in Art and Science, along with Structure in Art and in Science,"[6] are perhaps the most explicit illustrations of this widespread transdisciplinary dialogue between science and the arts. His tenure at MIT brought him into contact with figures such as Wiener and gave him a window into some of the scientific research going on at Cambridge. His own experiences with the war effort also provide a clear exemplar of the convergence between the visual arts and the science of optics, where Kepes' expertise was employed in the development of effective camouflage patterns for the US military.

Kepes' books highlighted Fuller, the Smithsons, Fumihiko Maki and Pier-luigi Nervi, among others, as designers deeply engaged with a systems-based and often prototypical understanding of design. Other contemporaries such as Ray and Charles Eames and Victor Papanek also contributed to models of design practice that were committed to a more systemic influence on society and were therefore also invested in a systems-based model of practice focused on new processes as well as new, scientifically informed material inventions. There were clearly shared motivations and design thinking underlying the great differences in outcomes in this period.

The modern standard & the design marketplace

Interestingly, despite the legacy of systems in design, the contemporary view on Modernism has been largely revised to diminish the importance of its prototypical and systemic ambitions. The Postmodern reaction against the dominance of the Modern convention of practice also brought with it a recalibration of the historical narrative of Modern architecture. In many ways, this would accelerate the impulses of the re-branding of Modernism as an International Style at the 1932[7] MOMA exhibition, seeing Modern design as another formal style within a historical continuum of changing styles. This promoted a more individualistic focus on the main protagonists of this International Style, placing greater emphasis on explicating distinct personalities and talents rather than following through on the larger shared systemic ambitions. Exceptional works and authors of the time were placed in the foreground at the expense of design systems. In many ways, this shattering of Modern history into many individual stories and a shift towards individuation and differentiation also resonates with larger cultural turns.

7. The New York MOMA exhibition and book was curated and authored by Philip Johnson and Henry Russel Hitchcock in 1932. It has been widely interpreted as a defining moment for Modernism into the United States. It has also been seen to be a revision of the Movement for an American audience, where the social and political ambitions of the movement were underplayed and minimized in favor of a more traditionally formal and stylistic representation of Modernism.

Modernism could be seen as a common base for a wide international spread of practitioners. Resonating with the creation of a shared international monetary system at Breton Woods aimed at postwar economic reconstruction, Modern architects who were scattered throughout the world principally developed practices pegged to the international Modern standard of practice. Although it operated as a broad consensus for design practice, this standard spanned a considerable cultural and political diversity between the planning and housing projects developed by Hannes Meyer and Ernst May for the Soviet Union to Mies Van Der Rohe's work for private real estate developments and corporate headquarters in the US.

The dissolution of the Bretton Woods "gold standard" by the 1971

"Nixon shock" shifted the global economy to a floating exchange rate and market-led system. The shift to a free-market economic model is a strong analogy for the shift in architectural practice over those same decades. The dominance of a singular framework for practice was jettisoned in favor of a plurality of competitive approaches. In place of Modernism, a steadily expanding repertoire of different design practices, as well as design cultures and smaller sub-cultures, has since proliferated.

The cultivation of identifiable signature practice styles has become the main currency for design practice, and most contemporary designers actively differentiated themselves through the development of a practice identity. A privileging of individual design languages has been a dominant model of practice for some time.

Patents & prototypes

Some historians and theorists have linked this transformation to the move to post-industrial economies in many of the world's developed markets, which resulted in a change of focus from manufacturing to services. Although designers were still very much linked to the delivery of products—whether they be industrial goods, construction systems or architecture—the role of design as a service in the economy was consolidated even further. Ideas and styles were elevated as the main currency in this economy; as such, a designer's responsibilities was to add value to commodities. One of the consequences of this development was that unique authorship also became something that could be exploited to add value to products. Adding a recognizable and marketable style to commodities was as lucrative for designers as technical invention.

However, despite the shift to signature styles and the individuation of the practice landscape, the industrial production associated with Modern design endured as the dominant model. Despite a stylistic "big bang," much of the production process and construction technology remained within the second industrial revolution model of mass production and standardization.

This industrial paradigm supports a proprietary model of design inventions. If the means of production involve the bulk replication of a standard, then the design is assumed to have been original and perfected. Under this supposition, there is a strong association of proprietorship between a designer and their designs. Patent protection has long supported this notion of an individual right to ownership of intellectual property.

Many of the design systems developed by Buckminster Fuller, the Eameses and other notable figures such as Miguel Fisac and Erwin Hauer were protected by patents, including the geodesic dome, the laminated wood splint, the Husesos beam construction system, and Continua light-diffusing

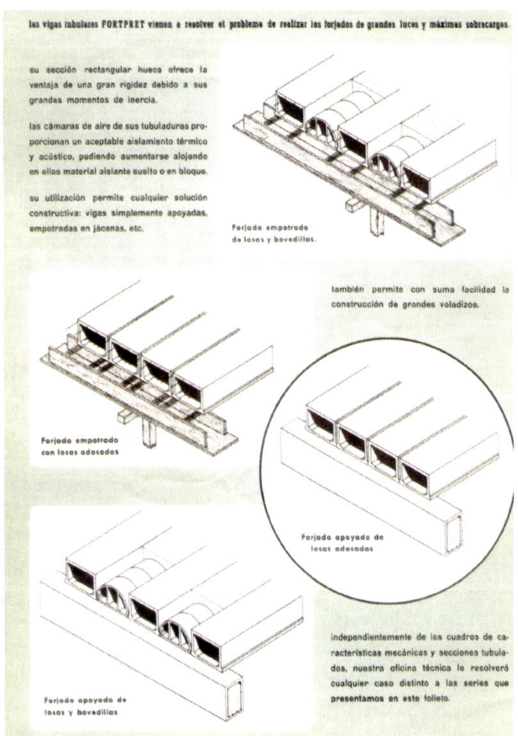

05_Miguel Fisac_Barredo and Peiro S.A beam advertisements

walls. Architects have long been associated with industrial invention; in fact, the first known patent was granted to the architect Filippo Brunelleschi in 1421 for his invention of a barge designed to transport building material.

Patents have also been adopted as a system to foster a wider culture of invention. The patent system is seen to serve two main functions: protecting the intellectual property rights of authors and providing a way to widely disseminate these novel creations for greater public benefit. The transfer of exclusive rights to the wider public occurs when these rights expire after fourteen to twenty years. Once expired, patented inventions subsequently enter the public domain. The patent office also operates as a single reference source for technology and inventions. The eventual expiration of patents allows for a widespread diffusion.

Of relevance to the design world is the distinction between utility and design patents. Utility-patented inventions must prove "novelty, usefulness and non-obviousness." A design patent, on the other hand, simply protects the ornamental aspects of an object. Looking at the array of Modern patents, this distinction can be illustrated by the difference between Buckminster Fuller's utility patent for the geodesic dome and Charles Eames' design patent for the Eames chaise longue. The geodesic dome itself is considered a technological invention, whereas the Eameses' chaise longue is a unique design variation on an already existing invention.

Design's intimate relationship to mass production, particularly industrial design, has ensured that patents have persisted as a dominant practice. Notable postmodern industrial designers such as Phillipe Starck, Ettore Sottsas and Alessandro Mendini all hold a formidable number of design patents. However, patents related to architecture by celebrated architects of similar periods, such as Robert Venturi and Densie Scott Brown, Aldo Rossi, James Stirling and Mario Botta, are few. These architects do hold design patents, but most are for stylized household products and furniture. In many ways, the evolution of design cultures after Modernism has been towards a growing dominance of styling, in architecture as much as in industrial design. It is likely that the economic demands for brand, product or institutional differentiation is related to the great importance of imbuing objects with character or style.

The importance placed on the uniqueness of architectural styles is exemplified by the patenting of the standard Apple store design, as well as its more specific Fifth avenue store in New York, to safeguard its brand

06&07_Miguel Fisac_Barredo and Peiro S.A beam advertisements

identity. Among its many utility patents for new technologies, the Apple corporation has also worked to ensure exclusive ownership over its corporate image [8] embedded in architecture, reflecting the importance of design styling to support brand differentiation in the contemporary economy.

In contrast to the predominance of design patents among Modern designers, Buckminster Fuller held twenty-four American utility patents, while Miguel Fisac, and Jean Prouvé are among a larger cohort of Modern designers who actively transformed their architectural innovations into patented construction products. More recently, architectural practices such as Foster and Partners, Shigeru Ban Architects, Renzo Piano Building Workshop, and designer Chuck Hoberman have all contributed to this more Modern tradition of patented architectural construction systems. This trend emerges out of a design focus offering novel technological solutions for various architectural construction elements such as a hung ceramic tile envelope system, a suspended glass wall construction method, and paper tube and transformable structural techniques.

Beyond patents

Other systems aimed at supporting innovation are emerging out of the so-called third and fourth industrial revolutions. [9] Alternatives to a range of conventions related to authorship or the proclivity for signature styles and industrial mass production are beginning to achieve wider recognition and

8. See Garcia M., (2016) Architectural Patents and OpenSource Architectures: The Globalization of Spatial Design Innovations (or Learning from 'E99'). In *Architectural Design* (Volume 86, Issue 5, Special Issue: *Digital Property: Open.Source Architecture*), pp. 92-99.

9. The Third Industrial Revolution has been described by the economist: Jeremy Rifkin as the convergence between three major innovations in technological networks. These are communications, transport and energy networks based on renewable energy, the internet and new innovations in transport such as autonomous vehicles. This revolution is supported by the prevalence of digital technology and the internet of things. For more information, see Rifkin J. (2011). *The Third Industrial Revolution*. London: St Martins Press. The term; Fourth

Industrial Revolution has been coined by Klaus Schwab of the World Economic Forum. This new revolution "*is characterized by a fusion of technologies that is blurring the lines between the physical, digital, and biological spheres.*" Schwab K. (2016). *The Fourth Industrial Revolution.* Retrieved from: https://www.weforum.org/agenda/2016/01/the-fourth-industrial-revolution-what-it-means-and-how-to-respond/

adoption. These challenges to the proprietary model of design authorship as well as industrial model are being taken up only gradually. However, there is growing recognition of the capacity for rapid systemic changes associated with these processes afforded by new computational technologies.
In parallel to the Modern explorations in patented system designs, another attitude and sensibility was also evolving at the same time. Victor Papanek, designer, educator and friend of Buckminster Fuller, along with the cybernetician Norbert Wiener and writer Stewart Brand, were vocal critics of patents and the notion of exclusive ownership over technological inventions. Papanek rejected patents for what he saw as their role in restricting innovation. At a hacker's convention in 1984, Brand famously stated, "information wants to be free." For his part, Weiner championed the free dissemination of scientific knowledge. Despite being contemporaries who were influenced by Fuller, these key figures and their positions stand in contrast with Fuller's zealous patent filings motivated by his resentment of others profiting from his inventions.

The other systems for innovation advocated by Brand and Papanek are based on ideas of collective authorship and contrast with the proprietary model. These approaches also suggest design processes that are more evolutionary in nature, as the design can be seen to remain unfinished or perpetually open to development. The outcomes may not necessarily be aimed at optimized design standards that provide absolute templates for mass production and deployment. Instead, an emphasis is placed on processes open to the engagement of many stakeholders and participants in the formation process.

With the rapid adoption of both digital design and fabrication by the design fields, the Modern paradigms of mass production and standardization no longer remain the dominant considerations and constraints for designers. Digital processes that allow for the rapid generation of design iterations are well established. Coupled with the possibility of mass-customization provided by digital fabrication, these innovations have begun to restructure some areas of the design economies and cultures.

However, many of the earlier ambitions for the more fundamental shift in design practice advocated by Papanek remain unfulfilled despite the ubiquity of digital design and manufacturing. The notion of an open-source design culture has been identified as one of the possibilities that may be enabled by the shift away from mass production and standardization. When industrial mandates and constraints are removed, design and production may be freed from the compulsion to achieve singular designs and standard products. These designs need not be actualized as redundantly mass-produced products. Design may see a shift in focus toward a preference for design codes that may be tinkered with to generate many possible adaptable design solutions.

Open source

> *"The basic idea behind open source is very simple: When programmers can read, redistribute, and modify the source code for a piece of software, the software evolves. People improve it, people adapt it, people fix bugs."*
>
> Open Source Initiative

It has been suggested that despite their differences, patents and open source share similar overall aims, namely the dissemination and advancement of inventions.[10] Nonetheless, the notion of open source put forward by the Open Source Initiative supports a more inclusive attitude toward cultivating a culture of innovation. Primarily concerned with software design, the initiative promotes a pragmatic proposition that the open and free, software development can be more efficient and can engage diverse participants who bring different expertise and approaches to the development process. The open-source route still aims to produce products with operability, but by making its underlying code available, the open-source approach keeps the development process open and transparent for customization and improvement. In effect, open source invites all stakeholders, including end users, into the development process. Despite the ambitions for public dissemination, patent documentation provides very few underlying technical instructions. Upgrading or simply replicating expired patented technologies will likely require a process of reverse engineering.

The notion of open source is associated with the free software movement, and both derive from hacker culture. Stewart Brand's engagement with the hacker movement and his advocacy for free information resonates with his support of alternative DIY communities and ethos through the publication of his Whole Earth Catalog and Review. The overlap between a more pragmatic attitude adopted by the Open Source Initiative to foster a more efficient innovation process and the more political motivations of the free software movement are very much part of this wider conversation. Kevin Kelly, the founding executive editor of Wired magazine and previously one of Brand's editors at the Whole Earth Review, has made arguments for a bottom-up and analogously biological approach toward innovation.[11] As a counterpoint to top-down directives, bottom-up

08_"The Last Whole Earth Catalog 1971" by scorzonera is licensed under CC BY-NC 2.0

10. See Garcia M., (2016) Ibidem. pp. 92-99.

11. Kevin Kelly's ideas on self-organization are most clearly presented in his book: Kelly, K. (1994) *Out of Control: The New Biology of Machines, Social Systems, & The Economic World.* New York: Basic Books.

processes clearly echo democratic ideals of a collaborative model of innovation or cultural production. The more politically motivated proponents of these movements emphasize the opportunity that these processes present for greater participation, inclusiveness, transparency and community building.

Open-source design

Returning to design practice, augmenting the process of prototypical design into an open-source model places a major emphasis on the distribution of the code that controls or describes the design and manufacturing processes. Because drawn or modeled documentation facilitate the mediation between design and manufacturing, they are also the most direct mediums that can be used in the dissemination of a design code. The importance of drawings in design can be exemplified by their legal significance.[12]

12. This significance can be seen through copyright laws in countries such as the US and Australia. An architect's design, as described in drawings, is what may be protected by law, not the buildings themselves.

In the case of an open-source model, it is the digital documents (drawings or digital models) that are made available to the public, often through creative commons licenses. With open source, the emphasis moves from providing standard products or commodities to devising codes that, in some cases, also offer user customization. It is significant that these new models signal a shared aim with earlier patent models in devising prototypical systems, where an ambition to effect wider systemic change informs many of these initiatives.

A tangible example is the decision by Elemental, a Chilean practice, to release four affordable housing plans for open-source use in 2016. Even though the practice may have garnered international recognition by delivering built instantiations of these prototypical designs, they have also taken the extraordinary step of releasing the design documentation of these prototypes to the public domain rather than protecting their exclusive rights to profit from these designs. The free dissemination of the prototype documentation creates the possibility of countless instantiations of these designs being delivered by many different agents. The motivation for this is to allow for a much wider and rapid adoption of their design innovations as a way to address global housing crises at scale.

Other comparable examples include Architecture 00's opensystems Lab WikiHouse system as well as Opendesk, an online marketplace for open-source furniture. Both provide downloadable digital fabrication files that can be manufactured locally, requiring only standard digital fabrication protocols and low-skill assembly. These open-source models allow for a more distributed network model for production in which these designs are devised to permit local, smaller-scale manufacturing. It also introduces an economic model that enables its products to be made on-demand or as needed, while the simple design tools used in the design of WikiHouse also offer users the ability to customize the designs to their specific needs.

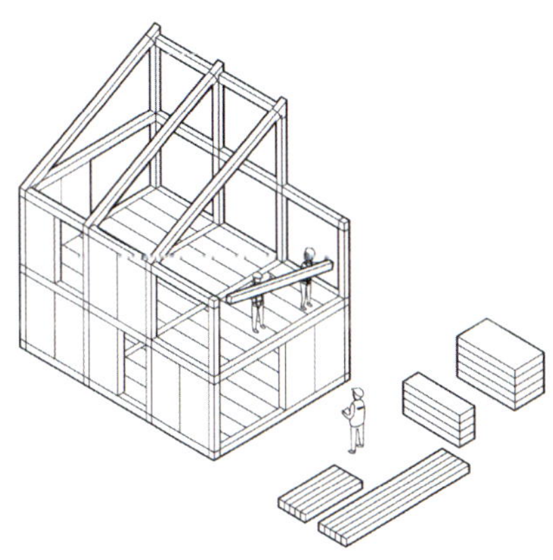

09_WikiHouse images by OpenSystems Lab (image by WikiHouse Foundation)

In 2011, a multi-authored article in Domus magazine presented a manifesto of sorts for an open-source architecture.[13] Its principal argument was for the radical restructuring of authorship, design, construction, funding, engagement and occupancies that an open-source model may bring to the conventions of architecture. One of the major takeaways from this piece was the capacity for reconsidering the economies and processes of manufacturing and distributing products. Either as a parallel system or as a potentially radical disruption of existing processes, an open-source model of architecture was recognized as being capable of systemic transformation.

13. The article was published in the magazine Domus on 15 June 2011. Contributors to the article included Paola Antonelli, Adam Bly, Lucas Dietrich, Joseph Grima, Dan Hill, John Habraken, Alex Haw, John Maeda, Nicholas Negroponte, Hans Ulrich Obrist, Carlo Ratti, Casey Reas, Marco Santambrogio, Mark Shepard, Chiara Somajni, Bruce Sterling. In the spirit of open source authorship, this article was subsequently made available on Wikipedia to allow for open editing.

From mass production to on-demand manufacturing

The industrial mass-production paradigm and the logic of on-demand manufacturing are obviously very different sets of practices. They also yield very different economies. To succeed, an industrial model generally must achieve economies of scale and can often involve substantial lead times. Large production batches are typical and come with the risk of overproduction. The model of standardization also works with a one-size-fits-all notion of product design.

The convergence of digital design with connected networks and computationally aided making in the so-called fourth industrial revolution allows for a manufacturing model based on flexibility rather than scale. In this model, designers could work on a multi-product, made-to-order logic. Customizable processes or systems are more likely than industrial products to take advantage of this model.

A business example of this approach is the UK-based fashion consultancy and brand Unmade (originally Knyttan). Operating on a made-to-order

10_"Opendesk" is licensed under CC BY-NC-SA 2.0 (laboratoriolinux)

model of production, the use of digital tools, networks and custom software has allowed the company to offer consultancy services as well as a range of customizable items that are digitally knitted on demand. Interestingly, with this model, relatively small businesses can offer a much wider range of designs and products than would have been possible under the older industrial paradigm.

The innovation demonstrated by the Unmade approach is as much related to the manufacturing process and its associated effect on the business model as it is to the actual designs themselves. The design emphasis on the development of software that controls the parameters of customization for a product is another relative novelty. French architect Bernard Cache established an earlier example of this approach through the Objectile software, which generated customizable furniture and architectural fixtures, devised with designer Patrick Beaouce in the early 1990s.[14]

14. Cache, B. (1995) *Earth Moves: The Furnishing of Territories.* Cambridge: MIT Press.

15. See Wu D., Rosen David W., Wang, L. & Schaefer D. (2014). Cloud-based Manufacturing: Old Wine in New Bottles?. In *Procedia CIRP* (Volume 17), pp. 94-99.

16. The opposite of offshoring.

Design and manufacturing ecosystems?

Another emerging trend associated with these technologies is manufacturing[15] platforms or cloud-based design and manufacturing. These networked production management systems are touted for their potential to increase the efficiency, productivity and flexibility of manufacturing and design processes.

An emphasis on networks is purported to enable the management and cultivation of more distributed, localized and nimble business ecosystems. An on-demand model of delivery, onshoring[16] and increased efficiencies are believed to emerge from an integrated management platform that

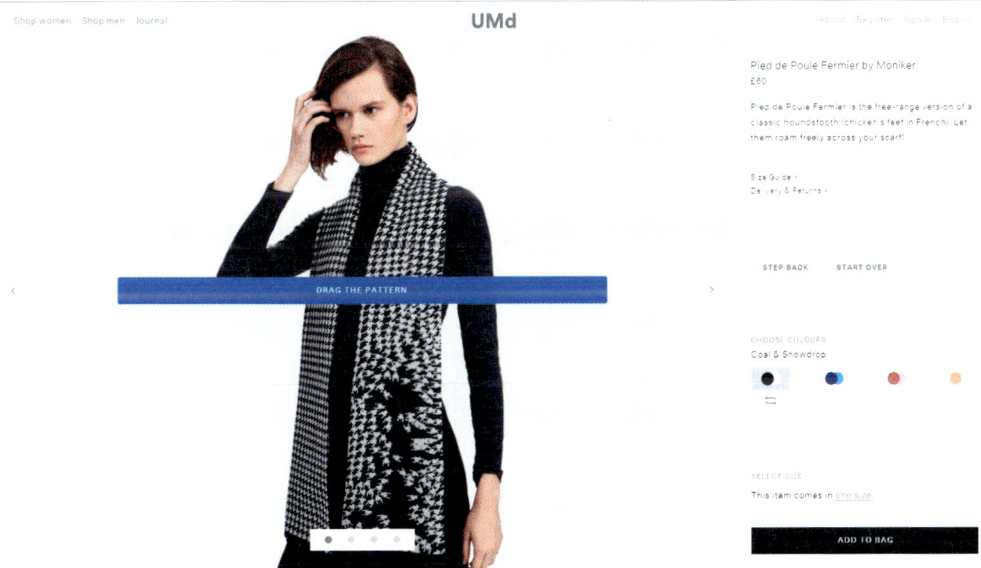

11_Unmade_webpage

tracks the whole process.[17] This approach is assumed to offer a range of advantages over mass production. The adoption of digital manufacturing and prototyping helps to accelerate the design to manufacturing lead times, while on-demand production can minimize inventory and redundancy. However, it is important to acknowledge that the adoption of automation and digital technologies does not directly equate to on-demand, open-source or customizable practices.

A comparison between the Unmade example and Byborre, a Dutch textile innovation studio, highlights the diversity of business models and motivations that may still be associated with the adoption of advanced digital design and manufacturing processes. In the case of Byborre, a greater emphasis is placed on material exploration and the production of sophisticated textiles produced by digital knitting machines for its own clothing line and other brands. Byborre markets itself as a textile innovation studio and appears to be adopting a more traditional design-atelier approach with small-batch and high-end products. Neither Byborre nor Unmade are necessarily aimed at mass audiences, and both seem to occupy niche markets.

Curiously, both companies' approaches can be seen to resonate with strategies employed by the Nike corporation. Their product lines, such as the Nike ID personalization service (now Nike By You) and the Flyknit range, are antecedents to Byborre and Unmade. Nike's mass customization service was first offered in 1999 and the use of digital weaving machines for the Flyknit range allows Nike to rapidly produce a line of sneakers that has the dual advantages of light and minimal-waste construction. However, the made-to-order service remains a very small component of the business.

17. The integration of a large database of manufacturers and suppliers allows for a more flexible supply chain. Automation allows for manufacturing to return to countries that have offshored their manufacturing, allowing for fabrication to occur locally.

Furthermore, although Flyknit sneakers are more materially efficient, they are still effectively sold as industrial products that sit alongside the vast range of other mass-produced sneakers the company offers.

The effects that these systems will have on wider practice are still evolving and ongoing. Larger corporations like Nike, Uniqlo and Adidas often have the capital to invest in new technologies and many have begun to integrate small-batch, on-demand production complimenting their mass production in order to remain competitive and agile in responding to consumer demands. Uniqlo is said to be investing in digital knitting for a mass-production capacity. Clearly this technology can still support older economic and business practices. However, while large, integrated organizations stand to benefit from these systems, these can also be favorable to networks or ecosystems of smaller agents.

The third and fourth industrial revolutions are widely touted as being more accessible. Their advancements are said to theoretically lower the cost of participation in the design and manufacturing economy, whether this be for smaller practices or in an open-source model. On-demand and manufacturing platforms, together with open-source online marketplaces, may help to reduce the typical overhead and investment that used to come with the older manufacturing paradigms. The proximity that comes with onshoring, together with the theoretical removal of the need for large inventories, is also said to make the process substantially more flexible and less wasteful.

The other effect of this wider participation is that niche may become the norm. Chris Anderson's "long tail business model"[18] of "selling less of more" highlights the opportunity to capture larger market shares by focusing on selling a wider range of products. This contradicts the bases of older industrial practices. Although mass-producing a few popular products will still be very profitable in Anderson's model, the aggregation of all the niche markets that occupy the long tail sustains a larger portion of the economy. Given the use of design codes, on-demand and networked digital manufacturing's capacity to support flexible, multi-product manufacturing businesses, a network of smaller participants in this new economy may be well placed to flourish.

18. See Anderson, C. (2006) *The Long Tail: Why the Future of Business Is Selling Less of More*. New York: Hachette Books.

In architecture, a wide diversity of models for practice and delivery have also emerged, with Architecture 00's WikiHouse project as well as Elemental and Architecture For Humanity's open-source release of building plans illustrating novel practice models enabled by these new processes. Smaller practices have also profited from these new technologies by identifying new niche markets for their retooled design practices. The Very Many and Ball-Nogues Studio are smaller practices that have been able to develop an expertise and business in digitally designed and fabricated installations and prototypes.

Conversely, larger, more established practices have also integrated these processes and systems into their offices in many different ways. Snohetta's robotic in-house workshop allows the practice to quickly and seamlessly produce mock-ups and prototypes, enhancing their capacity for exploration and problem-solving in the design and delivery process. Gehry and Partners[19] have also been industry leaders in engagement with these new technologies and capacities. Their technology wing expanded the core business of architectural design to include software development as well as consultancy services on digital design and delivery. (However, these capacities have since been acquired by Trimble Inc., a large software-as-service business). The culmination of these new processes contributes toward establishing a considerably different context than the one that supported the invention of Modern architectural prototypes. With the privileging of diversification, customization, and the "long tail" of niches, it is hard to imagine a central consensus of the sort that underpinned Modernism.

19. See Bruce, L. (2001) *Digital Gehry: Material Resistance, Digital Construction (The Information Technology Revolution in Architecture).* Rome: Skira.

20. See Papanek, V. (1984) *Design for the Real World: Human Ecology and Social Change.* Chicago: Academy Chicago Publishers

A new consensus?

How can the transformative capacities aimed for by the earlier Modern design systems be recast in this new economy and culture? The massive disruptions of industrialization and the world wars compelled a systemic transformation of political, cultural and economic conventions. A consistent and widely disseminated design culture emerged from the transformation of the design disciplines and professions in response to these larger international upheavals and crises.

Today, changes exemplified by the third and fourth industrial revolutions and a corresponding splintering of the larger body politic converges with a global environmental and climate crisis. These compounded concerns are threatening a systemic disruption similar to that faced by an earlier generation, and perhaps more ominous. The apparent absence of consensus and emphasis on individuation seems strikingly inopportune in this context. Given these instabilities and existential threats posed by the climate crisis, there would seem to be some urgency in determining whether a return to a common focus may be possible.

The conflation of major disruptive forces may be the trigger that helps to re-contextualize and reinvigorate an investment in design systems. Interestingly, we may return to the earlier Modern period to locate a sensibility that can help to significantly reframe creative practice. Victor Papanek[20] and Buckminster Fuller shared a common ecological mission that guided their prototypical and system designs. Their mutual premonition of environmental crises associated with the economic and cultural models of overconsumption was a primary concern for both designers. Papanek and Fuller also defined architectural and urban systems that were capable of and intended for widespread deployment; in other words, they were aiming for a wider systemic impact.

The impending anthropogenic climate crisis and technology-led disruptions signal the need for a deliberate shift in design culture to address these contemporary concerns with a systematic, technical and aesthetic capacity once more. There is a growing consensus that a global economic, technological and cultural transformation akin in scale to the campaigns during the world wars will be needed to adequately address these crises. Owing to the magnitude of the undertaking, designers responding to these concerns may seek to ensure that their design responses have the capacity to scale up and achieve extensive adoption.

It may be fruitful to pursue a different model of exploration that builds upon this early Modern project. A renewed engagement with systems design may adopt a position that engages and benefits from earlier research so that it may be recontextualized and upgraded. Devoid of any pretense to the avant-garde or radical originality, this process may build upon a legacy of material intelligence while also upgrading it away from older systems of authorship, design, making and dissemination.

In the same way that geodetics and geodesics were iterated upon by many different designers to address many different applications, the opportunities presented by digital tools and an open-source model of work could also foster a larger collective engagement with upgrading and repurposing existing systems. The re-contextualization of these systems may help in identifying flexible and nimble generative codes that may be used to produce many possible prototypes with equally diverse applications. This potentially massive virtual catalogue of designs enables a search to identify many other dormant potentials that have been latent in their generative codes. Although not strictly limited to a pursuit of optimal solutions that are reproduced ad infinitum, such a search is, of course, another potential of the process where adaptability is privileged.

Given the fractured long tail of niche audiences, users and constituencies, it may no longer be feasible that our designs follow the older strategies for production and dissemination. The capacity to rapidly generate multi-product lines on-demand allows for the efficient and flexible production of "less of more." Rather than aiming for enabling ever-growing consumption, a system for diversification also makes it possible to captivate a wider spectrum of audiences.

In this context, achieving a wider systemic reach will not be about optimums and perfection as it was for Modernism; rather, the focus will be on an efficient capacity for adaptation.

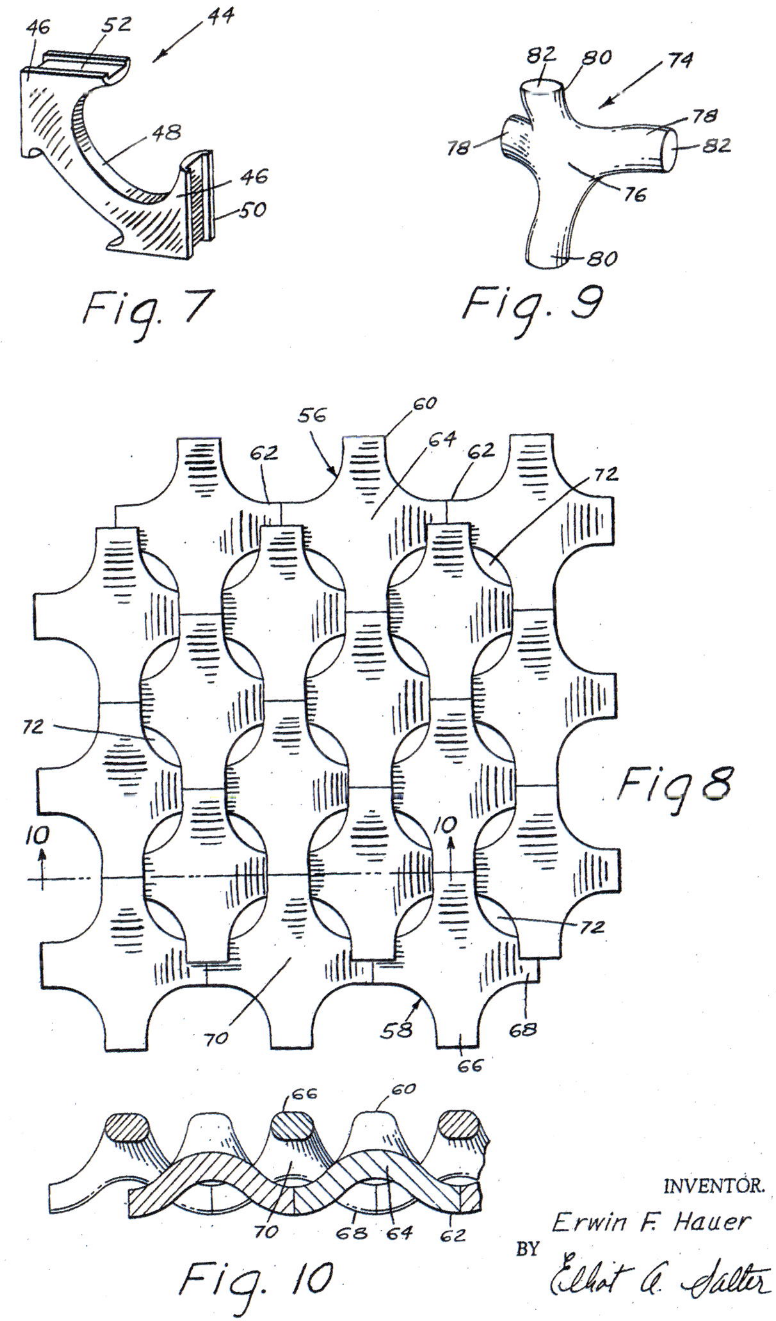

12_Erwin Hauer_Design 3 patent_1963

(Re)fabricating tectonics prototypes

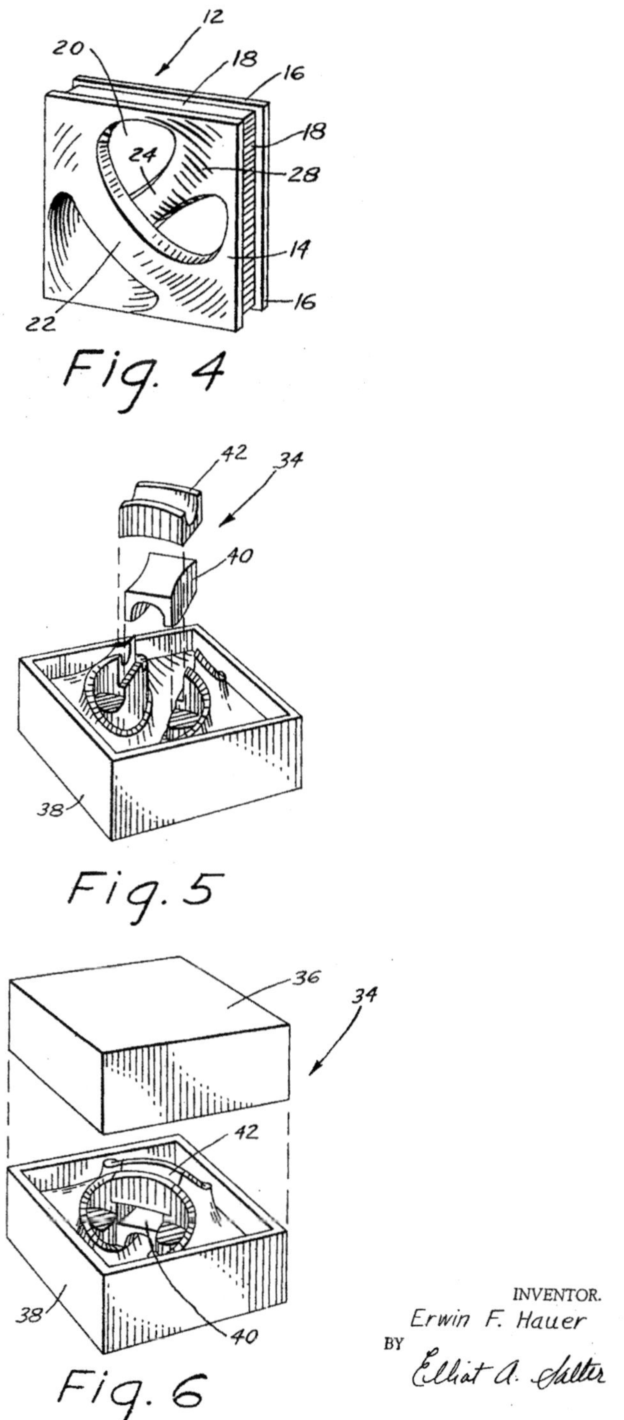

01_Erwin Hauer_Design 1 patent_1951

The work explicated in this book is part of a larger ongoing research agenda, involving academic investigation, practice and education undertakings. These efforts are framed by a wider motivation to contribute towards the development of contemporary creative practice approaches that are equally informed or enriched by historical precedent as they are by the mandate for a speculative and novel outlook. We have pursued this design research through a specific focus on the development of tectonic and construction systems in architecture.

This research has also focused on supporting the definition of creative practice approaches that leverage the systematic and material intelligence associated with both emerging and established digital techniques and workflows. But rather than assume the common misconception that new technologies disrupt creative practice in an ahistorical manner, these explorations assume that many valuable ideas and techniques that resonate with contemporary concerns may still be found in precedent.

By extracting lessons from the deep material analysis of exemplary legacy construction/tectonic systems, a bridge between earlier design research and contemporary practices may be forged. The migration of the material and design intelligence embedded in these precedents into computationally amplified design processes affords a rich knowledge and practice base for an extended life. This strategy is guided by the notion that the valuable extension of contemporary design capacities through the engagement with the third and fourth industrial revolutions may only really achieve efficacy as a creative practice if it deliberately builds on the embodied knowledge of preceding material practices.

This research builds upon the understanding of creative practice as an act of bridging precedent and future potential which has been crucial throughout design history. Even in the case of Modernism, a movement which has often been perceived and characterized as one of the more radical shifts in material and construction culture, innovative tectonic practices specific to the needs and sensibilities of their time were often developed while being equally informed by traditional forms and material practices as by technological innovations of the time. Consequently, the Modern transformations to prevalent design and material culture is a particularly abundant reference point for this research agenda.

A specific array of Modern construction and tectonic systems have been employed as subjects of study and reconsideration in these investigations so that they may inform the bases for new constructive prototypical systems. A particularly compelling example is the Danish architect; Jorn Utzon's exploratory investment in prefabrication. This extended focus benefited from the reconsideration of the applicability of traditional Asian tectonic systems such as the twelfth century Chinese building manual by Li Jie: the Ying Zhao Fa Shi into twentieth century applications. The Sydney Opera House and Kuwait National Assembly are perhaps the most renowned projects where these systems were creatively deployed by Utzon and his team.

Other contemporaneous constructive systems ranging from Miguel Fisac's precast concrete long-span Huesos structures and his flexible formwork system, Buckminster Fuller's adaptation of geodesic and tensegrity structures to Erwin Hauer's architectural mathematically imbued screen forms are significant in the way that they offer reference systems open for contemporary reconsideration and extension.

These are especially significant as instances where the design and art world actively developed construction systems or patented products intended for widespread deployment and application. Most of these systems were earlier promises for a radical restructuring of design, construction and delivery capabilities and expressed the promise for the potential systemic transformation of the built environment. Some of these inventions were even intended as socially transformative systems with the promise for reorganizing prevalent economic and social practices of their time. Buckminster Fuller's seemingly technical focus on enhancing structures for lightness offered a vision for transportable houses which questioned the notion of landed property. Erwin Hauer's continua series extend artfully composed mathematical forms into building light screening components which actively modulate the environment while the prefabricated structural innovations of Fisac and Utzon allowed for the comparatively swift assembly of long-span expansive and uninterrupted interior spaces.

Their resonance with the widespread concerns of their time can be reflected by the intentions of these creators for their systems to become standardized and routinely replicable architectural systems or components. In effect, these precedents were understood as mass-produced construction systems that would offer new ways for aggregating and deploying larger building envelopes. Replicability and standardization were design aims that mirrored the dominant industrial production of the time. Improvement in the performance and constructability of the structures afforded by these inventions also paralleled the emergence of compelling expressive and communicative sensibilities which exploited these new opportunities.

While these legacy systems may be recognized for their underlying potential for expansion into contemporary concerns and sensibilities, these should also be acknowledged for having been devised under different capacities and assumptions, whereby these systems and material forms were all conceived under the influence of an industrialized construction culture.

02_Photograph of "ceramic formations" course final review at Harvard, GSD 2016. Photograph by Anita Kan

One of the outcomes of the explorations described in this book has been the redefinition of the Modern tendency for standardization, mechanical reproducibility and optimization embedded in these systems.
The reconsideration of these systems and a subsequent proposal for upgrading them in light of our contemporary perspectives has been largely informed by a research framework that is focused on the operative phases of creative practice. This conceptual structure is divided into four phases that have been retooled by the widespread adoption of digital design and manufacturing tools in creative practice. These being: re-describing, re-designing, re-fabricating and re-contextualizing.

Re-describing / interpreting - associative modeling

The analysis of these existing systems and their associative geometric as well as material relationships initiate the development of a rigorous analytical understanding of specific construction and tectonic systems. This also establishes a proficiency of the base models that affords the possibility of their application to future creative practice. The vital process adopted in these research projects is the construction of reverse engineered associative/parametric digital design models of the precedent systems.

Exercises in re-constructing and re-describing these precedents into associative models formats are done to access the specific formal, organizational and material qualities of these systems. By reverse engineering exemplary material systems, the deep reading of the geometric definition of these artifacts can be more deeply scanned for transformational opportunities. In this process, the associative model operates as the technical geometric code that re-describes and interprets these precedents.

The rigorous geometric description of the precedents elaborated within the format of an associative model has been found to provide bridges between form and different kinds of material performance and behavior. In principle, the maturing practice of associative or parametric design is predicated on the coupling of the geometric design models to different performance criteria.

Since the geometric generation of an associative or parametric model is meant to be achieved through an indexing of performance, this design and modeling technique also offers the capacity of an inverse path. The production of specific visual effects, realizing material lightness through the minimization of structural elements, ensuring structural self-stabilization, intricate methods for aggregating tectonic units and enveloping spaces in materially resourceful ways are just a few of the exemplary qualities of these precedent forms which can be clearly associated with a strategic engagement with its geometric description.

A careful attendance to geometric definition has also been a crucial design practice adopted to strategize and regulate the translation of design ambitions into manufacturing and construction considerations. The associations between the geometric definition of a design and the formal, organizational and in some instances: material properties of its realized outcome can be carefully established by designers so that construction, performance and aesthetic concerns may be developed and imbued in the design during the description process. Compelling exemplars include Buckminster Fuller's development of his globular and dome structures through the geometric discretization of a sphere following geodesic lines of shortest distance. This geometric logic for efficiently subdividing a sphere is, at its lowest resolution base form; the icosahedron. Higher frequencies of segmentation further approximate a sphere at higher resolution. The primary choice of the sphere is informed by the low perimeter to area ratio of the geometry which best defines a spatial volume that also delivers a light-weight structure with minimized envelope surface.

The way the precedent systems may be reverse engineered is crucial in determining our capacity to identify the ways in which these artifacts may be transformed. Seemingly prosaic concerns such as the actual ways in which we choose to break down the definition of larger complex forms or organizations into smaller geometric components can have a significant effect on how are enabled to view the opportunities for formal or organizational variabilities.

Re-designing / trasnsforming

Coupled with re-description, design research projects exploring systematic re-design is another critical area of consideration in the wider research project. Across the majority of these research explorations, the knowledge and material intelligence embedded in precedent forms have provided the bases for re-design. Design processes made accessible through digital design tools have been adopted to systematically upgrade these exemplars through workflows that allow for the coupling of formal definition with processes of differentiation, transformation and adaptation.

A number of these computationally assisted practices have proven to offer the capacity to support the intelligent evolution of these material systems. As re-description has benefited from the use of associative models, the design processes and workflows related with these techniques are a seamless bridge between analysis and design. Only through the opportunities for geometric transformation facilitated by the associative model, many iterations of differentiated geometric arrangements may be generated. Large numbers of design instantiations may be produced with different branches of transformation types brokering a spectrum of iterations conveying the changes in variables of each stream. Geometric transformation alone affords designers the ability to proliferate a large sample of design possibilities however associative design also allows for other capacities which can frame the assessment of this production.

The connection between form, geometry and organization with different parameters central to these design techniques allows for the transformations or adaptations of these precedent systems to be tuned to material behaviors predicated on use or performance. An engagement with these associations through the preceding process of re-description already allows access to a range of possible transformations that can be measured against specific functional or use criteria. Other criteria and measures outside of the original considerations of the precedents can also be brought to bear on these systems and can evolve these systems into other applications beyond their original applications.

Unintended material behavior and effects of a design can often be identified in later phases of prototyping or even post-design. Many design processes

02_Photograph of "ceramic formations" course final review at Harvard, GSD 2016. Photograph by asensio-mah

have benefited from integrating knowledge from the evaluation of outcomes of earlier design iterations and prototypes into subsequent phases of design refinement or development. These inadvertent effects are opportunities for exploration which are certainly available to researchers and designers looking to upgrade revisited systems. The nature of associative models and design processes enables the possibility of a recursive process of design generation or evolution. Computation is fundamentally based on iterative and recursive operations. Linking this to the design process itself allows for many possible lines of design exploration and system transformation whereby specific lines of exploration can be pursued through a rapid-fire process that allows for iterative generation, evaluation, feedback and then recursion.

The capacity to rapidly generate large samples of design iterations also allows designers and researchers the ability to study design outcomes in the aggregate. This allows for a few advantages, one being the possibility of a much wider or extensive search for design possibilities while it may also allow for a more intensive search for options within a narrower focus. All these processes are certainly poised to benefit from developments in artificial intelligence developments such as machine learning which can assist in the identification of larger patterns and opportunities presented by large samples of possibilities.

Re-fabricating

These systems upgrades are also enhanced through the establishment of a dialogue between design and material prototyping explorations that utilize contemporary and emerging fabrication technologies. Opportunities for re-thinking these precedents may also emerge in the translations as well as transitions between design, description and making (or building), where the processes of materializing or making design intentions offer equally fertile ground for invention.

Much of the advancements in contemporary construction culture can be associated with the accessibility and relative ease of complex prototyping as well as mass-customization, the manufacturing correlate to iterative or recursive design.

Rapid prototyping allows for, as the name suggests, a speedy production of mock-ups and test models and its wide dissemination and adoption has made it more generally accessible to designers. Aided by computation, many fabrication processes have emerged to allow for prototyping which can also offer access to a complexity and families of forms previously excluded for being labor or cost-inhibitive in older processes. Rapid prototyping also allows for the more seamless integration of opportunities for testing design intentions in materialized forms more regularly throughout design and development phases. The capacity to fabricate, test and evaluate prototypes, also enhances the ability to feed these findings back as considerations back into the design process, embedding more construction and material know-how directly into the recursive creative process.

While distinct from standardization and industrialized production resonating with the Modern precedents, these contemporary and evolving construction opportunities should also be differentiated from the notion of bespoke or idiosyncratic one-off construction processes. Mass-customization allows for differentiation across a series or within systems, implicating the potential for customization, differentiation and adaptability but within a consistency.

The translation from design to prototyping also presents many openings for creative transformation and the reconsideration of likely applications of the experience embedded in the precedent models. An opportunistic transposition of tectonic know-how into new materials is one such possibility. Lessons from the analysis of precedent systems may constitute a frame of reference for addressing other material capabilities or guide their evolution into other materialities. The re-fabrication of these systems through new manufacturing processes alone can already offer its own potentials as the specifics of these techniques may provide windows into systems upgrades across the spectrum from larger aggregated possibilities offered by new robotic assembly right through to the micro-scale where new additive and subtractive processes provide prospects for higher resolutions of material definition.

The range of processes that were engaged with for the research ranged from subtractive processes (facilitated by CNC and robotic milling and waterjet cutting), additive processes (3d-printing), robotic assembly as well as composite workflows which also integrated more traditional methods such as mold-making, slip-casting.

Re-contextualizing - environment

The exploratory phase of re-contextualization involves placing design iterations within simulations or models or larger environments in order to evaluate and subsequently refine these designs against selected contextual criteria and indicators. This process can also involve reconsidering the design against conditions, themes and settings which had not been concerns in the development of the precedent systems. By re-contextualizing designs, there is the opportunity for the adaptation or evolution of the designs in order to adapt to these new constraints

Re-contextualization, in this research, primarily involves a deliberate consideration of how the proposed designs may contribute and become integrated into an environment or eco-system. This imposes a mindset that views the design proposals not simply as objects but as constituents that interact with and participate in an ecological process. Simulations related to wind, hydrology, daylighting, solar exposure and radiation are a sample of tools that have been used to re-contextualize and inform the redesign of older precedents. Digital tools ranging from computational fluid dynamics to solar analysis are integrated within the design environment and workflow, allowing for a continuous feedback loop between design, simulation, analysis and design reiteration.

Re-contextualization also signals the mandate to reconsider these Modern inventions and knowledge in light of major prevailing matters of concern today. One of the overbearing anxieties that occupies the public and professional imagination is climate change and a need for renewed sensitivity to the relationships between the built environment and wider ecologies. Consequently, environmental performance and ecological impact have been the primary focus in many of these research pursuits. This focus helps to foreground the awareness of these design prototypes as agents in the regulation of microclimates.

Another major preoccupation that emerges from this research is the theme of adaptation. The aim towards design adaptation is one of the major factors in these projects that propel design transformation. It also informs the search for the prospect of customizing designs to different environmental conditions and different localities. Environmental adaptation also extends these explorations into the possibility of differentiating systems to adjust to landscape processes such as surface hydrology as well as reorienting towards the exigencies of specific site conditions.

Conclusion

For the project showcased in this book, the ambition for engaging the legacy of Erwin Hauer's oeuvre is informed by the identification of the potential to extend his work into new digitally assisted design contexts as well as extending the focus of the legacy into environmental modulation. Hauer's continua screens provide a valuable model for pursuing an exploration into the transformative generation of new microclimatic and daylight/thermal modulating screens. This is an opportunity to rethink one of the layers in larger scale of architectural envelope systems, whereby a reconsideration and transformation of these artworks as larger constructive systems has the potential for extracting new facilities for how these upgraded systems may allow for other visual properties and material performance to appear in scales further upstream in the built environment.

And transforming these precedent tectonic components and their modalities of assembly (their part to whole relationships), there is the possibility of exploring how alternative configurations and functions of larger envelope systems may be garnered from an altered definition of its smaller components. Through an extensive exploration of the re-description, re-design, possible re-fabrication and re-contextualization of this seminal material legacy, a detailed explication of this process of upgrading systems is offered for general consideration.

Besides the direct effects of performance, these investigations also afford the profession and discipline the space to also consider how the challenge of architecture and construction's engagement with climatic concerns, at the scale of building components, may also be an avenue to locate specific design qualities and sensibilities that communicate this larger collective momentum.

Re-describing

Flake System. (Re)fabricating Nervi's mushroom column. Koutsenko, S._Martin, J._Staudt, J._Ugarte, JP._Spring 2013

From a single center support, Nervi's expressive roof structure forms a cantilevered mushroom column. The circular roof is made of prefabricated concrete components. The structural system was used by the engineer in many other structures (Terme Chianciano, 1952, or the Palazzetto dello Sport). The structure is characterized by sunflower shaped reinforcements. Nervi placed the reinforced elements following a specific geometry, not only optimizing the structural performance of the material, but providing the building with very recognizable aesthetics. The students undertook a detailed exploration of the system, using associative modeling to redescribe the system, allowing for the rapid generation of variations on this topology. (edited from student report)

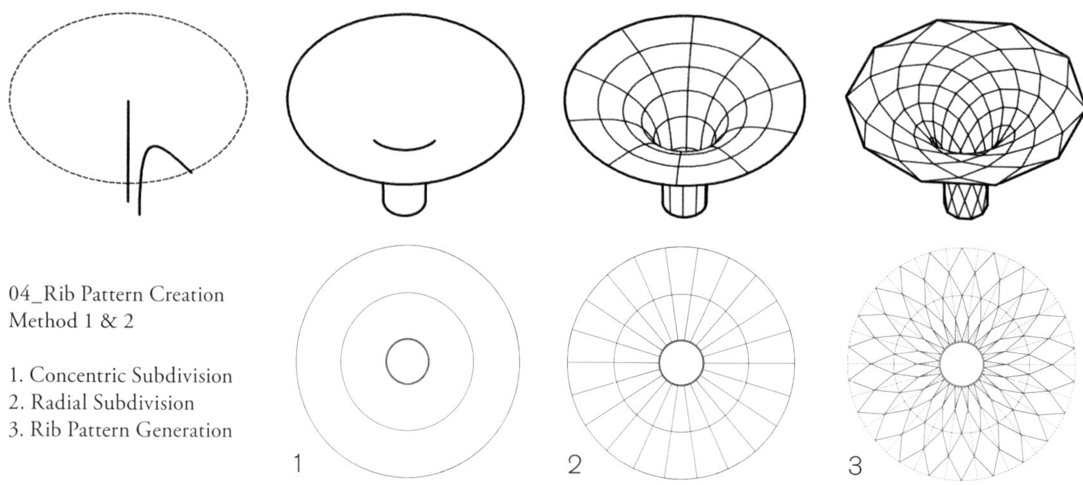

04_Rib Pattern Creation
Method 1 & 2

1. Concentric Subdivision
2. Radial Subdivision
3. Rib Pattern Generation

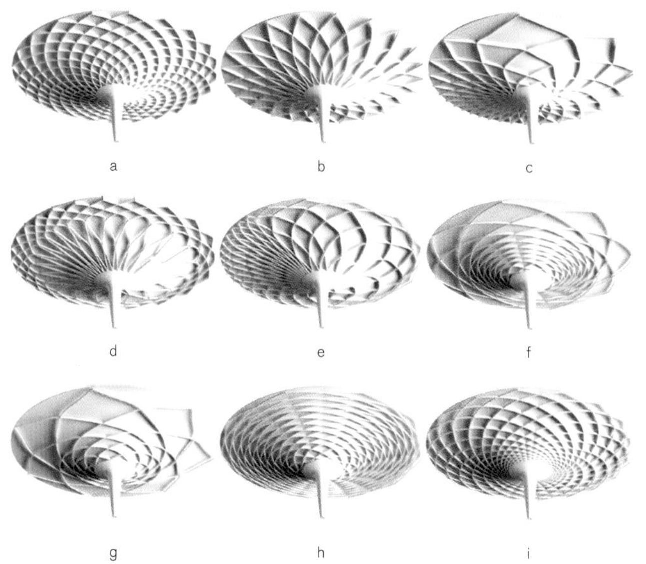

05_Section Profile Geometry Description

Re-describing

(Re)fabricating Fuller's fly's eye dome. Chung, H._Zhan, Y._Fall 2010

The original structure was intended as a light air-deliverable house. Its lightness and geometry were engineered to be cost, energy and materially efficient while also being able to harvest solar and wind energies. Chung and Zhan developed an associative model of the Fly's Eye Dome geodesic sphere enabling the possibility of generating a range of geodesic spheres by varying the parameters that rule the base geodesic sphere (the size of the base diameter, the base icosahedron, the different frequencies of the spheres and the depth of the geodesic skin). The two layers that constitute its thickness are linked by catenoids which are also modeled to be variable. (edited from student report)

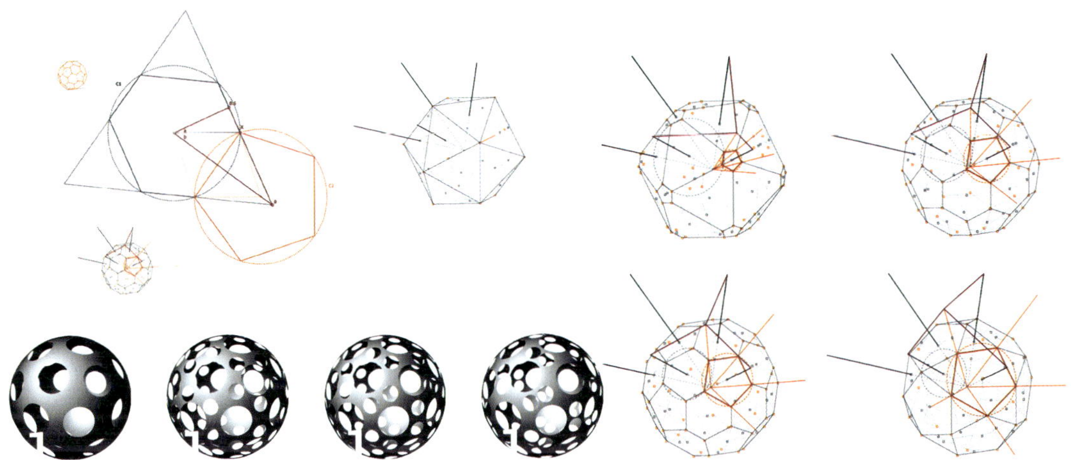

05_(Re)fabricating the Fly's Eye Dome_ Diagrams

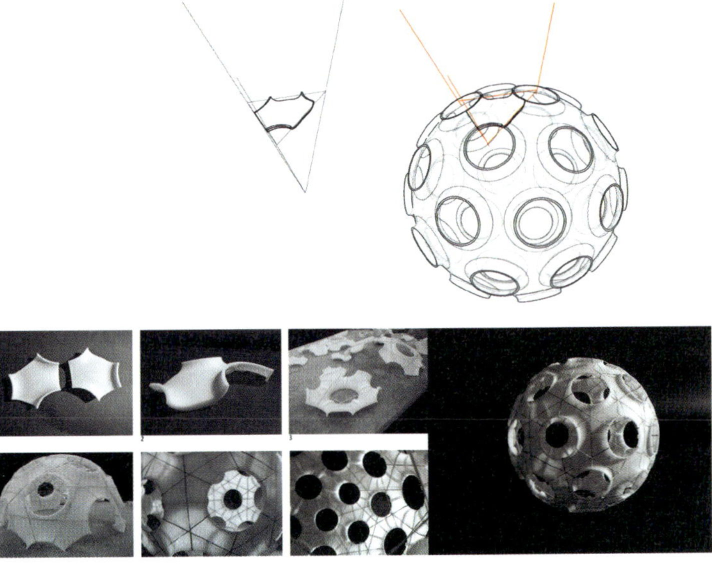

06_(Re)fabricating the Fly's Eye Dome_ Fabrication

Re-describing

(Re)fabricating Fisac
Choi, W._Imbern, M._Raspall Galli, F._Spring 2012

The Huesos structural system by Miguel Fisac was re-systematized by Choi, Imbern and Raspall by constructing a parametric 6-point system that could reproduce several different pieces. This system allows for a gradual variation and transition between these different pieces. It also allows for the specific control of the performance of these components, not just in terms of structures but also allowing for different light conditions and water drainage. The re-description of this precedent was determined by the aim of achieving this flexibility rather than an overtly faithful reproduction of the original system. (edited from student report)

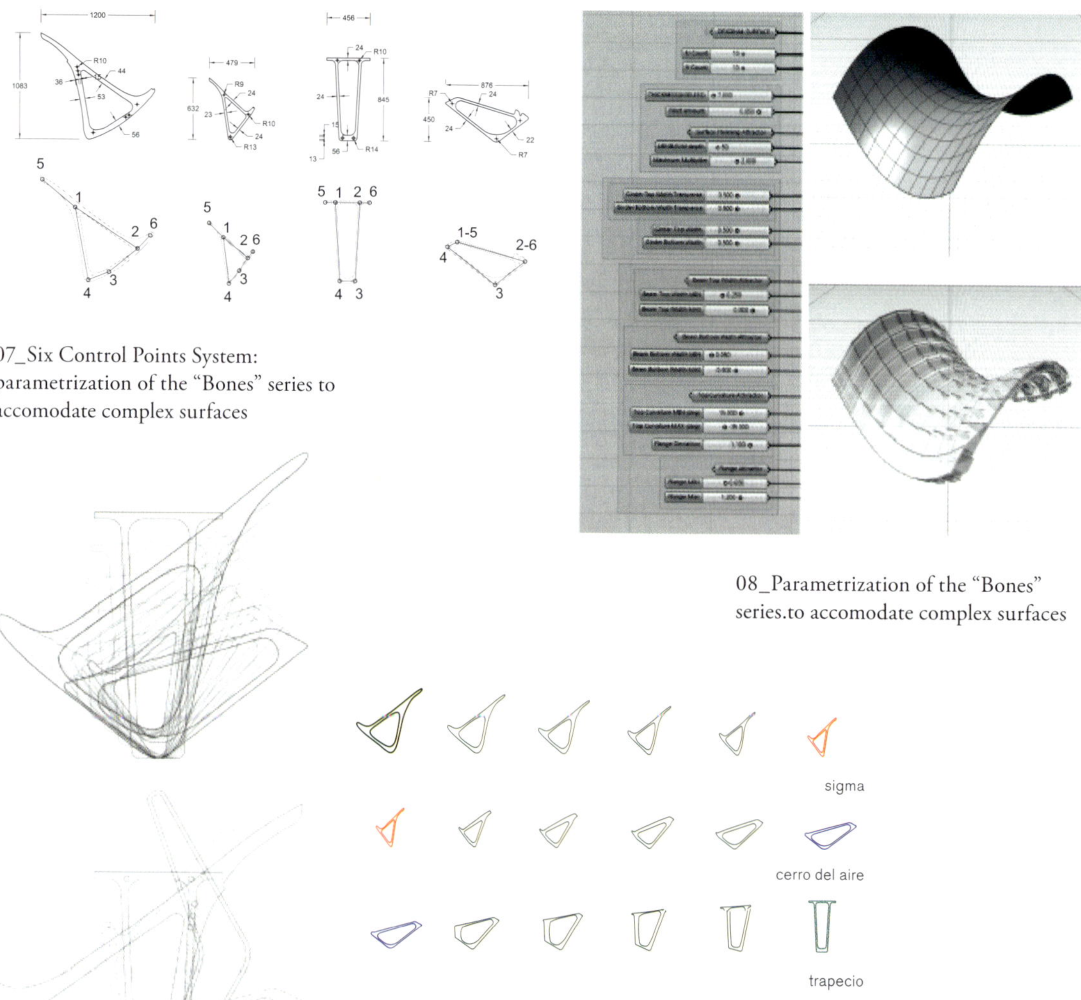

07_Six Control Points System: parametrization of the "Bones" series to accomodate complex surfaces

08_Parametrization of the "Bones" series.to accomodate complex surfaces

09_Original Fisac's "Bones" sections and examples of Fisac's Variations' interpolated range.

Re-describing

Systemic multi-formity on the pieza Valladolid
Becker, E._Chen, S._Hedberg, A._Tsui, W._Spring 2012

The team reverse engineered the geometric, material and constructive logic of the original. This knowledge was then translated into an associative model which also became the tool that supported the subsequent re-design phases. By transforming the geometry, orientation and position of the beam profile through calibrated formal operations, the students aimed to productively manipulate the originally linear beam element in order to demonstrate and test a broad range of architectural, spatial and phenomenological possibilities. (edited from student report)

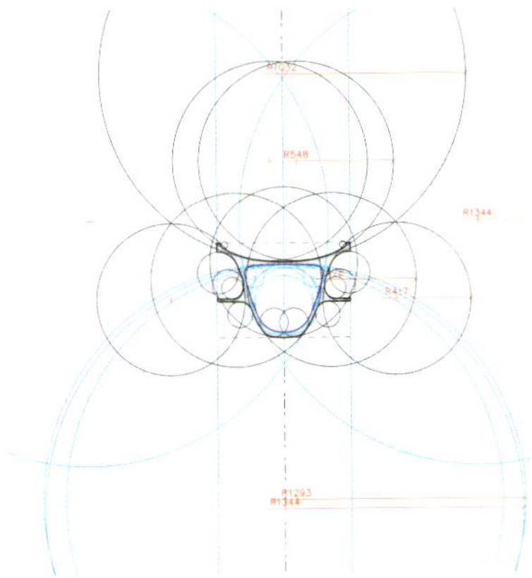

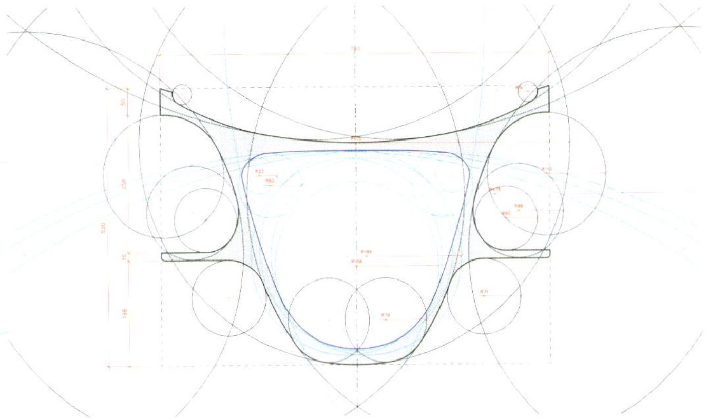

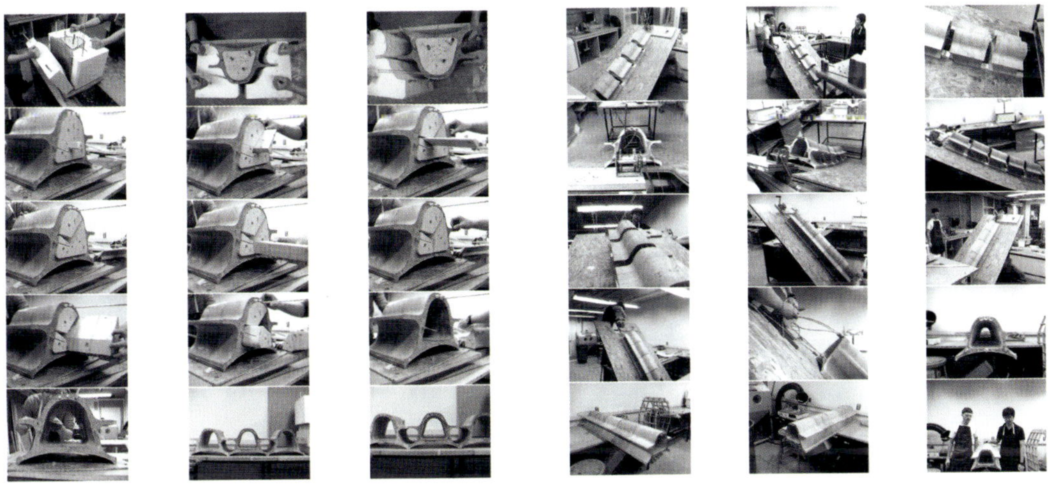

10_ Systemic Multi-Formity on the Pieza Valladolid_diagrams and fabrication

Re-describing

(Re)discretizing geodesic variables
Fu, Y._Lin, C._Solar, R._Yactayo, J. Spring 2013

To re-describe their precedent system, the team developed an associative model of the Fuller Fly's Eye Dome. This model was calibrated to allow for significant transformations to the precedent model. The dome was devised so that it may be transformed by multiplying the layers of surfaces in the dome buildup. Regularity and size of the dome openings may also be differentiated as well as sectional depth. Through the thorough re-description process, the team were able to identify opportunities within the construction system to introduce capacities for differentiation which were "natural" to the existing geometry. This reflects the overall ambition of the re-description exercise in the course, where latent opportunities for upgrading these systems were preferred over an imposition of an external system.
(edited from student report)

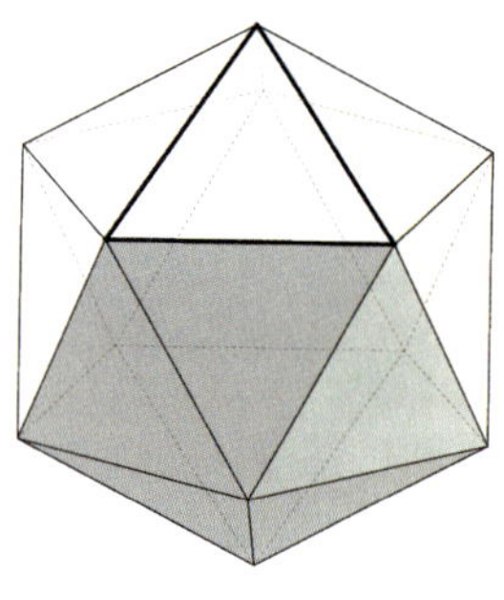

icosahedron

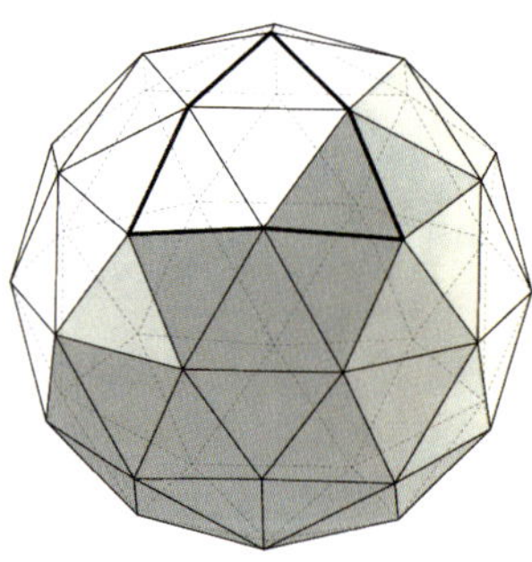

frequency 1

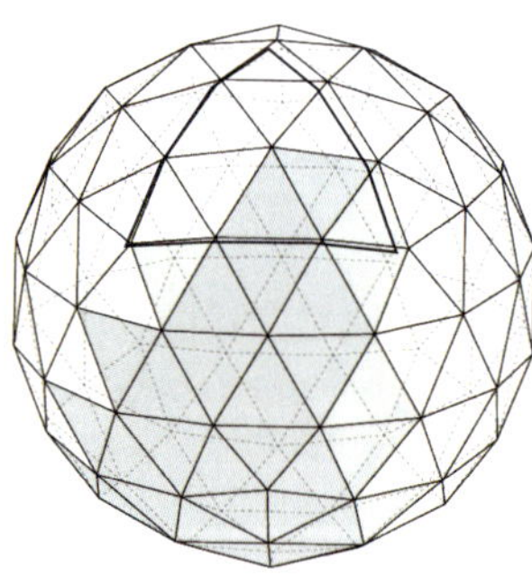

frequency 2

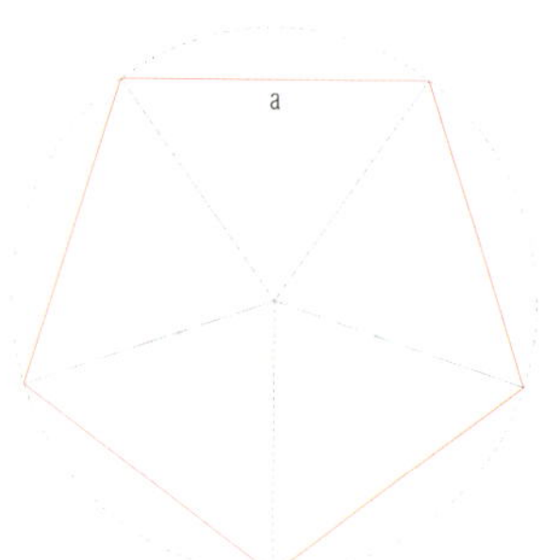

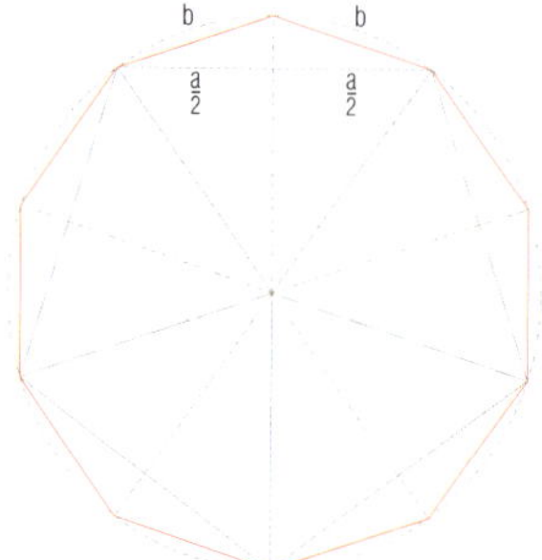

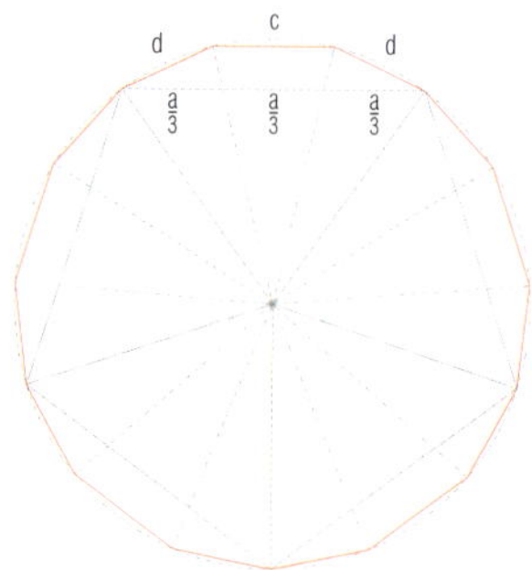

11_Discretization of the Geodesic Sphere_diagrams

Re-designing

Flake System. (Re)fabricating Nervi's mushroom column. Koutsenko, S, Martin, J, Staudt, J, Ugarte, JP._Spring 2013

Mushroom column definition

Generatrix definition

Revolution surface

Surface discretization

Diagrid

Panel geometric definition

P.01

P.02

P.03

P.04

Assembly sequence

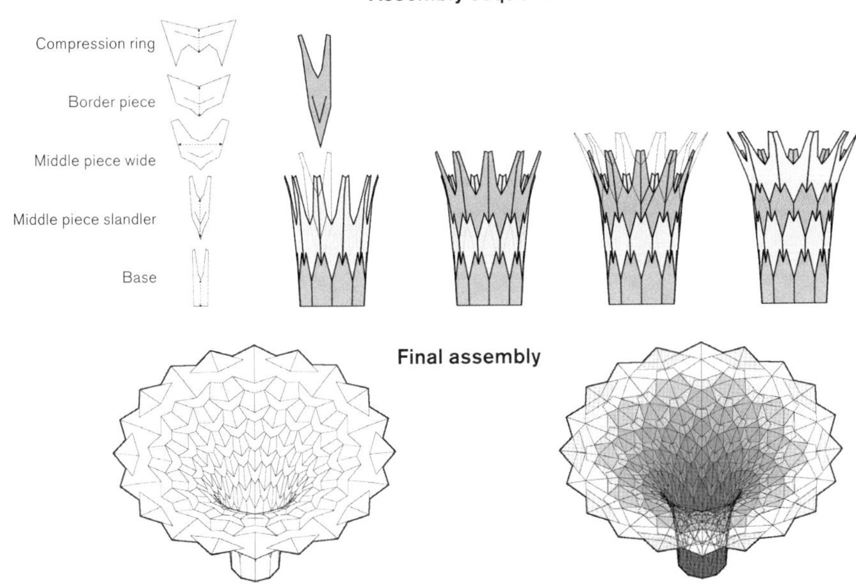

Nervi exposes the reinforcement elements within the mushroom-like geometry along the stress-line paths, thus considerably reducing the amount of material needed for the structure's overall performance and stability. The team departed from structural diagram and modularity of the precedent to produce a structural system that doesn't need mechanical connectors but rather follows a self-interlocking logic. This resulted in a reciprocal structure made of 1/8inch plywood material. The interlocking logic of a plywood module also allows for double curvature. The proposed geometric-based system is derived from different polygonal tiling patterns. (edited from student report)

12_Flake System_diagrams and model

Re-designing

(Re)fabricating Fuller's fly's eye dome
Chung, H._Zhan, Y._Fall 2010

The nature of the geodesic structure allows for the production of the whole sphere from a small number of modules. The team fabricated a portion of the sphere using two half modules that were able to generate the whole. Through their associative model, they were able to generate the digital files needed to fabricate prototypes of a potentially wide array of differentiated modules with variable thicknesses.
For the fabrication process, the team 3d-printed a positive form from of which a rubber mold was produced. The final prototypes were then cast in resin allowing for the fabrication of as many modules are required.

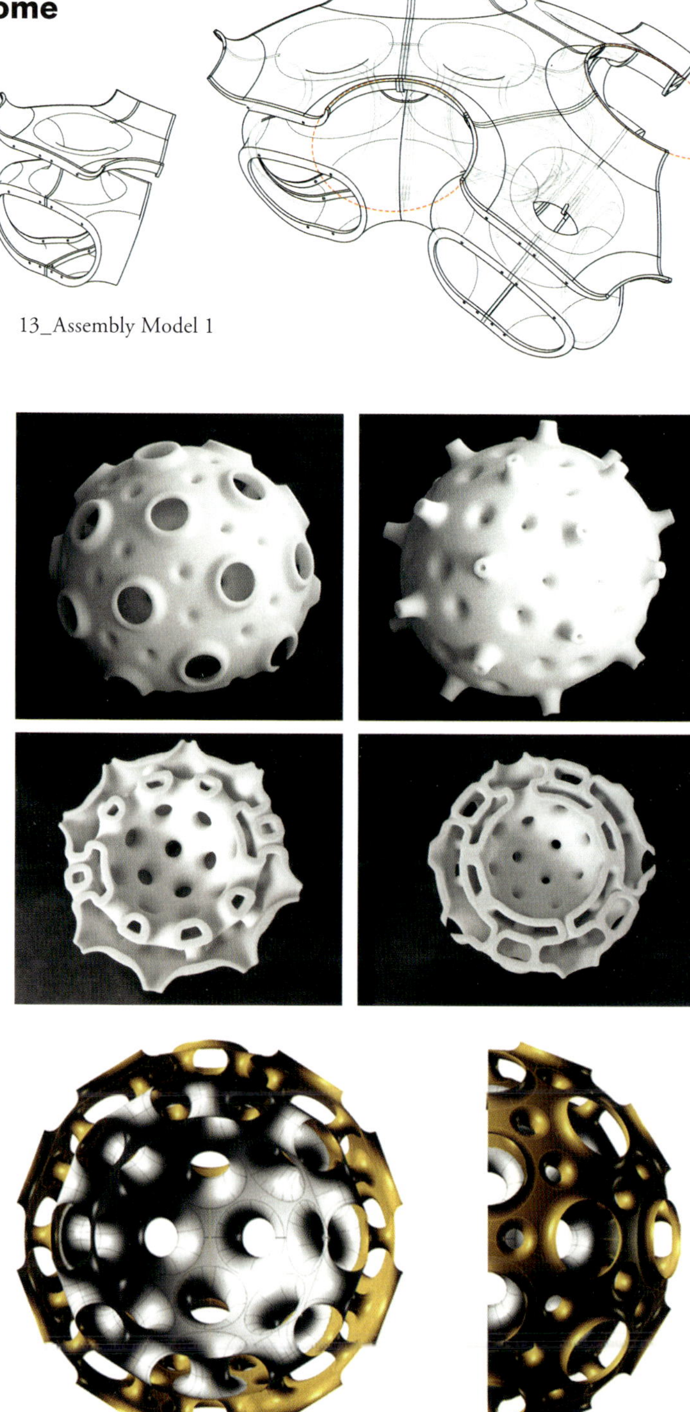

13_Assembly Model 1

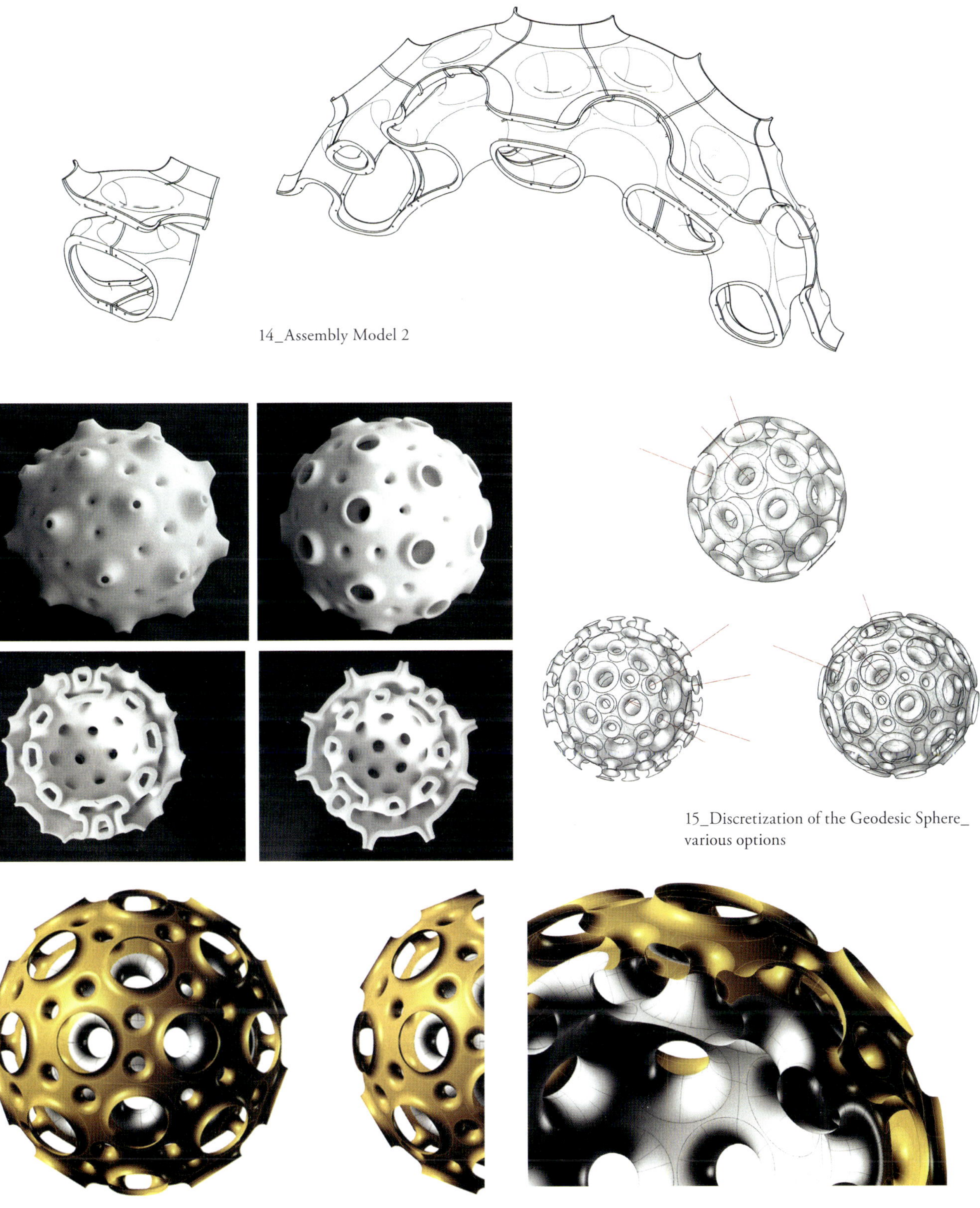

14_Assembly Model 2

15_Discretization of the Geodesic Sphere_ various options

16_Assembly Models_diagrams and 3D model visualizations

Re-designing

(Re)fabricating Fisac
Choi, W._Imbern, M._Raspall, F._Spring 2012

The team aimed to develop a new workflow that better integrated software linked to the control of fabrication machinery with digital design tools. This involved creating digital tools that could link robotic coding with parametric modeling software. The team deveoped a seamless connection between computer-aided design with advanced manufacturing, linking form-finding, structural analysis, geometric definition, CNC code generation and digital fabrication. This was done within a shared open-source computational environment. Using the associative model, the team explored a range of topological variations. The section of the beams were transformable between flat to non-zero Gaussian curvature. These differentiated sections could also be transformed along a section, allowing for the modulation of the geometry to address different structural, spatial and lighting performance. Through these explorations, the team was able to produce a structural system that could depart from the linear beam systems of Fisac and introduce a girder system; producing bidirectional slabs instead. This also allowed for the doing away of continuous linear supports. Remarkably, this exploration in geometric variation also yielded a transformation in the structural behavior of the system, allowing the students to discover alternative applications of the formal system in the structural domain. (edited from student report)

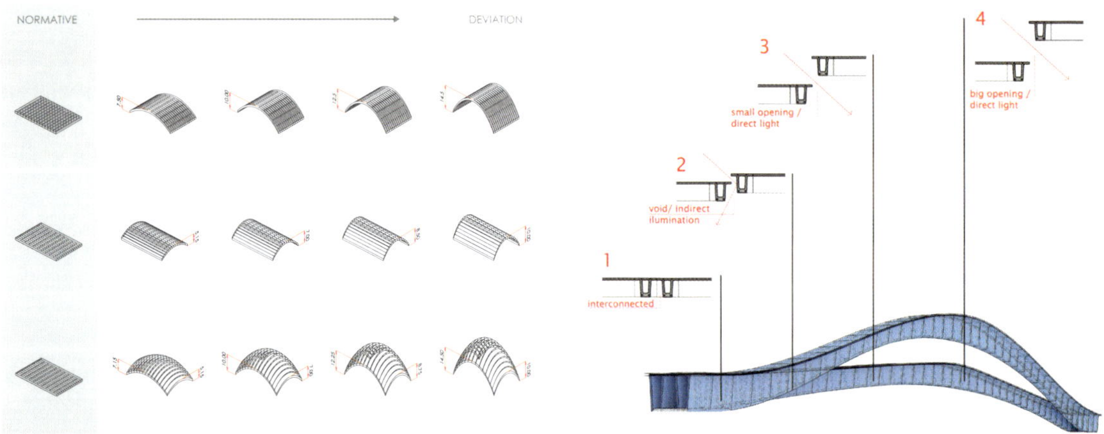

17_(Re)fabricating Fisac_section diagrams and quad definition

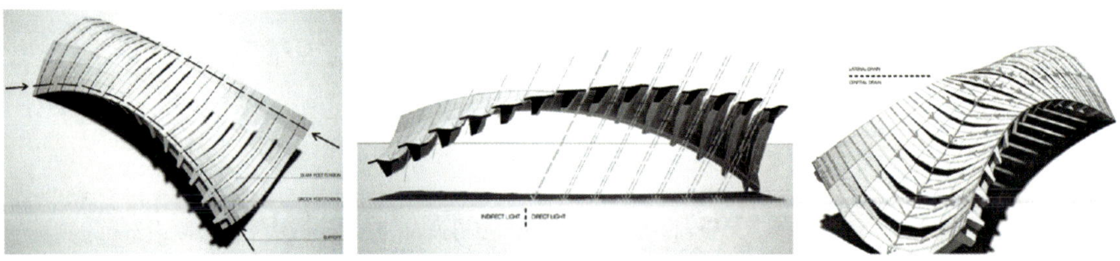

18_(Re)fabricating Fisac_stress, lighting and drainage diagram

Re-designing

Systemic multi-formity on the Pieza Valladolid
Becker, E._Chen, S._Hedberg, A._Tsui, W._ Spring 2012

By manipulating the associative model of the precedent, the students achieved a wider range of performances and spatial effects. Amplified performances such as improved cross-ventilation was studied by analyzing the response of different design instantiations to simulated wind-flows. Day-lighting was also studied with the production of variable aperture sizing, expanding the opportunities for applying the roof structural systems for different kinds of buildings with varying lighting requirements. The team also explored the capacity for a structural transformation. The linear, straight beam configuration is reconsidered as arch structures. They explore the possibility of making connections of the structure on different floor levels. (edited from student report)

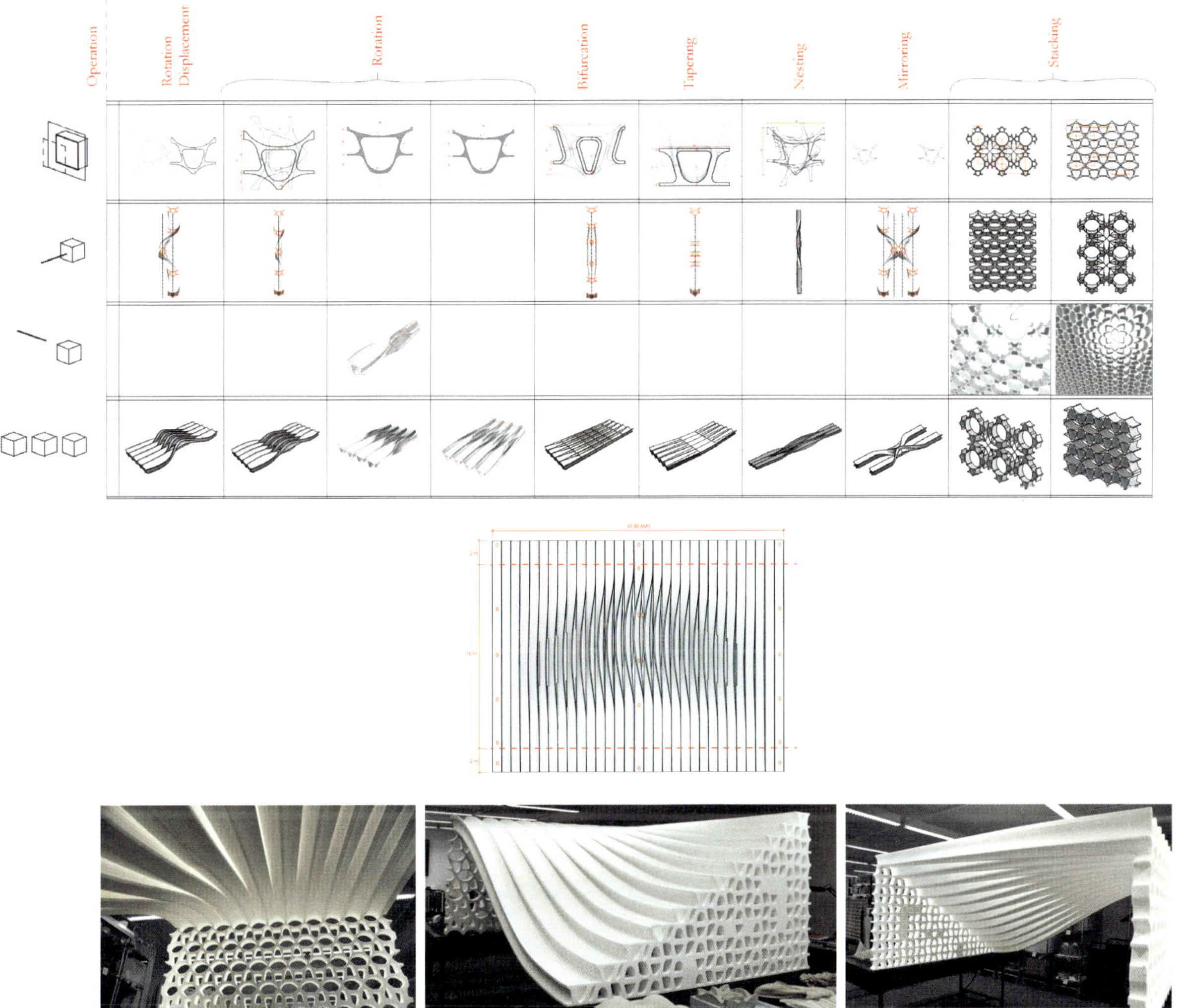

19_Systemic Multi-Formity on the Pieza Valladolid_diagrams and mock-up

Re-designing

(Re)discretizing geodesic variables
Fu, Y._Lin, C._Solar, R._Yactayo, J._Spring 2013

The team identified that the combination of frequency 2 and frequency 4 geodesic structures would produce planar surfaces in between. This would allow for the production of a thickened structure which could be manufactured from flat panels. This configuration also produced horizontal plane around the equator which allows the structure to rest on the ground easily. They developed a range of thickness for the structure based on the diameter of the outer and inner surface as well as a range of modes of differentiation for connecting surfaces between the outer and inner geodesic structure. While the different instantiations all had different performative and spatial capacities, the team decided to build a sample of the planar surfaces iteration.
(edited from student report)

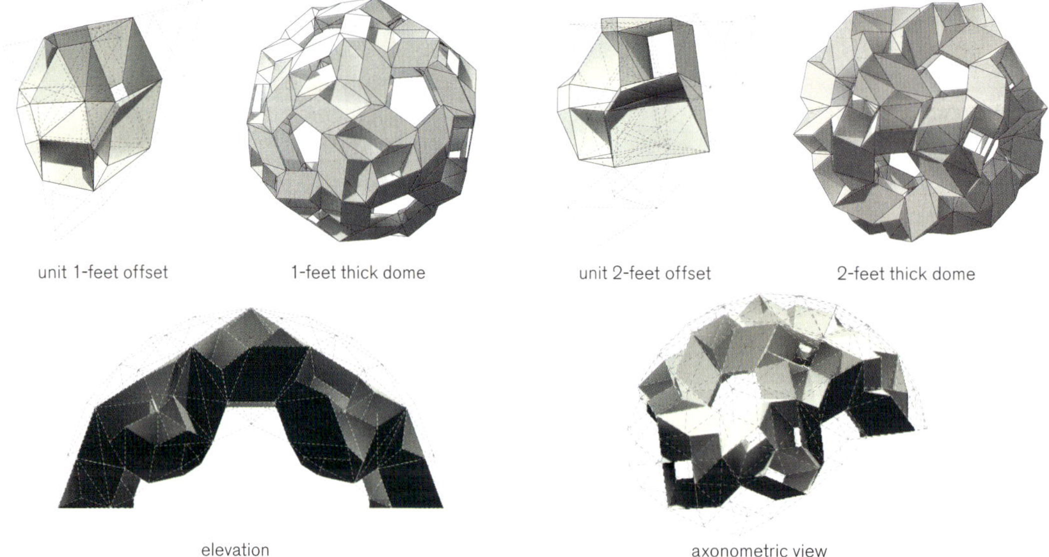

20_(Re)discretizing Geodesic Variables_various thicknesses based on frequency permutations

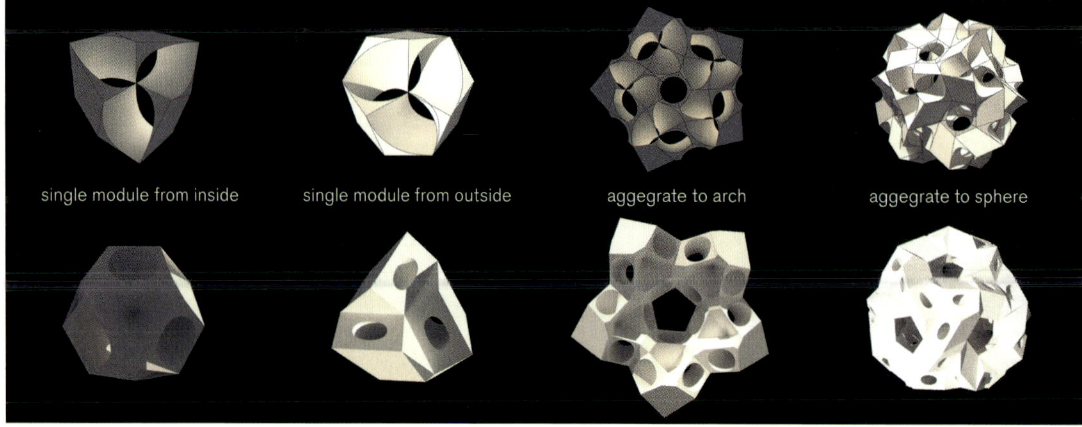

21_(Re)discretizing Geodesic Variables_light studies

Re-designing

On-site robotic assembly of double-curved self-supporting structures. Ariza, I._Gazit, M._Spring 2015

Using Nervi's cantilevered mushroom column as a precedent: a circular roof made of prefabricated concrete components, the team aimed towards establishing a protocol for constructing variations of this system using robotic assembly.

In order to do this, the team went through a rigorous process of a thorough discretization of its parts. The team devised a modular system that would be better accommodated by robotic assembly. These units are designed with an interlocking system of connections. The design of the units and the robotic assembly process was coordinated for the structure to be fully assembled as a unitized construction with a structural behavior inspired by Nervi's precedent.
(edited from student report)

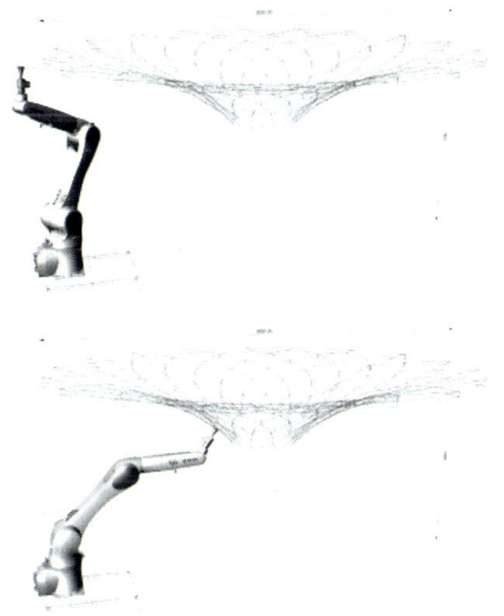

22_Re-modeling the mushroom structure to meet robot and fabrication constraints. Height: 1.4 meters / 4.6 feet at outer edge. Diameter: 3 meters / 9.8 feet.

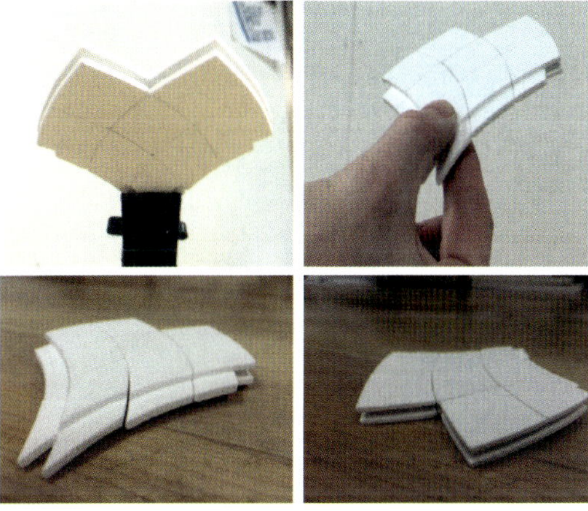

24_cantilevered components for a stacked self-supporting structure with male/ female cantilevered joints. small-scale prototype, 3d printed in ZCorp-

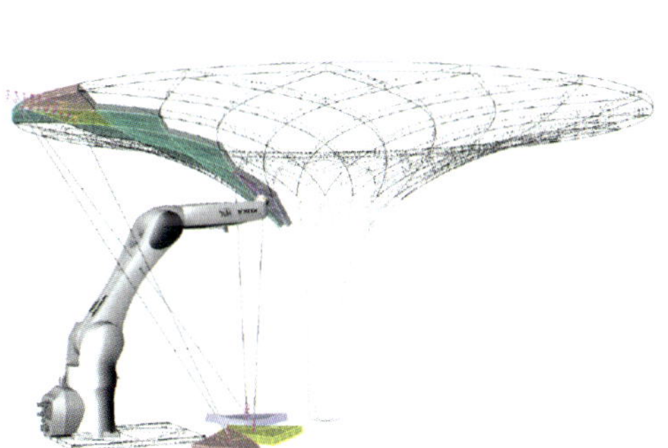

23_Simulation of assembly in accordance with the maximum reachable points of the robot's envelope space - full scale.

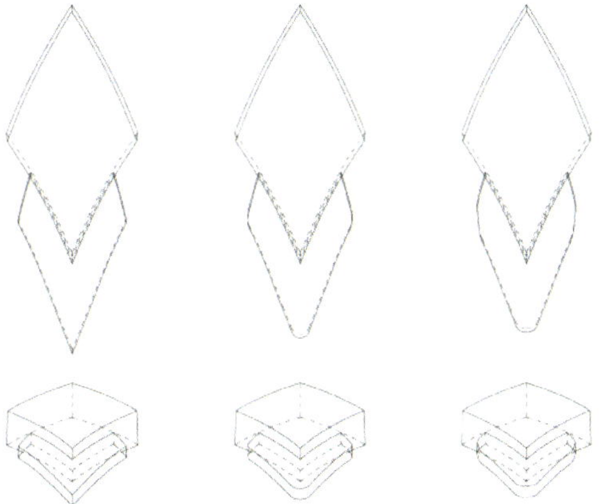

25_prototype for edge tolerance and smoothness tests.

Re-fabricating

Flake System. (Re)fabricating Nervi's mushroom column Koutsenko, S._Martin, J._Staudt, J._Ugarte, JP._Spring 2013

The team's re-designed structure was devised as a flat pack system that occupies minimal space to allow for ease of transportation. The devised manufacturing process operates on two levels:

1. Taking advantage of digital fabrication tools, the assembly process is made more efficient. The process takes into account major variables, such as the dimensions of the tool path (to optimize the cutting speed) and to achieve precise tolerances in the overlaps between the wood pieces.

2. It considers the material properties to improve the structural performance of each module relative to its location within the overall structure. This is possible when acknowledging the wood grain orientation relative to the individual pieces, and by working within the physical capabilities of the material. (edited from student report)

26_Assembled mock-up & volume of disassembled components. Photographs by Joe Staudt

27_Harvard, GSD_Spring 2013 Jury. Photographs by Anita Kan

Re-fabricating

(Re)discretizing geodesic variables
Fu, Y._Lin, C._Solar, R._Yactayo, J._Spring 2013

The team built a portion of their re-designed prototype using flat aluminum sheets. These sheets were cut using a robotic arm fitted with a water jet. These pieces were then folded into place. This system was initially tested using a larger cardboard mock up.
From the re-fabrication process and deep geometrical understanding of the Fly's Eye Dome, the students developed a critique of Fuller's design which came under two categories. First related to its limited thickness which results from using only one geodesic sphere and with one level of frequency. Secondly, the lack of resolution and clear intention for how the Fly's Eye Dome may engage with the ground.
Their main research interest laid in studying the interaction between multiple geodesic spheres, at different levels of frequencies. This was pursued as a method to generate thickness which can both, enhance the structural performance of the dome, as well as provide more control of the interior lighting performance.
Lastly, through the use of planar surfaces within this new thickness, the resulting dome can better address and adjust to different ground conditions.
(edited from student report)

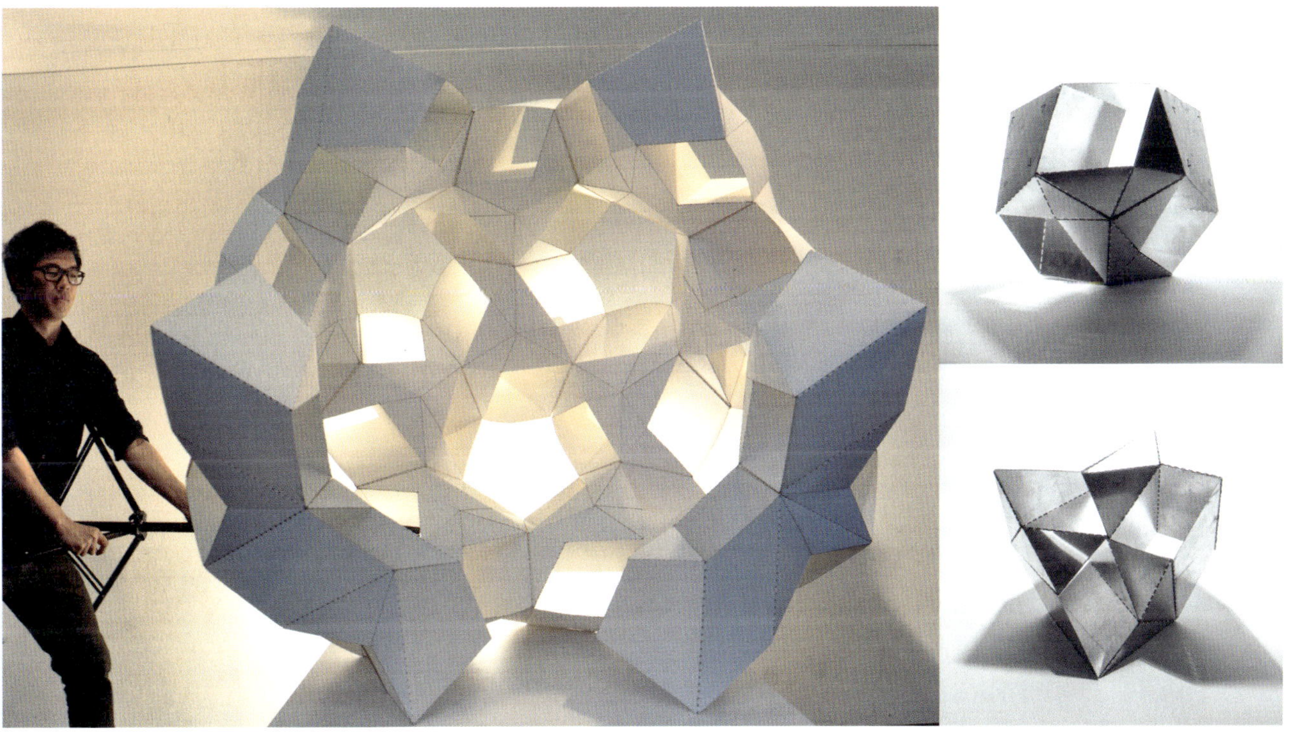

28_module fabrication_left image in card and right ones in aluminum.
Photograph by Ricardo Solar

Re-fabricating

(Re)fabricating Fisac
Choi, W._Imbern, M._Raspall, F._Spring 2012

The emphasis of this project was on the development of an automated process which converts the geometries developed by the associative design model into robotic code which instructs a hot-wire robotic arm to cut custom molds. Recyclable polystyrene was tested as a material which was cut by a hot-wire attached to the robotic arm using standard components. The process was developed to be rapid, precise, affordable and easily recyclable.

A complete cutting sequence for a full-scaled beam was calibrated to take 15 minutes to complete while a girder module of a meter length took 25 minutes. The units are cast from concrete within these customized molds.
High-tension and self-compacting concrete mixtures can be mixed with efficient assembly-lines to enable this process, affording for the production of differentiated beam elements (as opposed to the standardized system of Fisac's original.) In the assembly process, the units of the beam are arranged and then post-tensioned into place to assemble each beam. This process could be achieved in-situ or prefabricated. Once all the beams are assembled, the girders may be post-tensioned in a perpendicular direction to the beams to connect that beams into a single structural system.
(edited from student report)

29_Mock-up_Final Review at Harvard, GSD_Spring 2012

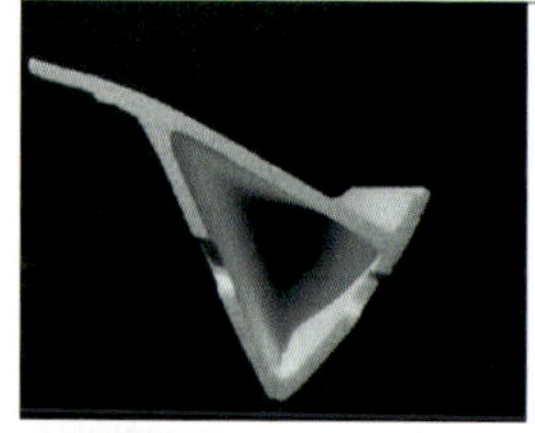

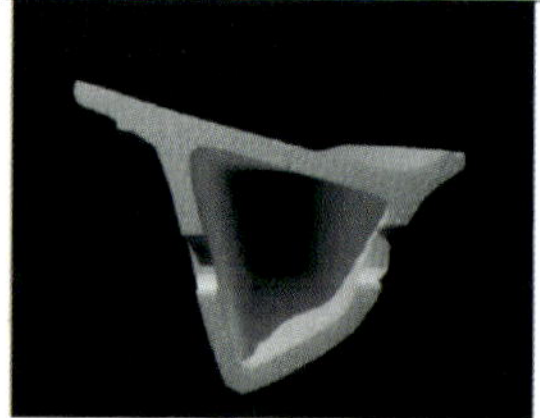

30_full scale voussoirs, wirecut EPS (left) and casted concrete (right).

31_wirecut diagram, cutting and assemblying sequence (next page).

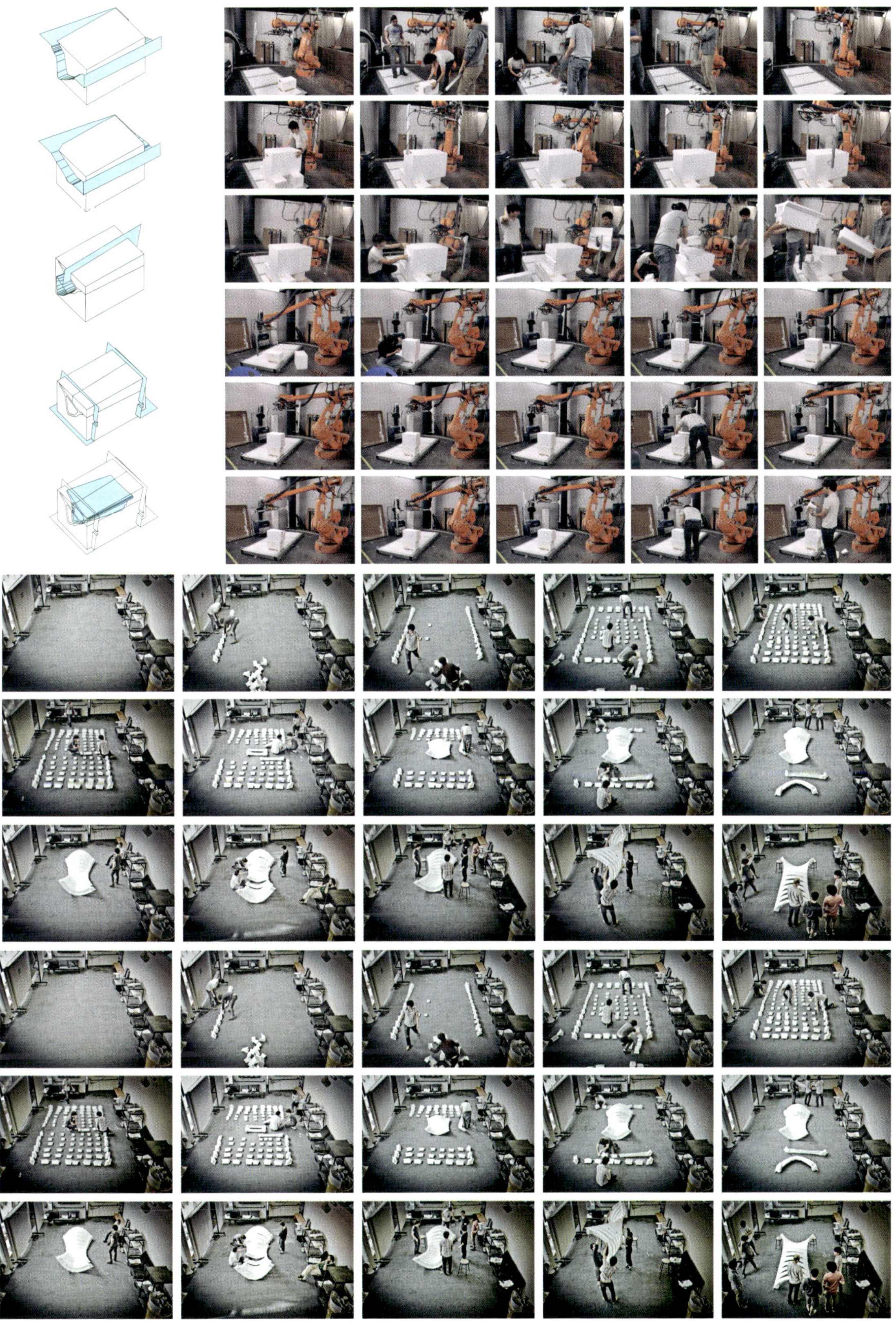

Re-fabricating

On-site robotic assembly of double-curved self-supporting structures. Ariza, I._Gazit, M._Spring 2015

The team produced numerous mockups with 3d printed modules to test assembly processes. However, the final prototype was acheived with larger milled pieces. In this project the team proposed a design-construction workflow by providing geometric information from the associative design model to an on-site robotic arm that performs the assembly process. The robotic arm is an important consideration and integrated part of the design process from its early stages, which in turn accounted for a more continuous and smooth design-construction workflow.
In many industries and for many years now, industrial robots have been crucial components in complex assembly lines (e.g. the car industry). As the ability of the designer to easily generate complex structures grows, there are also opportunities for developing an analogous assembly technology in the building industry. The automation of the assembly process can decrease the gap between design and construction processes, and between the initial architectural model and the final outcome. (edited from student report)

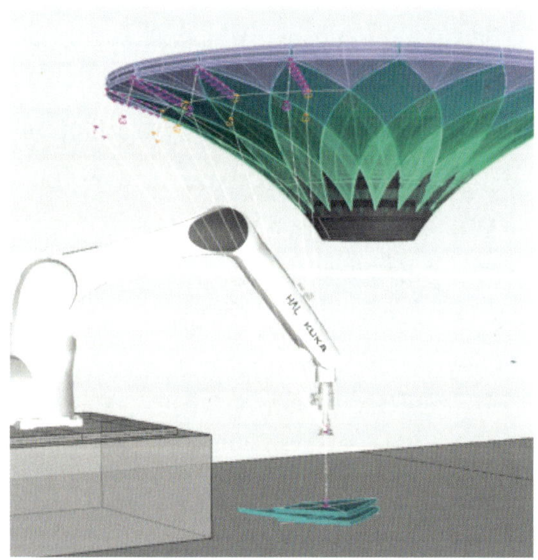

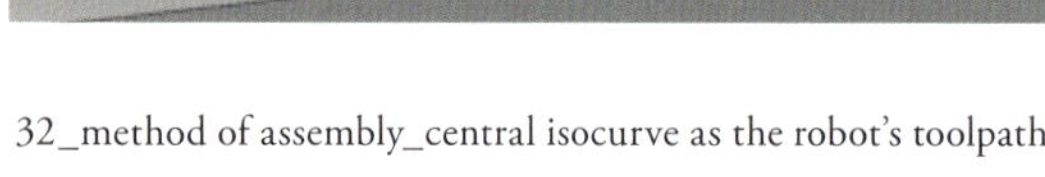

32_method of assembly_central isocurve as the robot's toolpath

33_Test assembly of self-supporting double curved structure

34_sequence of assembly, ring by ring. structure in compression, edge of structure (final ring) in tension. The structure is self-supported during each of the assembly phases, which omits the use of scaffolding.

Re-fabricating

Deformative matters.
Ampanavos, S._Santos, S._Jye, J._Stähelin, R._Fall 2014

The team started with a series of studies or analogue explorations where ceramic slabs were deformed through pinching and other techniques. At this point they realized that slabs pinched laterally allowed for consistency in the production of the "deformed" tiles while allowing them to have a series of simple pre-set parameters that controlled the mechanics of the pinching technique which could be easily translated to the digital fabrication environment. With this in mind they developed a slab machine that was controlled by a robotic arm. They also had to devise a series of linear magnets on the side of the clay and metal bays to keep the clay in place until it reached the leather hard state. This also helped in removing and transporting the pinched elements while maintaining their form. They also added a "conveyor belt" as well as a "cookie cutter" system to the robotic fabrication process in order to achieve dimensional precision to increase the fabrication efficiency.
(edited from student report)

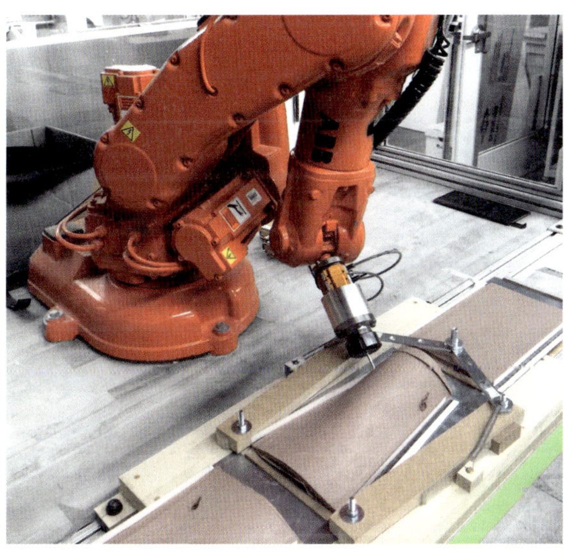

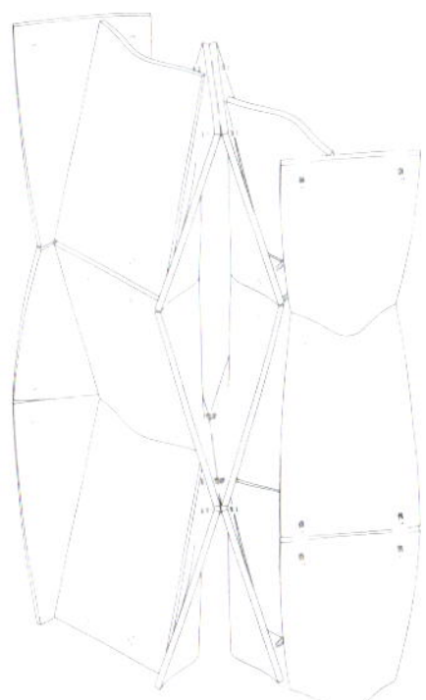

35_Deformative Matters_variability diagram, assembly fabrication and model

Re-fabricating

Pug Mill Parametrics.
Bucklin, O._Going, J._Sonnabend, K._Fall 2015

This team explored the possibility of customization in industrial brick production through the use of an automated wire-cutting system. An attachment to a ceramic pug mill that would use wires to carve two sides of the clay extrusion was developed, creating dynamic brick profiles and allowing for a large degree of variation and precision in brick geometry.

The tool allowed the team to control the brick geometry in two dimensions and ruled surfaces were particularly easy to achieve. The reciprocity between digital design tools, machine, and material in the fabrication process allowed them to make rapid adjustments to their design scripts to accommodate unforeseen material behavior during production.

The process allowed for structural assemblies that supported a consistent brick-laying pattern along a curved surface. (edited from student report)

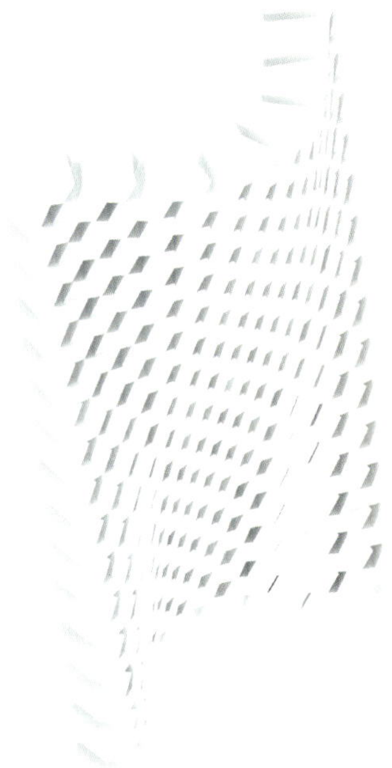

37_Pug Mill Parametrics_gaussian wall model

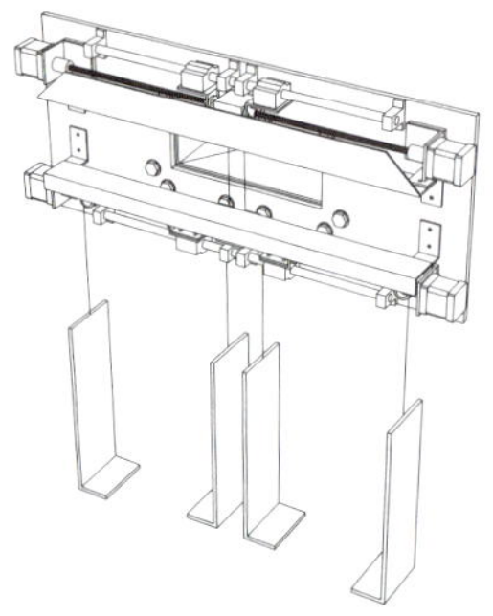

36_Pug Mill Parametrics_fabrication of pug mill attachment and customized bricks

Re-fabricating

RAse.
Kim, A._Qin, S._Mishra, T._Liao, Z._Fall 2015

This team developed a system for fabricating novel bricks by combining the functionality of a robotic arm with a turntable. The hand-manipulated processes of the potter's wheel were abstracted into simpler movements, which could then be translated into the robotic manufacturing process. The robotic technology combined with digital scripting tools was then used to expand the form-generation capabilities of the pottery-making process.

This merging of techniques of the 'old' and the 'new' not only introduced novelty in terms of forms but also made the structures more amenable to mass production. Mechanization of these manufacturing processes has allowed for speeding up the pace of manufacturing. The stages of manufacturing entailed a combination of analog and digital methods - involving the processes of extrusion, rotation, robotic carving, firing and assembly.

The pieces were shaped into slightly varying configurations of spiral forms. A mirrored aggregation method was developed to allow for lateral bracing of the individual columns with those that were adjacent to them. Some potential areas of application would be in designing expressive architectural screens, structures for evaporative cooling and porosity screens for privacy control or natural lighting control. (edited from student report)

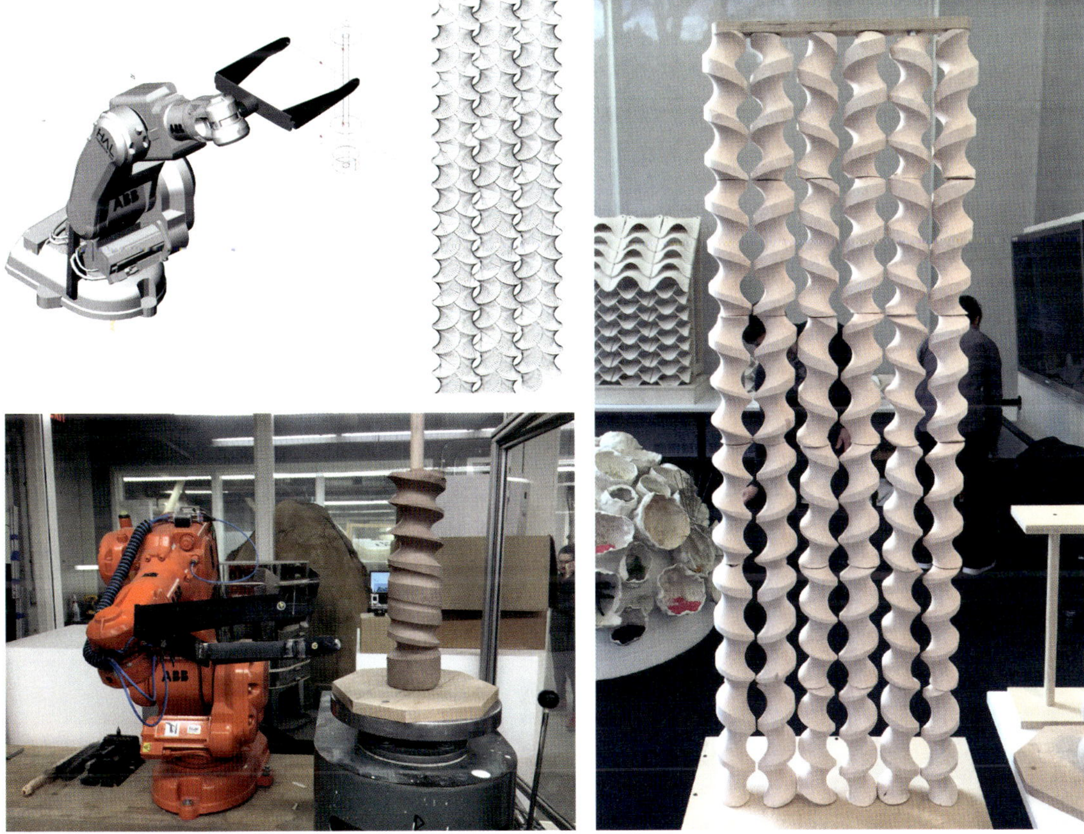

38_RAse_fabrication of components & assembled mock-up

Re-contextualizing

Systemic Multi-Formity on the Pieza Valladolid
Becker, E._Chen, S._Hedberg, A._Tsui, W._Spring 2012

While generating many other possible variants on the associative model based on the precedent from Fisac, the team also framed these explorations with an eye to daylighting and wind performance. To help them achieve this, they leveraged digital analysis tools that allowed them to re-contextualize and test their design iterations within a computationally simulated environment.

The proposed outcome of these manipulations is an expanded catalog of architectural components as well as a documentation of the variety of spaces these elements are able to produce. Using simulation and evaluation tools, the team test the ability this precedent holds for performing as a variable roofscape and natural lighting mechanism, a loadbearing facade element, and a means of transitioning or mediating between levels of a building section. By engaging with analytical tools that place their design models in a simulated environment, they aim to demonstrate the performative versatility that is latent in this simple structural beam element and to reveal the diversity of utility it may accommodate within the scope of architectural space making.
(edited from student report)

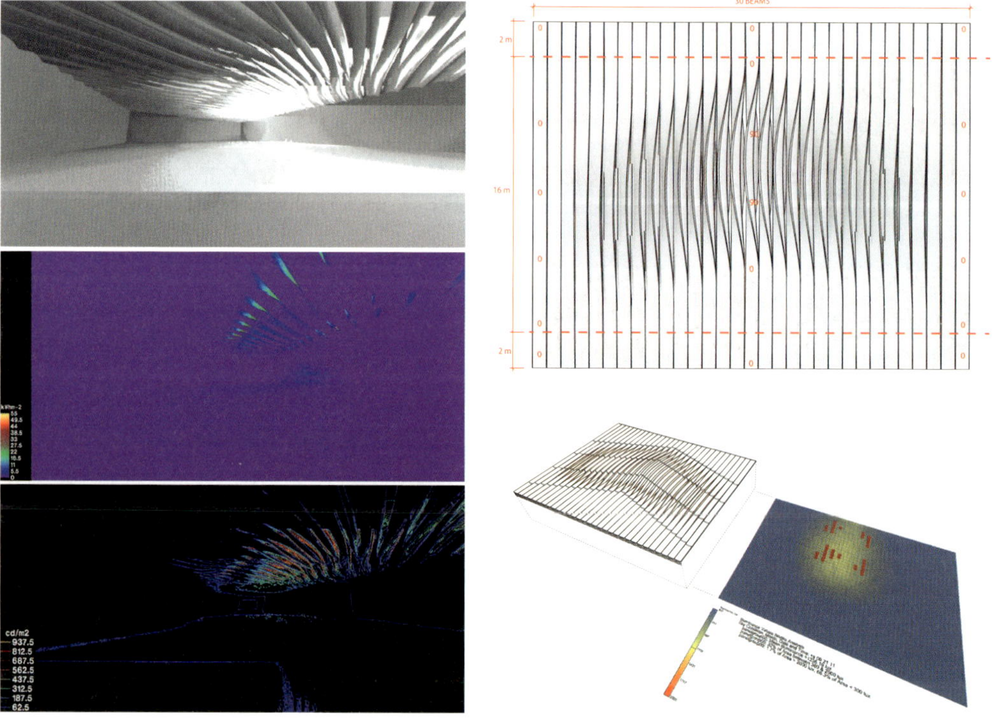

39_visualization, radiation map (kWh/m^2), surface illumination map (cd/m^2). (left)
40_plan, visualization, radiation map (kWh/m^2). (right)

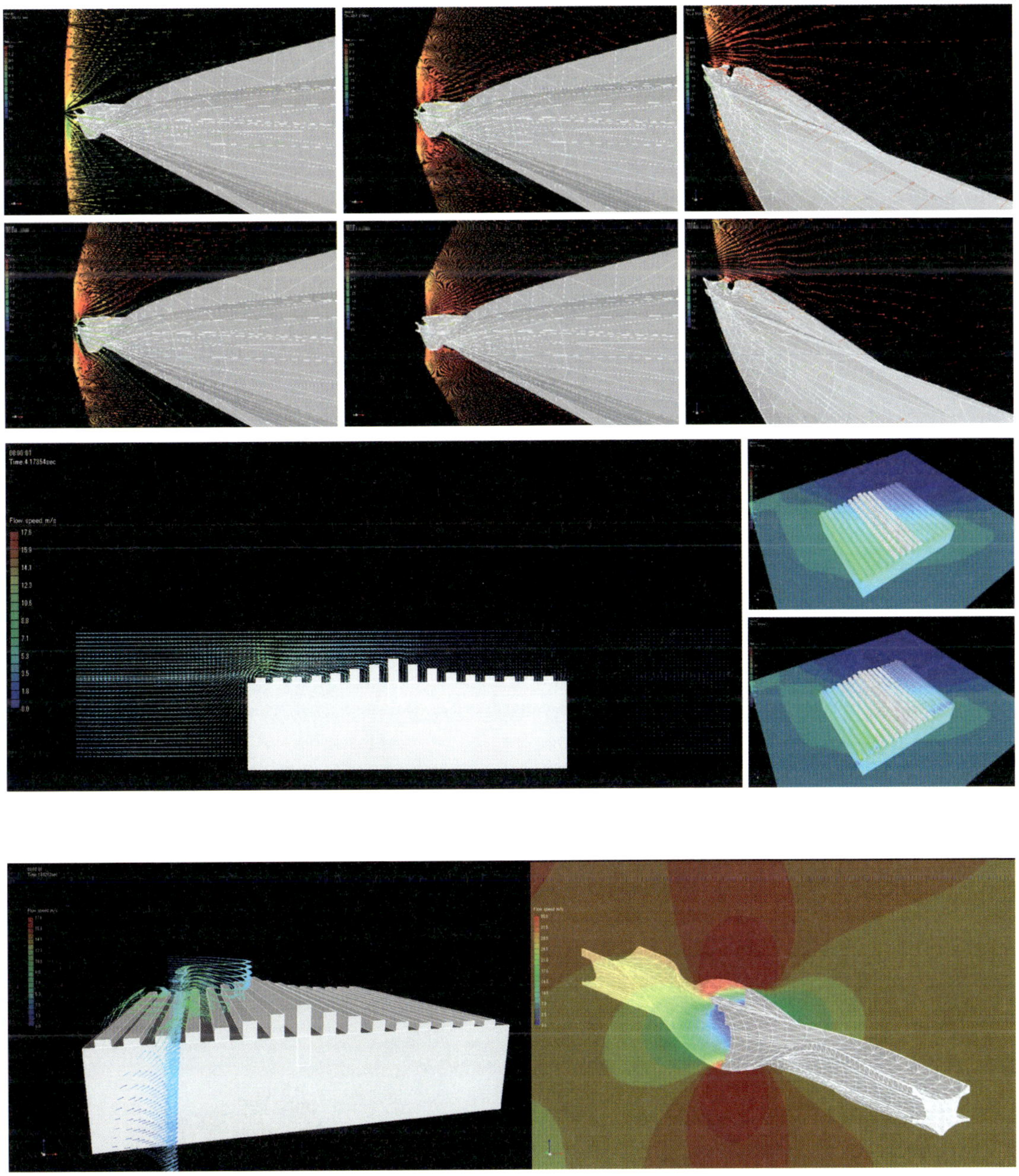

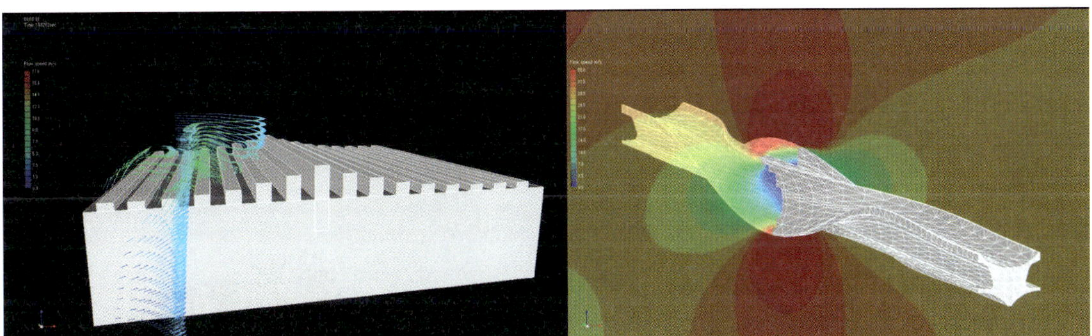

41_airflow analysis_chilled beam cooling, fluid simulation.

Re-contextualizing

Terracotta evaporative brick.
Akkineni, A._Jacobson, A._ Schecter, J._Papadopoulou, C._Fall 2014

These Terracotta brick prototypes are constrained within the dimensional constraints of a traditional brick so that they can be easily inserted as part of a traditional brick wall. Terracotta bricks use the material properties of ceramics to create an effective evaporative cooling system.
Each brick consists of five "wells," each holding a small amount of water. When air passes around these wells, the water evaporates and the air cools.
When aggregated the effects of the individual units can be felt over a larger area, contributing to an overall effect of cooling from one side to the other.
(edited from student report)

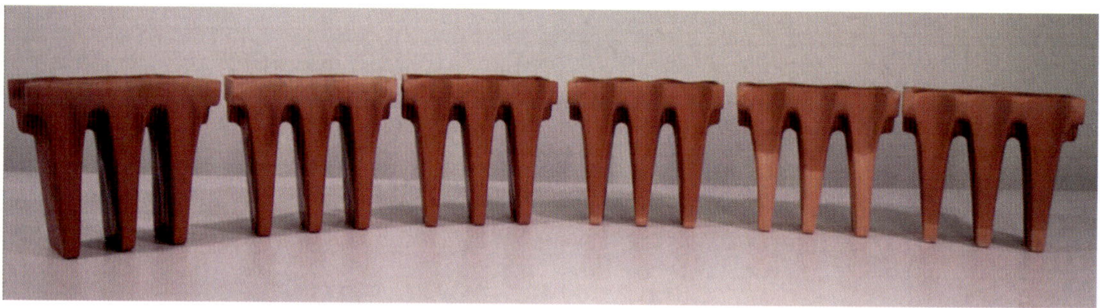

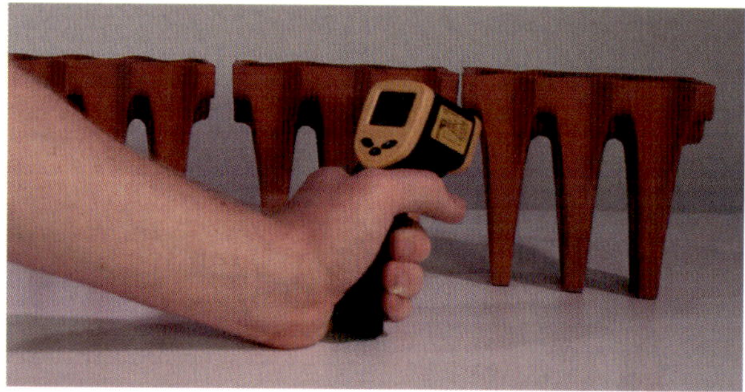

42_Terracotta Evaporative Brick_
Absortion & Temperature Test
(top and center left)

43_Terracotta Evaporative Brick_
Assembled mock-up (bottom images).
Photographs by Anita Kan

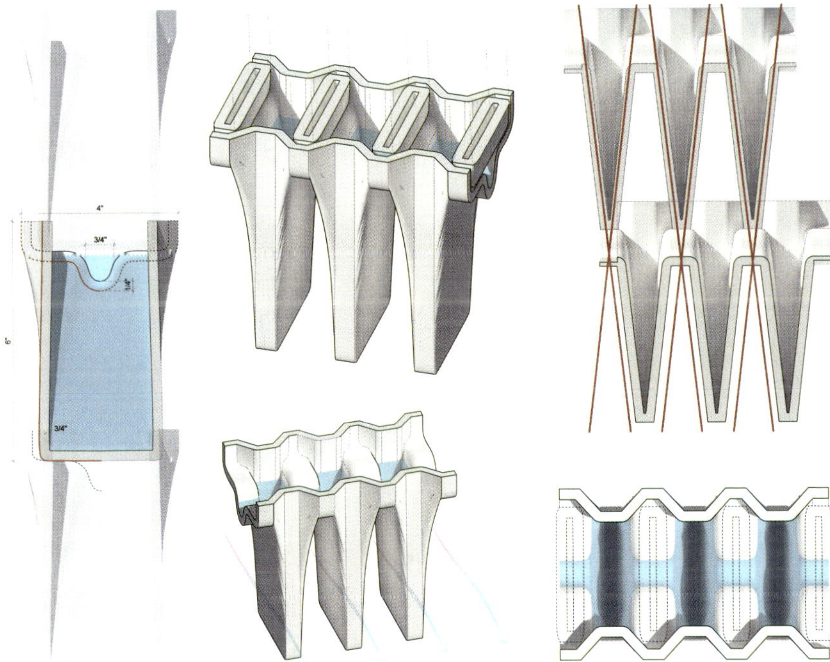

44_Terracotta Evaporative Brick_structure, air & water flow diagrams.
Structure stacking: the geometry that allows the circulation of air is manipulated to create a structural stacking system between bricks. Two distinct profiles allow the bricks to rest on top of each other, staggered for stability, while also permiting the passage of water from compartment to compartment. The individual unit attempts to maximize the surface contact between the surrounding air and the porous ceramic material.
This increases possible evaporation and the volume of air capable of being cooled.

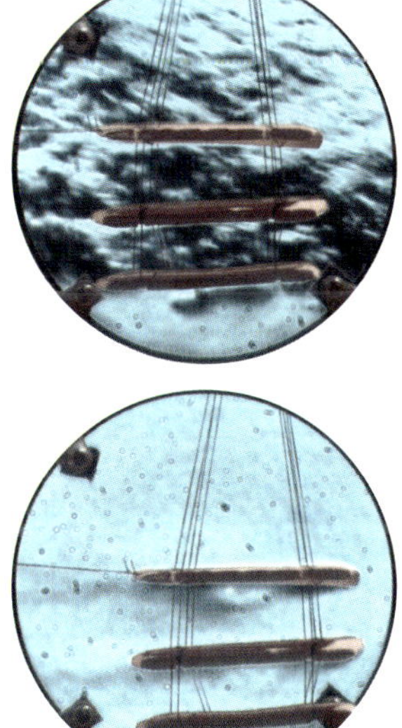

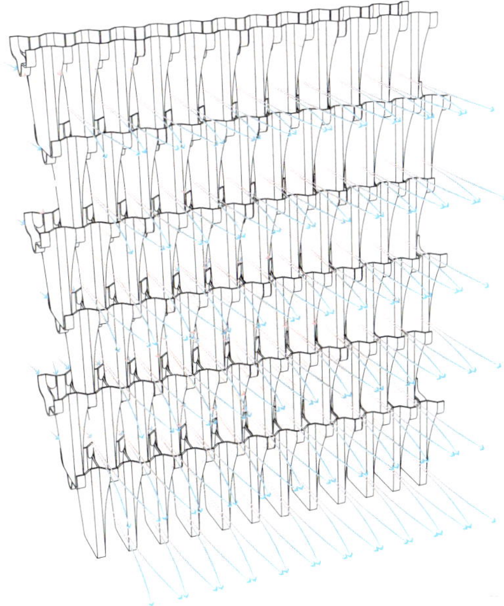

45_Terracotta Evaporative Brick_ schlieren test saturated ceramic tiles, heated with a heating gun, raising the temperature and causing the water to evaporate off the ceramic surface (top left image). The ceramic tiles with only a gentle breeze (bottom left image). Aggregation of units (right image)

Re-contextualizing

Terracotta tectonics.
Gadodia, P._Fernandez-Linares, A._Mendonca, A._ Muñoz Moreno, G._Serna, S._Fall 2015

CAD , CNC milling and slip casting techniques were employed to introduce hollow pathways for energy and matter flow through the structure. Using evaporative cooling strategies, the prototype is a reinterpretation of the common extruded brick. The truncated octahedron produces interconnected hollow terracotta pieces that mediate thermal and kinetic energetic flows. The damp earth structure is also suitable for growing moss which ingest airborne toxins and regulate humidity.
(edited from student report)

46_Terracotta Tectonics_mock-ups

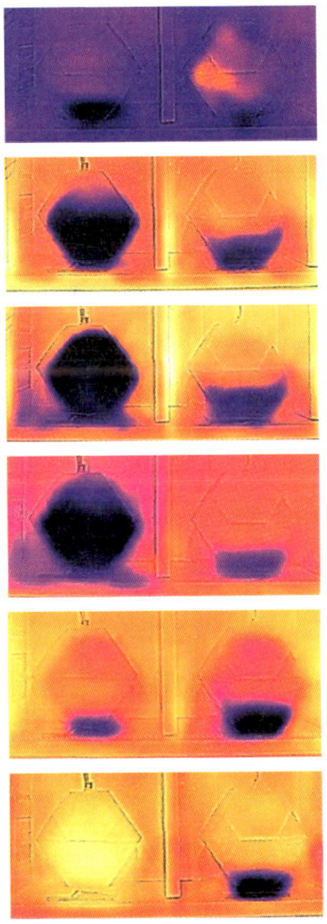

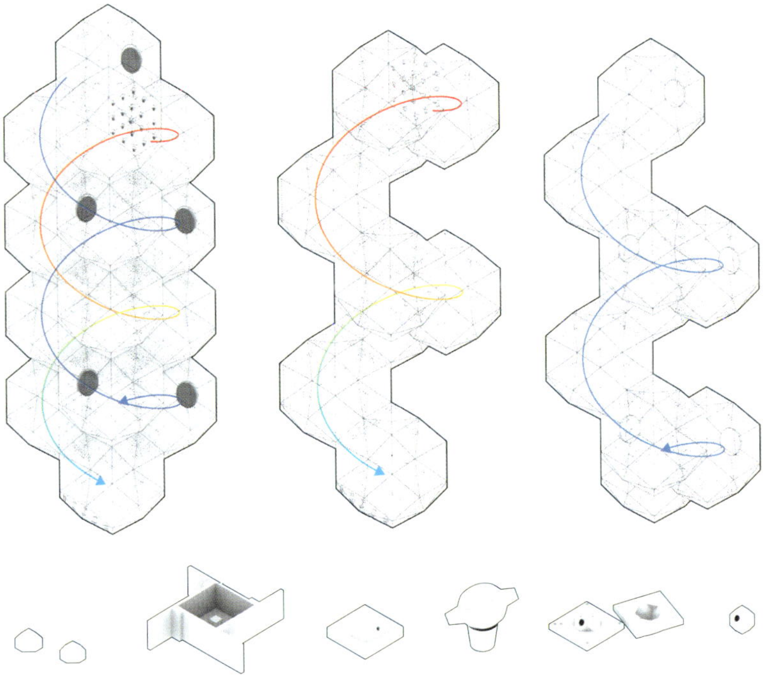

Thermal imaging and evaporative cooling

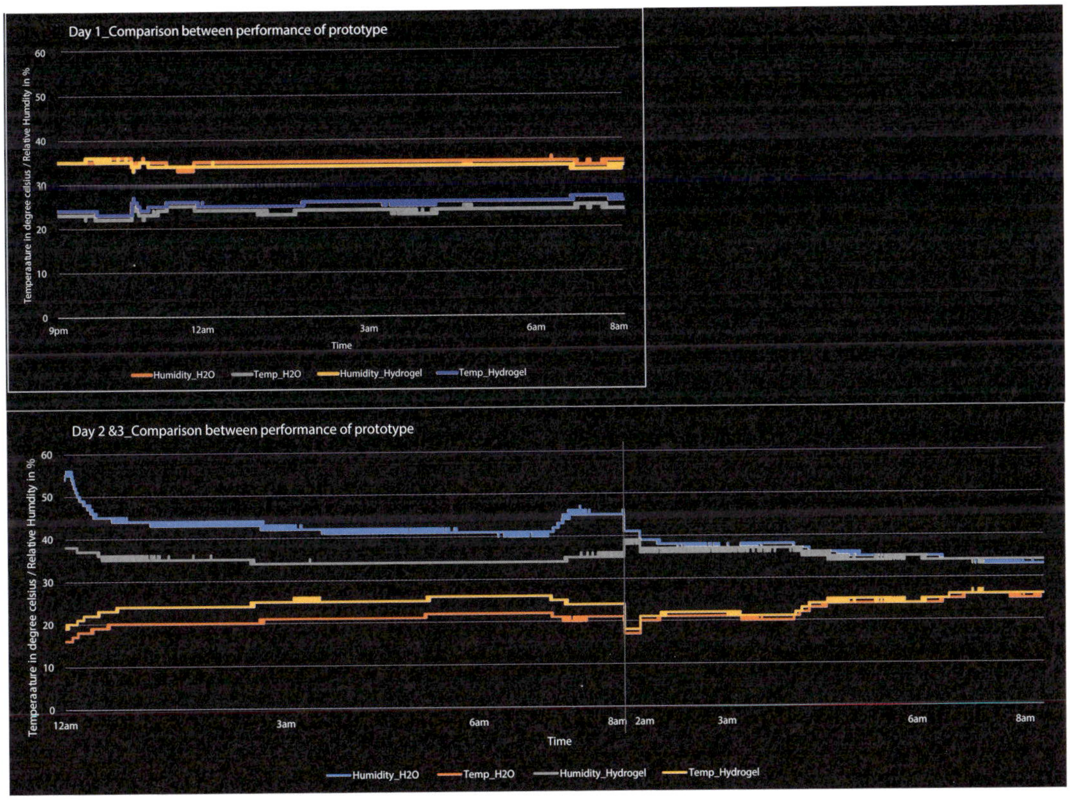

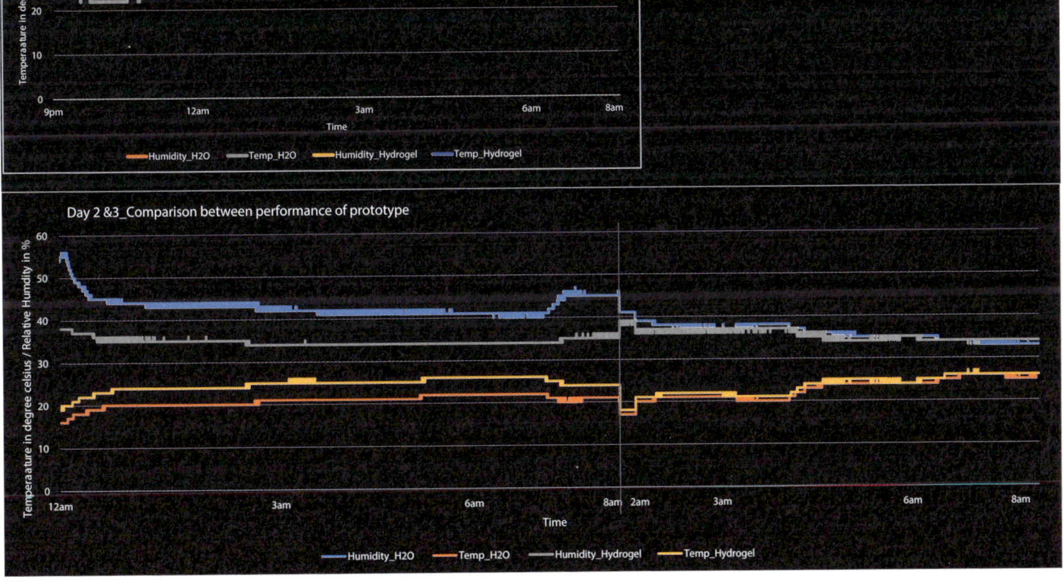

47_Performance comparison across prototypes throughout three days_temperature (°C)

Re-contextualizing

Curve Light.
Bang, E._Camacho, A._Kwon, H._Meyer, S._Pilz, D. Zuckerman, E._ Fall 2016

This exploration was motivated by the will to devise the production of specific visual effects, realizing material lightness through the minimization of structural elements, ensuring structural self-stabilization, locating intricate methods for aggregating tectonic units and enveloping spaces in materially resourceful ways.

A careful attendance to geometric definition has also been a crucial to strategize and regulate the translation of design ambitions into manufacturing and construction considerations. The associations between the geometric definition of a design and the formal, organizational and in some instances: material properties of its realized outcome can be carefully established by designers so that construction, performance and aesthetic concerns may be developed and imbued in the design during the description process.
(edited from student report)

48_Curve Light_final review at Harvard, GSD_Fall 2016

49_Curve Light_final review at Harvard, GSD_Fall 2016

50_Ceramic Formations Course directed by L. Asensio Villoria_final review at Harvard, GSD_ Fall 2015 (left image)

51_Ceramic Formations Course directed by L.Asensio Villoria & F.Raspall_final review at Harvard, GSD_Fall 2014 (right image). Photographs by Anita Kan

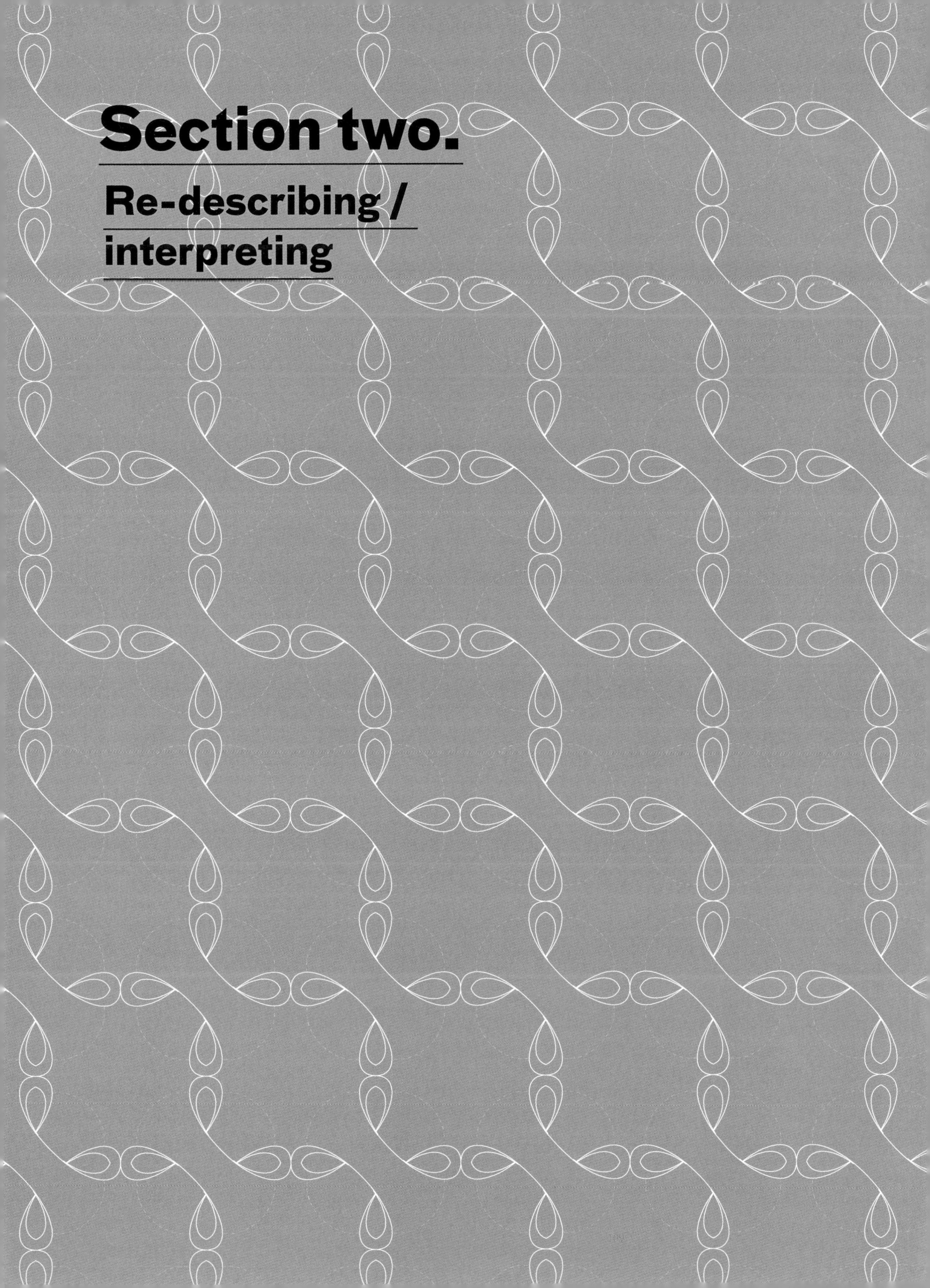

Section two.

Re-describing / interpreting

Erwin Hauer: An introduction

This research on Erwin Hauer's design legacy has been a long-spanning project for us. Our interest in his work was ignited far before we had the opportunity to actively study his creative practice. While the works captured our imaginations and always served as reference points for our own work, we lacked the capacity to rigorously pursue an immersion in the work until an opportunity presented itself in 2010.

Hauer's designs would be one of the recurring focuses of the elective course described in the preceding essay. While preparing the curriculum and teaching materials for the course, we had invested effort in defining the beginnings of a re-description exercise of Hauer's Continua series that would eventually span across several years of intermittent focus. The longer we invested in this effort, the more we became enthralled by the pairing of deep rigor and creative ingenuity embedded in the work itself.

For many years, our immersion in the work focused on studying the underlying geometries and modes of making associated with the material production of Hauer's artistic practice. It was very much aimed at getting closer to the operational intelligence exemplified by the work itself. Despite recognizing its place within a wider historical community of practice, we remained steadfastly committed to find opportunities through the work itself. For us, our interest in this historical research was motivated by a desire to extend design practice.

In 2011, we had the great privilege of meeting Erwin Hauer and his close collaborator: Enrique Rosado at their Connecticut studios. We also hosted them for a public lecture in 2012.

At the studio, the huge array of sculptural explorations spanning many decades was captivating. Equally engaging was the dense array of jigs, molds, templates, prototypes, milling machines as well as various sketches and drawings which populated every corner of their studios.

Hauer and Rosado's own efforts at upgrading the studio work to leverage digital documentation and fabrication tools were compelling. Hauer's sculptural forms had been translated into digitally modeled geometries while innovative CNC milling techniques were developed to compliment an earlier expertise in casting.

A focus on saddle surfaces, continuity and modularity sustained a very long and productive period of creative research for Hauer. What was evident to us was the possibility that these explorations were clearly not exhausted with the studio's legacy and there was a capacity and relevance for extending the search today.

Rather than leave this vital exploration to history, we endeavored to explore if there were opportunities to be found in the material evidence of Hauer's oeuvre. We explored the possibility of locating the underlying codes that may extend this creative research and vital legacy. The research outcomes described in this book provides the outlines for models of study that bridge across investigation and creative practice. Conducted through our own dedicated investigative efforts as well as through teaching, what follows is a detailed description of a particular process for upgrading systems. While we have been mindful about offering as precise a re-description of these works as possible, we fully acknowledge that these are interpretations and do not claim to be Hauer's and Rosado's actual processes.

Yale
Oil-free Air

01-06_Photographs of a visit to
Erwin Hauer's studio, 2011

Hauer's legacy

01_Erwin Hauer sharing his work with the class

Erwin Hauer (born 1926) was a sculptor known for his career-spanning focus on forms which were typified by modularized fields of continuous surfaces. He was born in Vienna, Austria and studied at Vienna's Academy of Applied Art, the Accademia di Belle Arti di Brera in Milan, the Rhode Island School of Design and was invited by Josef Albers to study and subsequently teach sculpture at Yale University. Hauer remained at Yale for thirty-three years until 1990, when he was named Professor Emeritus of Sculpture upon retiring.

In 1950, Hauer began producing his renowned Continua sculptural series. Designs 1, 2, 3 and 4 were all developed and manufactured using cast concrete, gypsum, limestone and acrylic resin in Vienna prior to his migration to the United States. In 1955, Hauer was a awarded a Fulbright Scholarship to study in the United States, where he first attended the Rhode Island School of Design and would subsequently join Josef and Ani Albers' renowned community of teachers and students at Yale University, which included Sheila Hicks and Eva Hesse.

Hauer's works were first developed for installation in several churches across Vienna and would later be manufactured under license by the New York based Mural Inc as building systems or products. These patented designs were sold for twelve years in the United States and other international markets.

Hauer's designs were adopted as room dividers or architectural screens by a few established architects and designers such as Philip Johnson, Edward Durell Stone, Gordon Bunshaft of SOM, and Florence Knoll and were used in the Coca Cola Pavilion at the New York World's Fair (1964-1965), the Canadian Imperial Bank of Commerce in Montreal and the Look magazine headquarters amongst others. More recently, Hauer's screens have been installed at high-profile buildings, including the Museum of Fine Arts East Wing extension in Boston by Foster and Partners, the Standard Hotel adjacent to New York's High-Line as well as at the Cobogo House in Sao Paolo, Brazil by Marcio Kogan. His work has also been included in the permanent collections of major art institutions such as the Museum of Modern Art in New York, Brooklyn Museum of Art, Art Institute of Chicago, Wadsworth Athenaeum and Museum of the National Academy of Design.

02_Erwin Hauer and Enrique Rosado sharing their work with the class.

Hauer's creative practice can be characterized by a remarkably consistent and intense focus on abstract sculptural forms that resonate with a mathematical rigor and sensibility. Hauer's creative output demonstrates a strong geometric precision but much of this was arrived at through a conversation between intuitive exploration and detailed refinement. His enduring exploration of complex surfaces and intricate continuities are a recognizable trait of this work and can also be defined as elaborations on modulated continuity or a potentially infinite spatial extension. The geometric sophistication demonstrated by the complex periodic minimal surfaces of Hauer's work reverberated with leading mathematical research of the time. Alan Schoen, the American physicist and computer scientist who is known for discovering the gyroid minimal surface, defined the I-WP (Inner-core wrapped package) surface through the documentation of Hauer's pieces.

In America, Hauer pursued his sculptural explorations in a Connecticut studio while teaching at Yale. His work has been academically categorized as "modular constructivism" and has been placed in association with the work of Norman Carlberg. In both cases, their work reveals an obvious shared commitment towards extensive forms resistant to closure that take on an extensive yet segmented formal logic. The work of the sibling protagonists of Constructivism: Naum Gabo and Antione Pevsner has also been known to be one of the most crucial formative influences on Hauer. Gabo and Pevsner's favoring of a more explicitly material focus on space and time can be seen to have been a notion which motivated both Hauer and Carlberg's own works.

03-05_Erwin Hauer and Enrique Rosado sharing their work with the class

06_Erwin Hauer sharing his work with the class.

Both sculptors have also shared a transdisciplinary relationship with architecture. Carlberg's own accomplished sculptures have also been installed in the buildings of established Modern architects; most notably the Viennese émigré architect: Harry Seidler in Australia. However, Hauer's entanglement with architecture can be seen to be more integrated and transformative, whereby Hauer's artistic practices can be said to have migrated directly into architectural applications.

Hauer's complex forms could be seen to have introduced novelty into the dominant design language of High Modernism. In place of the literal transparency of diaphanous glass in the open and dematerialized Modern façade, Hauer's screens brought a renewed investment in the idea of the building envelope as a filter. It also resonated with older traditions of screens, veiling interior from exterior rather than enabling seamless continuities. Despite its Modern forms, these screens also brought ornament, scale and texture back into a movement dedicated to stripping its forms back to the essential. Hauer's revision of the Modern envelope was explicitly expressive. For us, this illustration of the transformative capacity of the bridging or migration of concerns and practices across disciplinary spheres is one of the most compelling aspects of Hauer's legacy.

BIBLIOGRAPHY

Erwin Hauer, *Still Facing Infinity, Sculpture by Erwin Hauer* (Mulgrave: Images Publishing Dist Ac, 2017)

Erwin Hauer, *Continua – Architectural Screens and Walls* (New York: Princeton Architectural Press, 2007)

Erwin Hauer and Enrique Rosado – *Transformations*, public lecture at Harvard University Graduate School of Design, February 22, 2013

Anoka Faruqee, *Search Versus Re-Search: Recollections of Josef Albers at Yale*- Josef and Anni Albers Foundation - https://vimeo.com/207155945, 2015

07_Erwin Hauer's studio in Connecticut, 2011.

Like the Blaschka glass flowers at the Harvard Museum of Natural History, Hauer's work occupies an ambiguous position in relationship to its status as artifacts embodying sculptural, design and even mathematical merit and information. His Continua series straddles commitments to functional design, ornament, spatial and geometric exploration into complex minimal surfaces. It links across different disciplinary concerns and migrates different practices, such as sculpture and mathematics into the definition of industrial building components.

Through a new monograph and exhibitions; Hauer's extensive body of work was introduced to a new generation of designers and artists in the early 00's. Hauer enjoyed a reinvigorated esteem and attention, particularly from the design fraternity. This renewed demand for his work incited the dedicated effort in translating the work into digital design and manufacturing environments as well as workflows, upgrading them for contemporary processes of construction.

Erwin Hauer passed away in 2017 aged 91.

08_Erwin Hauer in Connecticut, 2011.

Transformations: Associative model 1 & 6

Based on lecture by Erwin Hauer and Enrique Rosado at Harvard University's Graduate School of Design on February 22nd, 2013.

Hauer's exploration of continua forms often took on an almost evolutionary process, whereby certain designs were revisited and refined over multiple decades. His Design 1, was first developed while still in Vienna. It is a case where the different instantiations of the design have evolved considerably in response to artistic refinement and most dramatically in response to technological changes. Design 1 was first conceived and developed in 1950 as casted masonry or hydrostone pieces in 8 inch modules. It took on a more solid and heavy appearance owing to its materiality and formal definition.

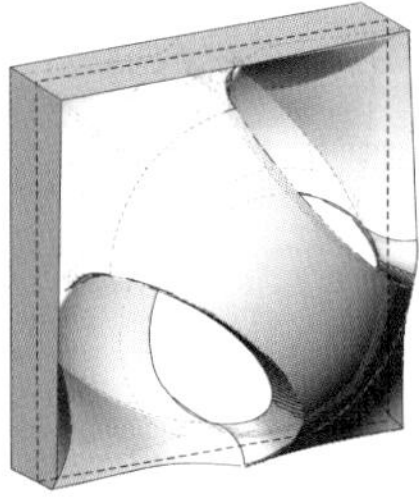

09 & 10_Design 1_high resolution_single module (left) and 3x3 matrix of modules_isometric (right)

Together with Enrique Rosado, Hauer refined Design 1 into new configurations which allowed for their materialization through the use of CNC milling techniques. The geometries of the design were adjusted to accommodate this change in manufacturing and the evolved design could be seen to achieve a lighter appearance.

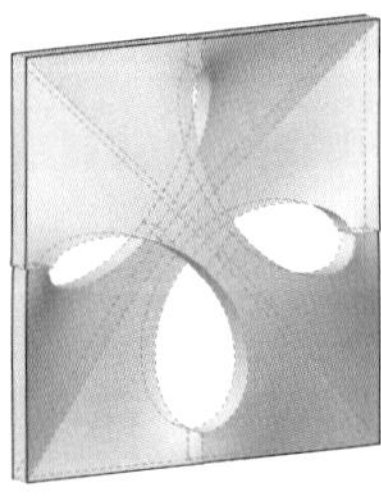

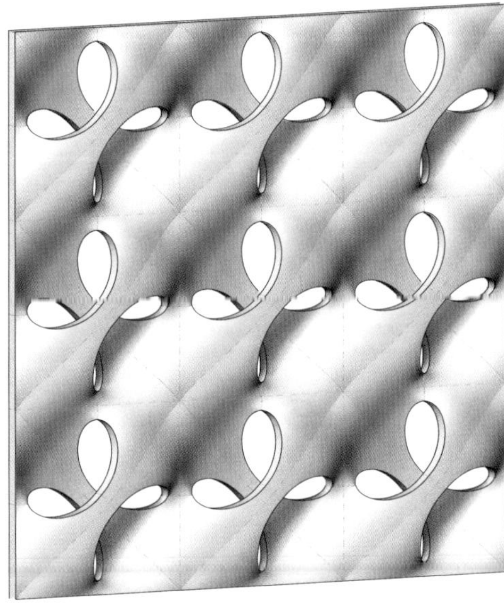

11 & 12_Design 1_milled_3x3 matrix of modules_isometric (left) and single module (right)

These drawings are interpretations of the original designs informed by publicly available drawings and photographs.

In 1954, Design 4 was conceived as a load bearing screen of stacked cast stone modules.
The modularization, load bearing performance and mode of construction were likely to be considerations that affected the heavier proportions of the design. Over the years, the geometric schema that informed Design 4 also provided the framework for Hauer's later design explorations such as Design 5. The refinement of the manufacturing processes also influenced their formal evolution, whereby the overall screen took on a lighter appearance.

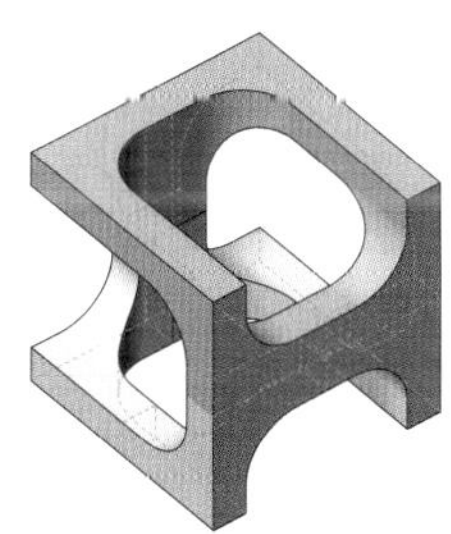

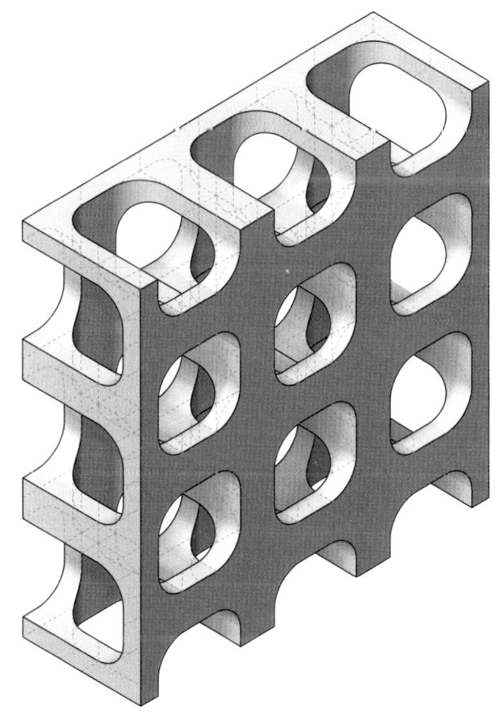

13 & 14_Design 4_3x3 matrix of modules_isometric (left) and single module (right)

This process of using underlying geometric associations and principles to refine instantiations or generate new designs has been a clear influence on our research. Our development of methods for re-describing or interpreting these designs into geometric associative models were compelled by a desire to enrich design practice knowledge with the embedded intelligence latent within these legacy precedents

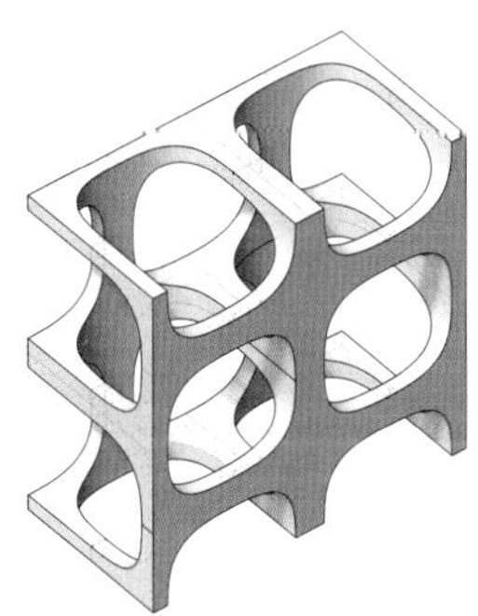

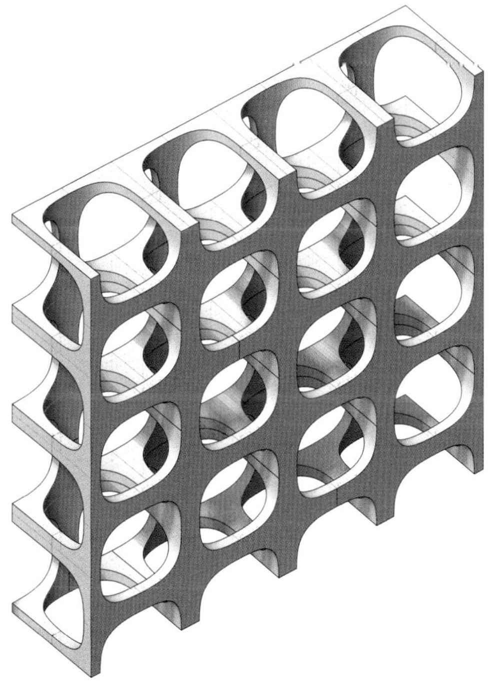

15 & 16_Design 5_single module (left) and 2x2 matrix of modules_isometric (right)

Re-describing - suture curve

The suture curve is an important geometric figure that underpins our interpretation of Hauer's Designs 1, 4 and 5. It is a three dimensional curve that may be used to partition the surface of a sphere into two identical halves. The value of this technique is both theoretical and also practical.[1]

Splitting a sphere along the Suture curve produces two handle-like surfaces.

The suture curve module that we used as a generative input for modeling comes from intersecting a sphere with both the Suture curve and two orthogonal planes at the meridian and equator. This produces a quarter of a Sphere split along the Suture curve. This approach has been the most consistent way to produce a base for the modeling of these designs in a manner that also allowed for variation.

In our modeling of the suture curve, we generally begin with the parametric definition of an enneper surface.

The geometric and mathematical definition of an Enneper Surface is communicated in figure 18.

In mathematics, in the fields of differential geometry and algebraic geometry, the Enneper surface is a self-intersecting surface that can be described parametrically by:

$x = u(1-u^2/3+v^2)/3$
$y = -v(1-v^2/3+u^2)/3$
$z = (u^2-v^2)/3$

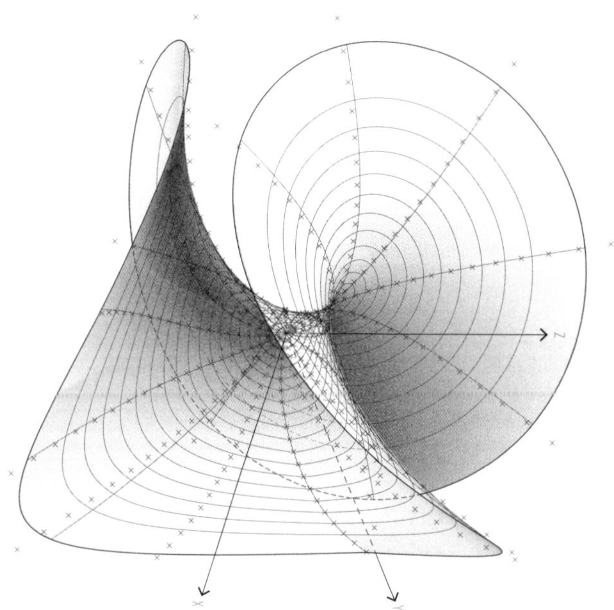

17_Enneper surface drawn by asensio-mah (assisted by Xun Liu)

1. Hauer E. (2007) *Continua, Architectural Screens & Walls.* Princeton Press. New York.

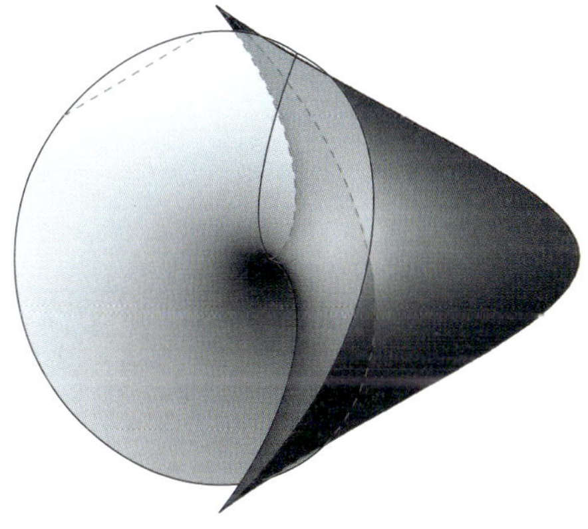

a. Enneper minimal surface

b. Sphere

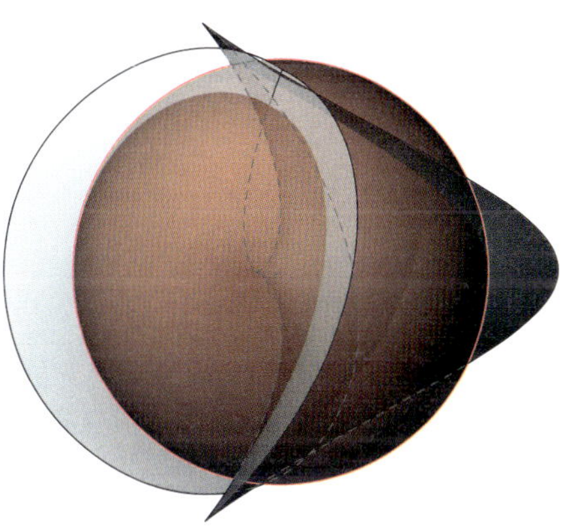

c. Intersection between Enneper and Sphere surfaces

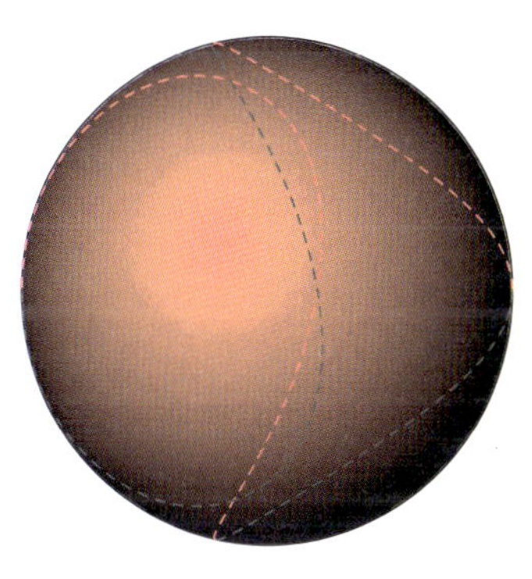

d. Suture curve on Sphere surface

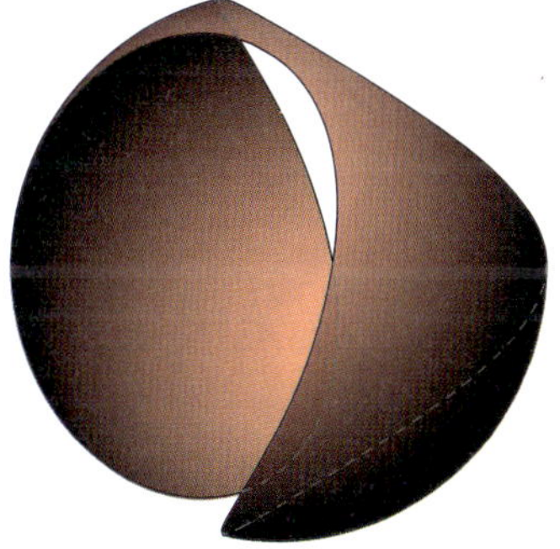

18_Enneper surface and Sphere intersection produces a Suture Curve

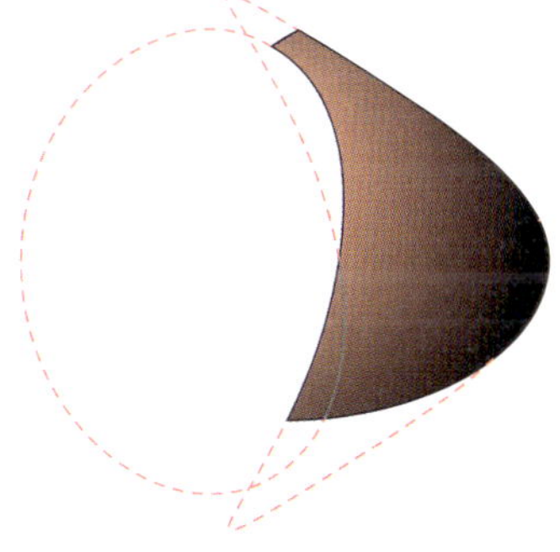

f. Quarter of a Sphere split along Suture curve

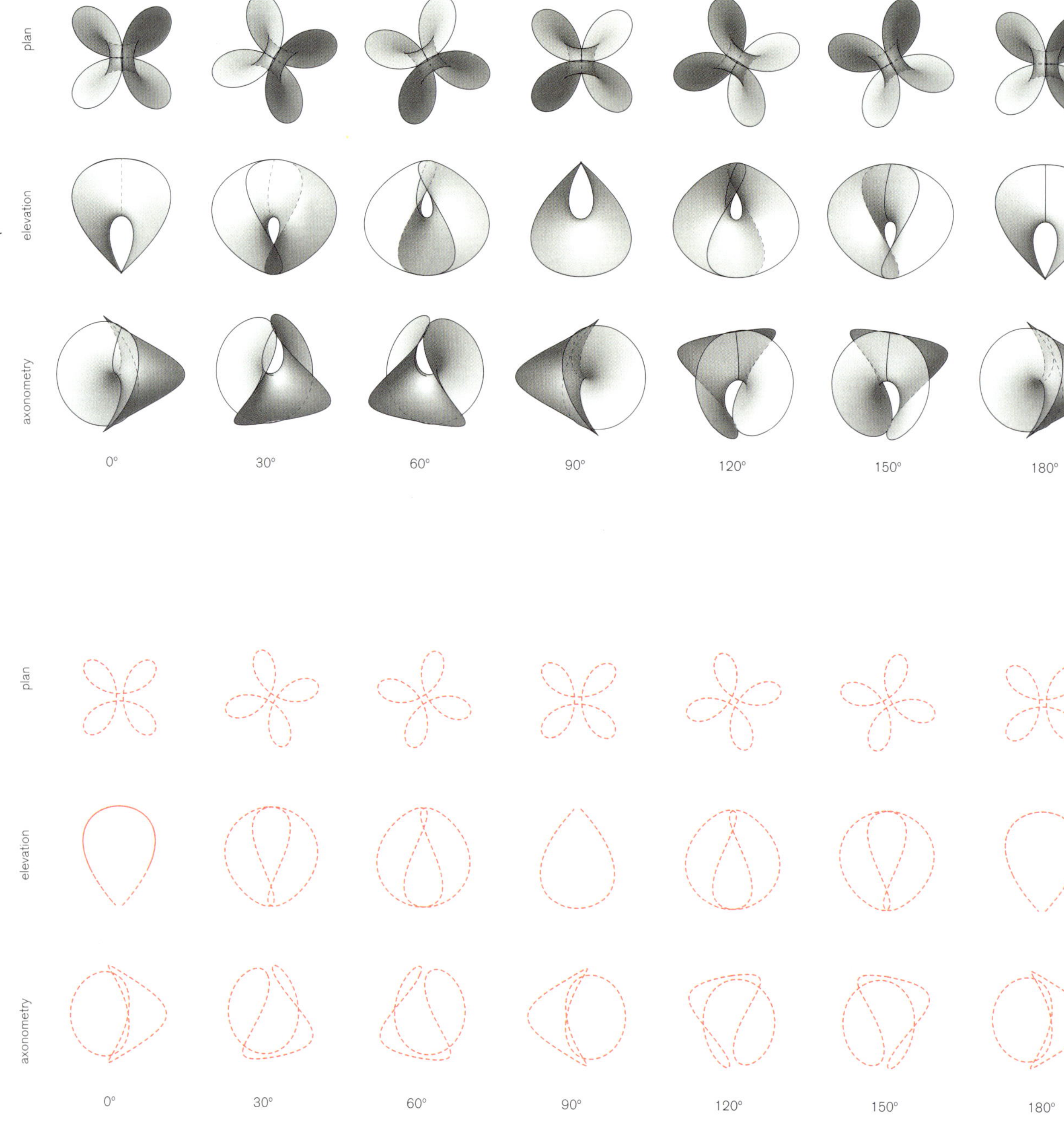

All photographs in this chapter were taken by asensio_mah unless otherwise stated.

All drawings in this chapter were produced by asensio_mah (assisted by Candela De Bortoli) unless otherwise stated.

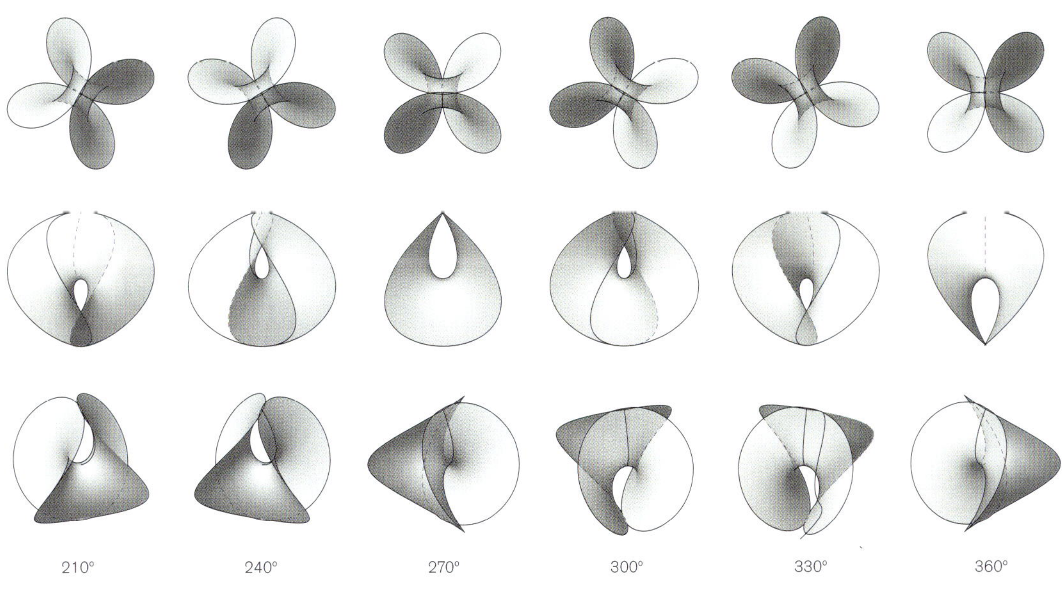

19_Enneper surface visualization of
30° rotations with rendered images.

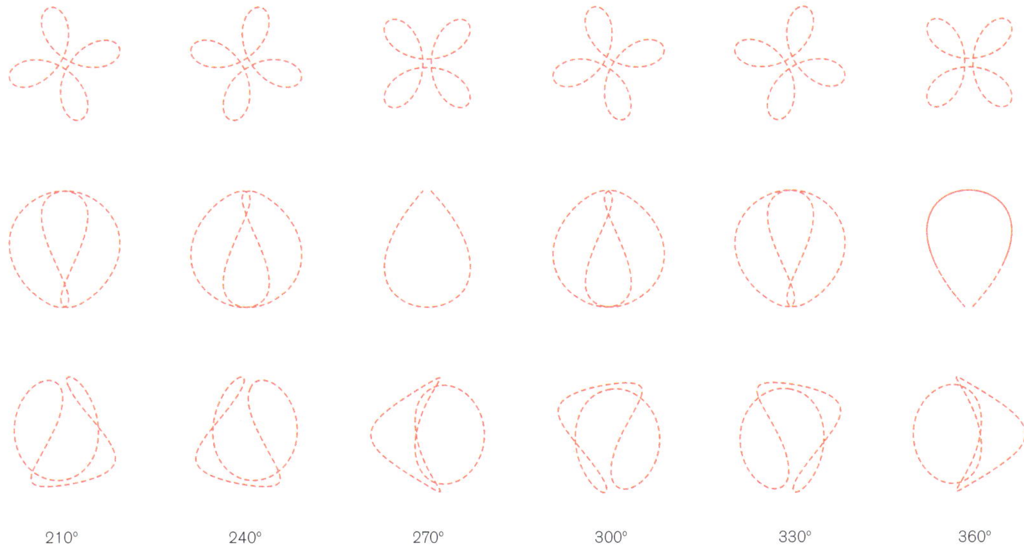

20_Suture curve visualization of
30° rotations.

Continua series

01 & 02_Design 1 and Intercircles at Hauer's Connecticut Studio

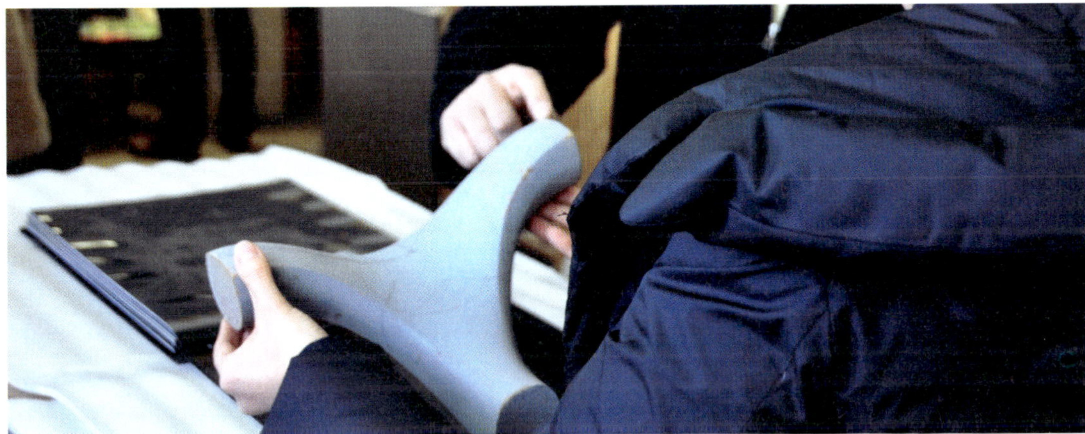

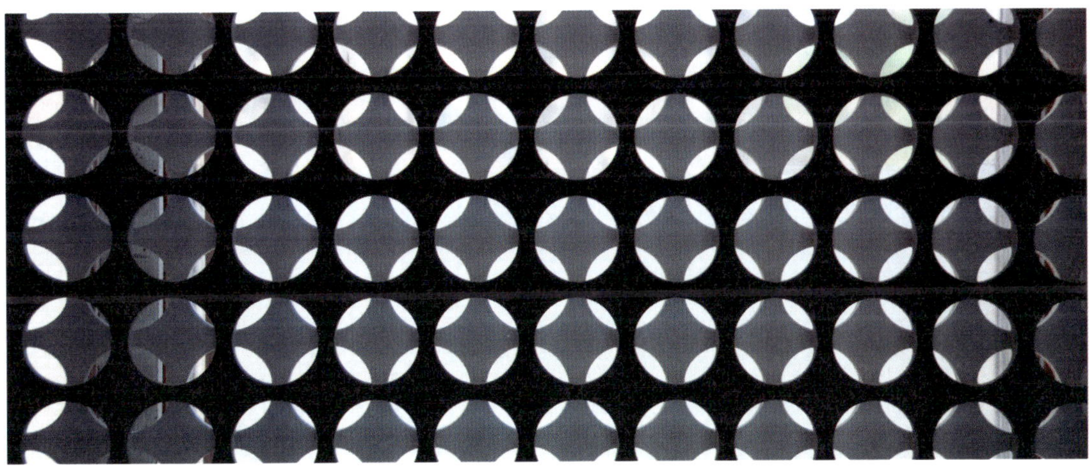

03-05_Design 2, 3 and 5 at Hauer's Connecticut Studio

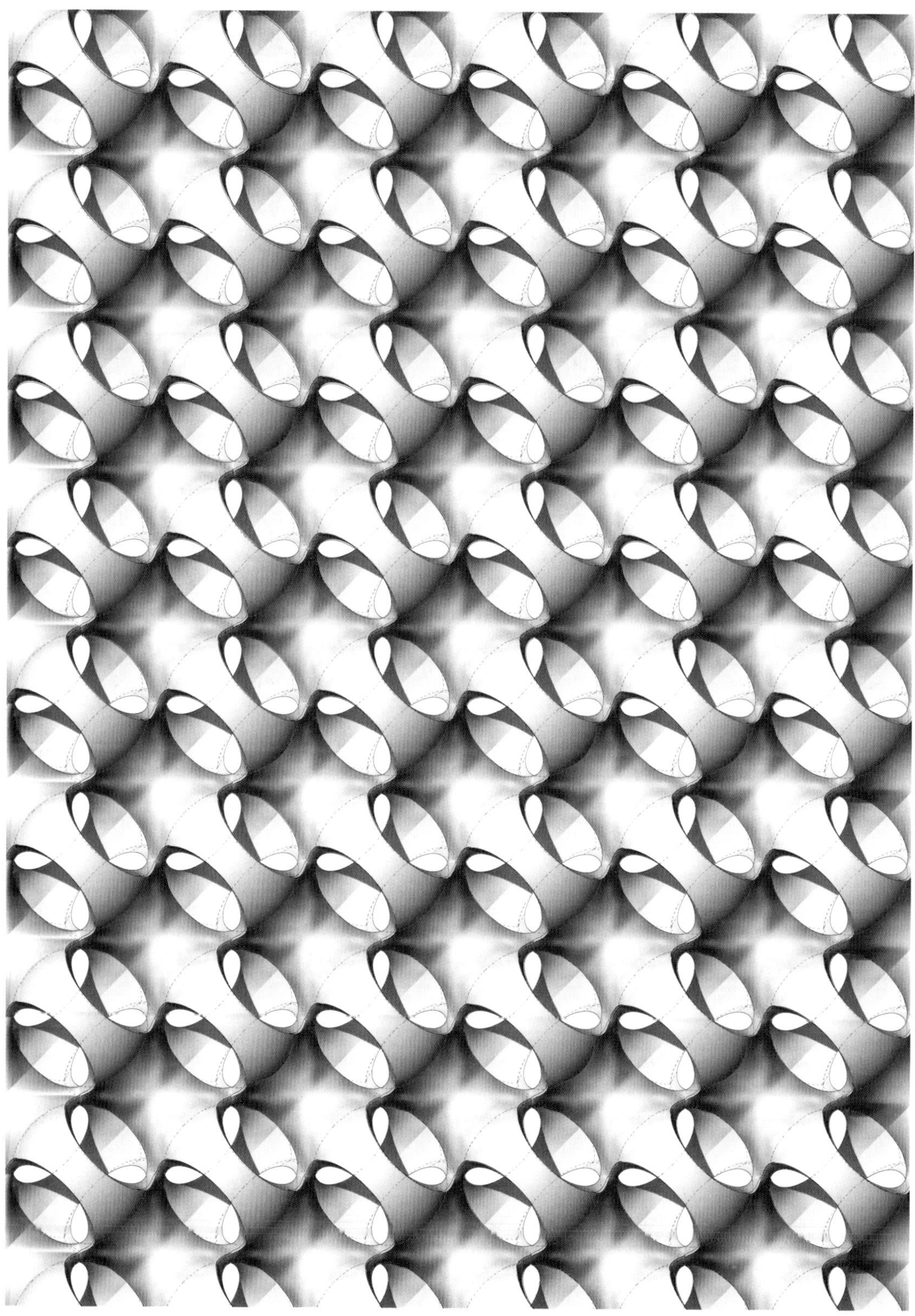

06_Associative model 1_matrix elevation

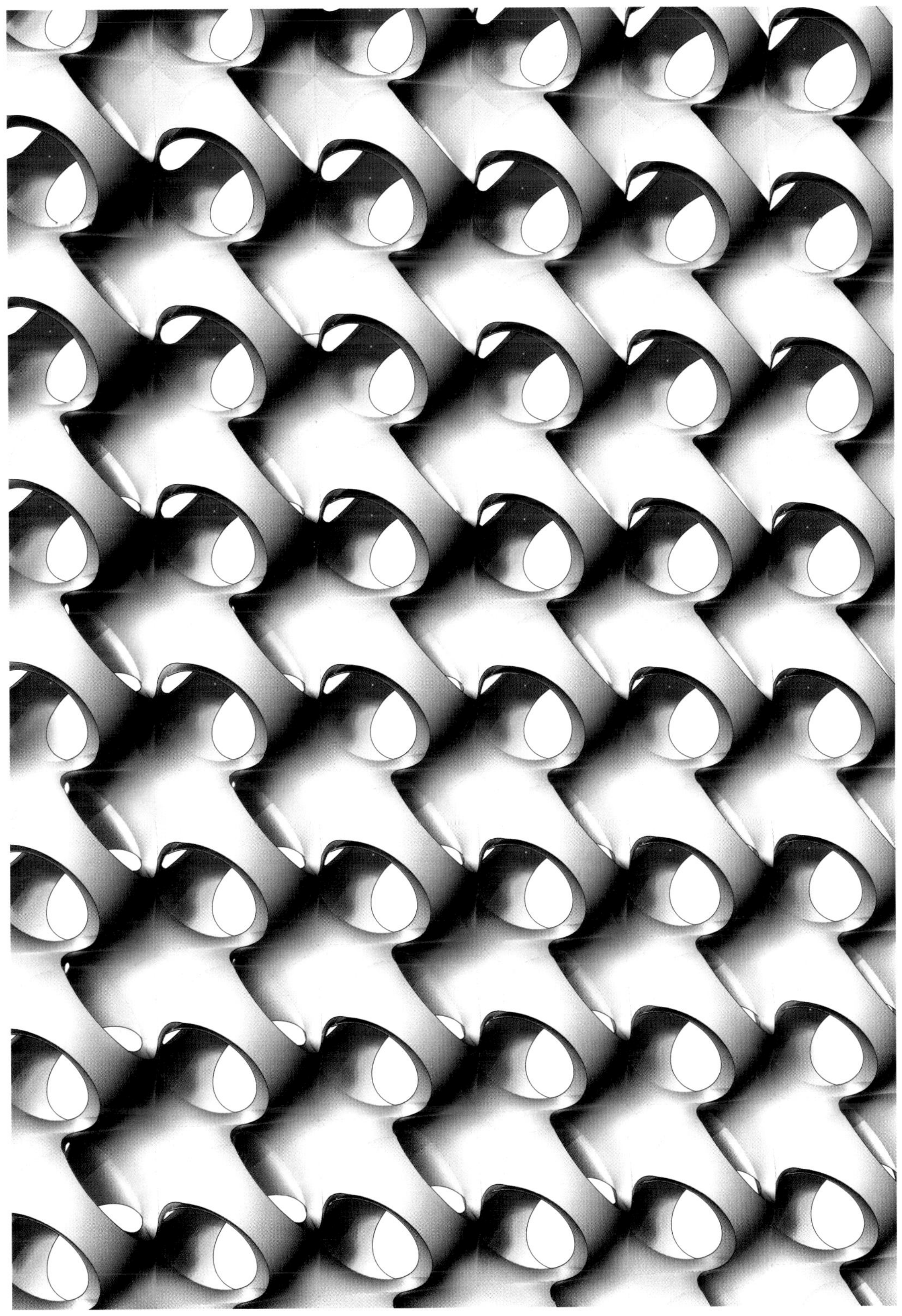

07_Associative model 1_matrix perspective

Associative model 1

Design 1 is the first design in Hauer's Continua series. Its geometry is primarily defined by compositing saddle and spherical surface components.

The formal concept of the design can be summarized through the image of a pair of bridges or handles arranged diagonally into a square tile.[1]

These handles inscribe a spherical space and define a module that can be tiled to create larger surfaces.[2]

In terms of fabrication, this design has been refined and produced several times over many decades. This particular interpretive model of Design 1 described here is defined by a geometry intended for casting.

The drawings in this section are interpretations of the original designs informed by publicly available drawings and photographs.

1. Hauer E. (2007) *Continua, Architectural Screens and Walls*, Princeton Architectural Press. New York
2.(ibid)

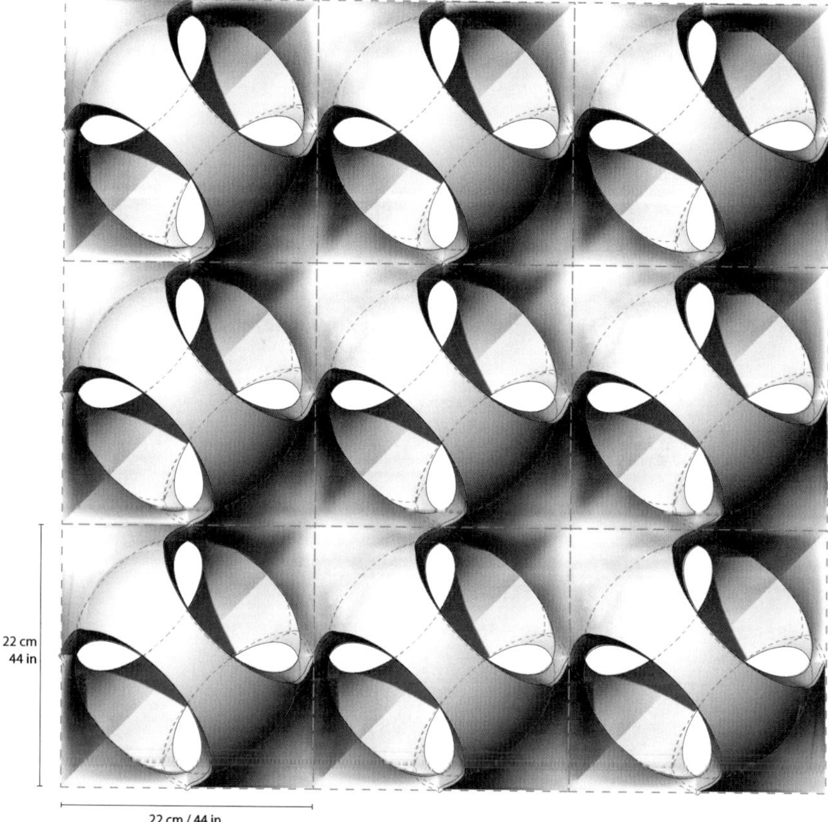

08_Associative model 1_3x3 matrix of modules_elevation, tile edges and axis

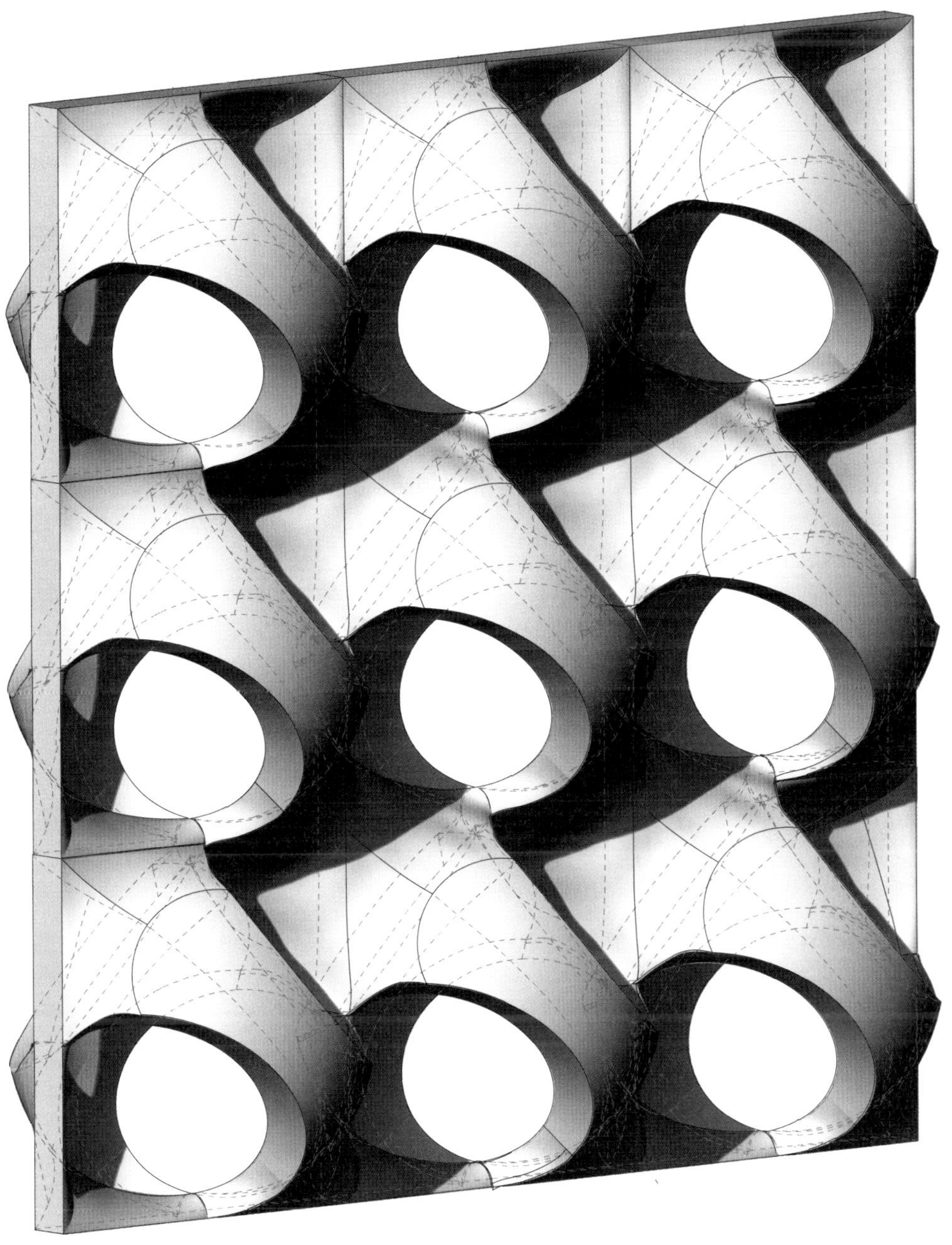

09_Associative model 1_3x3 matrix of modules_isometric

Assembly

This interpretive model of Design 1 is defined as a quadrilateral tile that can be proliferated in a square grid. Distinct from other models described in this book, it is not defined by arraying a module around a tile center. Instead, this model is defined through the re-conceptualization of the tile as a series of complementary surfaces that are re-assembled in an associative manner.

The sets of surfaces can be divided into three broad categories. Firstly, the spherical sections that make up the outer and inner shells of the handle. Then the surfaces that bridge the difference between the outer and inner shells, making its edges. Finally, the two complementary saddle-like surfaces that transition between the handle surfaces. The curves that define the edge surfaces are quarter sections of the ellipses and arcs that limit the inner and outer shells. The ends of the ellipse are the starting points of the transitional curves that bridges between the two adjacent outer shells. These curves together with other interpolated curves, make up the limits for the group of saddle-like surfaces. Finally, the upper edges of the saddle surfaces are shared with the lower edges of the outer shells. These are used as the edges to trim the primitive sphere.

10_3x3 matrix of modules_isometric.
Construction and assembly

Associative model overview

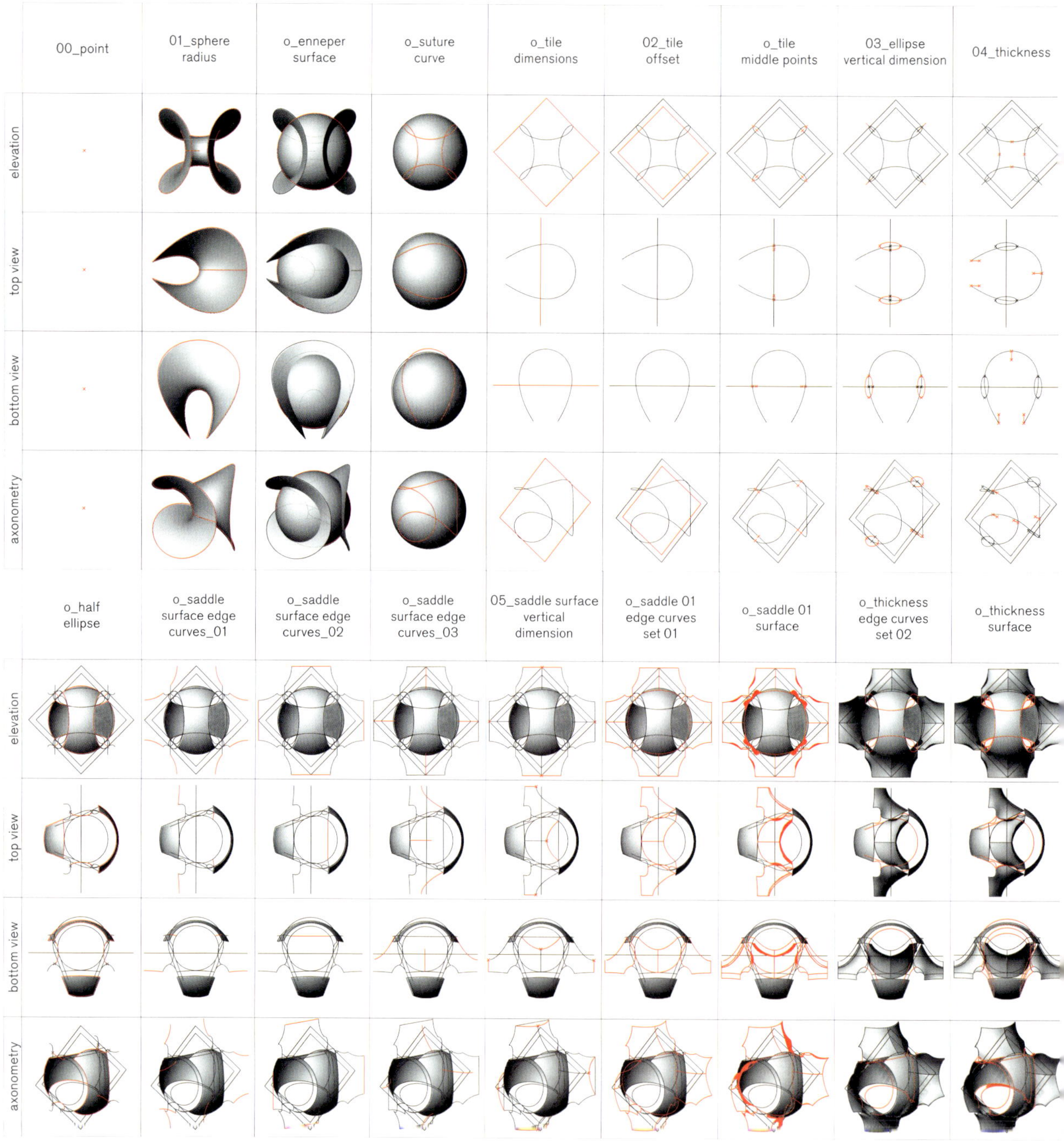

	00_point	01_sphere radius	o_enneper surface	o_suture curve	o_tile dimensions	02_tile offset	o_tile middle points	03_ellipse vertical dimension	04_thickness
elevation									
top view									
bottom view									
axonometry									

	o_half ellipse	o_saddle surface edge curves_01	o_saddle surface edge curves_02	o_saddle surface edge curves_03	05_saddle surface vertical dimension	o_saddle 01 edge curves set 01	o_saddle 01 surface	o_thickness edge curves set 02	o_thickness surface
elevation									
top view									
bottom view									
axonometry									

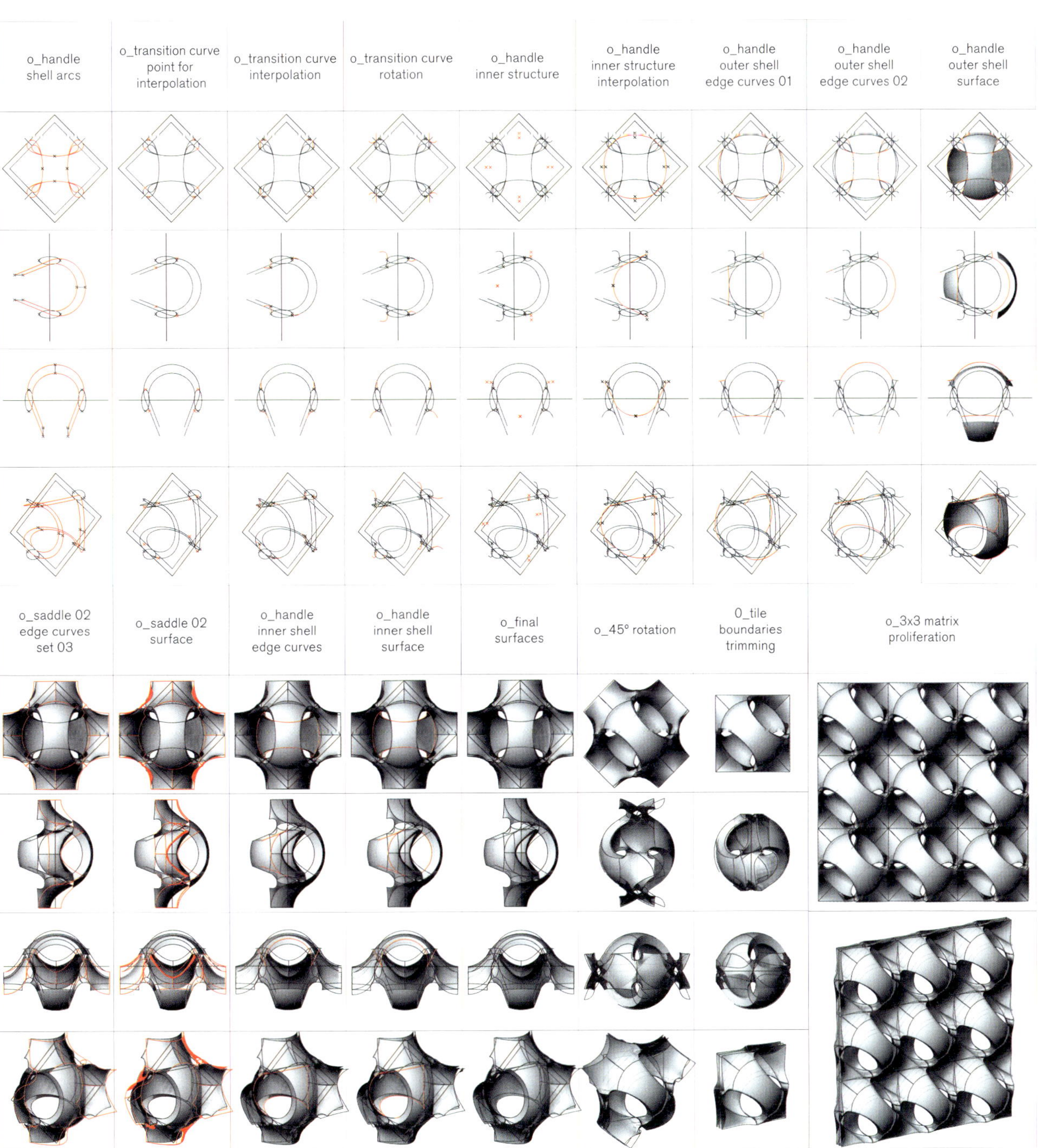

11_System construction_variables and operations

This model offers a geometric interpretation of a tile module which is then arrayed into a larger field. Each tile is constructed as a pair of mirrored and rotated thickened handles that enclose a spherical space with saddle-like surfaces that transition between them. These surfaces help to solve a tension between the spherical origin of the suture curve and the squared matrix within which the module is bounded by means of sharp orthogonal edges. The key to this smooth transition lies in the transitional curves and the ellipses that bridge between the adjacent tiles. The model developed for this version could be described as being more elaborate and detailed and consists of five variables and twenty-six operations. Using a shared centroid, a sphere (variable 01) and an Enneper surface are constructed. This point also constitutes the center of the tile. The resultant suture curve which is bounded in a cube controls the tile's dimensions. This square is offset at a variable distance (v02), determining one of the two lengths of an ellipse that will be constructed afterwards.
The midpoints of the tile edges and corresponding midpoints of their offsets are identified. The ellipse is a figure that is vital to the construction of the continuous surfaces that make up this model. It creates a vertical continuity between the convex and concave handles and in turn, produces volumes in an otherwise planar transition.
The two parameters of the ellipse are its two radii. One of these is already defined in the previous step through the vector between the midpoints of the tile and its offset edges. This third variable sets the second radius and therefore the vertical dimension of the ellipse.

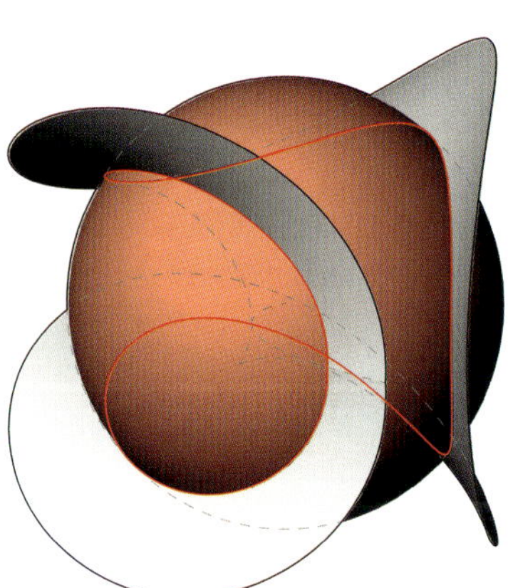

12_a. Intersection between the Enneper surface and the Sphere

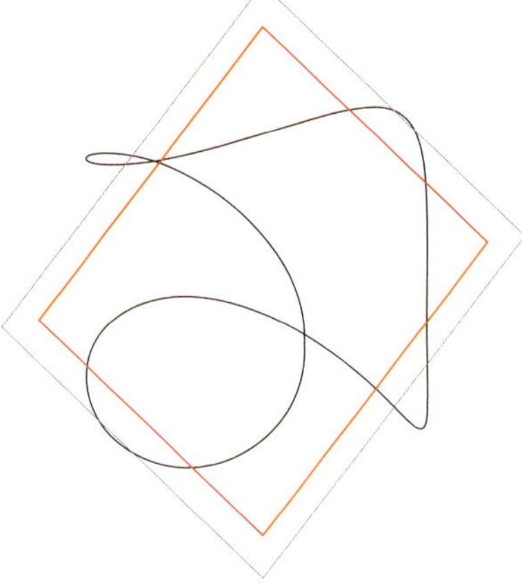

12_b. Tile offset from suture curve's bounds

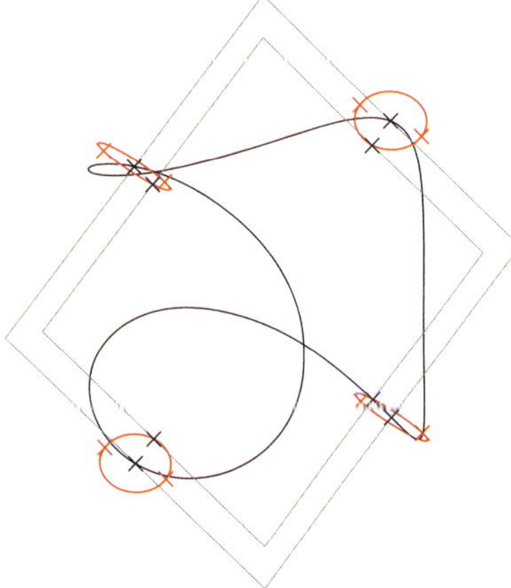

12_c. Ellipse dimensions at middle points of tile

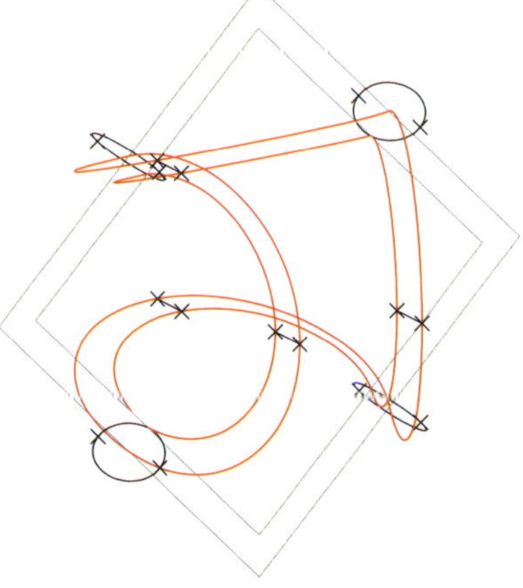

12_d. Handle outer and inner shell edges

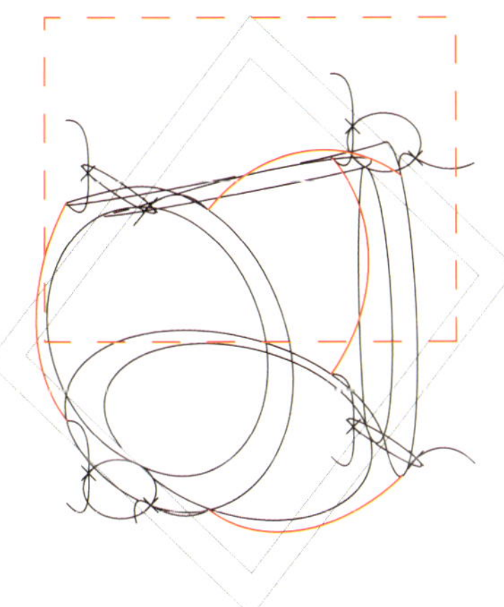

12_e. Outer shell tangent edges and transitional curves

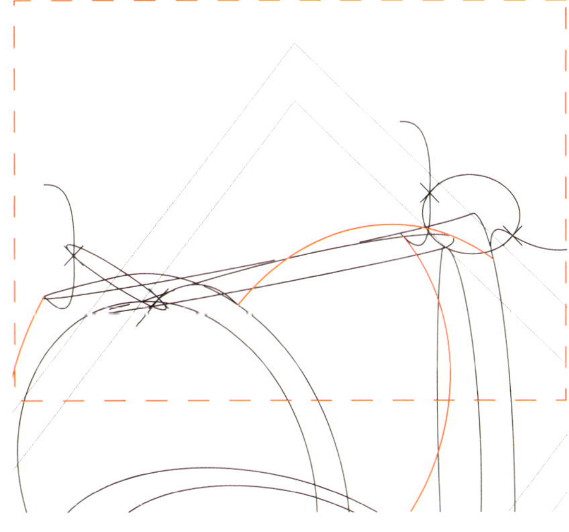

12_f. Outer shell tangent edges and transitional curves, zoom

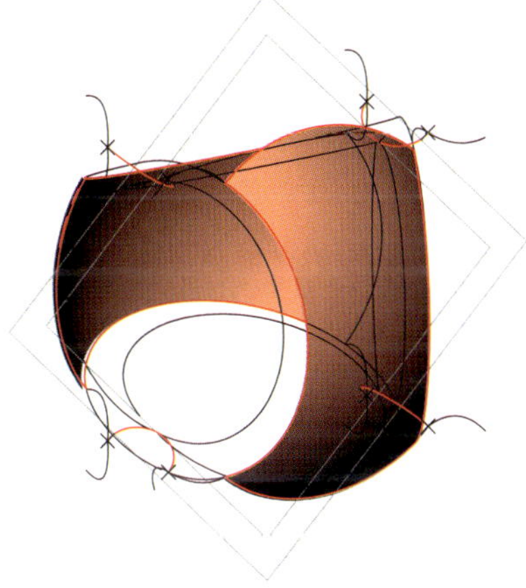

12_g. Handle outer shell surface from sphere trimming

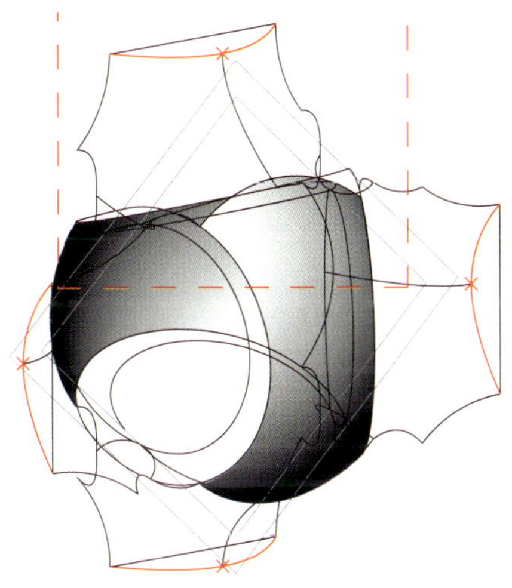

12_h. Primary saddle srf edge curves: rotated edges and curves

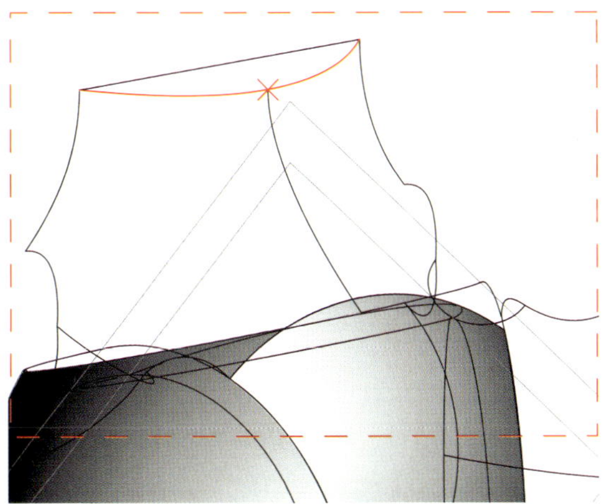

12_i. Primary saddle-like surface edge curve, zoom

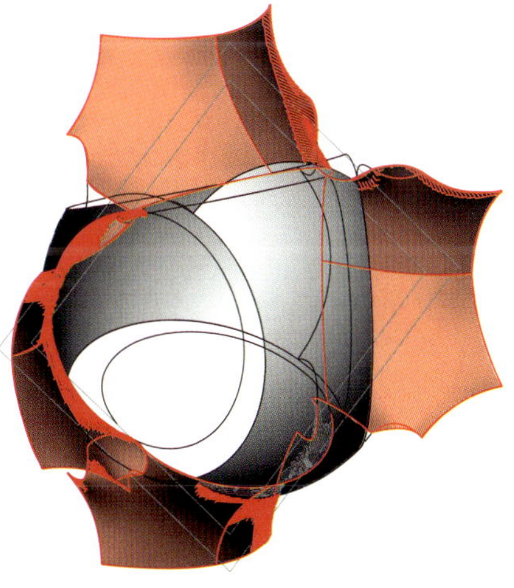

12_j. Primary saddle-like surfaces

The handle consists of an outer shell, an inner shell and a thickness surface. The thickness surface (v04) is constructed through two pairs of points that define these limits. These curves are intersected with extruded planes to identify the end points of transitional curves which connect two perpendicular handles. This curve is constructed from a series of primitive points and projected circles which are later on interpolated and rotated in space. This is done because the assembly logic is one of array rather than reflections. 180º rotations of the transitional curves produce continuity between two juxtaposed handles. The surfaces between handles are saddle surfaces. These are defined by means of edge curves, which are different to the structure of the handles. These correspond to the inner surface for the concave handles that will be related to the outer surface of the convex handle. Using the end points of the transitional curve between the outer surface of the convex handle and the ellipse together with the tangent point at each handle's axis, a three-point interpolated curve is constructed as the limit of the outer shell. From the tile corners, tangential lines are created to the central axis of the handles. Straight lines at the tangential point split the handles and become end points for the transitional curves that connect the handles with the ellipses. The arc defined as the limit for the outer shell of the handle is trimmed with the transitional curve. Once the middle point is defined, the curve is interpolated. Using the previously constructed limits, the primitive sphere is trimmed and two outer shell handle-like surfaces are isolated. The ellipse is divided using the extreme vertical points to identify the segments that are useful for the construction of the transitional surfaces between the saddle and the handles. The limits of the outer shell of the convex handle defines the extents for the saddle surface. The surface is constructed for this tile when rotated 180º from the midpoint on the tile edge. The curves are open, so a straight line is needed to closes the boundaries for surface construction. Later, this line will be part of a composite curve that defines the vertical proportion of the saddle surface. The other direction of the saddle surface is perpendicular to the outer limits of the shell. Midpoints are identified and a line between pairs of handles is constructed. The point that will be the midpoint of the edge of the other direction of the saddle surface is constructed by translating in the Z axis the corner point of the tile, correspondent to each middle point of the saddle surfaces.
For each tile, saddle surfaces should be constructed as quartered elements. This set of curves defines the construction for the first set of saddle surfaces. A number of different sets of curves define the construction for the surfaces between the inner shell and the outer shell of the handles, the second set of saddle surface and the second set of handle-like surfaces, the inner shells. Once this final surface is constructed, the tile's surfaces are complete. This group is rotated 45º and the excess surfaces are trimmed. This way, the surfaces achieve a much better curvature than if constructed directly as a squared tile.

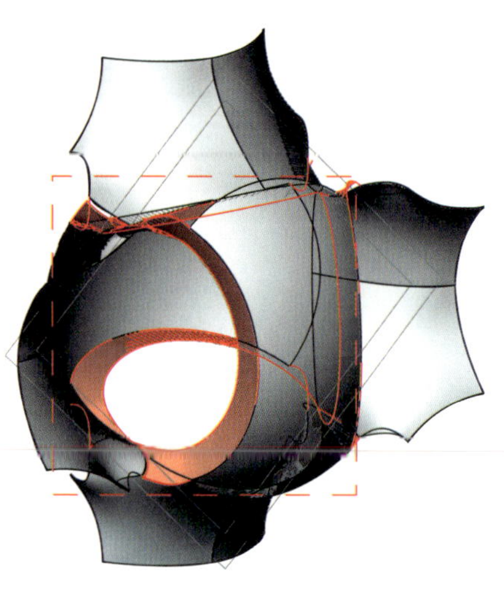

12_k. Handle thickness surfaces

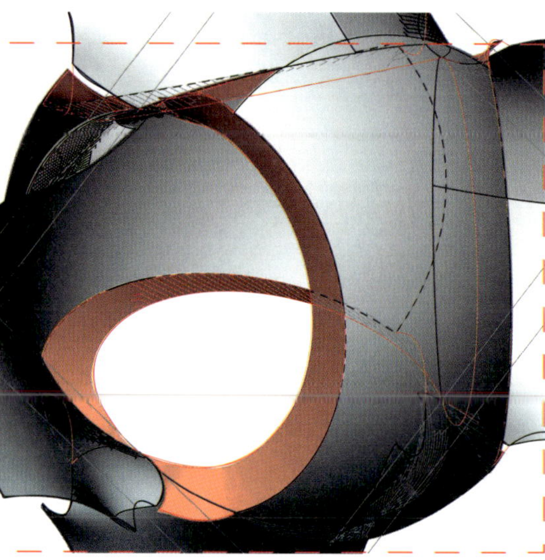

12_l. Handle thickness surfaces, zoom.

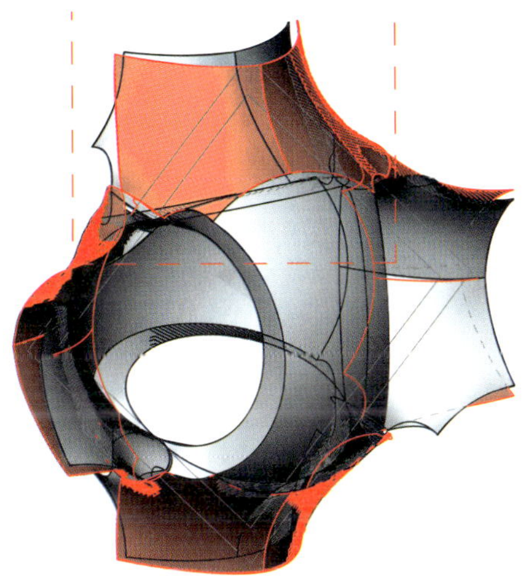

12_m. Secondary saddle srf from rotated primary surfaces

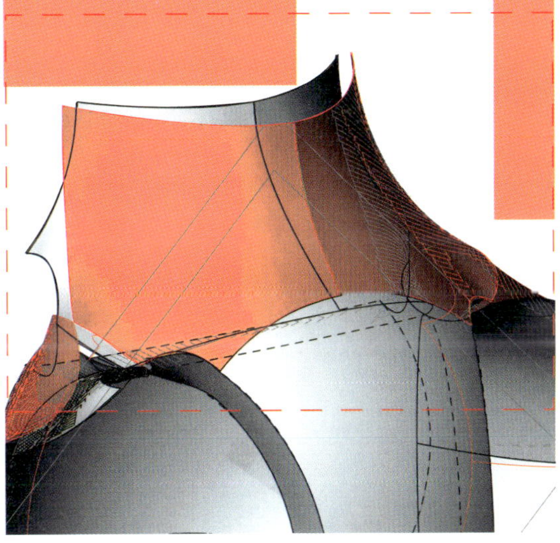

12_n. Secondary saddle srf from rotated primary surfaces, zoom

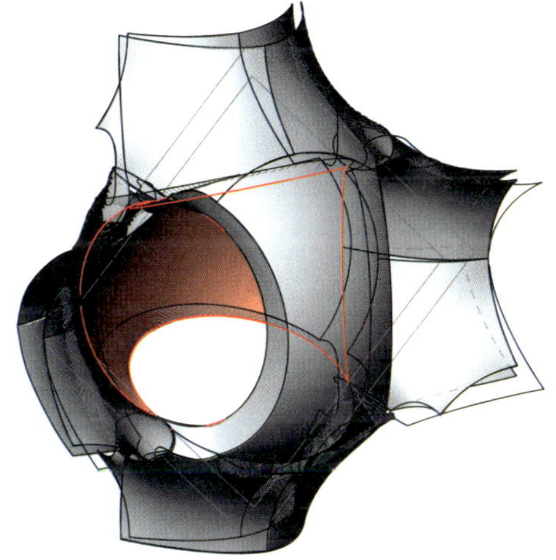

12_o. Handle inner shell surfaces

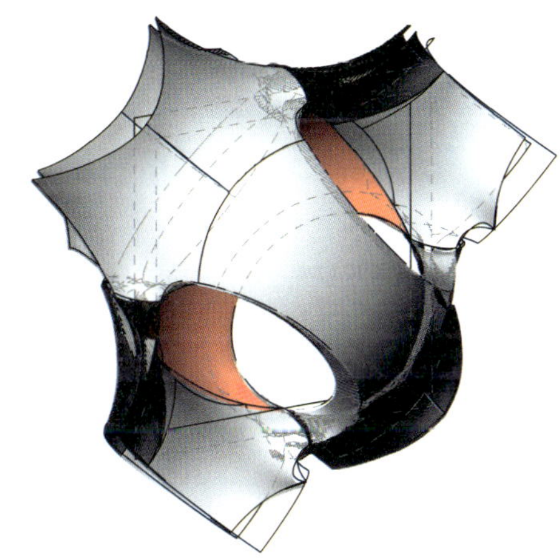

12_p. Tile rotation

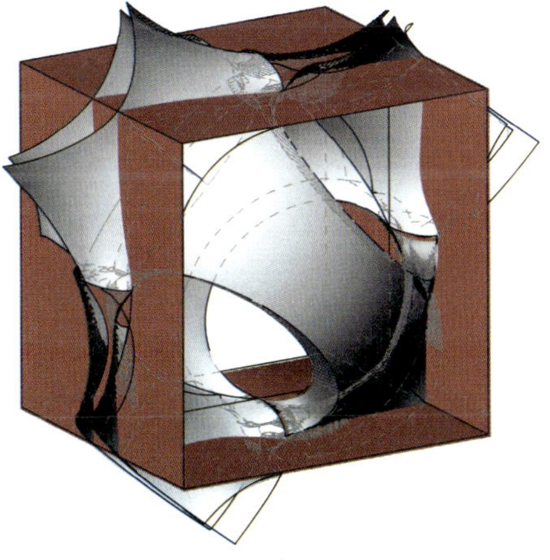

12_q. Tile secondary trimming, square fitting

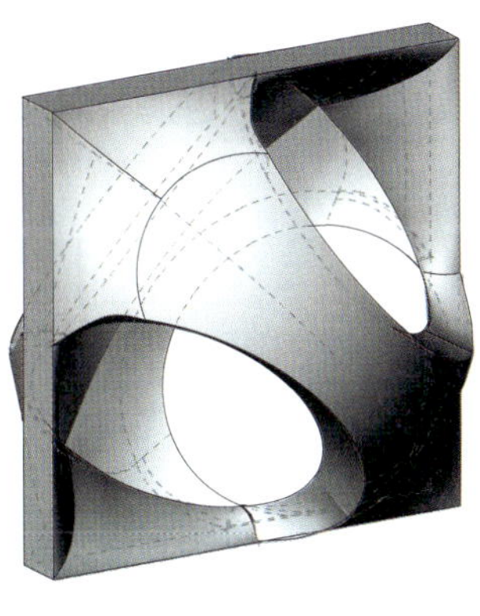

12_r. Final tile

13_Associative model 2_matrix elevation

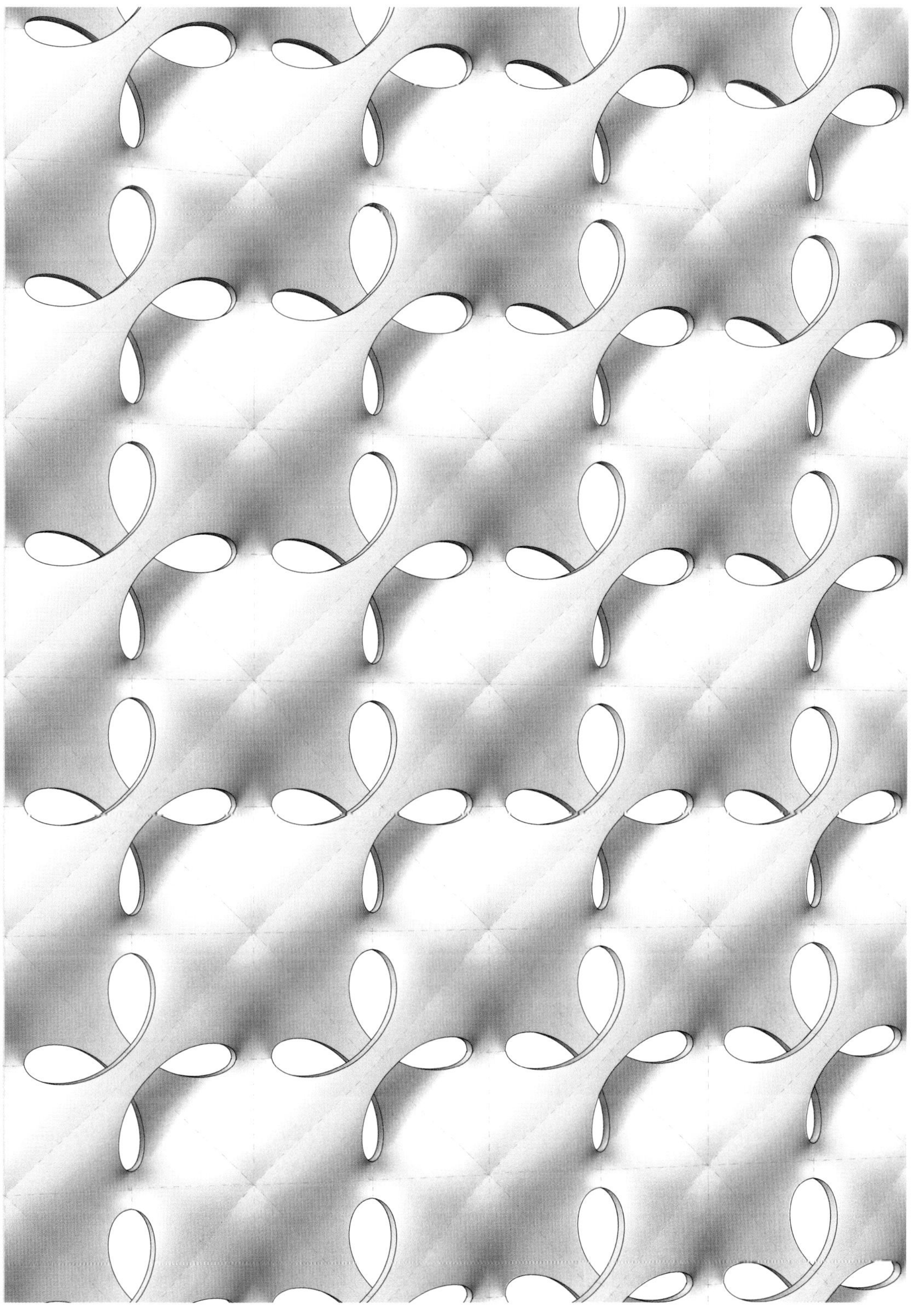

14_Associative model 2_matrix perspective

Associative model 2

The geometric complexity and over-determination of the associative model developed from the interpretive study of the earlier cast instantiations of Hauer's Design 1 limits its capacity for variability.

The associative model has higher intricacy but this has also limited its transformative possibilities. Another production method that was adopted late in Hauer's career for the materialization of Design 1 was CNC milling.

In lieu of the expressed volumes and more massive geometries achieved by means of complex molds, the topology of the design was reconsidered in light of the limitations of a subtractive process.

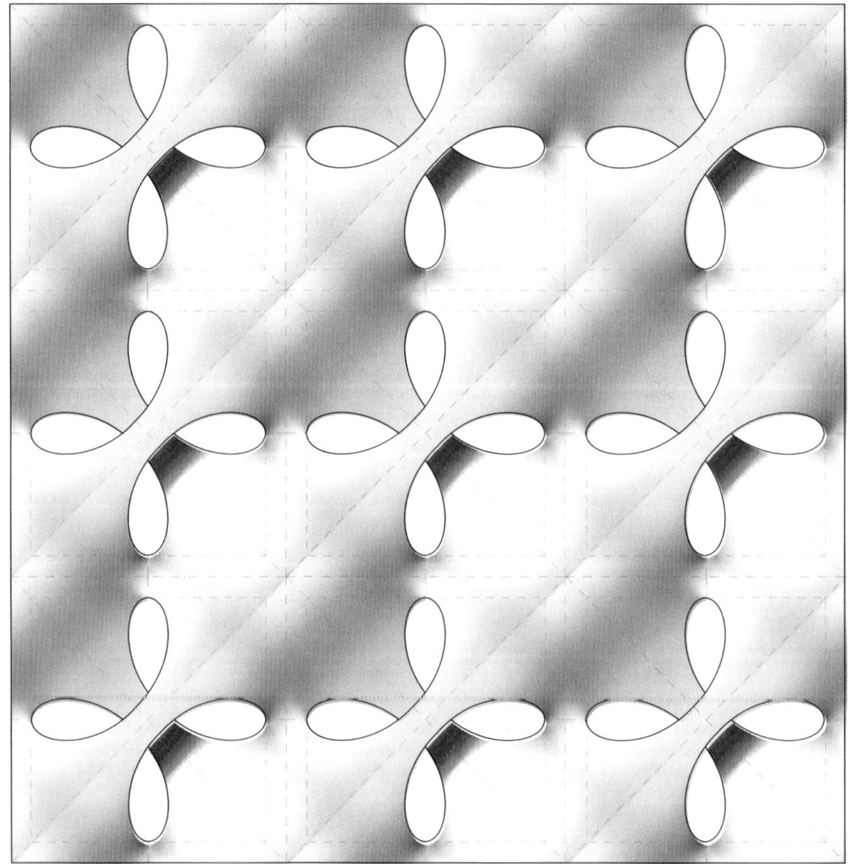

15_Associative model 2_3x3 matrix of modules_elevation

Consequently, this model, focuses on interpreting those geometries associated with a particular production method for Design 1 which generally resulted in a more surface oriented quality. Formally, we needed to reconceive the design as emanating from a module of a thickened suture curve bounded in a squared tile. One of the main points of difference between this and the previous model is the flattened nature of the surfaces. Overall, these geometries also resulted in an increase in the variability of the overall model. There was a higher capacity for generating a wider range of differentiated design instantiations from these geometric associations.

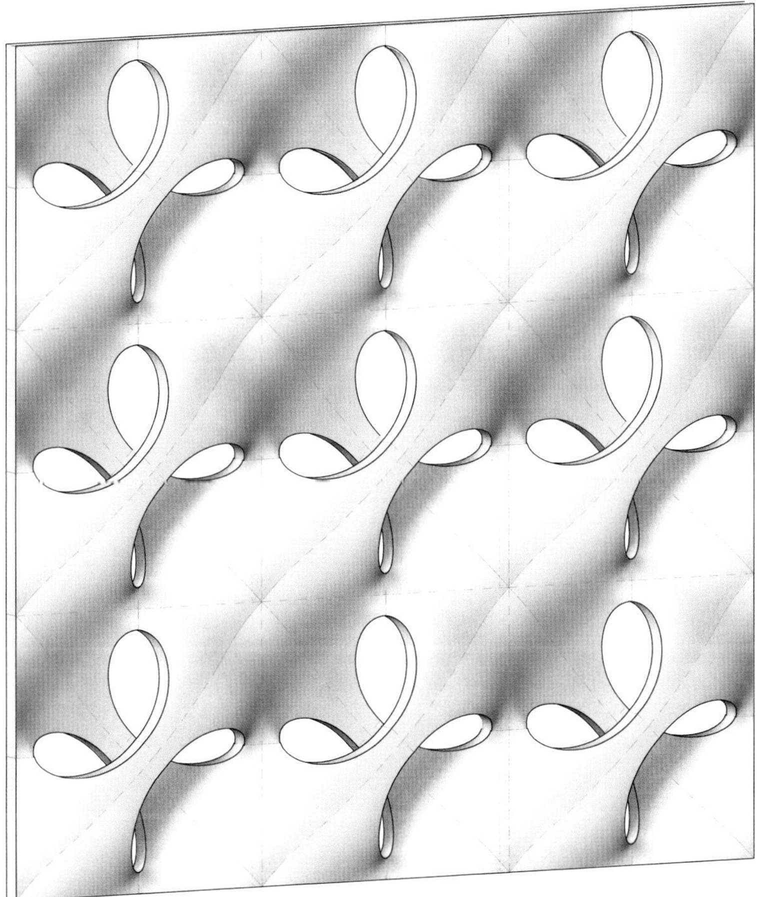

16_Associative model 2_3x3 matrix of modules_isometric

Assembly

In this interpretive model of Design 1, the conceptual module for the overall pattern is defined by a half-handle module which constitute a quarter of the tile which is subsequently arrayed in a grid. Distinct to the previous associative model, , saddle surfaces do not play a role in the construction of the surfaces.

Given the geometry of the tile and the spherical origin of its construction, both handles enclose a semi-spherical space, but this is proportionally flatter than other versions of this design. The continuity between handles is achieved by constructed tangential lines that mediate between the suture curve and the squared tile.

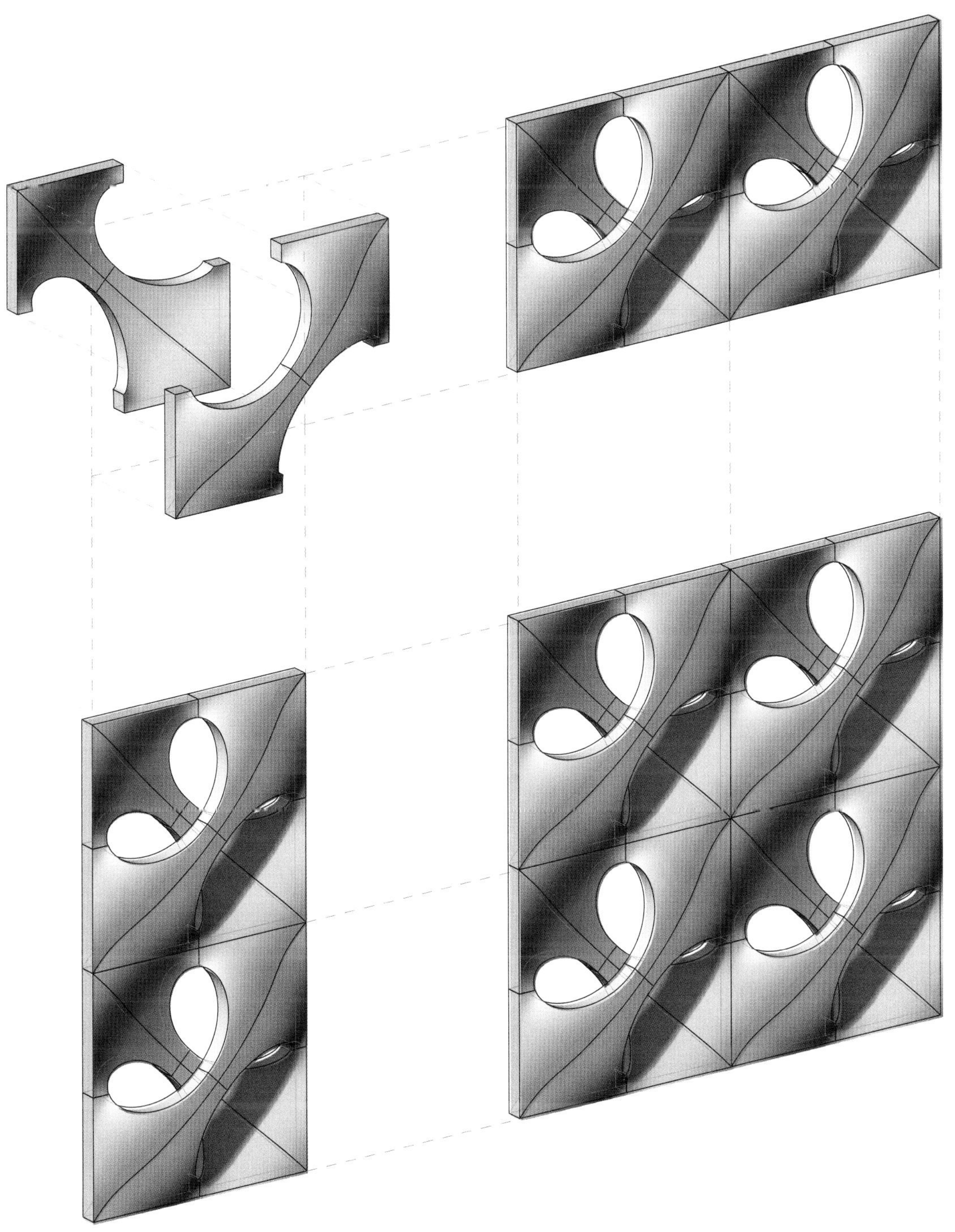

17_3x3 matrix of modules_isometric.
Construction and assembly

Associative model overview

Like the previous model, each tiled module is conceived as a pair of facing thickened handles that inscribe a semi-spherical space. The overall tile can be seen as the transitional surfaces that bridge between a suture curve and a squared edge. Continuity between tiles is achieved by producing a flat surfaces along the squared edge of the tile to ensure that modules are co-planar. These flat edges are blended with the three-dimensional suture curve by means of tangent lines from the four corners. This associative model is organized into four variables and eleven operations. From a shared centroid, a sphere (variable 01) and an Enneper surface are constructed. This point is also the center of the tiled module. A module from the suture curve is extracted as the basic module within the tile and from the original sphere, a diagonal axis is identified.

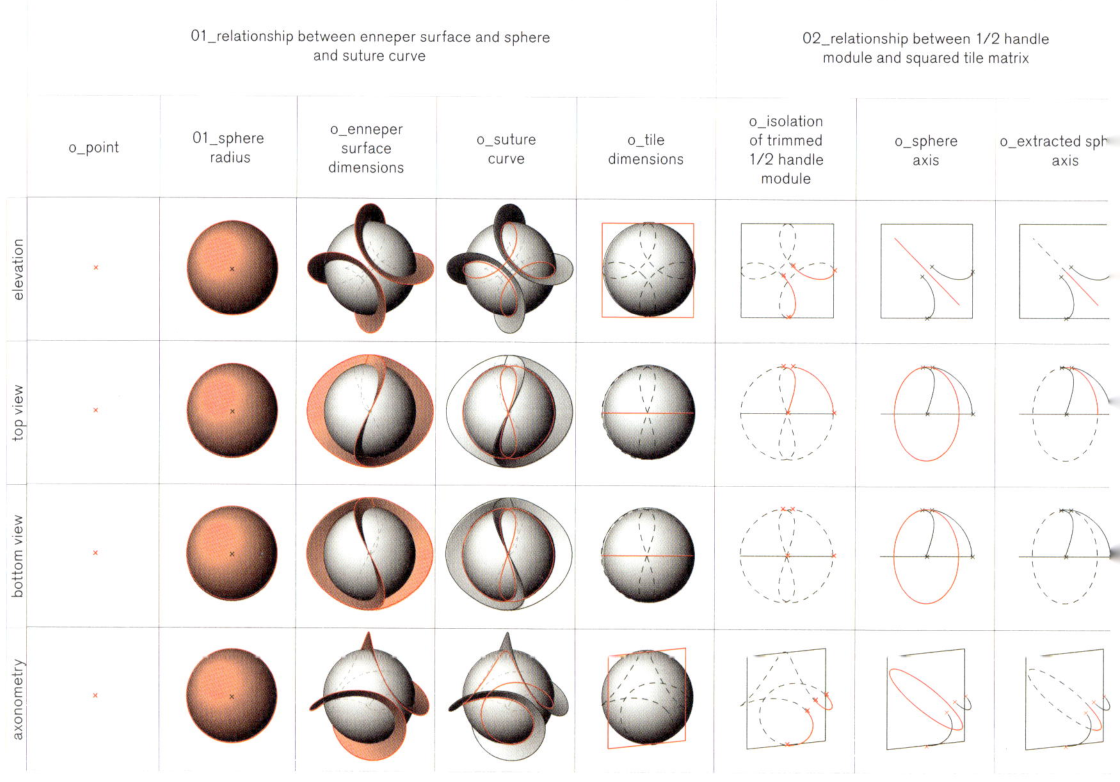

A second outer tile is constructed as an offset (variable 02) from the initial tile boundary. From the closest corner of this outer tile, a tangent line is drawn towards the diagonal axis. As previously mentioned, the vertical proportion of this associative model is significantly flatter than the previous version. The vertical scaling of the elements accounts for this difference in order to produce shallower surfaces. It is likely that these shallower surfaces are the result of limitations in height imposed by the drill and spindle dimensions associated with CNC milling (which preceded robotic arm milling) that also narrowed the capacity for significant undercutting. Once the basic half-handle module is generated, it is proliferated within the squared tile by means of reflections and rotations. Once the tile is complete, the continuous surface is extruded vertically to a specific dimension (variable 04). Finally, this tile is proliferated in a squared matrix.

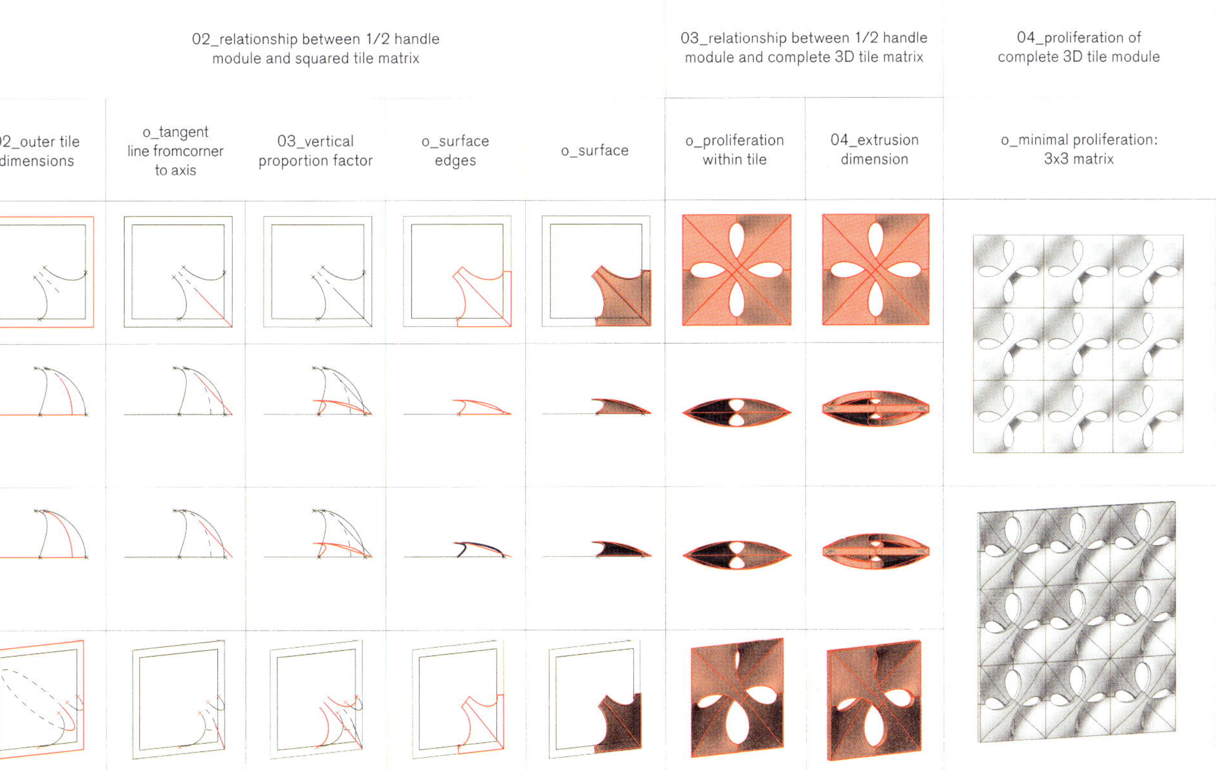

18_System construction_variables and operations

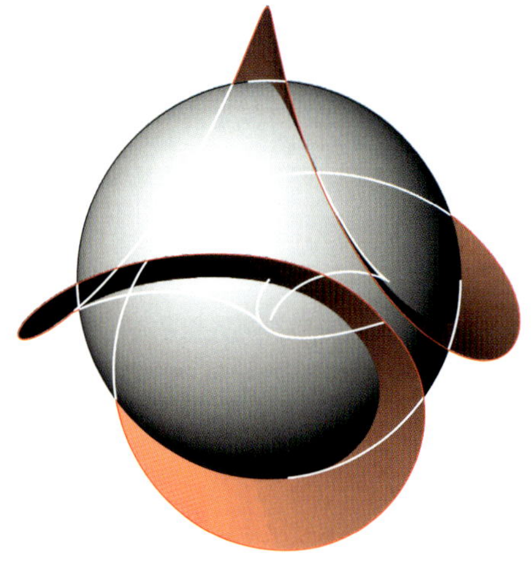

19_a . Intersection between the Enneper surface and the Sphere

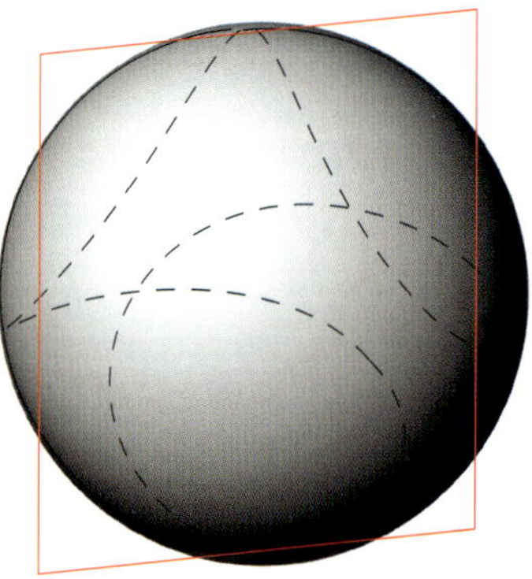

19_b. Suture curve on Spherical surface

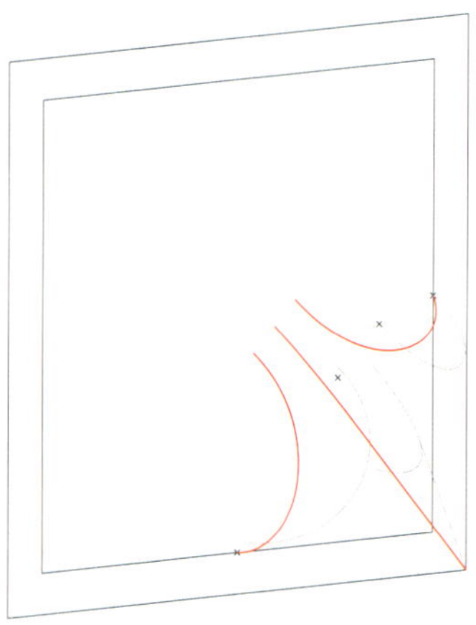

19_e. Vertical proportion

19_f. Half-handle surface

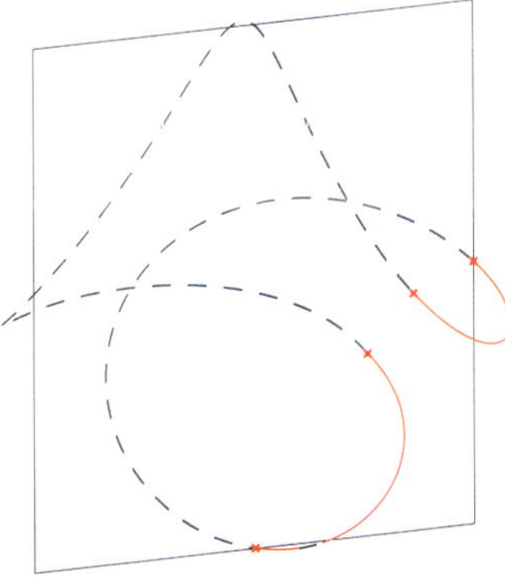

19_c. Extraction of half-handle module

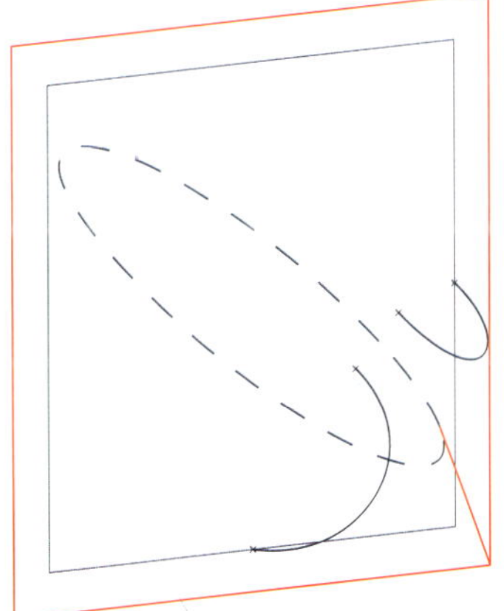

19_d. Tangent to sphere's axis and outer tile dimension

19_g. Proliferation within tile

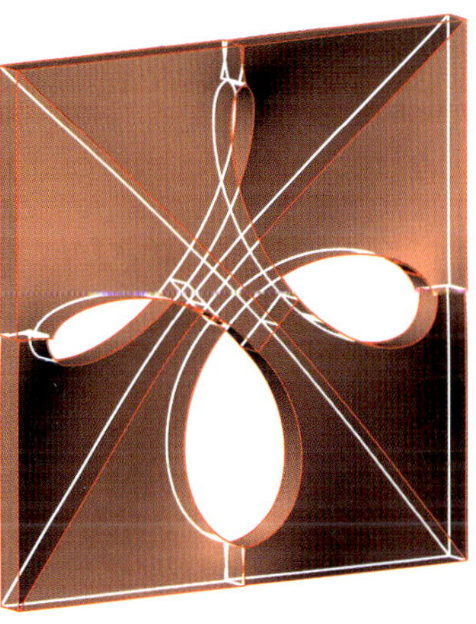

19_h. Extrusion of surfaces

20_Associative model 3_matrix elevation

21_Associative model 3_matrix perspective

Associative model 3

This third interpretive model of Hauer's Design 1 is an abstracted associative model that was constructed to offer a schematic approximation of the main qualities of the precedent. However, it was also constructed with the specific ambition to enable greater ranges of variability and differentiation within the model. The previous Design 1 based interpretative models were exercises in re-describing the existing forms which were differentiated by time as well as methods of fabrication. This model was explicitly developed to define an associative model that could afford much higher degrees of variation through a streamlining and schematization of the original geometries. Certain details and precision associated with the original surfaces were sacrificed for a model that was based less on the modeling of complex surfaces and more on the compositing of simple geometries into a framework

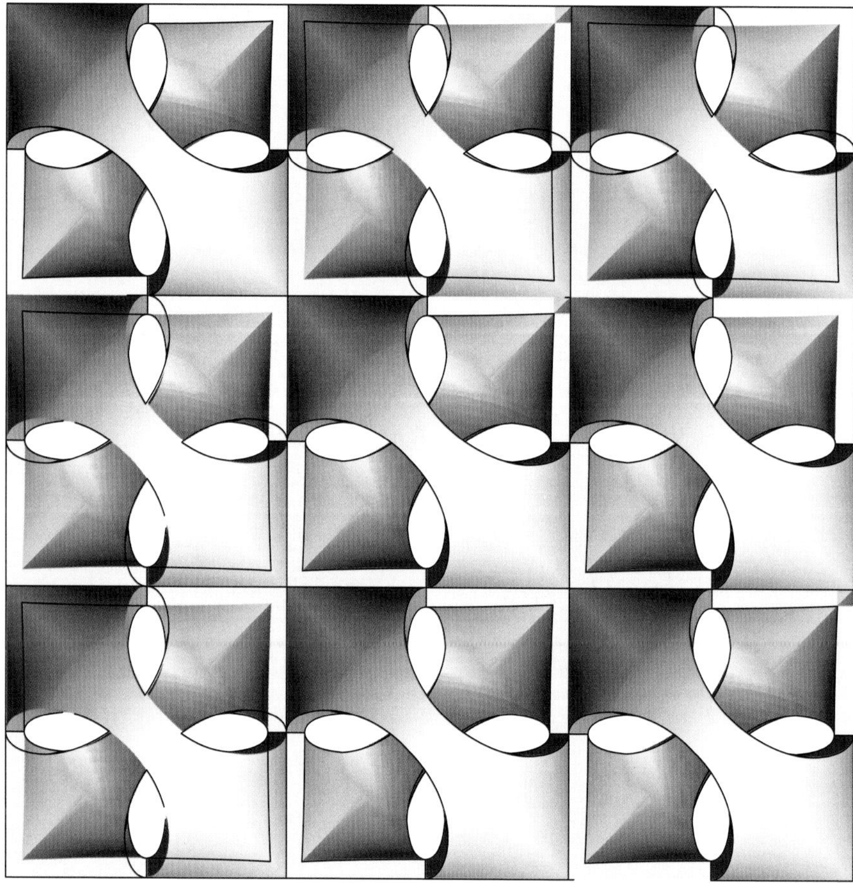

22_22_Associative model 3_3x3 matrix of modules_elevation

that described the originals in a diagrammatic manner. This leverages the general benefits of associative models for their ability to generate a large sample of design instantiations from geometric relationships that permit for a wide range of variables. Precision was less important than a more malleable topological arrangement.

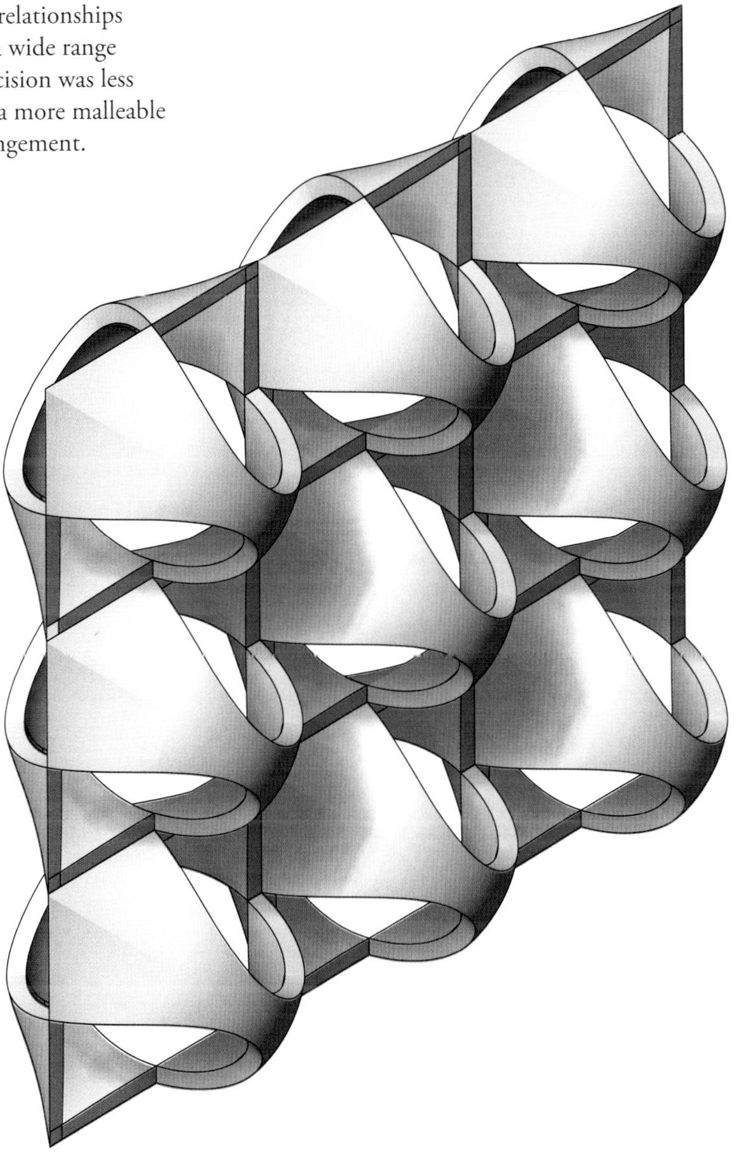

23_22_Associative model 3_3x3 matrix of modules_isometric

Assembly

Like the previous interpretative models of Design 1, it is generated by describing a basic module that is bounded by a square frame or tile and is subsequently proliferated in a square matrix. The basic module is a quarter of the overall tile and is composed of half a handle and a quarter of a saddle transitional surface. The overall matrix is achieved then by the translation of identical tiles into a matrix.

Given the geometry of the tile and the spherical origin of its construction, both handles are configured to enclose a spherical space. The deliberate construction of geometric continuity between the handle and the saddle surfaces is essential for a seamless reading of the overall mass.

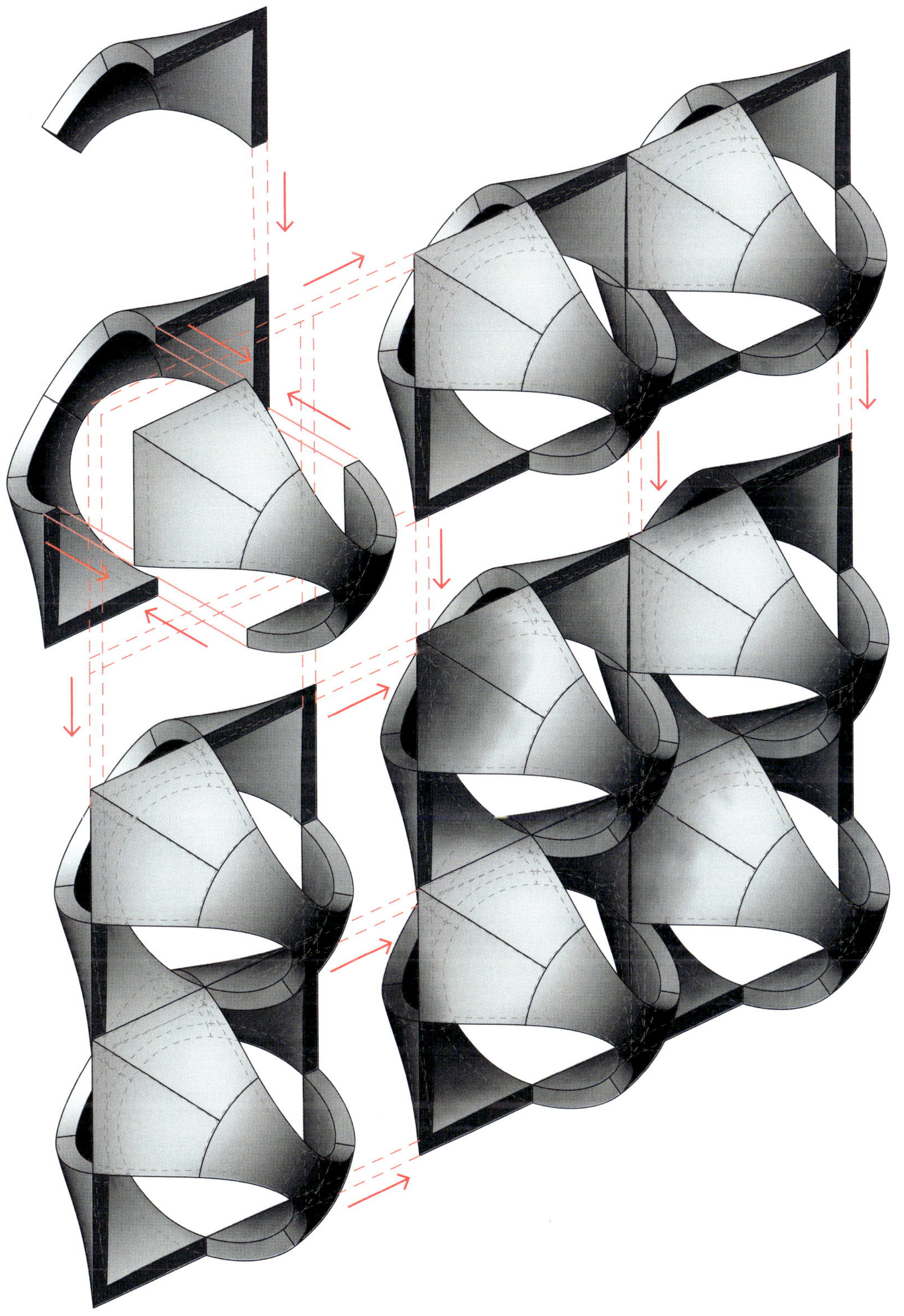

24_3x3 matrix of modules_isometric. Construction and assembly

Associative model overview

This process of constructing this model, as with all the associative models in this book, can be described through a linear series of variables and operations that have the capacity for ranges of variability. Each tile is produced by arranging four basic modules into a mirrored handle pairs arranged around the tile centroid. In this design, there is a constant tension between the spherical origin of the suture curve and the squared matrix imposed on the module. The mediation between the two is achieved by tangential lines drawn from the corners to the half-handle module.

This model is produced through the proliferation of a module at two scales: within a squared tile, by means of rotations and reflections of a quarter module; and within a potentially infinite squared matrix, by means of the translation of identical modules.

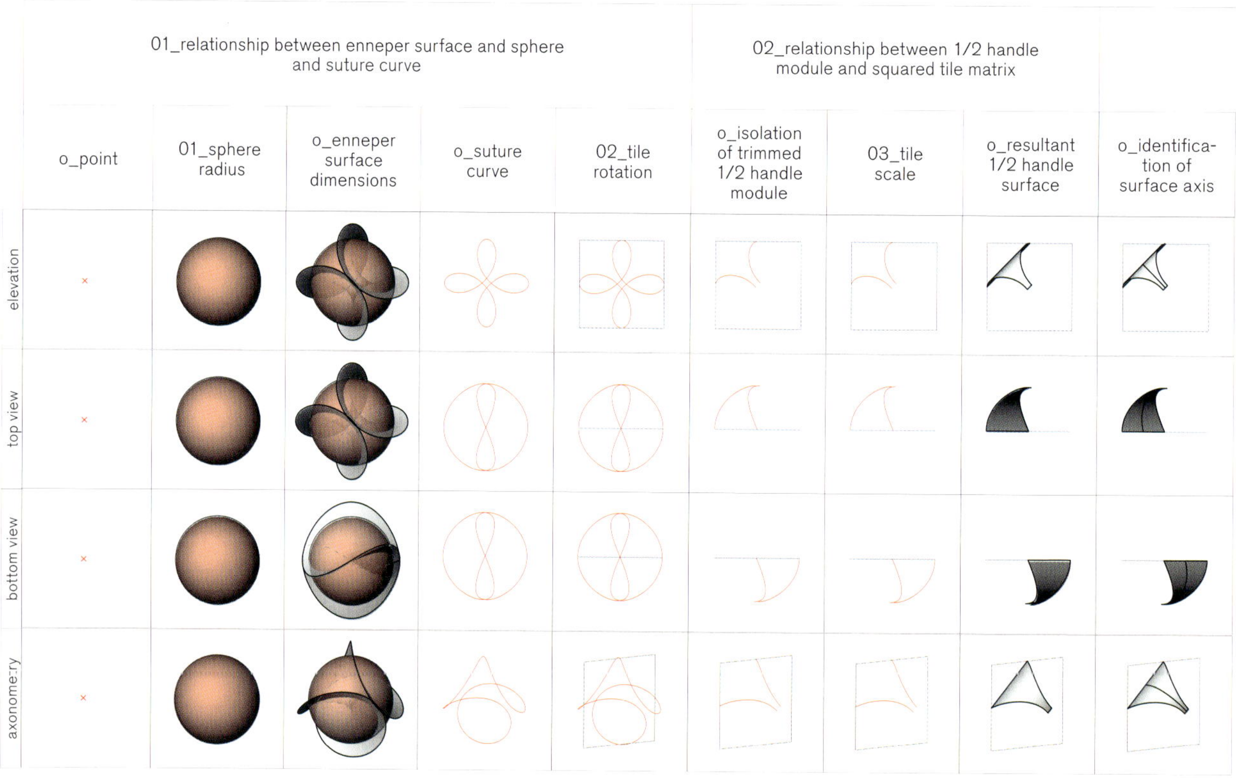

	01_relationship between enneper surface and sphere and suture curve					02_relationship between 1/2 handle module and squared tile matrix			
	o_point	01_sphere radius	o_enneper surface dimensions	o_suture curve	02_tile rotation	o_isolation of trimmed 1/2 handle module	03_tile scale	o_resultant 1/2 handle surface	o_identification of surface axis
elevation	x								
top view	x								
bottom view	x								
axonometry	x								

The steps of the construction for this model are conceptually divided into two parts. Firstly, there is an exploration of an intersection between two surfaces, a sphere and the Enneper, to produce the suture curve, which is used to generate a half-handle-like surface (see section "Suture Curve"). This surface is then bounded by a squared tile. The transition between the spherical surface and the squared plane is achieved through tangential lines from the closest corners.

The second part of the construction, once a continuous quarter module composed of a half-handle surface is achieved, is the thickness and proliferation of the module within the tile.

The model consists of four variables and eleven operations. From a shared centroid both a sphere (variable 01) and an Enneper surface are constructed.

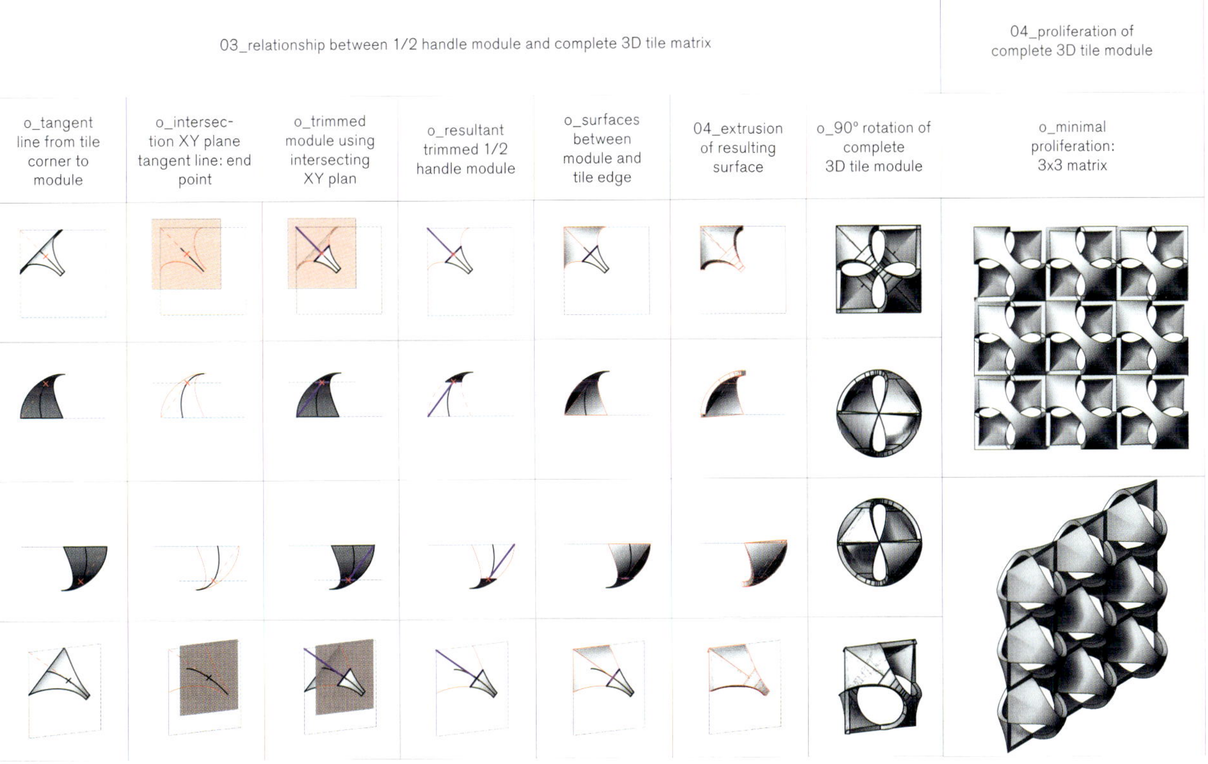

25_System construction_variables and operations

The result of the intersection between the sphere and the enneper surface is a suture curve. The sphere's scale determines a specific bounding volume, which is projected to produce a bounding square. This regular shape is the tile that will eventually be proliferated in larger matrices. The model is constructed in a manner that allows for a higher degree of variability. The possibility of rotating the bounding square in relationship to the resultant suture curve is one such capacity embedded in the model (variable 02). The possibility of scaling the tile becomes another variable (03). The resultant suture curve is a closed, symmetric and continuous curve. A basic module is derived from a quarter of its length.

The two resultant symmetric lines define a ruled surface that it is assumed to be a half handle and also defines its axis.

A line is traced from the closest tile corner to the tangent point on the handle surface, along the handle's previously identified axis.

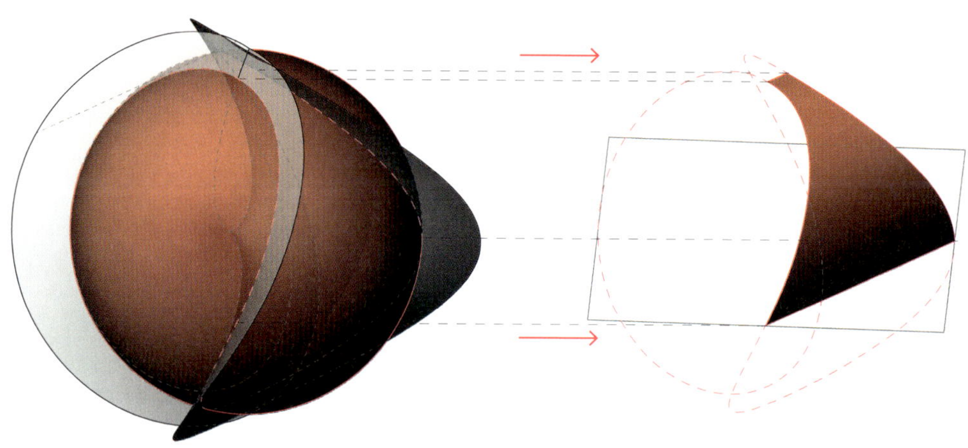

26_a. Intersection between the Enneper surface and the Sphere

26_b. Surface trimming along the sphere's equator and meridian

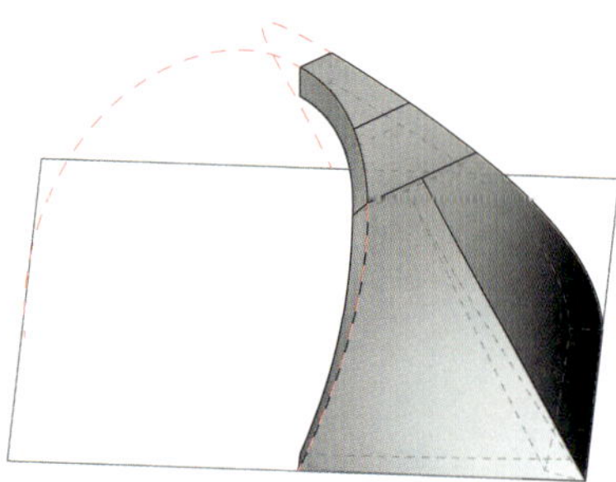

26_e. Surface thickness

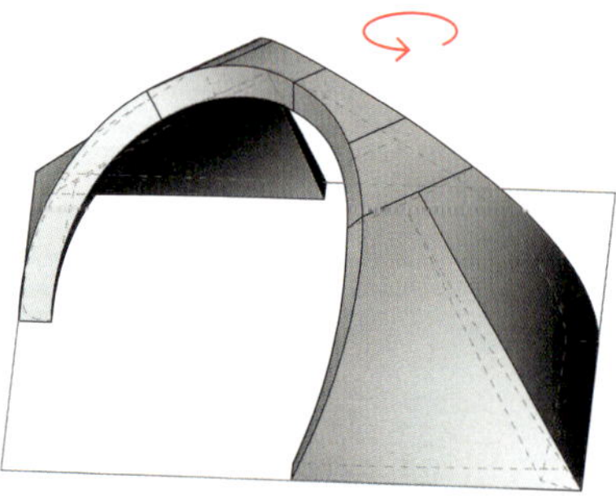

26_f. Module assembly. 180° degrees rotation from tile center

At this tangent point on the surface, an XY plane is constructed. The half-handle is trimmed using the intersecting XY plane.
The transitional surface is a mediation between the squared tile and a spherical surface and it is constructed from the edges of both the tile and the trimmed handle surface.

Finally, the extrusion of the surface (variable 04) determines a thickness for the material which introduces a certain weight (both physical and visual) to the tile.
Also, this can generate more surface area which can result in different light effects across the tile.

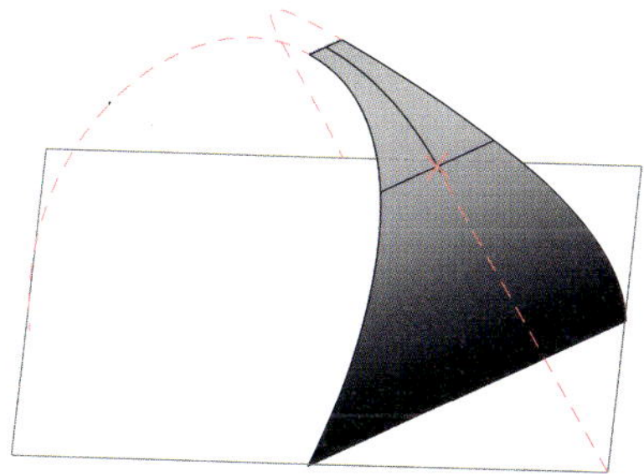

26_c. Tangent line from tile corner to half-handle surface

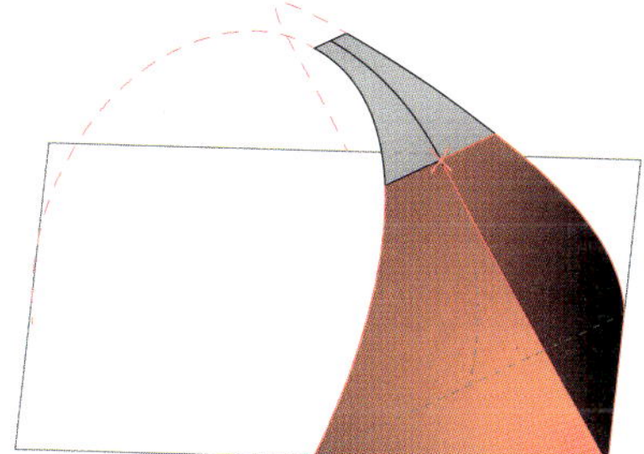

26_d. Transitional surfaces: half-handle surface and tile edges

26_g. Reflection along a XY plane from tile center

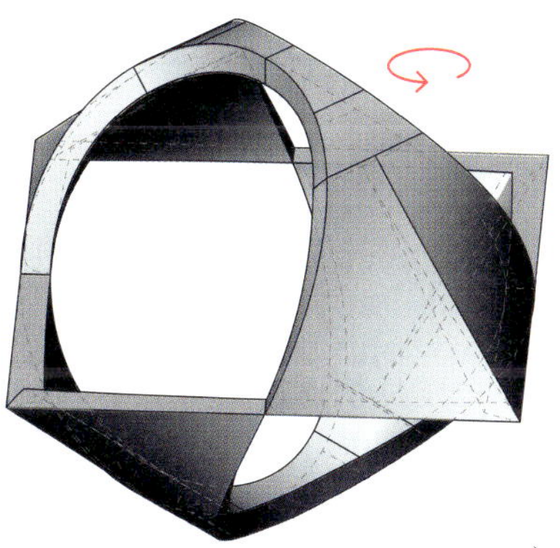

26_h. Module assembly. 90° degrees rotation from tile center

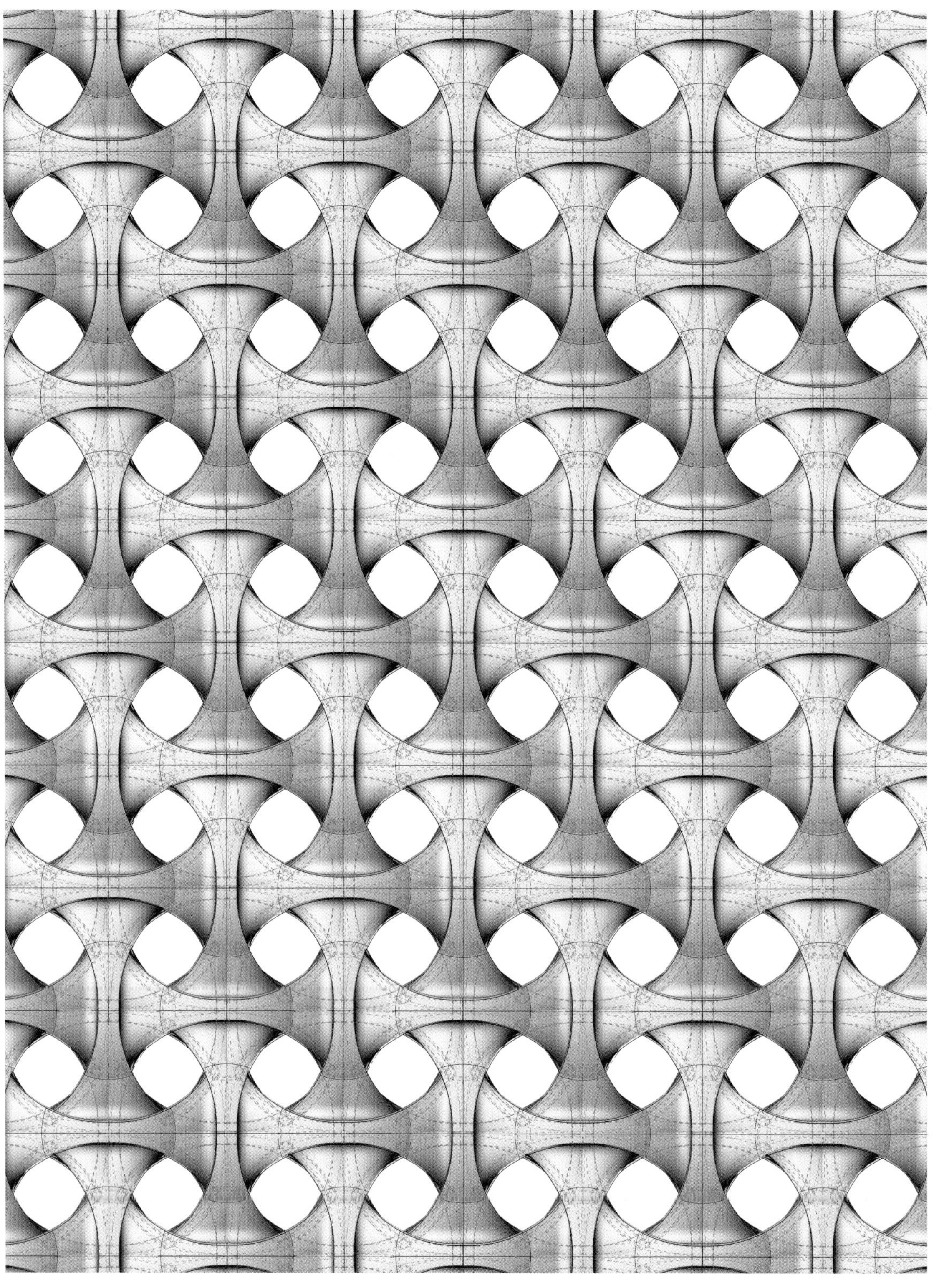

27_Associative model 4_matrix elevation

28_Associative model 4_matrix perspective

Associative model 4

Upon completing the first iterations of Design 1 in the 1950's, Hauer discovered the emergence of a pattern of great circles in the larger proliferation of the modules.[1] This model is an interpretation of his second design based on using "The Great Circles", as an effect produced from the assembling of modules. In a way, it is about constructing another scale of the design that is inherent to the module but it is only perceivable once a critical mass of tiles within a larger field is established.[2]

1. Hauer E. (2007) *Continua, Architectural Screens and Walls*, Princeton Architectural Press. New York
2.(ibid)

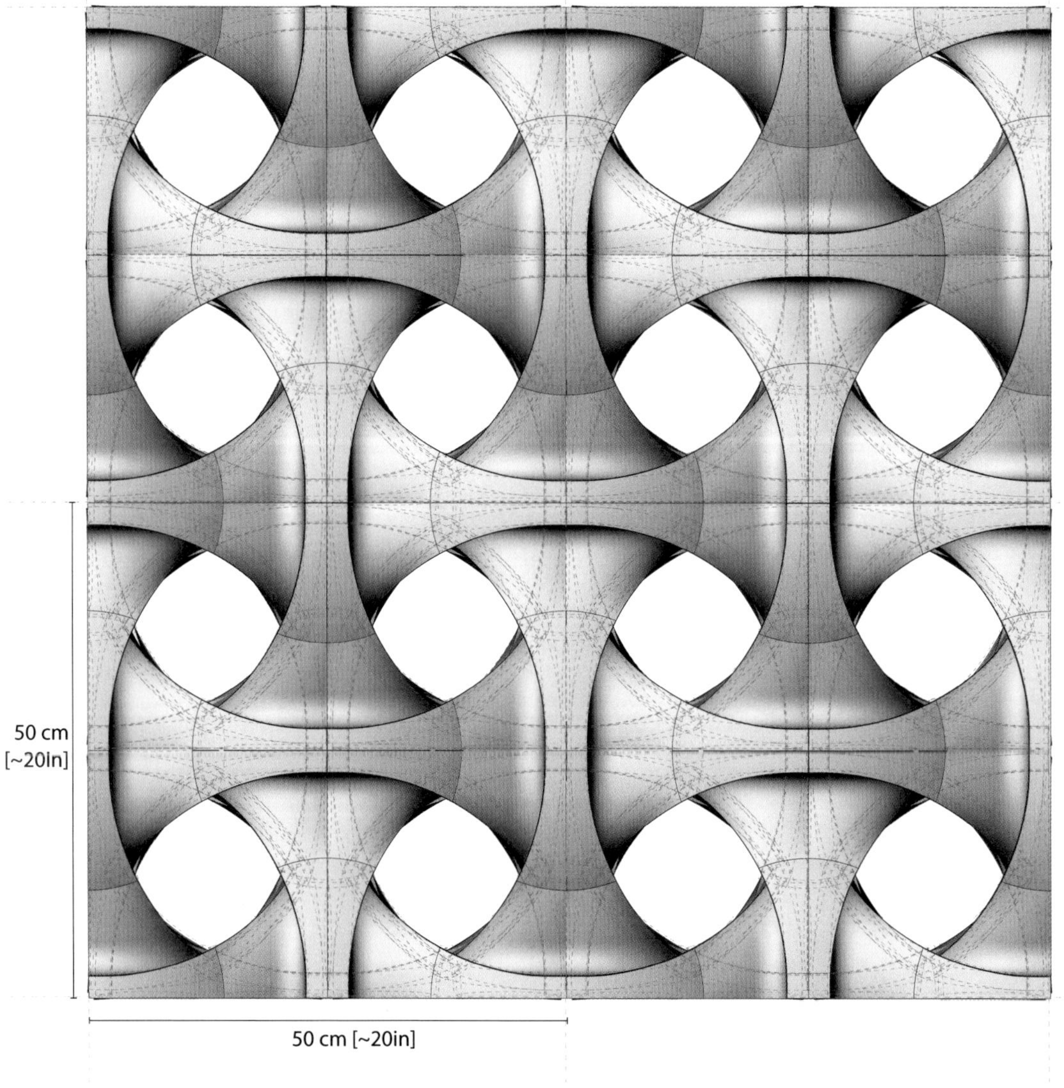

29_Associative model 4_3x3 matrix of modules

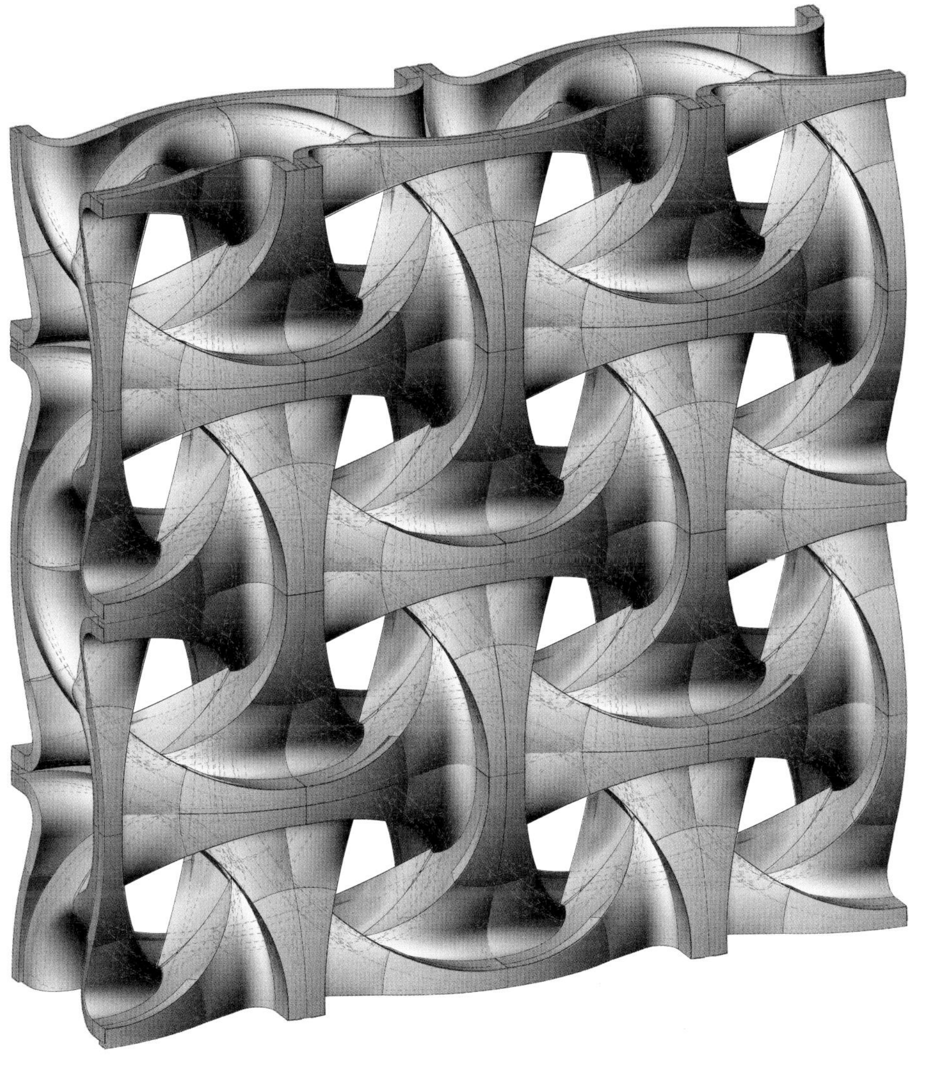

30_Associative model 4_3x3 matrix of modules_isometric

Assembly

This interpretive model of Design 2 can be modeled through the proliferation of a module at three scales:

a) using a basic module defined by a quarter of a squared tile, by means of polar arraying around the quarter's center.

b) using the complete square tile, by means of two reflections, along the two orthogonal axis of symmetry.

c) within a potentially infinite squared grid, by means of reflections of the tiles along the horizontal and vertical edges.

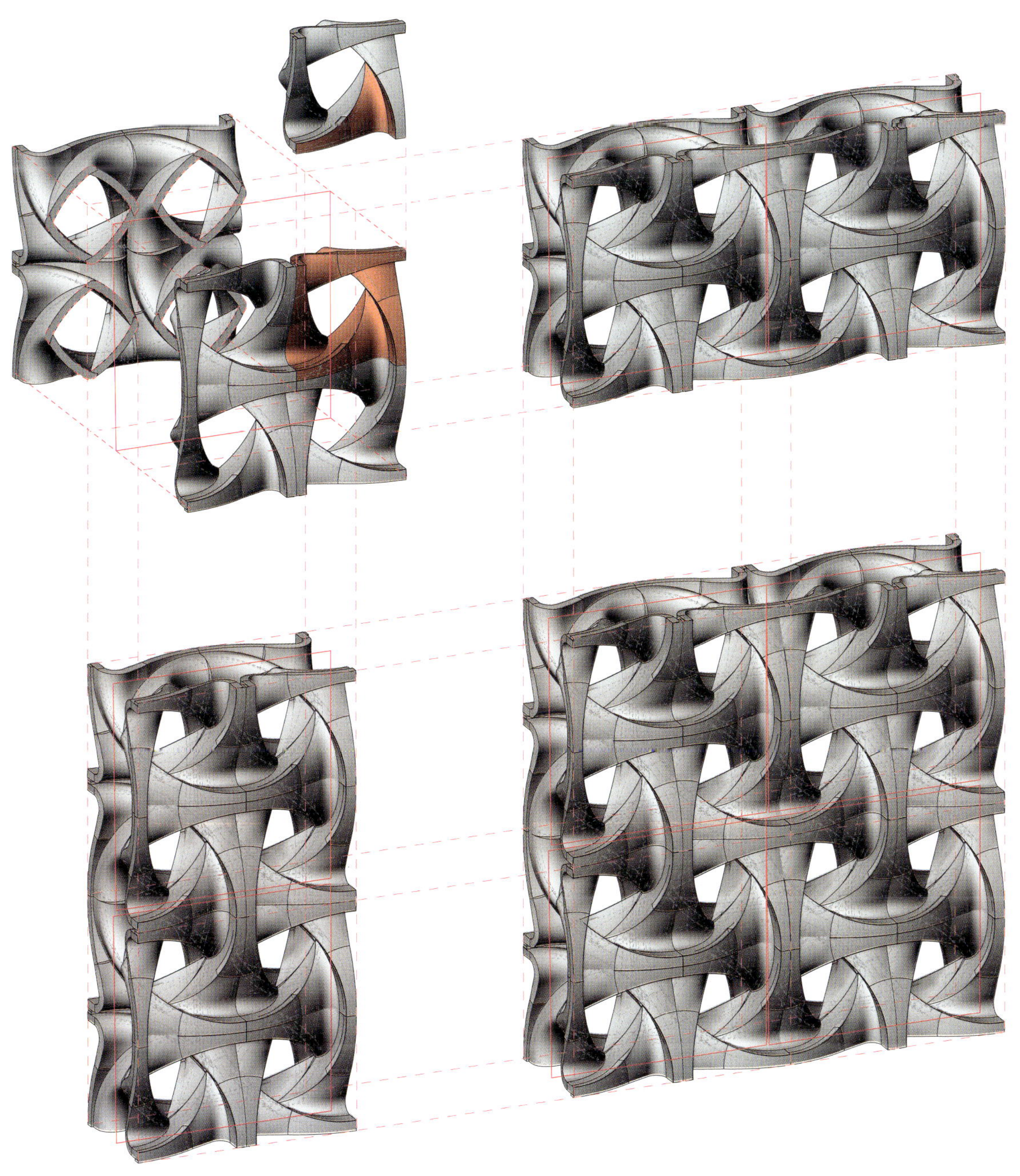

31_3x3 matrix of modules_isometric. Construction and assembly

associative model overview

This model begins with one basic module which is proliferated to produce a tile and finally, a matrix. Each complete tile is constructed using thirty-two similar basic modules. Like the earlier models, there is a tension between a spherical origin in the suture curve and the squared matrix that the module is bounded in. However, this matrix is also more complex than earlier models, as it incorporates another scale in the assembly of the final tile besides the simple replication of a basic handle-like surface module.

	o_point	01_sphere dimensions	o_enneper dimensions	o_intersection enneper srf / sphere	o_bounding tile	o_isolation of trimmed 1/2 module	o_resultant 1/2 handle surface	o_lateral circle centre position	02_lateral circle radius	o_lateral circ radius extrusion
elevation										
top view										
bottom view										
axonometry										

	o_1/2 module X traslation of handle	o_intersection: module and curve	o_resultant segment	o_subdivision of segment	o_start point of tangent line	o_identification: circle and surface points	o_tangent line from divided segment	o_intersection_ segment and tangent line	04_fillet radius_ segment and tangent line	o_resultant edge
elevation										
top view										
bottom view										
axonometry										

In the construction of this model, transitional surfaces between different modules are essential to achieve seamless continuity. The basic module consists of a transitional surface between two handle-like surfaces. This surface is then proliferated to fit a squared tile. Constructing the model can be conceptually divided into three parts. Firstly, the intersection between a sphere and the Enneper produces a suture curve, which is used to generate a half-handle-like surface (see section "Suture Curve").

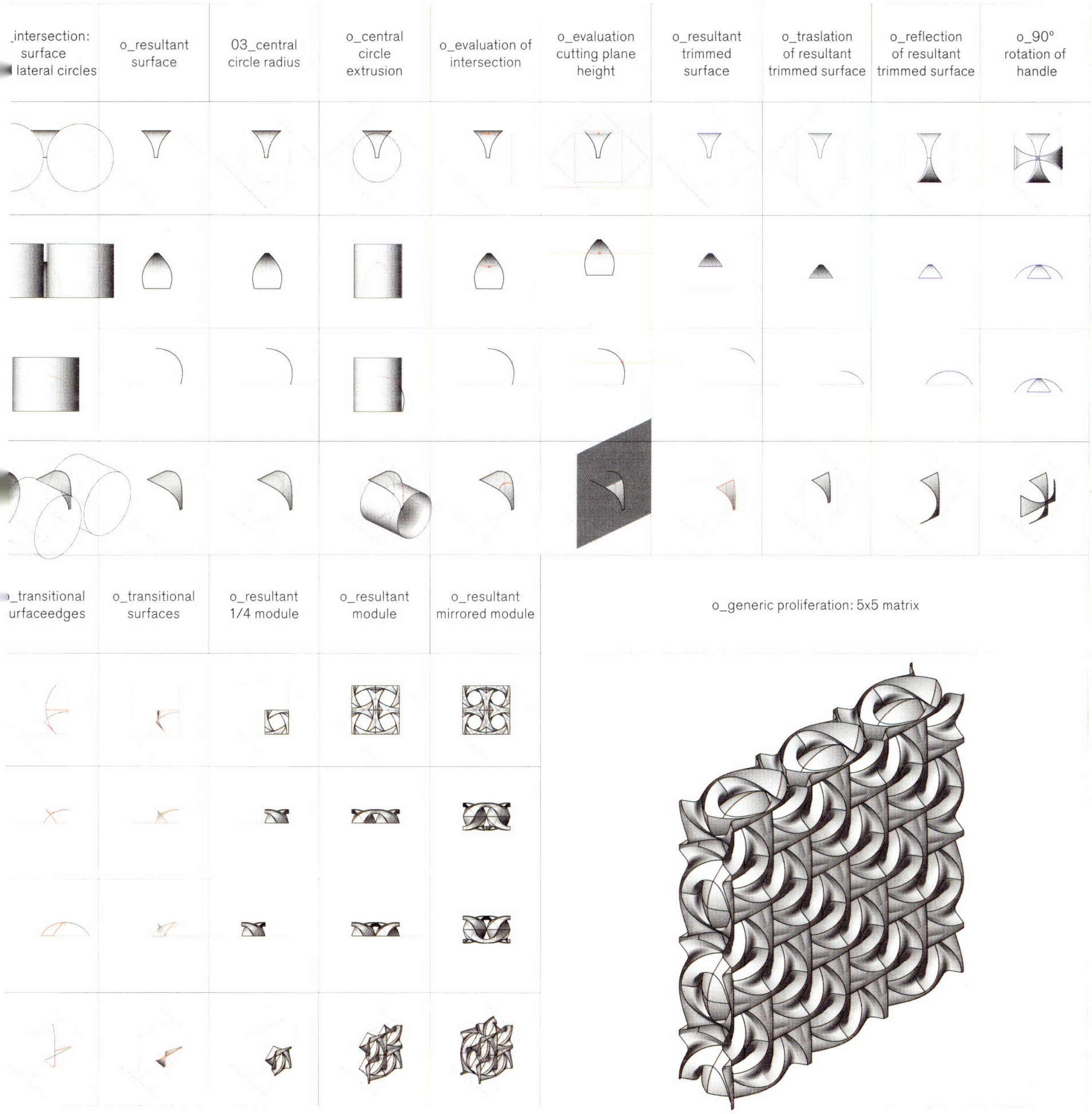

_intersection: surface lateral circles

o_resultant surface

03_central circle radius

o_central circle extrusion

o_evaluation of intersection

o_evaluation cutting plane height

o_resultant trimmed surface

o_traslation of resultant trimmed surface

o_reflection of resultant trimmed surface

o_90° rotation of handle

_transitional urfaceedges

o_transitional surfaces

o_resultant 1/4 module

o_resultant module

o_resultant mirrored module

o_generic proliferation: 5x5 matrix

32_System construction_variables and operations

This half-handle surface undergoes a series of operations to be positioned in the tile. The second part of the construction involves creating the transitional surface between two orthogonally placed handles.
This transition is achieved by defining each one of the surface edges by means of tangent lines and fillets. The final part of the construction involves proliferating the module across the previously mentioned scales of within a tile and arrayed in a matrix. The model consists of seven variables and twenty-six operations. From a shared centroid, both a sphere (v01) and an Enneper surface are constructed. This point is also the center of the tile. The sphere's bounding volume is projected to form the square that constitutes the limits of the tile and grid cell of the two dimensional matrix. The trimming of the sphere using a section of the suture curve produces a half handle surface. Two symmetrical points along one of the diagonals of the tile define the centers of the lateral circles with variable radius (v02).
Again from the center of the tile, a new circle of variable radius (v03) is constructed. The intersection between the trimmed surface and the extruded central circle is a curve. The evaluation along the curve's length (v04) results in a point from which an XY plane is constructed. The previously trimmed surface is once again

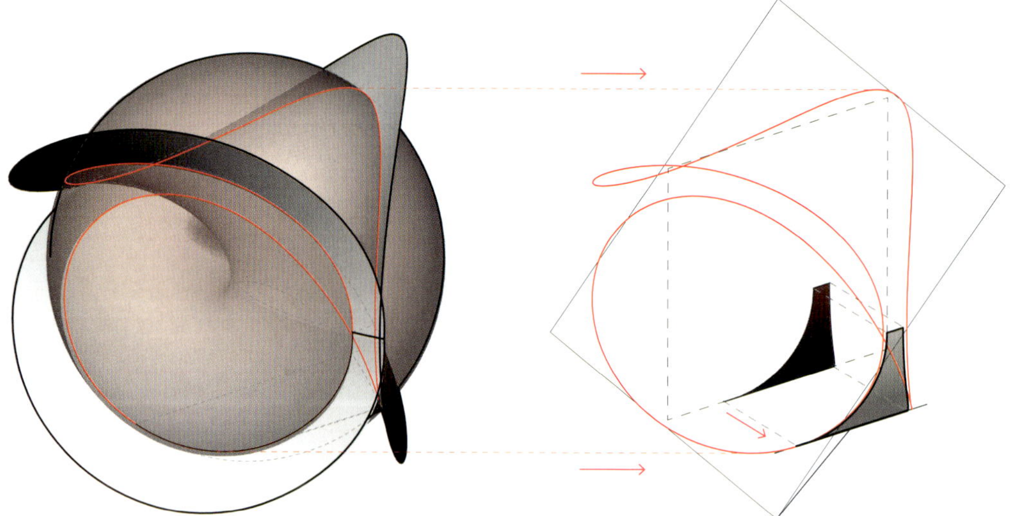

33_a. Intersection between Enneper surface and Sphere

33_b. Isolation of a half-handle module

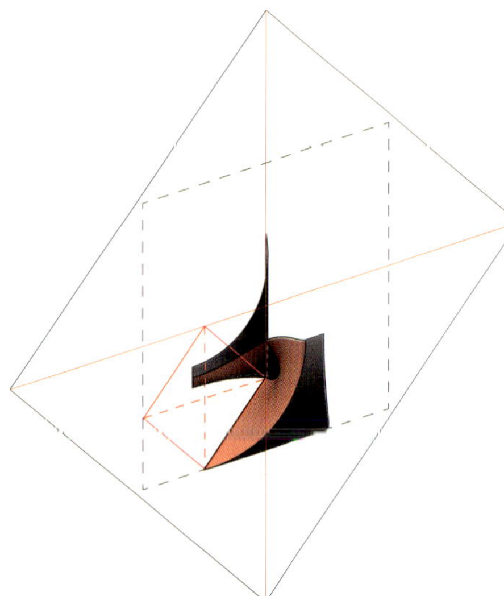

33_e. Transitional surface

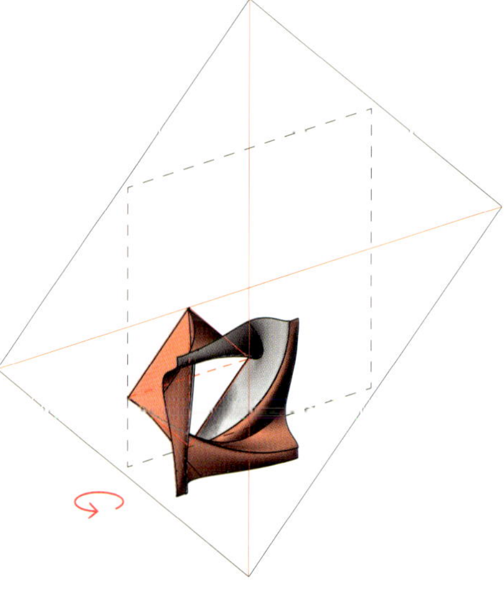

33_f. Polar array of an eighth of a module

trimmed using this cutting plane. Later, it is translated towards the tile plane such that the original cutting plane height is zero and mirrored to produce a whole handle and rotated 90º. Using one of the two half handles' edges as auxiliary curves, a line is constructed between two points. One of these points is the highest end point, while the other point is the middle point between the two lowest points of a complete handle. In other words, from one of the edges of the 1/2 handle with its two end points (Start (highest point), End (lowest point)), the two points of the line (A, B) are defined by A(x,y,z) = Start(x,y,z) and B(x,y,z) = Start(x) + End(y,z).

This straight line intersects the other half surface. The point of intersection is identified and used to trim the line into two segments. This segment is later subdivided (variable 05).

One of the resultant points is chosen (variable 06) as a starting point of a tangent line to the axis of curvature of the handle that is smoothened through a fillet radius (variable 07).
The resultant curves are identified as the edge curves and a surface is constructed. This defines the basic quarter module of the model. After several rotations and mirrors, the complete tile is produced.

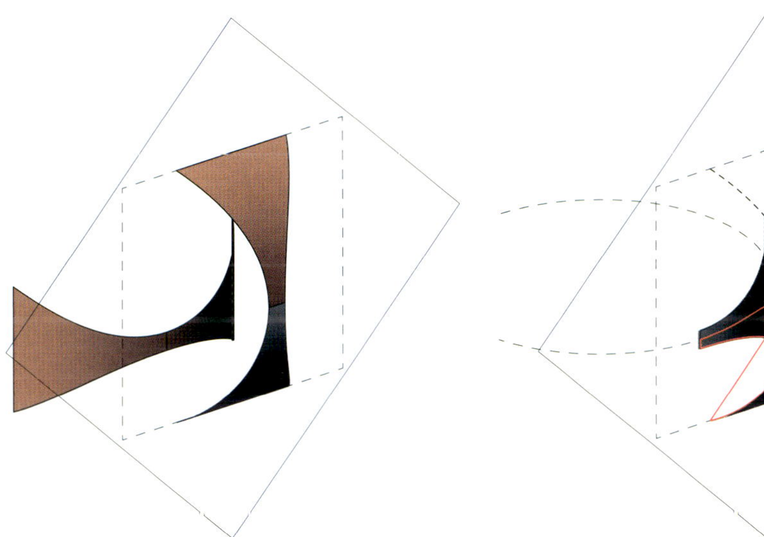

33_c. Orthogonal organization of handle-line surfaces

33_d. Construction of transitional surface edges

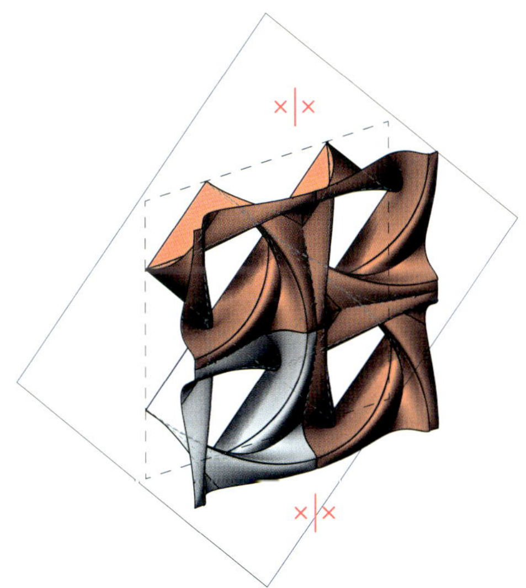

33_g. Polar array of a fourth of a module

33_h. Reflection along tile plane. 180° rotation from tile centre

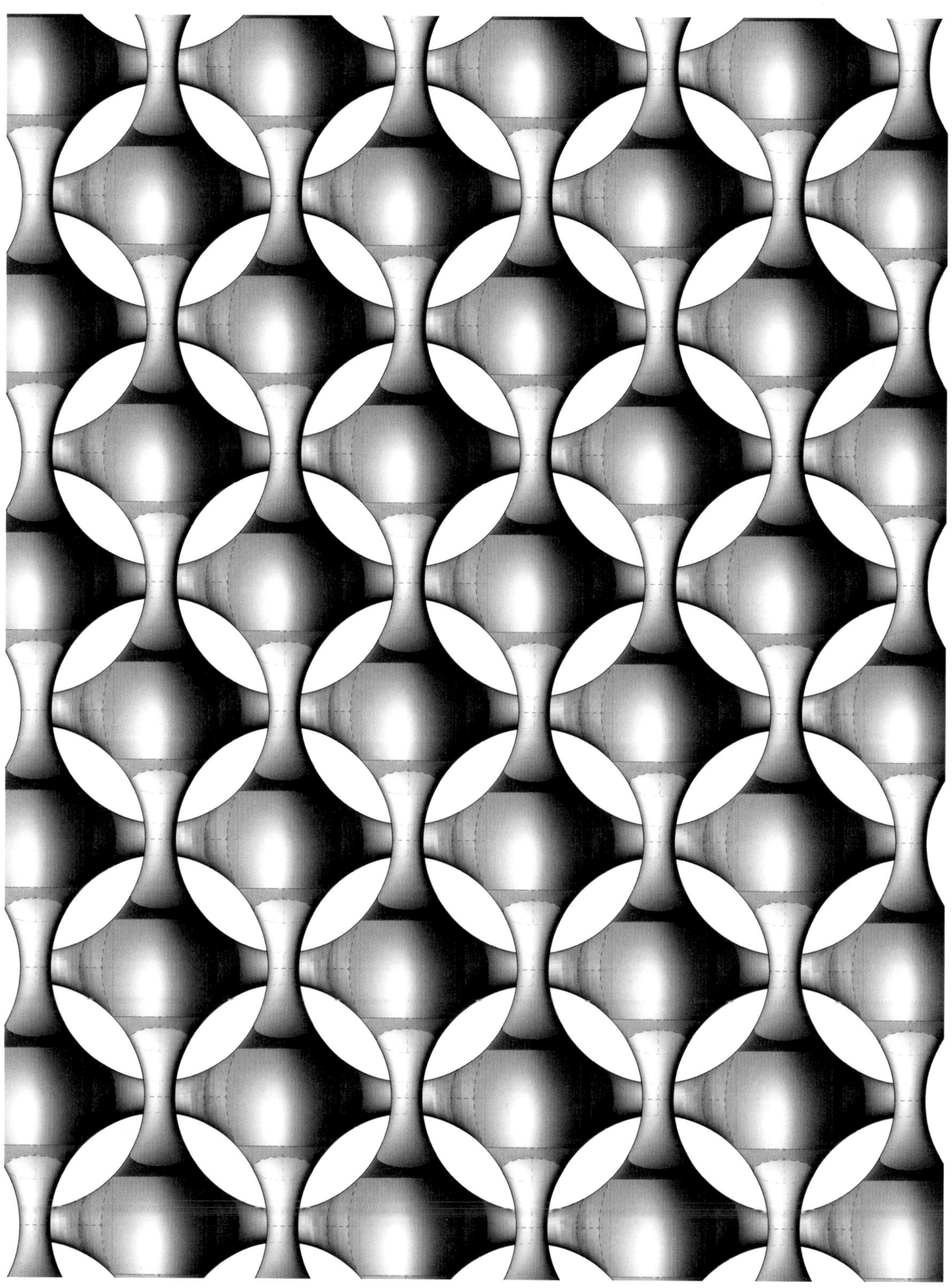

34_Associative model 5_matrix elevation

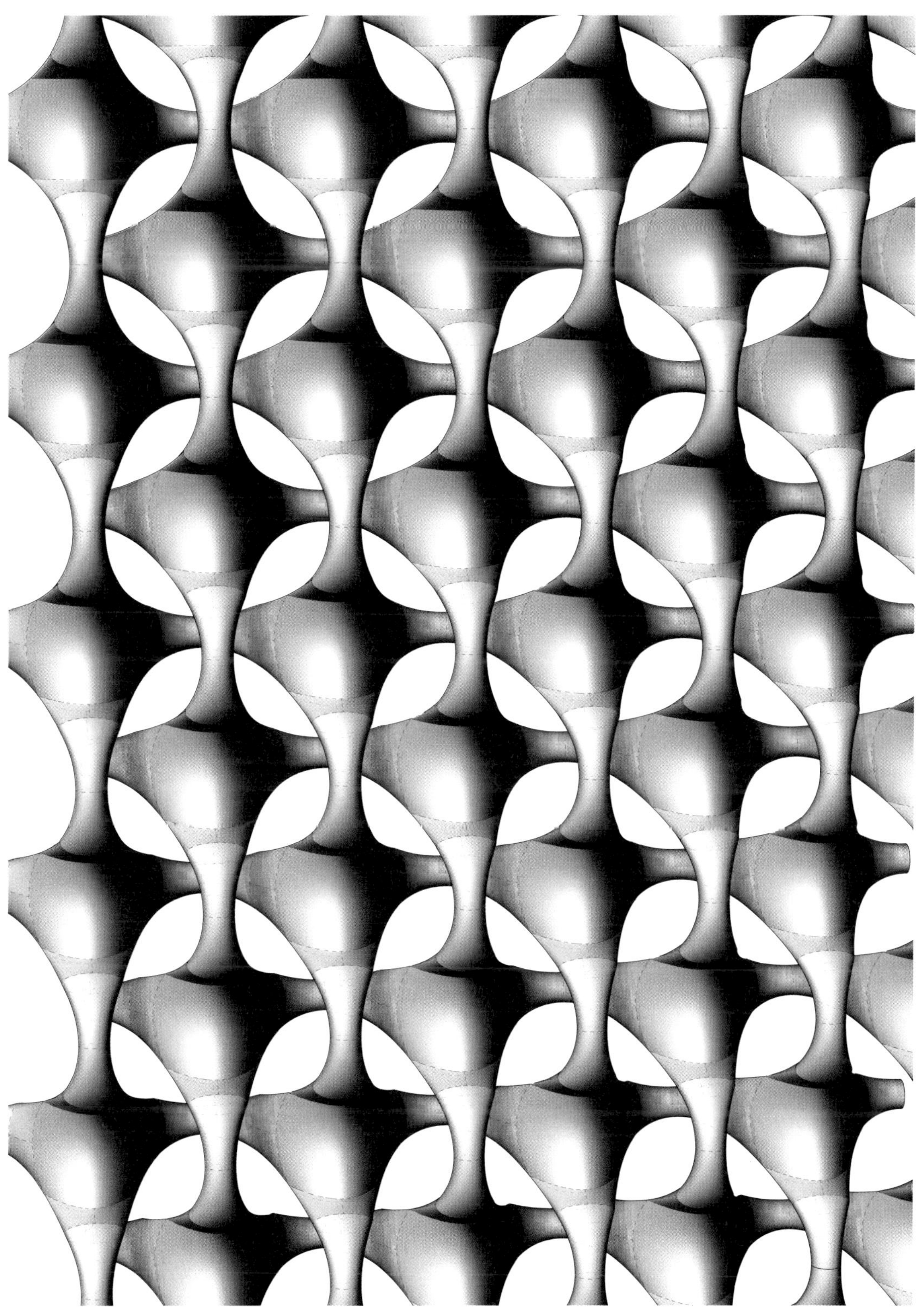

35_Associative model 5_matrix perspective

Associative model 5

When assembled, the greater composition of Hauer's Design 3 can be read as two separate matrices that are intertwined, two similar continuous masses that are interwoven within each other but never intersect.[1]
In this design, the proliferation of handle units takes on the organization of two offset and intertwining grids.
Like Design 2, these forms were conceived *"in 50-centimeter sizes as a split, hollow shell, using plaster molds for the lay-up of the cast stone grout, composed of white Portland cement and granular dolomite aggregate".* (Hauer E., 2004, Continua: Architectural Screens and Walls, The Princeton Architectural Press, New York, p. 95).

1. Hauer E., 2007, *Continua, Architectural Screens and Walls,* Princeton Architectural Press, New York.

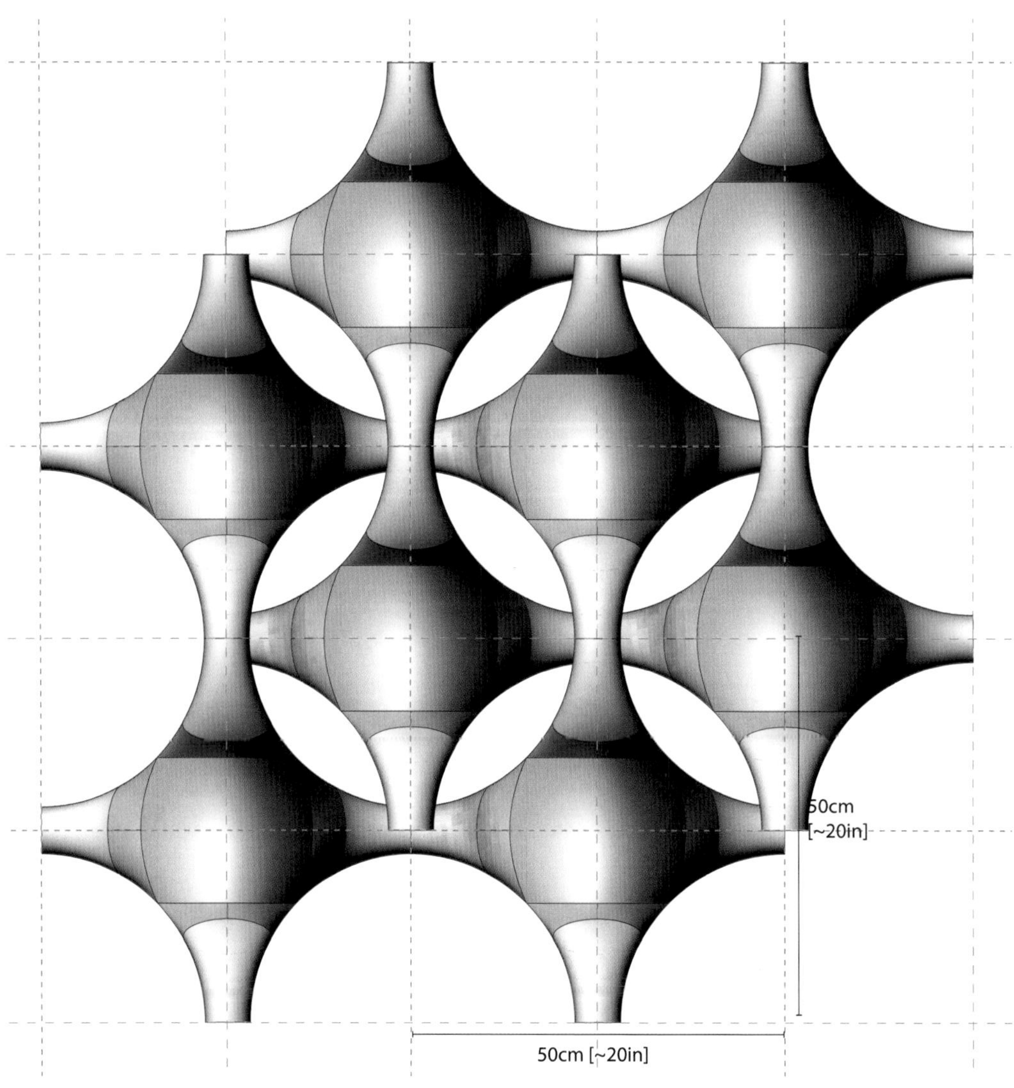

36_Associative model 5_3x3 matrix of modules

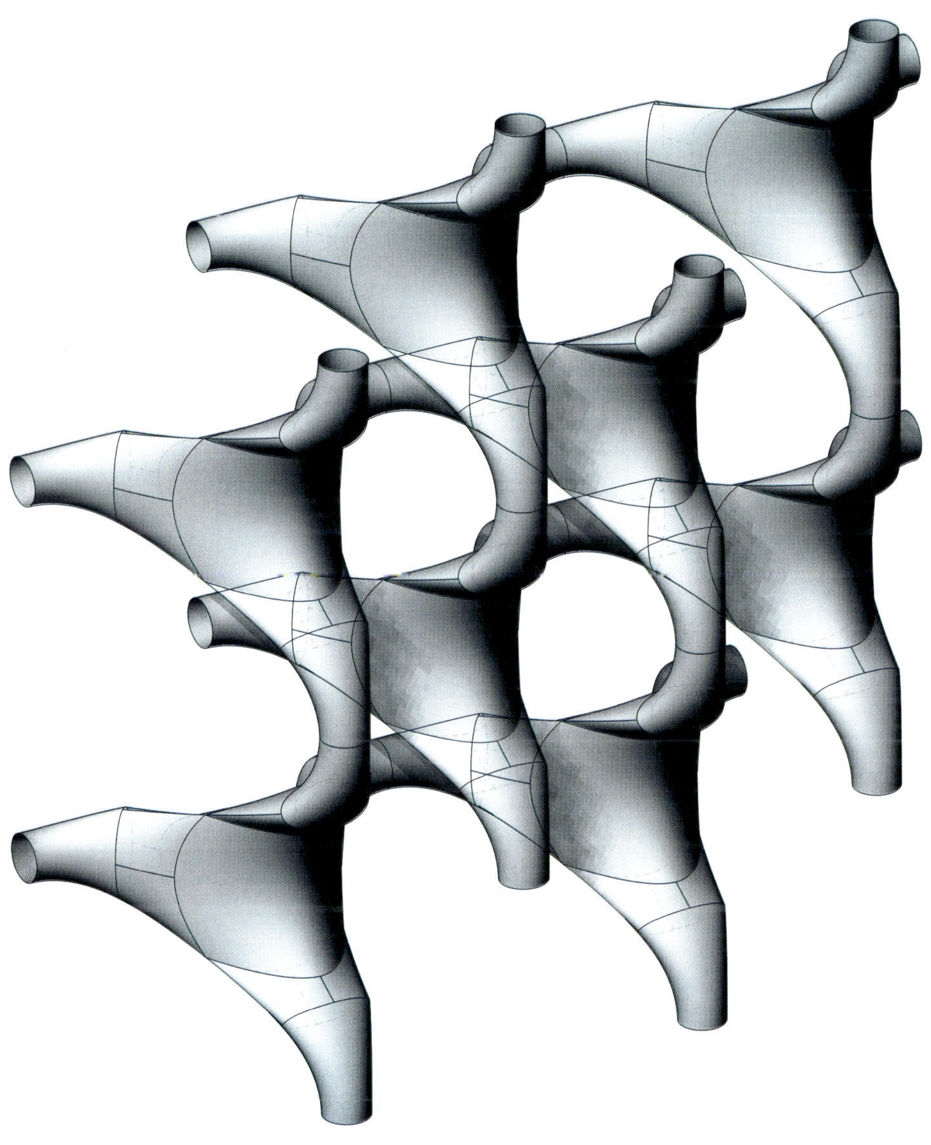

37_Associative model 5_3x3 matrix of modules_isometric

Assembly

This interpretive model of Design 3 can be described as the proliferation of a geometric tile module across two scales. This module involves the assemblage of three sets of surfaces.

The first group comprises of two complementary and facing saddle surfaces, which are reflected and share the same four corner points. The second set of surfaces, is composed of the half-handles that evolve from the spherical surface that characterizes the Design 1 interpretive associative model but produces a cylindrical surface that wraps this section of sphere. Finally, the third group is the construction of transitional surfaces between these two last groups. Once the tile is assembled, it is proliferated within a potentially infinite squared grid. This proliferation results in one matrix, which is the first arraying scale for this design.

The second scale is a second, offset and intertwining matrix that complements and interacts with the first matrix, but does not intersect it.

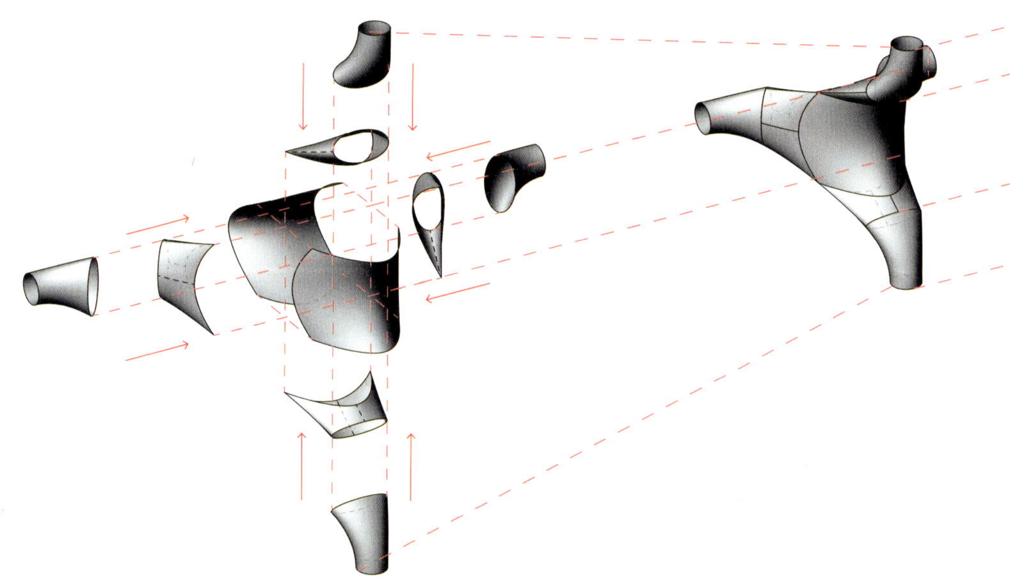

38_3x3 matrix of modules_isometric.
Construction and assembly

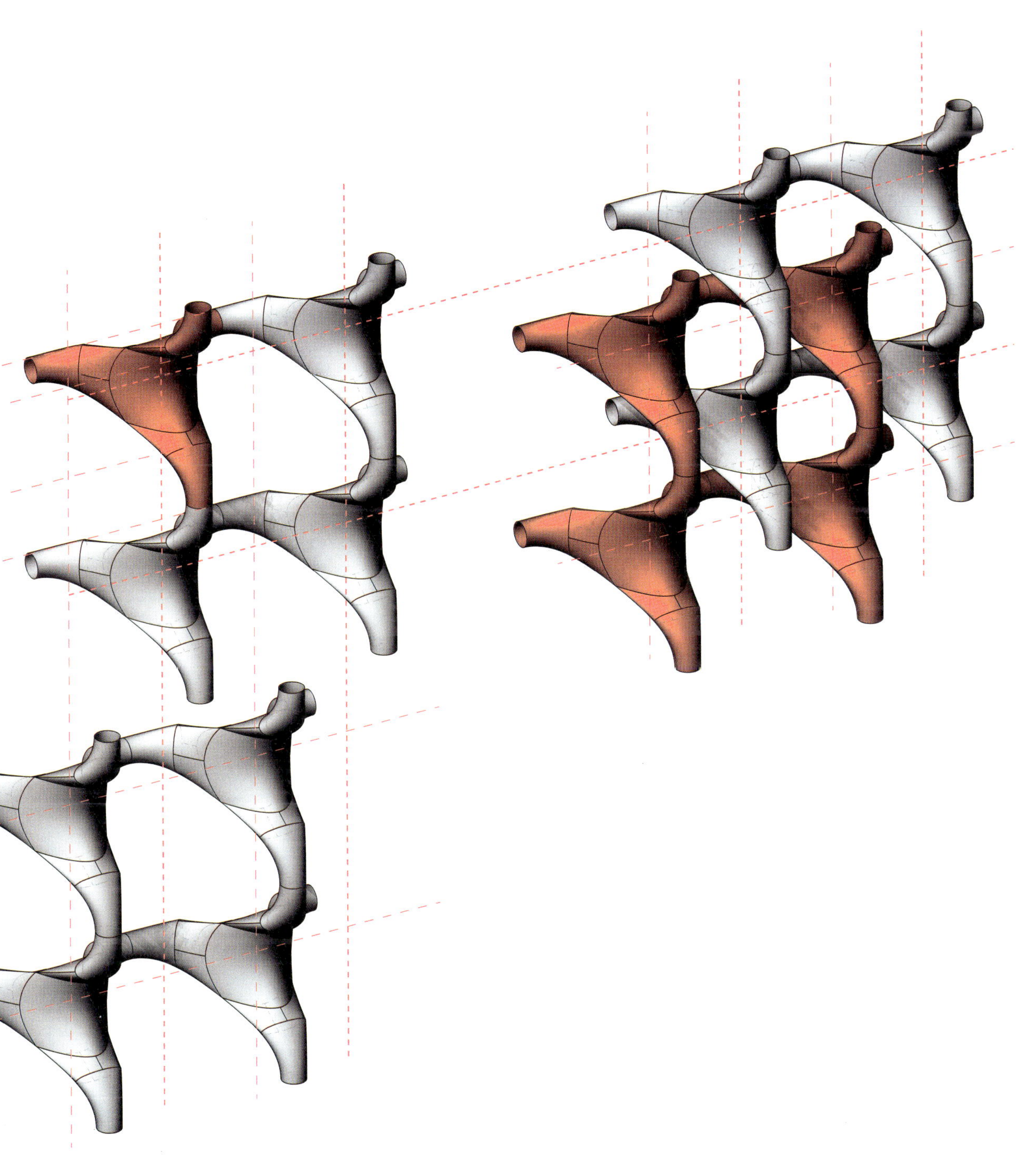

Associative model overview

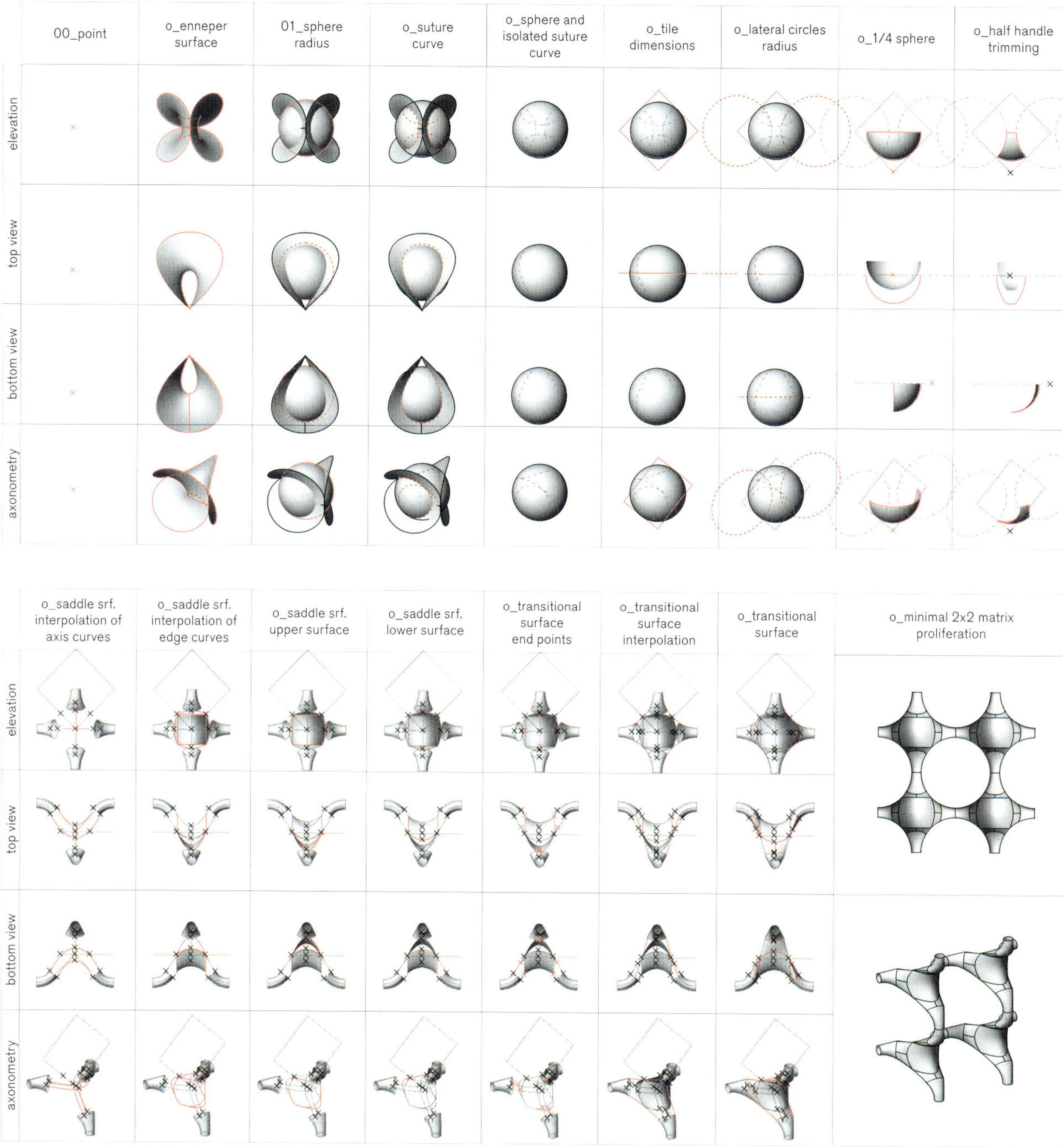

	00_point	o_enneper surface	01_sphere radius	o_suture curve	o_sphere and isolated suture curve	o_tile dimensions	o_lateral circles radius	o_1/4 sphere	o_half handle trimming
elevation									
top view									
bottom view									
axonometry									

	o_saddle srf. interpolation of axis curves	o_saddle srf. interpolation of edge curves	o_saddle srf. upper surface	o_saddle srf. lower surface	o_transitional surface end points	o_transitional surface interpolation	o_transitional surface	o_minimal 2x2 matrix proliferation
elevation								
top view								
bottom view								
axonometry								

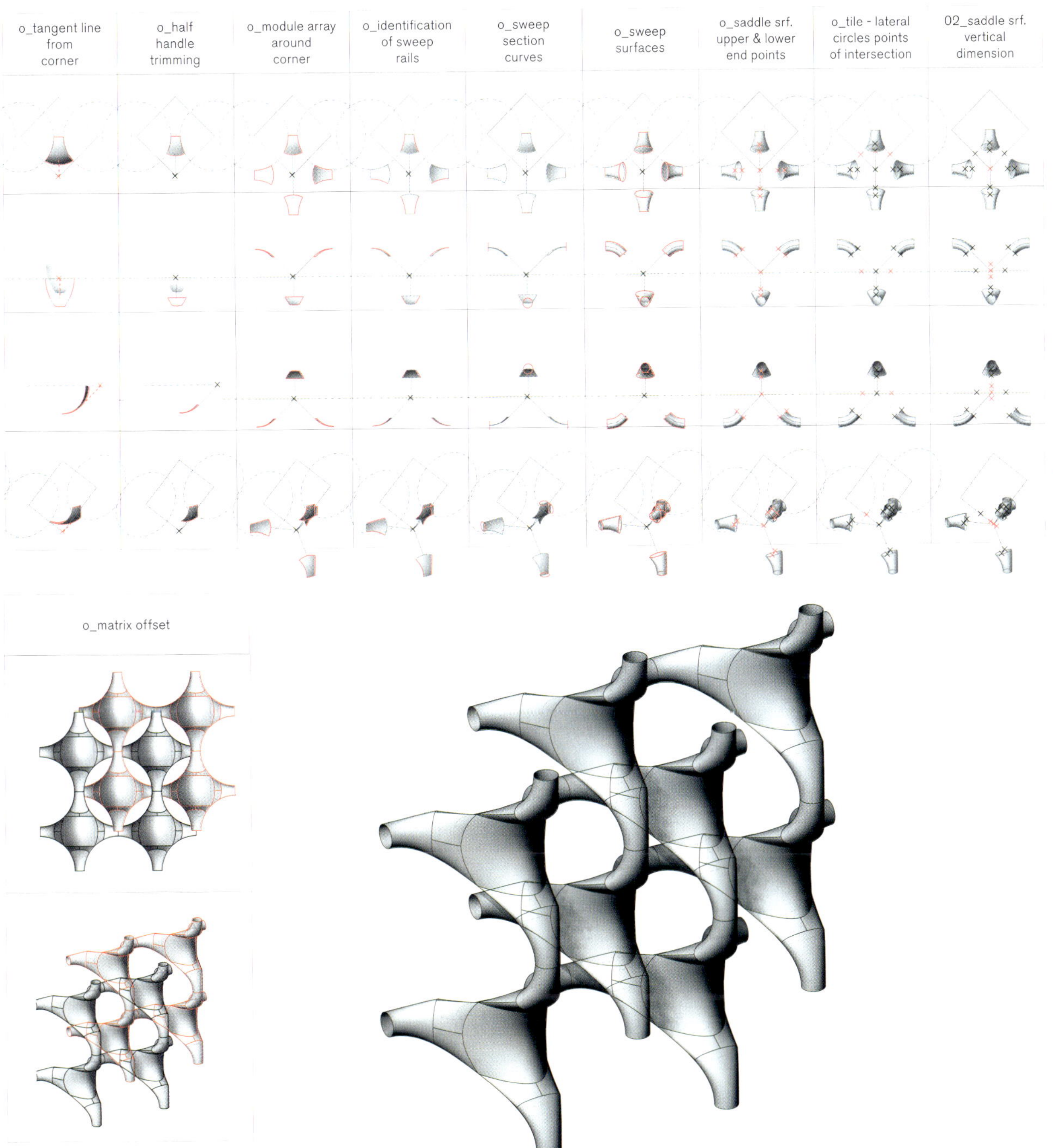

39_System construction_variables, operations and Final proliferation: 3x3 matrix_rendered isometric

In this model, one tile module is produced, which is later proliferated to produce a matrix and finally duplicated to produce an intertwining pattern between two offset matrices. Each tile consists of one rounded handle with an ellipsoidal section that inscribes a semi-spherical space; and a pair of complementary and facing saddle surfaces that transition between two adjacent sets of rounded handles. These surfaces solve a tension between the spherical origin of the suture curve and the squared matrix that the module is bounded by. This model is constructed as an assembly of three categories of surfaces. Firstly, the saddle surfaces in the center of each tile. Then, the rounded half-handles that are a result of the revolution of ellipses along a specific section of sphere. Finally, the transitional surfaces that mediate between these last two groups. The key to a smooth transition lies in a broader conception of the tile, where the center does not lie on the middle point of a handle, but rather in the center of the pair of saddle surfaces. Also, transitional surfaces solve the difference in nature between revolved and saddle surfaces.

The model consists of two variables and twenty-two operations. From a shared centroid, a sphere (variable 01) and an Enneper surface are constructed. The result of the intersection between the sphere and the enneper surface is a suture

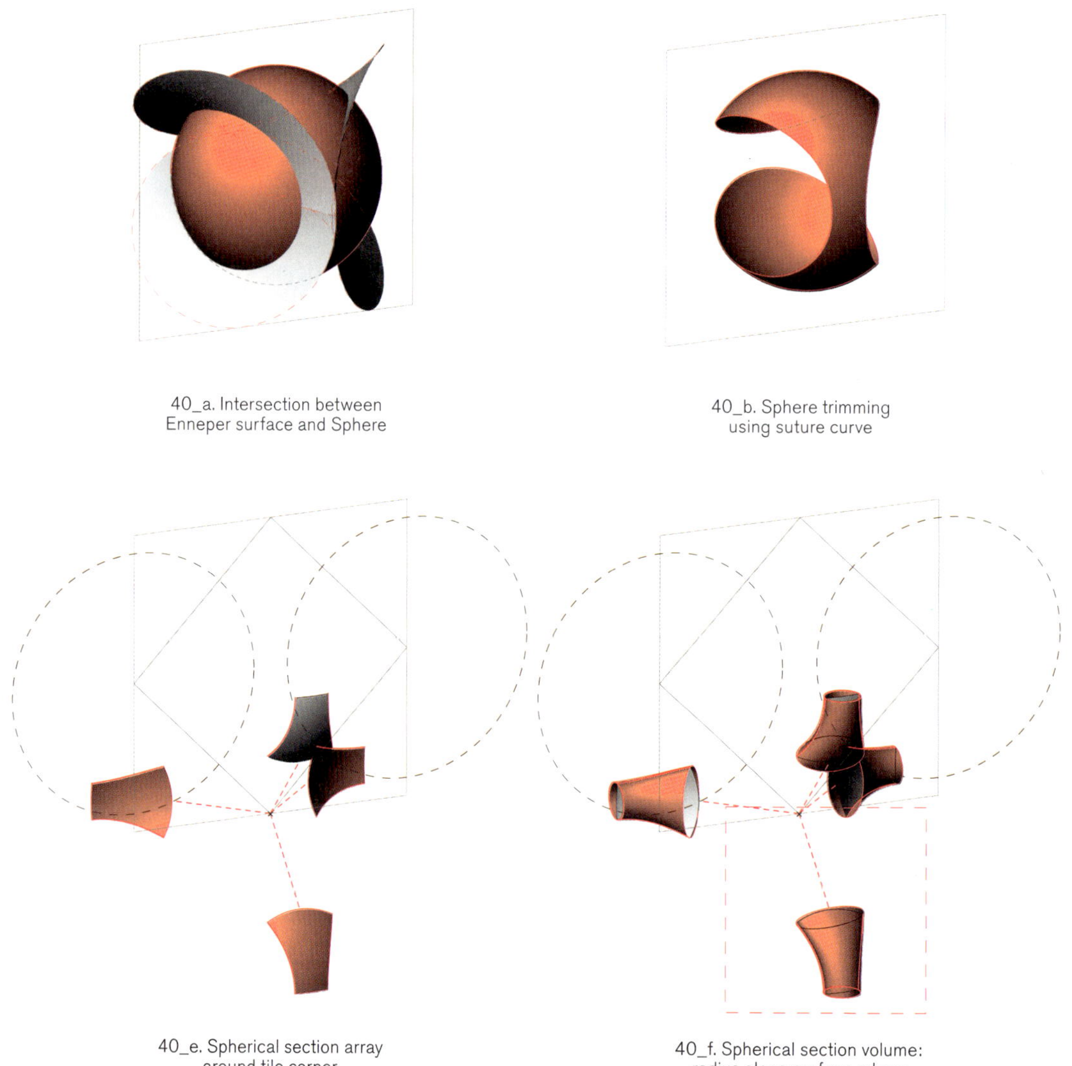

40_a. Intersection between Enneper surface and Sphere

40_b. Sphere trimming using suture curve

40_e. Spherical section array around tile corner

40_f. Spherical section volume: radius along surface edges

curve. The sphere's scale determines a specific bounding volume, which, when projected, becomes the bounding square for a tile module. This boundary is finally rotated 45º. In two opposing corners of the tile, a pair of circles of a specific radius are constructed. The center point is located on the tile corner and the radius is such that it intersects with the middle point of the suture curve in each half of the tile. These circles are useful guides for the construction of the handles. Once extruded, these will cut the sphere in a way that circles will be formed in the overall matrix, once a larger proliferation of tiles is assembled. The sphere is cut into twice until half of a semi dome remains. This spherical surface, once trimmed with the lateral circles, will result in a half-handle like surface.

A tangential line from the tile corner to the half-handle surface axis is constructed. Once again, a section of the sphere is trimmed, this time using an XY plane on the tangential point.

The remaining upper section of the half-handle surface is arrayed around the tile corner from which the tangent line was drawn.

Four modules, alternatively mirrored, form the primitive structure of the tile. For each surface two edges are essentially arcs since it has been previously cut using circles. This pair of curves are identified as the rails for the surface of revolution.

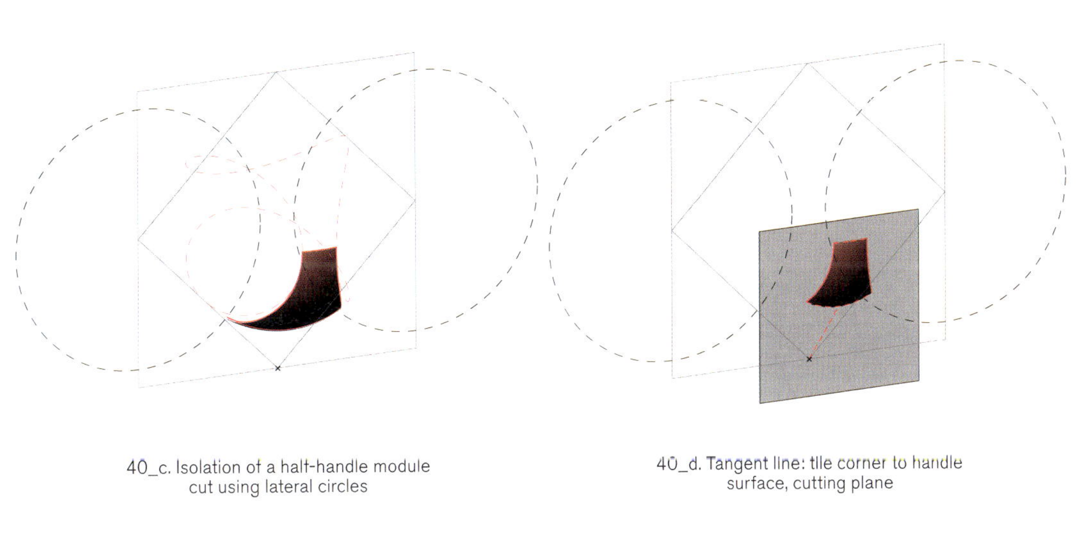

40_c. Isolation of a half-handle module cut using lateral circles

40_d. Tangent line: tile corner to handle surface, cutting plane

40_g. Spherical section volume, zoom

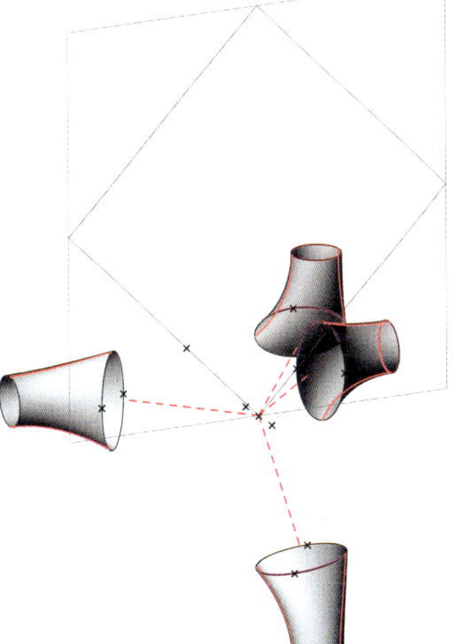

40_h. Identification of points for saddle surface edge curves.

The section for each revolution consists of a circle with diameter that is defined by the smallest projected width of the half-handle surface. At the middle of the handle, the section curve will be circular and transforms to an elliptical section at the end of the curve. For the transition to the saddle surface, the upper and lower end points of each ellipse are identified. These points are important for the definition of the saddle surface edges. The second and last variable of the procedure is the vertical dimension or distance between the centers of each saddle surfaces. The tile corner that has been the center of the array is duplicated in space to create the volume of the tile. Each saddle surface axis curve is constructed as a three-point interpolation. The two end points of this interpolation are the respective upper or lower points of the revolved surfaces. The middle point for the interpolations are the respective vertical dimensions. Following this logic, upper interpolated curves connect upper end points to upper vertical center points to upper end points on the other side and so forth.

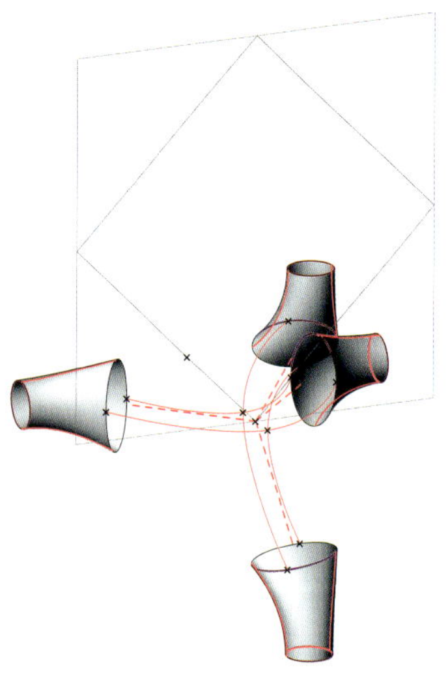

40_i. Saddle surface axis curves interpolation.

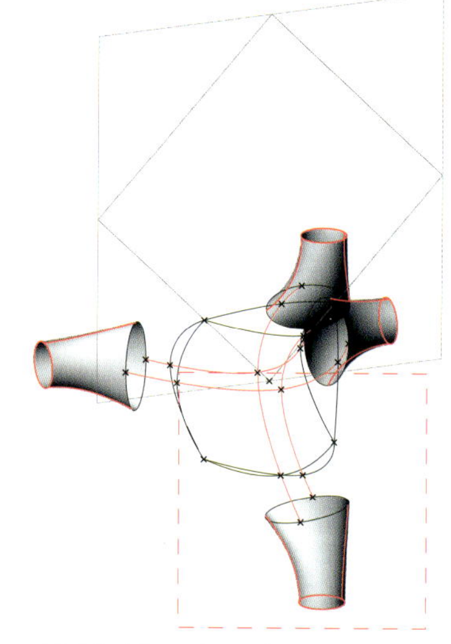

40_j. Saddle surface edge curves interpolation.

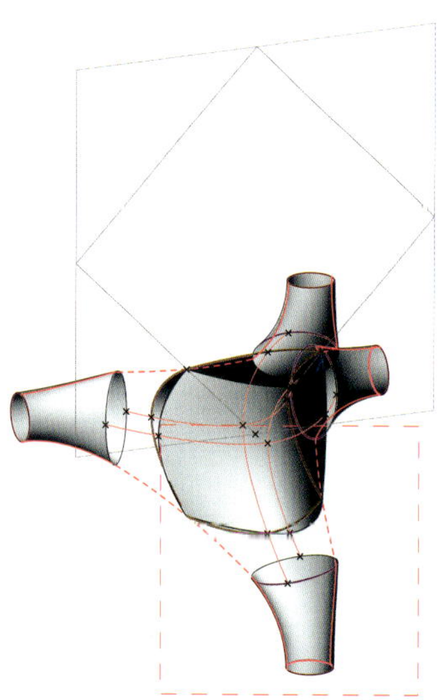

40_m. Transitional surfaces edge curves interpolation.

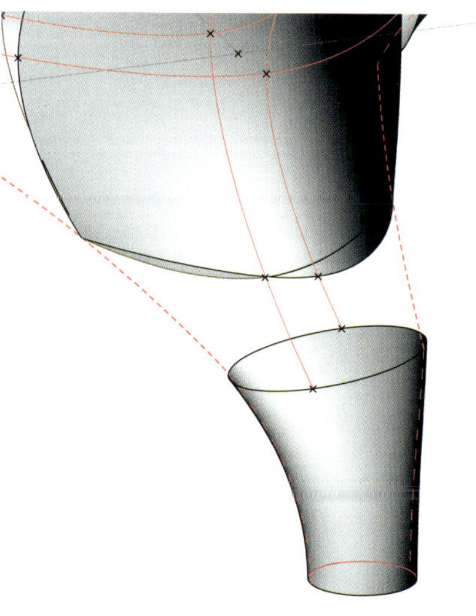

40_n. Transitional surfaces edge curves interpolation, zoom.

Each saddle surface is constructed using four edge curves and a pair of axis curves. The edge curves are also constructed as three-point interpolations. The end points are the intersections between the lateral circles and the tile. Then, the middle point is identified as the virtual intersection with the previously defined axis curves. The edge curves associated with the upper surface are used to construct the upper saddle surface and the edge curves correspondent to the lower surface are used to construct the lower saddle surface. The final part of the construction consists of defining the surface that mediates between the revolved and the saddle surfaces. This is called the transitional surface. Its edge curves are identified as the end section curve of the revolved surface, which is an ellipse; the saddle surface edge curves and finally an interpolated curve between the ellipse extreme points and the saddle surface corners. Using these edge curves, the transitional surface is constructed.

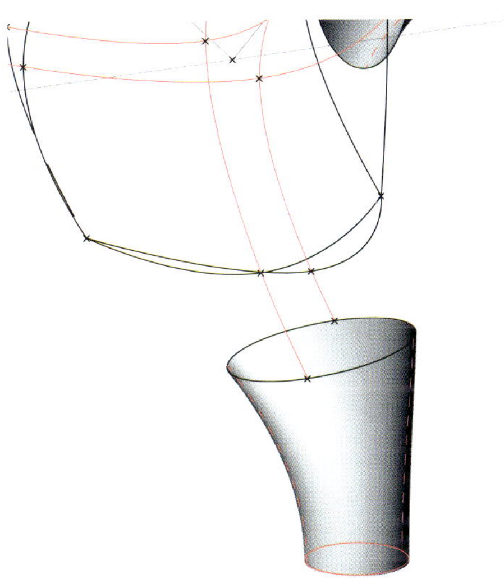

40_k. Saddle surface edge curves interpolation, zoom.

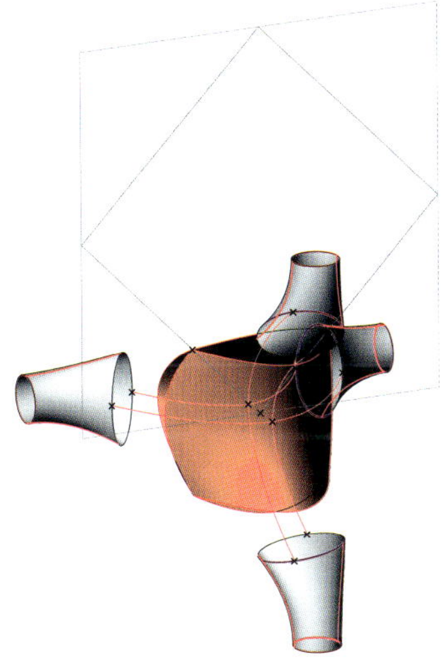

40_l. Saddle surfaces.

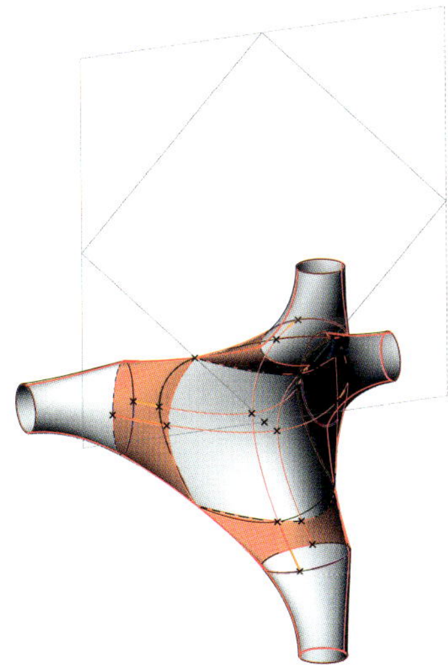

40_o. Transitional surfaces.

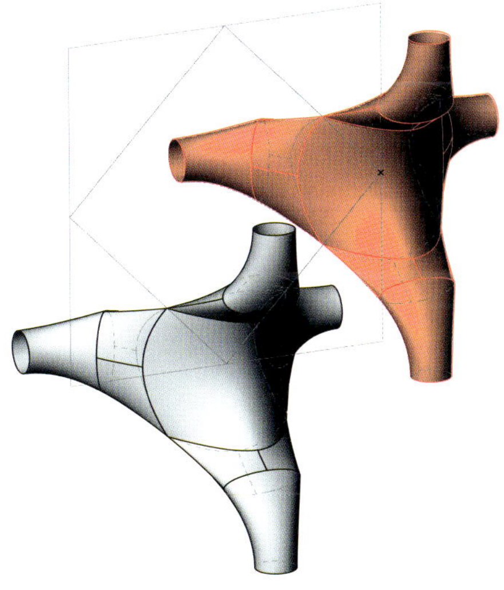

40_p. Tile proliferation into two matrices.

Correlations

Both Design 1 and Design 3 are works in Hauer's continua series that are constructed using saddle surfaces. This is the simplest type of minimal surface and it is used to produce a seamless transition between spherical handles. Saddle surfaces are generated through two sets of facing curves. Its formula reveals how dimensions (a, b) and curvature (x, y) are controlled, where:
z=(x2/a2)-(y2/b2)
Using the interpretive drawings and pictures, the geometric analogy becomes evident when both designs are superimposed. The different proliferation logics for each design are clear whereby a tile module in the Design 3 interpretive model is defined by a center point and in the Design 1 interpretive model it is defined by a squared tile. Their similar curvature can be attributed to the fact that both models work with spherical surfaces to extract surface sectors. These are also similar in the manner that these are given volume and also by means of their sharing of saddle surfaces.

1. Based on a discussion at Erwin Hauer and Enrique Rosado's studios in 2012.

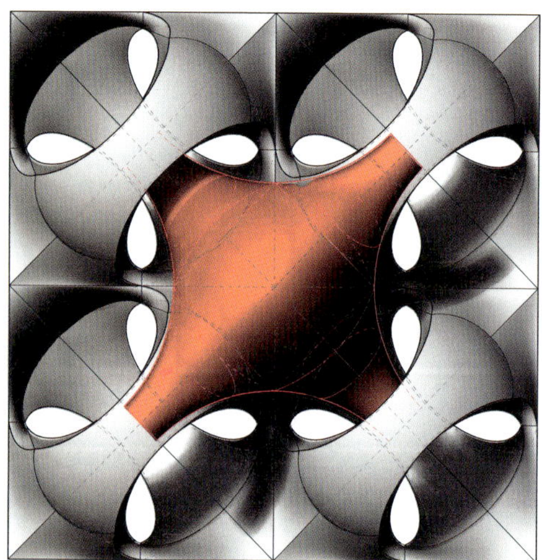

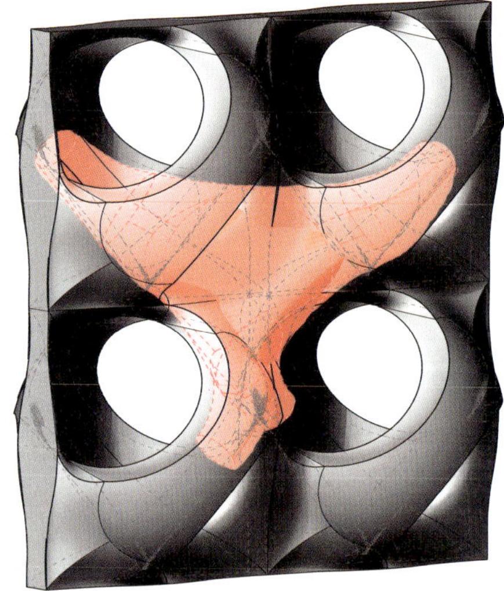

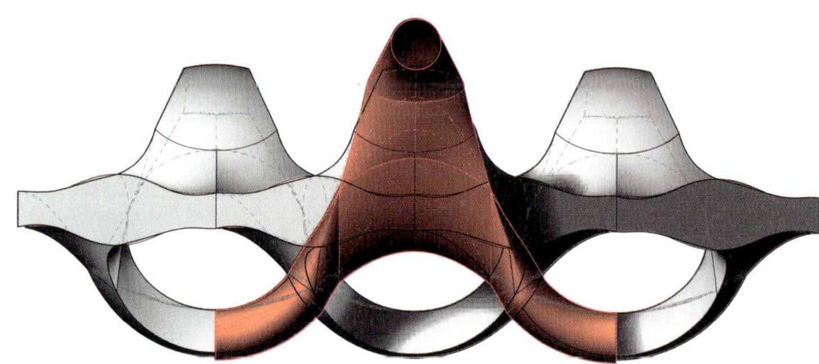

41_Interpreted drawings of Design 1 and 3_overlapping: elevation, plan and isometric views

42_Design 1 on Design 3_Erwin Hauer at his Connecticut studio

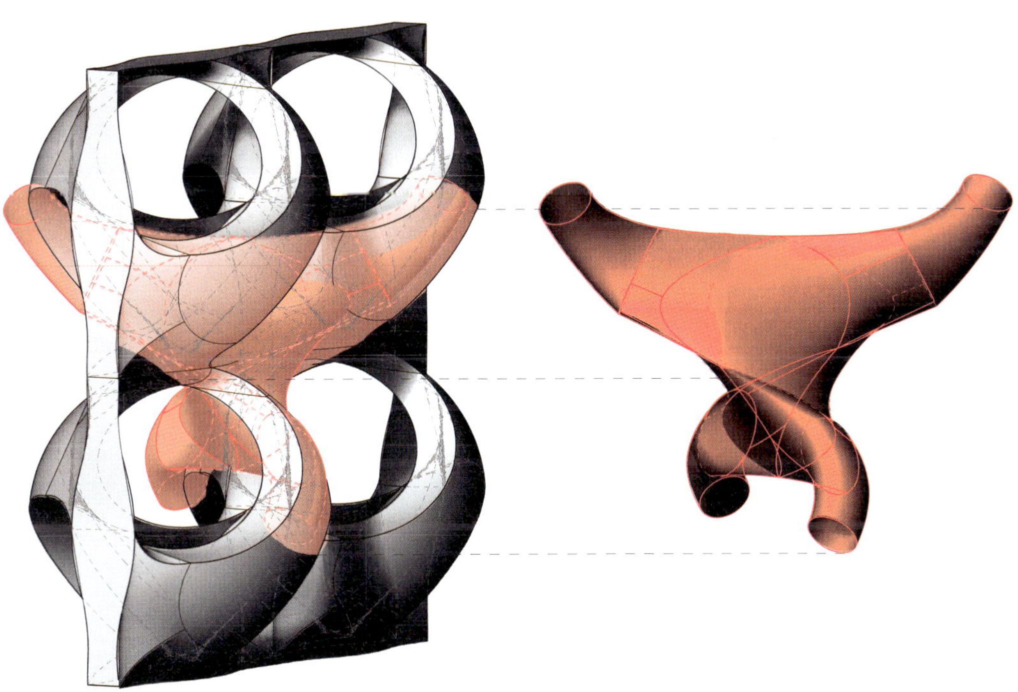

43_Interpreted drawings of Design 1 and 3_overlapping: perspective deconstruction

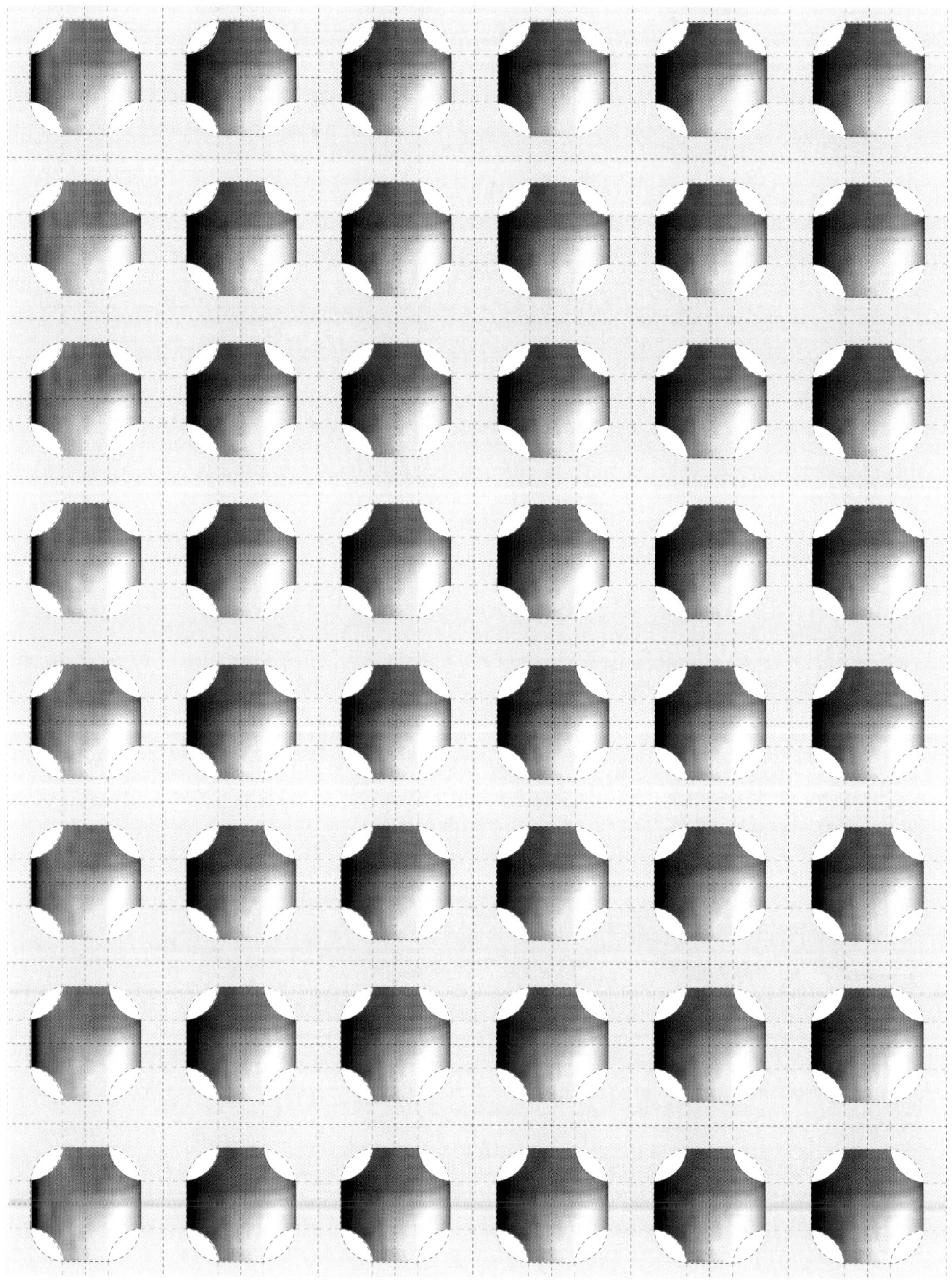

44_Associative model 6_matrix elevation

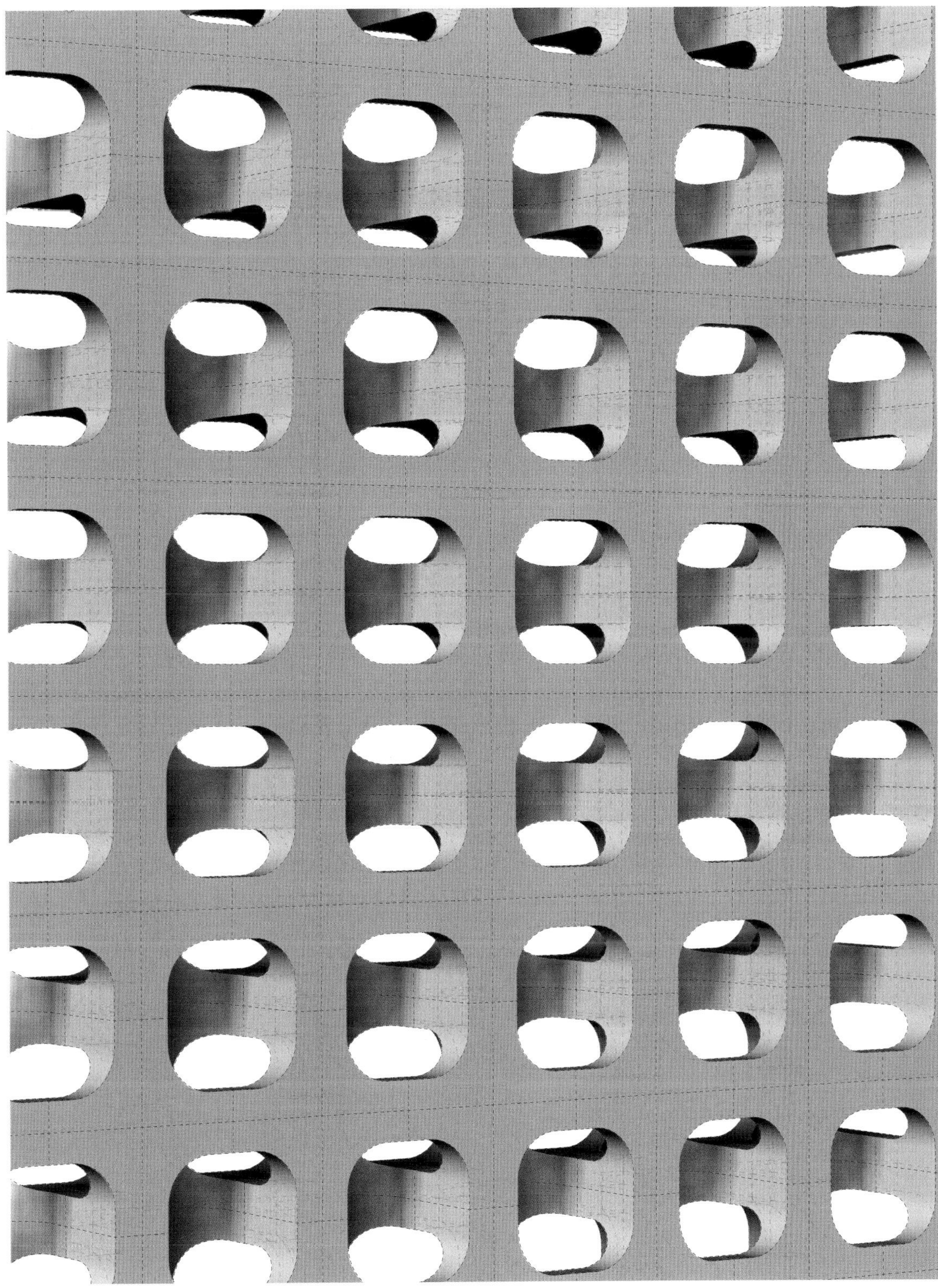

45_Associative model 6_matrix perspective

Associative model 6

As described by Hauer in Design 4, in this design two sculptural concerns converge. Firstly, an exploration of the Great Circle pattern as a structuring device, which first appeared to Hauer after assembling several tiles of Design 1. The design is also informed by a search for greater structural efficiency, which is likely to have been influenced by the challenges posed by the materialization process for Design 3.[1] This Design, according to the artist, generated a fundamental matrix that later on became the base for several other designs.

"The distance between outer circular grids and their relative position are maintained by structural connectors. These skins carry the tension and compression loads and a lightweight core material to act on a shear web". (Hauer E., 2004, Continua: Architectural Screens and Walls, The Princeton Architectural Press, New York, p. 32)

The double layered nature of the design produces light reflections and perceptual play. However, due to the simpler singly curved surfaces of the design, the diffuse light behavior on these forms

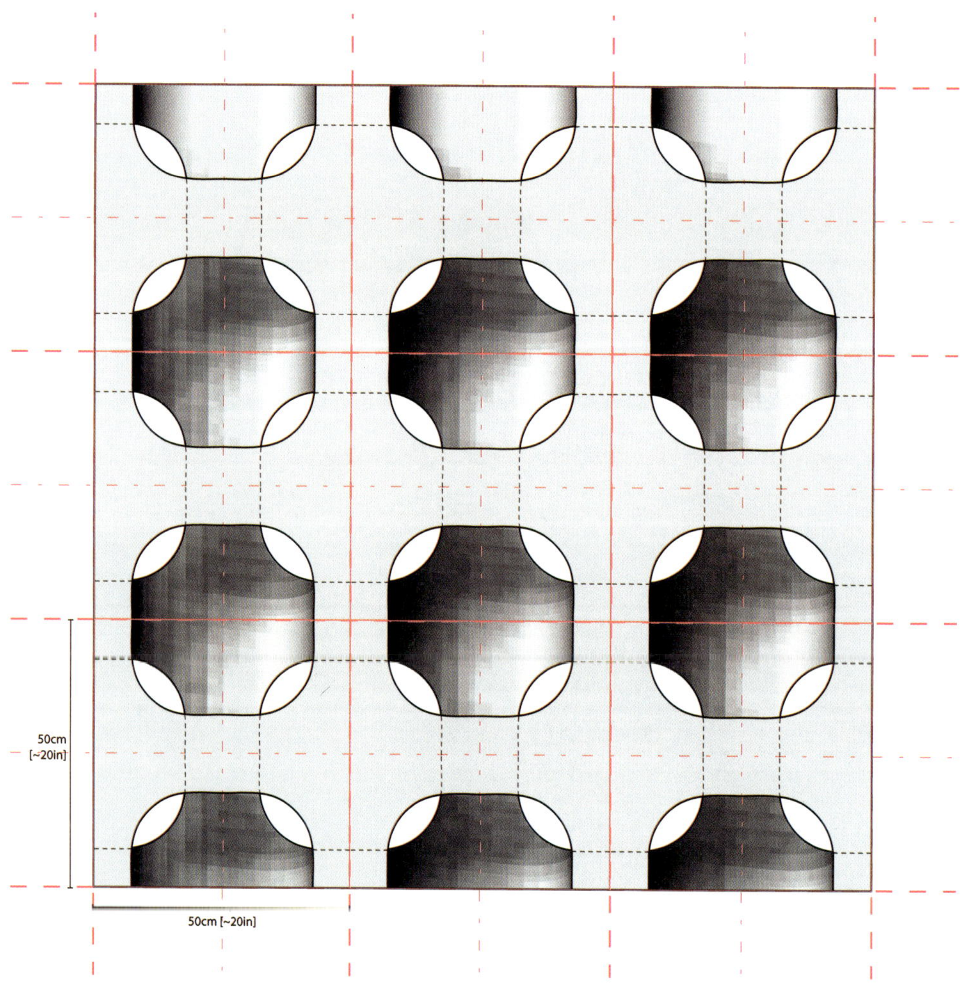

46_Associative model 6_3x3 matrix of modules

could be regarded as being less pronounced.[2] The molds for this design were easy to construct and *"consisted of four cast and fitted bronze components contained within a steel box."*
(Hauer E., 2004, Continua: Architectural Screens and Walls, The Princeton Architectural Press, New York, p. 95).

1. Hauer E., 2007, Continua, Architectural Screens and Walls, Princeton Architectural Press, New York.
2. (Ibid)

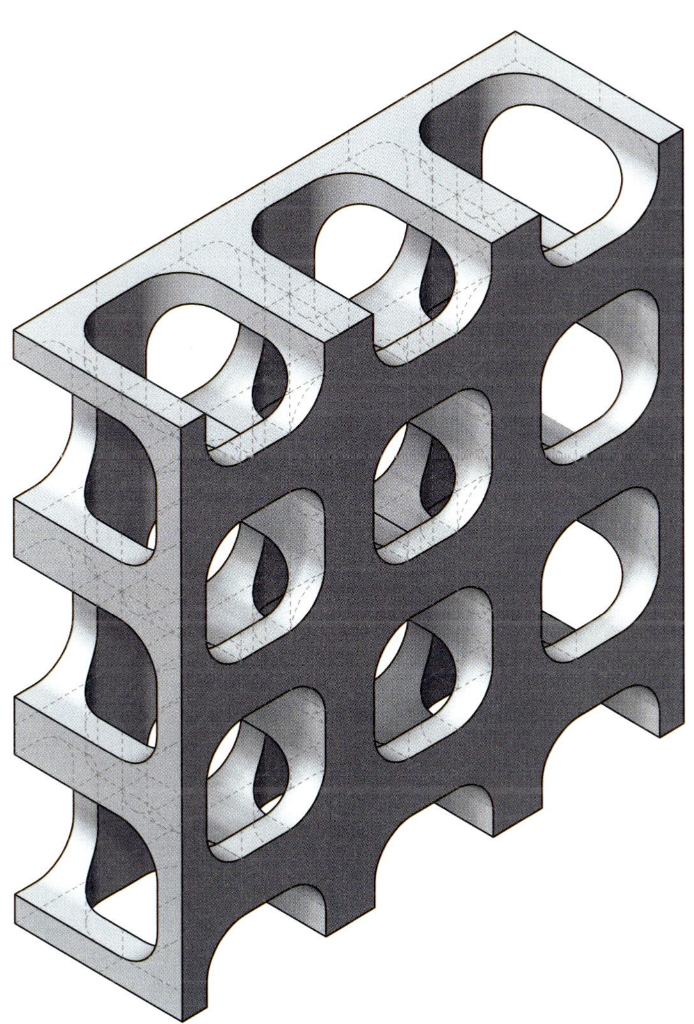

47_Associative model 6_3x3 matrix of modules_isometric

Assembly

The interpretive Design 4 model is conceived and generated through the proliferation of a geometric module at three scales:

a) within a square tile, by means of polar arraying around the center

b) within a virtual cube, by means of a horizontal reflection across the cube's center of mass.

c) within a potentially infinite square grid.

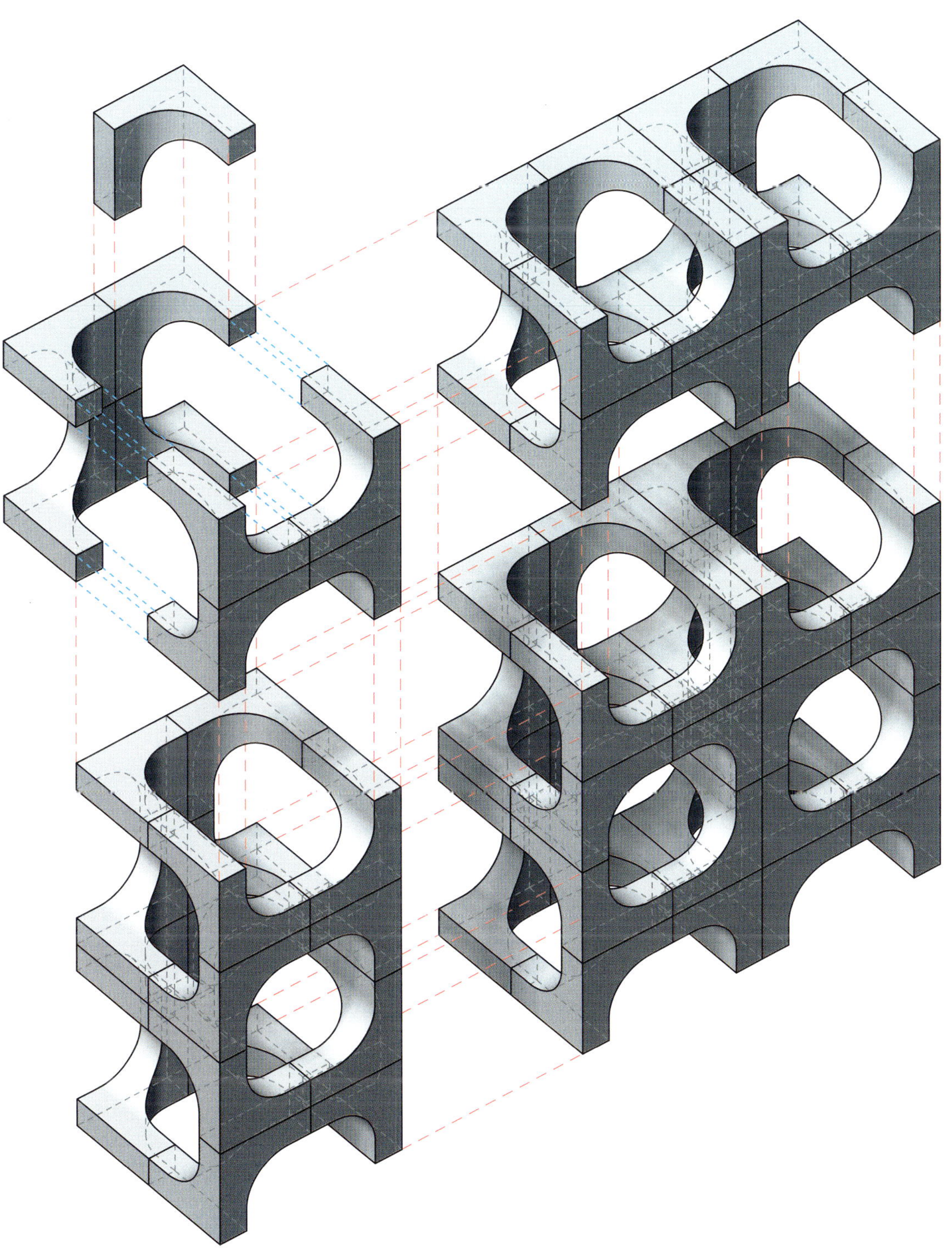

Associative model 6_3x3 matrix of modules_isometric. Construction and assembly.

Associative model overview

The construction of this associative model is organized into a series of geometric operations that constitute a linear process with variables. A single geometric module is defined in the process, which is then proliferated to produce a tile and finally, a matrix. This is the first model from this series that explores material continuity from the idea of volume or Boolean subtraction rather than from the arrangement and modification of half-handle-like surfaces. This model is not based on the construction of transitional surfaces but is defined through the construction and multiplication of modules. The final tile is produced using eight similar modules.
The square matrix is still an element in this model but unlike other models, where a square tile is determined as a polygonal boundary and arranging matrix for the final tile, it produces a square matrix using a cube as its basic volumetric unit. The dimensions of this cube determine the proportion of the final tile, which is then copied, mirrored and rotated to create two faces of the unit. This bounding cubic volume defines the sharp orthogonal corners and planar surfaces that are later used for a successful proliferation of the unit into larger fields.
The associative model for Design 4 is produced through the proliferation of a module at two scales: within a square

	00_start point	01_cube dimensions	02_circle radius	o_circle extrusion	o_intersection_ cylinder + cube	o_cylinder + cube_ end points	o_cylinder + cube_ symmetry lines	o_cylinder + cube_ mirrored end points	o_cylinder + cube_ extended tangent lines	o_cylin cub interse tangen
elevation										
top view										
bottom view										
axonometry										

tile, by means of polar arraying around the center; within a virtual cube, by means of a horizontal reflection across the cube's centroid. Once the tile is constructed, this is proliferated to produce a square matrix.
In this model construction there is an exploration of the intersection between two types of volumes, a cube and a pair of cylinder-like sections, to produce a seamless module.

This pair of surfaces are constructed from circles and tangential lines. These straight lines are important to mediate between a continuously curved surface like cylinders and the sharp edges of the cube. This ensures that the resultant module's faces are similar and a successful proliferation is possible.
The model consists of two variables and fifteen operations. From a centroid, a cube's dimension is determined (variable 01).

Two of the eight corners of the cube are identified. These two points belong to the same edge but they are also the same corner point for two adjacent faces. From each one of these points, a circle of a variable radius (variable 02) is constructed. These circles are coplanar in relationship to their respective faces and both planes are perpendicular.

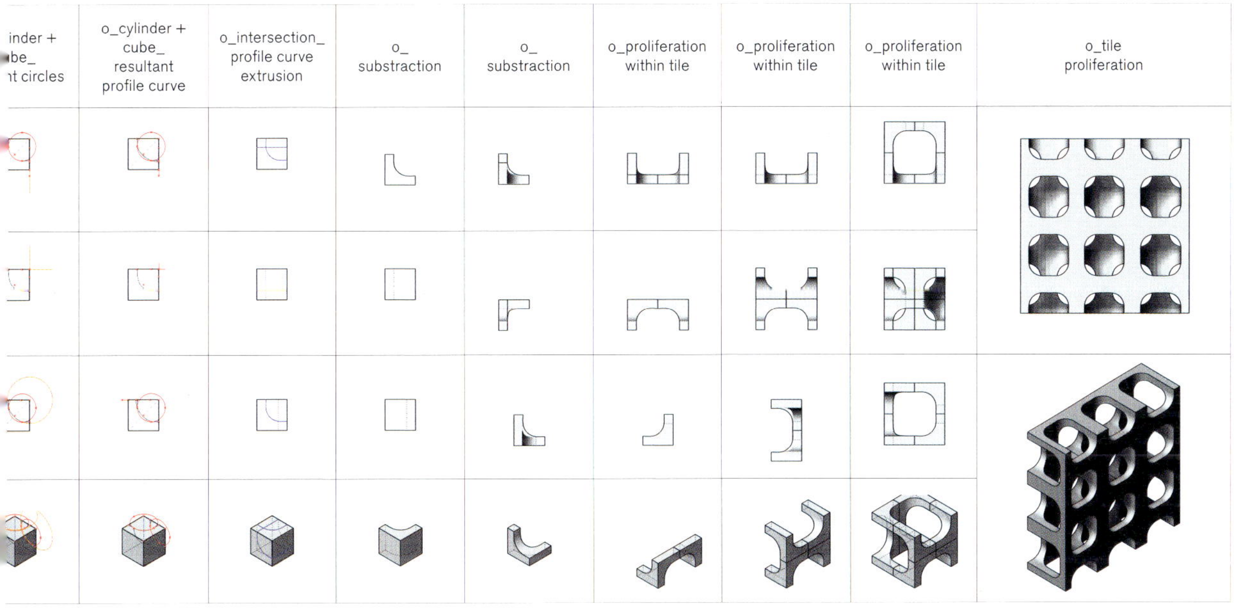

inder + be_ nt circles

o_cylinder + cube_ resultant profile curve

o_intersection_ profile curve extrusion

o_ substraction

o_ substraction

o_proliferation within tile

o_proliferation within tile

o_proliferation within tile

o_tile proliferation

49_System construction_variables and operations

This series of operations work with intersections and tangent lines to produce the necessary volumetric subtractions from the cube that constitute the final module. Both circles are extruded to a length that equals the cube´s edge. The intersection between both cylinders and the cube results in a sinuous curve.
The end points of this sinuous curve are identified. These points lie within the circles' curves.
A straight line coplanar to each one of these circles is constructed. These lines join the center of each circle with the opposite corner of the coplanar face.
Each end point of these lines are mirrored along a symmetry line to produce a pair of points for each circle. From each pair of points, lines are constructed towards its orthogonal projection at the closest edge of the cube, producing a pair of lines for each circle. The mirrored end points are once again mirrored using the original end point as a mirror plane. These planes are perpendicular to the face that each circle is coplanar to. The result of the two mirror operations are

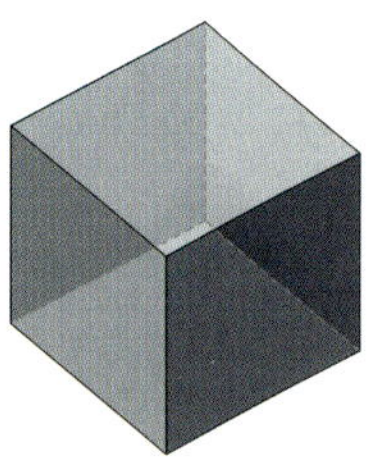

50_a. Cube.

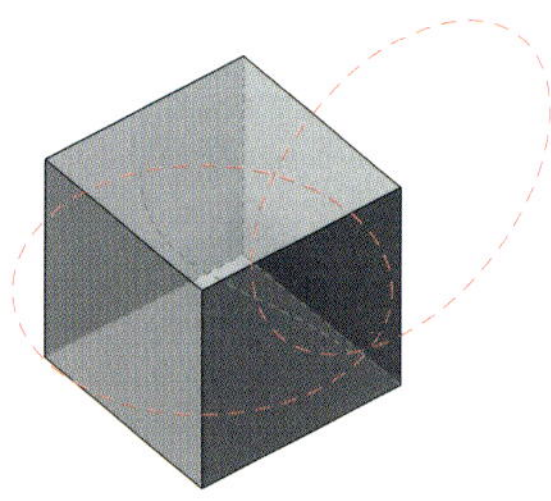

50_b. Radii from cube corners. Intersection: virtual cylinders.

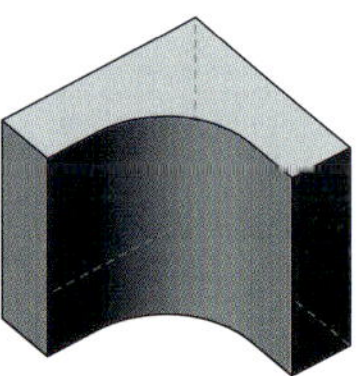

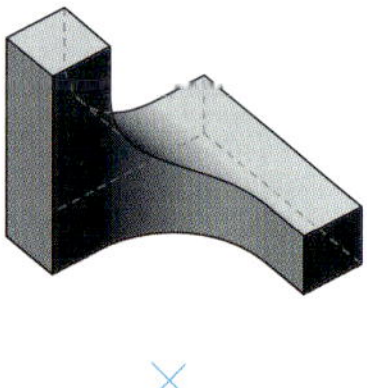

50_e. Subtraction of first extrusion from cube.

50_f. Second subtraction from cube. Final 1/8 module.

two sets of three points, one set per circle. These three points are used as inputs to define a new circle. By intersecting each new circle with the two previously created tangent lines and joining the pair of three resultant curves, two profile curves defined by a quarter of a circumference and two straight tangent lines to this arc are produced.

Both profile curves are extruded perpendicular to the plane each respective circle is coplanar to. The cube is intersected with one of the extruded surfaces. The intersected cube is once again intersected with the remaining extruded surface. The resultant form corresponds to an eighth of the complete tile. The module is mirrored in the two planes (YZ, XZ), then again in a XY plane and rotated to produce the complete tile. This volumetric unit can be proliferated in a planar quadrilateral matrix.

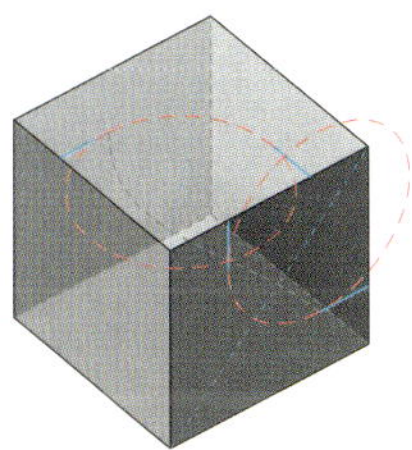

50_c. Construction of new radii and tangents.

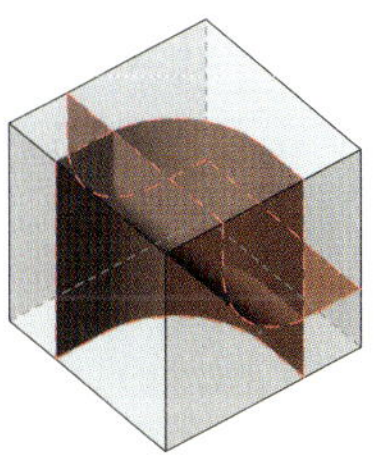

50_d. Extrusion of new radii.

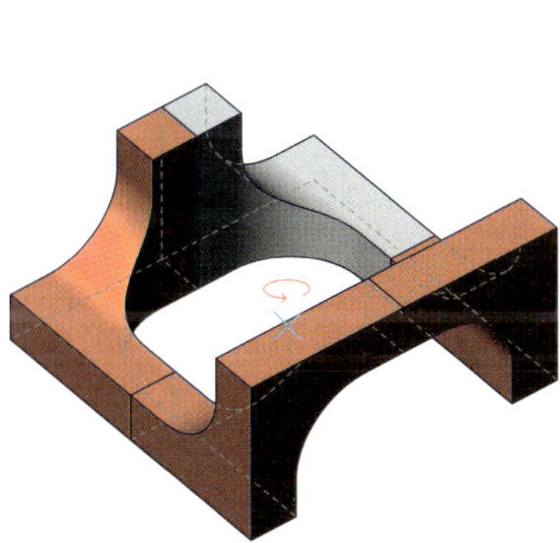

50_g. Rotation and reflection of 1/8 module.

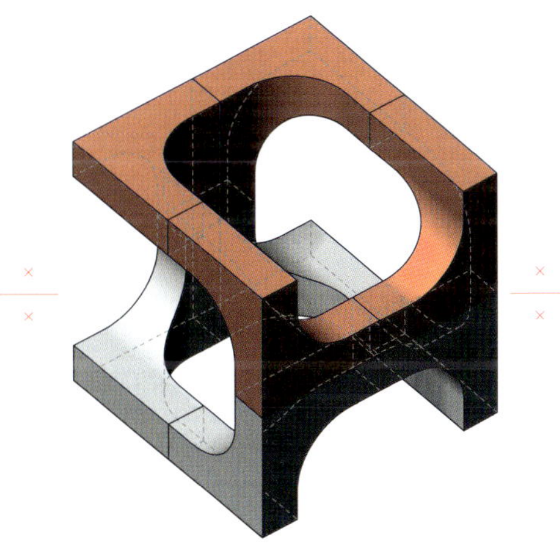

50_h. Horizontal reflection of 1/2 module.

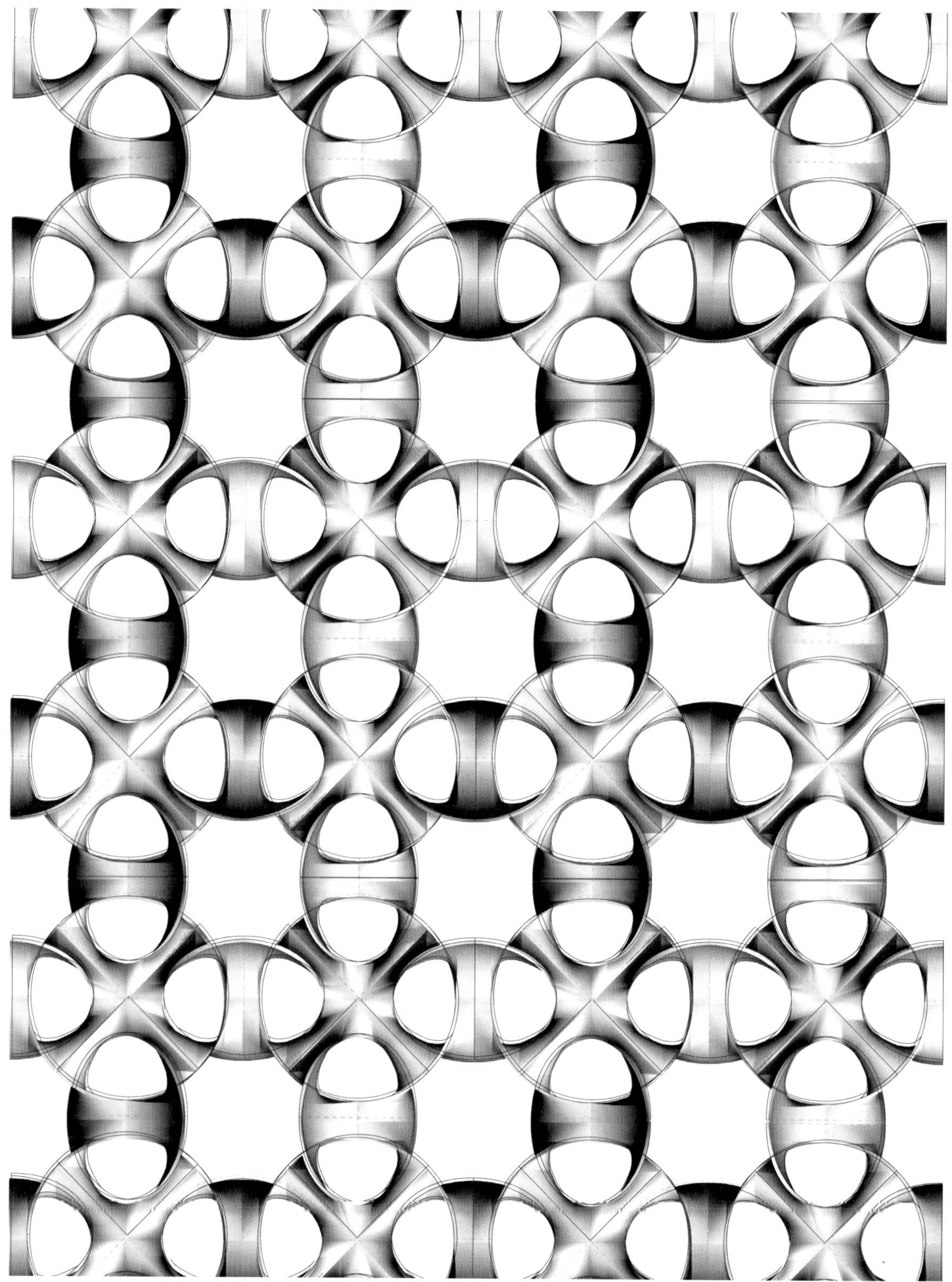

51_Associative model 7_matrix elevation

52_Associative model 7_matrix perspective

Associative model 7

Intercircles was created in 1957. It is defined by two overlapping grids of circles.
One of these grids is aligned with the screen plane, while the other grid is composed of oblique circles that are tilted at different planes.[1] The development of Intercircles involved a serendipitous redefinition of the Great Circle principle in Hauer's work which he called Finite Continua in the Plane. In lieu of a potentially infinite expansion characteristic of the other designs, Intercircles was conceived as a bounded and limited piece of 4 x 5 modules.[2]

1. Hauer E., 2007, Continua, Architectural Screens and Walls, Princeton Architectural Press, New York.
2. (Ibid)

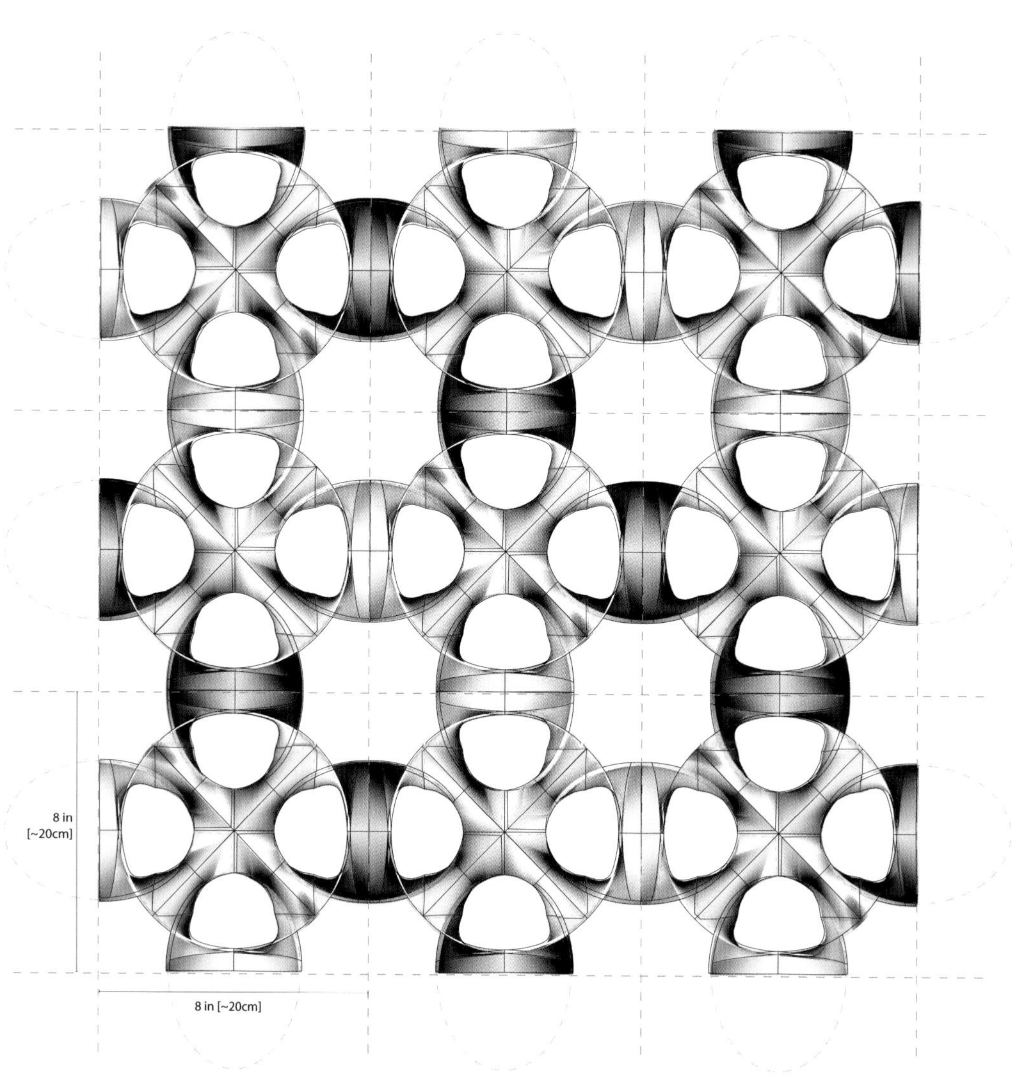

53_Associative model 7_3x3 matrix of modules

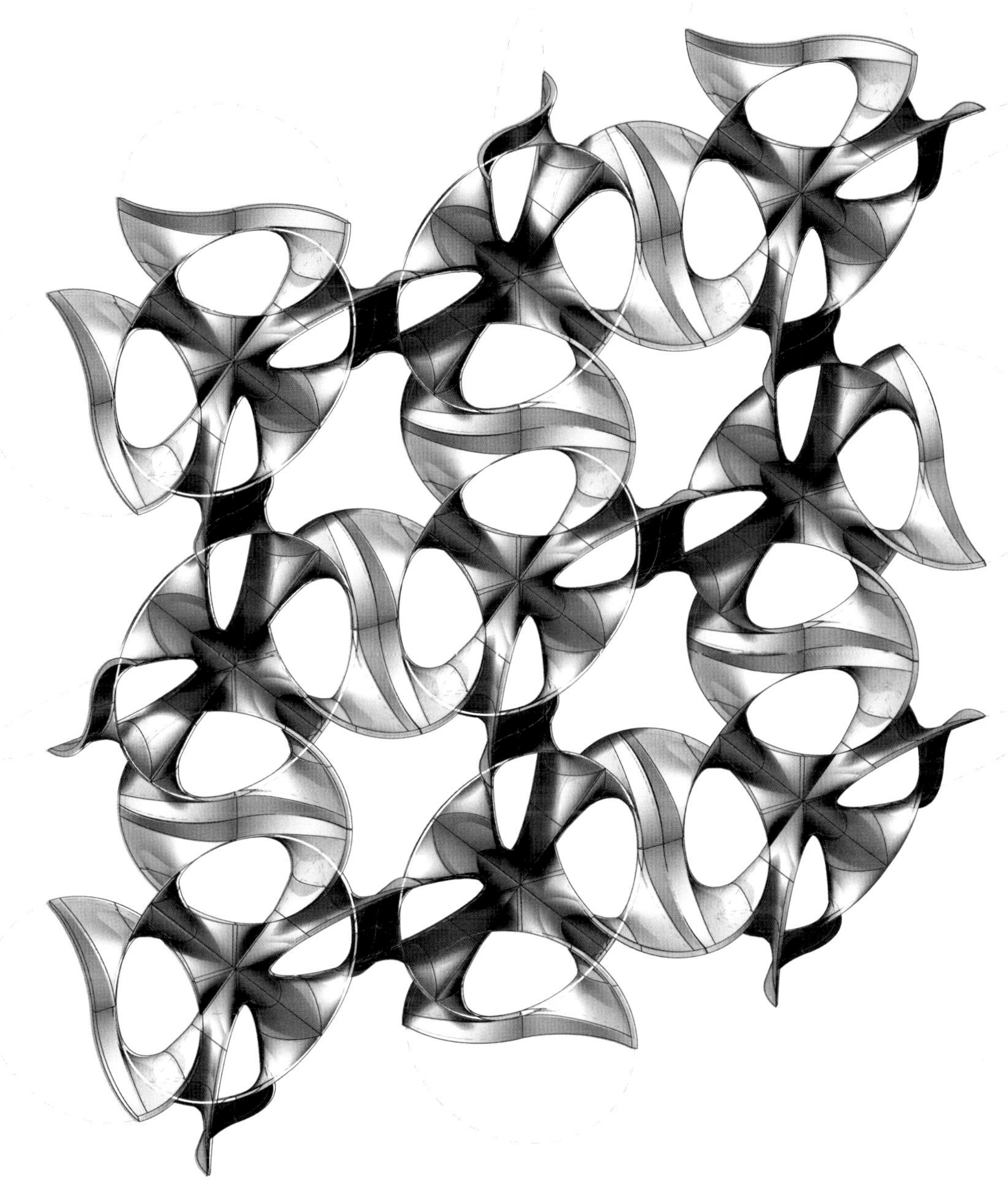

54_Associative model 7_3x3 matrix of modules_isometric

Assembly

The interpretive associative model of Intercircles is generated through the proliferation of a module at three scales:

a) within a quarter of a squared tile (or a 90 degree arc), my means of rotations

b) within the complete squared tile, by means of polar arraying

c) within a potentially infinite squared matrix, my means of reflections of modules along the edges.

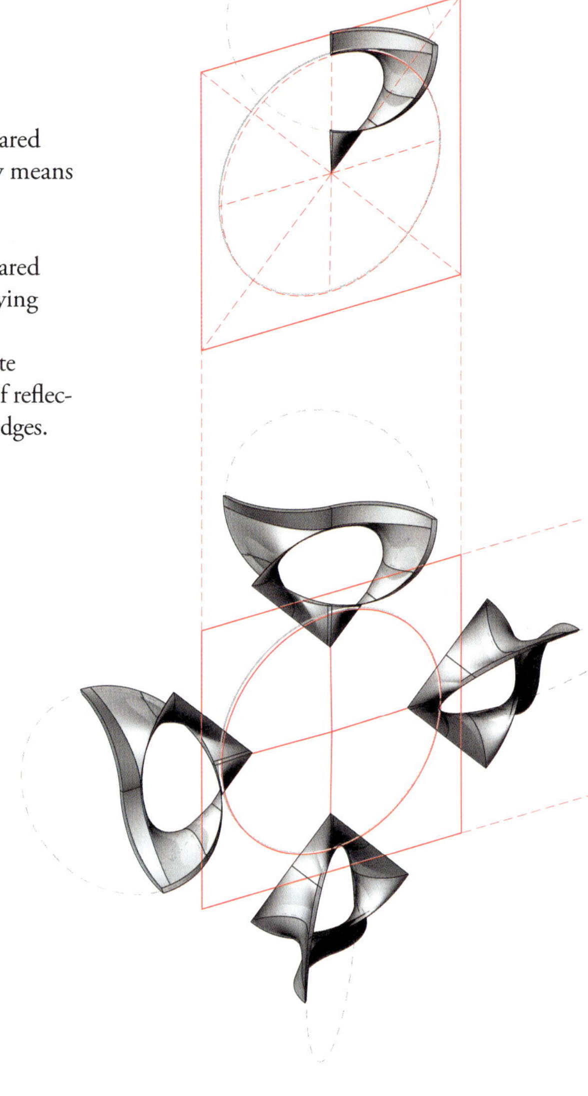

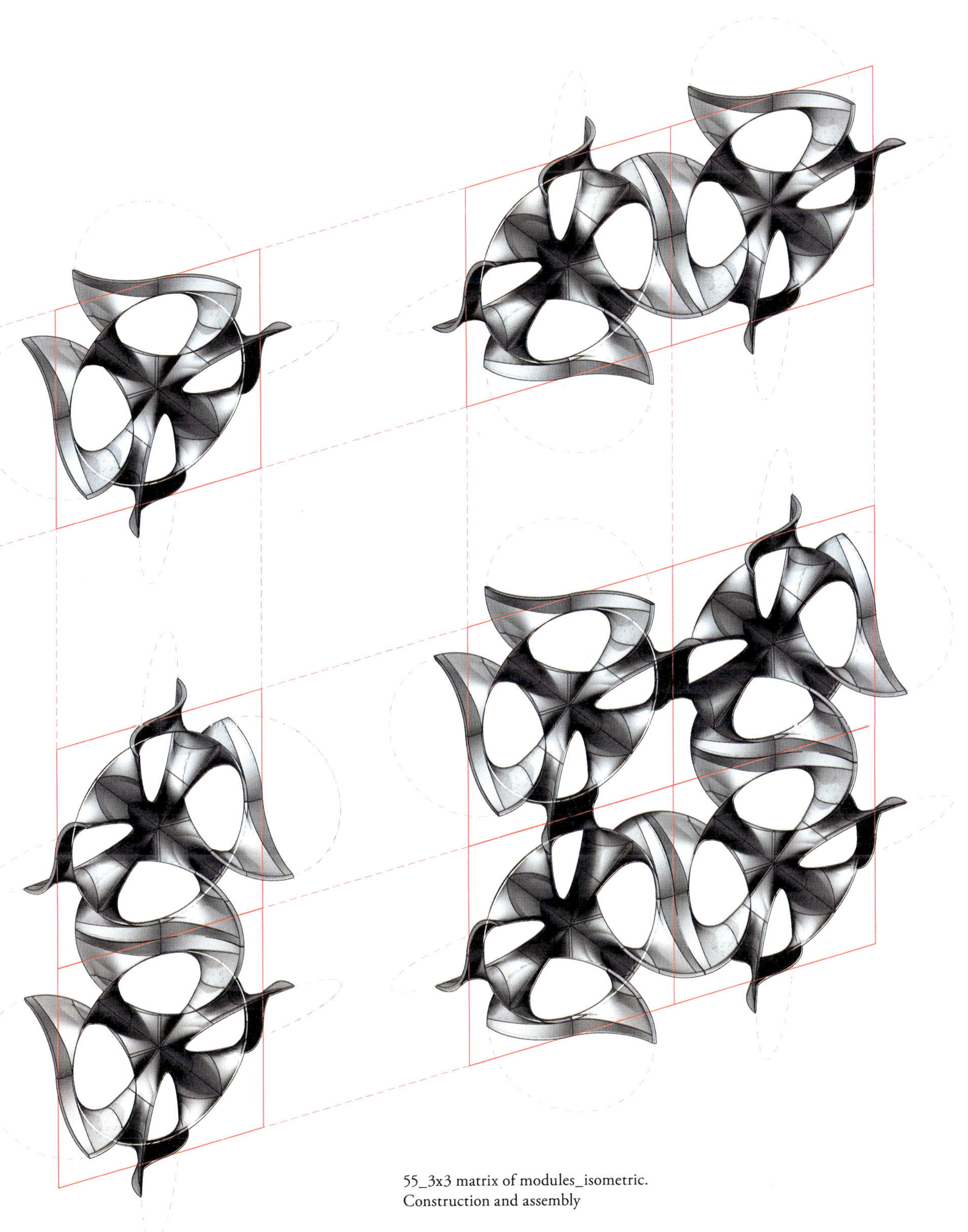

55_3x3 matrix of modules_isometric.
Construction and assembly

Associative model overview

The construction of this interpretative associative model is organized into a series of geometric operations that constitute a linear process with variables. A module is produced from this process and is later proliferated to produce a tile and finally, a matrix. Each tile is composed of eight similar modules.
This model also works with transitional surfaces to produce seamlessly continuous modules but it is unique in the series, being the only design that explores the construction of transitional surfaces between a pair of non-planar circles.
The simplicity of the model is related to the reduced amount of variables. The primary geometric structure of the model can be largely limited to the independent radii of both sets of circles, their rotation angle and the construction of transitional surfaces between them. The independence of these circles are what affords the flexibility of the model.

Each tile is defined by a central circle and four non-planar circles around it. Each pair of circles is mediated by two transitional surfaces. This means, each complete tile is produced with eight transitional surfaces, in four groups of two. As the lateral circles are arranged around the central circle in a square, the overall matrix is also based on a square grid.
The associative model is produced through the proliferation of a module at three scales: within a quarter of a squared tile (or

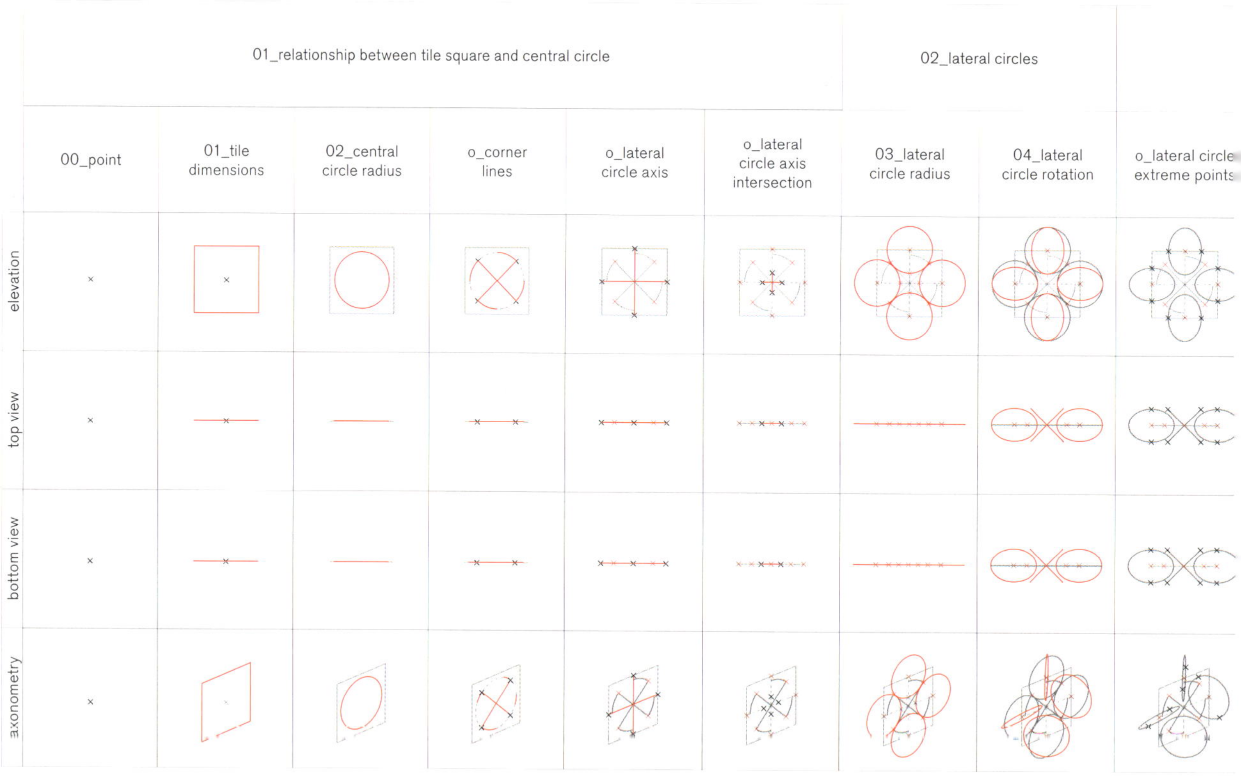

	01_relationship between tile square and central circle						02_lateral circles		
	00_point	01_tile dimensions	02_central circle radius	o_corner lines	o_lateral circle axis	o_lateral circle axis intersection	03_lateral circle radius	04_lateral circle rotation	o_lateral circle extreme points
elevation									
top view									
bottom view									
axonometry									

a 90-degree arc) by means of rotations, within the complete square tile by means of polar arraying. And finally, the last scale produces proliferations of the complete module within a potentially infinite square matrix. The steps of the construction for the model can be conceptually divided into three parts. Firstly, there is a segmentation of a square tile with a circle defined at its center. In the middle points of the square's quadrants, lateral circles are created. These four circles are then rotated in a way where pairs of facing circles are formed. Subsequently, the edges of the seamless surfaces are constructed. The final part of the construction involves proliferating the module across the previously mentioned scales.

The model consists of four variables and eleven operations. The square tile's dimensions (variable 01) determine the size of the final tile. The center of this tile is also shared by a central circle (variable 02), with a variable radius. Lines from the center of the tile to the corners of the square and from the center of the tile to the mid-points of the edges of the square are constructed. The intersection between these lines and the circumference as well as their mid-points, are identified. From these mid-points, lateral circles of variable radius (variable 03) are constructed. These rotate along their respective lateral circle axis. The angle of rotation is variable (variable 04) and the typical value is 45º.

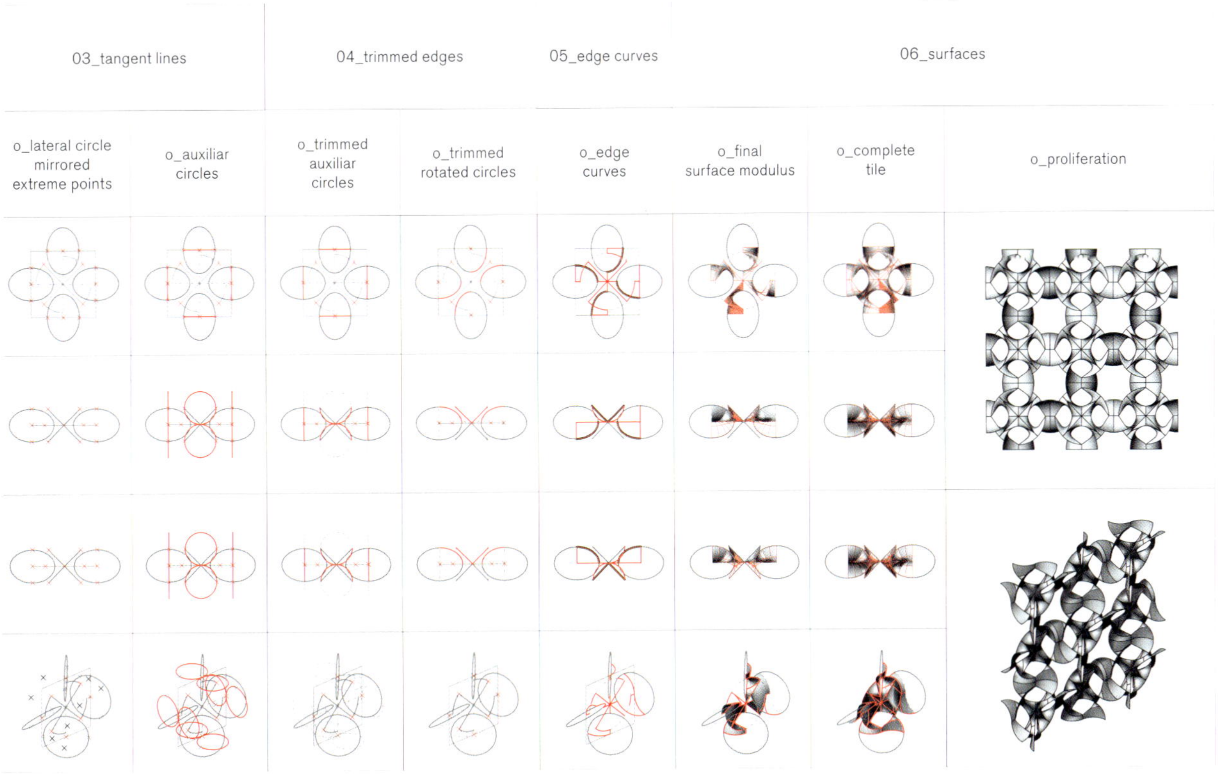

03_tangent lines
04_trimmed edges
05_edge curves
06_surfaces
o_lateral circle mirrored extreme points
o_auxiliar circles
o_trimmed auxiliar circles
o_trimmed rotated circles
o_edge curves
o_final surface modulus
o_complete tile
o_proliferation

56_System construction_variables and operations

Using a series of curves and points drawn from the existing geometry, auxiliary circles are defined, one pair for each rotated lateral circle. A quarter of each of these auxiliary circles is identified in order for each pair to produce a continuous curve that meet at the center of the lateral circles. Using the trimmed auxiliary circles and the central circle, the rotated circles are trimmed. The rest of the edge curves are identified (a quarter of the central circle and its correspondent corner line). Using these curves, a continuous surface is produced. These are rotated along the lateral circle axis to complete a tile, which is then rotated to create a vertical tile.

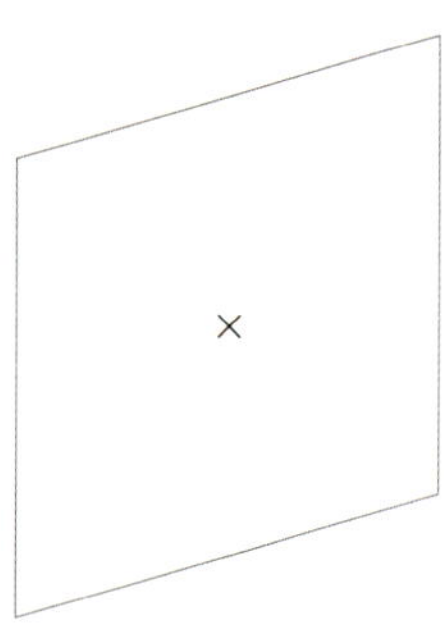

57_a. Tile dimensions and centre

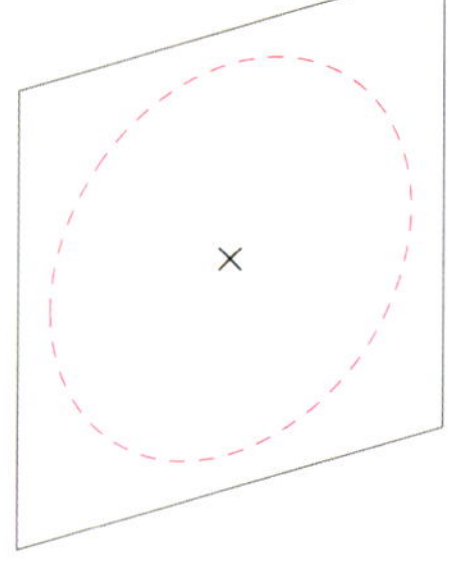

57_b. Central circle's radius

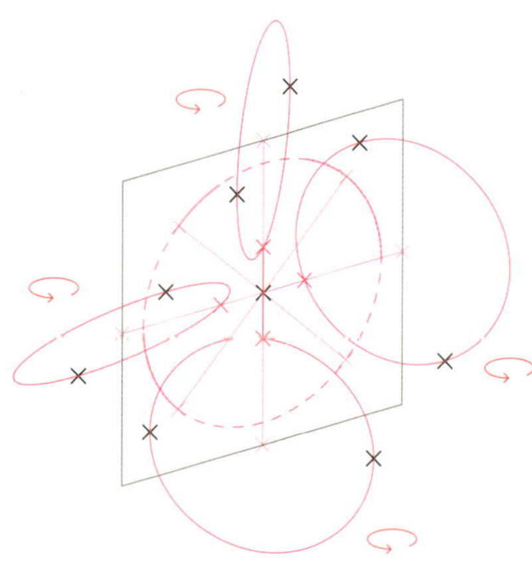

57_e. Lateral circles' rotation angle

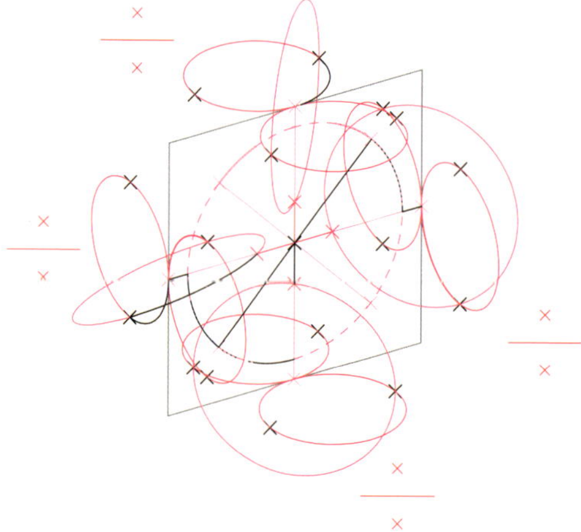

57_f. Construction of aligned auxiliary circles as surface edges

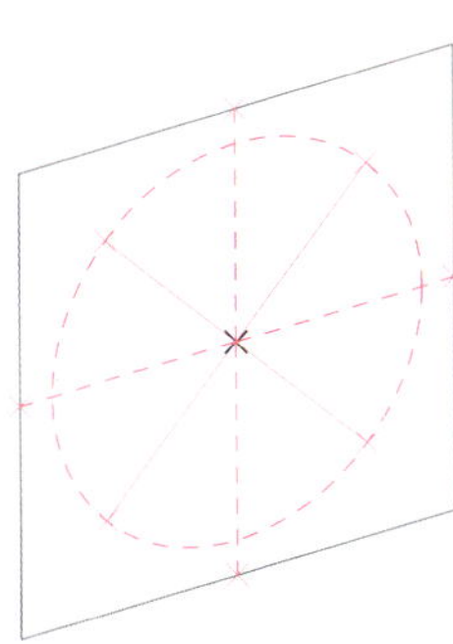

57_c. Axis and tile segmentation

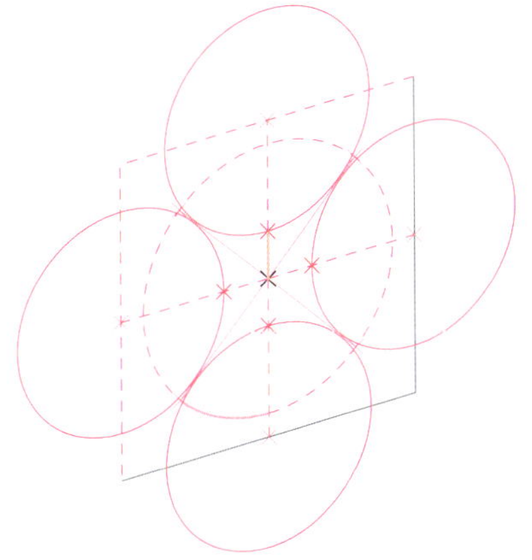

57_d. Lateral circles' radius

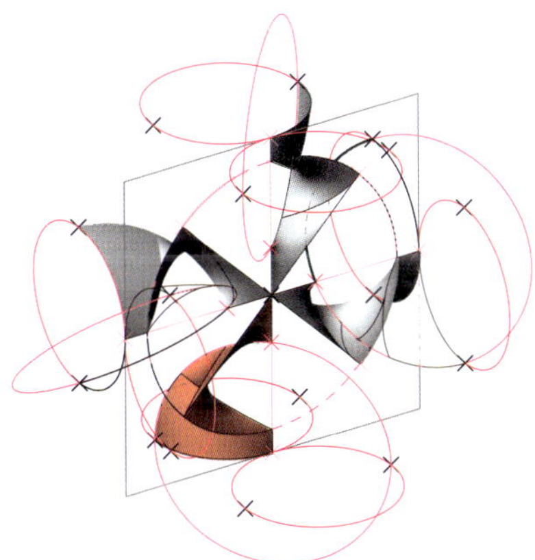

57_g. Construction of surfaces from edge curves

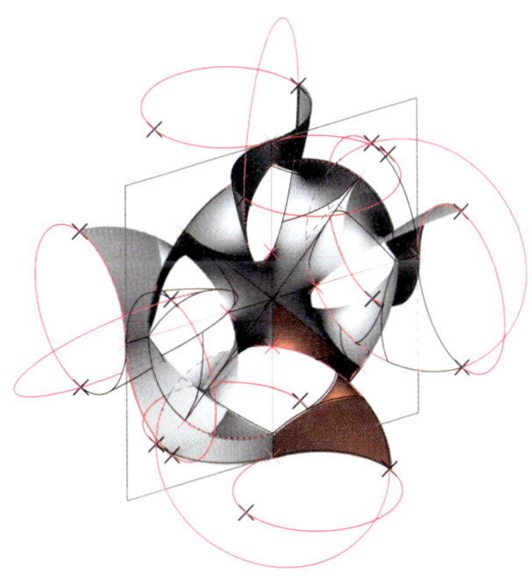

57_h. Rotation of surfaces and completion of tile

Bibliography

Erwin Hauer, Still Facing Infinity, Sculpture by Erwin Hauer (Mulgrave: Images Publishing Dist Ac, 2017)

Erwin Hauer, Continua – Architectural Screens and Walls (New York: Princeton Architectural Press, 2007)

Erwin Hauer and Enrique Rosado – Transformations, public lecture at Harvard University Graduate School of Design, February 22, 2013

Anoka Faruqee, Search Versus Re-Search: Recollections of Josef Albers at Yale- Josef and Anni Albers Foundation - https://vimeo.com/207155945, 2015

The drawings in this section are the author's interpretations informed by publicly available drawings and photographs on the precedents.

All drawings involved a process of interpretation which was processed through the construction of an associative digital model which were translated into 2d-drawings.

All drawings in this chapter were produced by asensio_mah (Candela De Bortoli) unless otherwise stated.

All photographs in this chapter were taken by asensio_mah (Leire Asensio Villoria & David Mah) unless otherwise stated.

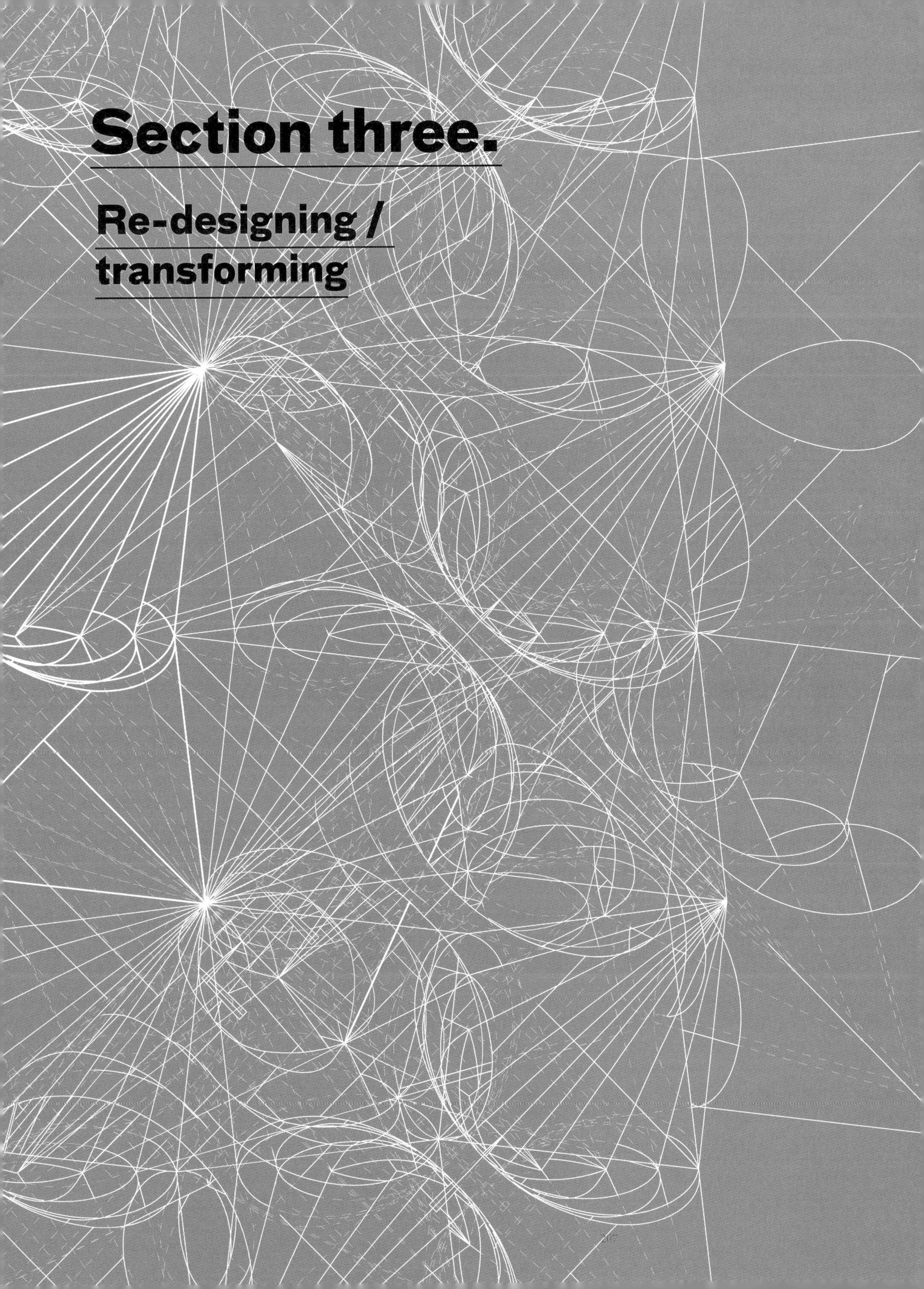

Section three.

Re-designing / transforming

01_Matrix of uniform differentiation.

More generic variations are arranged towards the center, while most differentiated one are arranged towards the periphery.

Some proliferations are selected as particular differentiations and are shown in full opacity.
New Modules developed later in this chapter are highlighted in light red. Each variation is named according to the variable and degree of differentiation.

The variables for Associative model 1 are:
(01) sphere radius,
(02) tile offset,
(03) thickness,
(05) saddle srf. central vertical dimension.

For Associative model 2:
(01) sphere radius,
(02) outer tile dimensions,
(03) vertical proportion,
(05) extrusion dimension.

For Associative model 3:
(01) sphere dimensions,
(02) tile rotation,
(03) tile scale,
(04) extrusion of resulting surface.

For Associative model 4:
(01) sphere dimension,
(02) lateral circle radius,
(02) central circle radius,
(02) fillet radius.

For Associative model 5:
(01) sphere dimension,
(02) saddle surface vertical dimension.

For Associative model 6:
(01) sphere dimension,
(02) tile rotation.

For Associative model 7:
(01) tile dimension,
(02) central circle radius,
(03) lateral circle radius,
(04) lateral circle rotation angle.

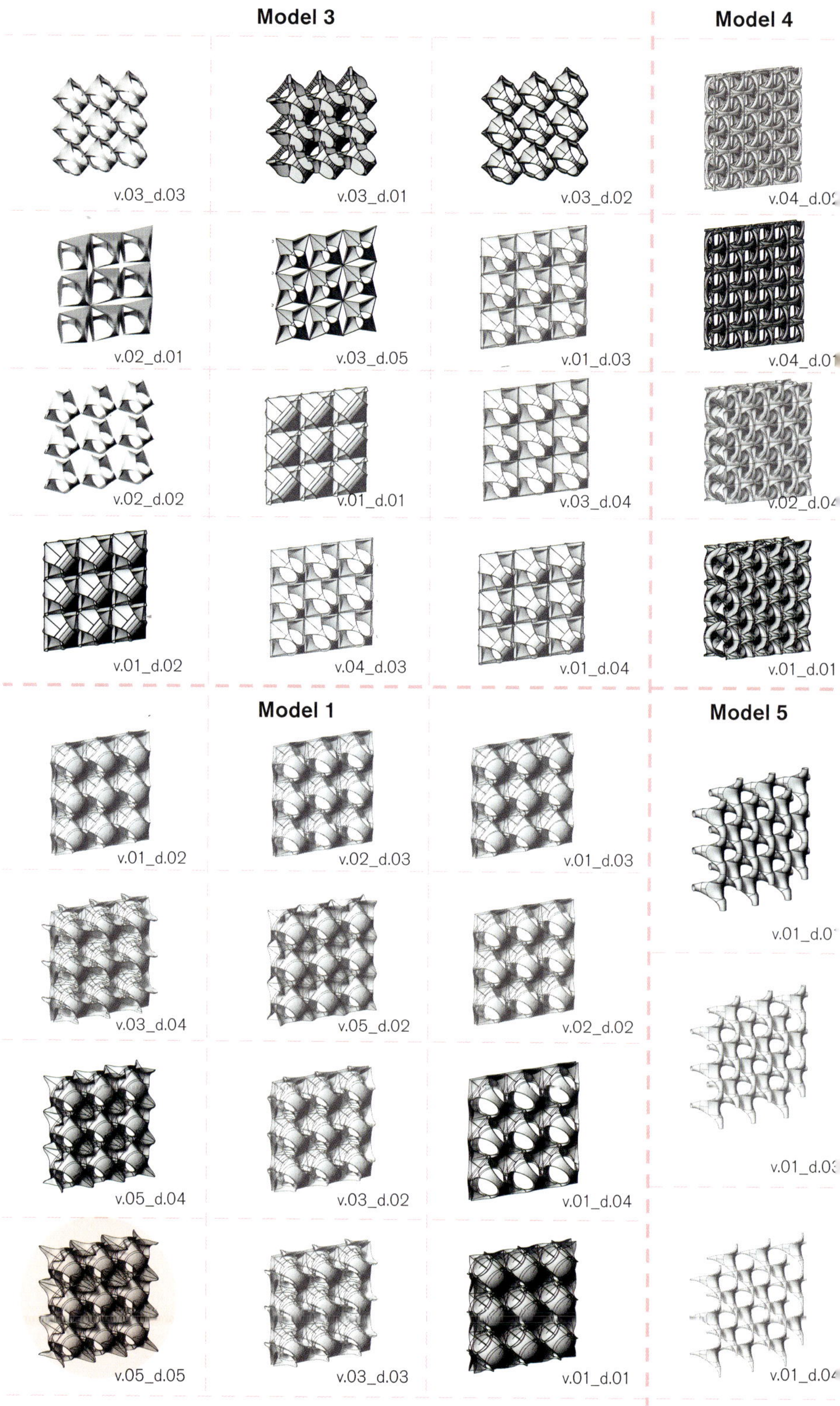

Model 3

v.03_d.03 v.03_d.01 v.03_d.02
v.02_d.01 v.03_d.05 v.01_d.03
v.02_d.02 v.01_d.01 v.03_d.04
v.01_d.02 v.04_d.03 v.01_d.04

Model 4

v.04_d.0
v.04_d.01
v.02_d.0
v.01_d.01

Model 1

v.01_d.02 v.02_d.03 v.01_d.03
v.03_d.04 v.05_d.02 v.02_d.02
v.05_d.04 v.03_d.02 v.01_d.04
v.05_d.05 v.03_d.03 v.01_d.01

Model 5

v.01_d.0
v.01_d.0
v.01_d.0

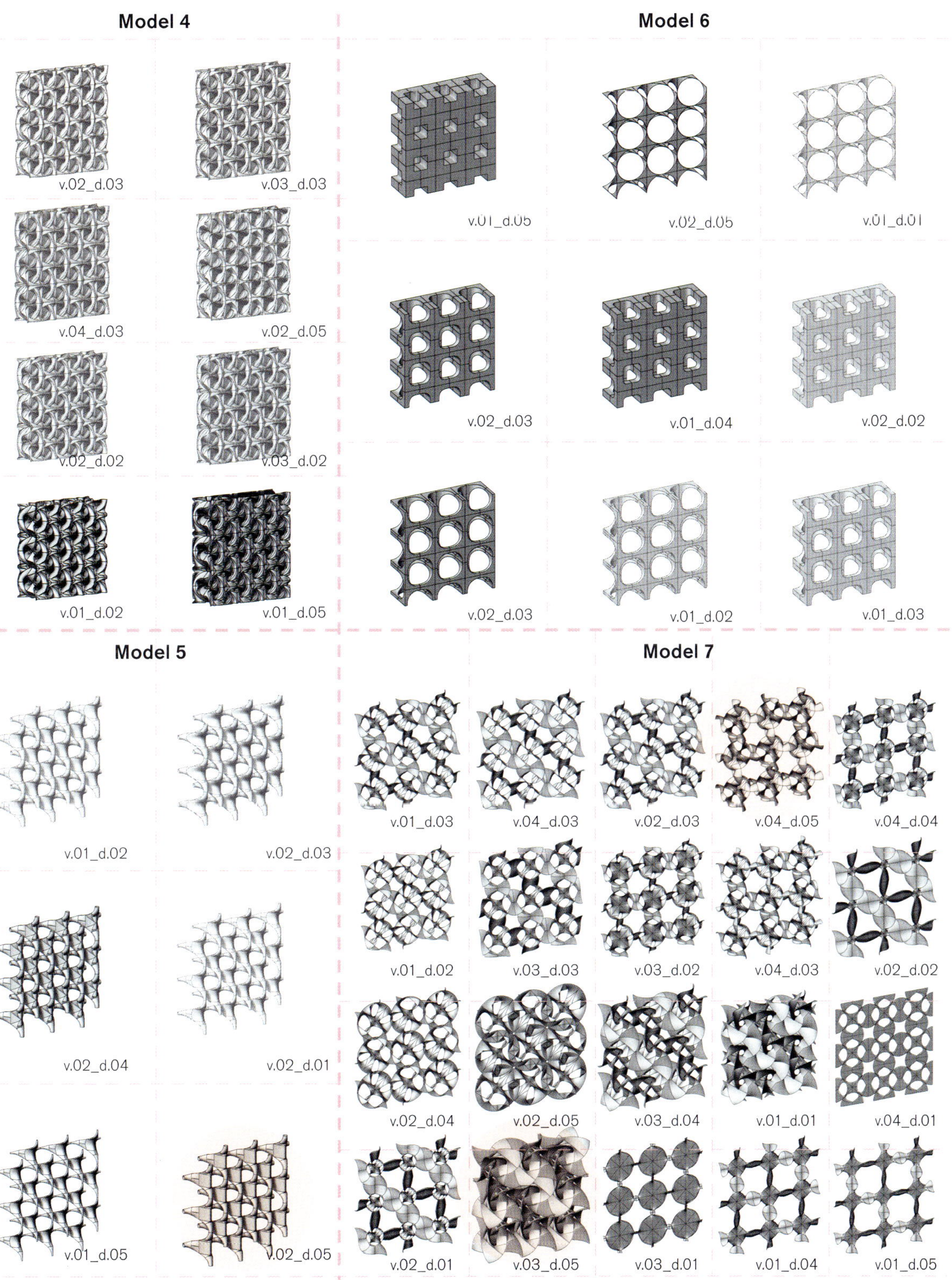
Model 4
v.02_d.03
v.03_d.03
v.04_d.03
v.02_d.05
v.02_d.02
v.03_d.02
v.01_d.02
v.01_d.05
Model 6
v.01_d.05
v.02_d.05
v.01_d.01
v.02_d.03
v.01_d.04
v.02_d.02
v.02_d.03
v.01_d.02
v.01_d.03
Model 5
v.01_d.02
v.02_d.03
v.02_d.04
v.02_d.01
v.01_d.05
v.02_d.05
Model 7
v.01_d.03
v.04_d.03
v.02_d.03
v.04_d.05
v.04_d.04
v.01_d.02
v.03_d.03
v.03_d.02
v.04_d.03
v.02_d.02
v.02_d.04
v.02_d.05
v.03_d.04
v.01_d.01
v.04_d.01
v.02_d.01
v.03_d.05
v.03_d.01
v.01_d.04
v.01_d.05

Uniform differentiation:

02_Overlapping of differentiated tiles_elevation

Associative model 1

Tectonic performances.
Variable 03_ellipse Z dimension: Varying this parameter of the ellipse also effects the transitions between adjacent tiles. However, this variable also has a direct effect on the extremities of the transitional curves and therefore transforming the overall edge curves of the outer shells of the handles.

Variable 04_saddle vertical dimension: This variable determines the distance between the centroids of the two complementary saddle surfaces. Varying this distance produces a difference in curvature for the transition between tiles.

03_Associative model 1_System variability

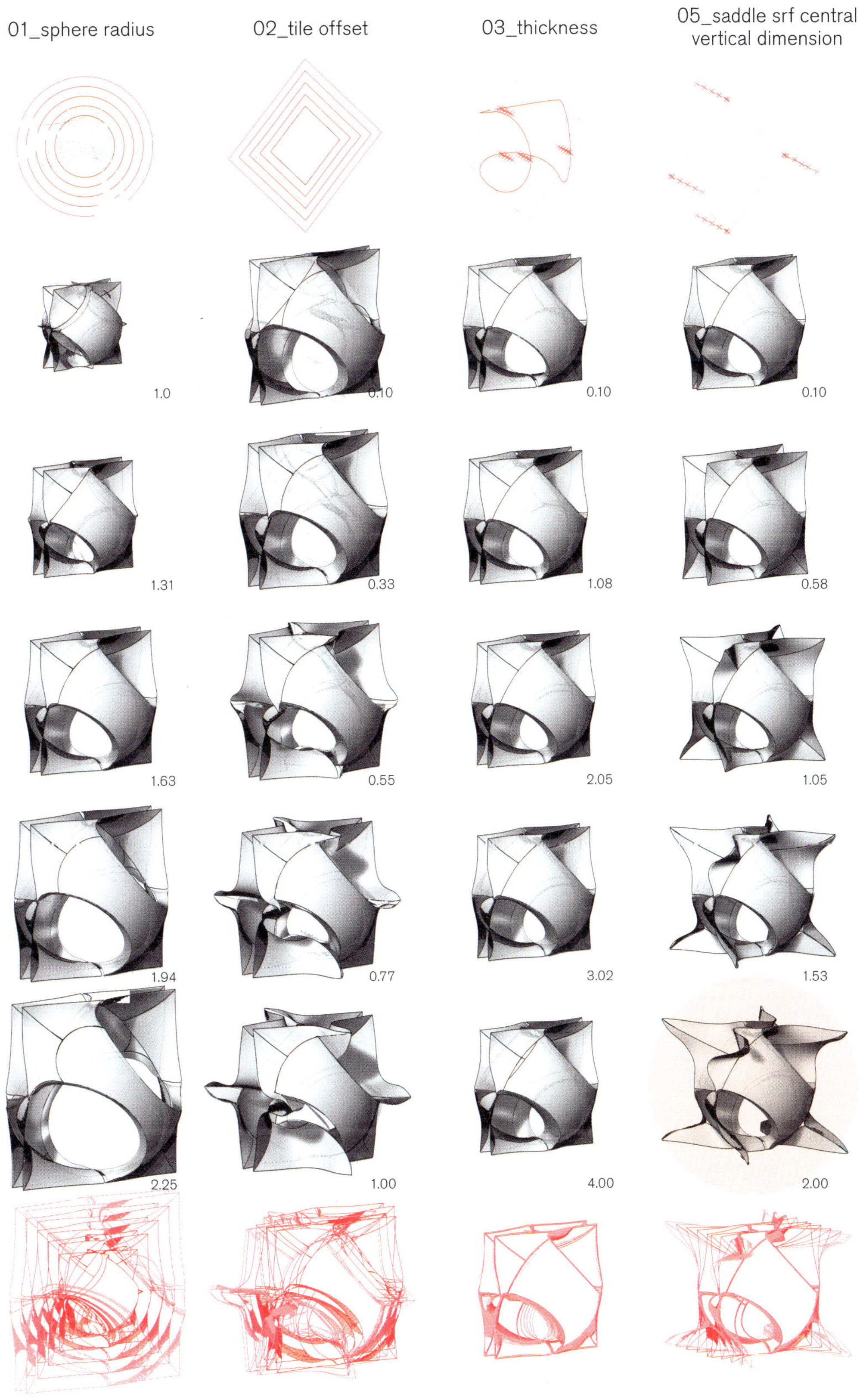

01_sphere radius	02_tile offset	03_thickness	05_saddle srf central vertical dimension
1.0	0.10	0.10	0.10
1.31	0.33	1.08	0.58
1.63	0.55	2.05	1.05
1.94	0.77	3.02	1.53
2.25	1.00	4.00	2.00

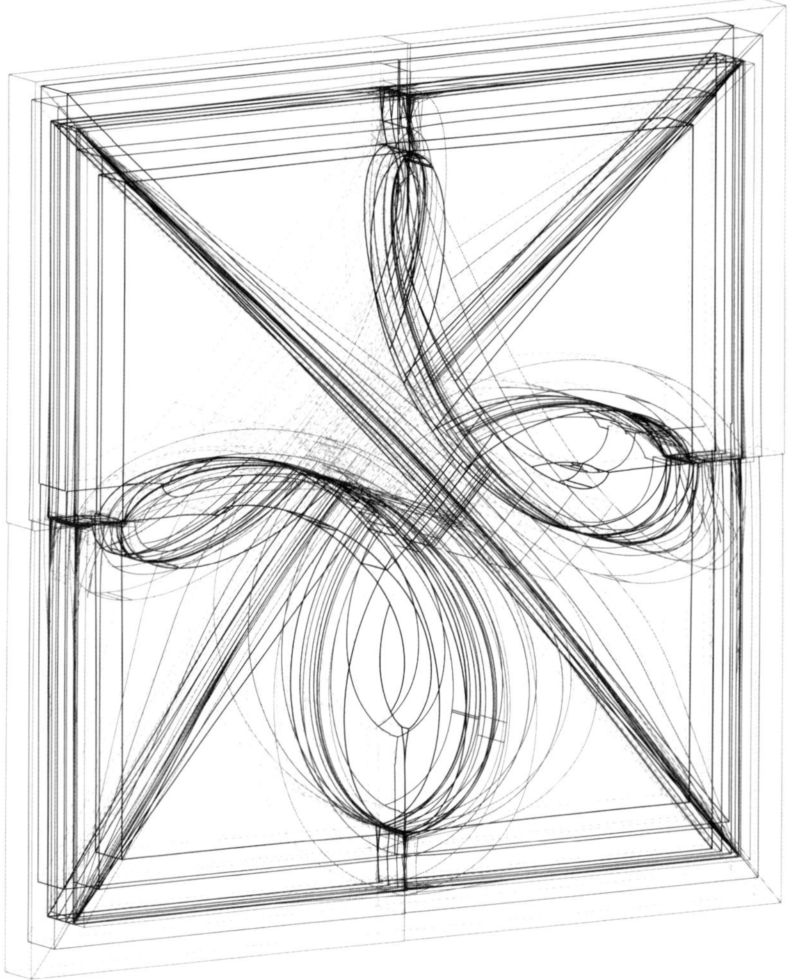

04_Overlapping of differentiated tiles_isometric

Associative model 2

Variable 01_sphere dimensions: Scaling the sphere results in a change of proportion for the suture curve and the overall tile. As in other interpretative models of Design 1, the bigger the sphere becomes, the thinner the handle and the deeper and more porous the tile.

Variable 02 _outer tile dimension: This variable determines scalar as well as proportional differences between the basic quarter tile and the full tile module. This is visible in the space between the suture curve quadrants and the tile edges. These variations result in a different perception of the whole pattern. Varying the offset distances of this model will result in more isolated handles and a shallower tangent curve.

Variable 03_vertical scale: This variable transitions between forming a spherical or flat space in between opposite handles.

Variable 04_extrusion of surface: This variable defines the proportion between the surfaces and their thickness.

05_Associative model
2_Systems variability

06_Overlapping of differentiated tiles_elevation

Associative model 3

Variable 01_sphere dimensions: Scaling the sphere results in a change of proportion for the suture curve and the overall tile.

Variable 02_tile rotation: This variable defines the rotational relationship between the tile boundary and the diagonally oriented handle. This ranges from its typical diagonal position and explores a 45-degree rotation in both directions.

Variable 03_tile scale : The typical ratio for the sphere to square tile dimension is 1:1. This can be varied to either a smaller and constrained or a flexed and stretched relationship. When the tile is smaller, its depth is greater than its frontal proportion. When the tile is wider than the sphere, it becomes shallow. Also, the tile edges are no longer orthogonal and therefore triangulate the tile either inwardly or outwardly.

These triangulations, once the tile is proliferated, produce local discontinuities and makes the overall field texture more porous.

Variable 04_extrusion of surface: This variable explores the proportion between surfaces and their thickness which affects porosity and tectonic performances.

07_Associative model
3_System variability

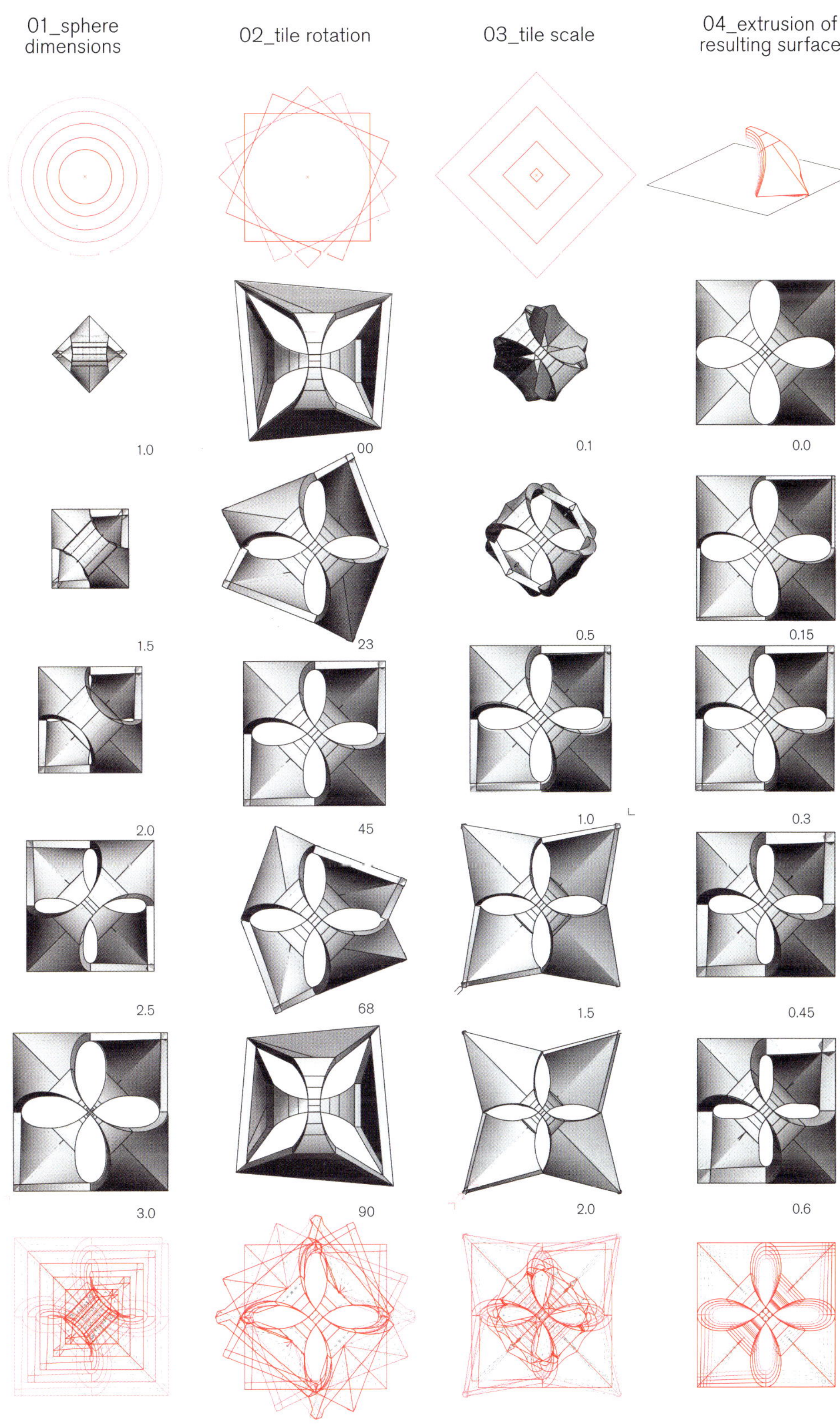

08_Overlapping of differentiated tiles_elevation

Associative model 4

Variable 01_sphere radius: Variations on the sphere radius produce either a more or less compact matrix, in which tiles become smaller or larger; varying visually permeable.

Variable 02_lateral circle radius: Variations on the lateral circles' radius produce either a thicker or thinner handle, which directly produces more or less visually permeable matrices.

Variable 03_central circle radius: This variable explores the proportion of the handle that will be eventually trimmed, so that is becomes wider or thinner to the end of the tile. This has a direct impact on the material continuity across the matrix and on the visual permeability.

Variable 04_fillet radius between segment and tangent line. Variations on the fillet radius define the curvature smoothness of the transitional surface. The extremes of the range produce either perpendicular, and thus maximum, changes in curvature; or smooth transitions, where continuity is maximum.

09_Associative model 4 System variability_ range of difference

01_sphere dimensions	02_lateral circle radius	03_central circle radius	04_fillet radius_ segment and tangent line
1.4	0.478	0.6	0.13
1.9	0.485	0.7	0.24
2.3	0.493	0.8	0.37
2.7	0.5	0.9	0.5

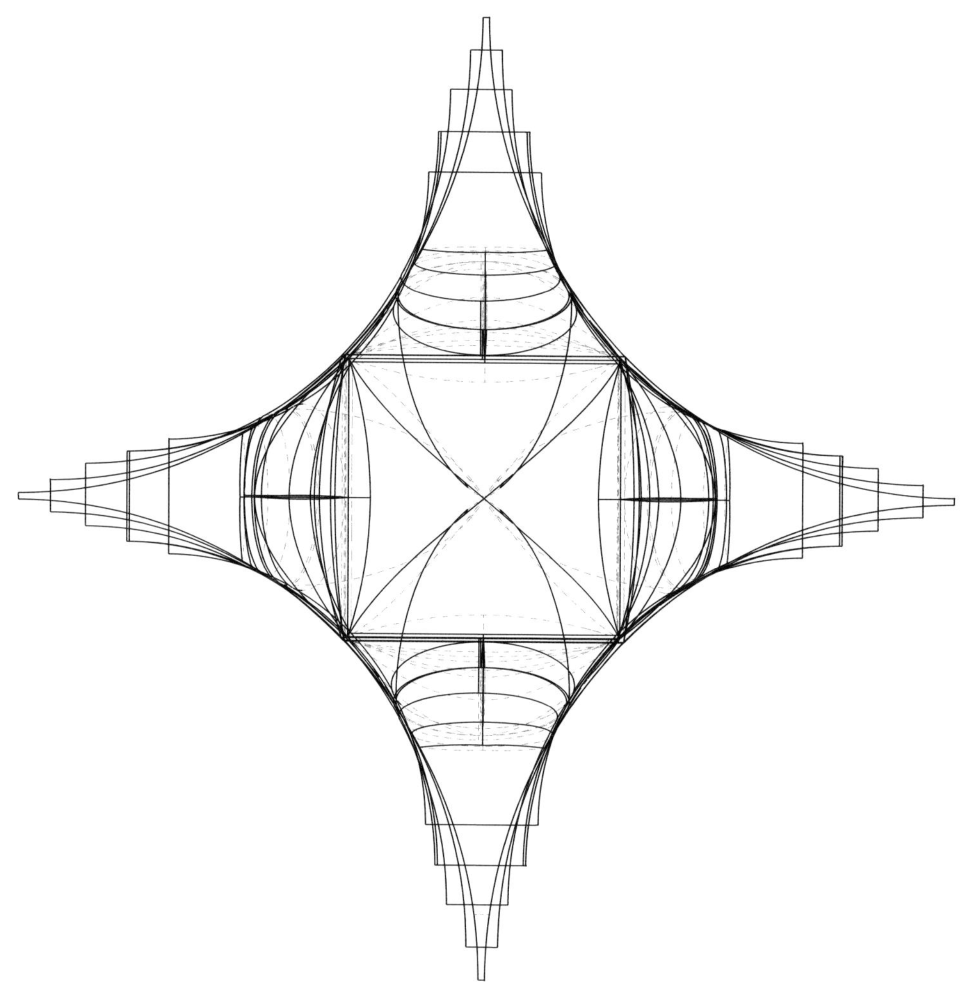

10_Overlapping of differentiated tiles_elevation

Associative model 5

Variable 01_sphere radius: The variation of the sphere radius has a direct effect on the tile dimension and therefore on the lateral radius of the circle. This proportion, however, is not reflected in the final tile, since an increase of the lateral circle's radius means that, after a certain threshold, circumferences will intersect themselves. As these curves act as surface cutting edges, once this threshold is reached, spherical surfaces are cut in a way that no width is produced and therefore sweep section radii will be minimum. This means that this variable has a direct effect on the proportion of the tile. In both extremes of the range we find either large tiles with thin handles that increase the porosity of the matrix or small flat tiles with thick handles that produce an opaque texture.

Variable 02_saddle surface's central vertical dimension: This surface explores the range of variability within the vertical dimension of the twin saddle surfaces. In ranges closer to the original model, the saddle surfaces have a curvature that is tangential to the sphere's curvature. As this dimension or distance becomes larger, the curvature of the saddle surfaces is flatter and the overall smoothness of the transition between handles is compromised.

11_Associative model 5_ System variability_range of difference

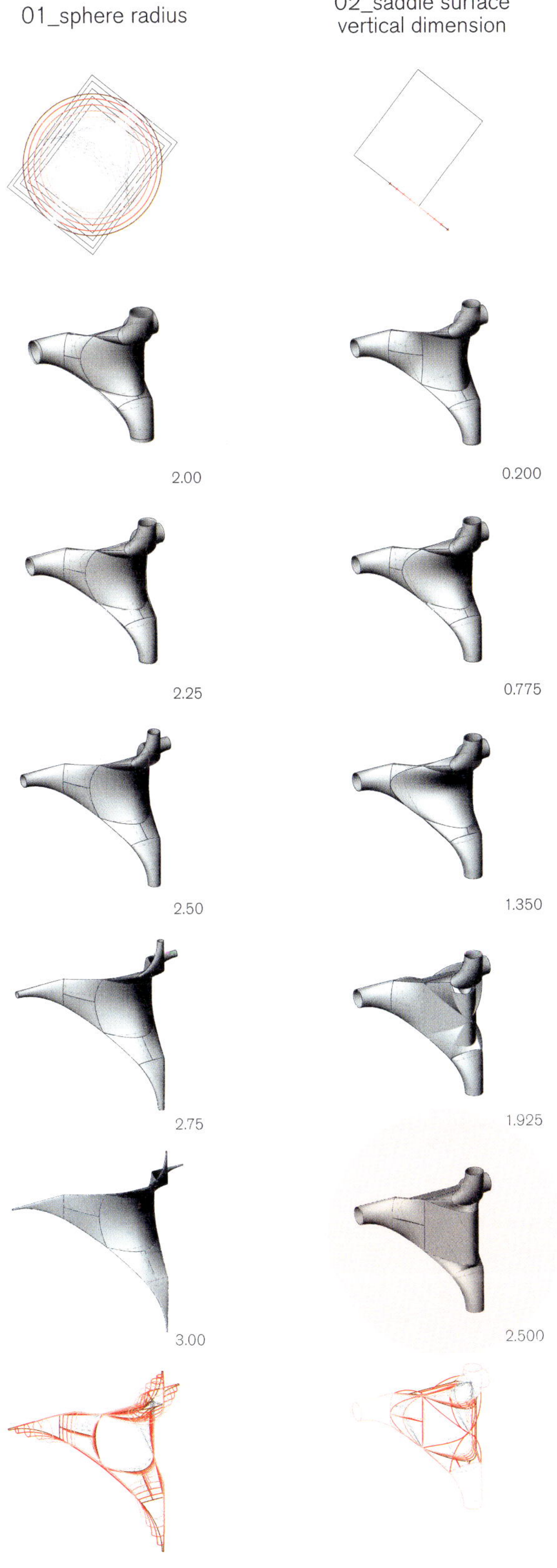

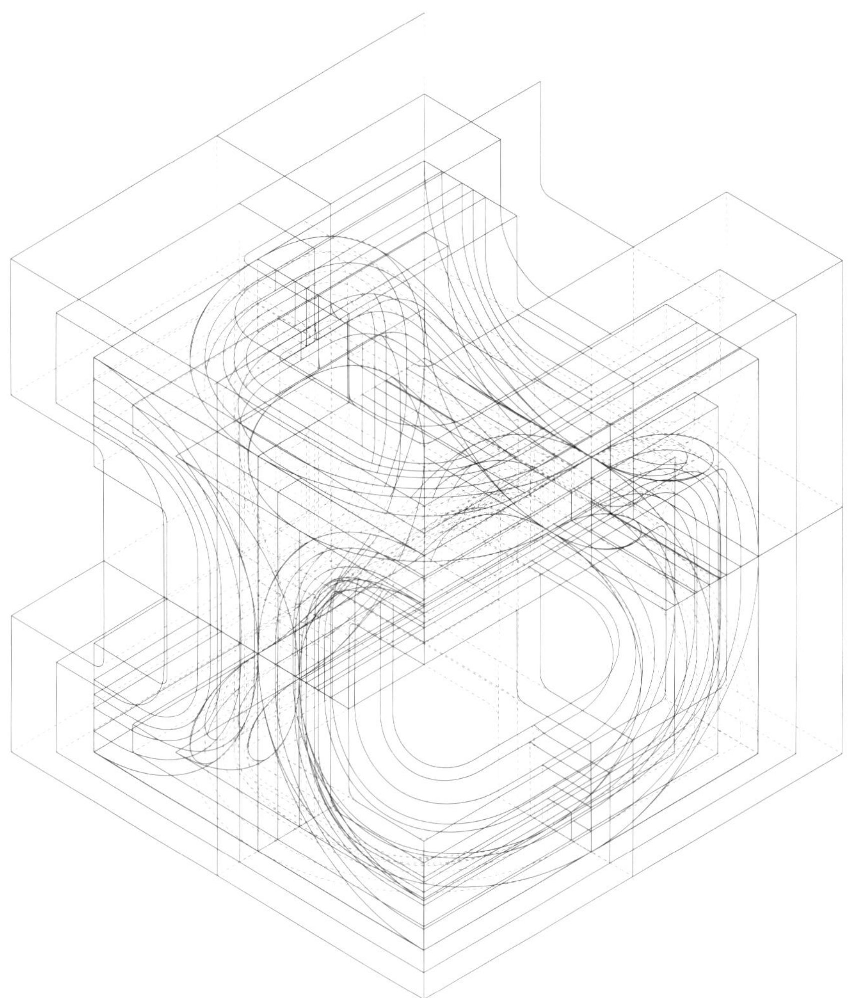

12_Overlapping of differentiated tiles_isometric

Associative model 6

Variable 01_cube dimensions:
Changing the relationship between the cube and the cylinder's radius produces either an almost complete or null perforation of the volume, resulting in differences in porosity, surface area and robustness.

Variable 02_circle radius:
This variable produces a proportionally inverse range of difference than the previous variable. Both variables produce differences in robustness, which is directly linked to stability. As the perforations become larger, mass decreases and tiles lose rigidity.

13_Associative model 6_
System variability_range
of difference

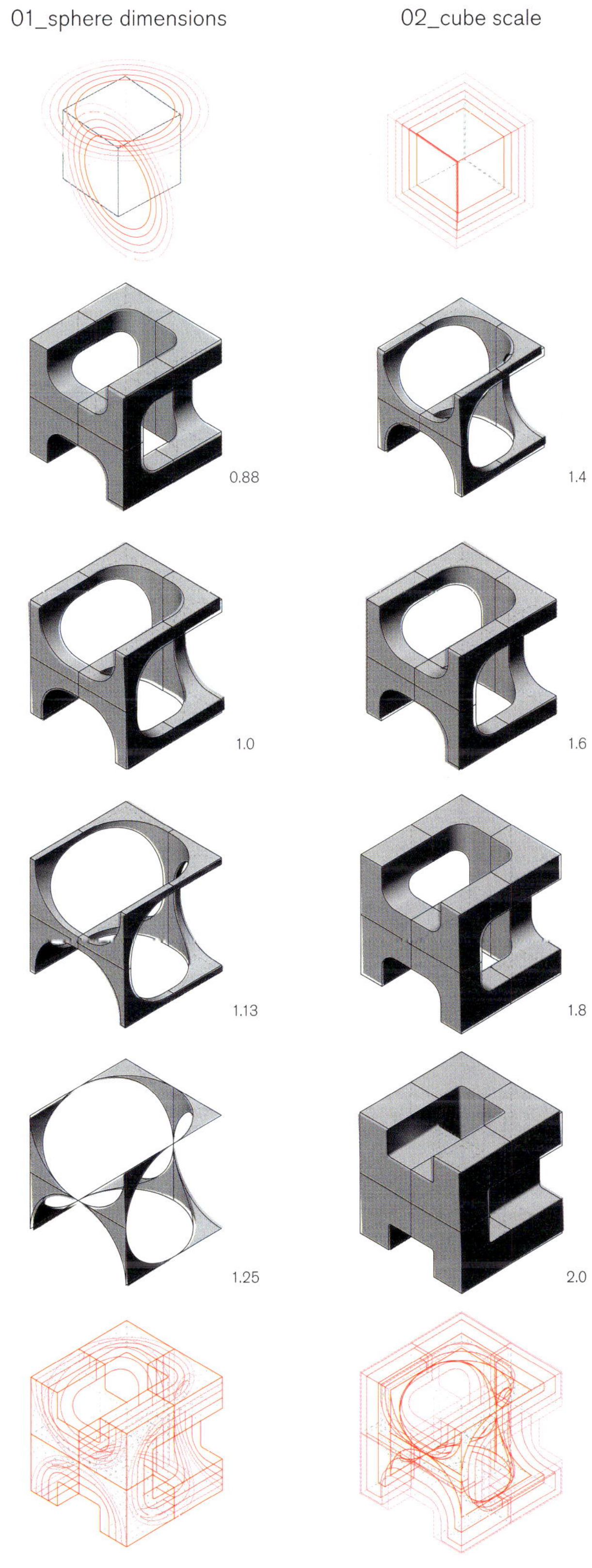

14_Overlapping of differentiated tiles_elevation

Associative model 7

Variable 01_tile dimensions: Changing the proportion between the tile and the sphere produces either a dense accumulation of overlapped steep curvatures or or a stretched, wide and porous matrix of not very steep curvature as extremes of the same spectrum.

Variable 02_central circle radius: This variable explores the proportion between central and lateral circles' radii. If central circles are significantly smaller, the vertically planar surfaces become minimized and changes in curvature are maximum. If central circles are larger, planar and warped surfaces overlap.

Variable 03_lateral circle radius: When central circles are fixed in size and lateral circles are significantly smaller, the vertically planar surfaces become maximized and changes in curvature are minimum. When lateral circles are significantly larger, planar and warped surfaces overlap.

Variable 04_lateral circle rotation angle: The variation of the rotational angle oscillates between a completely planar matrix, with zero change in curvature, in opposition to a perpendicular relationship between lateral and central circles, where curvatures are maximum.

15_Associative model
7_System variability_
range of difference

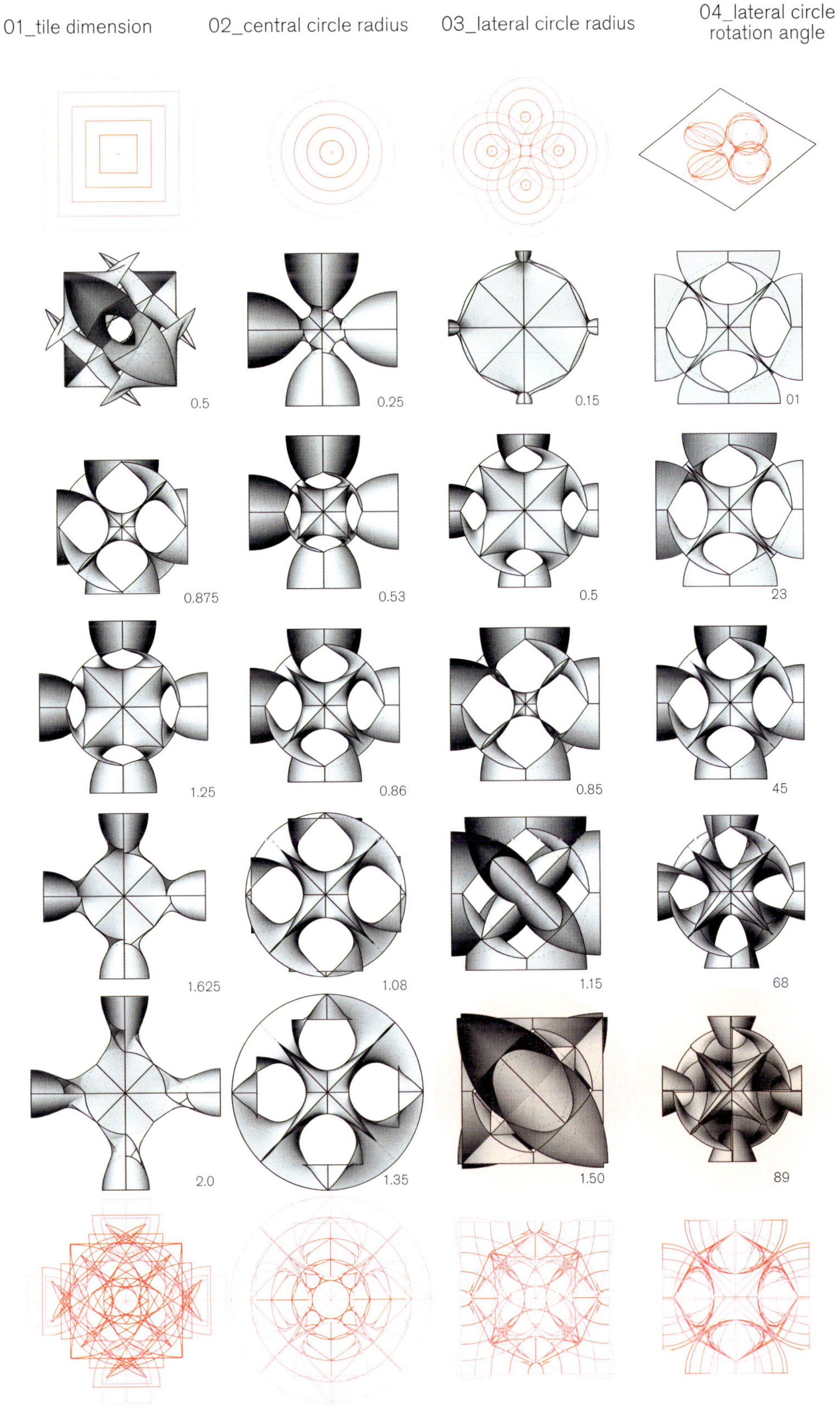

01_tile dimension	02_central circle radius	03_lateral circle radius	04_lateral circle rotation angle
0.5	0.25	0.15	01
0.875	0.53	0.5	23
1.25	0.86	0.85	45
1.625	1.08	1.15	68
2.0	1.35	1.50	89

01_Matrix of non-uniform differentiation explorations.

Top to bottom: non-uniform scaling of sphere, translation of sphere and Enneper surface variations in X, Y and Z components.

Each row shows a differentiation spectrum from a generic tile (right) to a differentiated one. A selection of particular differentiations and are shown in full opacity.

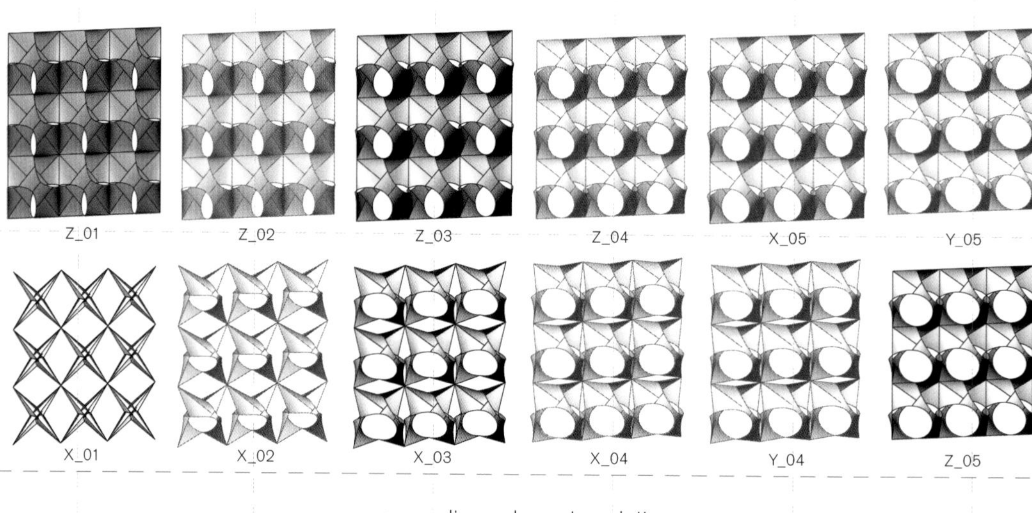

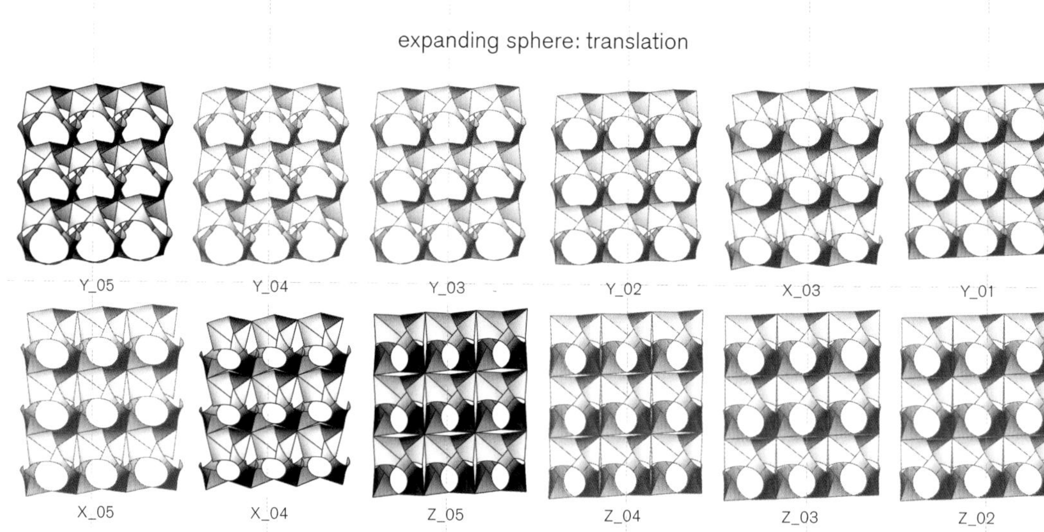

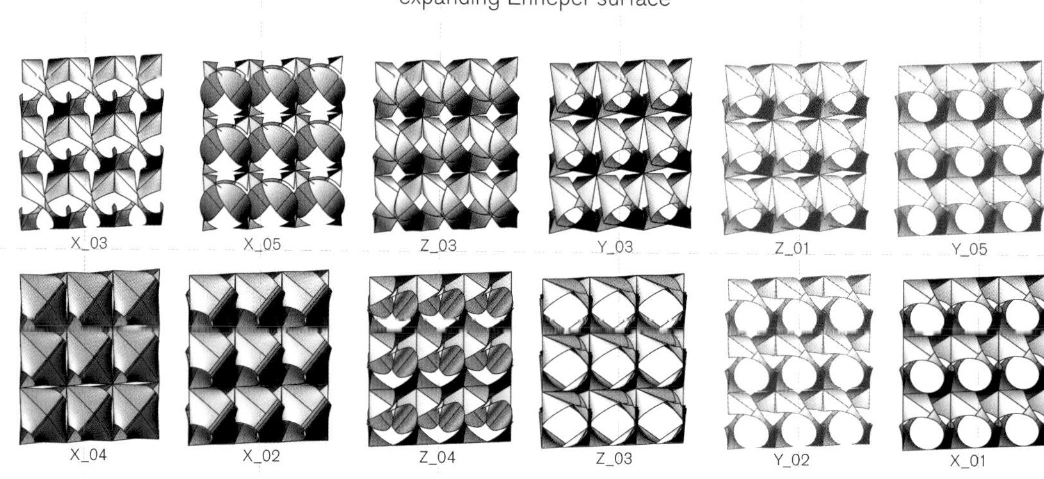

02_Matrix of tiling explorations based on non-uniform sphere scaling ("S") and translation ("T") tiles (in X, Y, Z).

Top to bottom: polygon fitting, varying contact edges and polar array matrices. "a" and "b" are two tiling alternatives.

A selection of particular differentiations and are shown in full opacity.

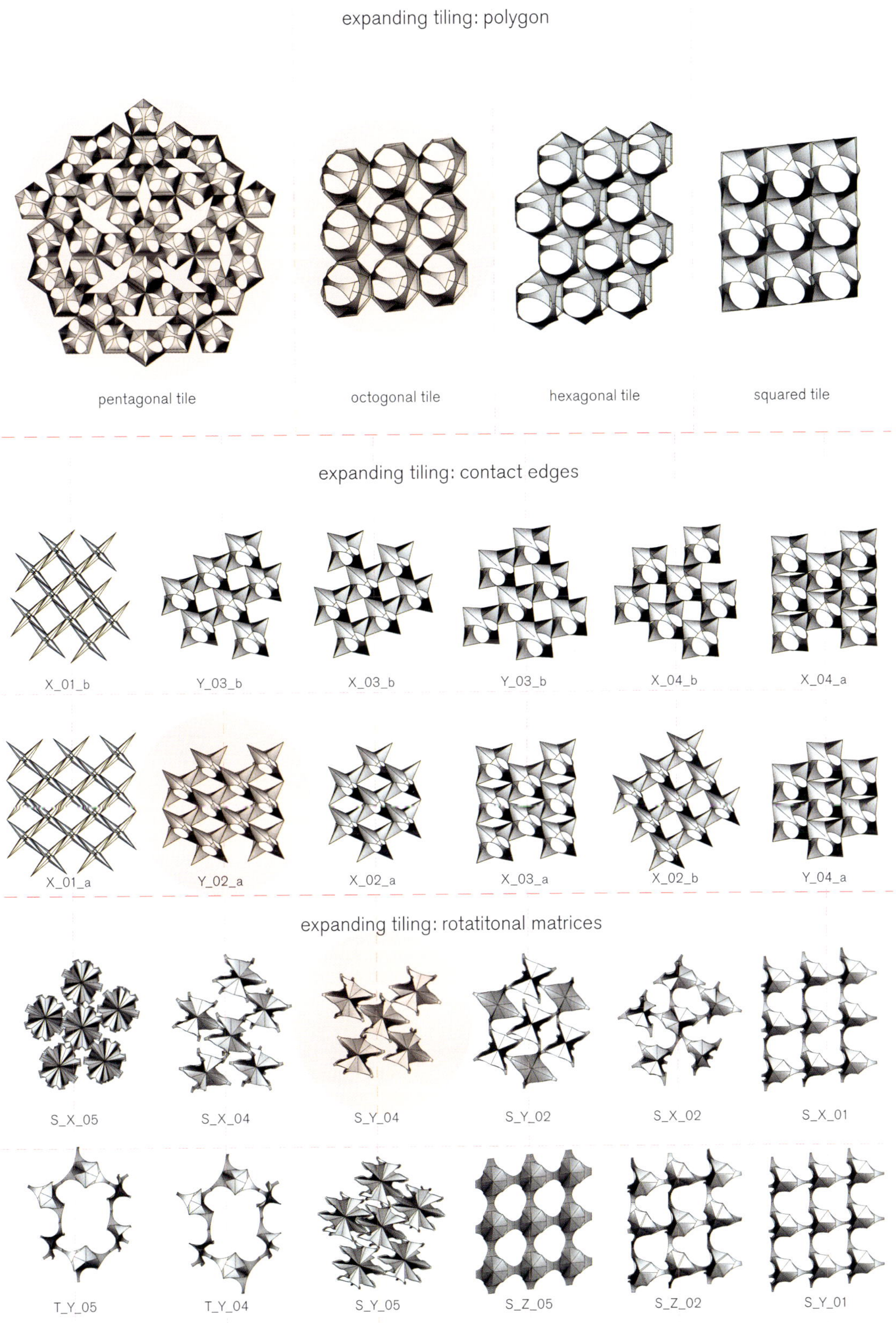

expanding tiling: polygon

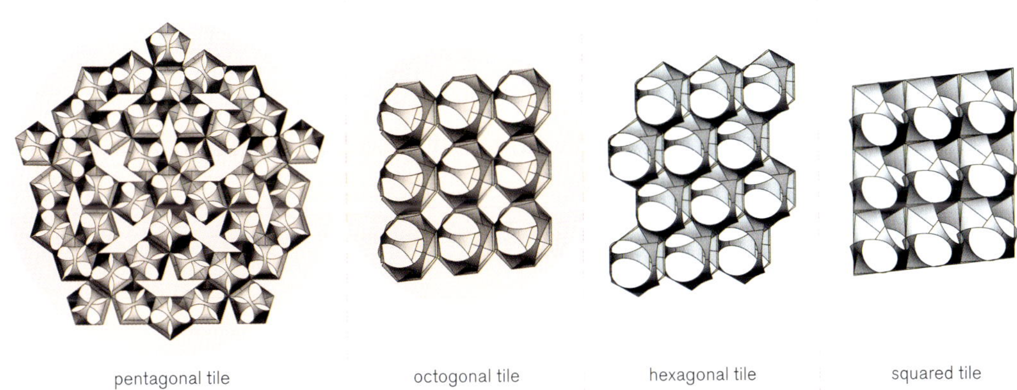

expanding tiling: contact edges

X_01_b Y_03_b X_03_b Y_03_b X_04_b X_04_a

X_01_a Y_02_a X_02_a X_03_a X_02_b Y_04_a

expanding tiling: rotatitonal matrices

S_X_05 S_X_04 S_Y_04 S_Y_02 S_X_02 S_X_01

T_Y_05 T_Y_04 S_Y_05 S_Z_05 S_Z_02 S_Y_01

Non-uniform differentiation

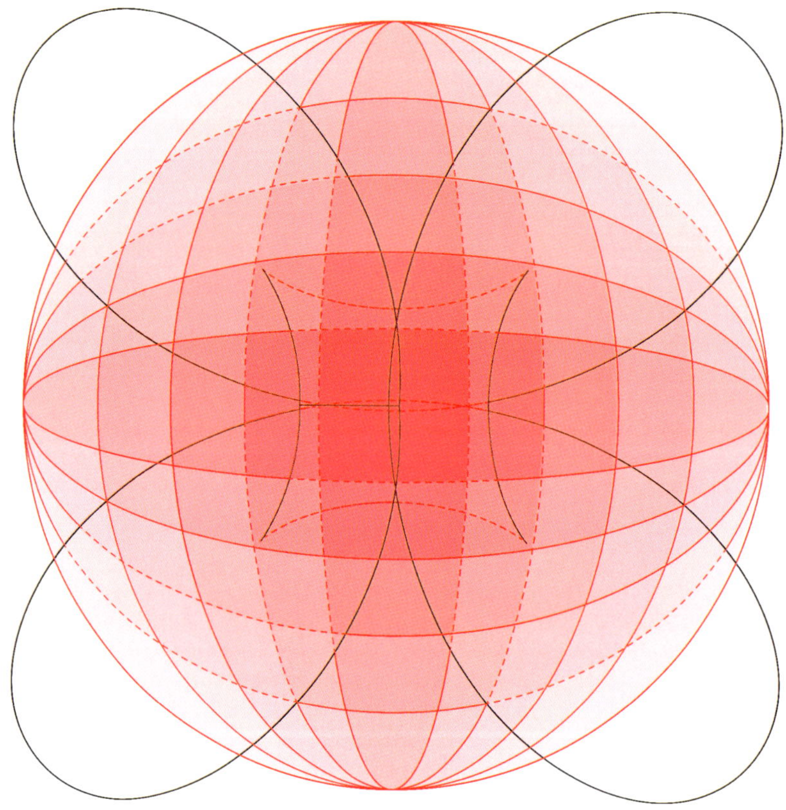

03_Overlapping of non-uniform scaled spheres_plan and isometric

Sphere: non-uniform scale & translation

These design iterations are made possible by differentiating the underlying sphere in the associative models. The sphere is differentiated in a non-uniform manner, transforming the sphere into different shapes with six variables. These are divided into two sets of three and each group is explored here within a specific range. In total there are 5 variations for each variable.

The first group of variables relates to scaling non-uniformly in three directions: X, Y and Z. This group of design iterations assumes the sphere's center is coincident with the Enneper surface's center.
The range is from no scaling (factor = 1) to a down-scaling (up to 0.2).
In non-uniform scaling, the resultant tiles tend to be symmetric given that both the sphere and the Enneper surface share their center point. Both X and Y scaling produce differences in the edge boundaries.
The corners still produce a squared tile, but the edges tend to split and triangulate towards the center of the tile. This opens up opportunities for other differentiation strategies that are explored in the tiling section.
Z scaling, however, does not

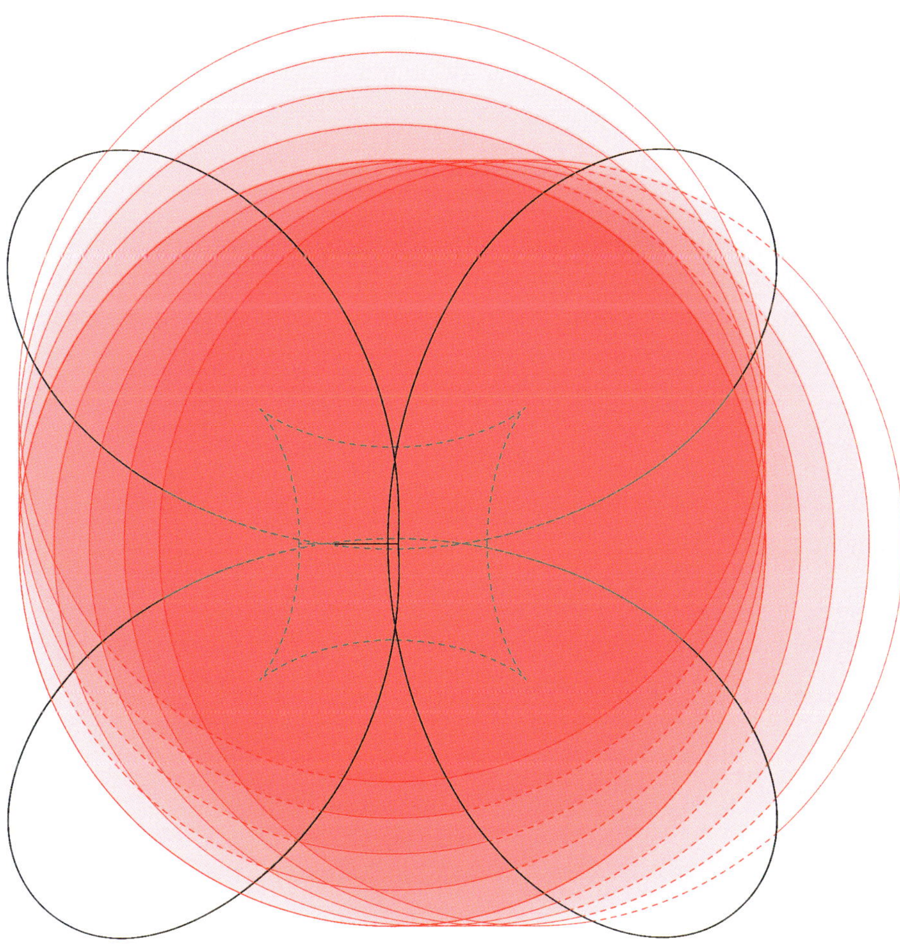

produce any differences in edge boundaries, but rather, affects the overall depth of the tile, producing flatter tiles for scaling under 1. As it was previously mentioned, the second group of variables relates to translation of the sphere in three directions: X, Y and Z and it assumes the sphere's radius is constant. The range is from no translation (factor = 0) to a maximum translation of 1.

In both X and Y translation variations, differences in the edge boundaries emerge. The resultant tiles tend to be asymmetric given that the sphere and the Enneper surface no longer share their center point and assembly of matrices tend to be unsuccessful to accomplish continuity. Z translations, however, do not produce any differences in edge boundaries, so tiles are still symmetrical and squared, but once again, these variations affect the overall depth of the tile, producing flatter tiles and therefore more opaque configurations.

05 & 06_ Matrices showing the resultant tiles from the sphere non-uniform scaling and translation explorations.

Each column corresponds to one of the non-uniform scaling or translation dirctions: X, Y, and Z.

Each row shows a degree of scaling or translation, from a scaling factor of 0.2 to 1 or 0 to 1 translation units.

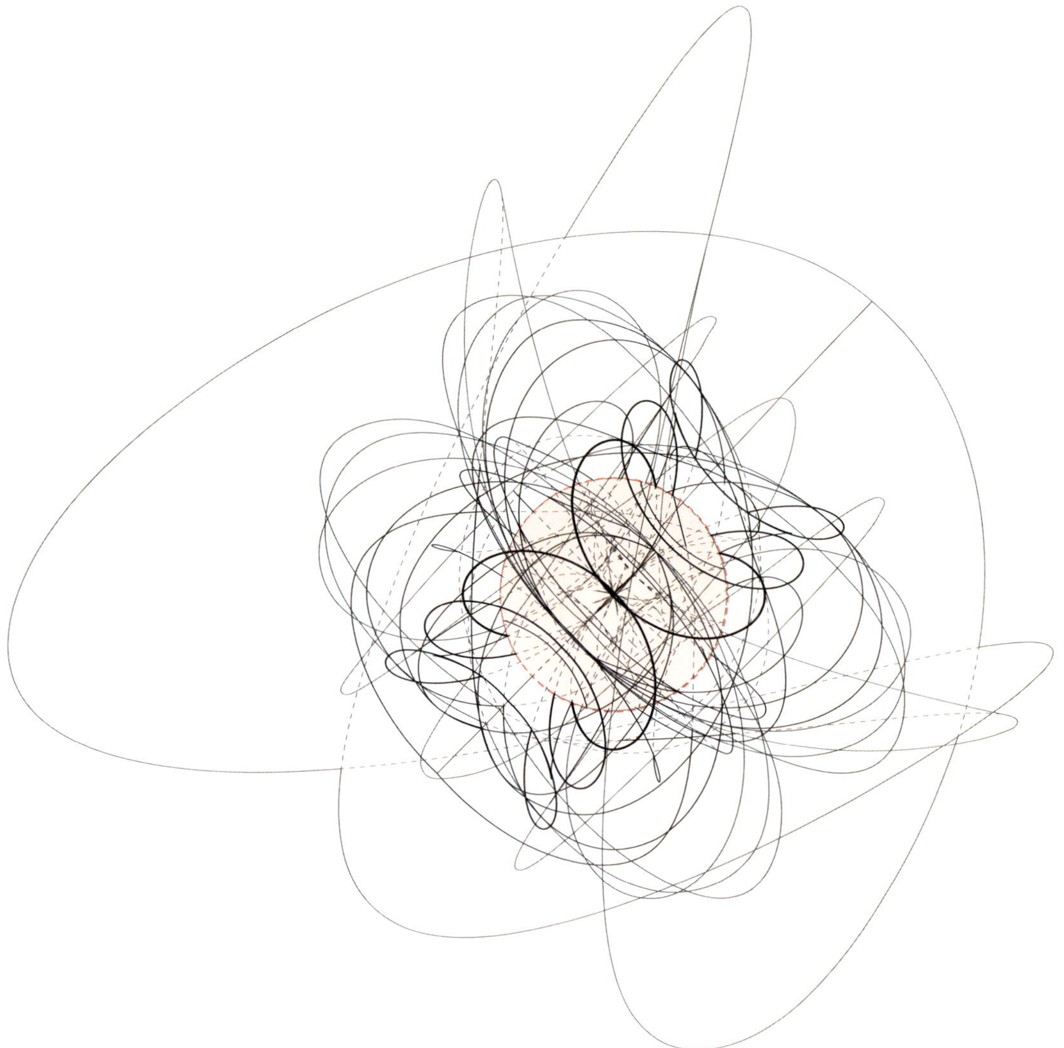

07_Overlapping of enneper surfaces_elevation

Expanding the Enneper surface

This section involves the differentiation of the Enneper Surface as a variable for the construction of associative model 1. The Enneper surfaces used to produce these variations are differentiated through variations in the parameters that determine X, Y and Z coordinates.

This exploration assumes that each Enneper surface variation intersects with identical spheres. The different suture curves generated from these variations produce new modules and therefore new tiles.

08_Matrix of Enneper surface variations, resultant tiles and variability_elevation.

Each column shows either a variation in the X, Y or Z component of the Enneper surface formula.

Tiling

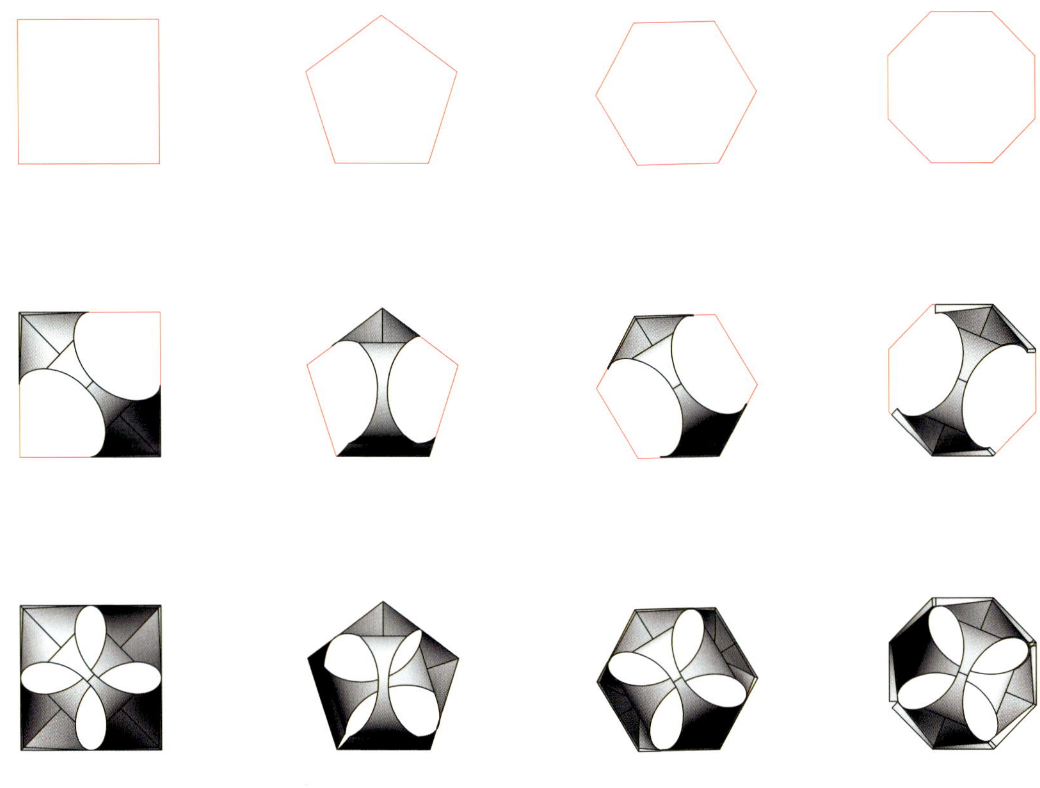

09_Polygon fitting matrix

Polygon fitting

These series of sections explore the concept of tiling. All variations are based on associative model 1. This first section focuses on tile bounding. The model is transformed to work in other polygons besides a square, such as a pentagon, hexagon and octagon. These polygons offer different kinds of tilling patterns. Octagonal tiles work very similarly to squared tiles, since the handles always relate to corner points and they meet perpendicularly in the center of the tile. The matrix produced by octagonal tiles, however, produces hollow squared spaces between tiles. Pentagonal tiles, being odd number of sides, produces unsatisfactory joints between handles. The resultant tiles are asymmetric and, when proliferated, larger shapes and spaces are formed.
The general perception of this matrix tends to be more chaotic and less continuous than other tiles. The hexagonal tile is satisfactory in the way it produces a continuous field with no spaces between tiles, but similar to the pentagonal tile, not being a multiple of four, there are two modules that make up the total tile.

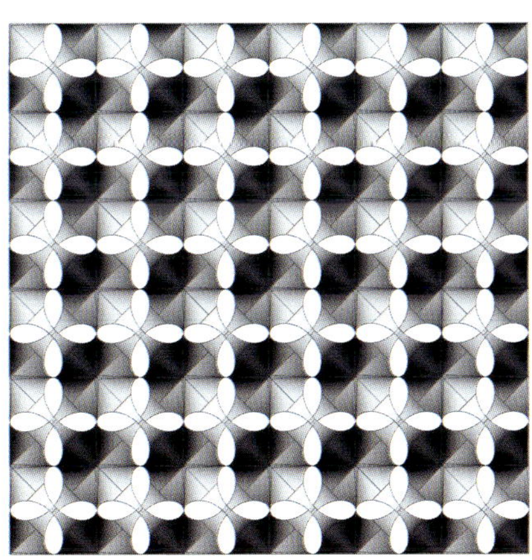

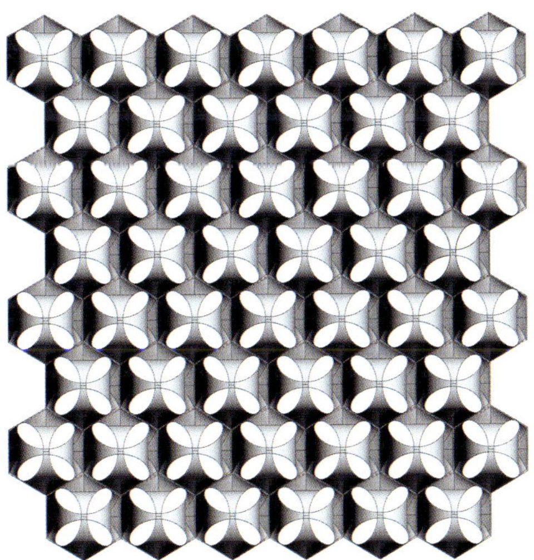

10_Expanding tiling_Polygon fitting_squared, pentagonal, hexagonal and octagonal tiles_proliferated matrix_elevation

11_Overlapping of contact edges exploration tiles_isometric

Contact edges

This section explores the production of new tessellation through the aggregation of identical modules. These options are created by defining different ways of assembling the matrix using shared edges.
Non-perpendicular edges are produced when the proportion between the sphere and the enneper changes due to a non-uniform scaling.
In generic cases, the proportion is 1 to 1, and the resultant tile is squared, so the corner angle is 90º. In scaling variations, angles diverge from orthogonal and the resulting tiles often have more than 4 sides.
New possibilities for assembling matrices emerge. The models used for this exploration are variations in non-uniform scaling of a sphere for associative model 1, in three sets of variations (non-uniform scaling in X, Y and Z).

12_Expanding tiling_Contact edges_selected proliferated matrices_isometric

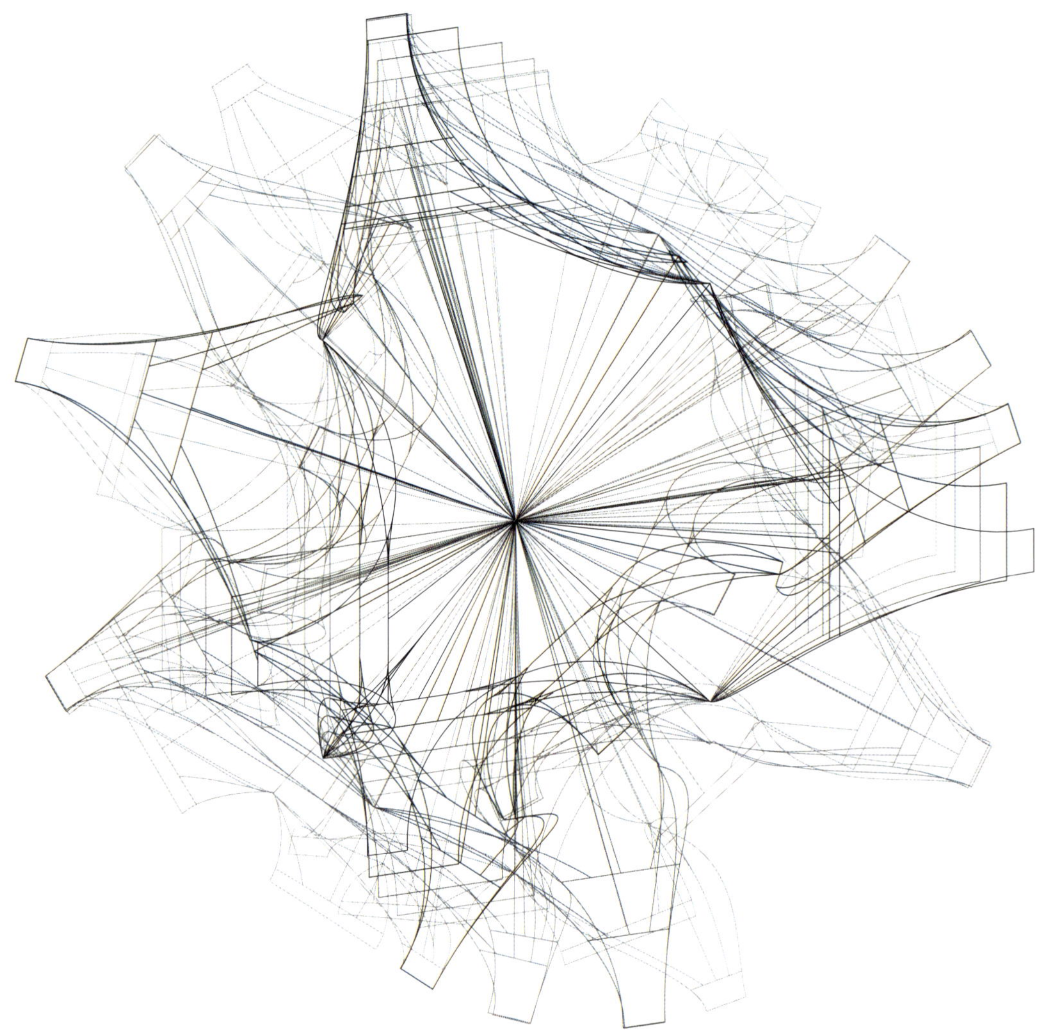

13_Overlapping of rotational matrices exploration tiles_isometric

Rotational matrices

This section explores the production of new tiles through the rotation of identical modules around a corner point. In generic cases the angle is 90° so exactly four modules complete the tile. In other variations, these are adjusted to be the closest angle that produces an integer number of modules to complete a tile. The models used for this exploration are variations in non-uniform scaling of a sphere for associative model 1, in three sets of variations (non-uniform scaling in X, Y and Z).

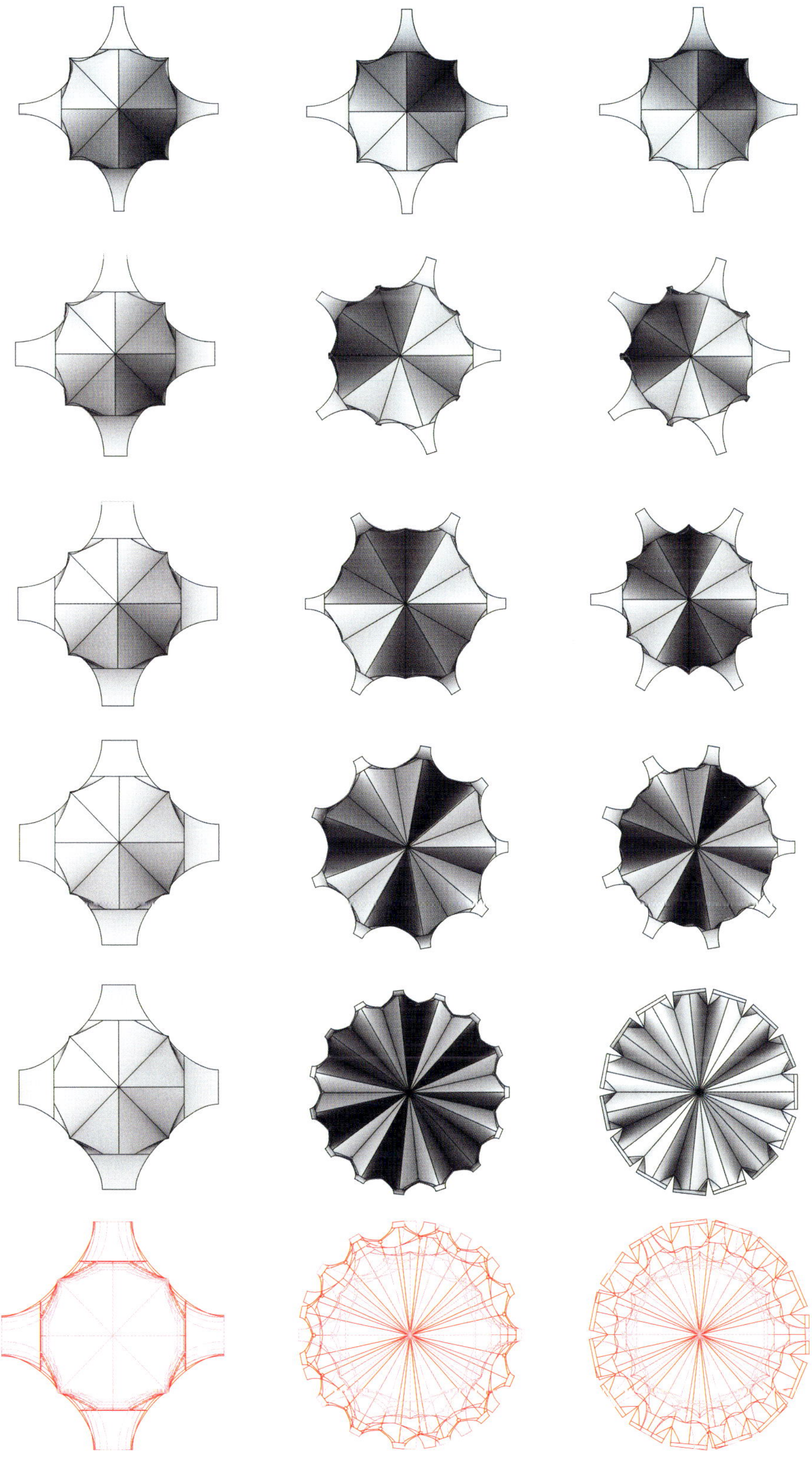

14_Matrix of tile variations_elevation Each row shows a variation in the X, Y or Z axis for a non-uniform scaled sphere.

Uniform differentiation: Series 1

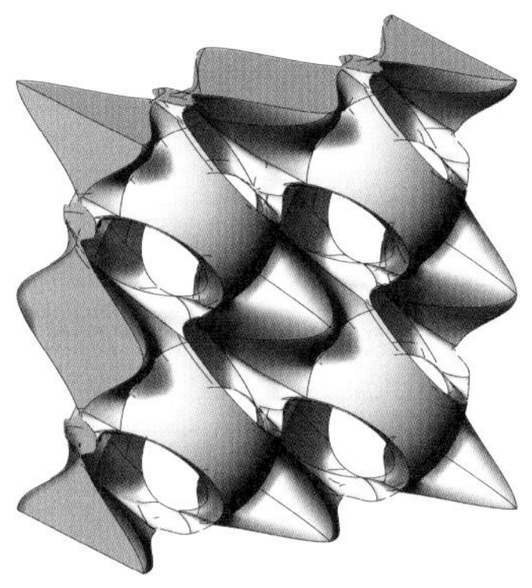

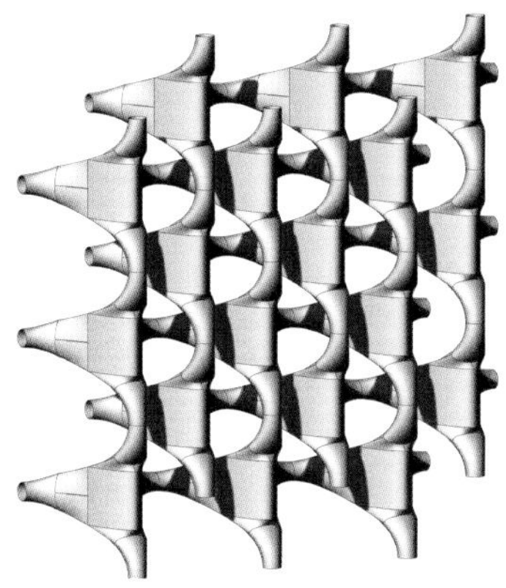

01_Matrix of selected tiles from New Modules

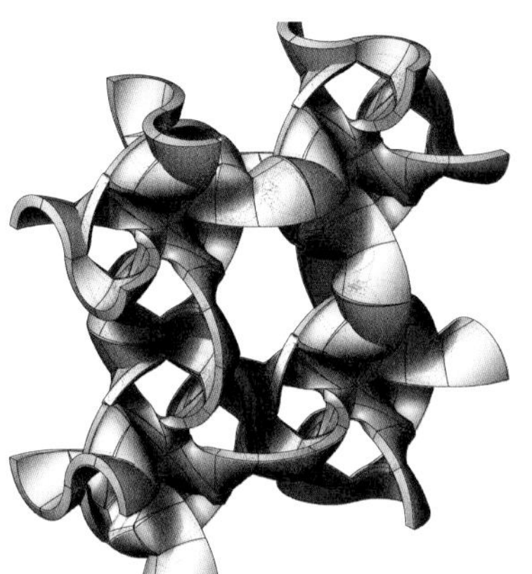

New modules from differentiation

This series of design iterations are generated through varying three formal attributes of the associative models of three particular designs. The associative model 7 has two variables that exacerbate some of the model's qualities. These two variables are (03) lateral circles radius and (04) lateral circles rotation angle. At the extremities of these variables, we find larger tiles and steeper rotations from the original Intercircles tile. These are two sets of associative models which transforms interpretations of Design 1 and 3. The first model versions were modeled in a manner that simplifies the geometries to allow for a higher degree of formal variation. These models produce a greater spectrum of variability but fail to reproduce the continuity of saddle surfaces. The second associative model focuses on describing the saddle and transitional surfaces, so the capacity for variability in the forms is minimized.

Non-uniform differentiation: Series 2

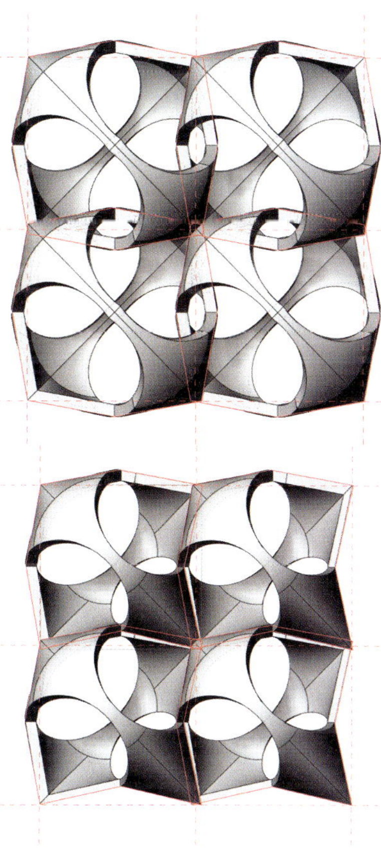

Tiling: Series 3

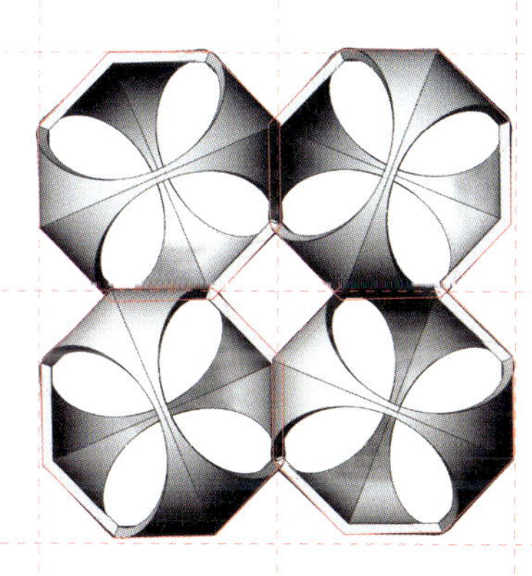

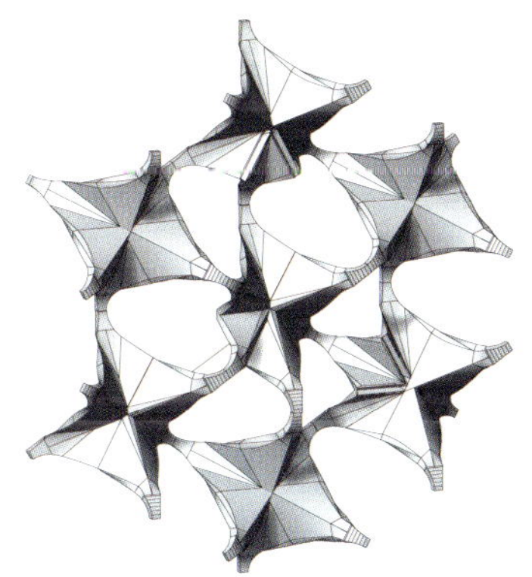

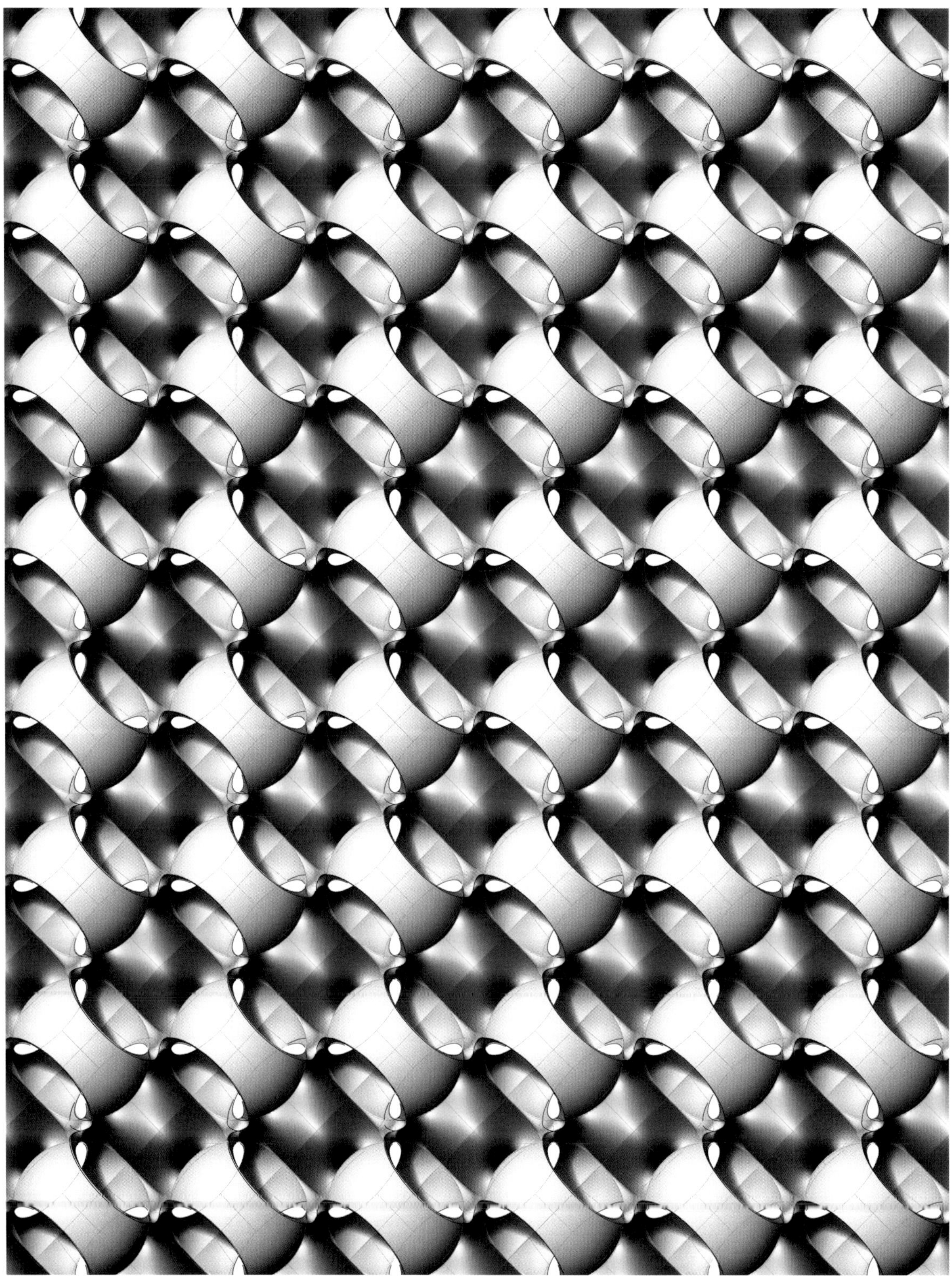

02_New Module 1.1_Design 1_Associative model 1 based_proliferated matrix_rendered frontal view

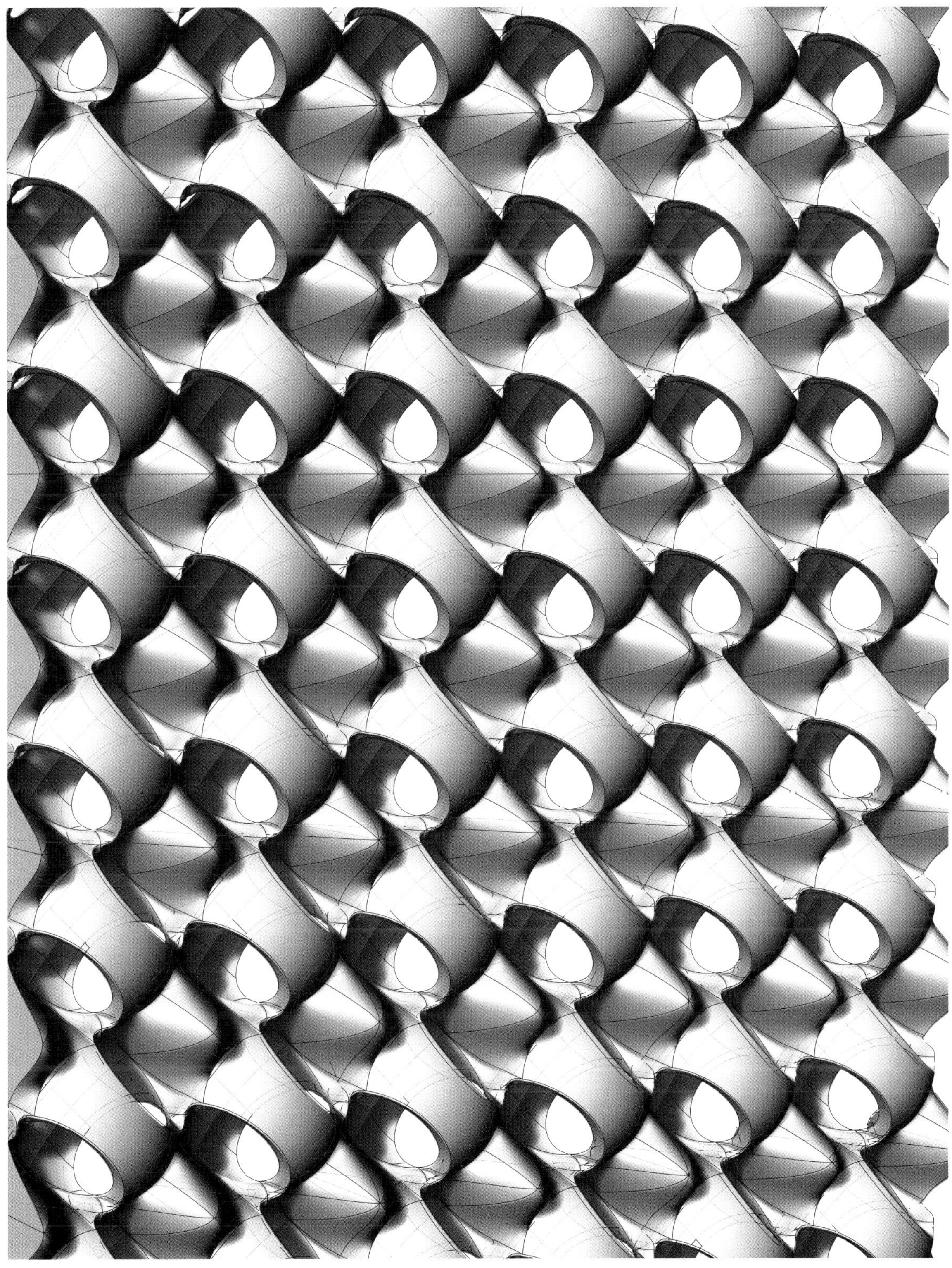

03_New Module 1.1_Design 1_Associative model 1 based_proliferated matrix_rendered perspective view

New Module 1.1: Associative model 1 based

This tile is selected from a larger sample of design iterations generated from associative model 1. The variable explored here relates to the vertical dimension of the transition saddle surfaces that bridge between handles.

The iteration represented here is the extreme end of this variable so as to illustrate an intensified instance of this range of transformation.

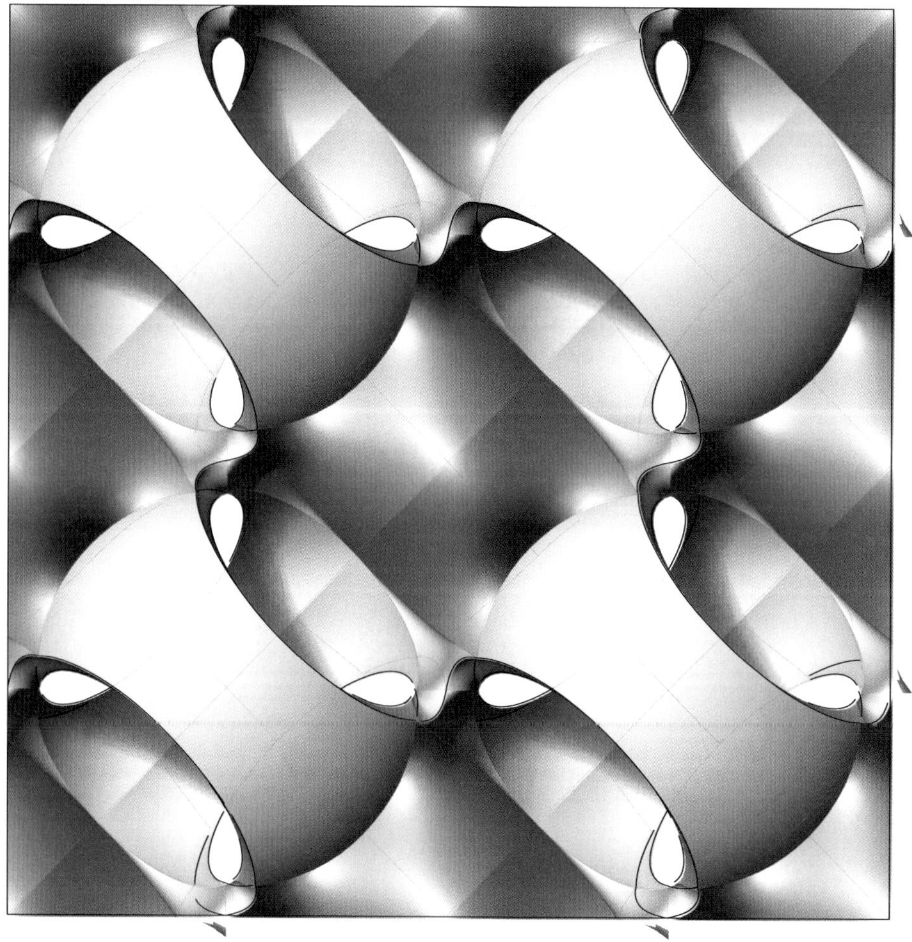

04_New Module 1.1: Associative model 1 based_ minimal proliferation_rendered frontal view

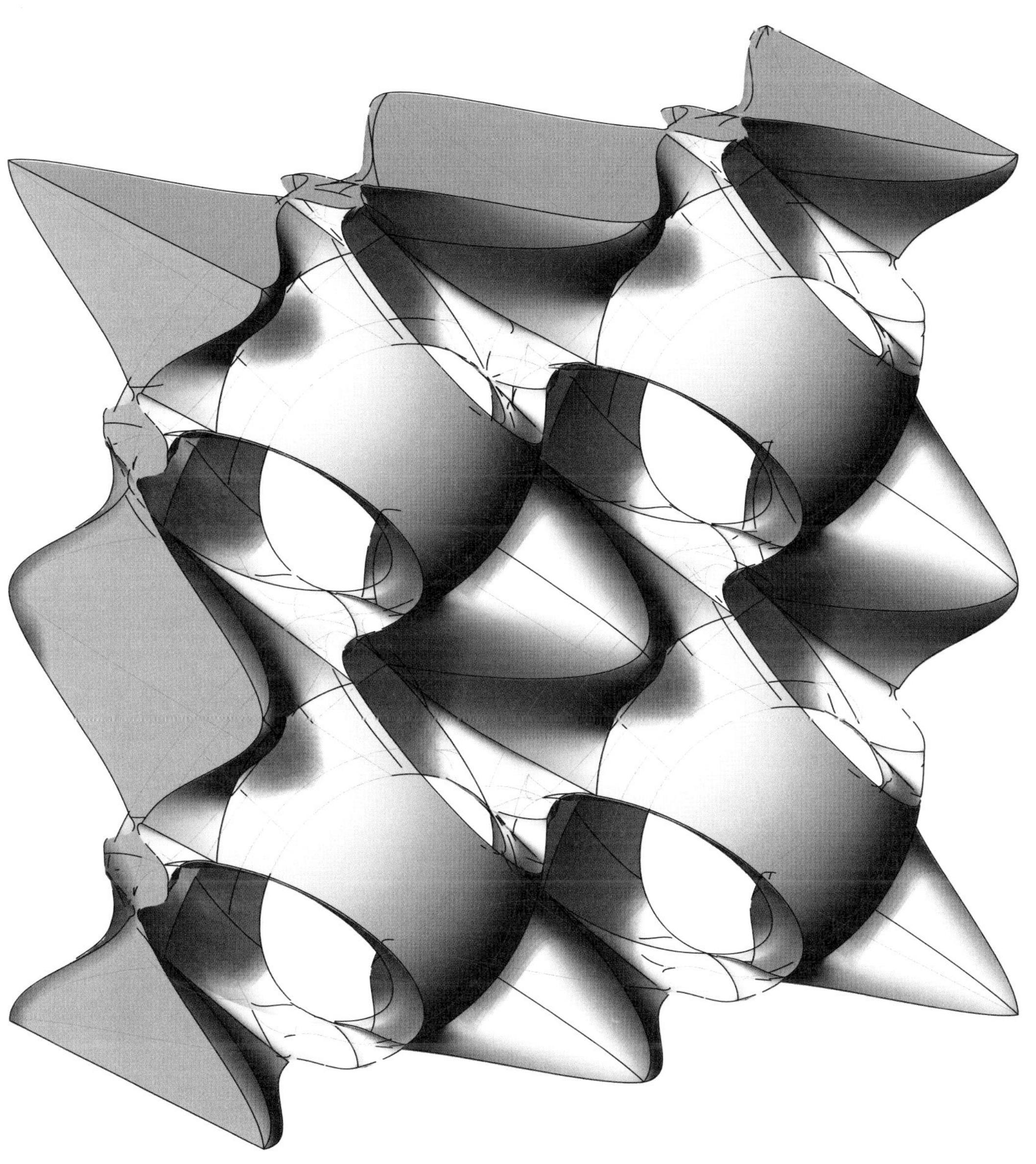

05_New Module 1.1: Associative model 1 based_minimal proliferation_rendered isometric view

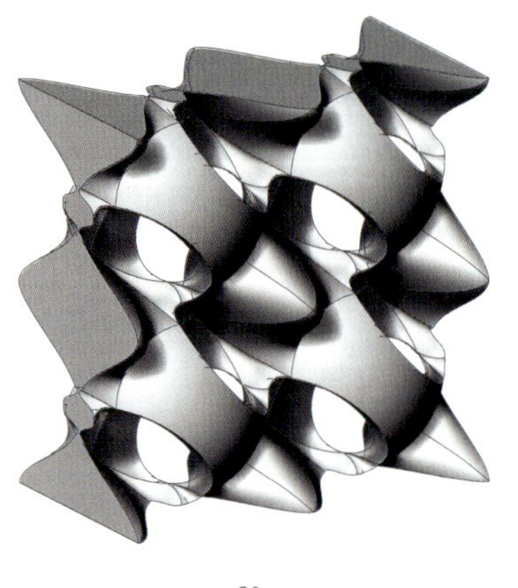

0°

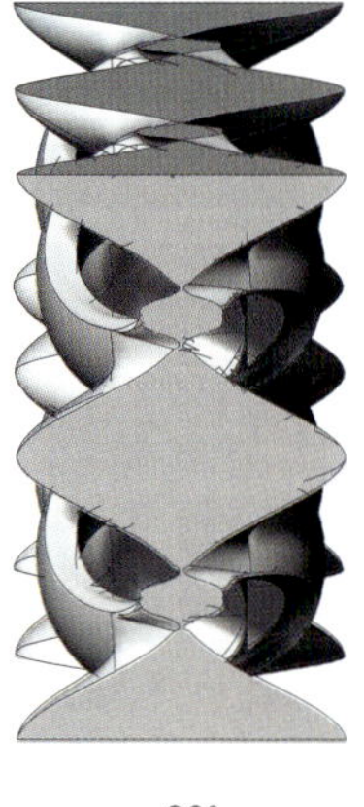

60°

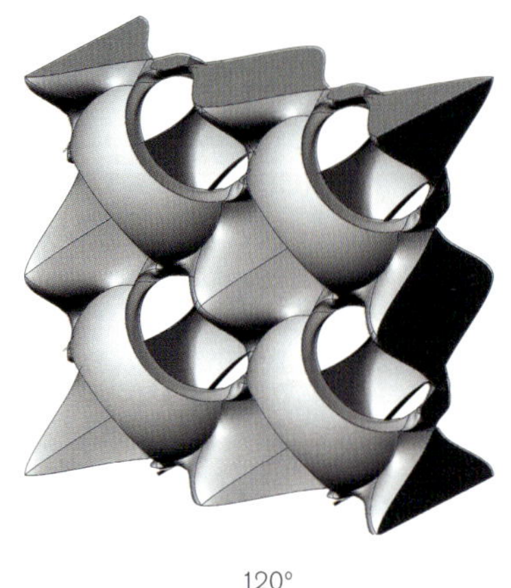

120°

06_New Module 1.1: Associative model 1 based_minimal proliferation_series of 60° rotations

The most prominent effect of this variable, as can be seen from the isometric view of a 3x3 matrix of tiles, is the formation of non-continuous surfaces between the handles. These, rather than achieving a smooth continuity between convex and concave handles, adds additional rippling in between modules.

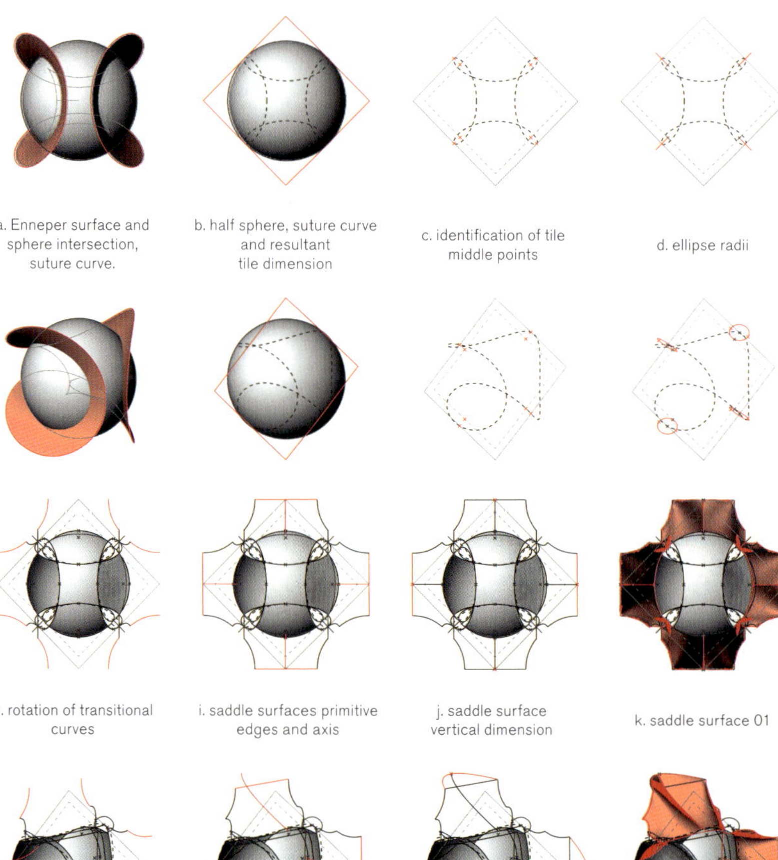

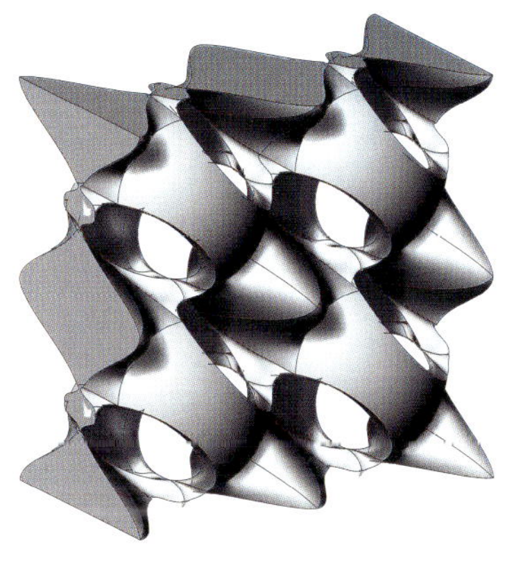

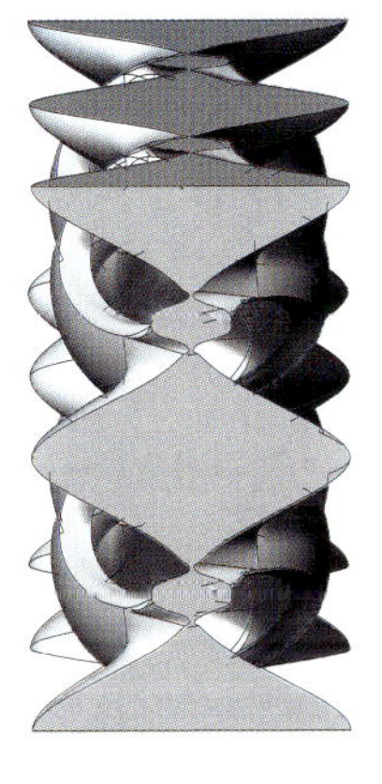

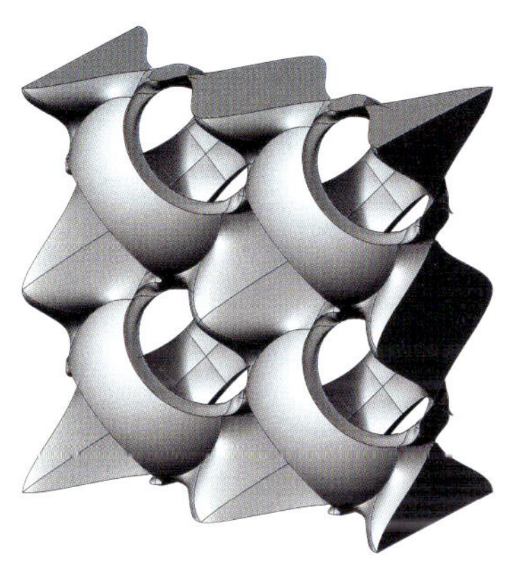

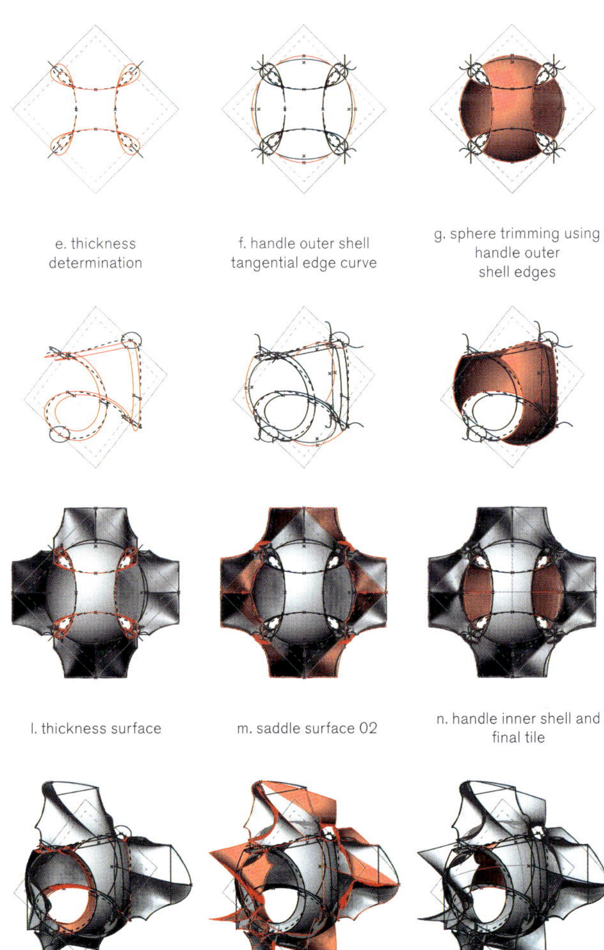

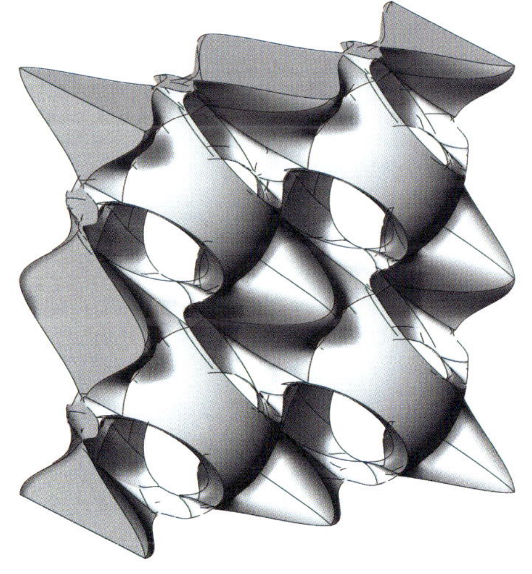

07-09_New Module 1.1: Associative model 1 based_tile construction

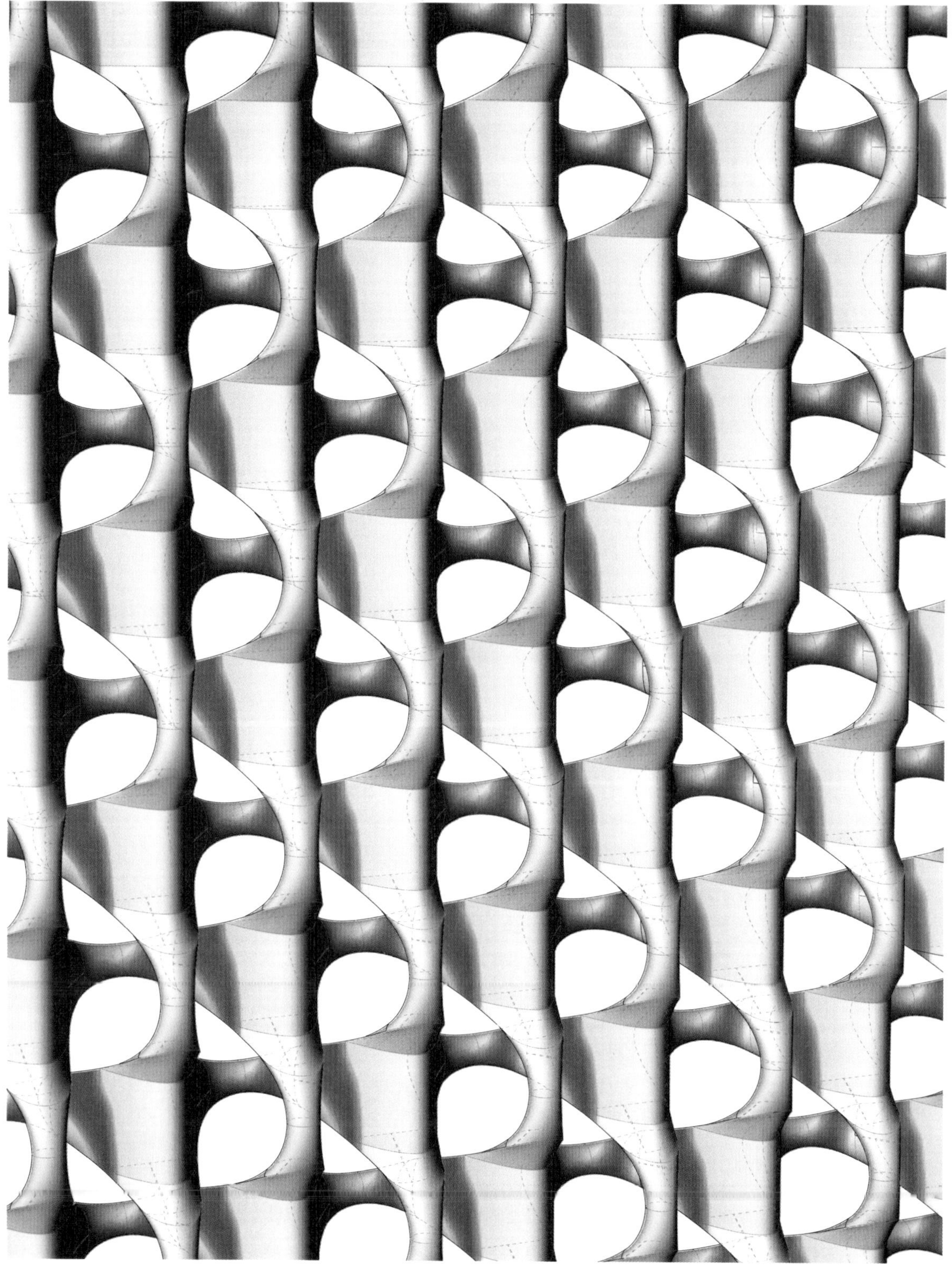

10_New Module 1.2: Associative model 5 based_proliferated matrix_rendered frontal view

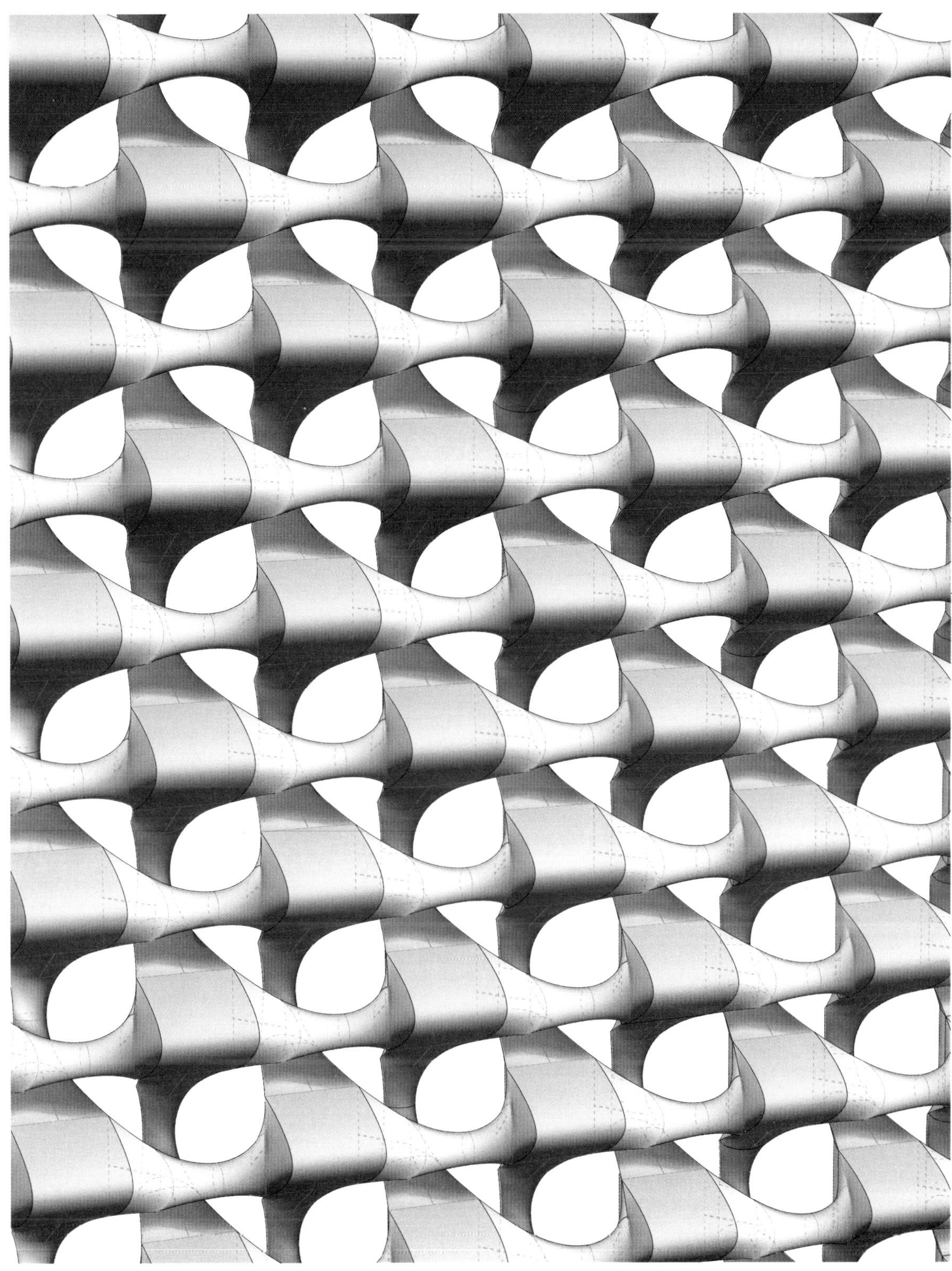

11_New Module 1.2: Associative model 5 based_proliferated matrix_rendered perspective view

New Module 1.2: Associative model 5 based

This iteration is generated from the associative model 5. The design is produced by determining the vertical dimension of the saddle surface curvature.
When this curvature is negligible, a revolved surface is achieved. This has a direct effect on the perception and symmetry of the tile.
The most extreme differentiation studied for this variable, produces a tile that, when proliferated, produces a distinctly vertical emphasis on one side and a horizontal patterning on the other. The symmetry which allows for a more uniform reading in its original form, is transformed into an asymmetrical module with a strong linear directionality.

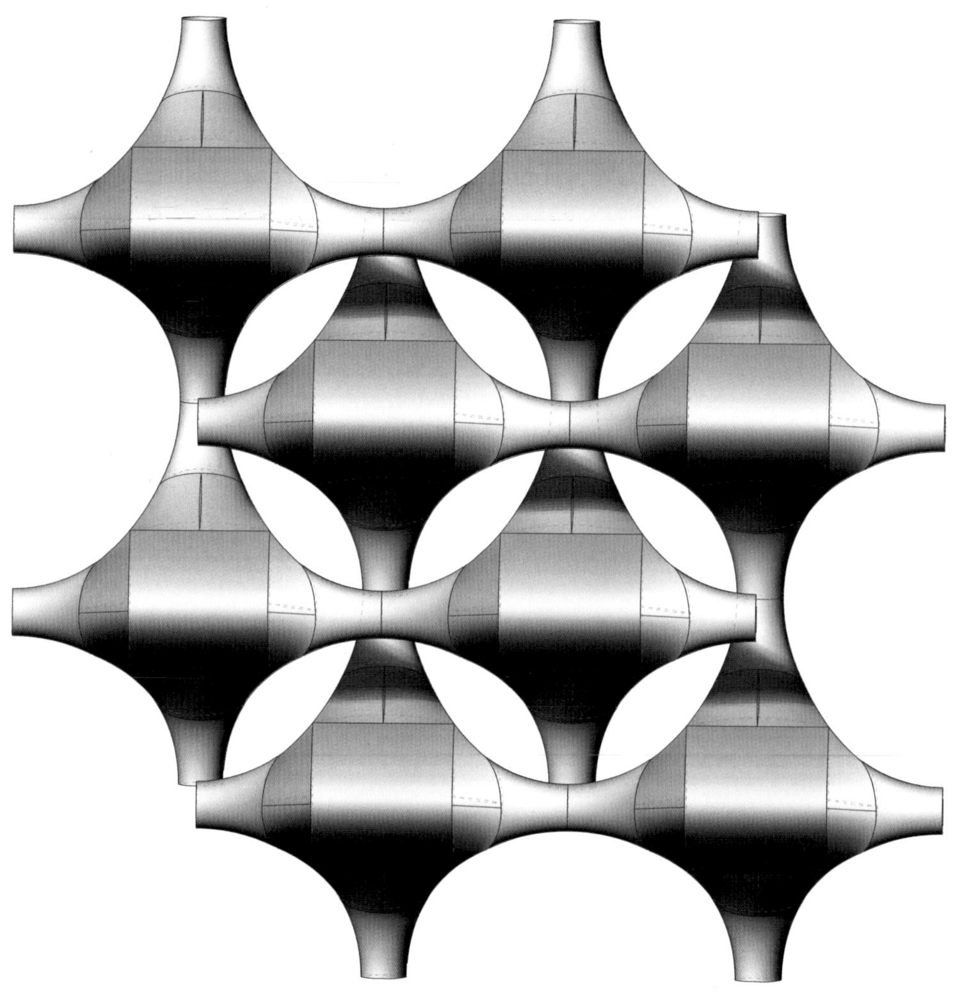

12_New Module 1.2: Associative model 5 based_minimal proliferation_rendered frontal view

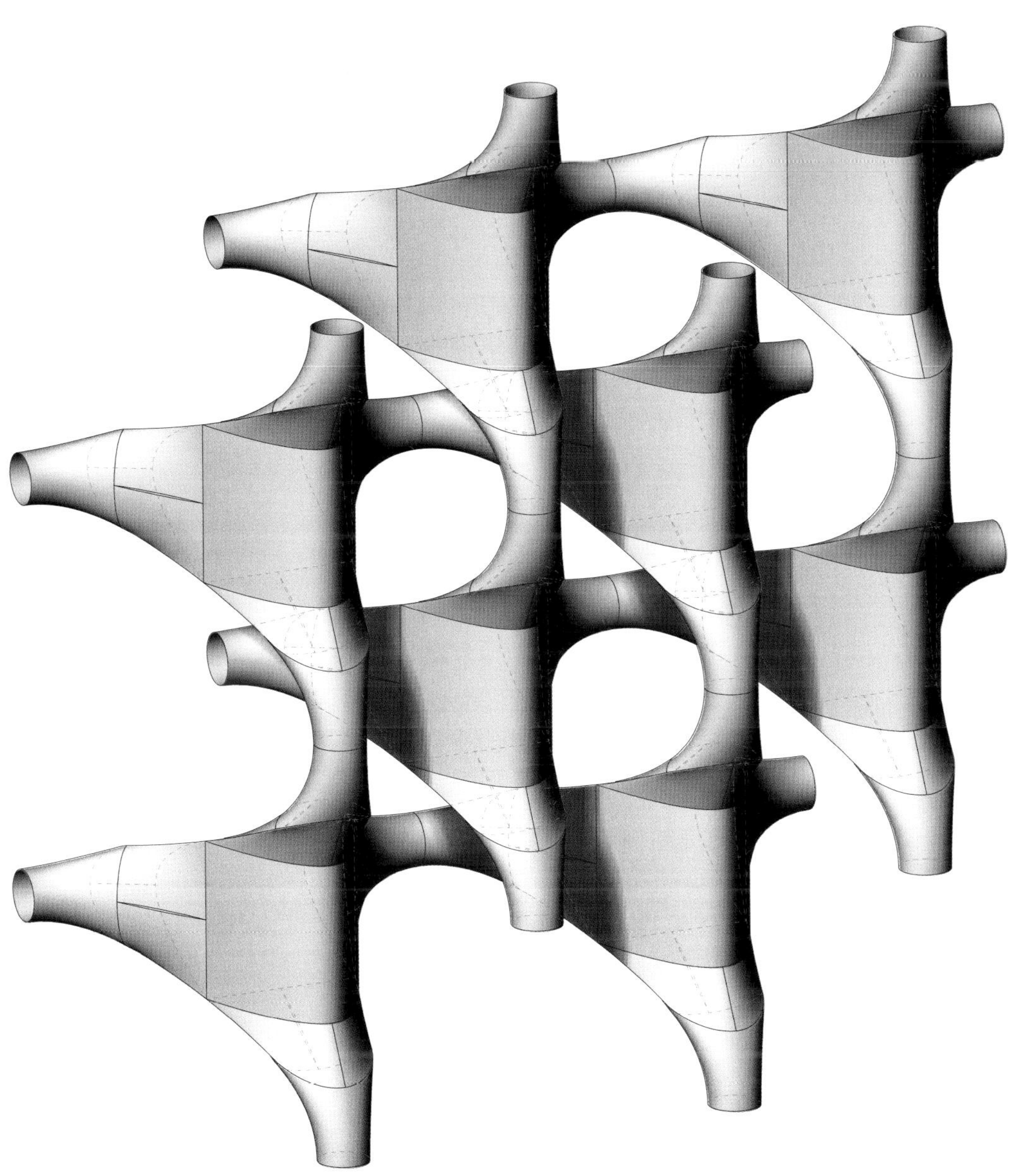

13_New Module 1.2: Associative model 5 based_minimal proliferation_rendered isometric view

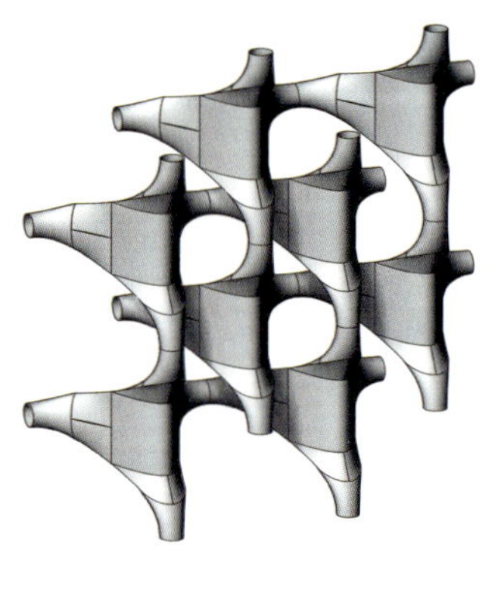

0°

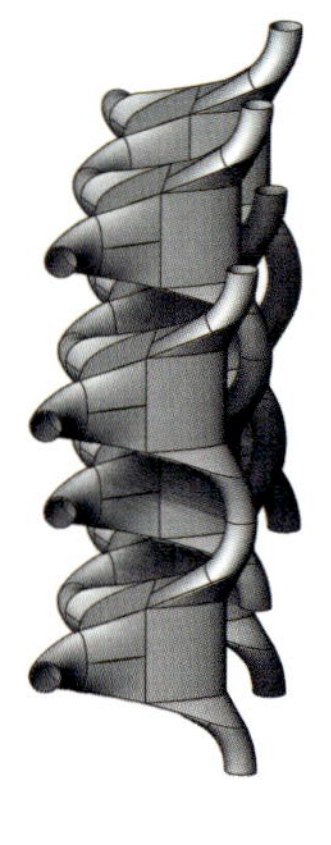

60°

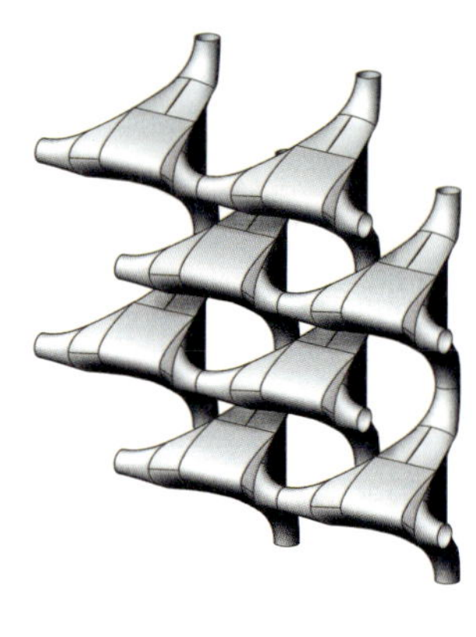

120°

14_New Module 1.2_Associative model 5 based_minimal proliferation_series of 60° rotations

The construction of this iteration is produced from the associative model 5. The spectrum of variables in this particular model is reduced, however the transformation of the design exhibits qualities which can be seen to be significantly different from the original model.

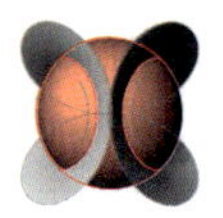

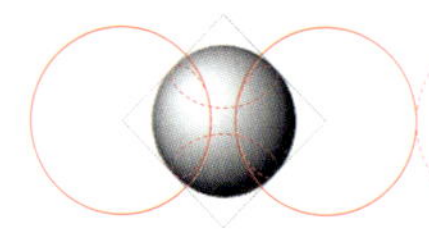

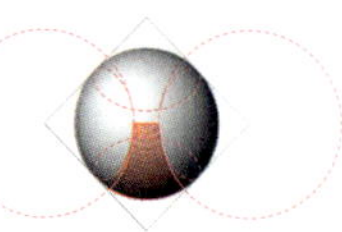

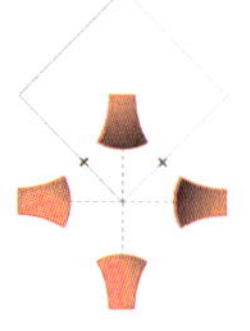

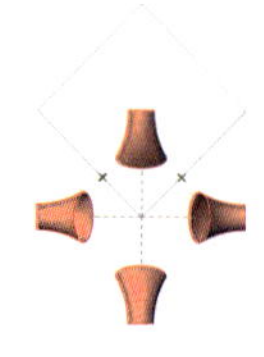

a. Enneper surface and sphere intersection, suture curve

b. hald sphere and lateral circles

c. trimming of sphere with lateral circles

d. tangent line from tile corner to resultant sphere sector axis

e. array of surface around tile corner

f. surface volume, surface of revolution of circular section

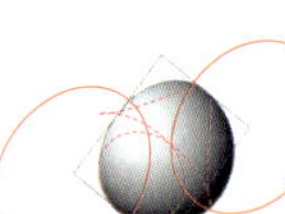

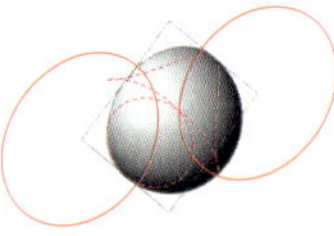

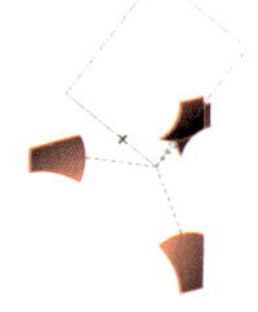

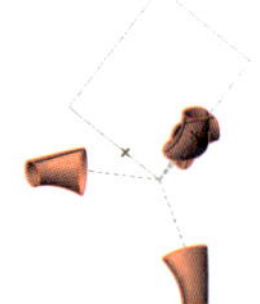

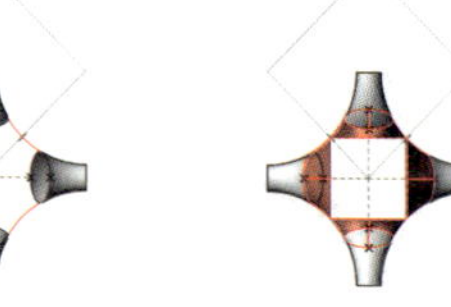

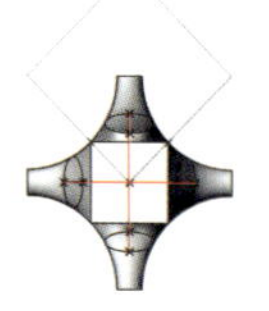

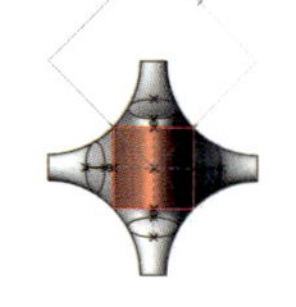

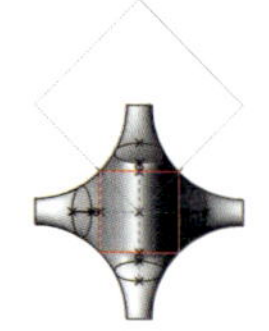

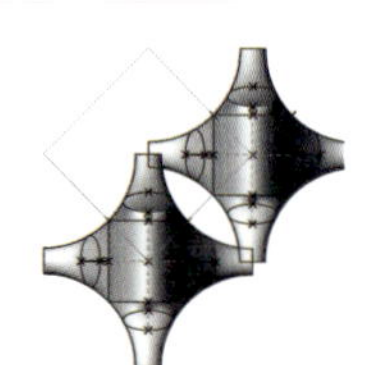

g transitional surfaces edges

h. transitional surfaces

i. saddle surface edge curves

j. saddle surface 01

k. saddle surface 02

l. proliferation of module within tile

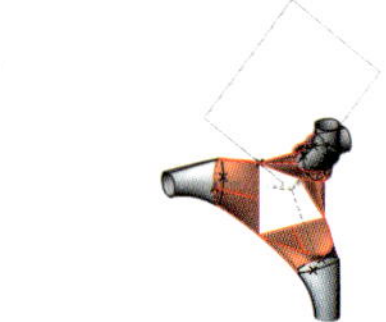

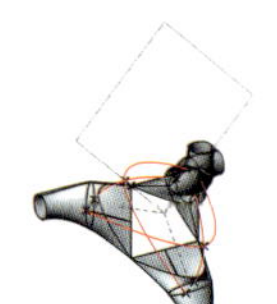

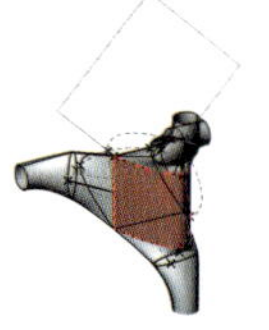

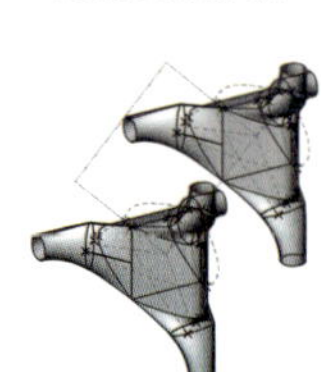

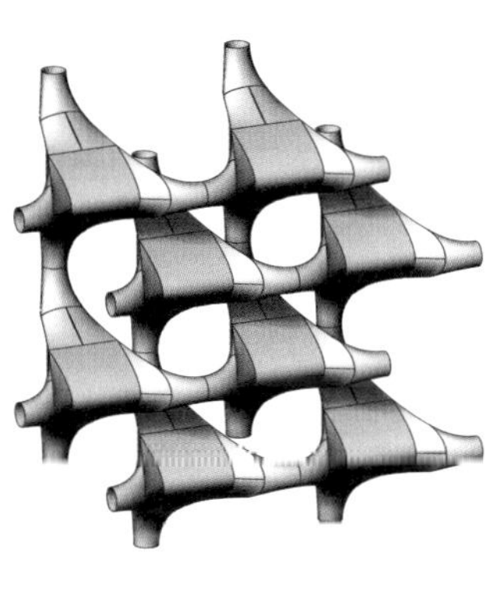

180°

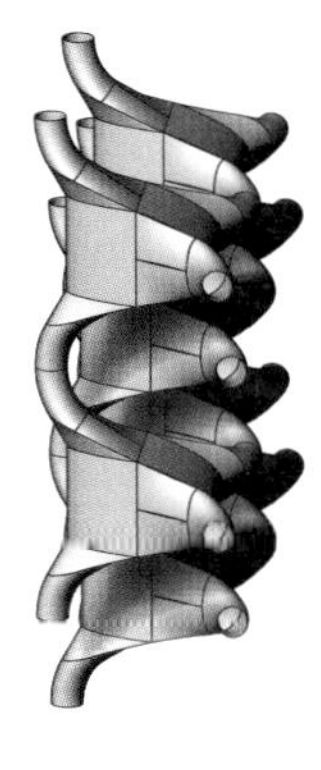

240°

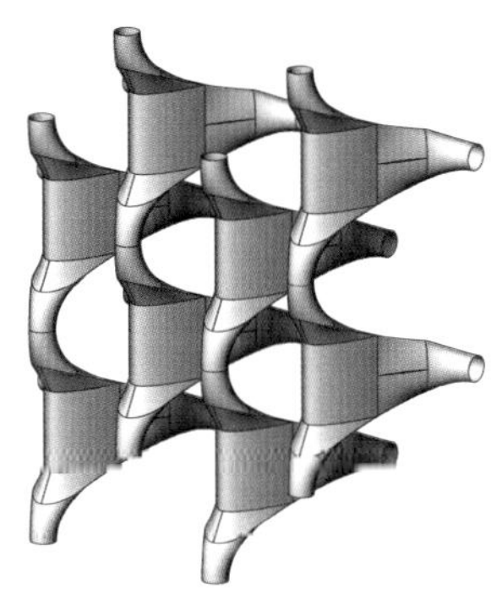

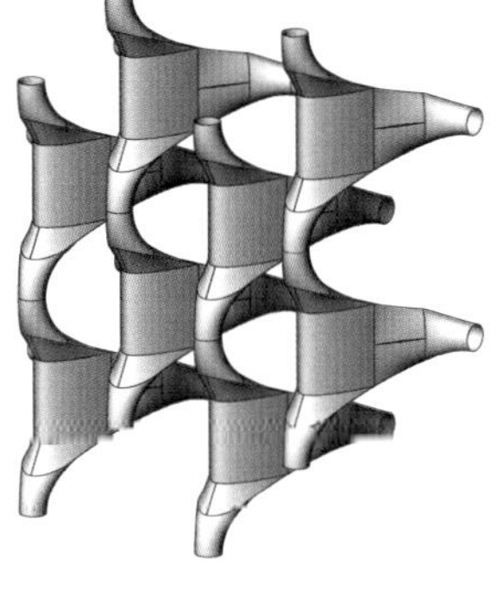

300°

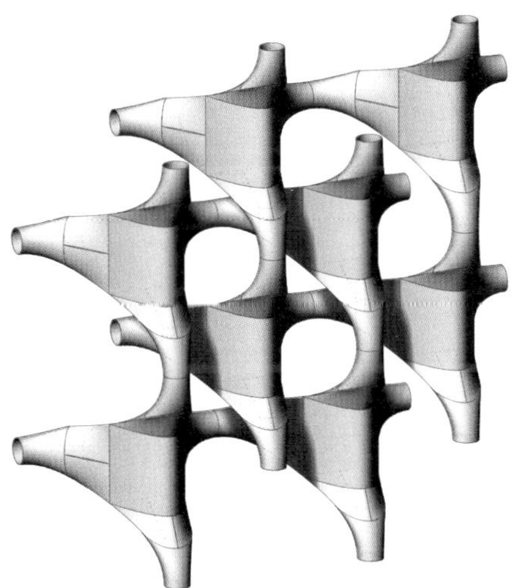

15-17_New Module 1.2_Associative model 5 based_tile construction

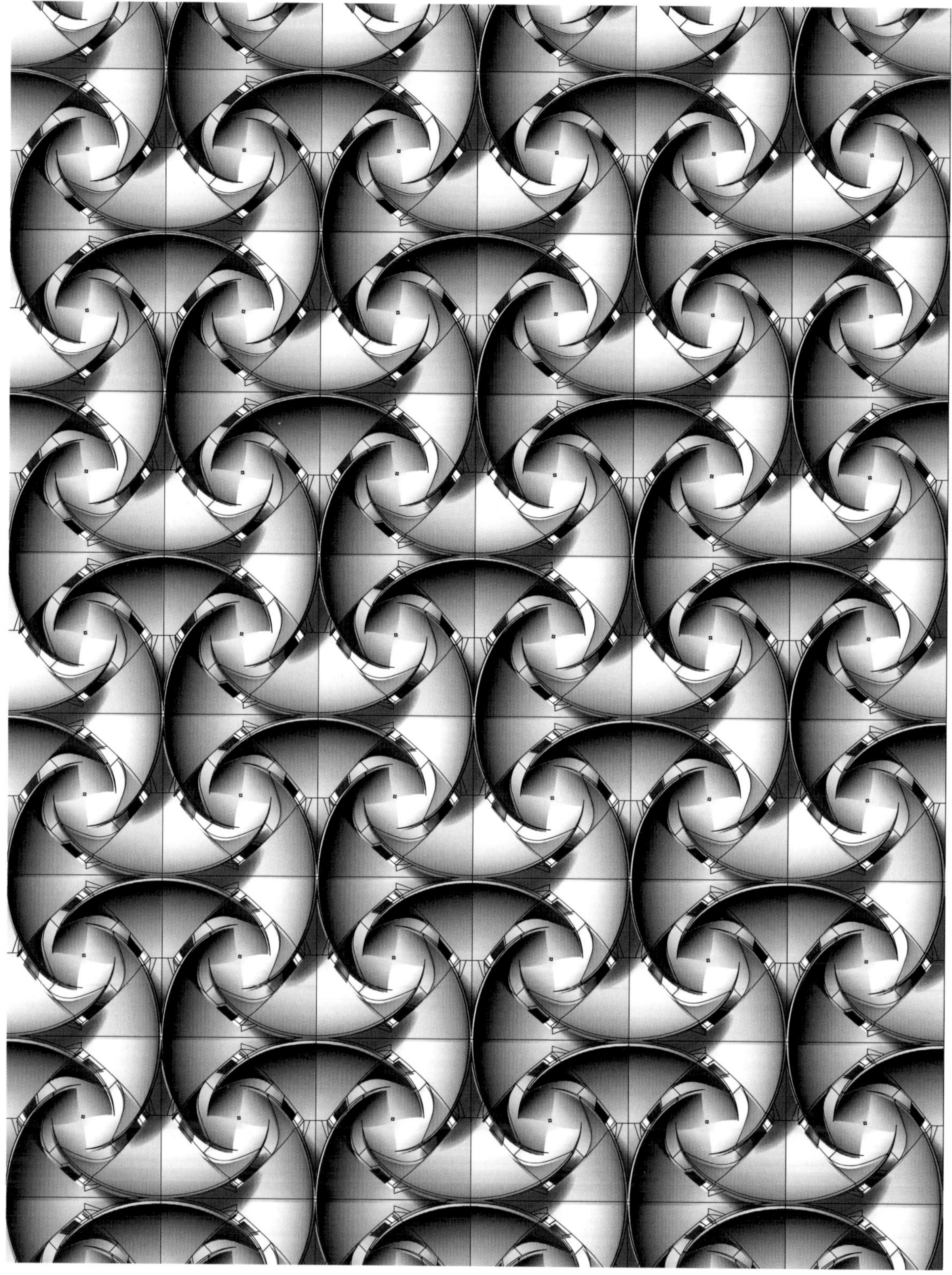

18_New Module 1.3_Associative model 7 based_proliferated matrix_rendered frontal view

19_New Module 1.3_Associative model 7 based_proliferated matrix_rendered perspective view

New module 1.3: Associative model 7 based_01

This design is an iteration produced by setting the highest possible value for the third variable which controls the scale of the lateral circles of the associative model 7. These lateral circles are the second set of circles produce the transitional surfaces with the central circles to define the tile. Changing the radius of either or both sets of circles would impact directly on the curvature of the transitional surfaces constructed between them. In this tile, lateral circles are made to be significantly larger than the original Intercircles tile. This means that surfaces do not maintain the same proportion as the central circle, but rather self-intersect as they become larger.

20_New module 1.3: Associative model 7 based_01_ minimal proliferation_rendered frontal view

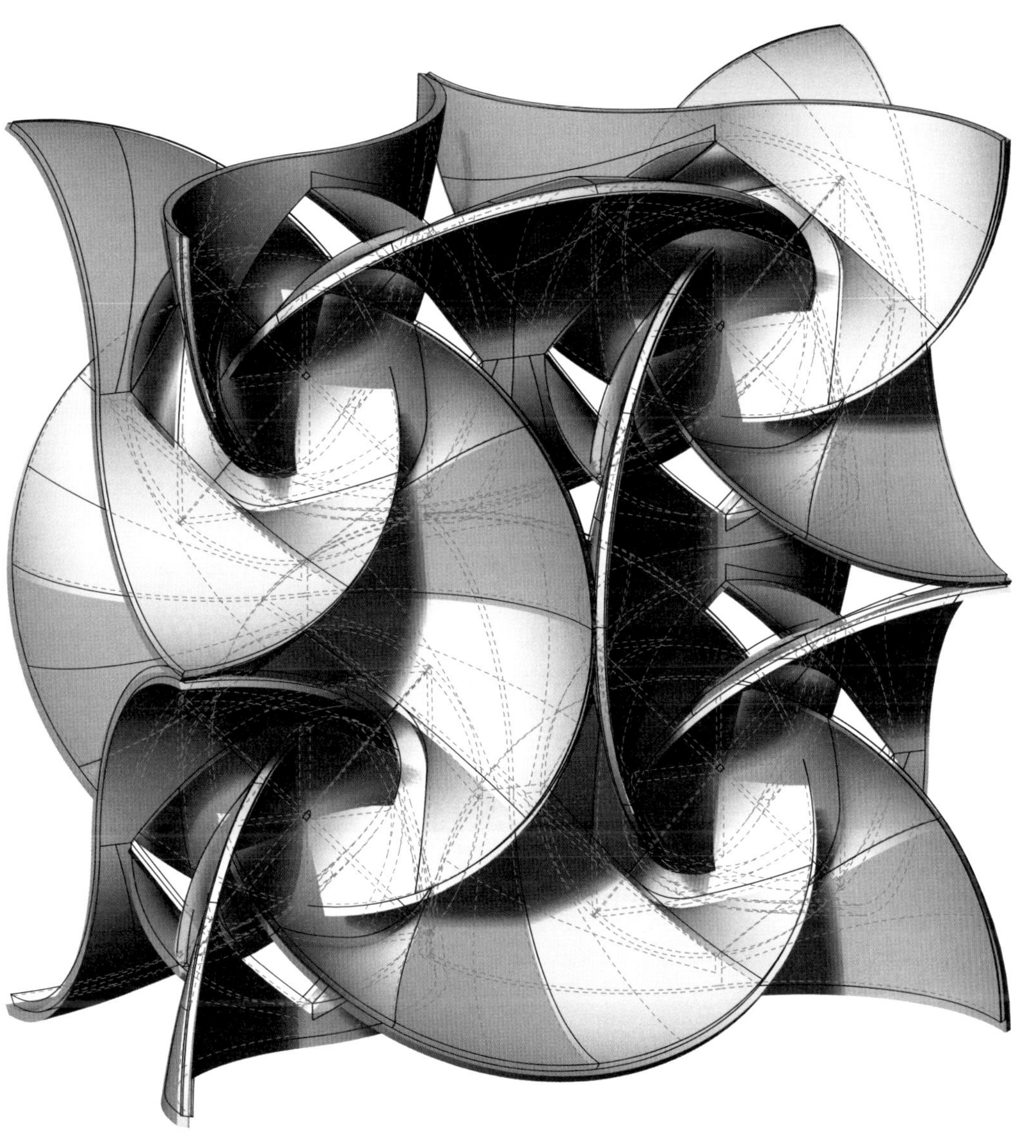

21_New module 1.3: Associative model 7 based 01 minimal proliferation_rendered isometric view

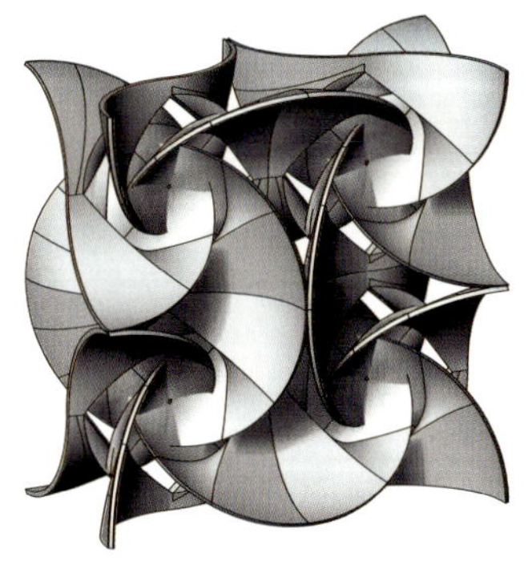

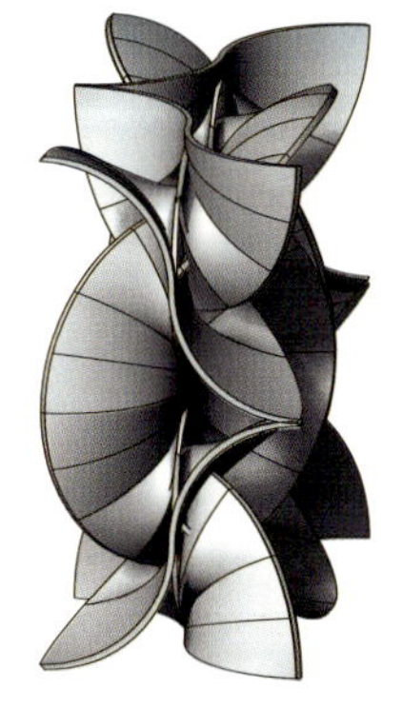

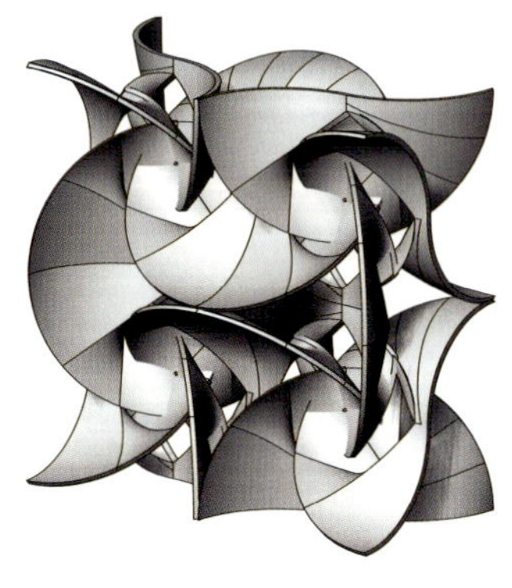

22_New Module 1.3_Associative model 7_minimal proliferation_series of 60° rotations

This first design in this series varies the lateral circle radius of the associative model 7. The construction below shows how this variation transforms the original model form and enlarges the surfaces to the point of self-intersection. The tile is assembled by mirroring a quarter of the tile along both orthogonal axes of symmetry.

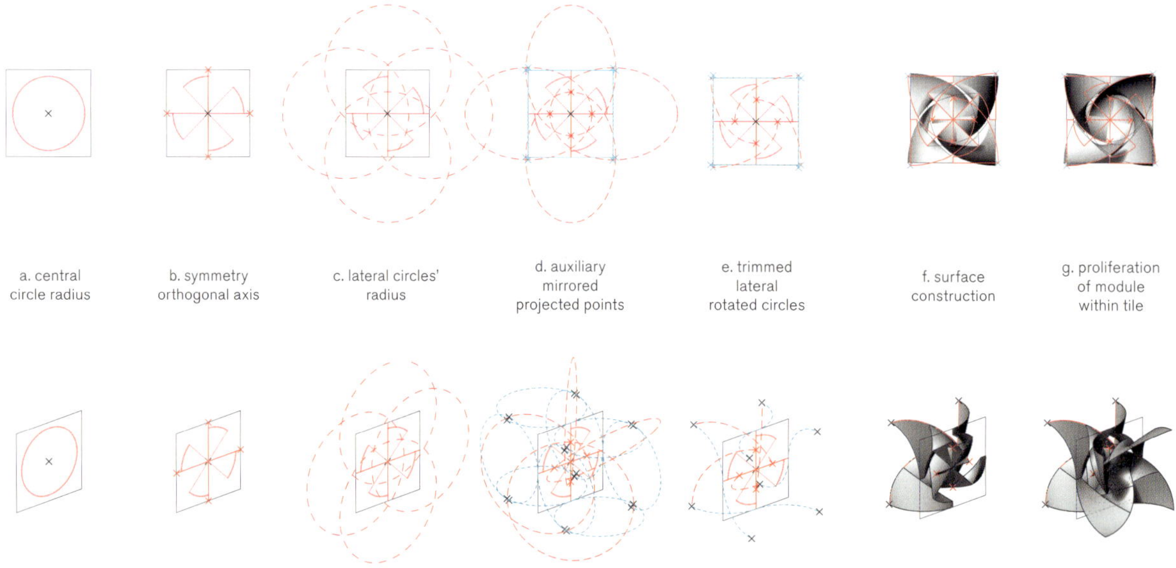

23_New Module 1.3_Associative model 7 based_01_tle construction

24_3x3 matrix_3d printed model_elevation

25_3x3 matrix_3d printed model_45° perspective

27_minimal proliferation_isometric view

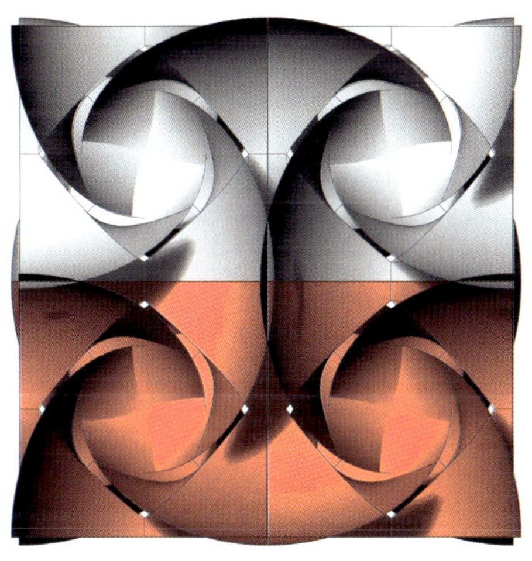

26_minimal proliferation_elevation

Top images show a 3d printed 3x3 matrix model for this New Module design. The resultant matrix is a very dense and opaque surface.

Bottom images show a 2x2 matrix as a minimal proliferation of this module. Modules are reflected and continuity is guaranteed.

28_New Module 1.4_Associative model 7 nased_02_proliferated matrix_rendered frontal view

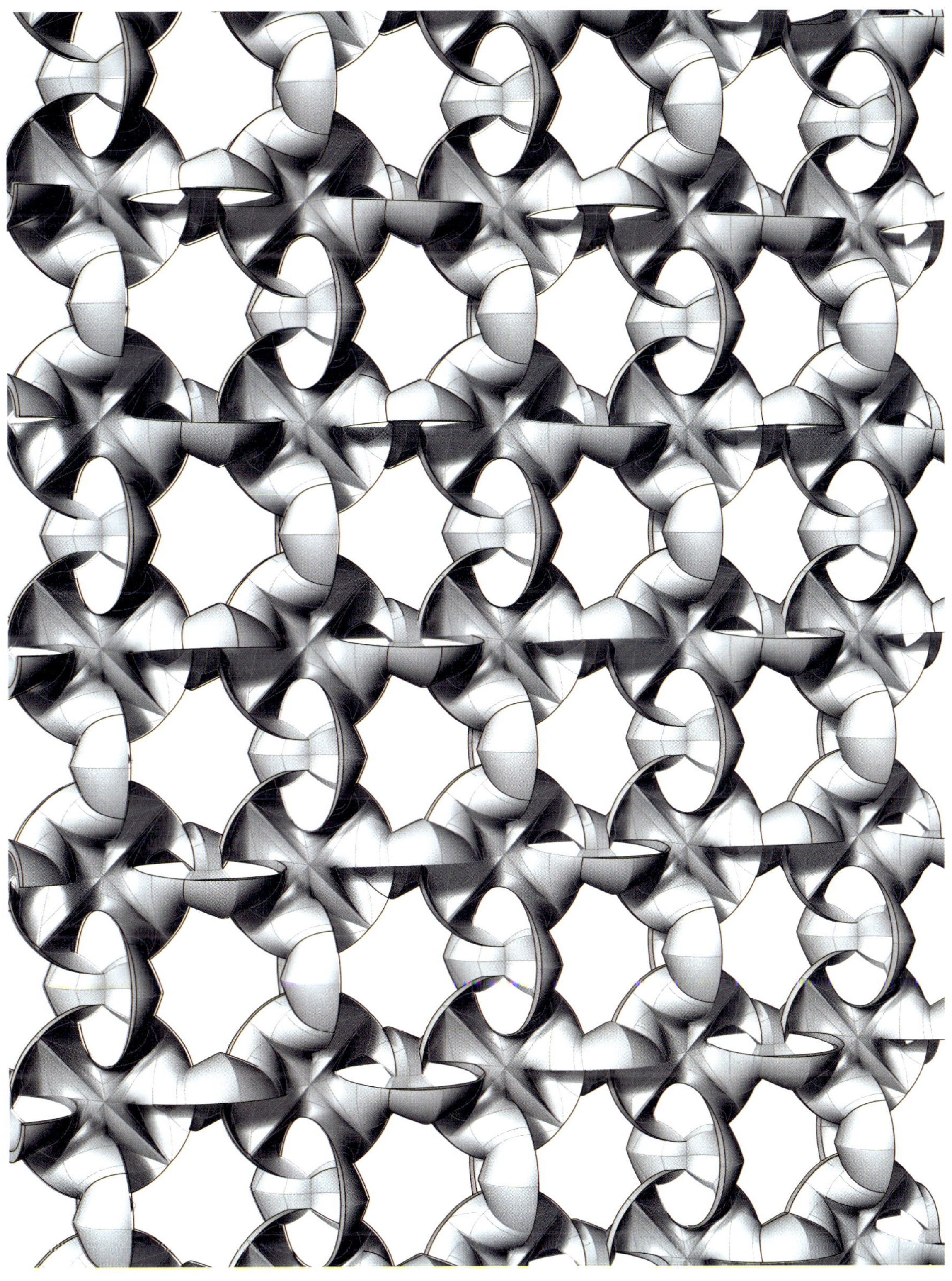

29_New Module 1.4_Associative model 7 nased_02_proliferated matrix_rendered perspective view

New Module 1.4: Associative model 7 based_02

This second design is another differentiation of the associative model 7.
The rotation of the lateral circles which define transitional surfaces with a set of central circles, influences the curvature of these surfaces.

This iteration is set to the largest radius in the model and rotated 90º, producing a significant formal departure from the original model. The lateral circles are oriented perpendicular to the central circle and the surfaces are more abrupt.

30_New Module 1.4: Associative model 7 based_02_minimal proliferation_rendered frontal view

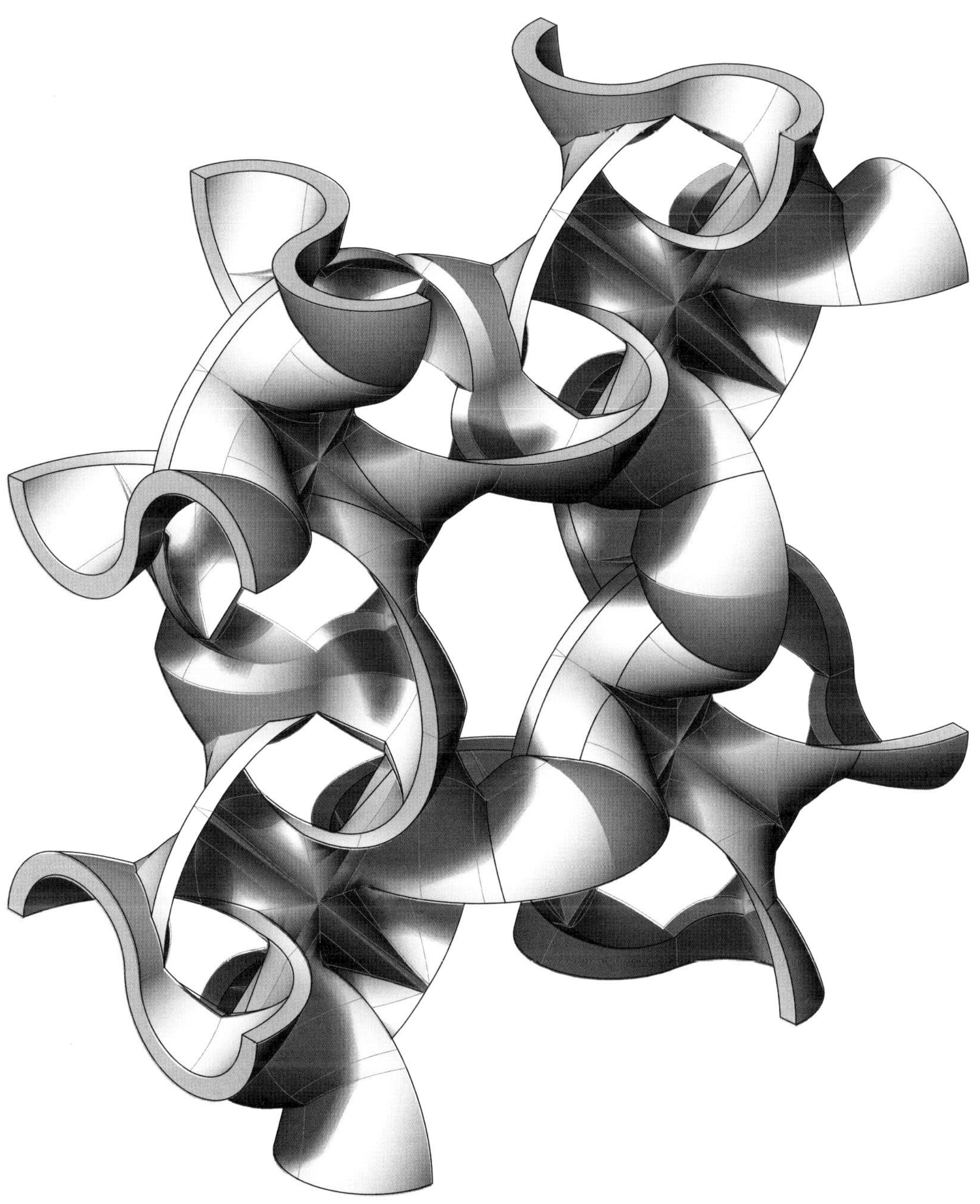

31_New Module 1.4: Associative model 7 based_02_minimal proliferation_rendered isometric view

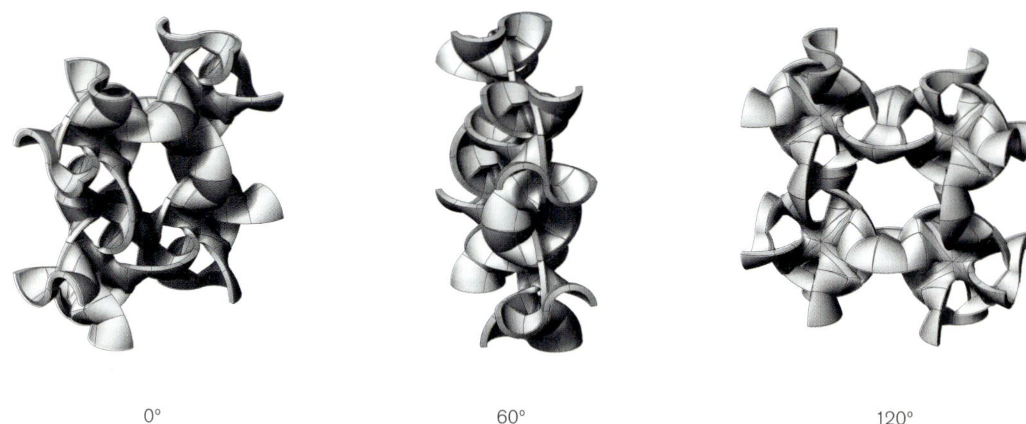

32_New Module 1.4: Associative Model 7 based_02_minimal proliferation_series of 60° rotations

This second design is also generated from a transformation of the associative model 7. This is produced through the differentiation of the lateral circle rotation. The construction diagram below shows how this variation differs from the original model, exacerbating the steepness of the surfaces. The tile is assembled by mirroring a quarter of the tile along both orthogonal axes of symmetry.

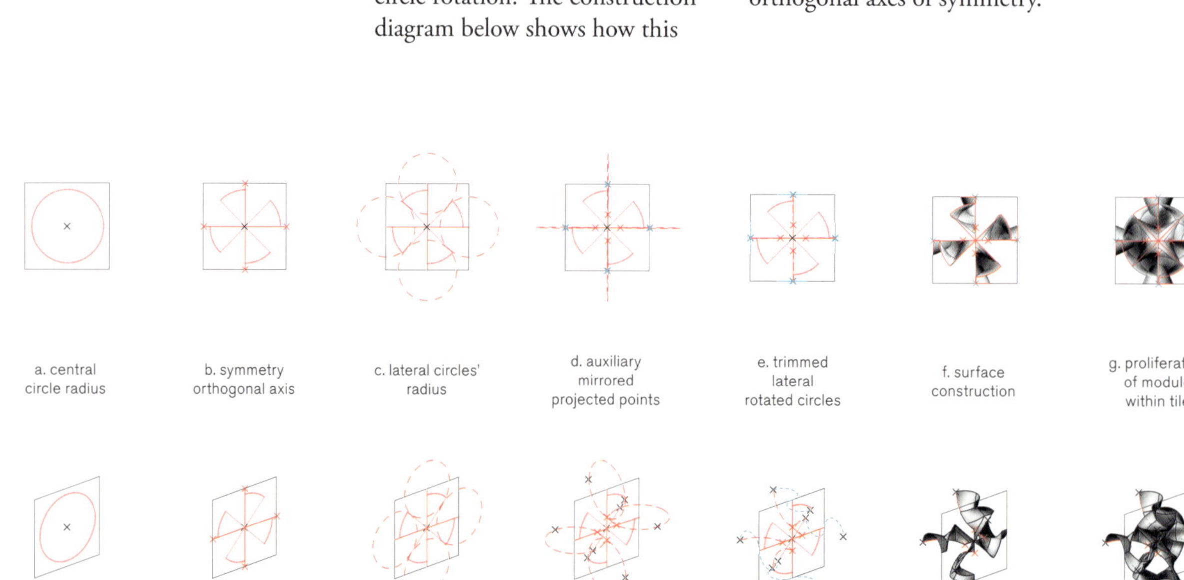

33_New Module 1.4: Associative Model 7 based_02_construction of tile from Intercircles associative model construction and final tile_ elevation and isometric views

34_minimal proliferation_3d printed model_elevation

35_minimal proliferation_3d printed model_45° perspective

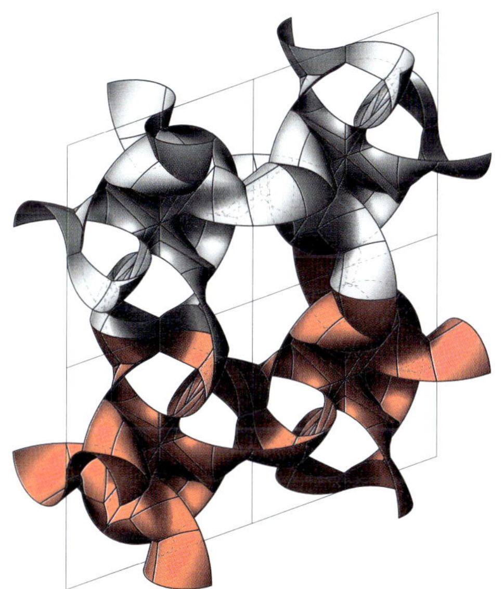

37_minimal proliferation_isometric view

36_module_elevation

Top images show a 3d printed 3x3 matrix model for this New Module design. The resultant matrix is a more permeable one than the previous variations.

Bottom images show a 2x2 matrix as a minimal proliferation of this module. Modules are reflected and continuity is guaranteed.

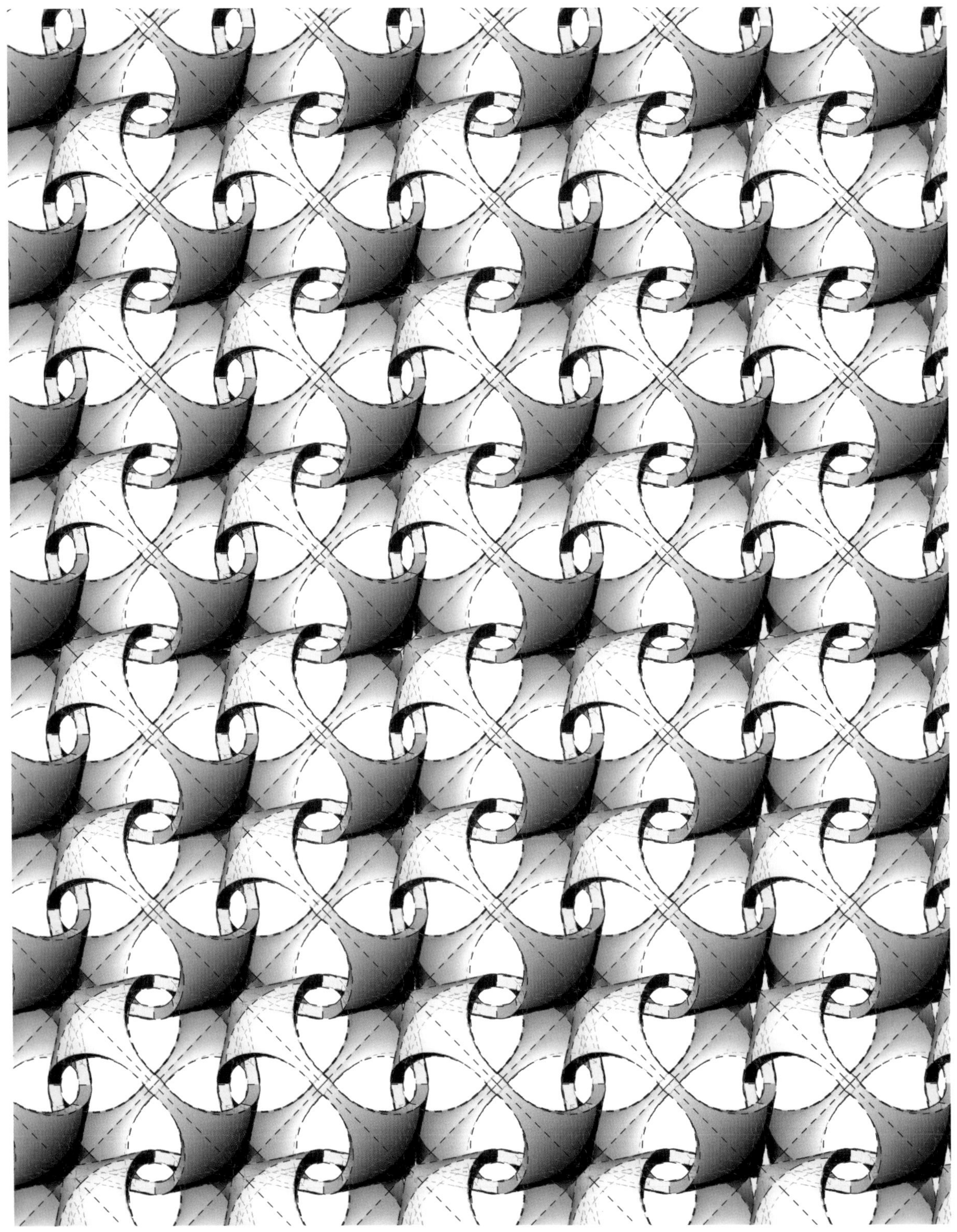

38_New Module_2.1_Intertwine_01_proliferated matrix_
rendered frontal view

39_New Module_2.1_Intertwine_01_proliferated matrix_
rendered perspective view

New module 2.1: Intertwine_01

This pair of designs is called Intertwine because of the formal qualities that the translation of the sphere produces in the module that is generated from the model. Intertwine has eight sides which expand outside the original square boundary and intertwine with its adjacent module.

This is produced by the misalignment between the sphere and Enneper surfaces, generating an asymmetric suture curve. This is also achieved by a translation in the y-axis. When the half-handle module is constructed and rotated along the center of the tile, the tile is created.

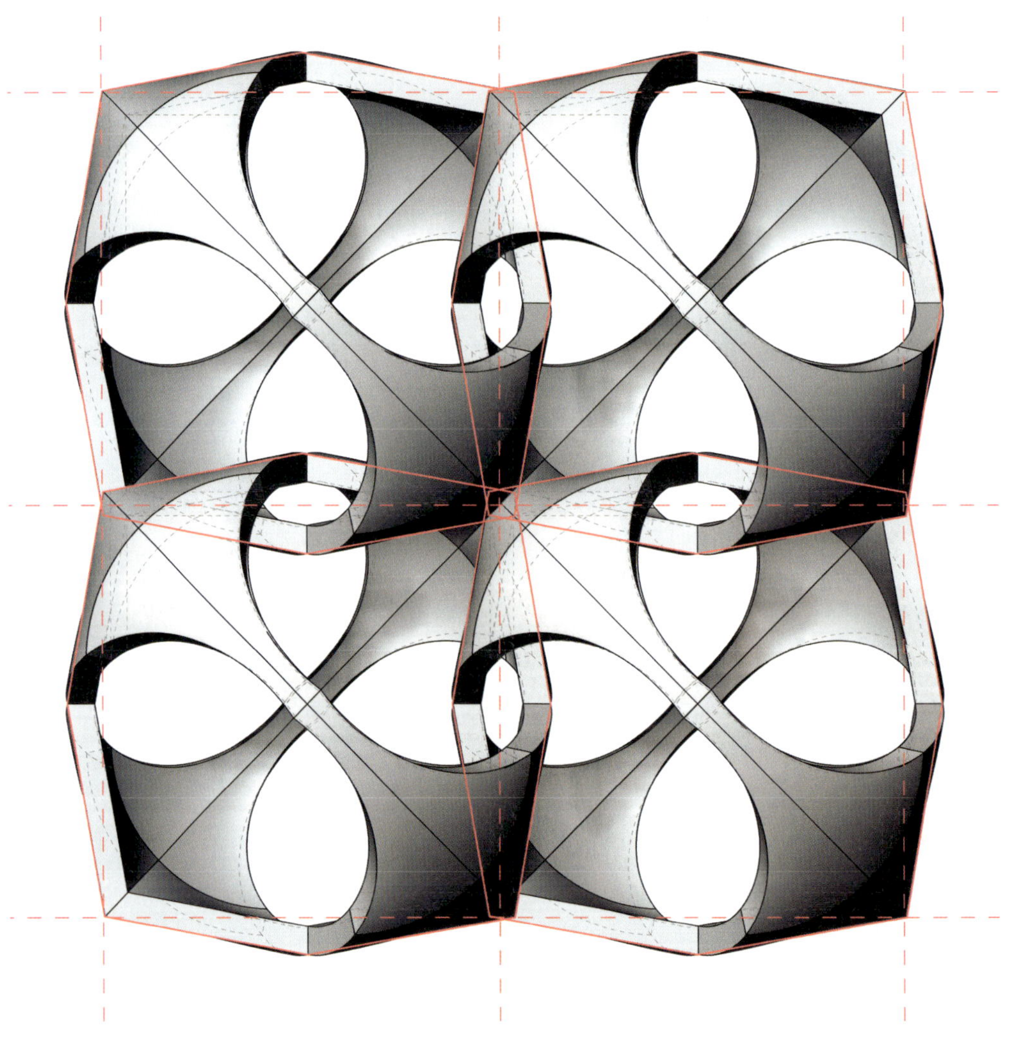

40_New Module_2.1_Intertwine_01_minimal proliferation_ rendered frontal view

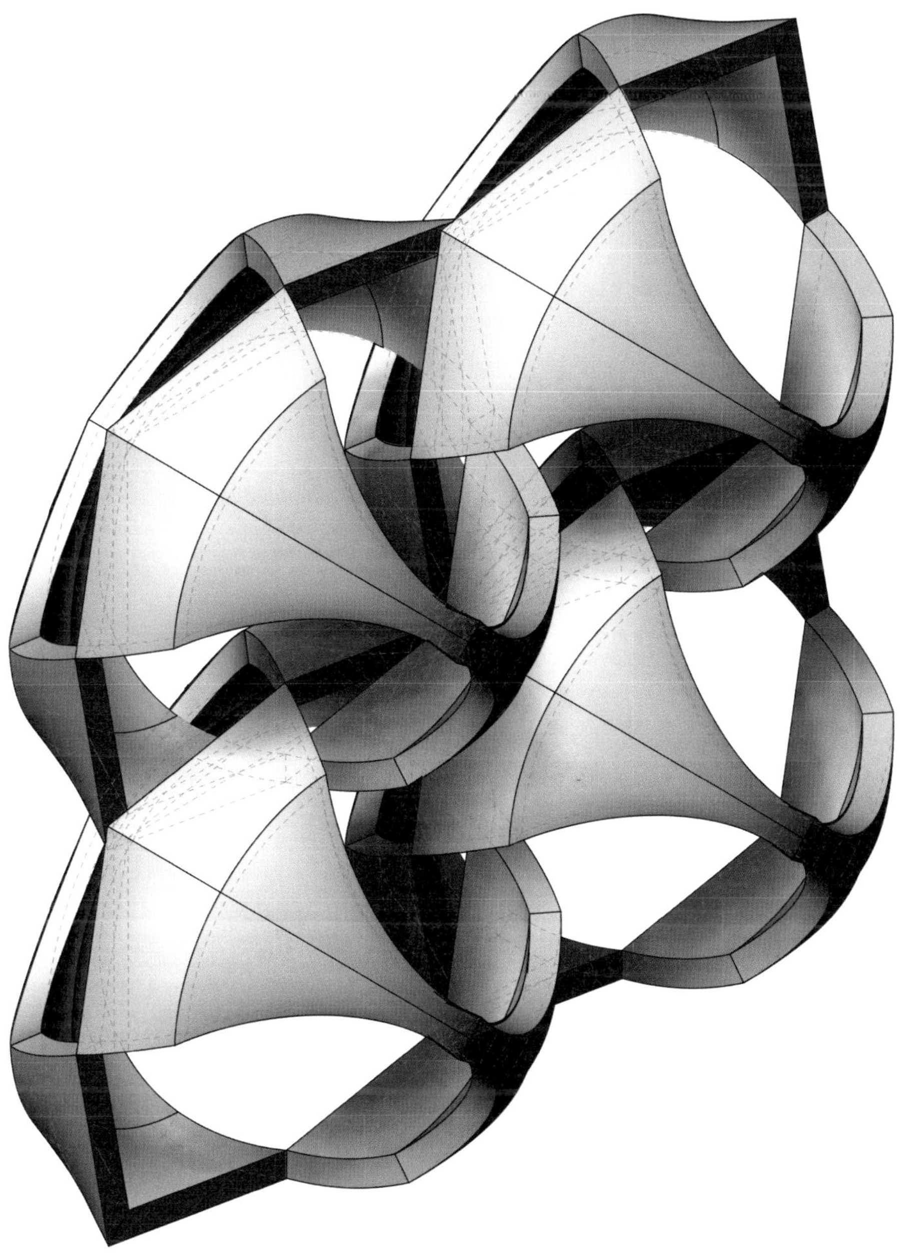

41_New Module_2.1_Intertwine_01_minimal proliferation_
rendered isometric view

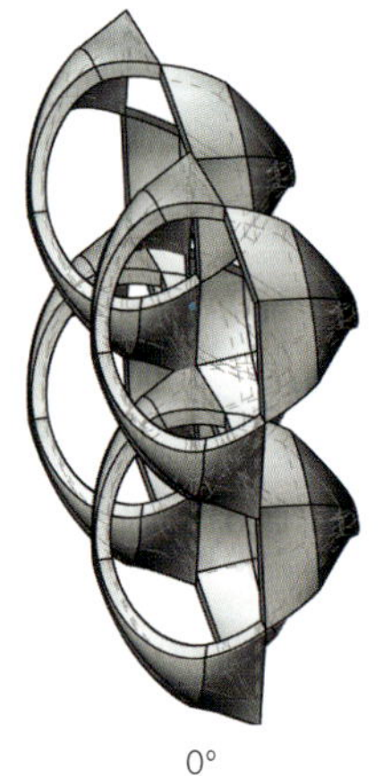

0°

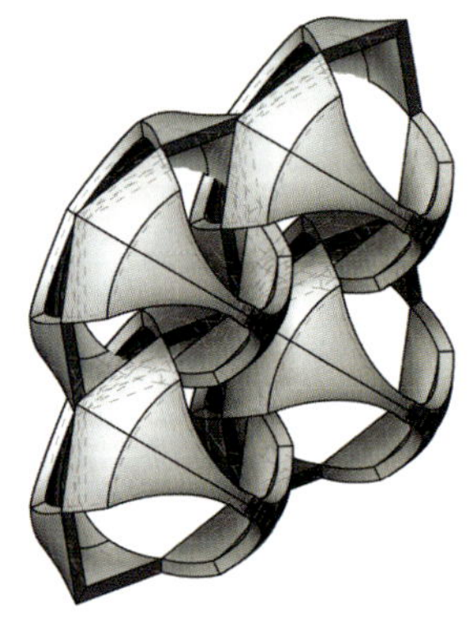

60°

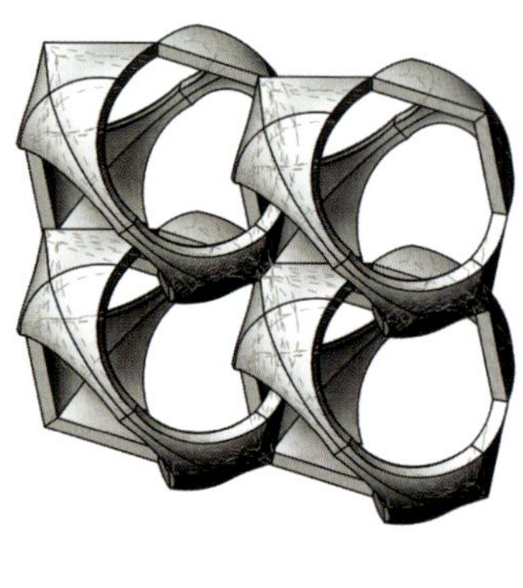

120°

42_New Module 2.1_Intertwine 1_minimal proliferation_series of 60º rotations

The design iterations in this section are based on transforming the associative model 1 by changing the relationship between the regular Enneper surface and the intersecting sphere is moved along the y-axis. This misalignment produces an asymmetric suture curve as shown below, which is then used to a produce a tile following the construction process of the model. The result is a tile with an octagonal border that overlaps with adjacent units when the tile is proliferated. This produces an effect of intertwining; as concave surfaces are paired to convex handles.

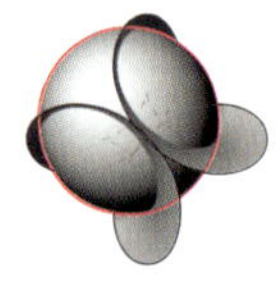

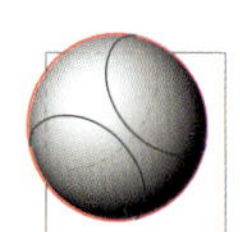

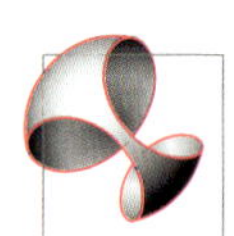

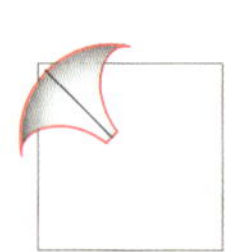

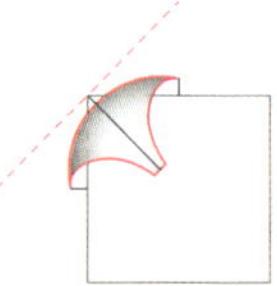

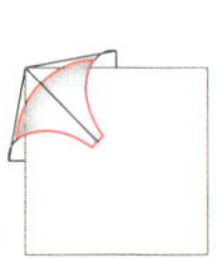

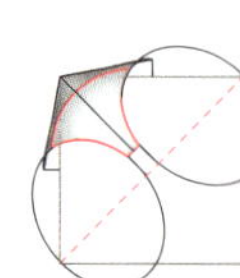

a. Enneper minimal surface and sphere.

b. Resulting intersection (suture curve)

c. Trimmed sphere using suture curve

d. Half-handle-like surface

e. Definition of perpendicular axis to corner point

f. Construction of edges

g. Auxiliary circles handle extensio

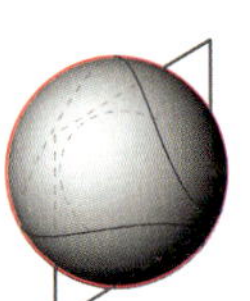

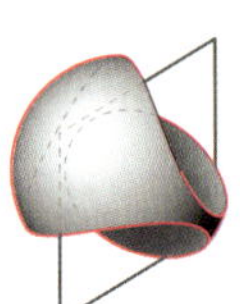

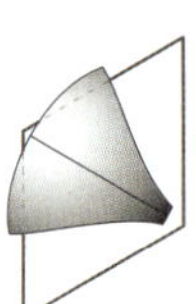

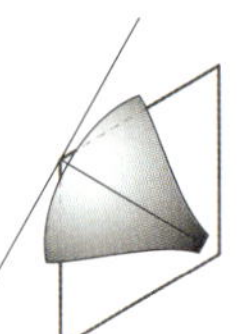

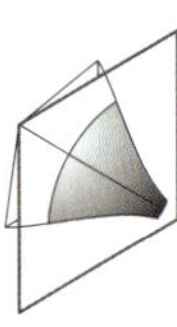

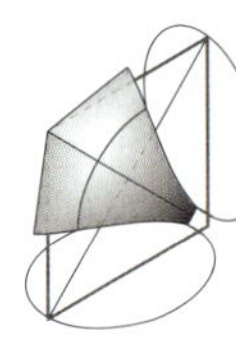

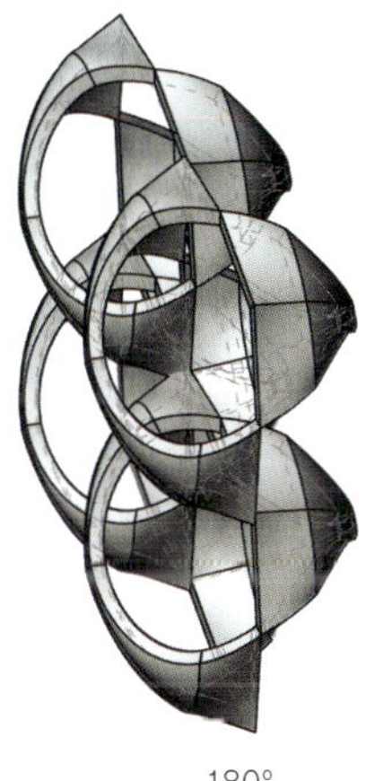

180°

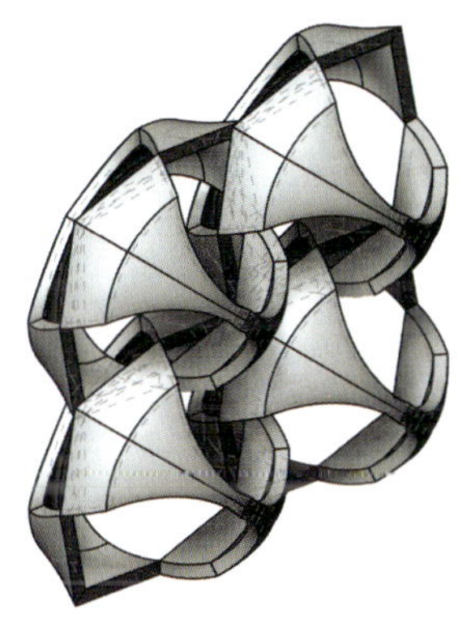

240°

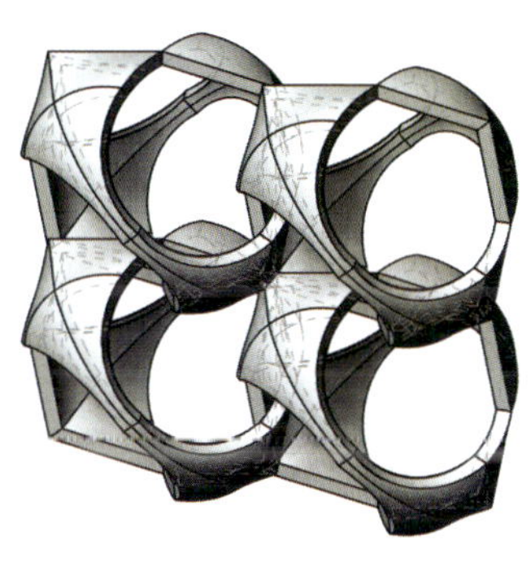

300°

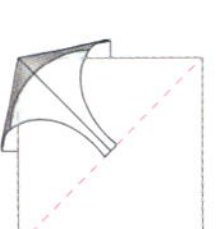

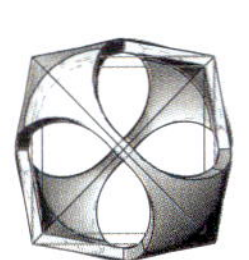

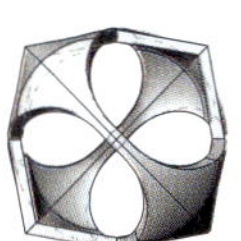

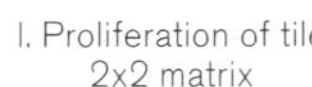

l. Proliferation of tile
2x2 matrix

h. Handle extension

i. Surface construction

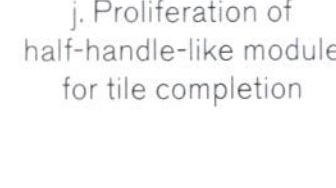

j. Proliferation of half-handle-like module for tile completion

k. Final tile

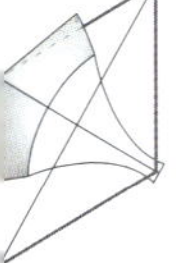

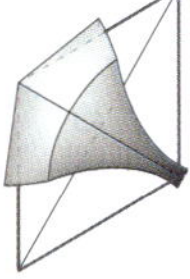

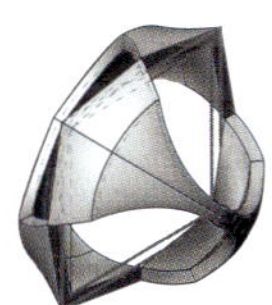

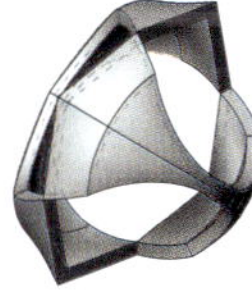

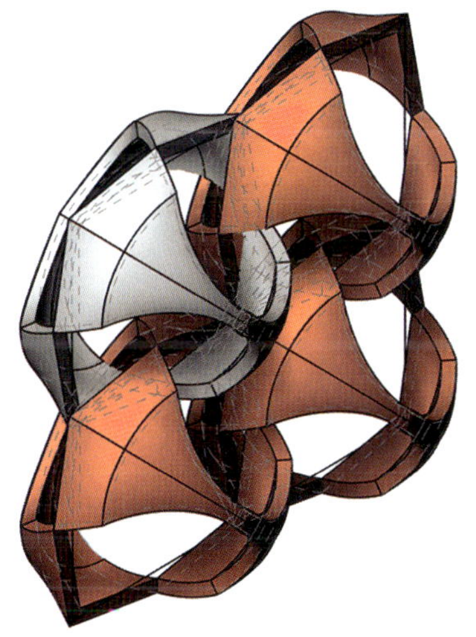

43-45_New Module_2.1 Intertwine_01_construction of tile from Intercircles associative model "proliferation and thickness

62_New Module 3.2_Octagon based_proliferated matrix_
rendered frontal view

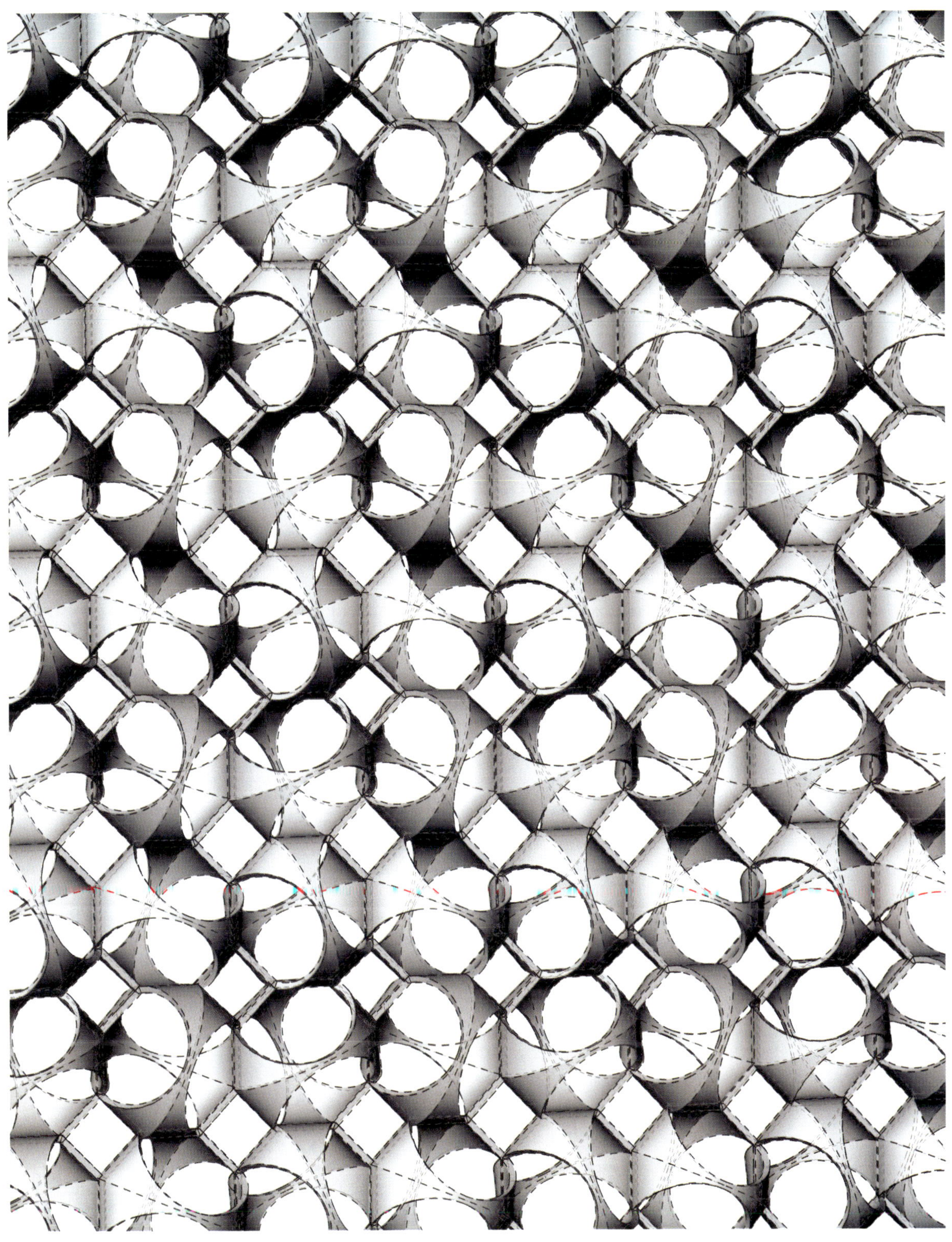

63_New Module 3.2_Octagon based_proliferated matrix_
rendered perspective view

New module 3.2: Octagon based

This design is produced by reorganizing the original model into other polygonal configurations. This is informed by a search for tessellations other than the quadrilateral tilling which defines many of the original designs. In this case, an octagon frames the module.

Instead of resolving the handle-like surface as a transition between the spherical surface and a corner point, this iteration constructs a transition between the spherical surface and two edges. The result of this variation is a polygonal tile.

Continuity is achieved in this design by arranging handles so that concave surfaces overlap convex handles. This way, tiles are disposed juxtaposing sides and leaving, in the process, squared empty spaces between them.

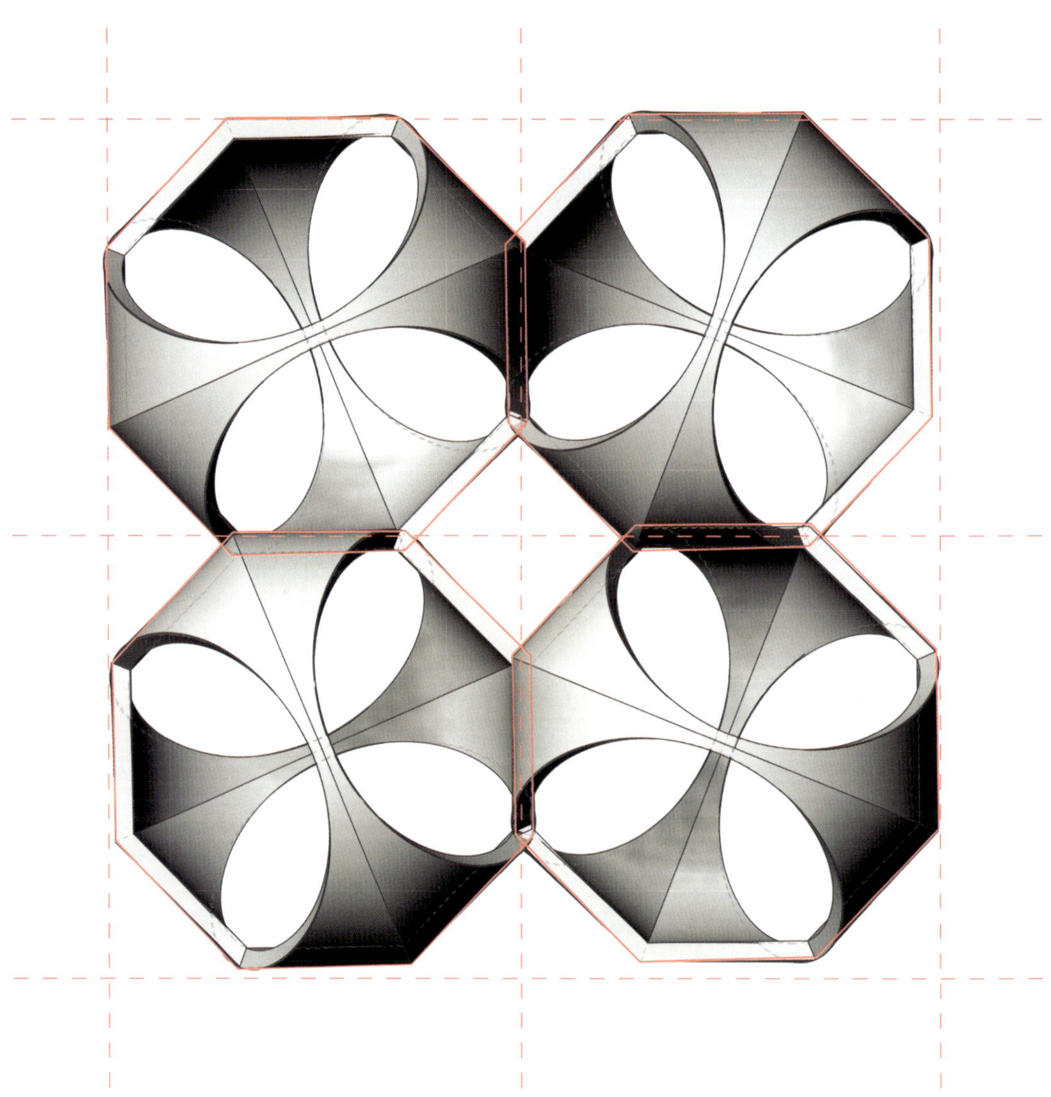

64_New Module 3.2_Octagon based_minimal proliferation_rendered frontal view

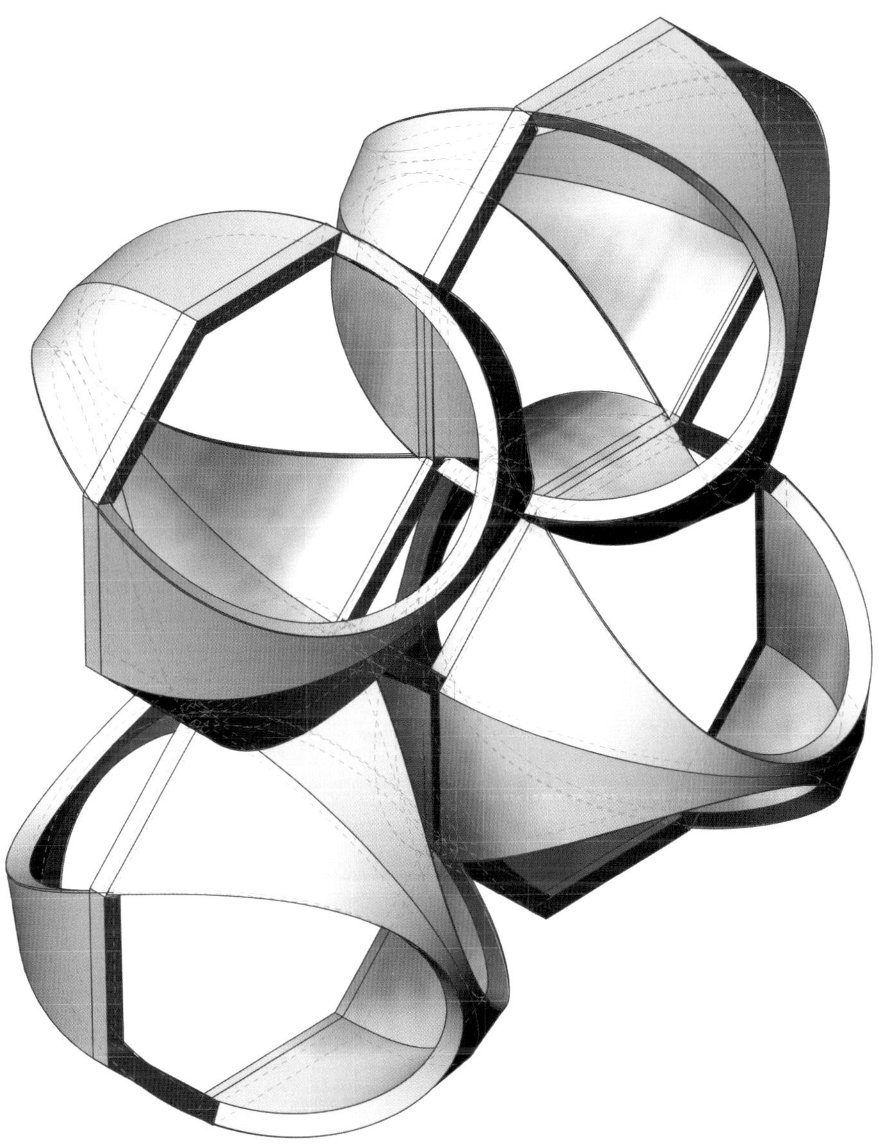

65_New Module 3.2_Octagon based_minimal proliferation_rendered isometric view

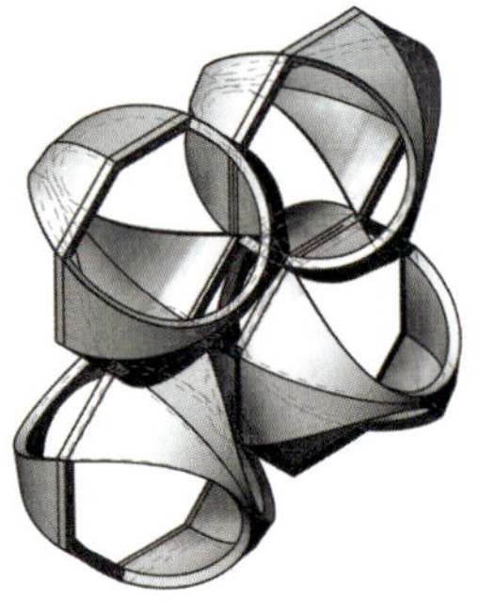
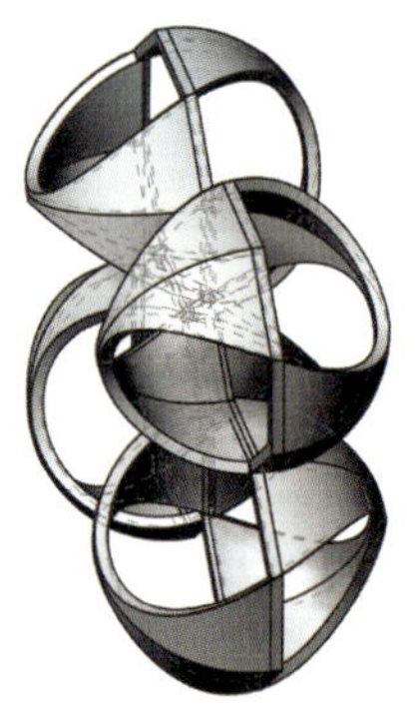
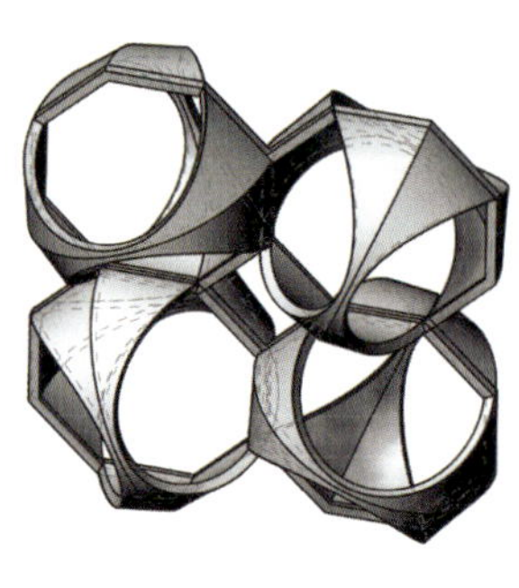

0°

60°

120°

66_New Module 3.2_minimal proliferation_series of 60° rotations

While the original Design 1 constructs transitional surfaces between the sphere and the four corners of the square tile through tangential lines, this octagonal design doubles the number of edges in the tile and therefore works with a ratio of two sides per half-handle.

This inevitably differentiates how the handles are constructed and impacts the overall form of the tile. The fact that octagons are a figure that cannot fill a matrix without leaving gaps spaces also produces a difference in the tilling when compared to the undifferentiated model.

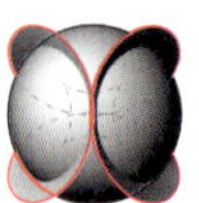
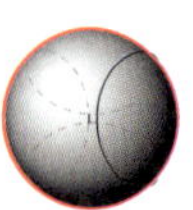
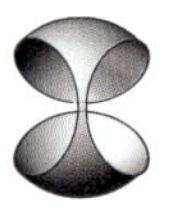
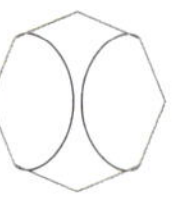

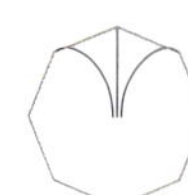

a. Sphere

b. Intersection between Sphere and Enneper surface

c. Resultant suture curve

d. Sphere trimming using suture curve

e. Hexagon fitting

f. Half handle isolation

g. Half handle axis

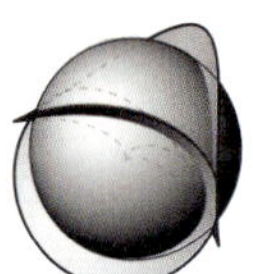
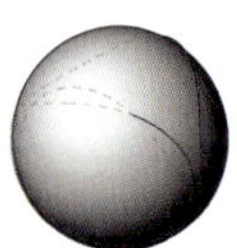
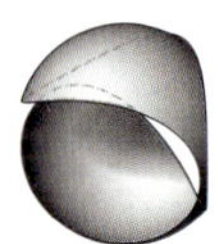

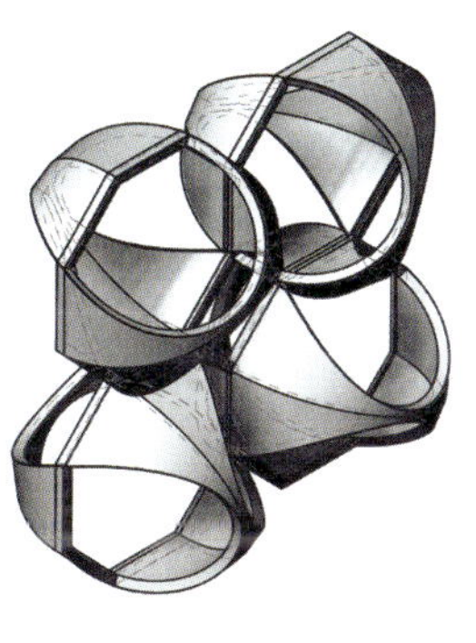

180°

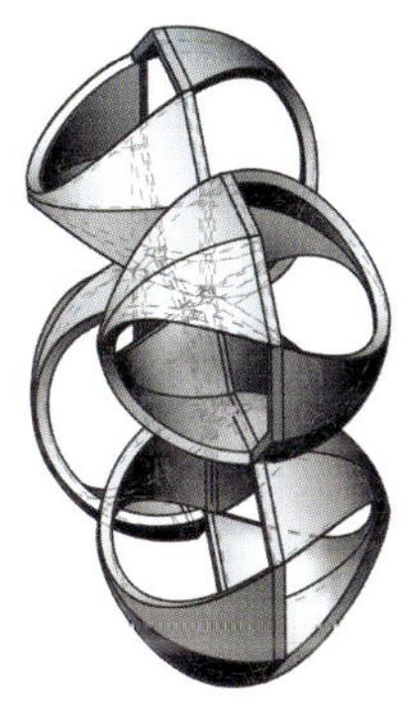

240°

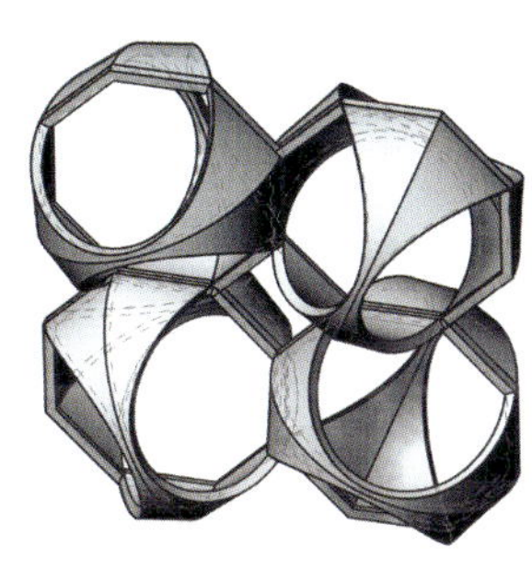

300°

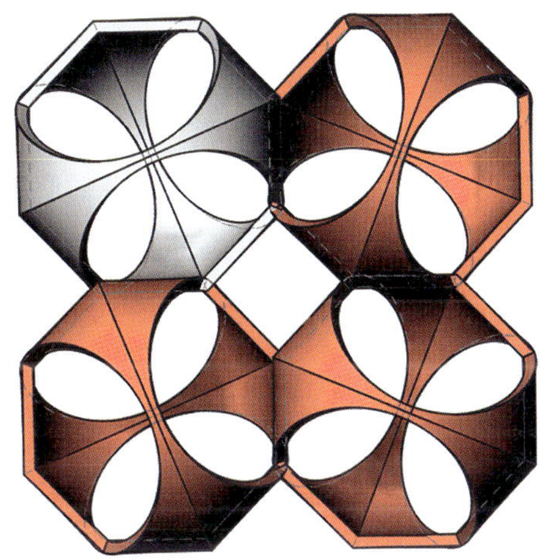

l. Minimal proliferation: 2x2 matrix

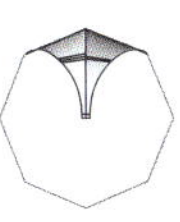

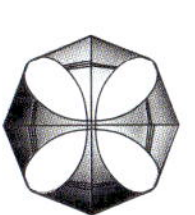

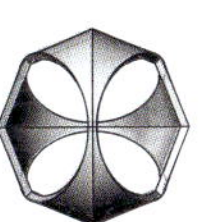

h. Half handle surface

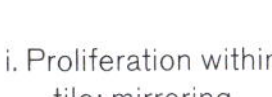

i. Proliferation within tile: mirroring

j. Proliferation within tile: rotation

k. Tile thickness

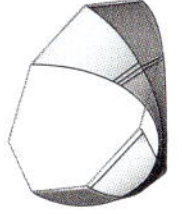

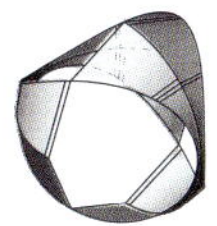

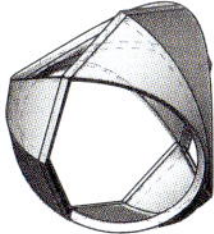

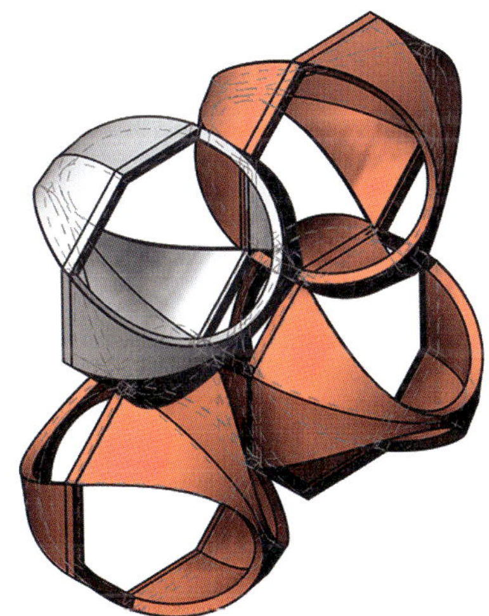

67-69_New Module 3.2_Octagon based_construction of tile from Intercircles associative model “proliferation and thickness”

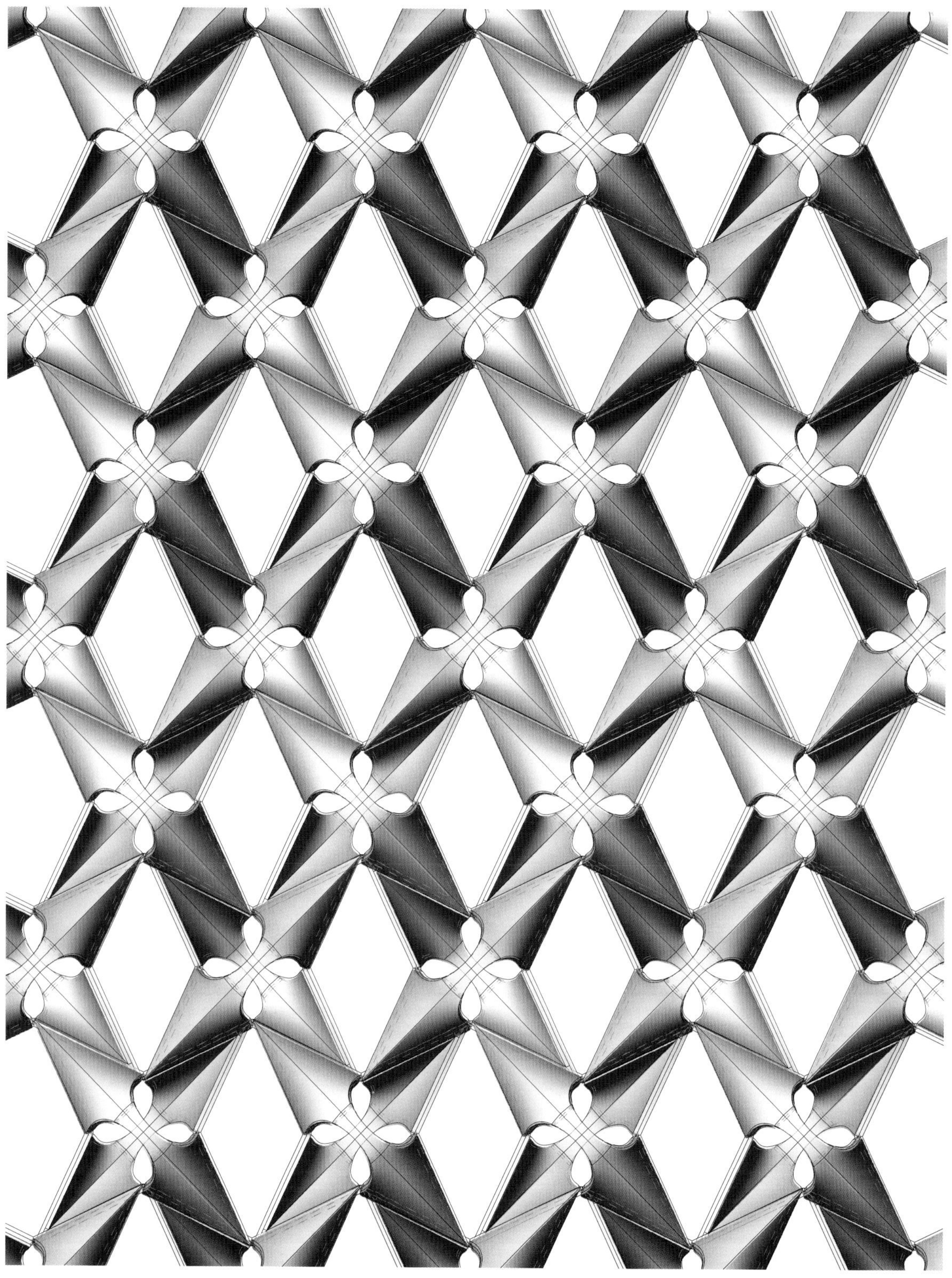

70_New Module 3.3_Contact Edges based_proliferated matrix_
rendered frontal view

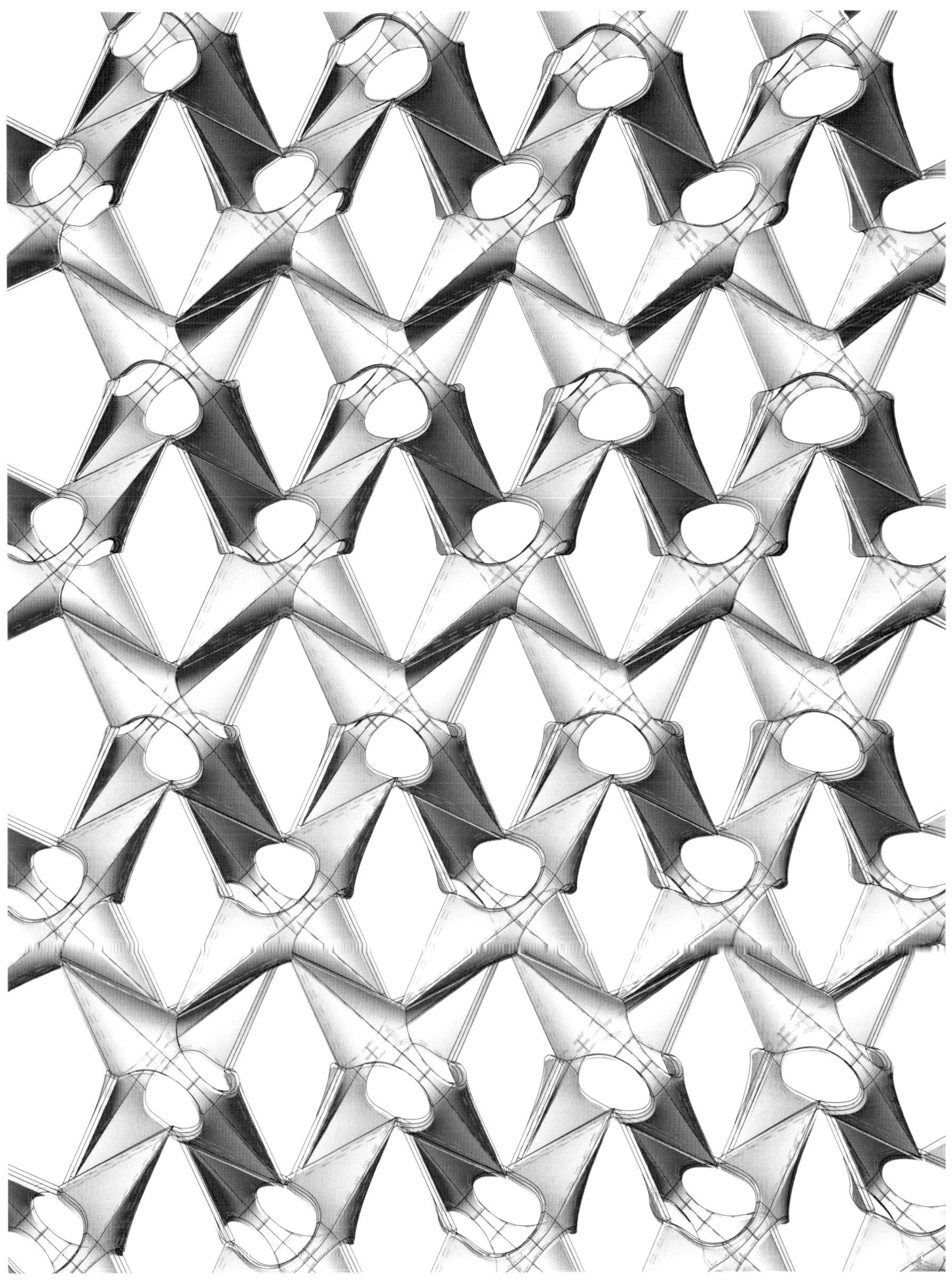

71_New Module 3.3_Contact Edges based_proliferated matrix_ rendered perspective view

New module 3.3: Contact edges based

This design is produced by generating elongated variants of the associative model 1 for Design 1. This design is an eight sided "star-shape" module.
The "stretched" quality is produced by a non-uniform scaling of the sphere. Non-perpendicular edges are produced due to this operation.

The tiling for this design does not follow the square tessellation of the original design but stacks the modules along the edges with the main contact surfaces between modules located on the frontal plane of the tile. The result of this stacking is the creation of rhomboidal gaps between tiles, adding another visual pattern as well as more permeability in the design. The result is an elongated version of the model where the number of sides have been doubled and the squared grid is shifted and overlapped.

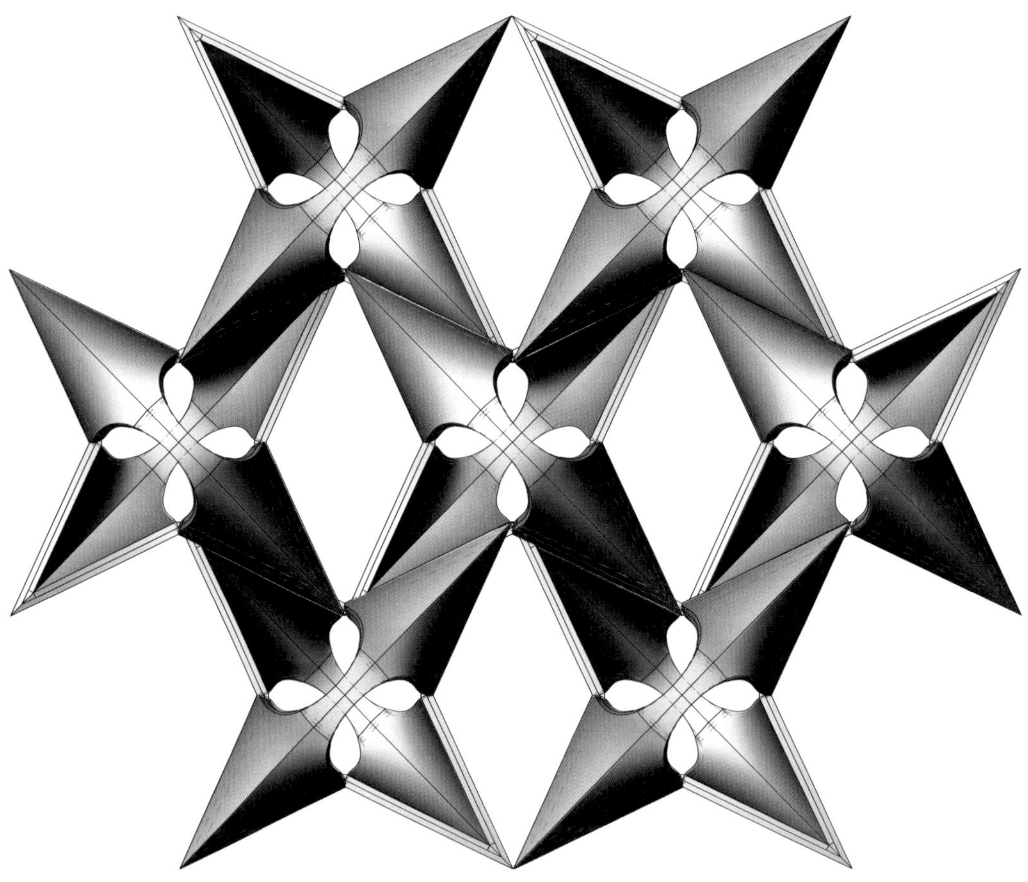

72_New Module 3.3_Contact Edges based_minimal proliferation_rendered frontal view

73_New Module 3.3_Contact Edges based_minimal proliferation_ rendered isometric view

0°

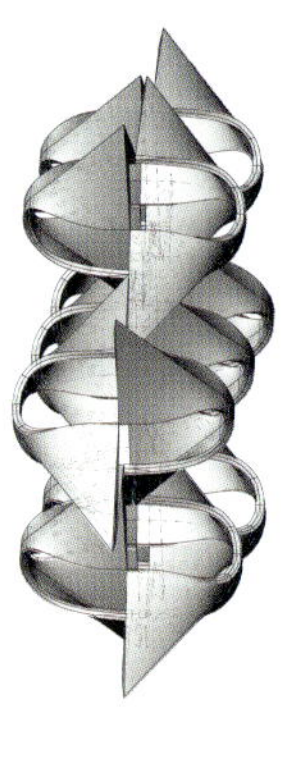

60°

120°

74_New Module 3.3_Contact Edges based_minimal proliferation_series of 60° rotations

This design investigates alternative tessellations based on the associative model 1. This is also produced by changing basically the relationship between the Enneper surface (which remains constant for this particular design) and the intersecting sphere, which, in this case, is non-uniformly scaled.

The construction involves producing new edge lines that connect the contracted suture curve with the square tile. Once the module is produced, it is proliferated to construct a symmetric tile, which is later stacked vertically and given volume.

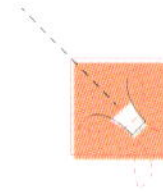

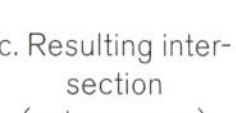

a. Enneper minimal surface and sphere.

b. Non-uniform scaling of sphere in X-axis

c. Resulting intersection (suture curve)

d. Resulting trimming of sphere with suture curve

e. Half handle like surface isolation

f. 45° rotation

g. Tangent line from tile corner

h. Cutting of surfac with plane at tange point

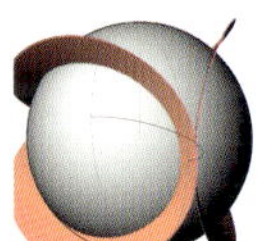
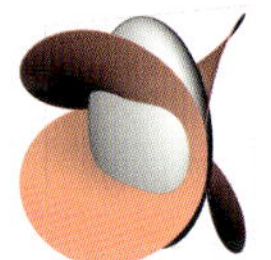
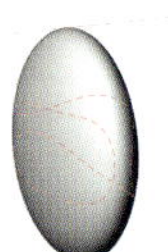
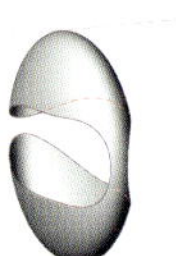

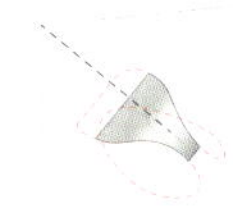
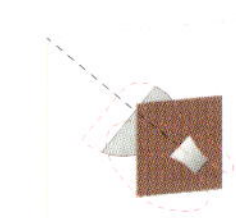

180°

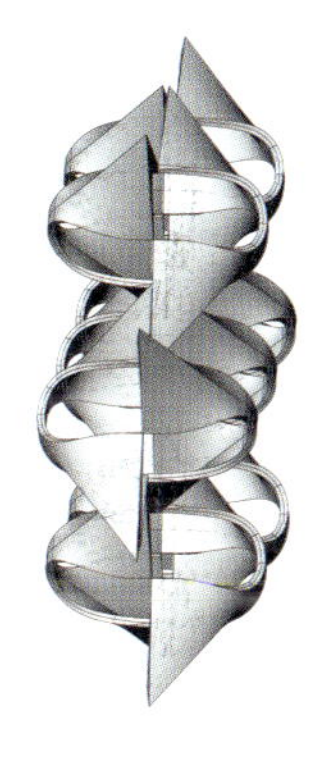

240°

300°

m. Proliferation of tile
Vertical stacking

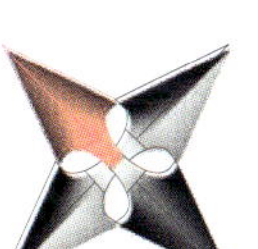
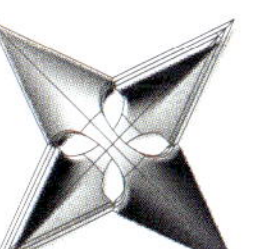

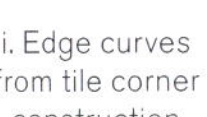

i. Edge curves from tile corner construction

j. Transitional surfaces

k. Proliferation within tile

l. Final tile

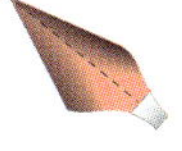
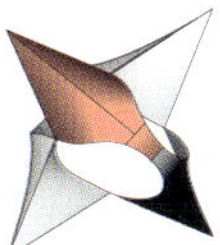
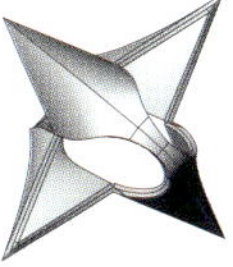

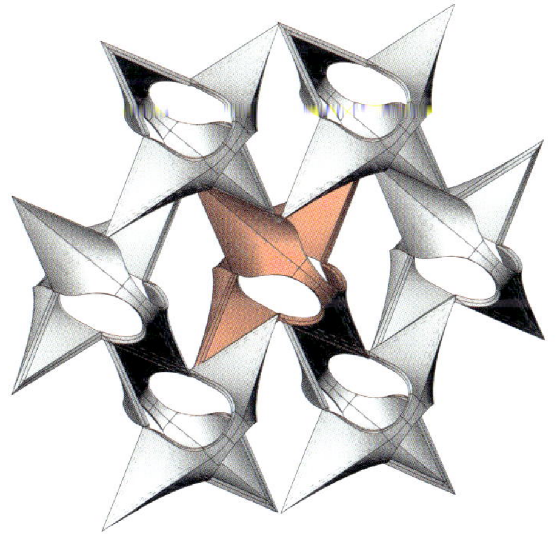

75-77_New Module 3.3_Contact Edges based_construction of tile from associative model 1"proliferation and thickness"

78_New Module 3.4_Rotational matrix based_proliferated matrix_rendered frontal view

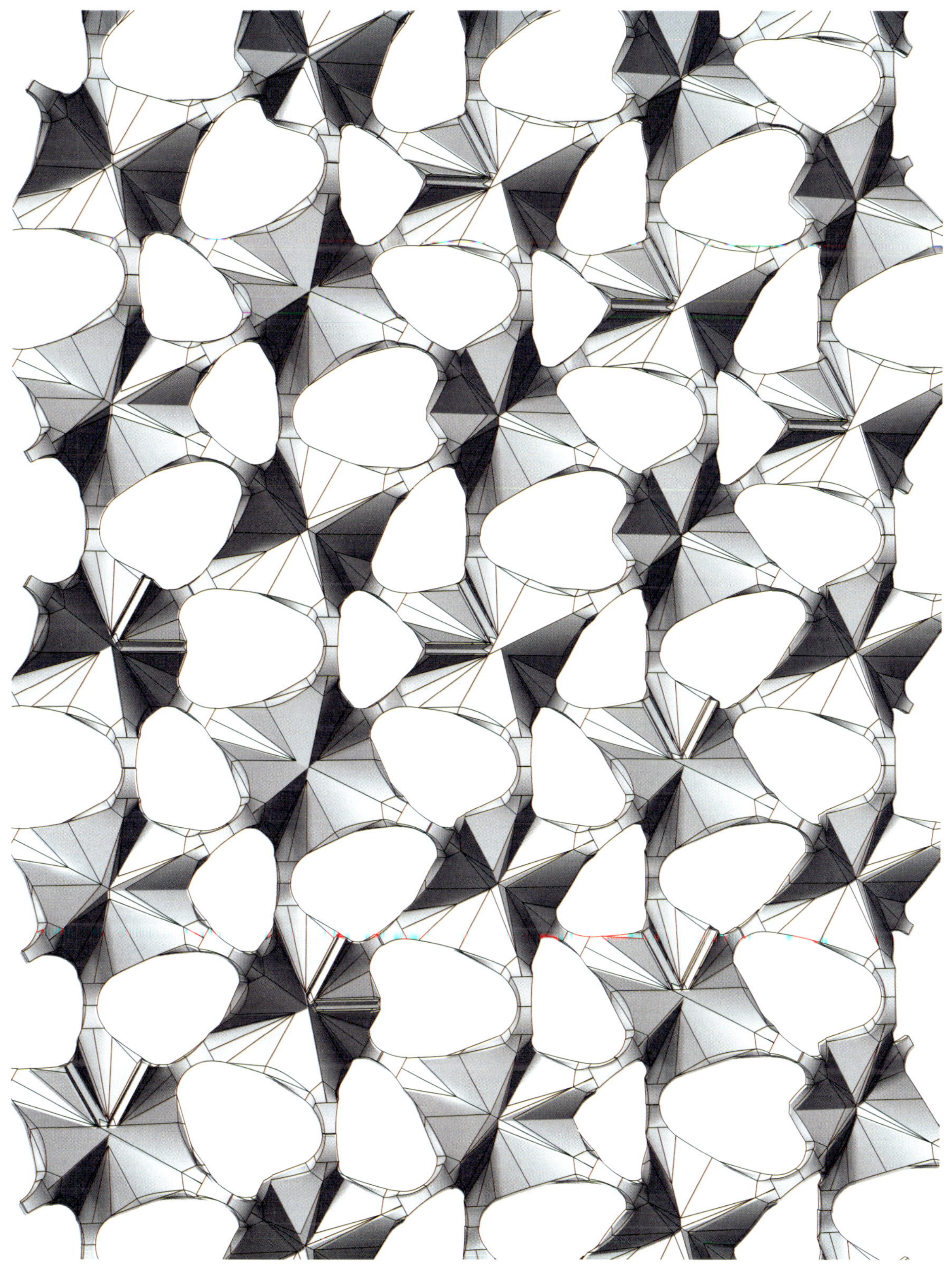

79_New Module 3.4_Rotational matrix based_proliferated matrix_rendered perspective view

New module 3.4: Rotational matrix based

This design is derived from the associative model 1 and also incorporates differentiation through non-uniform scaling of the sphere. This design is part of a series of explorations focused on rotational matrices. In these investigations, the tiles are not organized in a polygonal matrix but define their own matrix through a polar arraying of its handle. This means that the differences produced by non-uniform scaling observed earlier in the book, create deformed suture curves that no longer fit seamlessly into a squared tile.
These differences provide the opportunity to question the bounding by polygonal grids and uses the angles of the tiles and their rotation as the main operation that defines how these units can be tiled to produce continuity. This means that the amount of modules that complete a 360º tile around a tile corner is determined by the angle of the module's tapered form. In this case the angle is approximately 60º, so six handles are rotated around a corner to produce the final tile. The resultant grid for this particular unit is hexagonal.

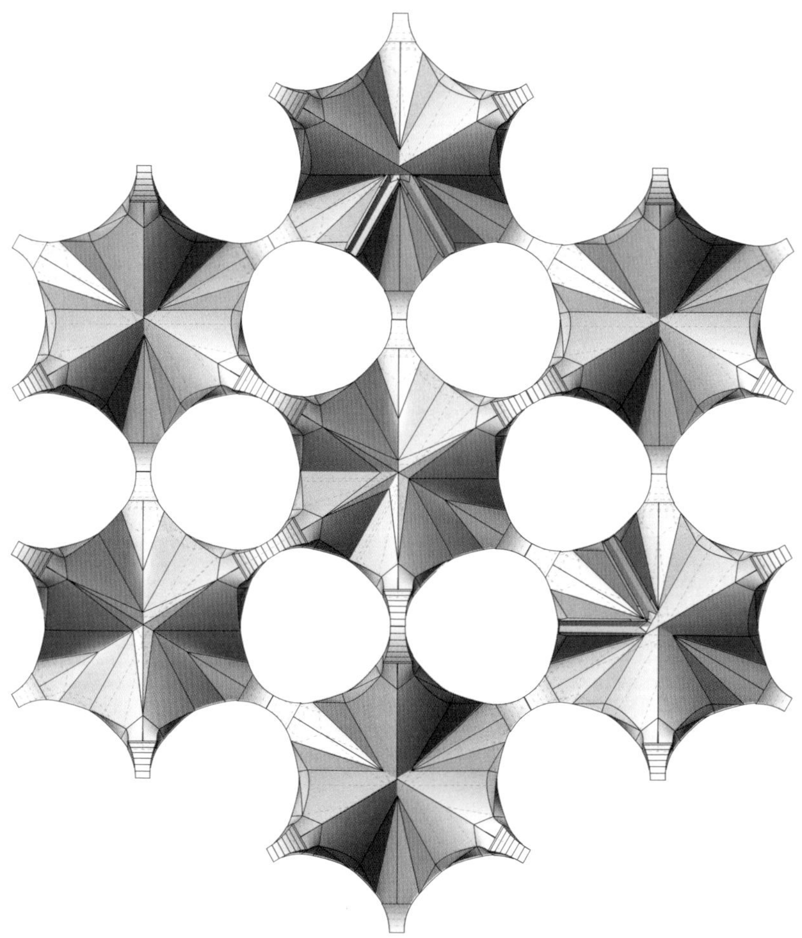

80_New Module 3.4_Rotational matrix based_minimal proliferation_rendered frontal view

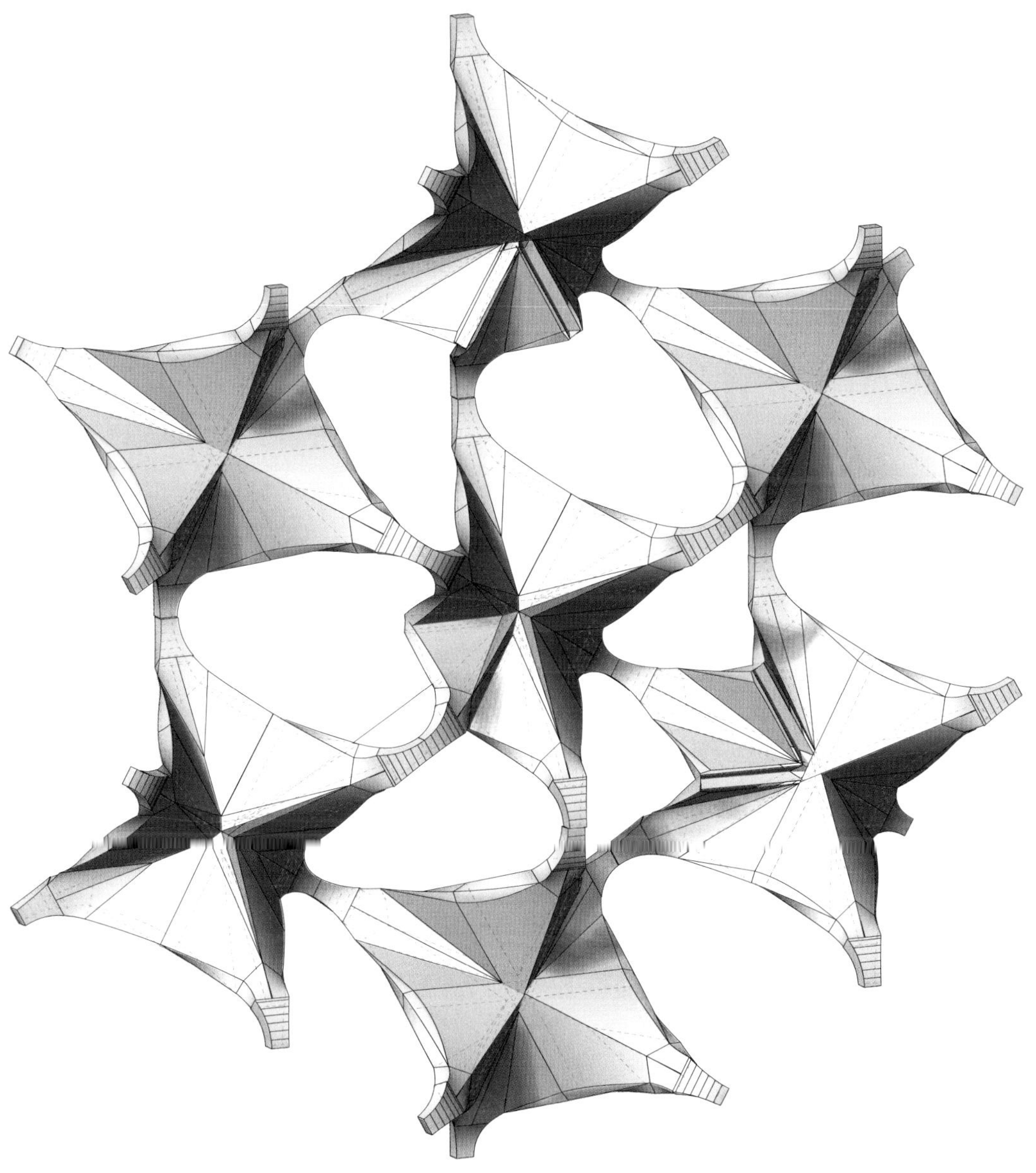

81_New Module 3.4_Rotational matrix based
_minimal proliferation_rendered isometric view

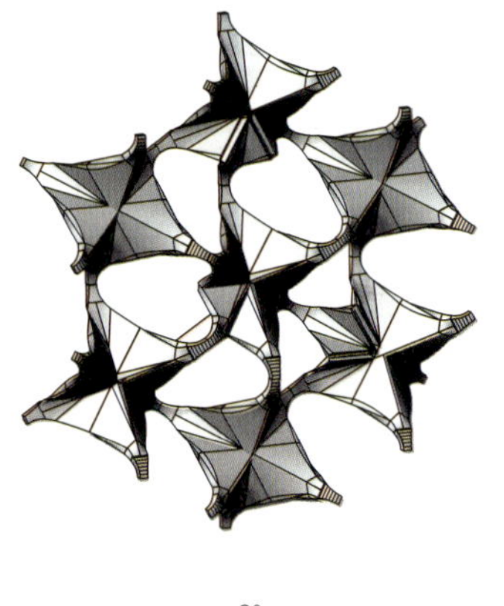

0°

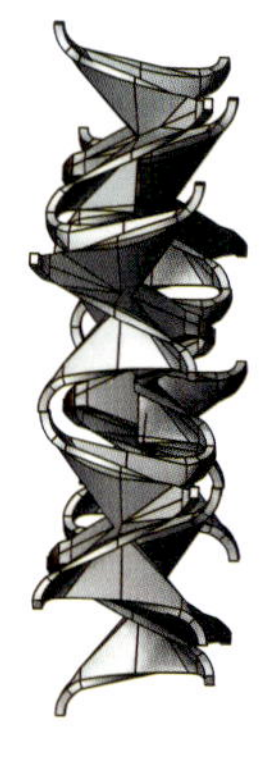

60°

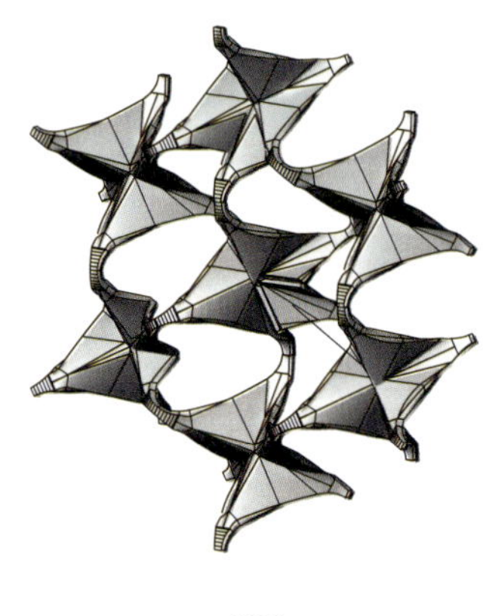

120°

82_New Module 3.4_Rotational matrix based_series of 60° rotations

When tiled as a larger field, a hexagonal tessellation is the most logical way to aggregate the modules. Because of the three-dimensional forms of these units, the tilling cannot be achieved without some degree of consideration to the sequencing of the handles as it is rotated about its centroid, where six modules are arrayed around the centre.
The handle modules will need to be flipped in an alternating pattern to allow for the three-dimensional connections of the units achieve a seamless field.

a. Enneper minimal surface and sphere.

b. Non-uniform scaling of sphere in Y-axis

c. Resulting intersection (suture curve)

d. Resulting trimming of sphere with suture curve

e. Half handle like surface isolation

f. 45° rotation

g. Tangent line from tile corner

h. Cutting of surface with plane at tangent point

i. Number of handles fitting around 360°

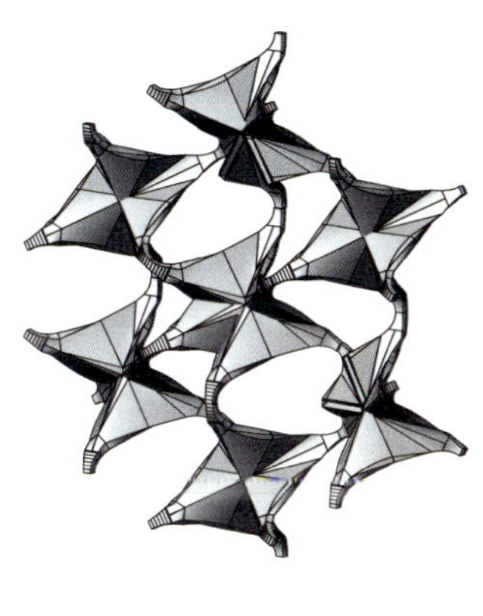

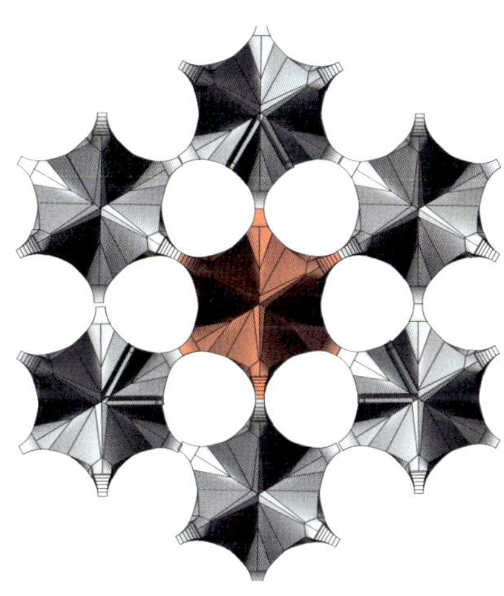

n. Proliferation of tile
Hexagonal matrix

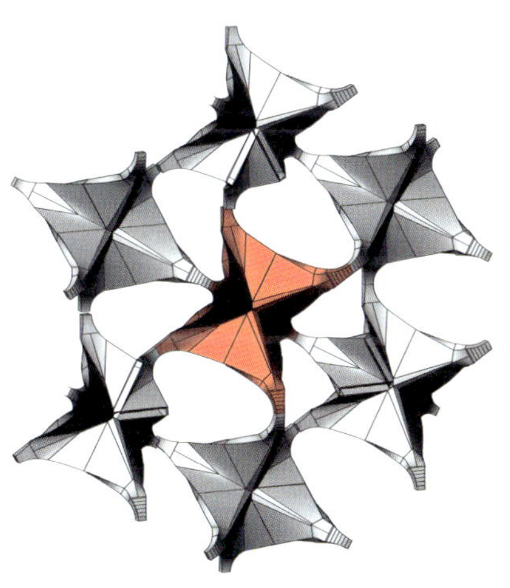

83-85_New Module 3.4_Rotational matrix based_construction of tile from associative model 1 "proliferation and thickness"

New modules from minimal surfaces

This section explores the opportunities for design instantiation made from one of the earliest steps in the process of constructing the associative models. These variations are produced by constructing new tiles from the intersection of the Enneper minimal surface with a series of different volumes. In this series of intersections, suture curves are not identified and they are not used to trim a sphere, but rather solid volumes are used to trim the Enneper surface itself. The resultant tiles do not need to construct transitional surfaces to produce continuity as they are inherently continuous in themselves being sections of a minimal saddle surface.

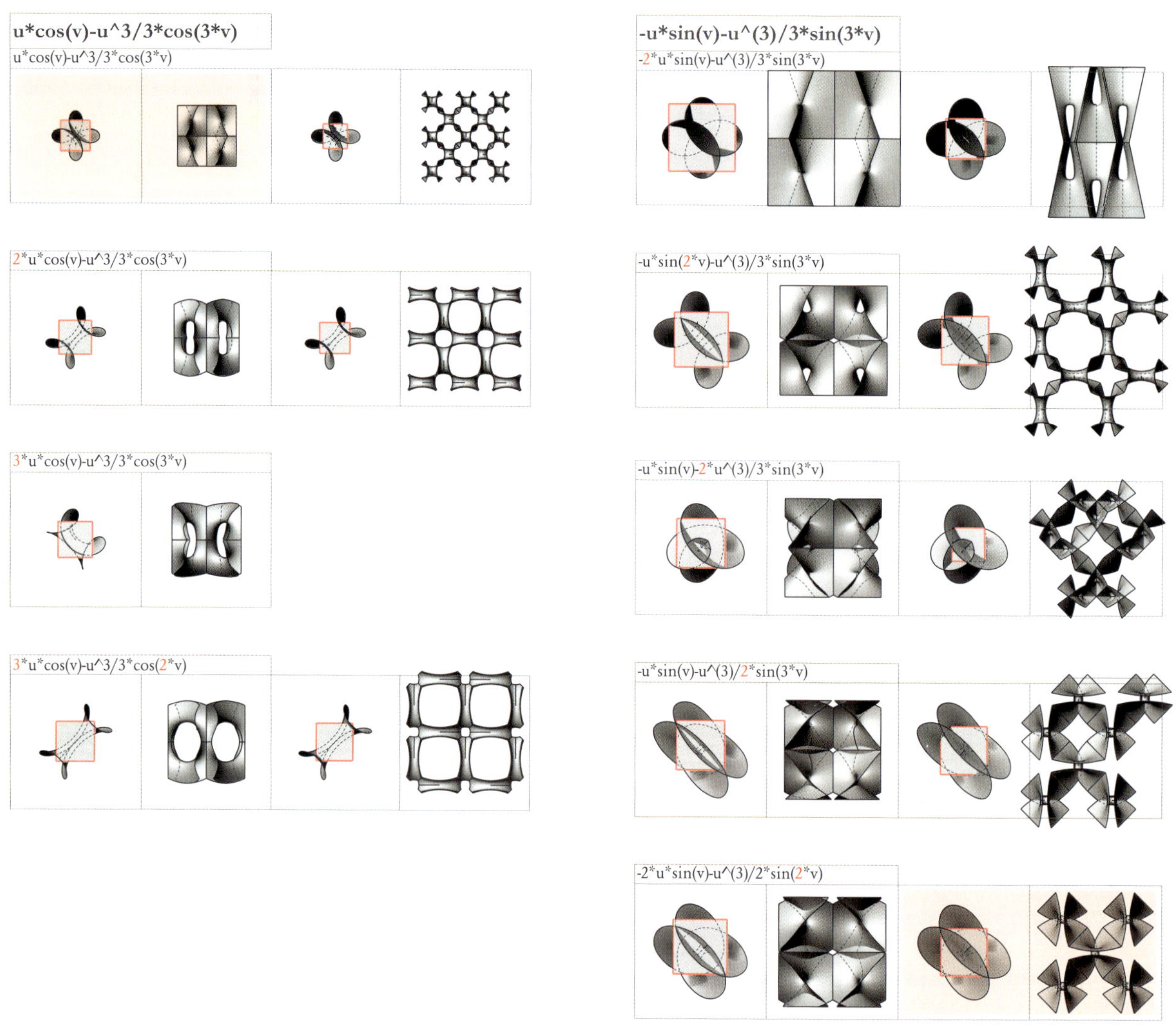

01_Matrix of intersections between cube (hexahedron) and Enneper surface variations_elevation.
Selection for New Continuas is marked in light red.

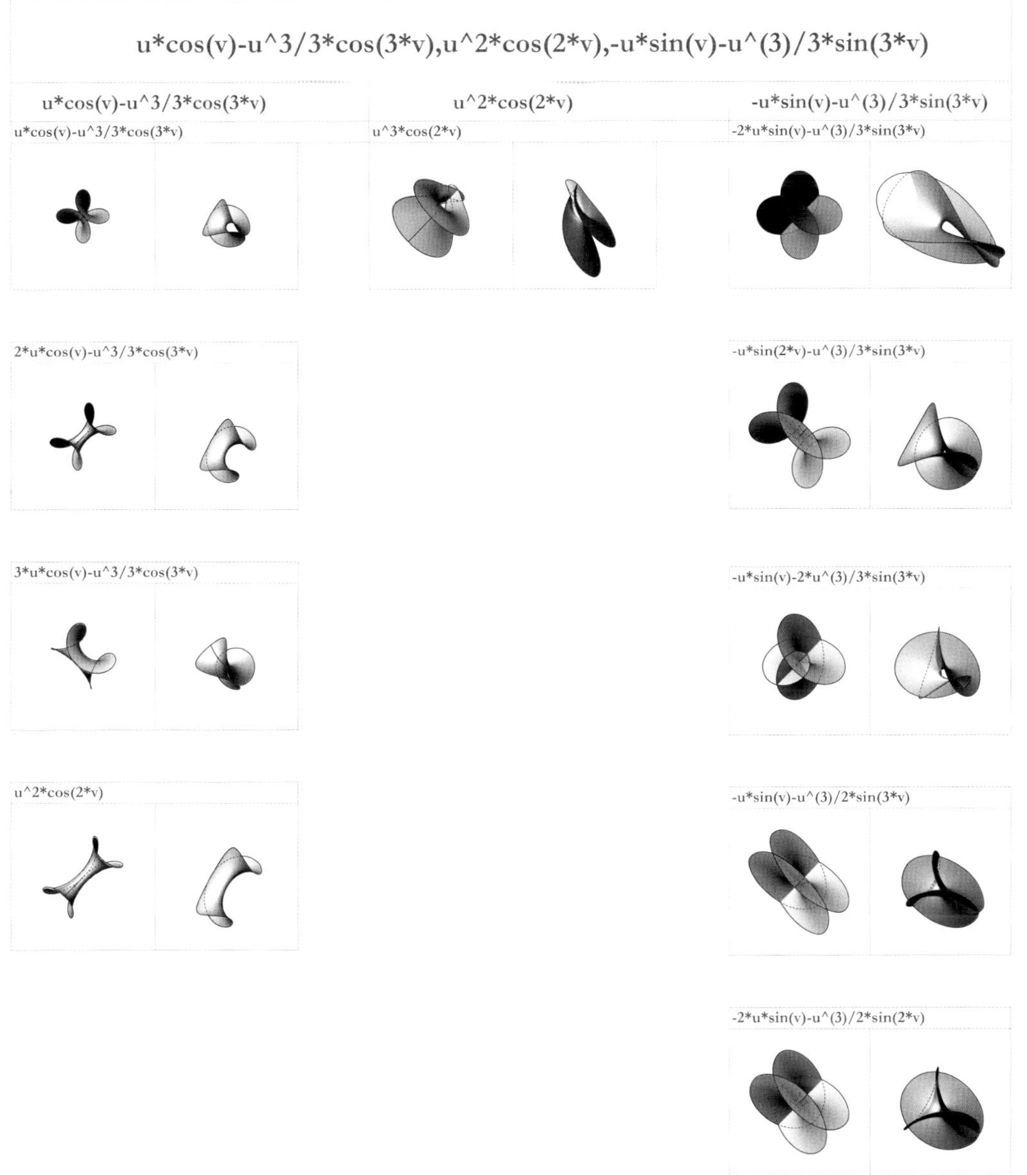

02_Matrix of Enneper surface variations_parameters in the x, y and z components rendered frontal and isometric views with varied formulas displayed.

The Enneper formula is a complex definition of three parameters: x, y and z, where:

{x}= u*cos(v)-u^3/3*cos(3*v)
{y}= u^2*cos(2*v)
{z}= -u*sin(v)-u^(3)/3*sin(3*v)

Each parameter in its turn is defined by a specific number of sub-parameters: 6 for x, 3 for y and 7 for z. A few of these variables are shown on the matrices and intersections have only been performed on x and z variations. The three intersections that are shown in these matrices are (a) a cube, (b) a pyramid (octahedron) and finally (c) a tetra-decahedron.

For each variation, two frames are displayed: (a) the intersection between the Enneper surface and the intersecting volume and (b) the resultant tile proliferated in a matrix. Also, some variations are studied further in terms of changing the proportion between the Enneper surface and the intersecting volume. In these

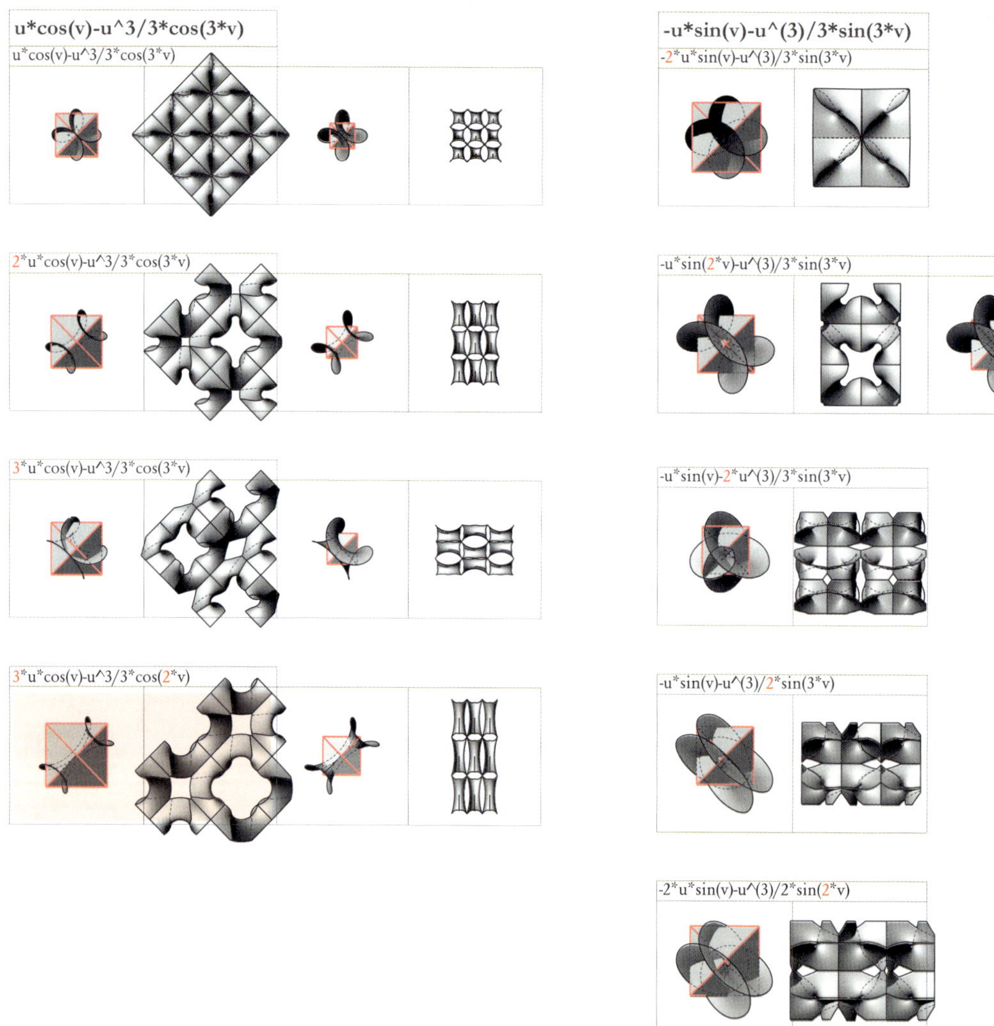

03_Matrix of intersections between double pyramid (octahedron) and Enneper surface variations

cases, a second group of frames (a and b) are shown, where the scale of the intersecting volume is either bigger or smaller. Varying the number of faces of each polyhedron in combination with the variation of both x and z components provide a wide number of possibilities.
Even in this relatively small catalogue, possibilities for other tiles emerge from understanding that every intersection offers a range of variability. This matrix aims to illustrate some moments of that variability.
The selected tiles for New Modules are highlighted using a light red mark.

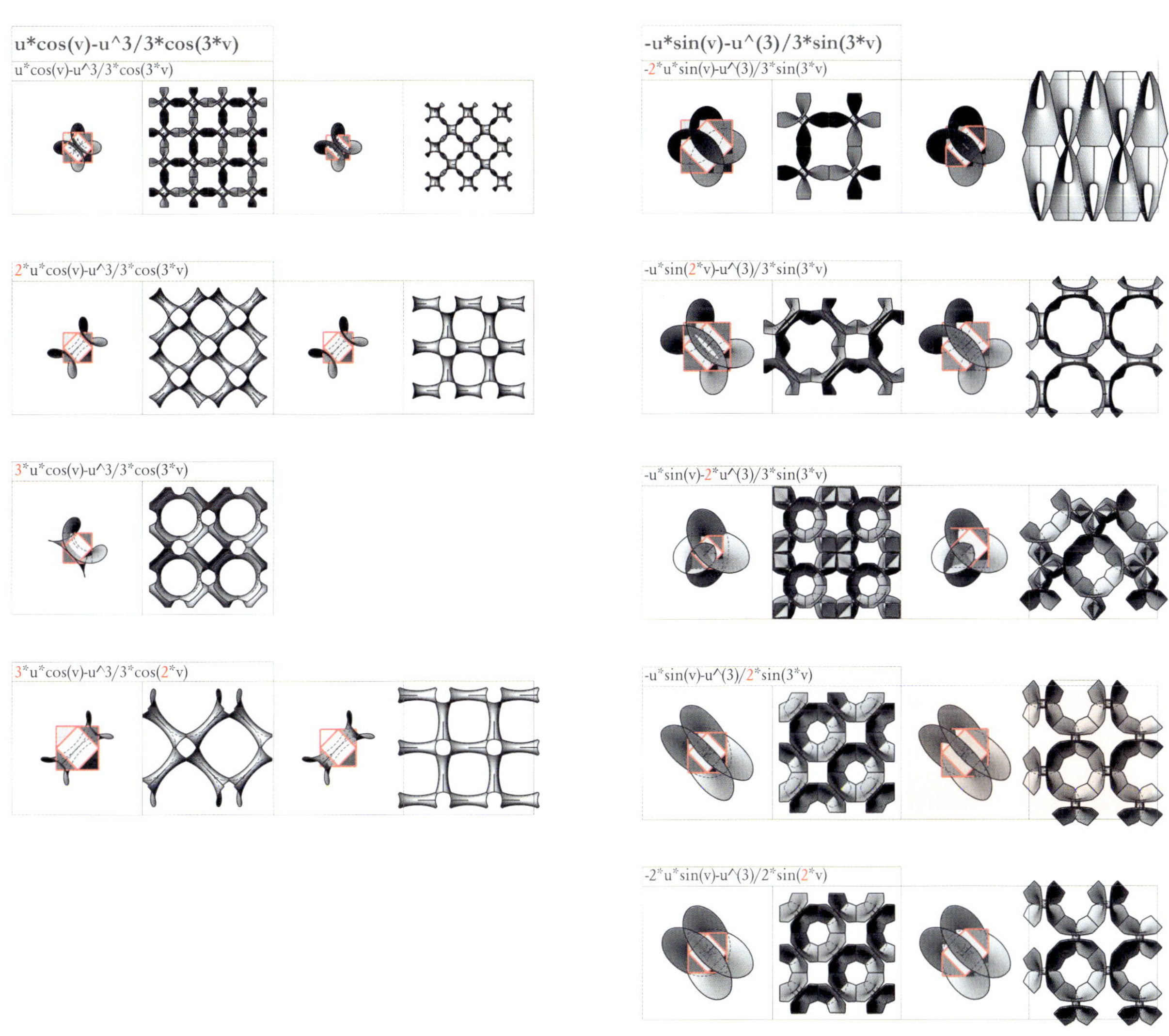

04_Matrix of intersections between tetradecahedron and Enneper surface variations

05_New Module 4.1_Generic cube based_proliferated matrix_ rendered frontal view

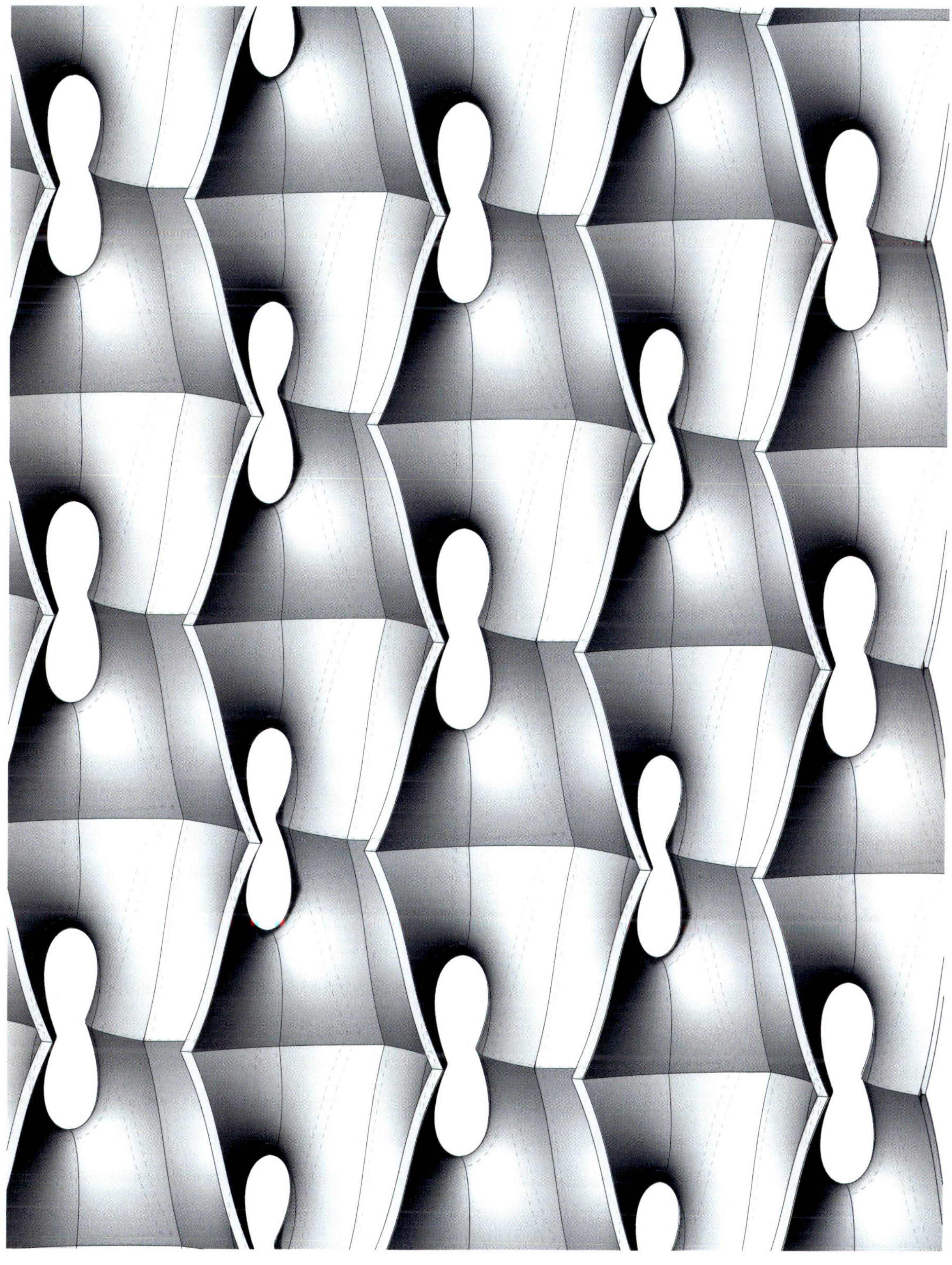

06_New Module 4.1_Generic cube based_proliferated matrix_ rendered perspective view

New module 4.1: Generic cube based

The Enneper formula for this design is:

{x}= u*cos(v)-u^3/3*cos(3*v)
{y}= u^2*cos(2*v)
{z}= -u*sin(v)-u^(3)/3*sin(3*v)

This means that the formula matches the generic Enneper surface used for associative models 1,2,3,4 & 5. However, as previously mentioned, the difference lies on how tiles are conceived as a solid intersection between the Enneper surface and a specific volume, in this case, a cube. This is, in a way, a new generic continua for this series.

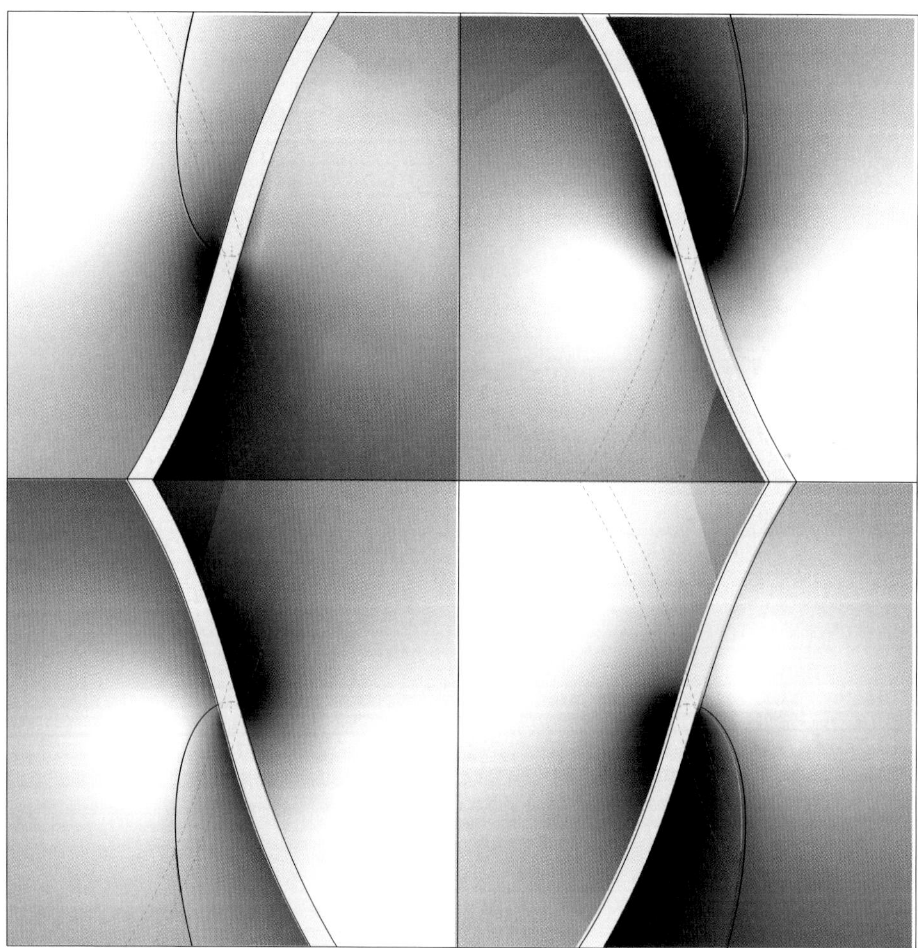

07_New Module 4.1_Generic cube based_minimal proliferation_rendered frontal view

08_New Module 4.1_Generic cube based_minimal proliferation_rendered isometric view

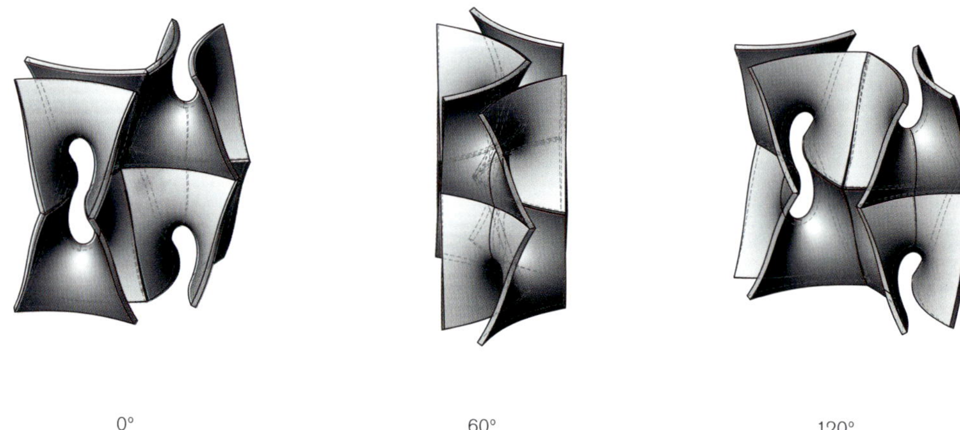

09_New Module 4.1_Generic cube based_minimal proliferation_ series of 60° rotations_isometric view

The resultant trimmed saddle surface fits a squared matrix. When trimmed, the Enneper surface's axis of symmetry is rotated 45° in relationship to the orthogonal axis of the cube and produces a particular form that generates vertical empty spaces between tiles (when seen from a diagonal point of view). Other possible variations from this generic form could further investigate how rotation plays a role in the definition and symmetry of the resultant tile. The solid cube used in the Boolean intersection could be scaled or translated to produce different tiles.

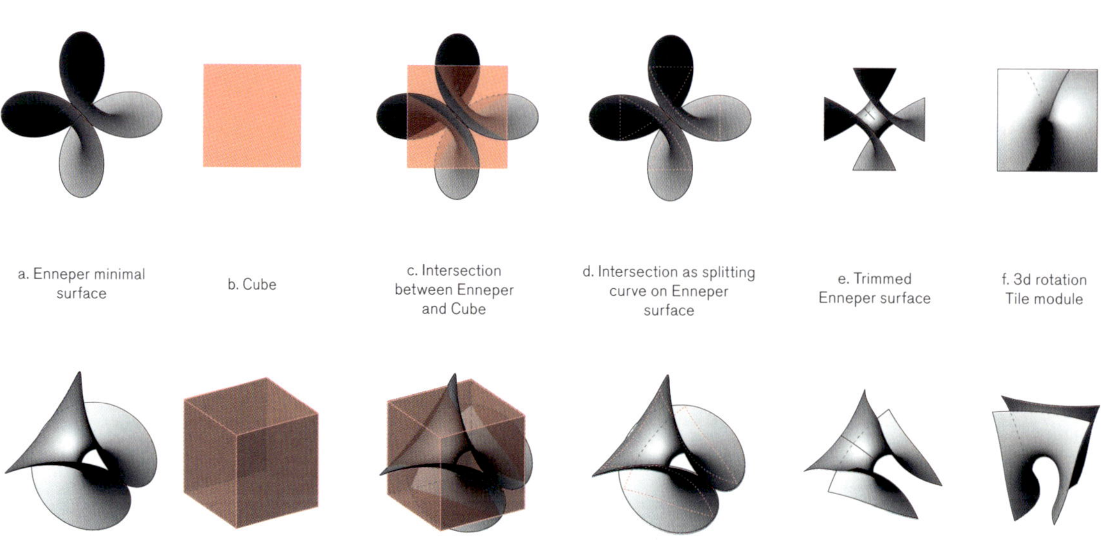

10_New Module 4.1_Generic cube based_ construction of tile from intersection between Enneper surface variation and cube

11_3x3 matrix_3d printed model_elevation

12_3x3 matrix_3d printed model_45° perspective

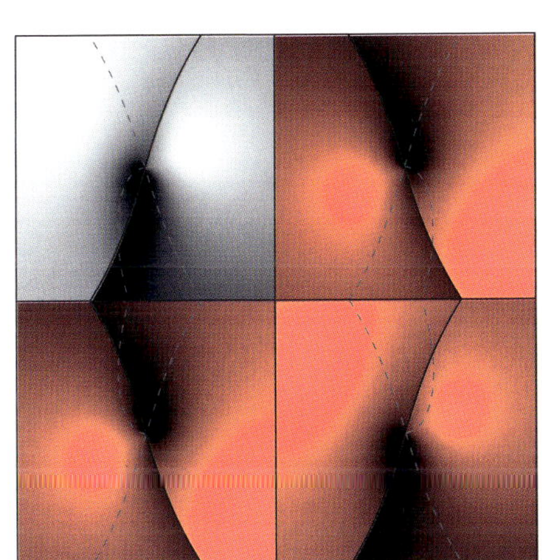

13_minimal proliferation_elevation

14_minimal proliferation_isometric view

Top images show a 3d printed 3x3 matrix model for this New Module design. The resultant matrix produces oblique openings.

Bottom images show a 2x2 matrix as a minimal proliferation of this module. Modules are reflected and continuity is guaranteed.

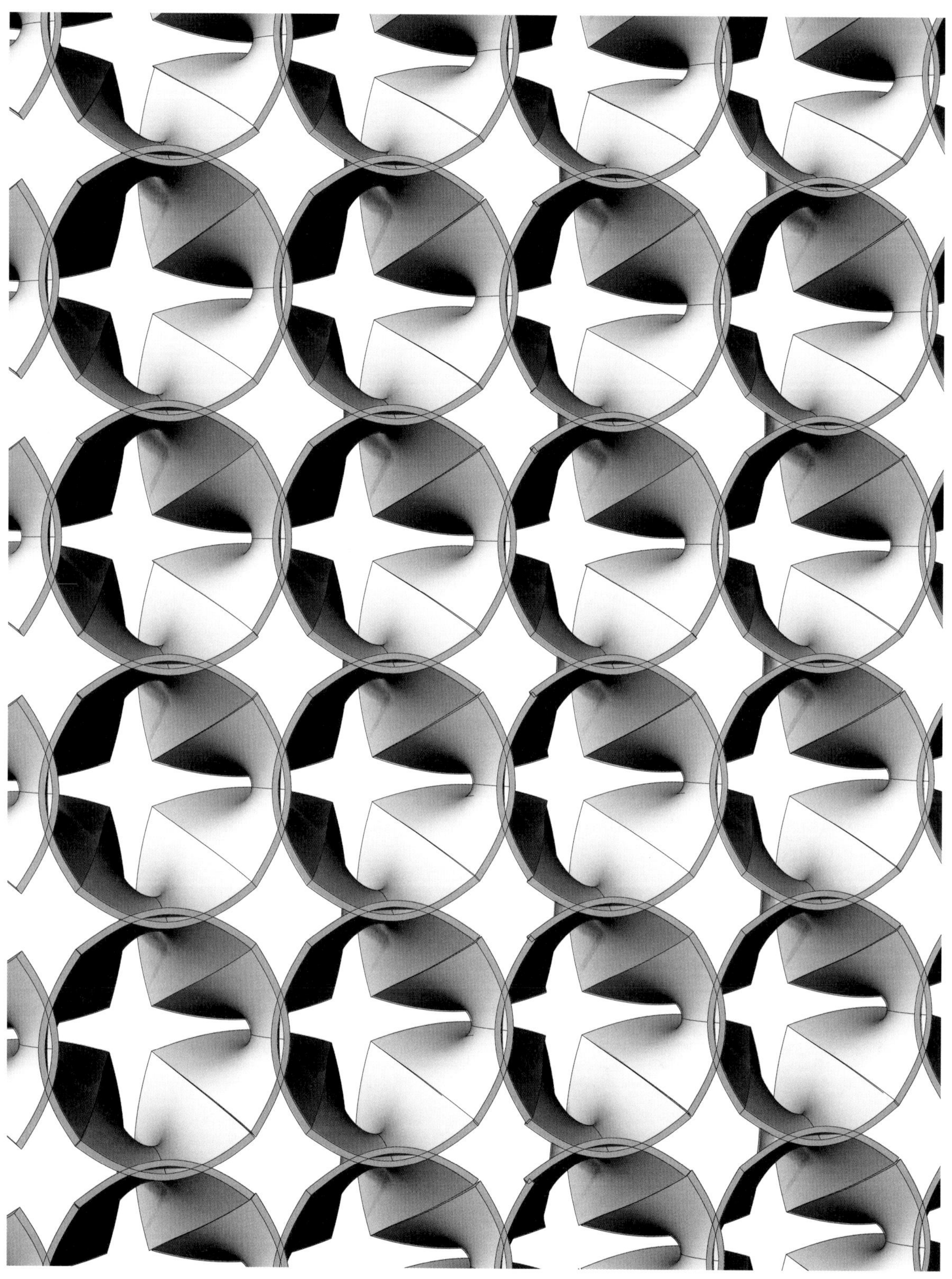

15_New Module 4.2_Differentiated cube based_proliferated matrix_rendered frontal view

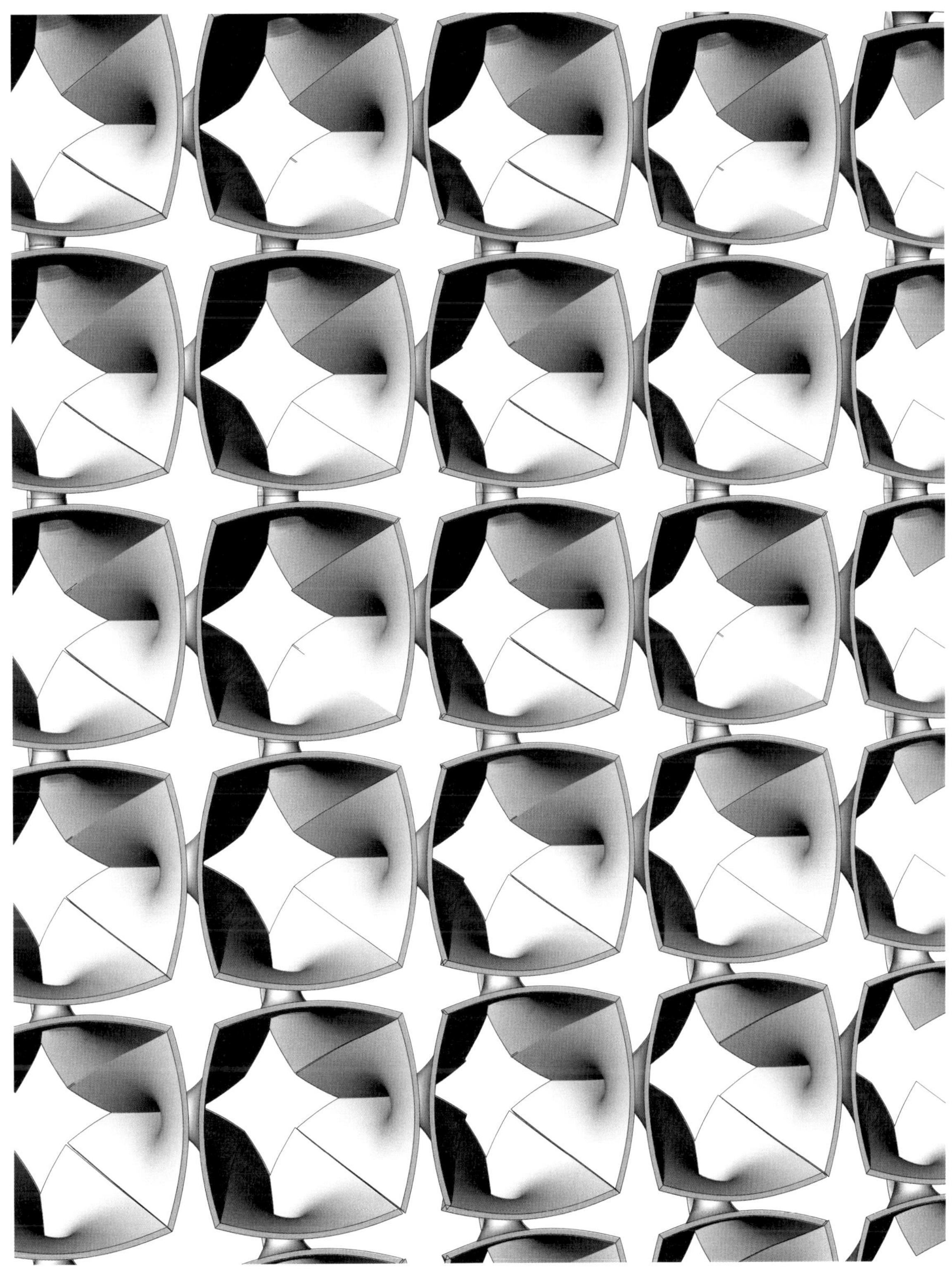

16_New Module 4.2_Differentiated cube based_proliferated matrix_rendered perspective view

New module 4.2: Differentiated cube based

The Enneper surface formula for this design is:
{x}= -2*u*sin(v)-u^(3)/2*sin(2*v)
{y}= u^2*cos(2*v)
{z}= -u*sin(v)-u^(3)/3*sin(3*v)

This formula is different from the generic Enneper surface used for the other associative models. The difference lies in changing one of the variables that define the x parameter of the formula. Marked in red, the v multiplier changes from 3 in the generic formula, to 2 in this surface. The result can be seen in the following spread, where the Enneper surface is lengthened in a unidirectional manner along its axis of symmetry. This produces a different minimal surface which, once trimmed with a cube generates a different tile.
The resultant trimmed saddle surface fits a square boundary; given its cubic origin.
Nevertheless, the resultant matrix is arranged along the diagonal corners of the tile. The matrix is a diagonal grid that generates empty spaces of different scales when the tile is proliferated. Once again, the Enneper surface's axis of symmetry is rotated 45° in relationship to the orthogonal axis of the cube.

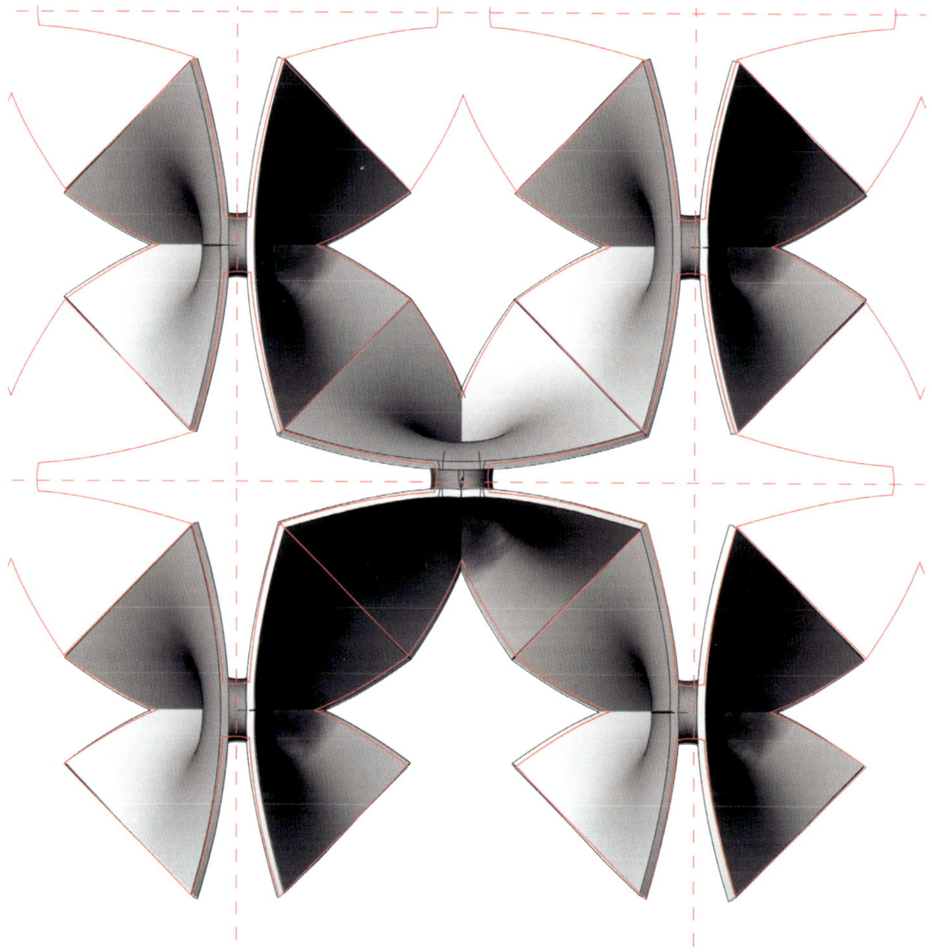

17_New Module 4.2_Differentiated cube based_minimal proliferation_ rendered frontal view

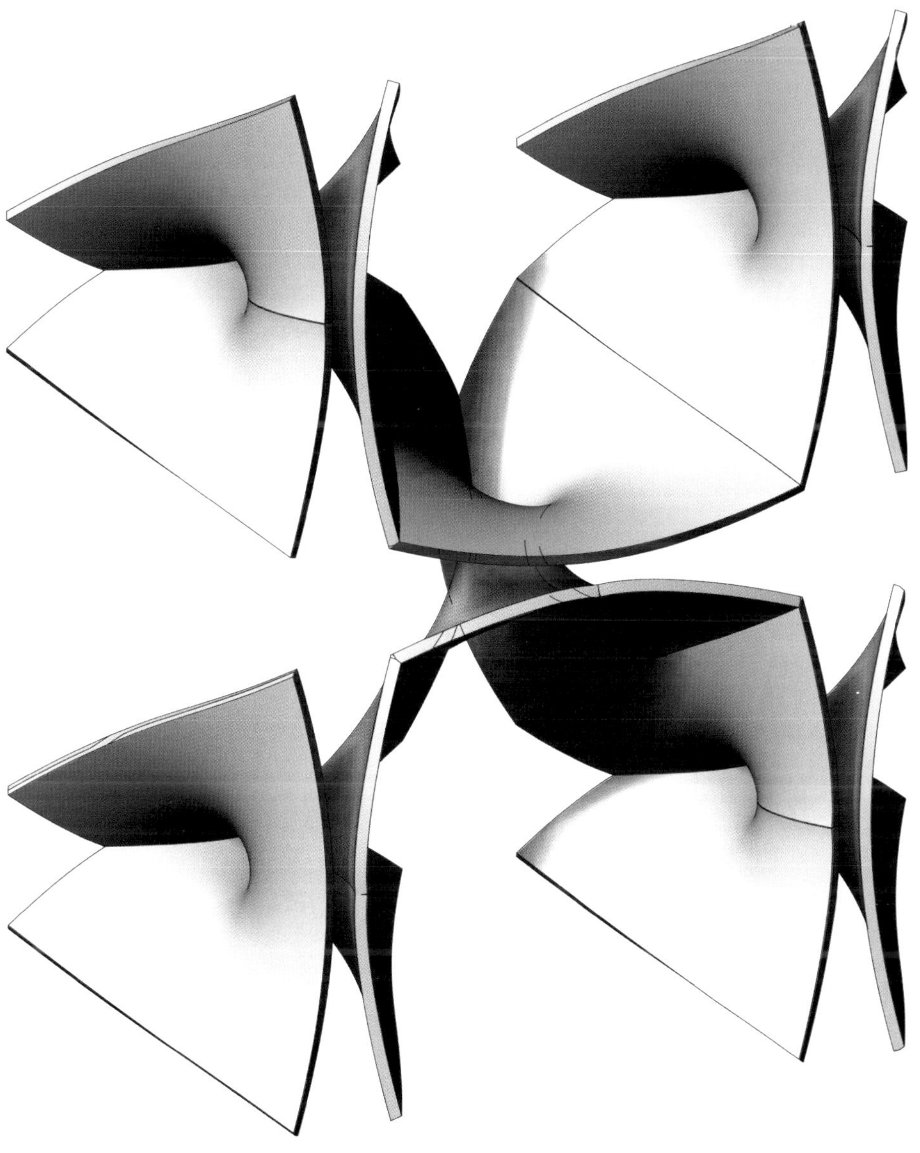

18_New Module 4.2_Differentiated cube based_minimal proliferation_rendered isometric view

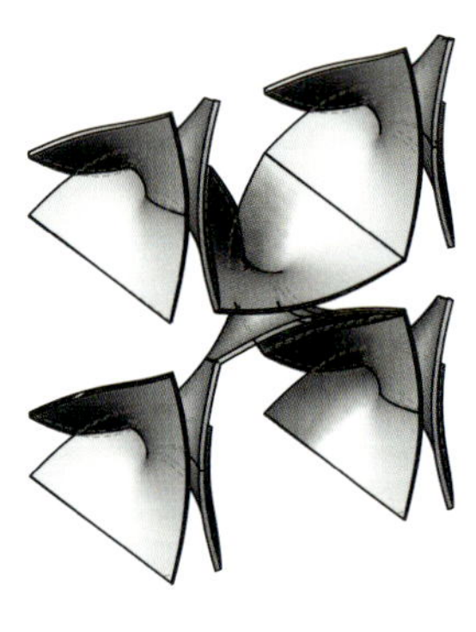

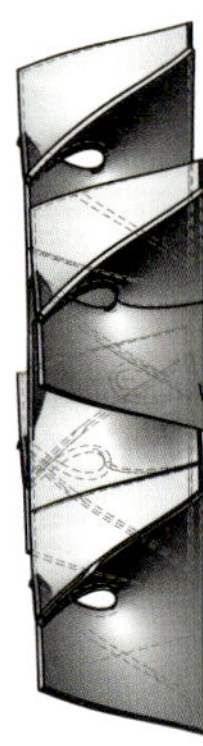

19_New Module 4.2_Differentiated cube based_minimal proliferation_series of 60° rotations

This design results from the intersection of a cube and a differentiated Enneper surface. This intersection produces a cubic boundary that clips the minimal surface in a manner that the remaining surface fits the cube. The tiles are rotated, arrayed and mirrored to test which type of proliferation produces the best continuity. In this case, mirroring the tile along its edges produces the best outcome. This is because the edges are not parallel to each other, so arraying is not possible.

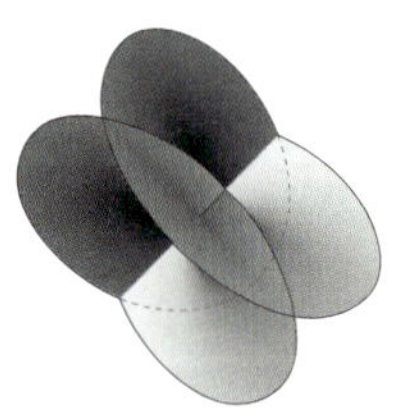
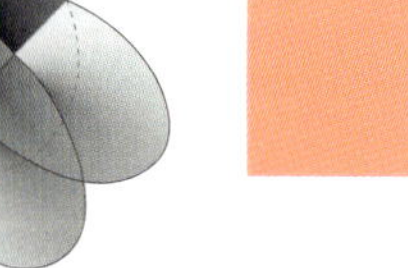

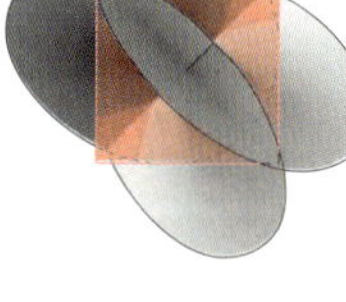
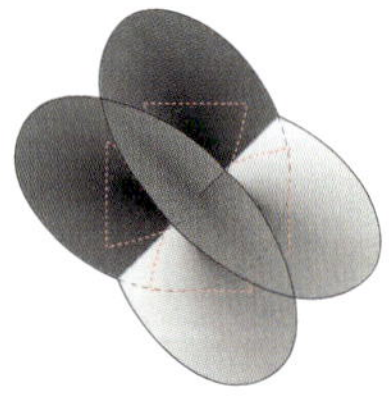

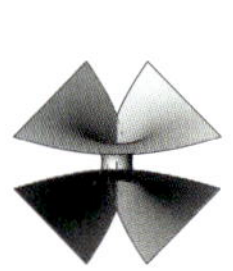

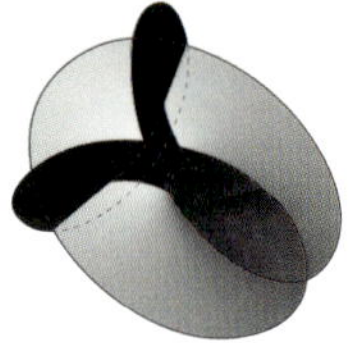

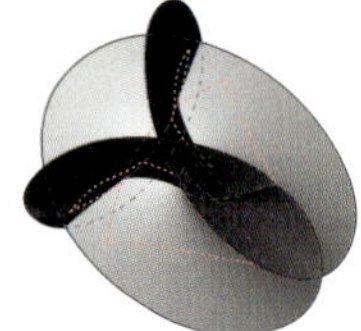

20_New Module 4.2_Differentiated cube based_construction of tile from Enneper surface variation and cube

21_3x3 matrix_3d printed model_elevation

22_3x3 matrix_3d printed model_45° perspective

23_minimal proliferation_elevation

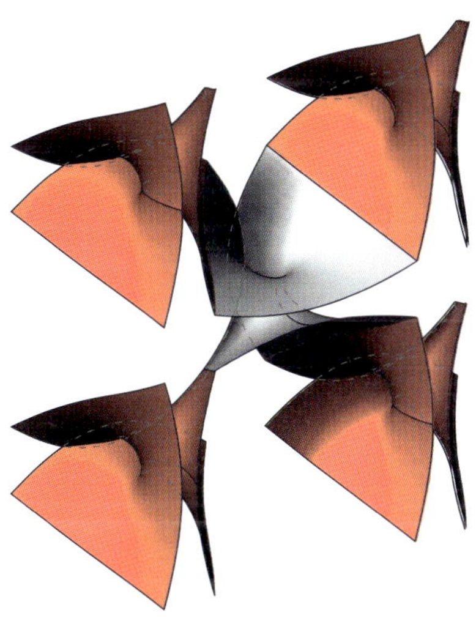

24_minimal proliferation_isometric view

Top images show a 3d printed 3x3 matrix model for this New Module design. The resultant matrix produces two faces, one where the limits of the surfaces produce diamond shapes, and another where the limits produce intersecting circular shapes.

Bottom images show a 2x2 matrix as a minimal proliferation of this module. Modules are reflected and continuity is guaranteed.

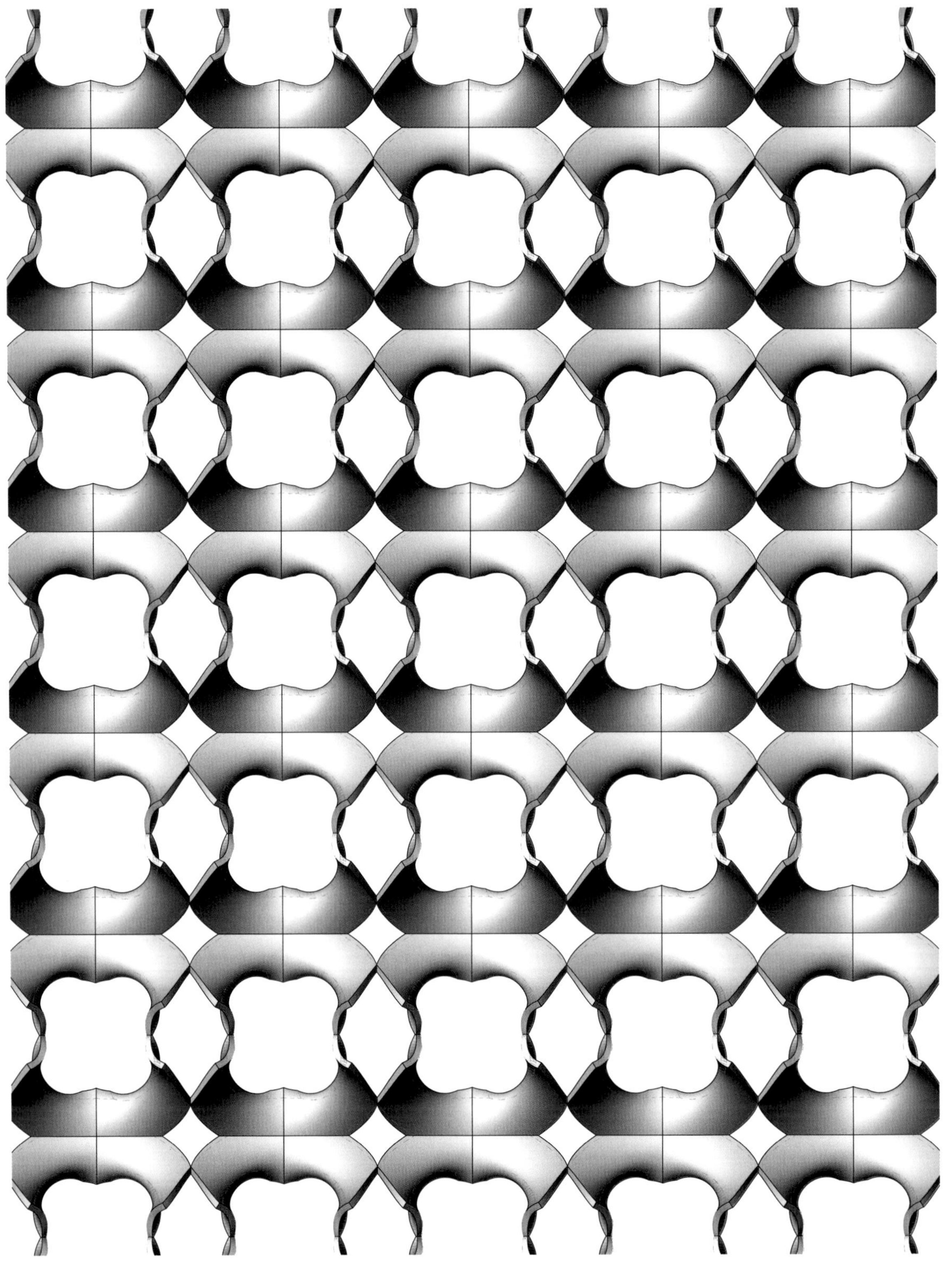

25_New Module 4.3_Octahedron based_proliferated matrix_ rendered frontal view

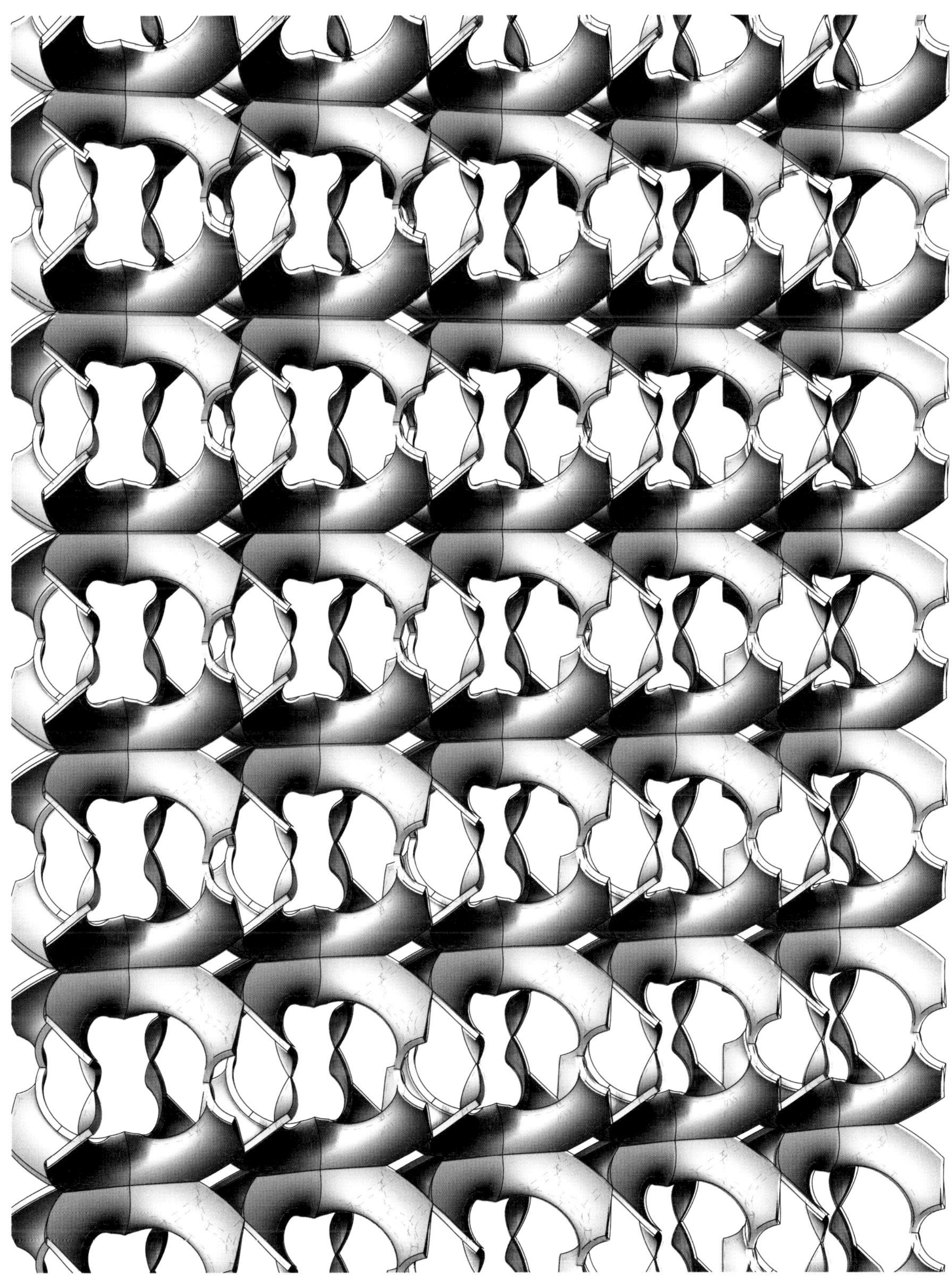

26_New Module 4.3_Octahedron based_proliferated matrix_
rendered perspective view

New module 4.3: Octahedron based

The Enneper surface formula for this design is:
{x}= 3*u*cos(v)-u^3/3*cos(2*v)
{y}= u^2*cos(2*v)
{z}= -u*sin(v)-u^(3)/3*sin(3*v)

This means that the formula is different from the generic Enneper surface used for earlier associative models. The difference lies in the intersecting volume, which instead of being a cube, is now a double pyramid or octahedron. Once again, the changed variable in the Enneper surface formula is the v multiplier, which changes from 3 in the generic formula, to 2 in this surface, as it is marked in red. The resultant surface, as it can be seen on the previous design, exhibits a unidirectional stretching along its axis of symmetry. This produces a different minimal surface which, once trimmed with an octahedron, generates a different tile and therefore a new matrix. Once again, the Enneper surface's axis of symmetry is rotated 45º in relationship to the orthogonal axis of the octahedron, which produces, when trimmed, the particular form of the tile.

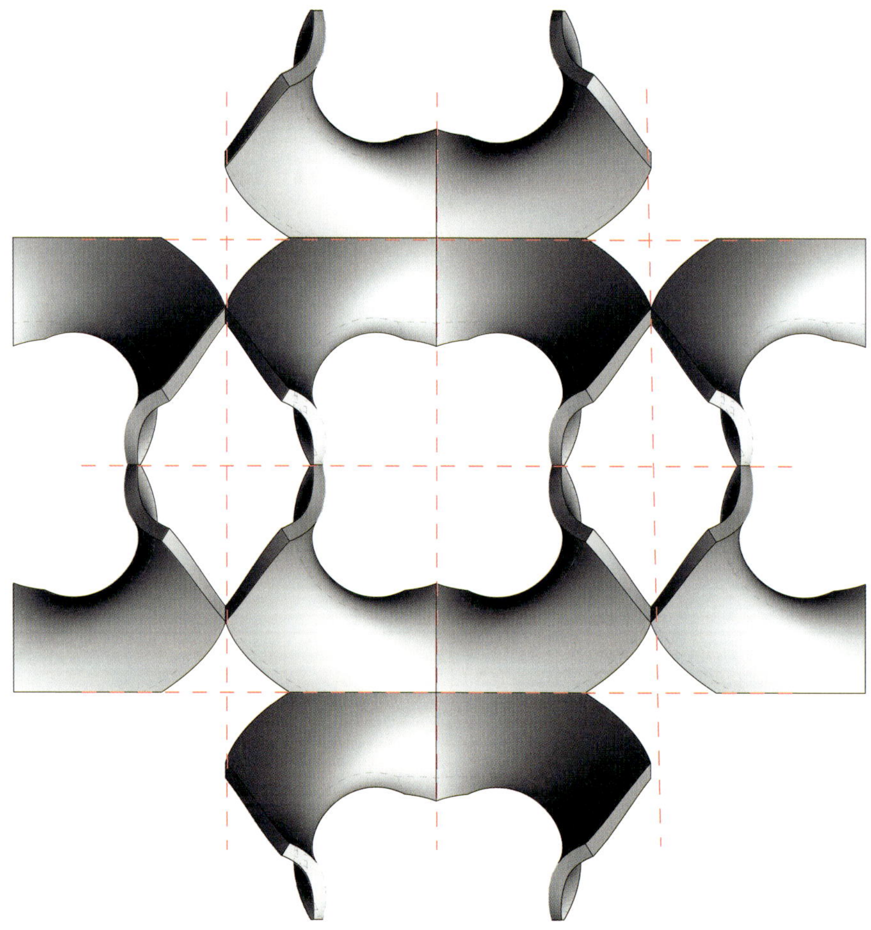

27_New Module 4.3_Octahedron based_minimal proliferation_rendered frontal view

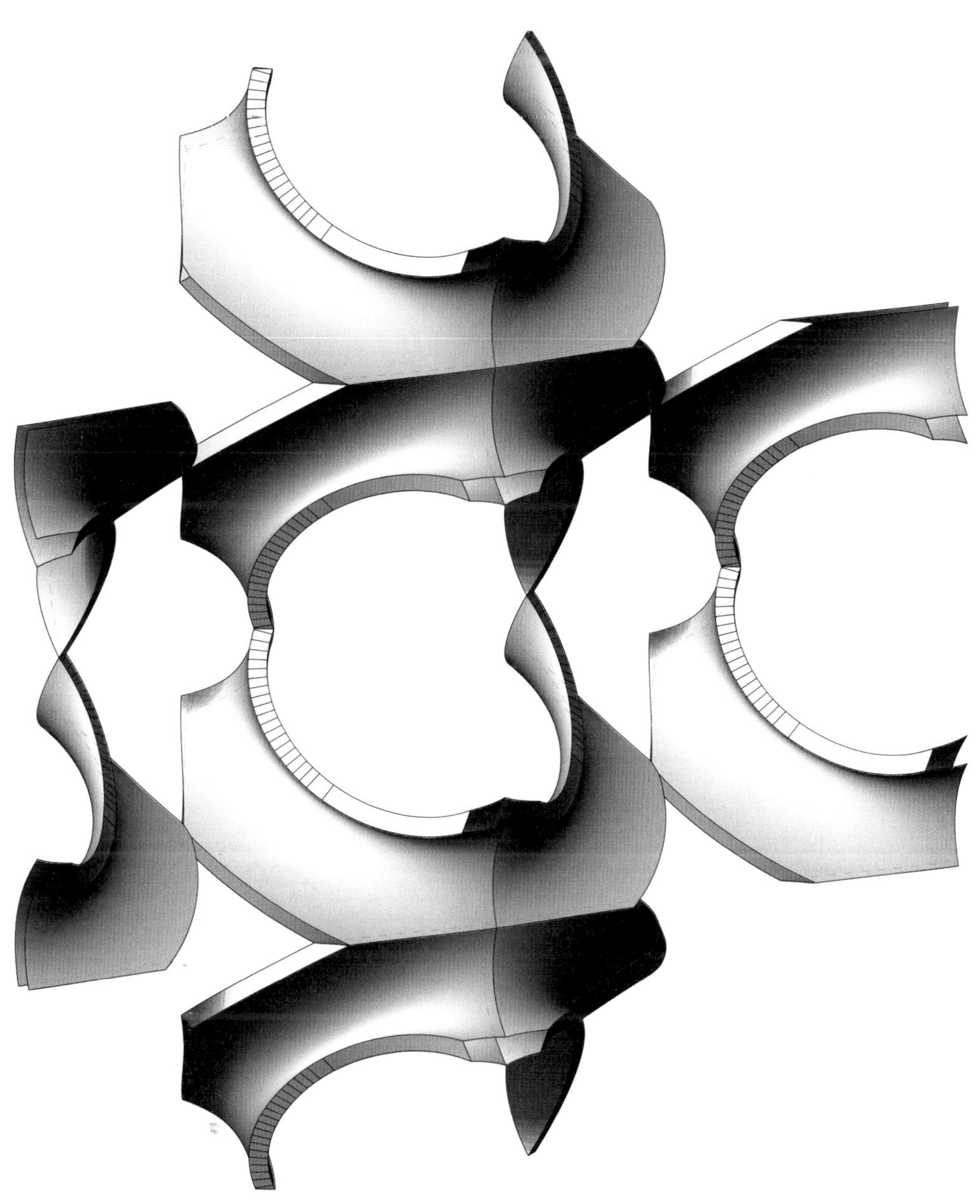

28_New Module 4.3_Octahedron based_minimal proliferation_rendered isometric view

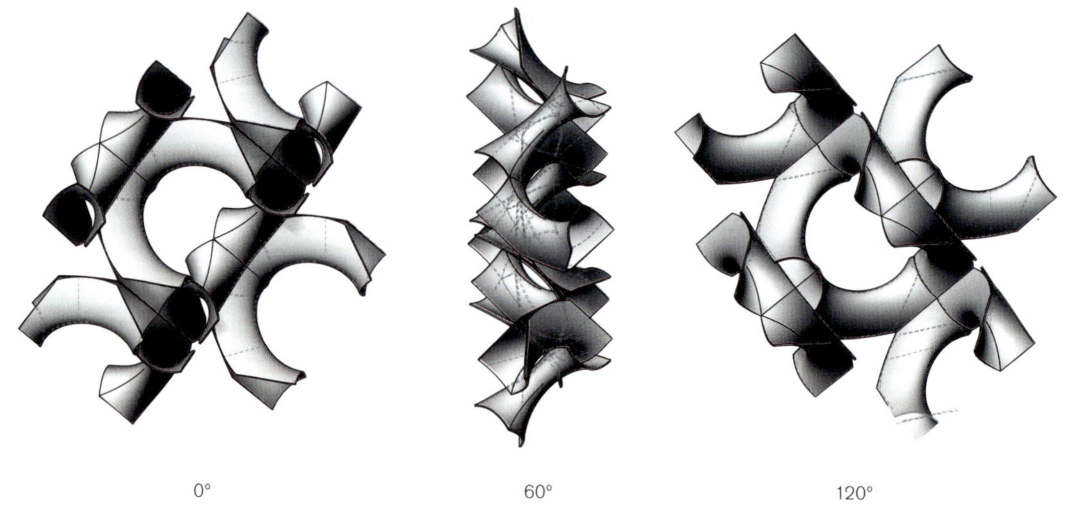

29_New Module 4.3_Octahedron based_minimal proliferation_series of 60° rotations

The construction works on the result of the intersection between an octahedron and a varied Enneper surface. This intersection produces an octahedral boundary that cuts the minimal surface such that the remaining surface fits the solid. Tiles are rotated, arrayed and mirrored to test which type of proliferation produces the best continuity. In this case, the matrix is arranged as reflected tiles along some edges, creating rotated squares with empty spaces in the middle. These are later mirrored along its sides for proliferation.

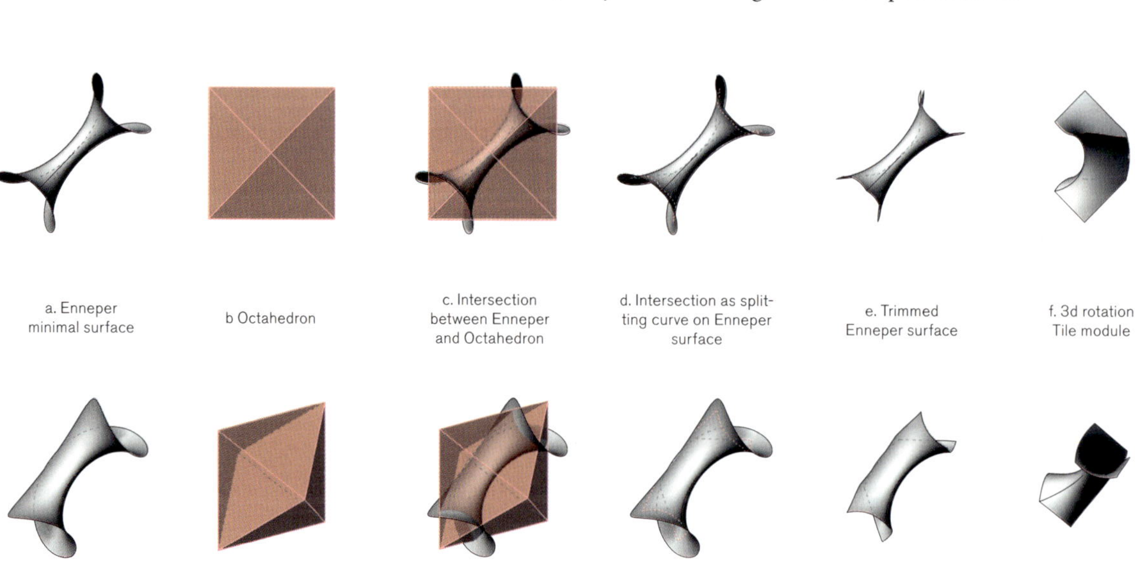

30_New Module 4.2_Octahedron based_ construction of tile from Enneper surface variation and octahedron.

31_3x3 matrix_3d printed model

32_3x3 matrix_3d printed model_45° perspective

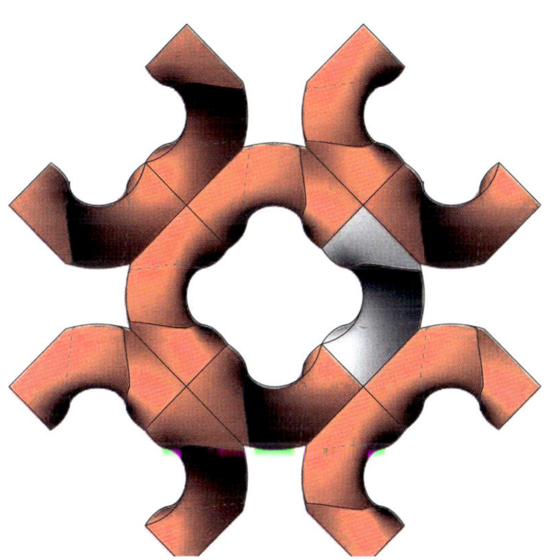

33_minimal proliferation

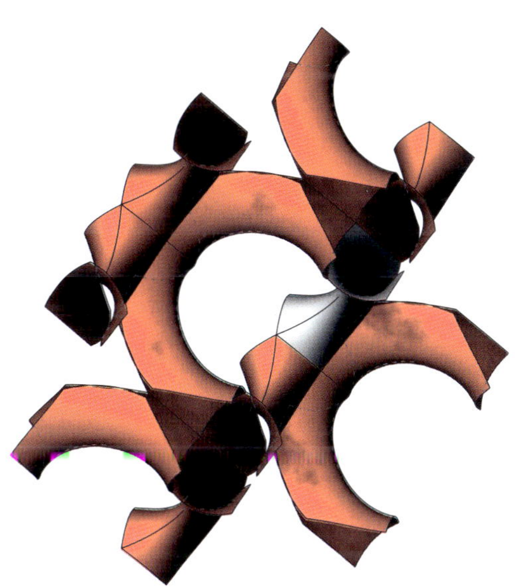

34_minimal proliferation_isometric view

Top images show a 3d printed 3x3 matrix model for this New Module design. The resultant matrix produces wide openings with twisting vertical supports.

Bottom images show a 2x2 matrix as a minimal proliferation of this module. Modules are reflected and continuity is guaranteed.

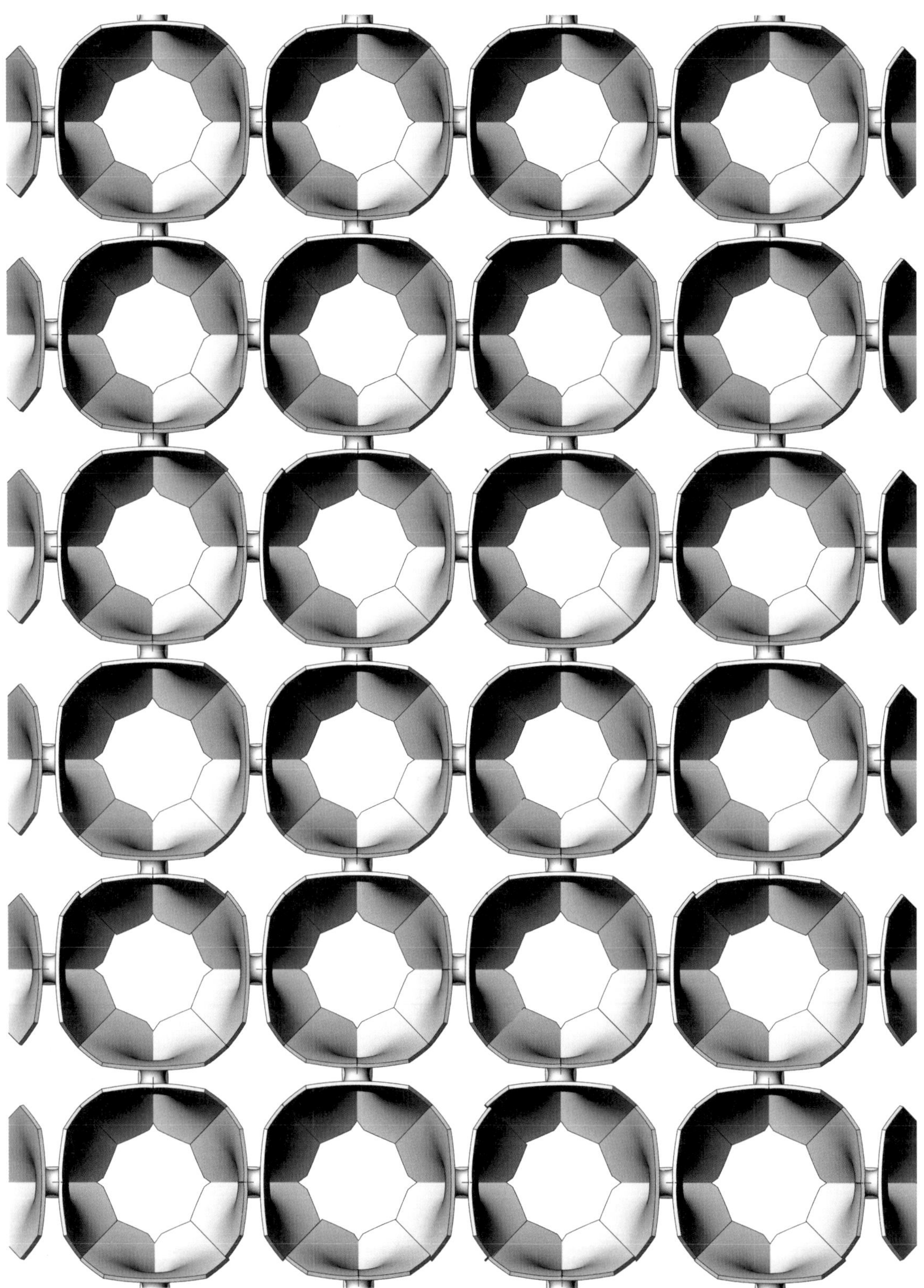

35_New Module 4.4_Tetradecahedron based_proliferated matrix_rendered frontal view

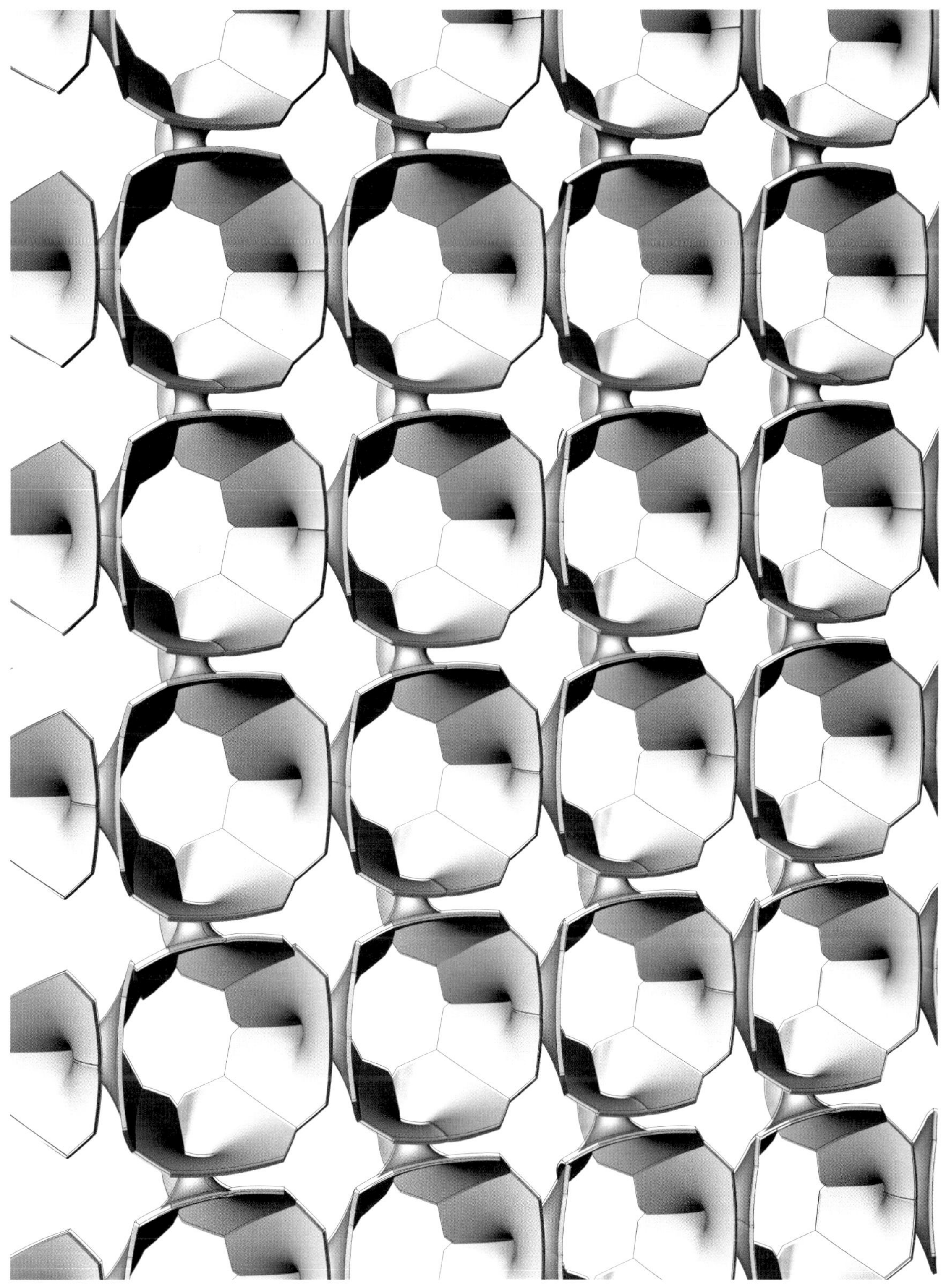

36_New Module 4.4_Tetradecahedron based_proliferated matrix_rendered perspective view

New module 4.4: Tetradecahedron based

The Enneper surface formula for this design is:
{x}= 3*u*cos(v)-u^3/3*cos(3*v)
{y}= u^2*cos(2*v)
{z}= -u*sin(v)-u^(3)/2*sin(3*v)

This is the only design in this series in which the Enneper surface is varied in z rather than x. It is different to any other Enneper surface formula used so far.

The variation is the sine multiplier, which changes from 3 in the generic formula, to 2, as it is marked in red. The resultant surface, as seen on the following spread, produces a scaling and exacerbation of its curvature, producing self-intersection. This variation produces a particular minimal surface which, once trimmed with a tetradecahedron, generates a unique tile and therefore a new matrix. Once again, the Enneper surface's axis of symmetry is rotated 45º in relationship to the orthogonal axis of the tetradecahedron. Other variations of this component in the x parameter of the Enneper surface formula could further investigate how curvature or rotation plays a role in the definition and symmetry of the resultant tile.

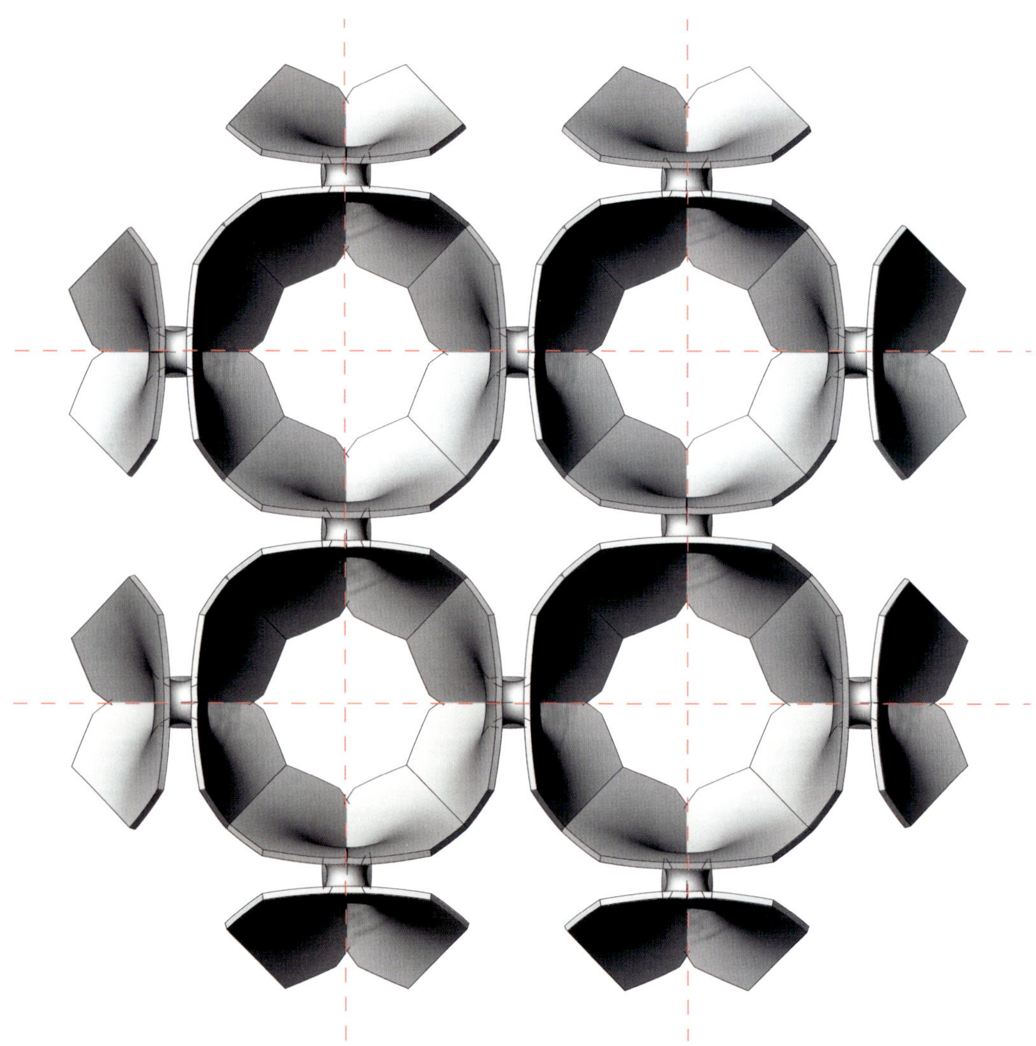

37_New Module 4.4_Tetradecahedron based_minimal proliferation_rendered frontal view

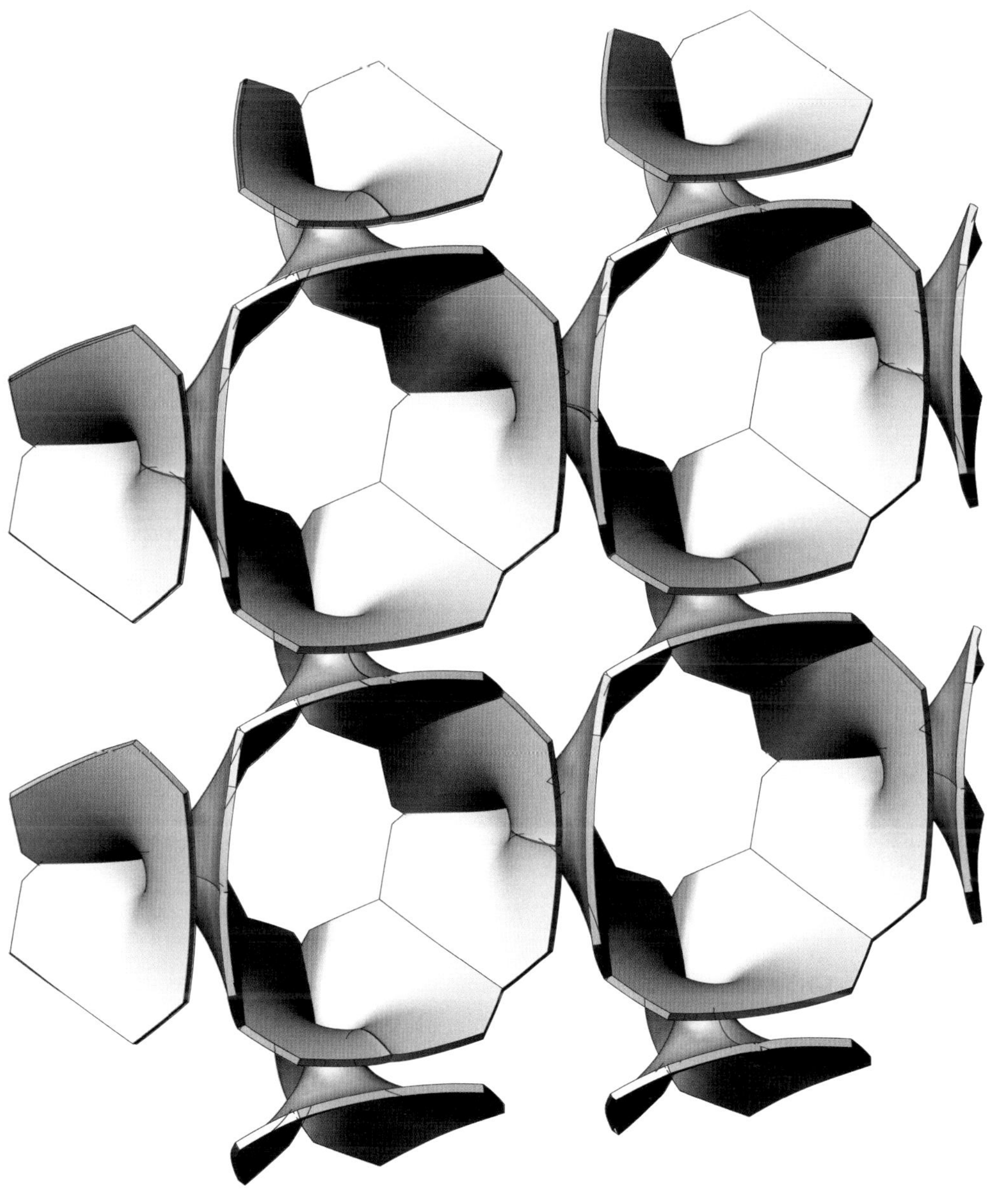

38_New Module 4.4_Tetradecahedron based_minimal proliferation_rendered isometric view

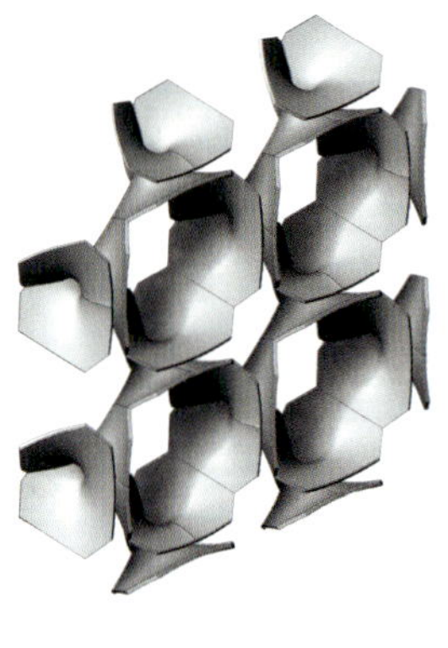

0°

60°

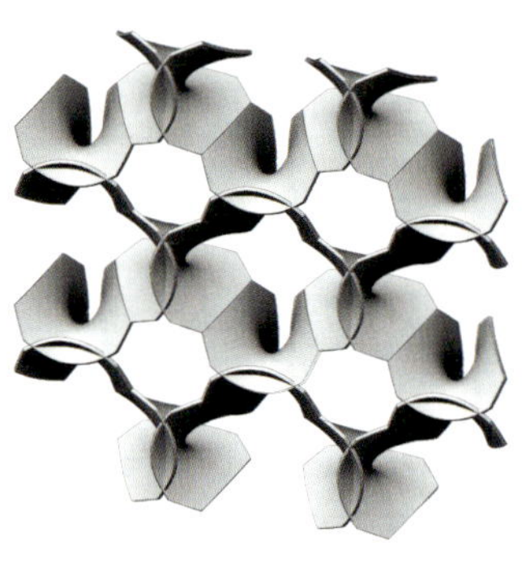

120°

39_New Module 4.4_Tetradecahedron based_minimal proliferation_series of 60º rotations

The geometric construction is produced through the intersection between a tetrahedron and a varied Enneper surface.

Once the minimal surface is trimmed, it is given a thickness and rotated 45º so that its edges are oblique and the tile can be proliferated through a diagonal grid.

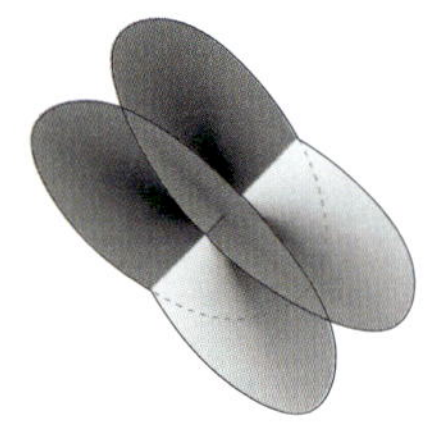

a. Enneper minimal surface

b. Tetradecahedron

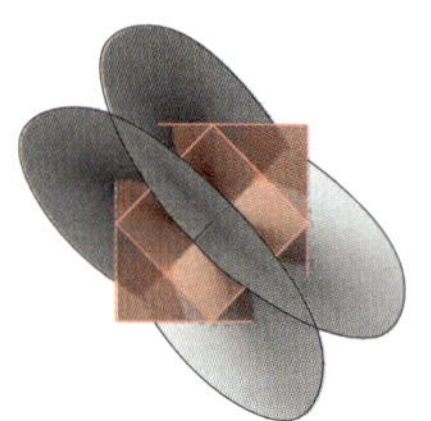

c. Intersection between Enneper and Tetradecahedron

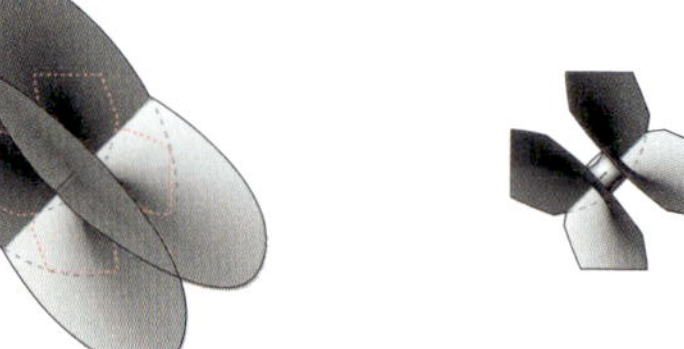

d. Splitting curve on Enneper surface

e. Trimmed Enneper surface

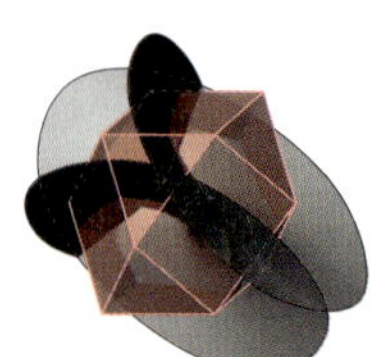

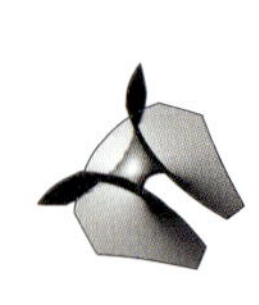

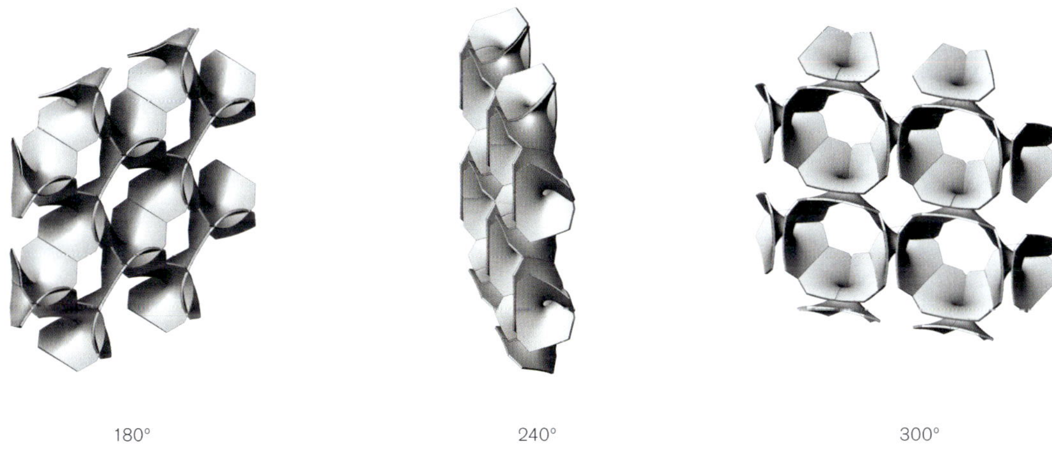

40_New Module 4.4_Tetradecahedron based_ construction of tile from intersection between Enneper surface variation and octahedron; proliferation and thickness

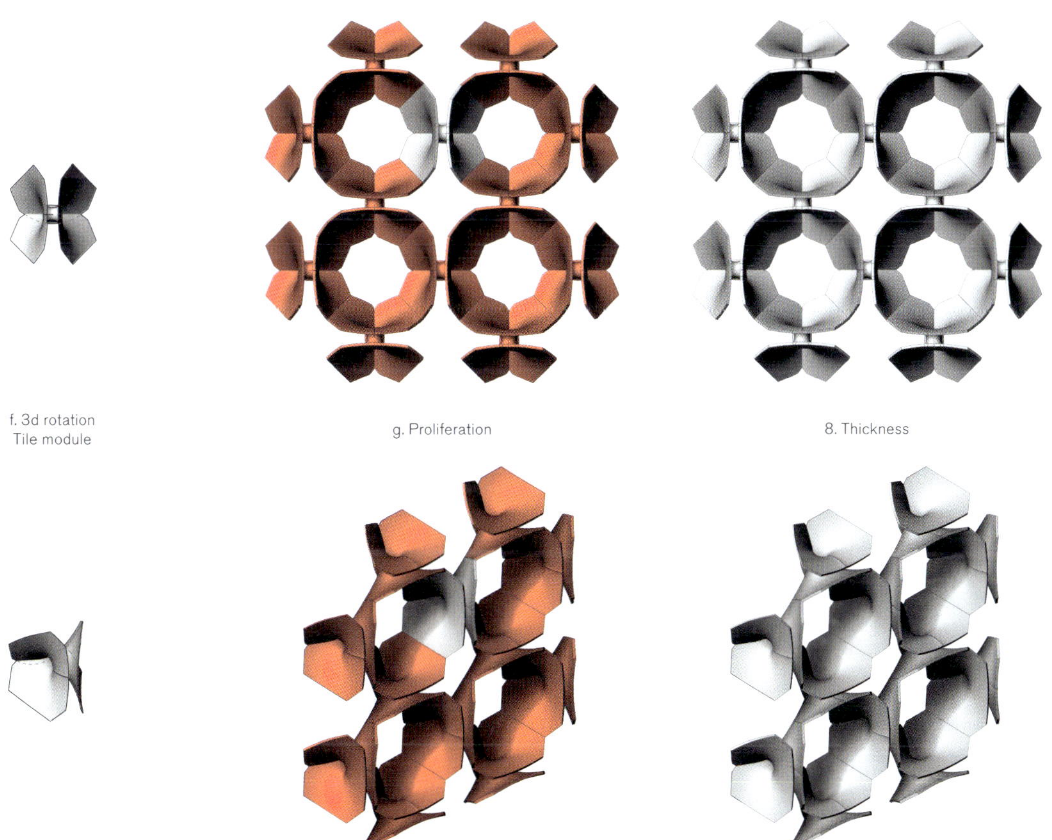

41_New Module 4.4_Tetradecahedron based_alternatively tiled proliferated matrix_rendered frontal view

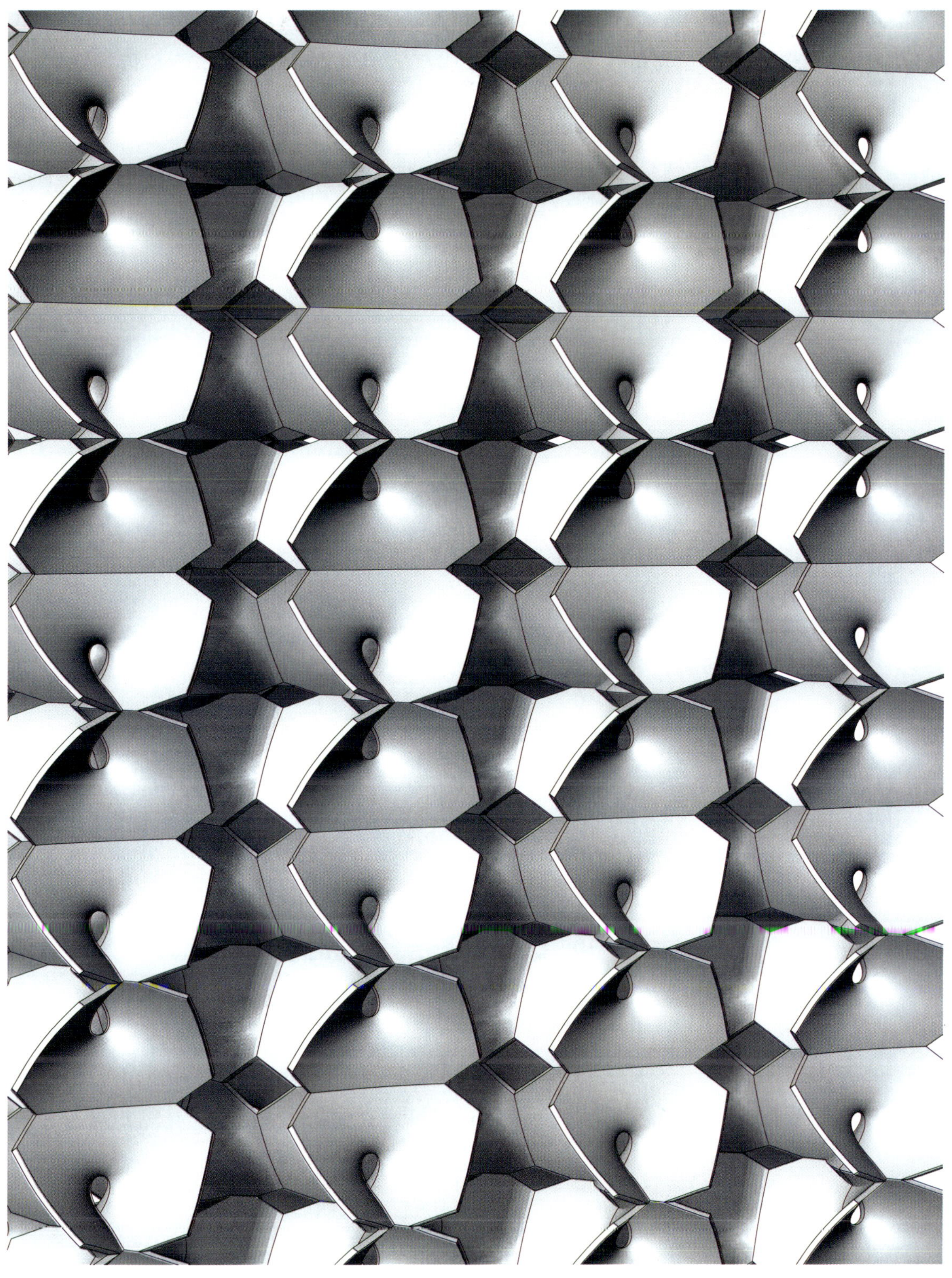

42_New Module 4.4_Tetradecahedron based_alternatively tiled proliferated matrix_rendered perspective view

New module 4.4: Tetradecahedron based_ tiling variation

The aggregative tiling in this design produces a thicker matrix of three-dimensional surfaces that provide different readings of the geometry as the viewer moves around the assembly.

Once again, the Enneper surface's axis of symmetry is rotated 45° in relationship to the orthogonal axis of the tetradecahedron, which produces, when trimmed, a particular form. Other variations of this component in the x parameter of the Enneper surface formula could further investigate how curvature or rotation plays a role in the definition and symmetry of the resultant tile.

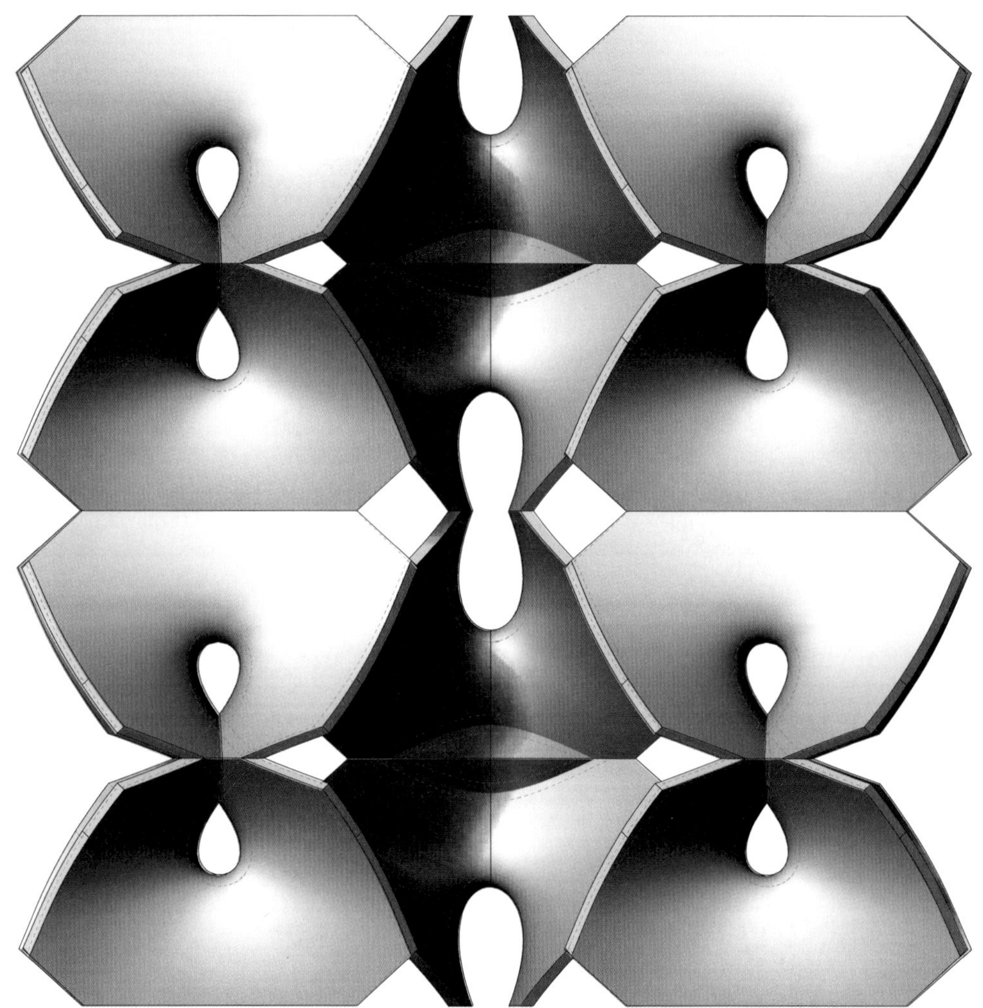

43_New Module 4.4_Tetradecahedron based_alternatively tiled proliferated matrix

44_New Module 4.4_Tetradecahedron based_alternatively tiled proliferated matrix_rendered isometric view

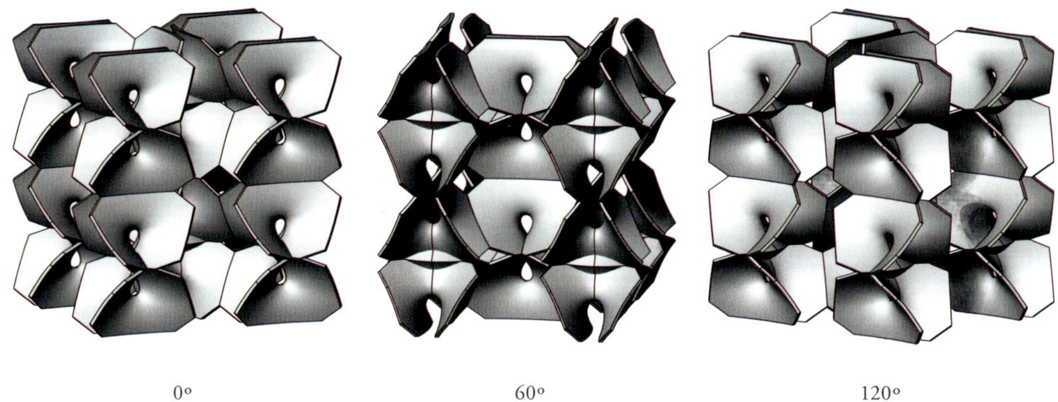

45_New Module 4.4_Tetradecahedron based_alternatively tiled minimal proliferation_series of 60° rotations

The construction for this design is almost identical to the Tetradecahedron based, but it is tiled differently. It works on the result of the intersection between a tetrahedron and a varied Enneper surface. Tiles are rotated, arrayed and mirrored to test which type of proliferation produces the best continuity. In this case, the matrix is arranged as aggregations of the module alternatively rotated so that the edges coincide. The result is a much more tridimensional assembly than any of the other designs in the New Module series.

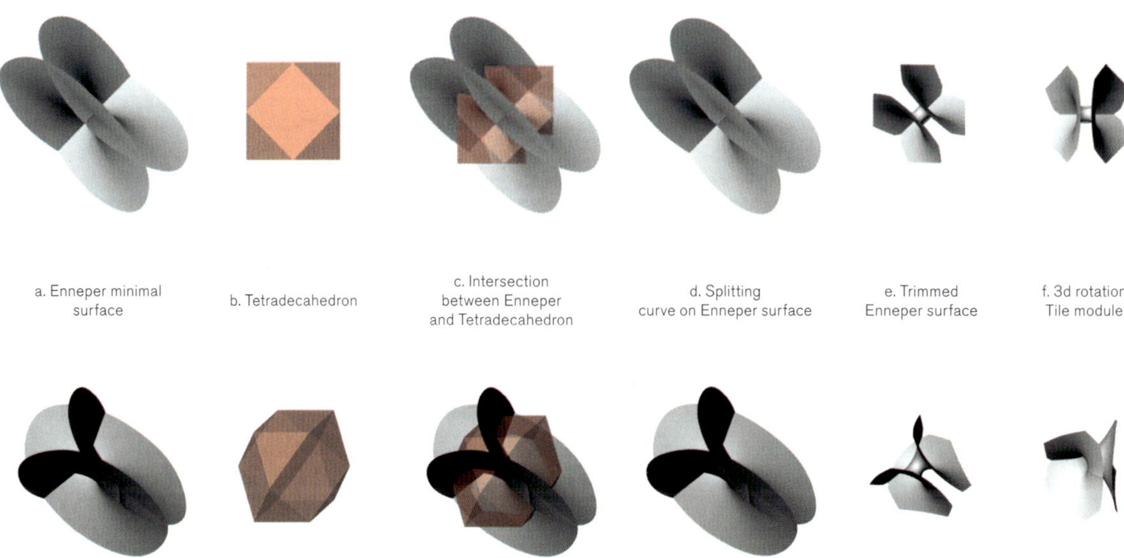

46_New Module 4.4_Tetradecahedron based_ construction of tile from intersection between Enneper surface variation and cube

47_3x3 matrix_3d printed model

48_3x3 matrix_3d printed model_45° perspective

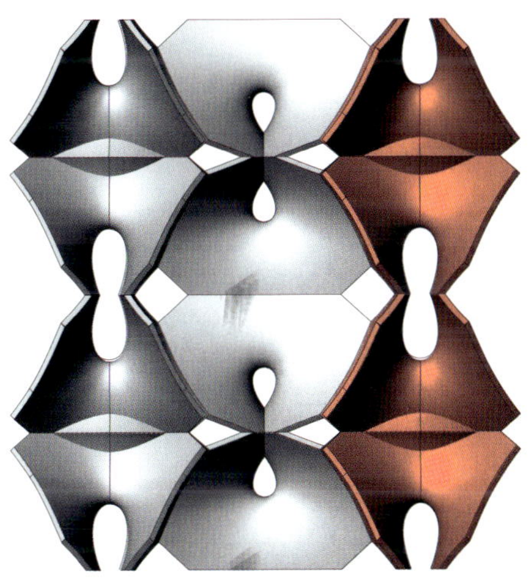

49_minimal proliferation

50_minimal proliferation_isometric view

Top images show a 3d printed 3x3 matrix model for this New Module design. The resultant matrix produces wide openings with twisting vertical supports.

Bottom images show a complex matrix as a possible proliferation of this module. Modules are reflected and continuity is guaranteed. The different tiling arrangement produces a denser and compact matrix.

New Module 4.1_Cube based_proliferated matrix

Section four.

Re-contextualization & Re-fabrication

Re-contextualization

The process of upgrading legacy design knowledge for contemporary creative practice benefits from deliberate reflection and a study of how it may re-contextualized. This is likely to span across a spectrum of considerations. From the opportunities enabled by contemporary design and fabrication for transforming this legacy to the migration of these earlier practices into concerns that it may not have been explicitly associated with. Such a re-contextualization may also involve a deliberate extension of the earlier ambitions which guided the precedent models, whereby an upgrade may be pursued by building upon and extending this earlier research through contemporary means and frames of reference.

The possibilities for bridging historical and contemporary design practice through this process of re-contextualizing design practice legacies is made explicit in the outcomes of the teaching explorations discussed in the (Re)fabricating Prototypes chapter of this book. Through directing and establishing the pedagogy of the course, a methodology and practice-based research culture focused on upgrading material history was cultivated over several years. The dedicated research into the study and re-contextualization of Erwin Hauer's modular constructivist works discussed in this book builds upon those earlier explorations. One of the most compelling characteristics of Hauer's work is the manner in which the complex surfaces of his pieces create masterful effects with light. Given this luminous capacity, it was perhaps self-evident that his sculptural explorations could be so seamlessly translated into architectural screens and envelopes. The environmental modulation and visual effects afforded by Hauer's forms still offer contemporary practice an unsurpassed exemplar of expressive lambent surfaces. The re-contextualization of Hauer's legacy may still profit from a deep engagement with this interplay between surface and light.

Staying within the realm of Hauer's intended architectural applications, explorations in extending the performance of these screens or envelopes in association with other environmental considerations can be readily supported by contemporary design processes and workflows. Reconsidering these intricate surfaces in light of thermodynamic performance is a complimentary line of re-contextualization that extends our design knowledge on the potentials of these surfaces.

Re-contextualizing this legacy within contemporary cultures of manufacturing and dissemination also supports the reframing of this material legacy. The possibilities associated with the third (or fourth) industrial revolution present a challenge to older notions of authorship as well as production that characterized earlier work. Rather than singular authorship and centralized production, the transformation of historical systems could be more explicitly evolved through a more shared and collective effort.

Re-contextualization of the work may also focus on extending this embedded material intelligence towards addressing and expressing an acute awareness of the environmental consequences of our design and building practices. The following speculations on avenues of re-contextualizing designs generated from the models offers a view of how we might work towards the upgrading and evolution of the intelligence and knowledge embedded in legacy design systems.

01_New Module 4.1_Generic cube based_proliferated matrix_
rendered perspective view

Double plane

Current visualization and simulation tools also provide a seamless workflow that enables testing the interplay between light and different surface iterations prior to physical prototyping. This allows us to visualize the effects produced by the interplay of light with complex surfaces of different generated iterations while also allowing for a more quantitative testing for their variations in light levels.

Design 4 by Erwin Hauer offered a good benchmark for a compelling visual effect produced by the interplay between light and Continua forms. The production of two different visual planes in this original Hauer design is apparent when the screen receives light, transforming a continuous form into two different planes of differentiated luminosity.

A series of design instantiations were tested in digital simulations to search for their effects on diffusing light and to envision their visual qualities.

Striking visual qualities which only become apparent when seen in their interaction with light could be identified in a number of the new design instantiations through this capability.

New module 4.1 was one such case that was found to produce a novel visual patterning which was not legible from its formal properties alone. The seamless, minimal surfaces took on an appearance which was more discretized, differentiated and patterned by emergent geometric shapes that were formed by diffuse light.

02_Erwin Hauer_Design 4_frontal view

03_New Module 4.1_Generic cube based_proliferated matrix _scale 2_rendered frontal view (summer, 16h)

Scale

Using New Module 4.1, the outcomes from testing the variations in the scale of the modules allowed us to identify two immediate effects. The first is the obvious variations in visual patterning and readings of scale. Another effect is the overall light levels that are achieved. Digital visualization and simulation supports the quick testing of different scalar variations of a wide spectrum of design types, allowing for a more customizable and specific definition of the design scale in association with lighting criteria as well as visual effects.

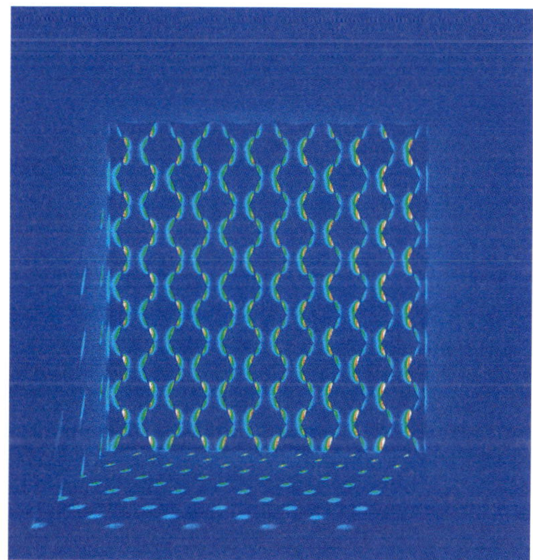

04_New Module 4.1_Generic cube based_proliferated matrix_scale 1_rendered frontal view and lighting analysis (summer, 16h)

05_New Module 4.1_Generic cube based_proliferated matrix_scale 2_rendered frontal view and lighting analysis (summer, 16h)

New effects - two faced

New Module 4.2 is an illustration of the capacities for the generated design iterations to produce very different patterning or readings on opposite sides of the screen/envelope. The proliferated tetrahedral unit matrix forms a complex section that transitions from an isolated "diamond" patterning on one side to a field of overlapping circular figures on the other. The resulting screen offers the possibility of providing a very different experiences on the interior face from its reading on the exterior facade. On the interior face, the screen achieves a double-planed condition as the inner surfaces take on a more darkened, silhouette-like condition while the exterior surfaces are significantly lighter. This strong contrast creates the illusion of the diamond units "floating" while the exterior surfaces recede into the background. This asymmetrical condition introduces novelty into the series.

06_New Module 4.2_Tetrahedron based_proliferated matrix_ rendered frontal views: interior (summer, 16h)

An explicit asymmetry such as this is a clear departure from Hauer's Continua series. New Module 4.2 exhibits formal characteristics which depart from symmetry and regularity. These formal departures help to produce significant new qualities and effects.

This capacity for asymmetry is also seen in other design instantiations.

New Module 1.2 is another iteration which produces an explicit difference between opposite faces of the screen, where one side has a strong vertical emphasis in the patterning while the other side is more horizontal.

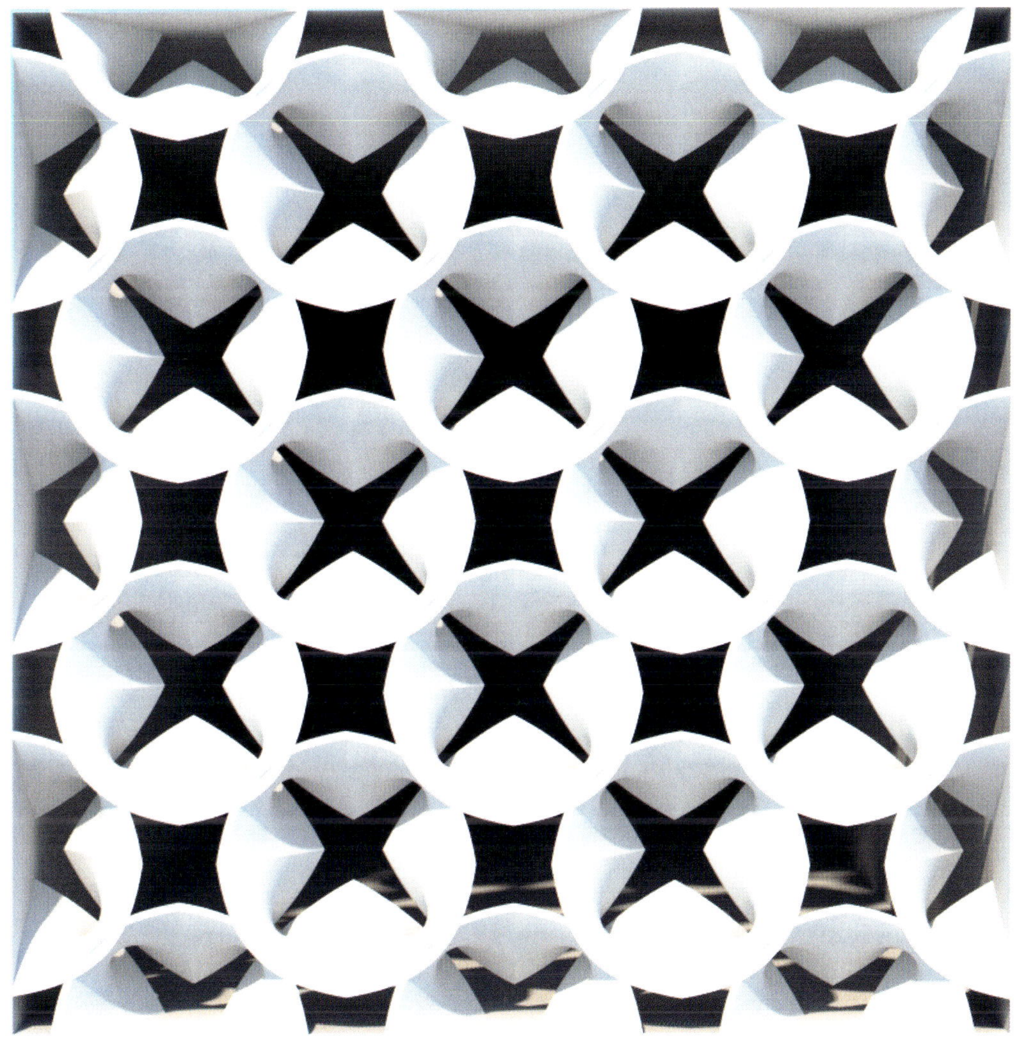

07_New Module 4.2_Tetrahedron based_proliferated matrix_ rendered frontal views: exterior (summer, 16h)

Light

A small sample of visualizations and analysis of design instantiations generated by the associative model is presented here to demonstrate how one may assess the ways in which these designs filter and interact with daylight, prior to investing in physical prototyping. Today, a range of widely accessible digital tools affords designers a seamless work flow between generative design platforms and simulation or visualization environments.

08_a. New Module 4.1_Generic cube based_rendered perspective view

08_b. New Module 4.2_Tetrahedron based_rendered perspective view

08_c. New Module 4.3_Octahedron based_rendered perspective view

08_d. New Module 1.3_Associative model 7 based 01_rendered perspective view

08_e. New Module 1.4_Associative model 7 based 02_rendered perspective view

08_a

08_c

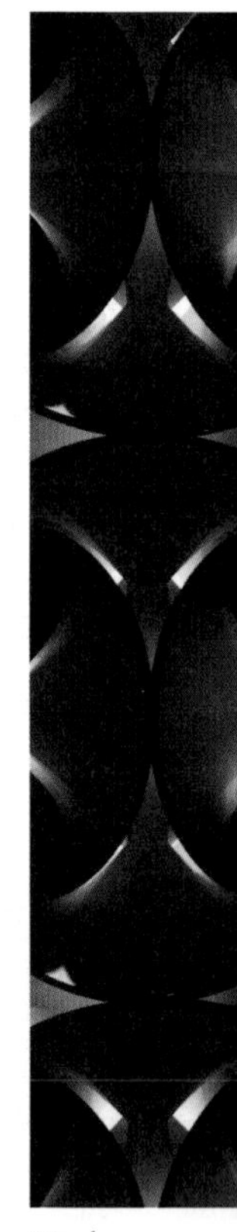

08_d

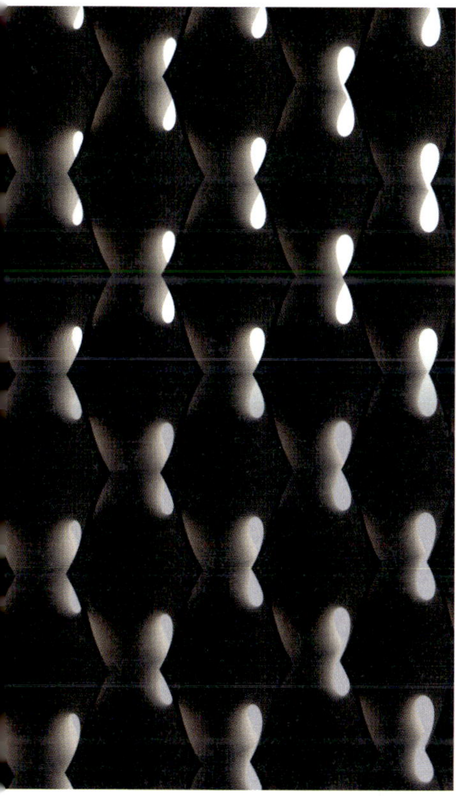

08_b

08_e

In the same way that we may use these digital tools to help study each individualdesign, the opportunity for a seamless feedback relationship between formal iteration and evaluation also allows for the study of large samples of different design instantiations in the aggregate. Computational lighting analysis allows for the consideration of these large samples of design iterations according to a systematic study of the light effects and screening performance that each form offers.
A re-contextualization of these designs extends this earlier formal and artistic endeavor into searching processes for different classes of screens based on a focus on measurable performance.

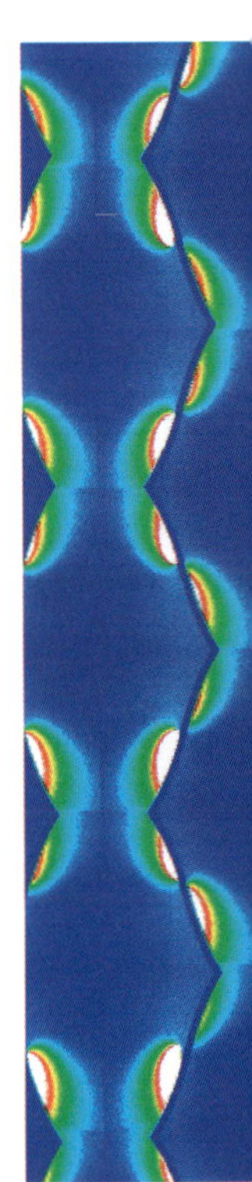

09_a. New Module 4.1_Generic cube based__lighting analysis

09_b. New Module 4.2_Tetrahedron based_lighting analysis

09_c. New Module 4.3_Octahedron based_lighting analysis

09_d. New Module 1.3_Associative Model 7 based 01_lighting analysis

09_e. New Module 1.4_IAssociative Model 7 based 02_lighting analysis

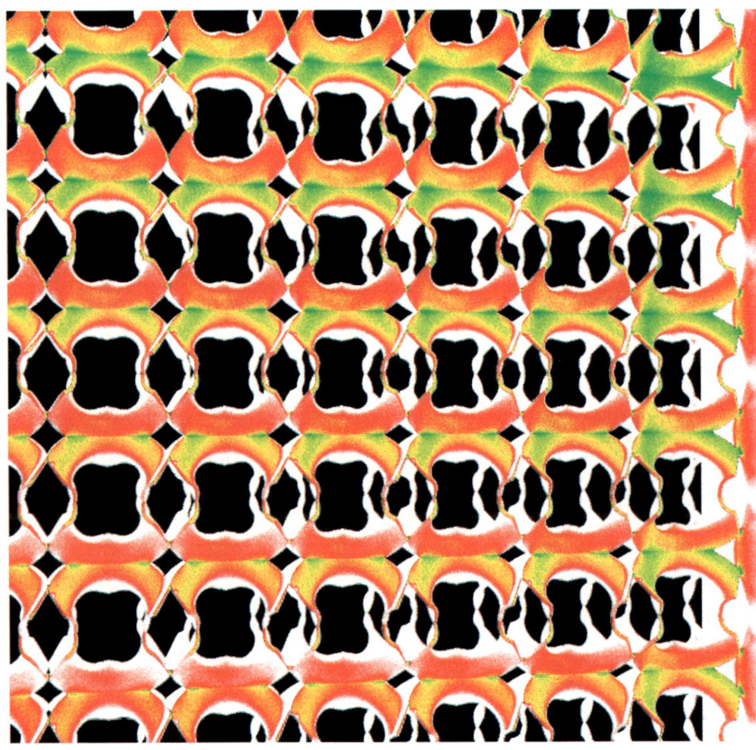

New Module 4.3_Octahedron based_ proliferated matrix_lighting analysis

New Module 4.1_Generic cube based_proliferated matrix_lighting analysis

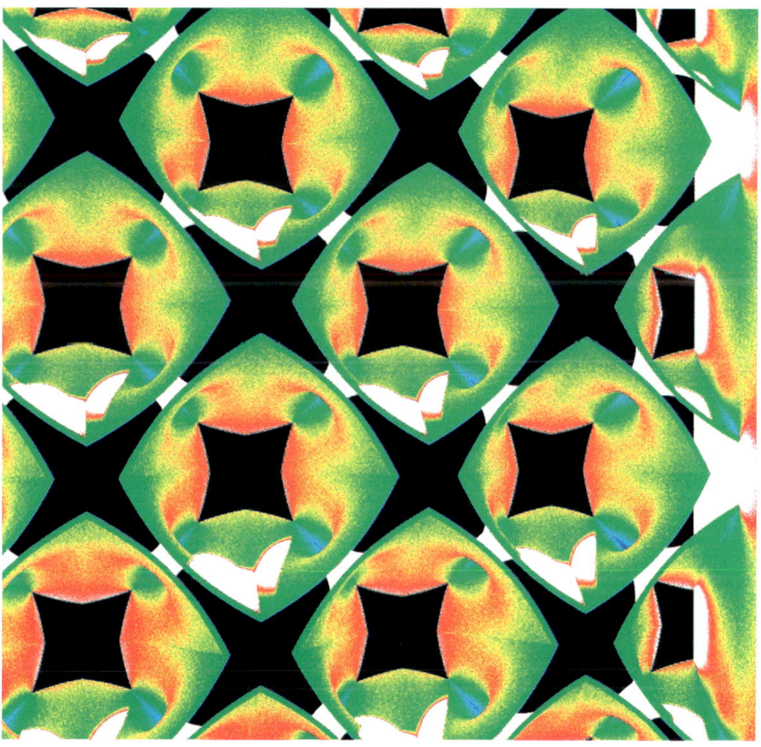

New Module 4.2_Tetrahedron based_proliferated matrix_lighting analysis

New Module 1.3_Associative Model 7 based 01_proliferated matrix_lighting analysis

New Module 1.4_Associative Model 7 based 02_proliferated matrix_lighting analysis

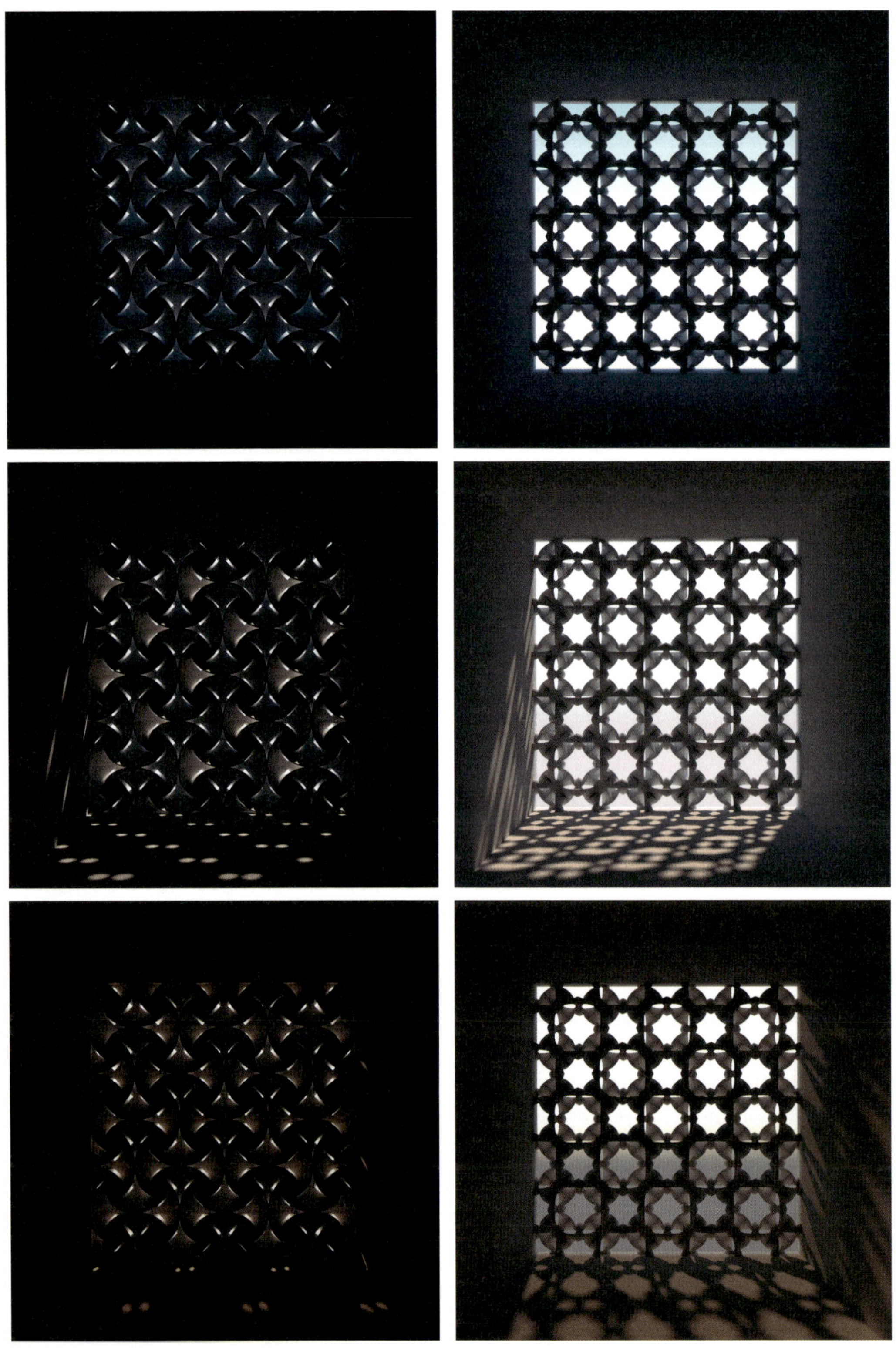

Matrix of rendered frontal views (summer: a_12h, b_16h and c_18h). From left to right: 10_New Module 1.3_Associative model 7 based 01, 11_New Module 1.4_Associative model 7 based 02

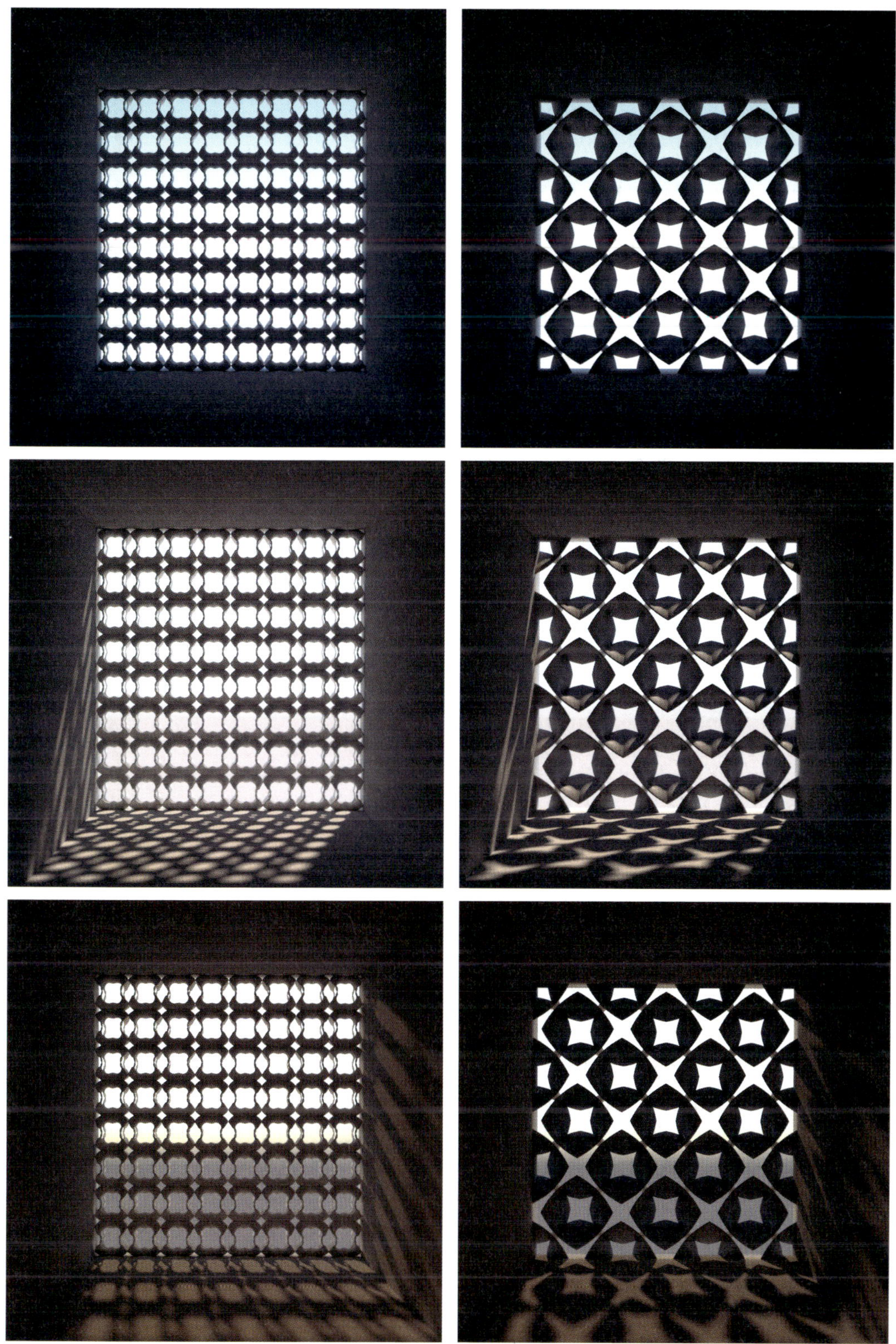

12_New Module 4.2_Tetrahedron based and 13_New Module 4.3_ Octahedron based

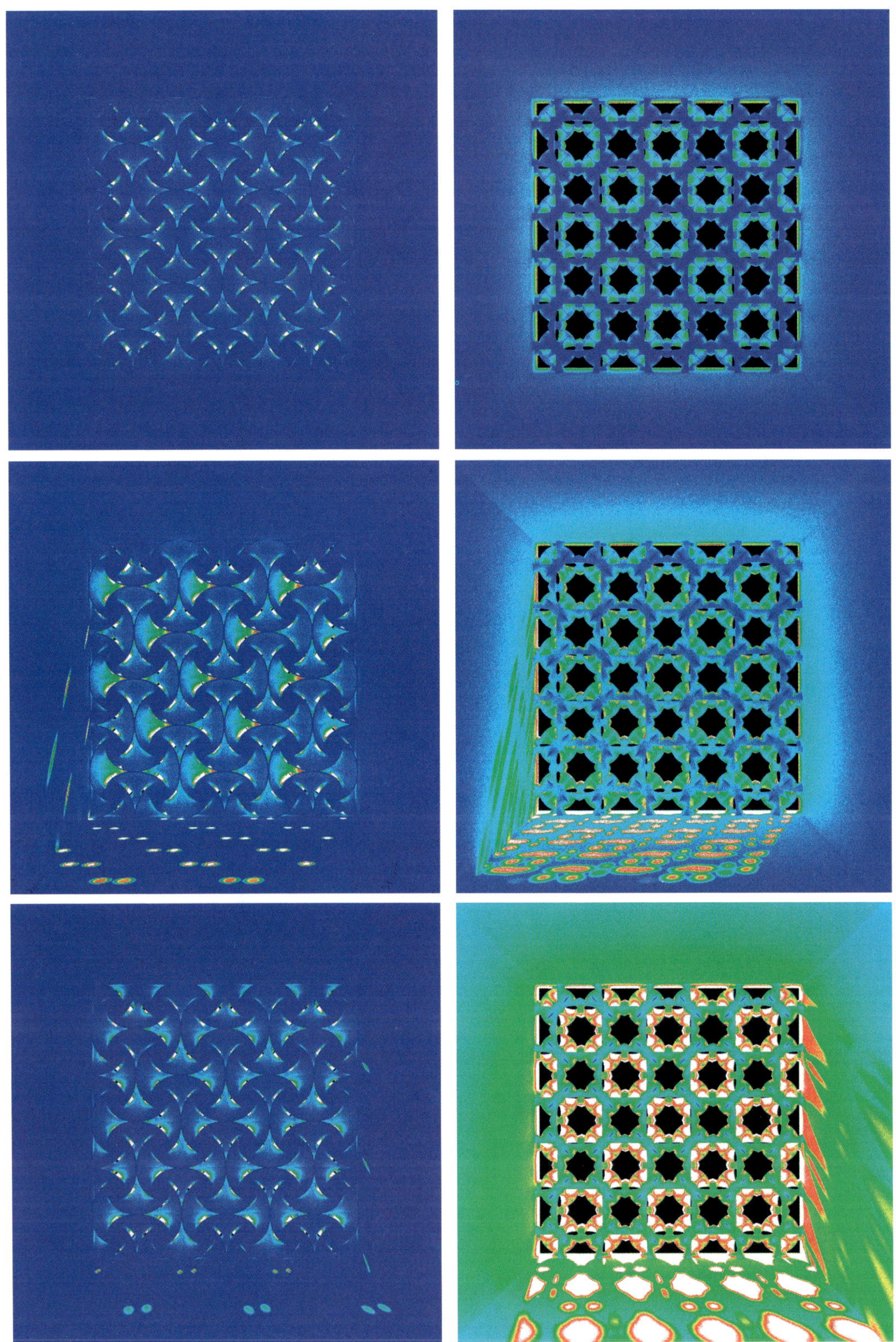

Matrix of lighting analysis (summer: a_12h, b_16h and c_18h). From left to right: 14_New Module 1.3_Associative model 7 based 01, 15_New Module 1.4_Associative model 7 based 02

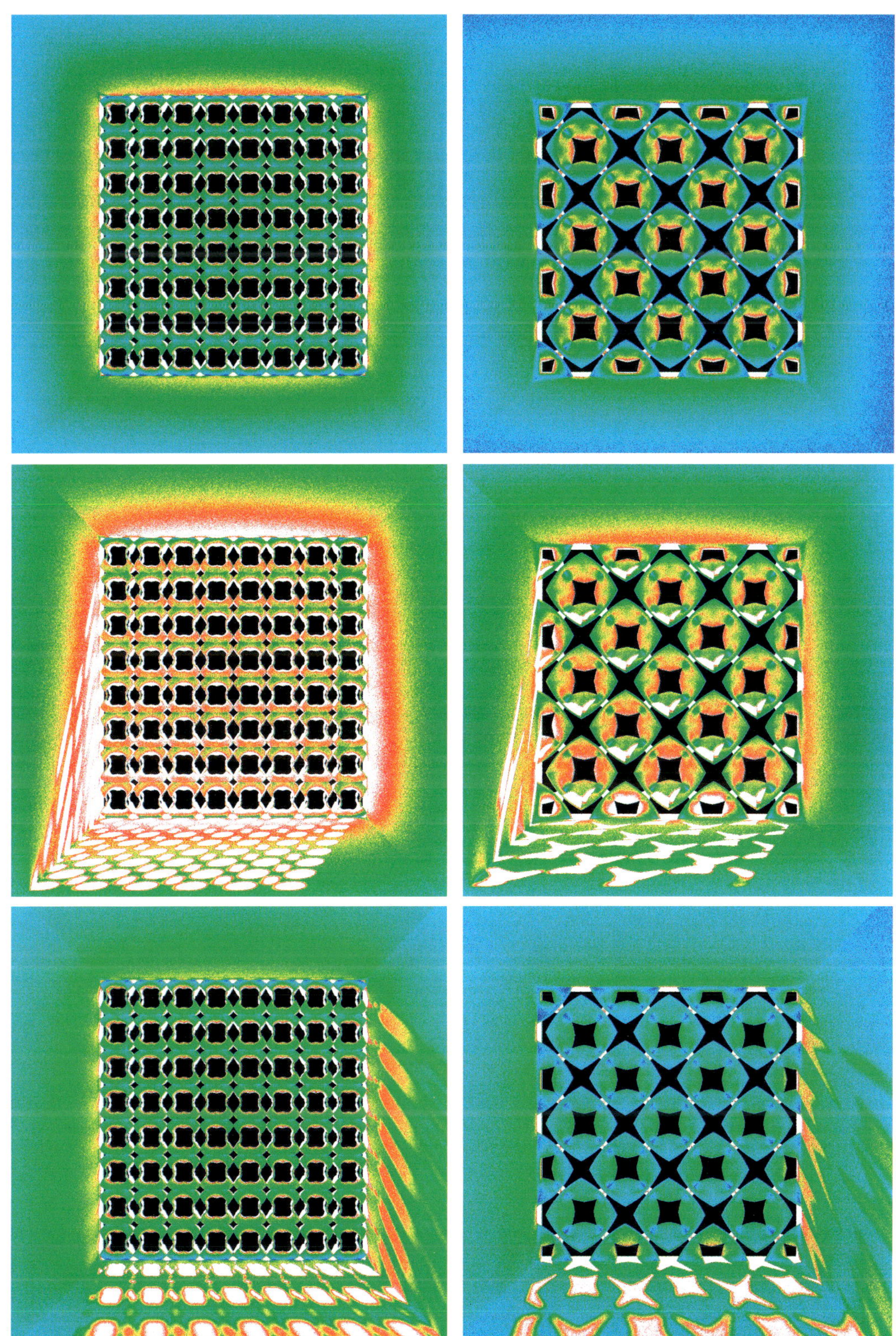

16_New Module 4.2_Tetrahedron based and 17_New Module 4.3_ Octahedron based

Fields & transitions

New module_associative 5 based_v02_d05

01_small scale_rendered frontal view

02_large scale_rendered frontal view

These designs have the ability to achieve seamless corner transitions. Transformations were explored where the design plane may transition from a horizontal to a vertically emphasized field. These possibilities are afforded by the new geometries and suggest a range of potential applications including architectural envelope systems.

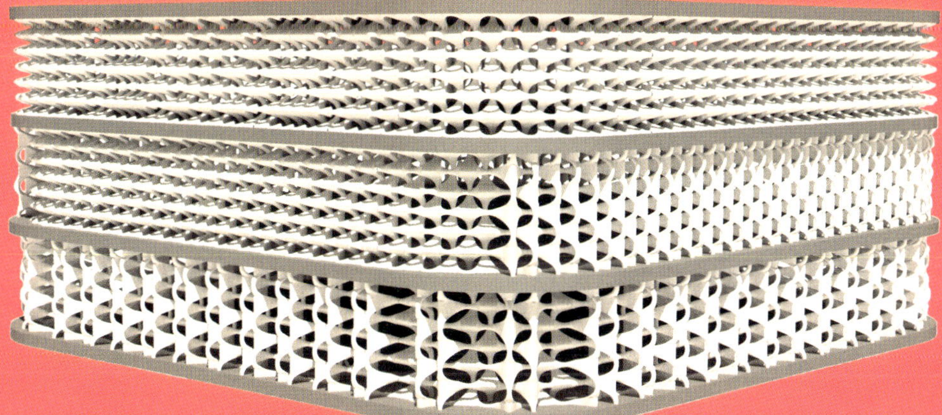

03_small scale_corner rendered perspective view

04_large scale_corner rendered perspective view

New module_cube_permeable

05_small scale_rendered frontal view

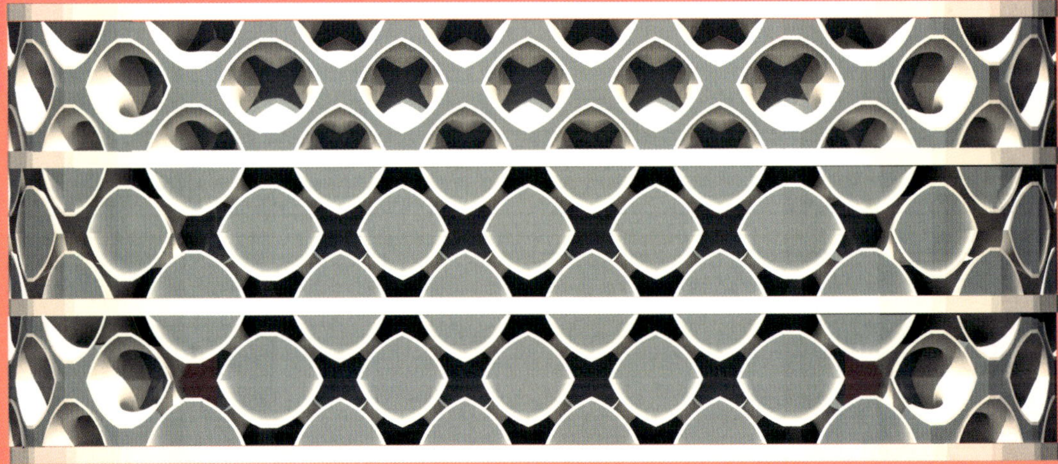

06_large scale_rendered frontal view

The volumetric nature of the designs, especially when scaled up beyond Hauer's originals, allows for producing different planar alignments within the thickness of the same modules.

The addition of glazing into this envelope thickness could be integrated at different points within its depth, producing very different performances and visual appearances.

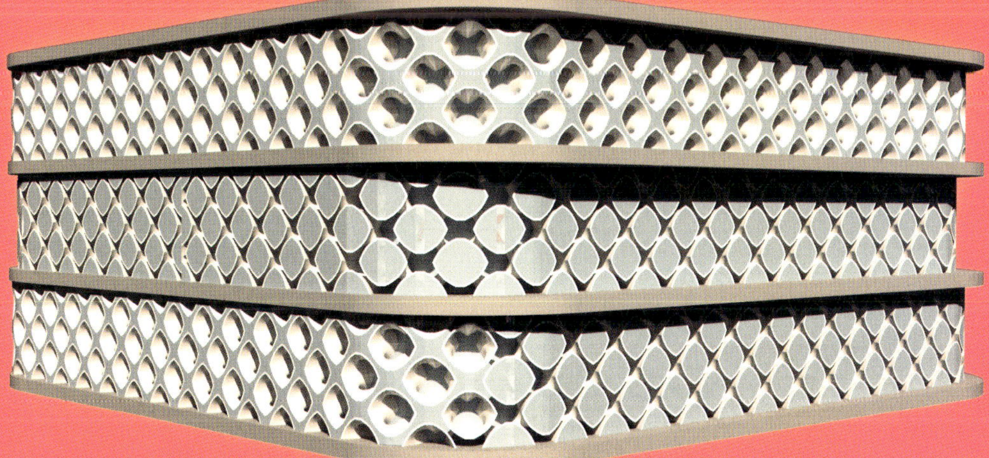

07_small scale_corner rendered perspective view

08_large scale_corner rendered perspective view

New module_cube_structural

09_small scale_rendered frontal view

10_large scale_rendered frontal view

Design instantiations, may be studied at different scales, considered at different sizes such as full-height modules resonating with Miguel Fisac's precast stabilizing envelope Boomerangs systems used at the IBM office building in Madrid, Spain.

11_small scale_corner rendered perspective view

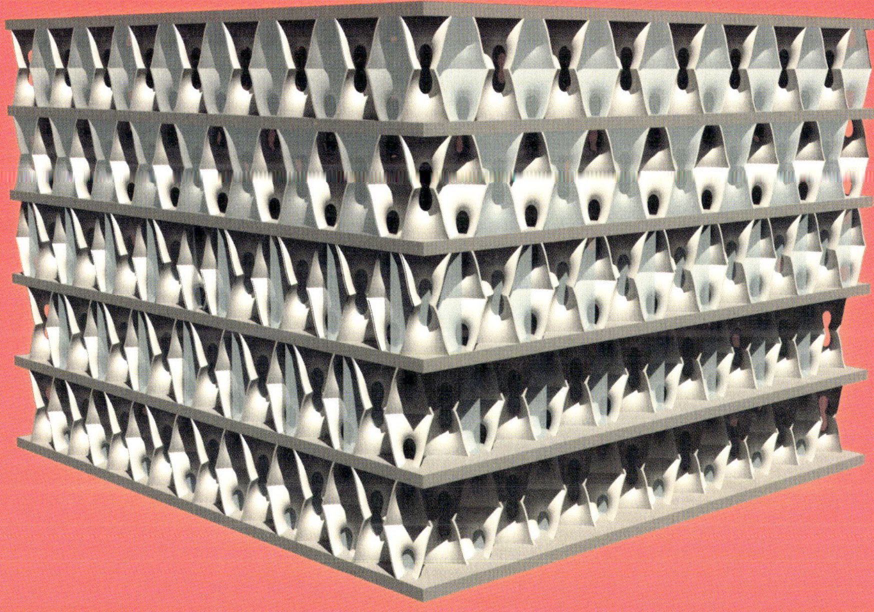

12_large scale_corner rendered perspective view

Thermodynamic forms

At a time when Modern architecture had been focused on the dematerialization of facades enabled by the industrialization of glass manufacturing, Erwin Hauer's screens were a clear expression of the building envelope as a multilayered material filter acting between different spatial and environmental spheres. The Continua screens reignited an older understanding of the building envelope as an interface modulating the exposed environment from a circumscribed micro-climate. Rather than sheltering, insulating, revealing or implicating an interior from exterior, these could be seen as a site where vision and light are active animated constituents. These conditions are reorganized through and on the surface. These screens may be transformed through a deliberate engagement with their capacities as thermally modulating envelopes. In addition to light, the screen systems may also be re-contextualized by actively pursuing their thermodynamic performance. To extend their role as environmental filters, it may be fruitful to explore the less visible atmospheric properties of warmth, cooling, humidity and dryness. Computational tools for simulating and analyzing the amount of solar irradiance received by buildings have become more accessible and easily

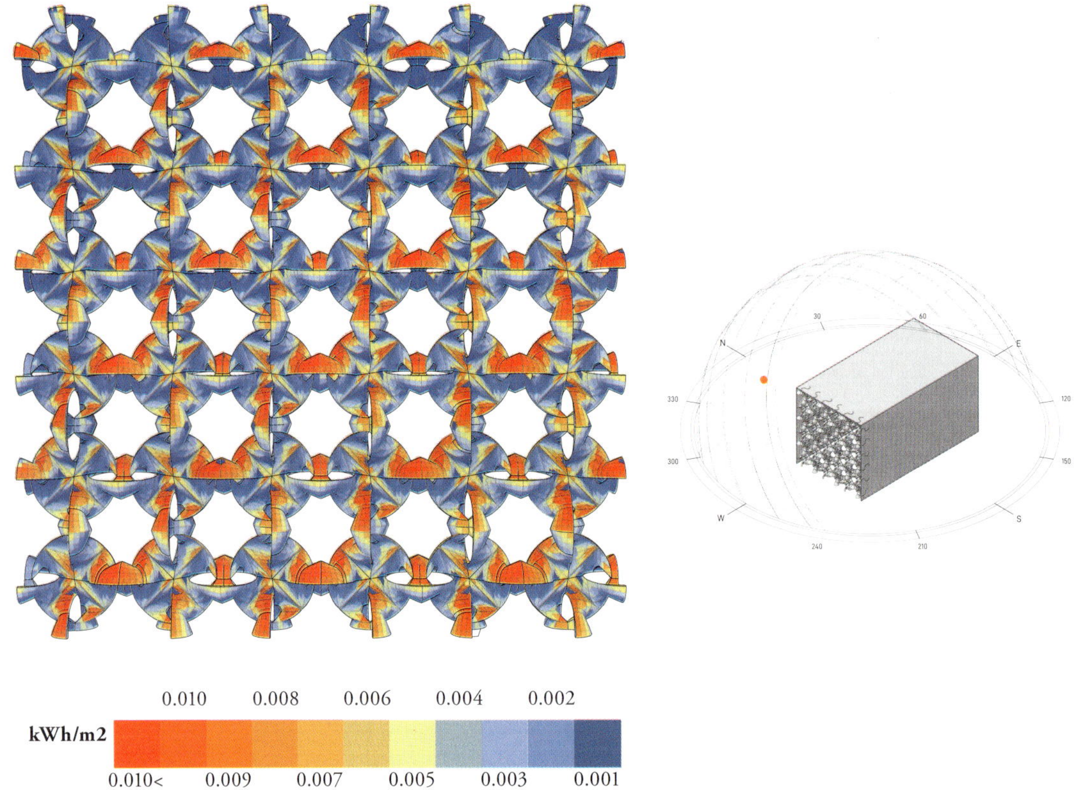

01_New Module 1.4_Associative model 7 based 02_proliferated matrix_summer radiation analysis (Melbourne, Victoria, Australia; February 14th, 15:00h to 17:00h)

integrated into a work-flow with digital design processes. Screen instantiations may be analyzed, allowing for an evaluation of these large samples of designs in accordance with the ways in which they may reduce solar heat gain through envelope design. Through this process, we could begin to pair technical considerations with a search for a formal language that could be associated with thermodynamic construction and expression in architecture, particularly in this realm of passive solar design. Passive and evaporative cooling are another process which can redirect this formal search.

At the detail level, the surfaces may be studied through a mapping of geodesic lines, to approximate how the natural micro-flow of water may be directed over its surfaces. This study affords us the possibility for designing the material textures on these surfaces to cultivate either hydrophilic or hydrophobic properties. Moisture that is collected on the surfaces or directed into cavities within the screen allow for passive cooling when oriented to cross ventilation through the screen in a manner akin to breeze blocks. The formal intricacy of these screens could also be restructured to dissipate radiant heating or cooling through a strategic increase in surface area. Thickened envelopes or columns of aggregated units could be defined with cavities that store or transfer fluids of varying temperatures. Cold or hot air conducted through these surfaces could then recondition environments.

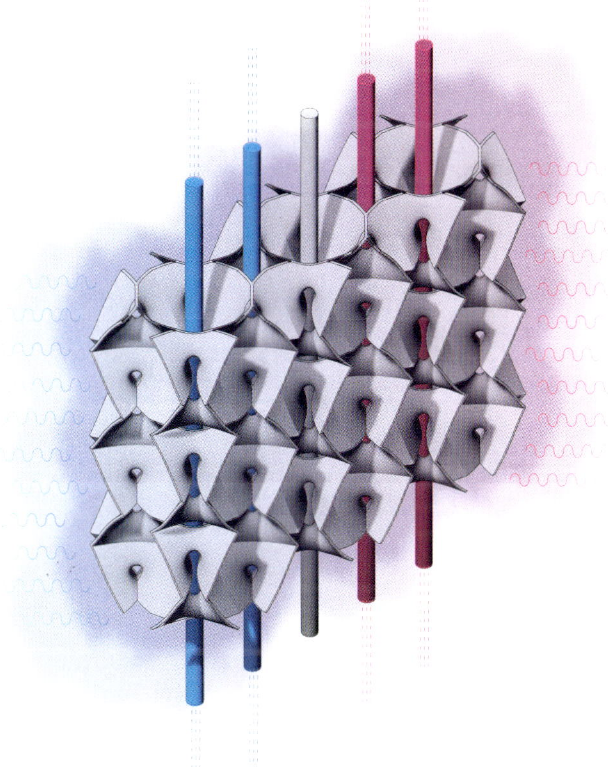

02_New Module 4.4_Enneper_Tetradecahedron based_ proliferated matrix_geodesic lines analysis

Re-fabrication: Continua screen

Jiang, G._Park, D._Perezamado, V._Tew, B. Fall 2010.

This group project, developed in the Fall 2010 (Re)Fabricating Tectonic Prototypes course at the GSD, involved a focused exploration of how formal concepts derived from a study of Hauer's Continua series could be used to define new geometric models capable of generating novel designs.

The students dedicated considerable effort in developing a workflow that allowed them to produce a number of physical prototypes of these new designs using digital design and fabrication tools paired with the more traditional practices of casting. Processes involving the construction of rubber molds from 3d-printed templates were developed by the team.

The intricacy of the design geometries also required a level of ingenuity and rigorous study to define and produce complex molds. (edited from student report)

06-08_(Re)fabricating Hauer_molds, diagrams and prototype

(Re)fabricating Hauer

Díaz, M._Kim, J._Koepcke, C._Omidfar, A._Zhang, L. Fall 2010

Also developed in the 2010 course, this student project culminated in a system for differentiating the Intercircles design developed by Hauer. The differentiations to the original Hauer geometry were directed by searches for configurations which could be structurally more robust (thicker pieces towards the base), or have variable visual porosity (depending on the angle of rotation of the great circles that form the piece). This was also complimented by a thorough investigation of the light screening capabilities that the different rotation angles of the great circles would afford.

Their explorations also involved the development of fabrication processes which reverberate with the earlier project using 3d-Printing to construct complex molds. The group cast multiple resin pieces from this process. (edited from student report)

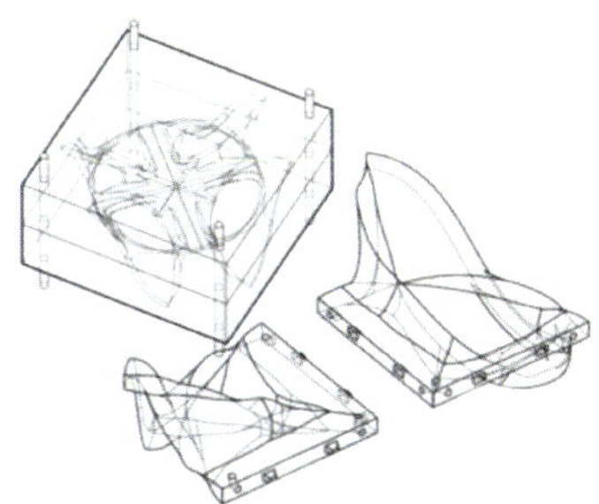

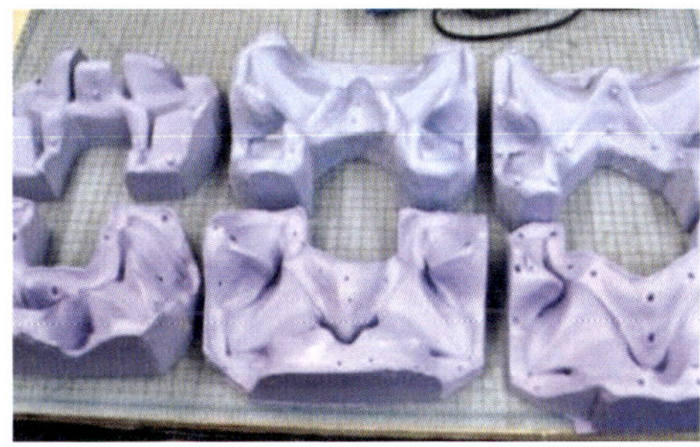

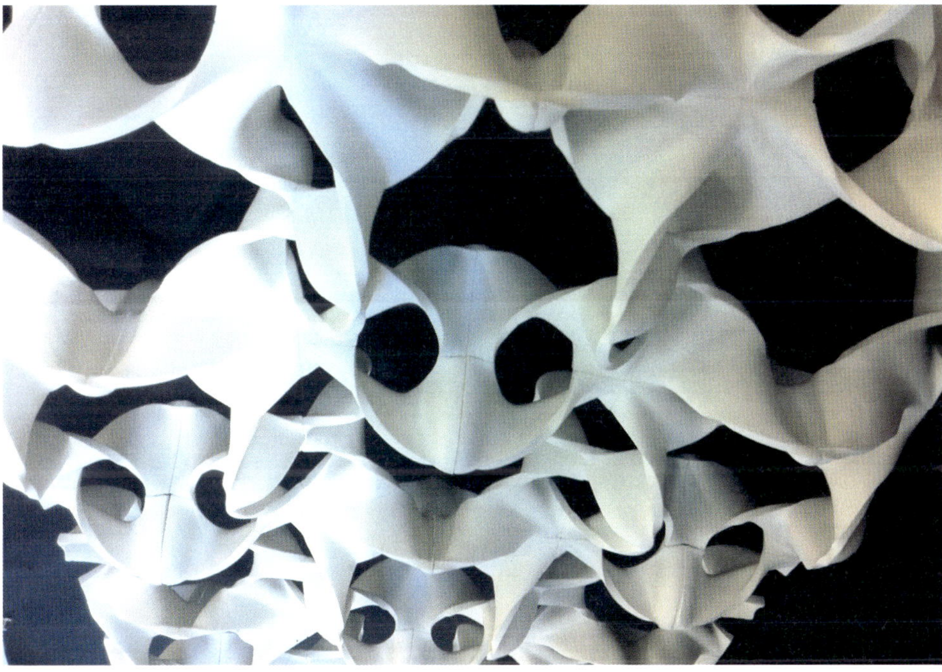

06-08_(Re)fabricating Hauer_molds, diagrams and prototype

Perforated columns

Campshure, J._Moen, S._Zhou, Z. Spring 2013

This team project produced in the Spring 2013 iteration of the course used Hauer's Design 4 as a reference. Their associative model allowed for differentiation in thickness to produce different visual porosity as well as loading capacity.
The fabrication of their units involved the production of a four-part mold with a predefined male/female interlocking system for ease of assembly. An ingenious system consisting of three variations of the module could be made from four unique parts. The center piece remains the same, while each variation has a different dimensional characteristic, such that the interior vertical load is carried through 1/2", 3/4", or 1" of material.
(edited from student report)

09_View of final mockup

10&11_Perforated column_casting process and prototypes

Tessellated diaphragm walls

Dickey, R._Mesa, O._Tse, L.L._Li, X. Spring 2014

The team aimed to learn Hauer's Design 1. They located some of the opportunities for transforming the precedent into a structurally self-supporting system. By developing an interconnected two-leaf system, the new prototype is able to operate as a diaphragm wall which could be assembled in plain, reinforced or pre-stressed configurations.
The team also explored the possibility of expanding the module of the system to afford a higher capacity for differentiation across the units of a wall. This would allow for a higher degree of visual variety and could be extended into providing a more performative screen. These screens could vary the porosity or aperture sizing of units to respond to specific solar radiation analyses.
(edited from student report)

12_View of final mockup

13_Tessellated diaphragm walls_casts

Open source

Technologically enabled disruptions to typical forms of authorship, production as well as dissemination are perhaps the most transformative factors in recontextualizing the material legacies and practices from Modern history. The wide adoption of digital tools in design practice and culture has given rise to design cultures and practices which depart from long-standing conventions.

While challenges remain for the mainstream adoption of open-source processes in architectural design, the efficacy of this model has been illustrated by the early response from the design fields to the Covid-19 pandemic. The challenges faced by the global medical field in sourcing protective equipment was met by a rapid response from designers and design institutions. Forgoing the usual proprietary relationship to design as well as industrial models of production, many design practices and education institutions of all sizes were able to share and collectively 3d-print open-source design files of protective medical equipment at scale.

At the early stages of the pandemic, this approach acheived agility through a distributed network of localized manufacturers enabled by automated fabrication. By adopting an open-source and distributed approach to disseminating design and manufacturing, this allowed for the expedient production and supply of protective equipment to medical workers at an immediate and local level while still acheiving extensive global reach.

While this example occured well outside of typical practice contexts, this event has provided a view into the possibilities for a shared and distributed logic towards design and production that may have the potential for a rapid and wide reach. Simmilar approaches had already been initiated by other organizations. Alejandro Aravena's Elemental group's release of housing plans under creative commons licences as a means to rapidly address housing crises is one such case. Victor Papanek's rejection of patents for a more open and shared understanding of design was underpinned by his dislike of the restrictions on dissemination imposed by a proprietary model of authorship. His motivation came from a sense of urgency for addressing the rapid environmental degradation caused by industrialized mass production.

In all these cases, the mandates have all been the compulsion to address crises of varying scales The Covid-19 pandemic has been described as a once in a century event. The risk of collapses to medical services as well as high mortality rates gave a common cause which mobilized a wide network of actors to openly share their design as well as manufacturing knowledge.

However, the societal risks posed by the Covid-19 pandemic of 2020 is likely to be surpassed by the challenges associated with the projected effects of climate change. The anticipated scale of mobilization needed to

01_Facade showing from top to bottom, left to right: 4.2_Tetrahedron based, 4.4_Tetradecahedron based_tiling variation, 4.1_Cube based, 4.3_ Octahedron based, 1.3_Associative model 7 based 02, 1.2_Associative model 7 based 01.

address climate change has been likened to the reorganization of national economies aimed at addressing the war efforts during World War Two. A significant social, cultural, technological, political and economic shift emerged out of this period and the design fields were also active agents in this transformation.

The research described here aims to establish bridges between Modern design systems legacies for upgraded creative practices that leverage established and emerging technological networks and capabilities.

While this can profit from a re-engagement with the Modern investment in design systems, a reorientation of the roles and agency of designers towards formulating protocols for generative creation systems resonates more clearly with digital culture and technology rather than exclusively remaining authors of standardized material artifacts.

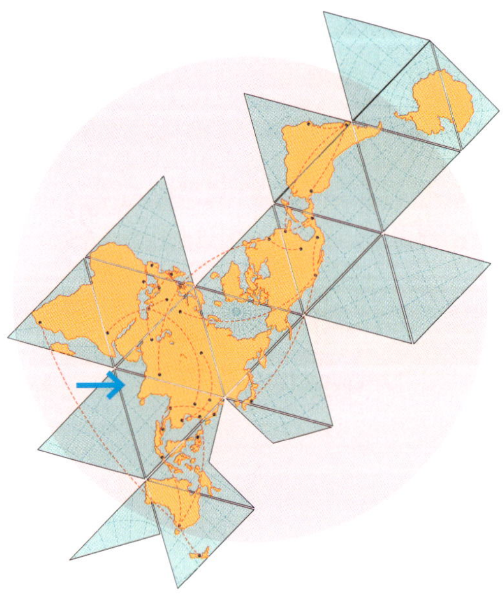

a_coding
Designers and researchers create or reverse engineer design systems. Associative models or generative codes are established that allow for the generation of large samples of different design instantiations based on these underlying codes.

b_global distribution
Design codes may be distributed as open-source codes, allowing for the free adoption and transformation of the codes. It may also be disseminated in a traditional manner through online stores offering large or customizable product ranges.

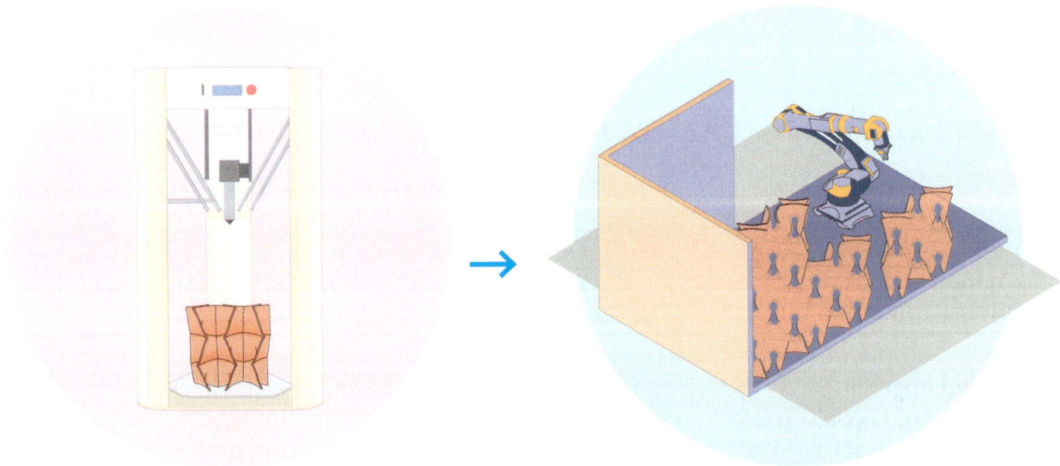

e_printing on demand
Rather than stockpiling inventories and large production runs associated with industrial production, digital fabrication may enable large product lines and customization without the associated waste.

f_assembly
Simple assembly may be designed into the system, allowing for unskilled installation. Alternatively design systems may be designed for automated assembly to enable easy and rapid implementation to facilitate widescale adoption.

02_transformation of the design, manufacturing and delivery process

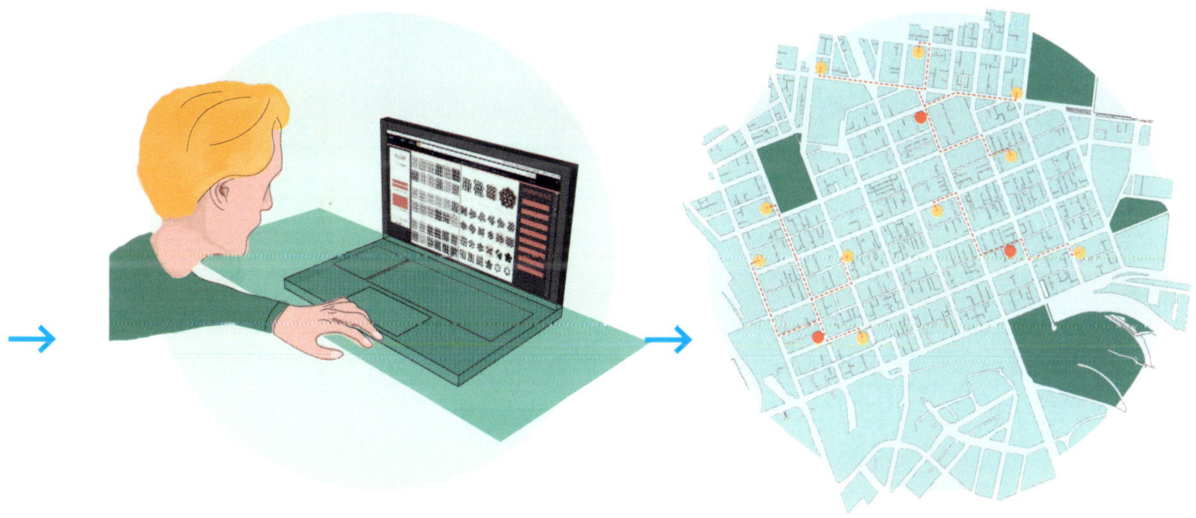

c_user interface / open source variability
Customization may be facilitated by a user-interface which allows for the generation of a large array of possible products without the burden of a matching inventory. Artificial Intelligence may also be employed to streamline this process.

d_local distribution and producers
Automated manufacturing may facilitate limited returns to local manufacturing. Reversing offshoring and industrial production, digital fabrication may cultivate a network of smaller and local producers.

The research offers a model of creative practice that links digital archaeological investigation with a vision for upgraded creative systems. It migrates earlier design practices focused on authored forms and notions of an authenticated production into a new agile and networked sensibility for design and creativity.

This also moves the conversation on the wide influence of design systems from centralized industrial deployment to open-source processes with proliferation also operating through viral crowd adoption.

The ambition behind upgrading systems is to locate another model of creative practice that circulates and opens up the possibility for transforming the design process itself. It also offers us another way to operationalize design histories so that it may still generate other design capacities. Established disciplinary knowledge and professional practice have been largely informed by the presumption of stabilized contexts and environments. But given the scenarios put forth by climate change and technological disruption, shouldn't the design community acclimatize itself to new concerns and opportunities? The design community is in need of upgrading its creative and delivery practices in order to articulate projective practices which engage with these crises and shifts with an agility and intentionality.

3d printed models

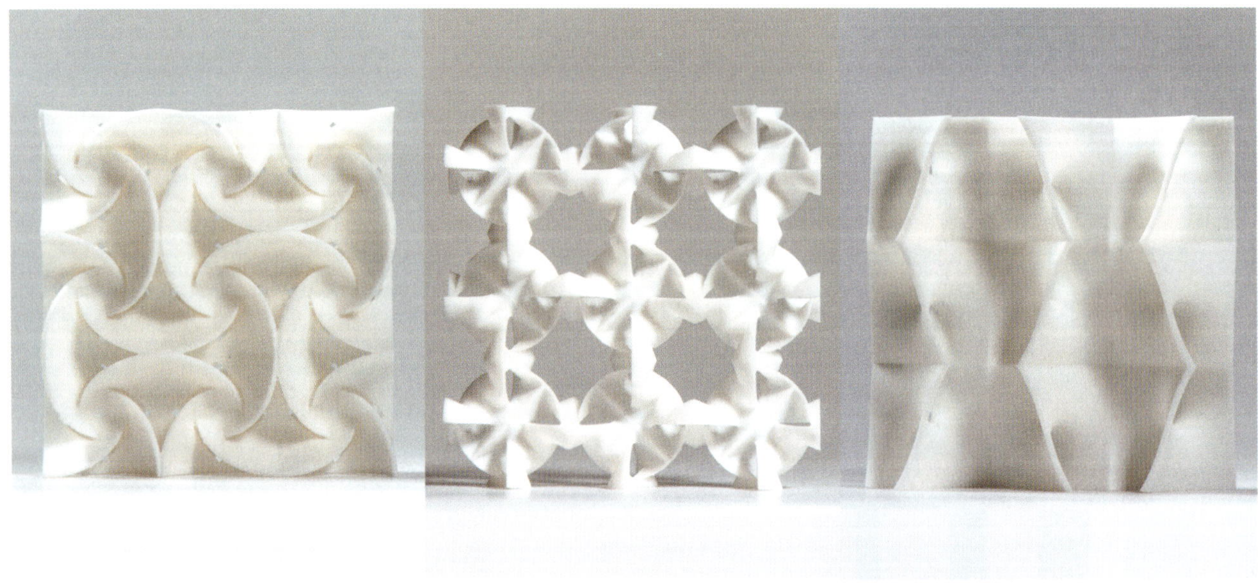

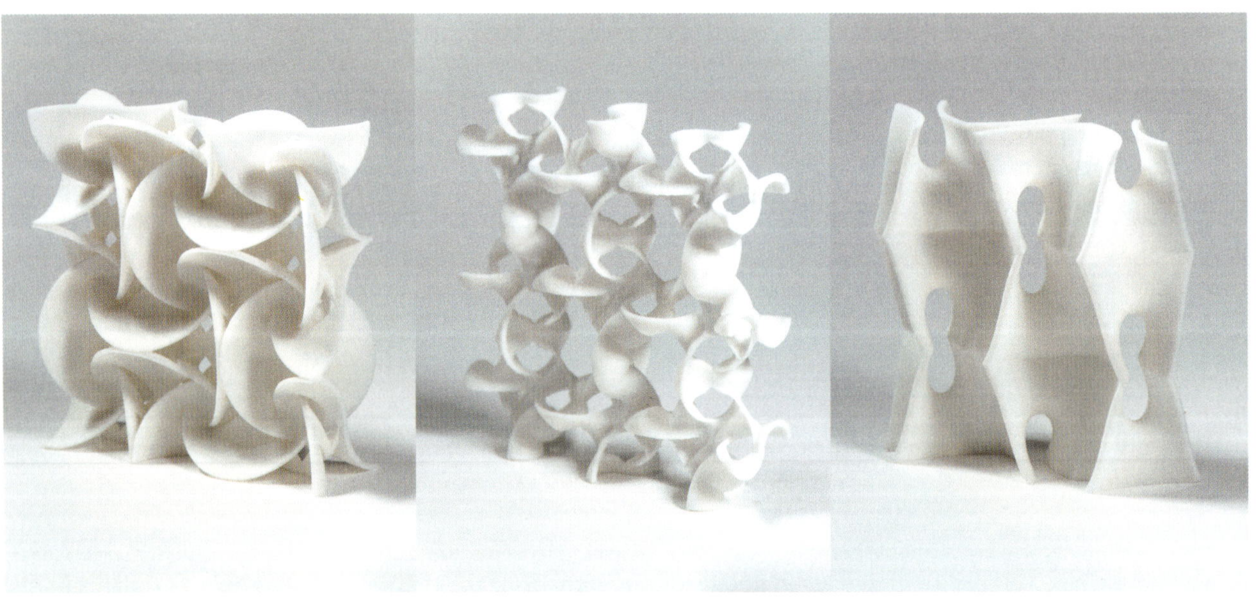

03_New Module 1.2
_Associative model 7 based_01

04_New Module 1.3
_Associative model 7 based_02

05_New Module 4.1
_Enneper + Cube

06_New Module 4.2
_Enneper + Tetrahedron

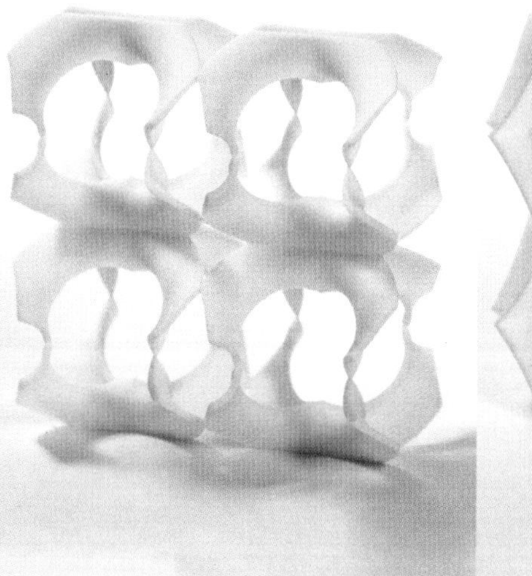

07_New Module 4.3
_Enneper + Octahedron

08_New Module 4.4
_Enneper + Tetradecahedron

New Module 1.3_ Associative model 7 based

New Module 3.1_Pentagon tile based

Biographies

Leire Asensio Villoria

Leire is a Senior Lecturer in Architecture and Urban Design at the University of Melbourne's School of Design. She is a co-director of the ADD+F Research Hub at the MSD, focused on advanced digital design and manufacturing. Leire has taught and led research teams at Harvard GSD, the Architectural Association and at Cornell University's AAP.

Leire is author and editor of the books:
Kara H., Asensio Villoria L. & Georgoulias A., 2017, *Architecture and Waste: A (Re)Planned Obsolescence*, Actar.
Mah D. & Asensio Villoria L., 2016, *Lifestyled: Health and Places*, Jovis.
She is an honors graduate from the Architectural Association and has been collaborating with David as asensio_mah since 2002.

David Syn Chee Mah

David is a Senior Lecturer in Architecture and Urban Design at the University of Melbourne's School of Design. David has taught and led research teams at Harvard GSD, the Architectural Association and at Cornell University's AAP.

David's is author of the book:
Mah D. & Asensio Villoria L., 2016, *Lifestyled: Health and Places*, Jovis.
He is a graduate of the Architectural Association (Landscape Urbanism) and has been collaborating with Leire as asensio_mah since 2002.

Acknowledgements

This book emerged out of a sustained investment of energy and effort over a period spanning between 2010 and 2020. We benefitted greatly from the support, conversations, and feedback from many friends and colleagues. This research has its early origins in the construction and teaching of a long-running elective course led by Leire: Refabricating Tectonic Prototypes, offered at Harvard's GSD between 2010 and 2016. The research was also extended in another course at the GSD on ceramic formations which Leire led between 2015 and 2016.

We would like to thank Mohsen Mostafavi, Inaki Abalos, Martin Bechthold and Preston Scott Cohen for supporting these courses at the GSD. The courses benefitted greatly from continued collaborations with Hanif Kara, the Office for the Arts' Ceramics lab at Harvard University (especially Kathy King, Mark Burns and Kyla Toomey) and was partly supported by the ASCER, the Spanish Ceramic Tile Manufacturers' Association of Spain. We also need to thank all the course TA's and students of these courses, of which there are too many to name individually here. Conversations with Ciro Najle, Panagiotis Micahalatos, Salmaan Craig have been motivational engines for the research. Xun Liu's efforts in assisting us are also greatly appreciated.

We would also like to thank friends and colleagues in Melbourne who have supported our capacities to continue this research in our new base in Australia. We would like to thank Alan Pert, Donald Bates, Hélène Frichot, Justyna Karakeiwicz and Dean Julie Willis at the Melbourne School of Design, University of Melbourne. We are also grateful to Dean Martyn Hook, who also afforded us a space to extend these explorations through the practice-based research hosted at RMIT. Thank you also to Candela de Bortoli for her assistance during the "Melbourne-phases" of this investigation.

We would like to specially thank Erwin Hauer and Enrique Rosado. Hauer and Rosado visited the course at the GSD in 2013 and gave a public lecture on "Transformations". They also very kindly hosted us at their Connecticut studios and workshop in 2012. Hauer's work and his collaborations with Rosado remain inspirational and singular to us.

Systems upgrade. (Re)fabricating tectonic prototypes

AUTHORS
Leire Asensio Villoria &
David Mah

PUBLISHED BY
Actar Publishers
New York, Barcelona

INTRODUCTION TEXT
Hanif Kara

COPY-EDITING
William C. Shipley

GRAPHIC DESIGN
Leire Asensio Villoria, David Mah and Ramon Prat Homs

DISTRIBUTION:
Actar Distribution Inc.

New York
440 Park Avenue South,
17th Floor
NEW YORK, NY 10016, USA
T +1 2129662207
salesnewyork@actar-d.com

Barcelona
Roca i Batlle 2-4
08023 BARCELONA, Spain
T +34 933 282 183
eurosales@actar-d.com

ISBN: 978-1-63840-971-7
PCN: Library of Congress Control Number: 2021943415
Printed in Europe, 2022

The authors and Actar Publishers are especially grateful to these image providers. Every reasonable attempt has been made to identify owners of copyright. Should unintentional mistakes or omissions have occurred, we sincerely apologize and ask for a notice. Such mistake will be corrected in the next edition of this publication.